WARFARE IN HISTORY

Elite Participation
in the Third Crusade

WARFARE IN HISTORY
ISSN 1358-779X

Series editors
Matthew Bennett, Royal Military Academy, Sandhurst, UK
Anne Curry, University of Southampton, UK
Stephen Morillo, Wabash College, Crawfordsville, USA

This series aims to provide a wide-ranging and scholarly approach to military history, offering both individual studies of topics or wars, and volumes giving a selection of contemporary and later accounts of particular battles; its scope ranges from the early medieval to the early modern period.

New proposals for the series are welcomed; they should be sent to the publisher at the address below.

Boydell & Brewer Limited, PO Box 9, Woodbridge, Suffolk IP12 3DF

Previously published titles in this series are listed at the back of this volume

Elite Participation in the Third Crusade

Stephen Bennett

THE BOYDELL PRESS

© Stephen Bennett 2021

All rights reserved. Except as permitted under current legislation no part of this work may be photocopied, stored in a retrieval system, published, performed in public, adapted, broadcast, transmitted, recorded or reproduced in any form or by any means, without the prior permission of the copyright owner

The right of Stephen Bennett to be identified as the author of this work has been asserted in accordance with sections 77 and 78 of the Copyright, Designs and Patents Act 1988

First published 2021
Paperback edition 2024
The Boydell Press, Woodbridge

ISBN 978-1-78327-578-6 (Hardback)
ISBN 978-1-83765-208-2 (Paperback)

The Boydell Press is an imprint of Boydell & Brewer Ltd
PO Box 9, Woodbridge, Suffolk IP12 3DF, UK
and of Boydell & Brewer Inc.
668 Mt Hope Avenue, Rochester, NY 14620–2731, USA
website: www.boydellandbrewer.com

A CIP catalogue record for this book is available
from the British Library

The publisher has no responsibility for the continued existence or accuracy of URLs for external or third-party internet websites referred to in this book, and does not guarantee that any content on such websites is, or will remain, accurate or appropriate

Contents

List of Illustrations	vi
Preface and Acknowledgements	vii
List of Abbreviations	x
Notes on Sources, Names, and Coinage	xiii
Introduction	1
1. Faith and Finance: Religious Foundations, Ecclesiastical Leaders, and Fraternity	29
2. Family and Heritage: Lineage, Kinship, and Tradition	90
3. Locality and Fellowship: Territory, Trade, and Tournaments	121
4. The Household of King Richard I at the Time of the Third Crusade	159
Conclusion: Personal, Spiritual, and Communal Influences on Participation in the Third Crusade	213
Appendices	
1. The Noble Network: Crusaders from North-Western Europe, 1187–92	220
2. King Richard I's Household, 1189–92	353
Bibliography	397
Index	437

Illustrations

Maps

1.	North-Western Europe	xiv
2.	Routes to the Holy Land	xv
3.	The Holy Land	xvi

Figures

1.	Nodes and Ties	17
2.	Dyads and Triads	18
3.	Bridges and Centrality	19

Tables

1.	Connections by Religious Affiliation and Notable Events	17
2.	Numbers of Known Crusaders from North-Western Europe Associated with Religious Houses that Participated in the Third Crusade	50
3.	Family Heritage and Participation in the Third Crusade	103
4.	Kinship and Participation in the Third Crusade	108
5.	The Geographical Composition of Richard's *Mesnie* 1189–1194	185
6.	The Social Composition of Richard's *Mesnie* 1189–1194	187
7.	The Background of Richard's *Mesnie* 1189–1194	190

Preface and Acknowledgements

Despite being more akin to a cultural history or perhaps even a genealogy of the Third Crusade than a traditional military history, this book grew out of my interest in unit cohesion, or the bonding together of warriors in a military organisation to sustain them in combat. In particular, it was inspired by Jan-Frans Verbruggen's view that the *Règle du Temple* was in part an attempt to replicate the bonds found in lay military households, which were arguably based on established social bonds – on family and locality.[1] However, the base assumption on the composition of lay households required, in my view, more investigation before it could be safely used to consider this question.

Recent debate on unit cohesion has featured a distinction between the components of social cohesion and task cohesion – the commitment to working together on a shared goal.[2] Since some studies have concluded that unit effectiveness is determined more by task cohesion than social cohesion, I thought it important to focus on a period in which various households from across Christendom were brought together for a common goal, such as in the attempted reconquest of the kingdom of Jerusalem.[3]

Like any such endeavour, researching and writing this book has benefited from the support of various bodies, as well as the goodwill and generous help of my own kinship and friendship network. Though it is impossible to repay many of the debts incurred, it is my pleasure to recognise them and to publicly offer my thanks for the help I was given during this project. Among the many debts of gratitude to individuals that I have incurred over the years whilst researching and writing this book the first is due to Tom Asbridge, who throughout the whole time has been an unfailing source of wisdom and support. Without his diligent guidance and unceasing encouragement, this

---

[1] See J.F. Verbruggen, *The Art of Warfare in Western Europe During the Middle Ages*, 2nd edition, trans. (Woodbridge, 1997), p. 65.

[2] See, for example, G. van Epps, 'Relooking Military Cohesion: A Sensemaking Approach', *Military Review* (November/December, 2008), 102–10.

[3] This debate about the relative importance, or even need for, social cohesion and task cohesion is exemplified by an exchange between Anthony King and Guy Siebold in *Armed Forces and Society* in 2006–2007: A. King, 'The Word of Command: Communication and Cohesion in the Military', *Armed Forces and Society*, 32/4 (2006), 493–512 and 'The Existence of Group Cohesion in the Armed Forces: A Response to Guy Siebold', *Armed Forces and Society*, 33/4 (2007), 638–45; G.L. Siebold, 'The Essence of Military Group Cohesion', *Armed Forces and Society*, 33/2 (2007), 286–95.

may have stalled early on. I wish to express my profound thanks to Matthew Bennett for his keen insights and encouragement throughout the process. Similarly, I am also grateful to Caroline Palmer, Judith Everard, and Nick Bingham for their patience and support.

I am grateful to those many friends and colleagues who offered guidance and support at important junctures in my research: Nicholas Vincent for generously sharing King Richard's *acta*; Benjamin Kedar, Helen Nicholson, Jonathan Phillips, and Kelly DeVries who offered fruitful criticism and helpful suggestions to my work on the battle of Arsuf; the stalwart members of the Antioch Dining Club, Martin Hall, Ian Wilson, Gary Ramsell, and Ahmet Hilmi; Stuart Buxton and Richard Dagnall.

I am especially indebted to Carsten Selch Jensen for reading through the manuscript and providing many useful comments and observations, causing me to hone my arguments and providing much-needed encouragement through the final stages of writing and revision. Other people who have offered advice and corrections on substantial portions of this work include: Mike Carr, Stephen Church, Bernard Hamilton, John D. Hosler, Andrew Jotischky, Jochen Schenk, and Kat Tracy. Likewise, my thanks go to the team at Queen Mary's: Andrew Buck, Belinda Guthrie, Stephen Spencer, and especially Peter Denley; to Ane L. Bysted, Janus Møller Jensen, Kurt Villads Jensen, Palle Rasmussen, Thomas Heebøll-Holm, Torben K. Nielsen and to the medieval societies at Aarhus University and at the University of Southern Denmark for welcoming me into their scholarly communities.

I am deeply indebted to the Queen Mary Fund and St John Historical Society for endowments to support my research, as well as the generous assistance of a grant from Isobel Thornley's Bequest to the University of London to produce this book. I wish to express my gratitude to the staff of the Bibliothèque Nationale and the Archives Nationales of France in Paris, the National Archives in Kew, the British Library and, of course, Senate House and the Institute of Historical Research.

My greatest debt of gratitude is to my parents and to my sister, who have provided me with strong roots and countered my occasional desperation with love, understanding, and good humour, to my children and, especially, to my beautiful wife, who has never stopped believing in me and has been my inspiration and joy, as well as my fiercest reader. All mistakes, naturally, remain my own.

Stephen Bennett
Odiham, 2020

This book is produced with the generous assistance of a grant from
Isobel Thornley's Bequest to the University of London

Abbreviations

Acta	*Acta of Henry II and Richard I*, Vol. 2, ed. N. Vincent (Kew, 1996).
AD	Archives départementales
Ambroise	Ambroise, *The History of the Holy War, Ambroise's Estoire de la Guerre Sainte, I. Text*, ed. M. Ailes and M. Barber (Woodbridge, 2003). Followed by line number.
AN	Archives Nationales (France)
ANS	*Anglo-Norman Studies*
Baha' al-Din	Baha' al-Din ibn Shaddad, *The Rare and Excellent History of Saladin*, trans. D.S. Richards (Aldershot, 2002).
BL	British Library
BN	Bibliothèque nationale de France
Barbarossa	*The Crusade of Frederick Barbarossa, The History of the Expedition of the Emperor Frederick and Related Texts*, trans. G.A. Loud (New York and London, 2010).
Cal. Charter Rolls	*Calendar of Charter Rolls Preserved in the Public Record Office*, Vols. 1–5 (London, 1903–27).
CCR	*Calendar of Close Rolls of the Reign of Henry III Preserved in the Public Record Office: Prepared under the Superintendence of the Deputy Keeper of Records* (London, 1902–37).
CDF	*Calendar of Documents Preserved in France, Illustrative of the History of Great Britain and Ireland, Vol. 1, AD.908–1206*, ed. J.H. Round (London, 1899).
Chronica	Roger of Howden, *Chronica magistri Rogeri de Houedone*, 4 vols. ed. W. Stubbs (London, 1868–71).
Coggeshall	Ralph of Coggeshall, *Radulphi de Coggeshall Chronicon Anglicanum; De expugnatione Terrae Sanctae libellus;...*, ed. J. Stevenson, Rolls Series (London, 1875).
Conquest	*The Conquest of Jerusalem and the Third Crusade, Sources in Translation*, trans J. Edbury (Aldershot, 1998).
CPR	*Calendar of Patent Rolls Preserved in the Public Record Office, 1388–92* (London, 1891–1982).
CRR	*Curia Regis Rolls, Richard I–Henry III*
Crusade Charters	*Crusade Charters, 1138–1270*, ed. C.K. Slack, trans. H.B. Feiss (Tempe, AZ, 2001).

Devizes	Richard of Devizes, 'The Chronicle of Richard of Devizes', *Chronicles of the Reigns of Stephen, Henry II and Richard I*, Vol. 2 ed. R.G. Howlett (London, 1886).
Diss	Ralph of Diss, *Ymagines Historiarum, Opera Historica*, ed. W. Stubbs, 2 Vols. (London, 1876).
EHR	*English Historical Review*
EYC	*Early Yorkshire Charters*, Vols. 1–3, ed. W. Farrer (Edinburgh, 1914–16), and Vols. 4–12, ed. C.T. Clay (Leeds, 1935–64).
Gerald of Wales	Gerald of Wales, *Giraldi Cambrensis Opera*, 8 Vols, ed. J.S. Brewer, J.F. Dimock and G.F. Warner (London, 1861–91).
Gesta Regis	Roger of Howden, *Gesta Regis Henrici Secundi Benedicti Abbatis: The Chronicle of the Reigns of Henry II and Richard I A.D. 1169–1192, Known Commonly under the Name of Benedict of Peterborough*, 2 Vols, ed. W. Stubbs (London, 1867).
Gilbert of Mons	Gilbert of Mons, *La chronique de Gislebert de Mons*, ed. L. Vanderkindere (Brussels, 1904).
HdB	*Histoire des ducs de Bourgogne de la race capétienne*, 9 Vols, ed. E. Petit (Paris, 1885–1905).
HGM	*Histoire de Guillaume le Maréchal History of William Marshal, Vol. 1 – text and translation (ll. 1–20031)*, ed. A.J. Holden, trans. S. Gregory, historical notes D. Crouch (London, 2002).
HSJ	*Haskins Society Journal*
Itinerarium	*Chronicles and Memorials of the Reign of Richard I, Vol. 1: Itinerarium peregrinorum et gesta regis Ricardi, auctore, ut videtur, Ricardo, canonico Sanctæ Trinitatis Londoniensis*, ed. W. Stubbs (London, 1864).
JMH	*Journal of Medieval History*
Landon, *Itinerary*	L. Landon, *The Itinerary of King Richard I with Studies of Certain Matters of Interest Connected with his Reign* (London, 1935), followed by charter number.
Newburgh	William of Newburgh, '*Historia Rerum Anglicarum*', *Chronicles of the Reigns of Stephen, Henry II and Richard I*, 2 Vols, ed. R.G. Howlett (London, 1884–9).
PL	*Patrologiae Cursus Completus: Series Latina*, ed. J.P. Migne (Paris, 1841–1855).
PR	Pipe Roll, followed by number and king's monogram; published by the Pipe Roll Society (Kew).
TNA	The National Archives – formerly Public Record Office
RCR	*Rotuli Curiæ Regis*, ed. F. Palgrave (London, 1835).
RHF	*Recueil des historiens des Gaules et de la France*, ed. M. Bouquet et al. (Paris, 1869–1904).

Rigord	*Oeuvres de Rigord et de Guillaume de Breton, historiens de Philippe-Auguste*, Vol. 1, ed. H.F. Delaborde (Paris, 1882).
RRRH	*Revised Regesta Regni Hierosolymitani Database*: http://crusades-regesta.com
Wendover	Roger of Wendover, *Flores Historiarum*, Vol. 1, ed. H.G. Howlett (London, 1886).

Notes on Sources, Names, and Coinage

Unless otherwise indicated, translations of primary sources are mine, although I have endeavoured to provide references to standard editions where appropriate; for the reader's convenience references to editions translated into English are provided whenever possible. I have sought to include details of recent or standard editions of primary sources where possible, although references to sources originally cited by the authors have generally been retained.

Proper nouns have been anglicised whenever possible, except where the non-English form is so well established as to render any other usage inappropriate. In the same way, unless another form has been customary, or an anglicised name is too different from the original or too anachronistic, the most suitable form of name has been selected for its bearer, for instance, William of Newburgh, but Baldwin le Carron and William des Barres.

Finance in High Medieval north-western Europe was based on the silver penny – known as a *denier* in France. For the purposes of accounting, people also used shillings (*sols*), pounds (*livres*), and *marks*. There were twelve pennies to a shilling, 240 pennies in a pound, and 160 pennies in a *mark*. A pound equated to that weight in silver, but there were a number of versions of that measure in use. The original Roman *libra*, for example, weighed approximately 328.9 grams, a Troy pound weighed 373.2 grams, and the Tower pound weighed about 350 grams. Such variation meant that a *denier parisis* (Paris penny) was worth 1¼ *deniers tournois* (Tours pennies). By way of context, a professional infantryman was paid two pennies a day in the Angevin realm at the time of the Third Crusade.

Map 1. North-Western Europe

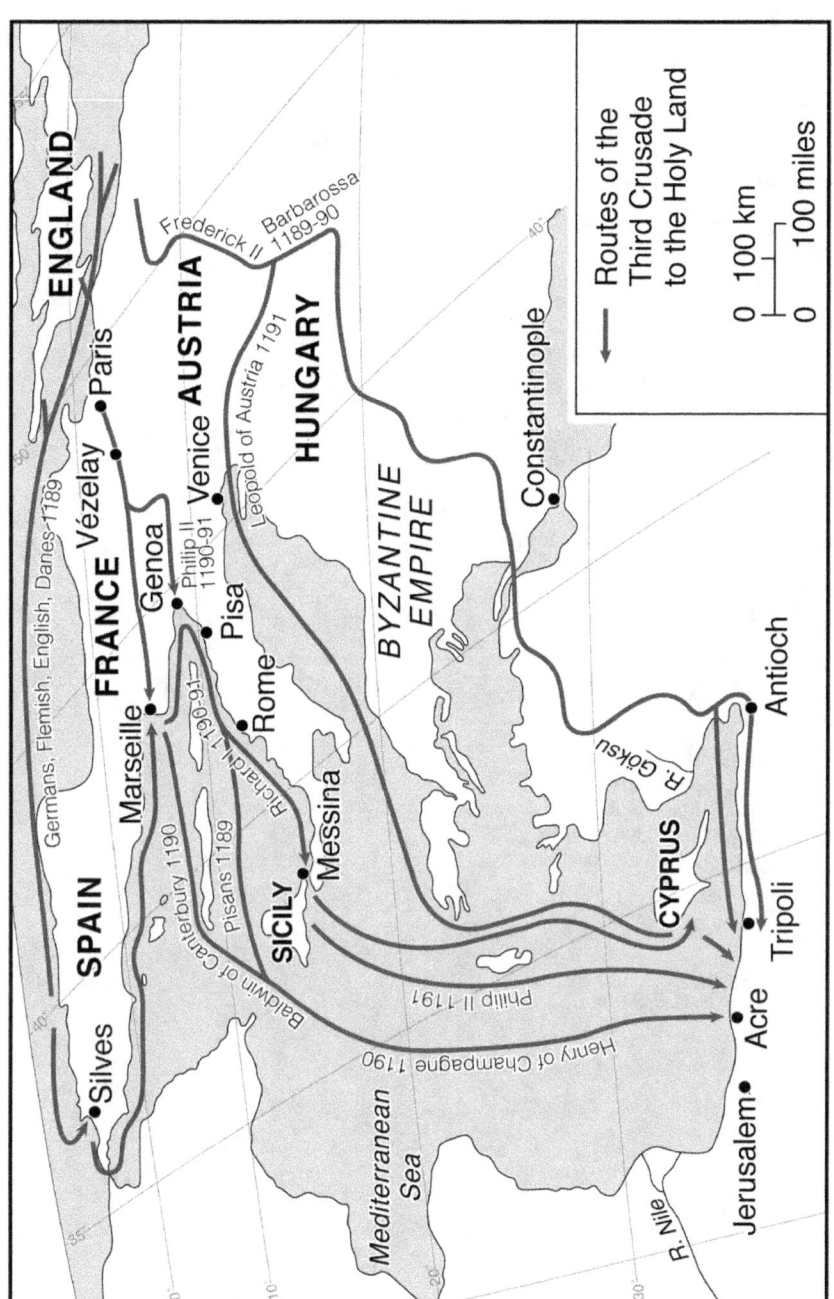

Map 2. Routes to the Holy Land

Map 3. The Holy Land

Introduction

> Let those who for long were brigands now become soldiers of Christ. Let those who once fought against their brothers and blood relatives fight lawfully against barbarians. Let those who until now have been mercenaries for a few coins achieve eternal rewards.
>
> Pope Urban II, Clermont, 1095[1]

The response to Pope Urban II's call to arms at Clermont in 1095 was overwhelming and the subsequent campaign to aid Byzantium and liberate the Holy Land established a number of new states in western Asia. This campaign came to be known as the First Crusade and its conquests as the Latin East, the Crusader States, or *Outremer* – the lands over the sea.[2] The greatest of these polities was the kingdom of Jerusalem based on the Holy City captured in the final stages of the First Crusade in July 1099.

Over the next hundred years, Latin settlers aided by waves of crusaders sought to defend their conquests against growing Muslim pressure. Whilst Edessa had fallen to Muslim forces in 1144, the remaining Crusader States seemed relatively secure. Yet, in 1187, Salah ad-Din Yusuf (Saladin r.1174–1193) annihilated Latin forces under Guy of Lusignan, king-consort of Jerusalem, at the battle of Hattin (4 July 1187), and seized control of the majority of Guy's kingdom, including its capital. The Third Crusade (1187–1192) sought to recover Jerusalem and re-establish Latin control over the Holy Land.

When word reached Europe of Saladin's destruction of the army of the kingdom of Jerusalem at Hattin and his capture of the True Cross, Pope Urban III was said to have fallen dead in shock.[3] Even before Archbishop

---

[1] An excerpt from Pope Urban II's sermon at Clermont in 1095 as related by Fulcher of Chartres, 'Nunc fiant Christi milites, qui dudum exstiterunt raptores; nunc iure contra barbaros pugnent, qui olim adversus fratres et consanguineos dimicabant; nunc aeterna praemia nanciscantur, qui dudum pro solidis paucis mercenarii fuerunt': *Fulcheri Carnotensis Historia Hierosolymitana (1095–1127)*, ed. H. Hagenmeyer (Heidelberg, 1913), pp. 136–7.
[2] For a discussion on the use of terms relating to the Latin East, see A.D. Buck, 'Settlement, Identity, and Memory in the Latin East: An Examination of the Term "Crusader States"', *EHR*, 135 (2020), 271–302.
[3] The True Cross is the name for the physical remains of the cross on which Christ was crucified. What was claimed to be a fragment of the True Cross was recovered during

Joscius of Tyre had spread the news of the fall of Jerusalem, hundreds across Latin Christendom rushed to take the Cross – to pledge themselves to a crusade. Amongst their number was Richard 'the Lionheart', duke of Aquitaine and heir to the throne of England (1157–1199), who risked the ire of his father, Henry II, in taking the vow without permission. Tens of thousands more joined them in response to a call for a crusade by the new pope, Gregory VIII, and the efforts of his preachers at mass cross-taking ceremonies.

At Gisors in January 1188, Kings Philip II of France (r.1180–1223) and Henry II of England (r.1155–1189) pledged themselves to the crusade, as did the Holy Roman Emperor, Frederick Barbarossa (r.1155–90), at Mainz in May of the same year. They were joined by the great lords of their realms: dukes, counts, earls, and landgraves mustered their retinues, along with prominent clerics like the archbishops of Besançon and Canterbury. In line with the First Crusade, this was not an expedition confined to kings and magnates; familial bands, knightly neighbours, artisans, and common folk – men and women – from across Europe responded in their tens of thousands to the call to recover Jerusalem. Many more, however, while they did not take the Cross and did not journey to the Holy Land, felt its influence through taxation, inflation, and social disruption. Improving our understanding of the people that embarked on an endeavour that had a significant impact on late-twelfth-century Europe is at the heart of this book.

In order to analyse the communal and cultural factors that influenced nobles from north-western Europe (the Angevin realm, Capetian France, and the Low Countries) who embarked on the Third Crusade, this book reconstructs a complex societal system (social network) through the creation of a database of participants and the application of Social Network Analysis.[4] This approach improves our understanding of the motives, dynamics, and extent of elite participation in the Third Crusade, and places that participation in the broader social and geographical context of crusading and medieval life.

---

the First Crusade. It was placed within a golden cross and carried as a sacred banner by the army of the kingdom of Jerusalem. See T.S. Asbridge, *The First Crusade, A New History* (Oxford, 2004), pp. 293, 322–3.

[4] The Angevin realm is taken here as the kingdom of England, the duchies of Aquitaine, Brittany, Cornwall, Gascony, and Normandy, the counties of Anjou, Auvergne, Limousin, Maine, Le Marche, Nantes, Périgord, Poitou, Quercy, Touraine, and Saintonge, and the lordship of Ireland. Due to the scarcity of data, the handful of crusaders from other parts of the British Isles have been included in the Angevin figures. The use of realm is not intended to indicate that these territories formed a singular polity or that they were subject to the same laws and customs. France is those areas of medieval France not forming part of the Angevin Realm. The Low Countries centre on the delta of the Rhine, Meuse, Scheldt, and Ems rivers, i.e., the counties of Flanders, Hainaut, and Holland, as well as Artois, Brabant, Gelders, Luxembourg, Namur, and the bishopric of Liège. Frisia, however, has been excluded.

This is the first study to tackle motivation in relation to participation in the Third Crusade in detail, which is arguably one of the biggest questions in relation to crusading – why did people go on crusade? In doing so it also revisits the question of how Richard I succeeded in attracting members of the nobility to his contingent whilst ensuring the stability of his realm. Participation in the Third Crusade was based on established crusader benefits, such as the plenary indulgence and papal protection of property.[5] This book, however, demonstrates the continuing importance of the concept of *imitatio Christi* – following in Christ's footsteps – to many of those taking the Cross.

In addition to an enduring view of crusading as a spiritual vocation, the data also shows that significant numbers of participants in the Third Crusade were descended from crusaders and indicates that the majority of them travelled to the Levant in the company of friends, family, and neighbours, as well as through membership of a military household. It shows that this was not an expedition made up of landless younger sons seeking their fortunes. It detects key individuals – both male and female – who influenced participation in the expedition from north-western Europe (as mediators), as well as identifying the significant role played by particular religious institutions in the diffusion of crusading ideology (as intermediaries), such as the Cistercians and the Order of St Lazarus, in the Third Crusade noble network.

Social Network Analysis

The precise personal, spiritual, and communal motivations of individual crusaders are notoriously difficult to uncover given the nature of the evidence they left behind, but Social Network Analysis is a remarkably apt tool for mapping patterns of human behaviour. A noble network is a social structure that is primarily composed of elite human actors (monarchs, magnates – both lay and ecclesiastical – barons, and knights, as well as their spouses and children), but also non-human actors (objects, artefacts, or structures that interact in a network with people, such as religious foundations or holy relics).

The main goal of Social Network Analysis is detecting and interpreting patterns of relationships between subjects of research interest. As an analytical approach, it is based on the concept of complex cultural systems (networks), specifically the study of the interactions between the many elements of a social structure, that is, actors are viewed as interdependent rather than

---

[5] See A.L. Bysted, *The Crusade Indulgence: Spiritual Rewards and the Theology of the Crusades, c.1095–1216* (Leiden, 2015), pp. 156–62.

independent.⁶ In Social Network Analysis, quantitative and mathematical methods and models are used to analyse cultural/social processes and structures, and to provide insight into the dynamics of real-world phenomena. When data permits, these techniques allow for research into such issues as kinship groupings and regional patterns of recruitment, indicating the importance of social factors in the mobilisation of crusades.

The formidable data requirements, however, can present significant challenges for a historian of the Middle Ages. Methodologically, it demands a broad range of high-quality and trustworthy records that evidence social interaction, and that locate activities in time and place. Balancing an incomplete historical record and an imperfect understanding of the precise social relationships between the subjects of a study with this requirement can be deeply problematic: gaps in the data can produce distorted results and lead to erroneous conclusions. I accepted at the outset that it would be impossible to capture all essential relations between actors in the social system. Indeed, only a proportion of the crusaders from north-western Europe were likely to be identifiable.⁷

A more egocentric approach compensated for the fragmentary nature of the data, that is, by studying the ties of single individuals, and focusing on the quality and nature of those ties to re-create a community network. This also addresses potential criticism that, in focusing on structural relationships through taking a sociocentric approach, there is a risk of overlooking the importance of individual agency. Community network analysis treats people as acting consciously and with purpose, that is, that their relationships are instrumental, rather than solely focusing on structures of groups as predicators of group-level outcomes.⁸

The study of the resulting community networks is then based on prosopographical methodology, which also helps reduce the risk of distortions

---

⁶ Network analysis is rooted in graph theory, from which it adopts techniques for identifying, examining, and visualising patterns of relationships. See J.A. Barnes and F. Harary, 'Graph Theory in Network Analysis', *Social Networks*, 5 (1983), 235–44; and F. Harary and R.Z. Norman, *Graph Theory as a Mathematical Model in Social Science* (Ann Arbor, MI, 1953). A graph represents the structure of a network of relationships, while a network consists of a graph and additional information on the vertices or the lines of the graph. It consists of a set of vertices (also called points or nodes), which represent the smallest units in the analysis, and a set of lines (or ties) between these vertices, which represent their relationships. See W.D. Nooy, A. Mrvar, and V. Batagelj, *Exploratory Social Network Analysis with Pajek* (Cambridge, 2005), pp. 6–7.

⁷ For more on overcoming the challenges of fragmentary evidence in historical Social Network Analysis, see C. Wetherell, 'Historical Social Network Analysis', *International Review of Social History*, 43 (1998), 125–44.

⁸ For a similar approach for the late medieval period, see *The Soldier Experience in the Fourteenth Century*, ed. A.R. Bell, A. Curry, A. Chapman, A. King, and D. Simpkin (Woodbridge, 2017).

caused by incomplete data. Prosopography is an investigation into the common characteristics of an historical group of people by means of a collective study into their lives, which in this case is designed to shed light on the networks of complex relationships that were created during the Third Crusade.[9]

The collective study is a precondition for comparative analysis of the various contingents and key individuals, but only the comparative study of the links between personal biographies allows for analysis of the noble network, identifying, for example, those best placed to transmit ideas between groups, such as Baldwin of Forde, archbishop of Canterbury (r.1185–90).[10] The resulting network is a complex, three-dimensional web with vertical (feudal, economic), horizontal (familial, neighbourhood or nearness, i.e., *propinquity*), and *homophilios* (shared) connections, including gender, age, values, status, and common activities – like participating in tournaments.[11] In its use of Social Network Analysis this book is heavily influenced by the concepts of collective identity construction and social interaction.

Collective Identity Construction and Social Interaction

Most modern historians of France dismiss Albert Sorel's teleological argument for a 'geography determined French policy' and the steady and inevitable expansion of France's borders to reach the Atlantic, Rhine, Pyrenees, and Alps laid out in 'the limits that Nature has traced' attributed to Cardinal Richelieu (1585–1642).[12] However, natural borders appear as a strong feature within the changing arrangement of images and symbols that make up an ideal unity of 'France' as well as other imagined spaces. Such ideal unities draw on ideas like a common history, a shared language, and a delimited space.[13] In its cultural, legal, and linguistic diversity, the Angevin realm challenges the narrative borders that underpin collective identity and, particu-

---

[9] See G. Beech, 'The Scope of Medieval Prosopography', *Medieval Prosopography*, 1/1 (1980), 6.
[10] L. Stone, 'Prosopography', *Historical Studies Today*, ed. F. Gilbert and S. Graubard (New York, 1972), p. 134.
[11] For the role of gender, see M. McPherson, L. Smith-Lovin, J. Cook, 'Birds of a Feather: Homophily in Social Networks', *Annual Review of Sociology*, 27 (2001), 415–44.
[12] A. Sorell, *Europe et la Revolution française*, Vol. 1: *Les Moeurs politiques et les traditions* (Paris, 1885), p. 246; P. Sahlins, 'Natural Frontiers Revisited: France's Boundaries since the Seventeenth Century', *The American Historical Review*, 95/5 (1990), 1423–1451. See also G. Zeller, 'La monarchie d'ancien régime et les frontières naturelles', *Revue d'histoire moderne*, 8 (1933), 305–33.
[13] For the symbolic construction of France see C. Beaune, *Naissance de la nation de France* (Paris, 1986), and P. Nora, *Les Lieux de mémoire: La Republique* (Paris, 1984); *La Nation*, 3 Vols. (Paris, 1986). On French space and national territory see D. Nordman, 'Des limites d'État aux frontières nationales', *Les Lieux de mémoire, La Nation*, Vol. 2 (Paris, 1986), pp. 35–61, J.W. Konvitz, 'The Nation-State, Paris, and Cartography in 18th and 19th Century France', *Journal of Historical Geography*, 16 (1990), 3–16; and D.

larly, collective memory in north-western Europe.[14] Indeed, the geographical divisions adopted in this study to assist in the analysis are in no way intended to suggest they were cohesive polities in the mould of early-modern nation-states – quite the contrary.

Identity refers to the definition of group membership, whereas memory concerns a group's shared past experiences.[15] Collective identity and collective memory are, therefore, connected by an experience of the present that is mirrored in a narrative of the past. Matthew Bennett has argued persuasively that chivalry, for example, was based on memorialisation: returning to an imagined past of moral and martial virtue and recreating it through ceremonial, games, and military practice both in secular and holy war, in order to gain glory for individuals, communities, and even nations.[16] These concepts are particularly valid in approaching the nature of a network and, in particular, the bonds that link individuals and families within an elite network such as those being analysed here.

The definition of who belongs to the in-group or 'Us' and the experience of what delineated out-groups or 'Others' have done to 'Us', arguably creates cultural bonds. These hold people together beyond personal interests that might otherwise unite or divide individuals in a given situation. This cultural embedding of economic and social life is central to approaching group identity and memory. Here, collective identity is taken to mean what people share and take as their identifying marks as a 'collectivity' or a group of people acting as a body.[17] Collective memory is the reference to a past that people share and that fundamentally shapes the way these people relate to each other. Collective identity construction creates commonness and difference depending on how the past is constructed and reconstructed among people. It can act as a link between actors within a large and diverse elite network that lacks more intimate connections.

A collective identity is arguably needed when cultural techniques (such as bureaucratic formula, written texts, etc.) serve to mediate social interaction. Social interaction refers to the relationship between two or more individ-

---

Nordman and J. Revel, 'La Formation de l'espace français', *Histoire de la France*, Vol. 1 (Paris, 1989), pp. 29–169.

[14] For the importance of the memory of the Angevin realm in the later Middle Ages, see M. Vale, *The Angevin Legacy and the Hundred Years War, 1250–1340* (Oxford, 1990).

[15] K. Eder, 'Remembering National Memories Together: The Formation of a Transnational Identity in Europe', *Collective Memory and European Identity: The Effects of Integration and Enlargement*, ed. W. Spohn and K. Eder (Aldershot, 2005), pp. 197–220.

[16] See, for example, M. Bennett, 'Remembering Chivalry', paper given at the 25th International Medieval Congress, University of Leeds (UK), July 2018.

[17] S.N. Eisenstadt and B. Giesen, 'The Construction of Collective Identity', *European Journal of Sociology*, 36/1 (1995), 72–102. See B. Stråth, 'A European Identity, To the Historical Limits of a Concept', *European Journal of Social Theory*, 5/4 (2002), 387–401 for the counter-argument to the concept of identity in social sciences.

uals, groups or organisations that form the basis of a social structure.[18] The resulting social network is made up of the actors and the dyadic ties between them. Each actor is represented by a node, which is the smallest unit in the network. A line is a tie between two nodes and represents any social relationship. The ties through which any given agent connects represent the convergence of the various social contacts of that agent.[19] It is possible to consider the degree of social cohesion enjoyed by a network by analysing the social network through shared interests, common goals, norms and values, the development of accepted sanctions, representations, ethnic/social backgrounds, and kinship ties. In this case, it can be used to consider the degree to which elite actors across north-western Europe formed a social unit.

The importance of belonging is arguably a cultural constant and, in order to belong, people seek a socially shared understanding.[20] David Crouch has argued that whilst lacking a self-conscious codification of noble behaviour, in the late twelfth century there existed a shared expectation of behaviour that operated in the same way as a code. This he calls 'the noble habitus' which he draws from the ideas of the French sociologist, Pierre Bourdieu.[21] A *habitus* is the environment of behavioural and material expectations that all societies and classes generate. It is the all-important explanation of how a mental construct like society can act on the people within it. The expectations a *habitus* imposes can be very powerful, but it is not written down and members are expected to acquire their understanding of it through their upbringing and social contacts; and the norms can themselves slowly or abruptly shift and be very different for men and women.[22]

Social norms are the rules that a group uses for appropriate and inappropriate values, beliefs, attitudes and behaviour.[23] Both David Crouch and Matthew Bennett also highlight the importance of the *preudomme*, where *preuz* means all that is noble, meritorious, and reliable in a man's behaviour. As William Marshal's biography exemplifies, to be considered a *preudomme* (man of worth – a man who has been tried and tested) was most probably considered the highest of accolades amongst our elite subjects, with its essential characteristics of *mesure*, *preuz*, and *largesse* (self-control, merit, and generosity). In this study, I draw out intermediaries responsible for the

---

[18] A.P. Hare, *Handbook of Small Group Research* (New York, 1962).
[19] M. and C.W. Sherif, *An Outline of Social Psychology* (New York, 1956), pp. 143–80.
[20] A.P. and S.T. Fiske, 'Social Relationships in Our Species and Cultures', *Handbook of Cultural Psychology*, ed. S. Kitayama and D. Cohen (New York, 2007), pp. 284–5.
[21] P. Bourdieu, *L'Amour de l'art* (Paris, 1966), fn 751.
[22] D. Crouch, *The Birth of Nobility: Constructing Aristocracy in England and France, 900–1300* (London, 2005), pp. 52–7. See also D. Crouch, *William Marshal*, 3rd edition (Abingdon, 2016), pp. 177–87.
[23] S.N. Durlauf and L.E. Blume, *New Palgrave Dictionary of Economics*, 2nd edition (London, 2008), pp. 476–9.

diffusion of such values, but more importantly, mediators that influenced participation in the Third Crusade, and consider what effect they had on individuals on the periphery of a network or who were party to more than one network.

Donald Campbell's 'realistic conflict theory' and, especially, the experiments of Muzafer Sherif on intergroup behaviour and identity formation are particularly useful in considering group dynamics.[24] Campbell's theory explains how intergroup hostility can arise as a result of conflicting goals and competition over limited resources, such as within the Angevin realm, as well as relations with neighbouring polities. In addition, it explains the feelings of prejudice and discrimination towards non-group members that accompany intergroup hostility, examples of which were highlighted by Pope Urban II in his sermon at Clermont in 1095, as well as in Gregory VIII's *Audita tremendi*.[25]

Sherif's study on intergroup behaviour was conducted over three weeks in Robbers Cave State Park, Oklahoma in 1954. The experiment was divided into three stages: 'in-group formation', 'friction phase', and 'integration stage'. On arrival, twenty-two eleven- and twelve-year-old boys were split into two approximately equal groups. Each group was unaware of the other group's presence. In the 'friction phase', the groups competed with one another in various camp games, which caused both groups to show hostility towards each other. During the 'integration stage', inter-group tensions were reduced through cooperative inter-group tasks. Sherif concluded that, because the groups were created to be approximately equal, individual differences are not necessary or responsible for intergroup conflict. He noted that aggressive attitudes toward an 'outgroup' arise when groups compete for resources that only one group can attain. Sherif also deduced that contact with an outgroup is insufficient, by itself, to reduce hostility. Finally, he concluded that friction between groups could be reduced, and positive intergroup relations maintained, only in the presence of superordinate goals that promoted united, cooperative action.

Those familiar with the background to the First Crusade may have already noted how this concept resonates with Pope Urban II's aim for that expedition to reduce internal strife in Christendom by focusing on a higher purpose, which was mirrored by Gregory VIII in *Audita tremendi*. As far as I am aware, however, it has not previously been employed in studying individual crusades or, indeed, crusading as a whole.[26] During this analysis,

---

[24] D.T. Campbell, *Ethnocentric and Other Altruistic Motives* (Lincoln, NE, 1965), pp. 283–311.

[25] Groups may be in competition for a real or perceived scarcity of resources such as money, political power, military protection, or social status. See Campbell, *Ethnocentric*, pp. 283–311.

[26] See M. Sherif, *In Common Predicament: Social Psychology of Intergroup Conflict and*

the Third Crusade is considered in the role of Sharif's superordinate goal, promoting united, cooperative action.[27]

As the chronicler Gilbert of Mons wrote of the participants at the assembly held near Gisors on 21 January 1188 at which the kings of England and France committed themselves to a crusade to the Holy Land, 'they caused truces to be arranged and confirmed between them concerning their conflict until after their return from Jerusalem'.[28] Similarly, Gregory VIII travelled to Pisa to broker peace between the rival Italian city-states and, his successor, Clement III (r.1187–91), secured a settlement with Frederick Barbarossa to ensure all sides would be free to collaborate in the Third Crusade.[29]

As is discussed in greater detail below, analysis of social structures has recently emerged as a popular field of study within medieval historiography. Scholars have begun exploring relationships as a means of tackling difficult issues such as the motivation and cultural make-up of crusaders. In doing so, we also discover new areas of interest that demand investigation, such as the cultural and motivational differences between various crusading expeditions to the Holy Land and other destinations, like Iberia.

Studying Crusaders

Prosopography provides the opportunity to investigate previously inaccessible areas for research by studying the common characteristics of a group of people. As a technique, prosopography in medieval studies focuses on evidence drawn from charters, letters, and narrative sources and uses traditional critical methods to test that data. The importance of using prosopography has been firmly established in studies of the crusades and the Latin East, significantly by James Powell whose research into the social impact of the Fifth Crusade explored the social structure of the expedition, as well as the effects of recruitment and the underlying religious climate.[30] Jonathan Riley-Smith drew from a broad range of source material for his comprehensive prosopographical analysis of members of the First Crusade, highlighting

---

Cooperation (Boston, 1966), pp. 24–61. On Pope Urban II and the First Crusade, see Asbridge, *The First Crusade*, pp. 55–65.

[27] Sherif, *Common Predicament*, pp. 24–61.

[28] 'et super discordiis suis usque post reditum suum a Jherosolimis treugas inter se ordinari et firmari fecerunt': Gilbert of Mons, p. 206. They were joined in taking the Cross by the counts of Blois, Clermont, Flanders, and Sancerre, as well as many other members of the north-west European noble elite. Rigord, p. 82, gives the alternative date of 13 January, but Roger of Howden also places the meeting on 21 January 1188; *Gesta Regis*, Vol. 2, pp. 58–9.

[29] Under the Peace of Strasbourg (1189), Barbarossa agreed to withdraw his forces from the Papal States without giving up his authority over the region. In return, the pope promised to make Frederick's son, Henry VI, emperor.

[30] J. Powell, *Anatomy of a Crusade, 1213–1221* (Philadelphia, 1986).

the importance of family amongst lay motivations to take the Cross, such as amongst the Montlhéry kinship group, and significantly damaging claims that crusading was the preserve of landless younger sons – an argument we will revisit in Chapter Two.[31] In his study of the kingdom of Jerusalem, Alan Murray examined the identity and background of 140 crusaders and settlers who were connected to its first two rulers, Godfrey of Bouillon (r.1099–1100) and Baldwin I of Jerusalem (r.1100–18), to provide new evidence on the kingdom's German social context.[32] Michael Lower's particularly relevant work considered the preaching, planning, recruitment, and conduct of a series of French and English expeditions to the Latin East between 1239 and 1241 which later became known as the Barons' Crusade.[33] Finally, Jonathan Phillips' research into Crusader motives rested on his identification of 350 individual participants in the Second Crusade (1147–50) and their pedigrees to highlight the familiar strands of kinship and patronage alongside faith and an opportunity for gain. Phillips also considered the challenges inherent in financing participation, as well as securing the hearth when absent on crusade, which I cover in relation to the Third Crusade.[34]

Studies into crusaders from late-twelfth-century Normandy and the Low Countries have broadened our understanding of regional participation in the Third Crusade, as has Tyerman's research into England and the Crusades and Jochen Schenk's work on familial associations with the Templars in France.[35] And yet, despite intense interest among modern scholars and Alan Murray's ongoing research into Frederick Barbarossa's contingent, there has been no monograph dedicated solely to members of the Third Crusade from north-western Europe.[36]

Following on from the prosopographical studies on the First and Second Crusades, this book is also well placed to consider the development of

---

[31] J. Riley-Smith, *The First Crusaders, 1095–1131* (Cambridge, 1997).

[32] A. Murray, *Crusader Kingdom of Jerusalem: A Dynastic Study* (Oxford, 2000).

[33] M. Lower, *The Barons' Crusade: A Call to Arms and Its Consequences* (Philadelphia, PA, 2005).

[34] J. Phillips, *The Second Crusade: Extending the Frontiers of Christendom* (London, 2007).

[35] F. Vielliard, 'Richard Coeur de Lion et son entourage normand: le témoignage de l'Estoire de la guerre sainte', *Bibliotheque de l'École des chartes*, 160 (2002), 7–26; M. Billoré, 'La noblesse normande dans l'entourage de Richard Ier', *La cour Plantagenêt (1154–1204): Actes du Colloque tenu á Thouars du 30 avril au 2 mai 1999*, ed. M. Aurell (Poitiers, 2000), pp. 151–68; C. Tyerman, *England and the Crusades, 1095–1588* (Chicago and London, 1988); and H. van Werveke, 'La contribution de la Flandre et du Hainaut à la troisième croisade', *Le Moyen Age*, 78 (1972), 55–90; J. Schenk, *Templar Families: Landowning Families and the Order of the Temple in France, c.1120–1307* (Cambridge, 2012).

[36] Thomas Madden highlights the surprising lack of a monograph on the Third Crusade, but he does not explain why no attempt has yet been made to cover this expedition in detail, *The New Concise History of the Crusades* (Oxford, 2006), p. 236.

crusading. The Third Crusade took place on the cusp of major changes in the movement that occurred around 1200. Historians such as Christopher Tyerman have attributed these changes to Pope Innocent III (r.1198–1216), but how many of those innovations were evident some ten years earlier?[37] Indeed, one of the central goals of this book is to consider whether the Third Crusade was a natural progression from earlier expeditions to the Holy Land or a foreshadowing of the innovations that were to come under Innocent III. To investigate the potential motivations of crusaders from the nobility, this study draws upon gifts to religious foundations and accounts of preaching activity in order to consider local variations and broader developments in devotional practice.[38] The approach of Penny Cole on the preaching of crusades is crucial in the search for the reality of devotional practice that lies hidden behind textual representations.[39]

Evidence for the identity and role of crusaders in primary sources makes investigation into non-noble groups problematic. For example, commoners are often only used as exemplars in narrative accounts of the Third Crusade, such as Ambroise's *Estoire de la Guerre Sainte*.[40] They remain in the shadows of historical accounts and official records, and are not yet reliably identifiable in sufficient numbers. Therefore, meaningful prosopographical research on the Crusades is largely restricted to noble elites and their retinues, of whom the sources offer fascinating insights. Indeed, David Crouch's work on an Anglo-Norman household and my own research into King Richard's *mesnie* on crusade support the suggestion of the multinational, pluricultural make-up of military households.[41] The members of elite groups are also the focus of this book and they provide valuable perspectives on complex medieval elite networks, and how they relate to crusading.

In focusing on the noble elite, this study engages with the knotty question of the *miles*. The Latin term, *miles* (singular, plural *milites*), is most usually

---

[37] C. Tyerman, *The Invention of the Crusades* (Basingstoke, 2000); J. Sayers, *Innocent III: Leader of Europe, 1198–1216* (London and New York, 1994); and B.M. Bolton, *Innocent III: Studies on Papal Authority and Pastoral Care* (Aldershot, 1995).

[38] For similar research on the First Crusade see M. Bull, *Knightly Piety and the Lay Response to the First Crusade: The Limousin and Gascony c.970–c.1130* (Oxford, 1993), and 'Views of Muslims and of Jerusalem in Miracle Stories, c.1000–c.1200: Reflections on the Study of First Crusaders' Motivations', *The Experience of Crusading: Western Approaches*, ed. M.G. Bull and N.J. Housley (Cambridge, 2003), pp. 13–38.

[39] P. Cole, *The Preaching of the Crusades to the Holy Land, 1095–1270* (Cambridge, MA, 1991).

[40] Ambroise, *Estoire de la Guerre Saint, Histoire en vers de la Troisième Croisade*, ed. G. Paris (Paris, 1897).

[41] Crouch, *William Marshal*, 3rd edition, pp. 227–40; S. Bennett, 'La mesnie de roi Richard 1er lors la troisième croisade', *Richard Cœur de Lion, Entre mythe et réalités*, ed. M. Aurell and C. Vital (Gent, 2016), pp. 70–8.

translated into knight in modern English.⁴² From the importance given to the horse, such as in the use of *chevaliers* (Old French), *caballero* (Spanish), and *Ritter* (German) to describe *miles* in medieval vernacular languages, it is clear that the term had evolved by the eleventh century from its Classical Latin meaning of 'soldier' into that of a cavalryman (*caballerius*).⁴³ That is not to say that *milites* were not capable of dismounting to fight on foot, such as at Brémule (1119) and Lincoln (1141), to stiffen the cohesion and fighting power of the foot. However, they identified themselves by their role as heavily armoured horsemen, delivering shock action in battle.⁴⁴ Moreover, knights were seemingly distinguished from other cavalrymen that might be similarly armed and equipped through a formal ceremony in which they were girded with a sword and made a knight.⁴⁵

In the eleventh and early-to-mid twelfth centuries, the term covered a broad spectrum of individuals. Distinct from magnates and barons, Jean Scammell divided Anglo-Norman knights at the turn of the twelfth century into four categories based on their ownership of land and arms.⁴⁶ Richard Abels demonstrated that, drawing on data contained in the *Domesday Book*, knights with money-fiefs were outnumbered by those without feudal obligation.⁴⁷ However, Jonathan D'Arcy Boulton argued that knighthood became a social rank during the twelfth century, in which *milites nobiles* were distinguished from the non-noble *milites gregarii*.⁴⁸ The *Dialogue of the Exchequer* (c.1180), for example, illustrates the approach of King Henry II's officials,

---

⁴² While the earliest use of *cnihtas* to describe armed retainers appeared in the Laudian version of the Anglo-Saxon Chronicle (composed c.1100), it was not seemingly established in Angevin England until around 1300.

⁴³ J.D. Hosler, *John of Salisbury, Military Authority of the Twelfth-Century Renaissance* (Leiden and Boston, 2013), pp. 12–22.

⁴⁴ S. Morillo, 'The "Age of Cavalry" Revisited', *The Circle of War in the Middle Ages: Essays on Medieval Military and Naval History*, ed. D.J. Kagay and L.J.A. Villalon (Woodbridge, 1999), pp. 46–56; M. Prestwich, '*Miles in Armis Strenuus*: The Knight at War', *Transactions of the Royal Historical Society*, 6th ser., 5 (1995), 204.

⁴⁵ See, for example, the description of William Marshal being dubbed a knight and girded with a sword, HGM, lines 817–26. For the process of being knighted, see also, M. Lieberman, 'Knightings in the Twelfth and Thirteenth Centuries: A New Approach', paper given at the Battle Conference on Anglo-Norman Studies 2020: A Virtual Workshop, July 2020.

⁴⁶ J. Scammell, 'The Formation of the English Social Structure: Freedom, Knights, and Gentry, 1066–1300', *Speculum*, 68 (1993), 595, 600.

⁴⁷ R. Abels, *Lordship and Military Obligation in Anglo-Saxon England* (Berkeley, CA, 1988).

⁴⁸ D'A.J.D. Bolton, 'Classic Knighthood as Nobiliary Dignity: The Knighting of Counts and Kings' Sons in England, 1066–1272', *Medieval Knighthood V, Papers from the Sixth Strawberry Hill Conference 1994*, ed. S. Church and R. Harvey (Woodbridge, 1995), pp. 48–9.

who used *miles* to mean 'anyone who had ever possessed the knightly belt'.⁴⁹ It went on to extricate social rank from the knightly profession of arms. If a knight was unable to pay his debts, he could retain his horse, as befitted his rank. If he was also an active warrior, however, he could retain all his personal armour and the necessary horses, so that he could pursue his profession. This is reinforced by evidence drawn from the writings of John of Salisbury, bishop of Chartres and clerk to the archbishops of Canterbury, such as his *Policraticus* (c.1159), a treatise on political and courtly affairs. According to John Hosler, Bishop John saw a *miles* as 'a person of honour given the particular task of defending both commonwealth and Church'.⁵⁰

From this evidence and the Angevin King Henry II's Assizes of Clarendon (1166) and Northampton (1176), we can conclude that, along with *barones* and their kin in the Church, by the time of the Third Crusade the *milites* formed part of the noble elite in north-western Europe.⁵¹ Knighthood did not become closely associated with the ideals of chivalry based on an identifiable code of conduct until the later Middle Ages. Yet Matthew Bennett has argued that chivalry was 'essential to military professionalism' in the eleventh and twelfth centuries – that it was already a legitimate and socially respectable code for Christian warriors.⁵² Moreover, David Crouch has established that although the twelfth and early thirteenth centuries had no formal codification of noble behaviour, there was a shared expectation of (courtly) behaviour that operated in the same way as a code.⁵³ In addition to the evidence from John of Salisbury, the ideal of the *preudomme* runs strongly through the biography of William Marshal, with his father introduced as a *chevaliers proz e loials* (brave and trustworthy knight) and William himself as *plus prodome* (worthiest man).⁵⁴ In this book, I illustrate how crusading formed an intrinsic part of late twelfth century noble culture in north-western Europe.⁵⁵

---

⁴⁹ *Dialogus de Scaccario*, ed. C. Johnson (Edinburgh, London, and New York, 1950), pp. 111–12.
⁵⁰ Hosler, *John of Salisbury*, p. 13.
⁵¹ See also, J.D. Hosler, *Henry II: A Medieval Soldier at War, 1147–1189* (Leiden, 2007), pp. 104–13.
⁵² M. Bennett, 'Why Chivalry? Military "Professionalism" in the Twelfth Century: The Origins and Expressions of a Socio-Military Ethos', *The Chivalric Ethos and the Development of Military Professionalism*, ed. D.J. Trim (Leiden, 2003), pp. 41–64. See also, M. Bennett, 'Manuals of Warfare and Chivalry', *A Companion to Chivalry*, ed. R.W. Jones and P. Coss (Woodbridge, 2019), pp. 268–72.
⁵³ Crouch, *Birth of Nobility*, pp. 52–7 and D. Crouch, *William Marshal*, 3rd edition (London and New York, 2016), pp. 177–87.
⁵⁴ *HGM*, lines 16, 27; Crouch, *William Marshal*, 3rd edition, pp. 182–6.
⁵⁵ For detailed coverage of Anglophone and Francophone historiography of chivalry, see, P. Coss, 'The Origins and Diffusion of Chivalry', *A Companion to Chivalry*, ed. R.W. Jones and P. Coss (Woodbridge, 2019), pp. 7–38.

Regarding debate on the crusading movement, as an expedition launched by a papal bull, whose members took the Cross and were focused on the liberation of Jerusalem, the Third Crusade sits firmly within traditional definitions of a crusade and provides the opportunity to test contrasting perspectives. Giles Constable laid out a series of unofficial categories for these perspectives, which are widely accepted as a useful model.[56] 'Traditionalist' views, such as those of Hans Mayer, focus predominantly on the Levant, whilst 'pluralists' like Jonathan Riley-Smith regard the Crusades more as an approach to war in general as opposed to simply the liberation of the Holy Land.[57] In analysing the Third Crusade, this book considers whether or not there was a qualitative distinction in a crusade's destination, that is, whether a crusade to the Latin East was held in higher esteem than those conducted elsewhere, such as along the Baltic coast. The identification of any crusaders who returned home after fighting in Iberia but before reaching the Holy Land is invaluable in considering this question.

By focusing on the nobility and their potential motivations, I touch upon the view of the 'populist' school, represented recently by Gary Dickson in *The Children's Crusade*, that crusading was an eschatological act of the masses and part of the religious revivals that occurred during the central Middle Ages.[58] It has been established that the crusading movement lay within a context of repentance, penance, and pilgrimage – following Christ by being willing to fight in his cause and for the Holy Land, which was seen as his heritage.[59] However, by looking at the relationship between the crusader elite and religious foundations, as well as outbreaks of anti-Jewish violence, it is possible to demonstrate that aspects of the Third Crusade presaged the religious revival and enthusiasm overseen by Pope Innocent III. In relation to social factors, this book considers the degree to which crusading permeated the fabric of elite culture and its place in class structures against the emerging social frame proposed by Ernst-Dieter Hehl and especially the interaction between lay nobles and their relations in the Church.[60]

From this review of the academic context, it can be seen that analysis of participation in the Third Crusade allows for consideration of key questions regarding the development of crusading and Christianity, as well as the

---

[56] The terms, traditionalist, pluralist, populist, and generalist are discussed by Giles Constable in his influential article 'The Historiography of the Crusades', *The Crusades from the Perspective of Byzantium and the Muslim World*, ed. A.E. Laiou and R.P. Mottahedeh (Washington, DC, 2001), pp. 1–22.

[57] H.E. Mayer, *The Crusades*, 2nd edition, trans. J. Gillingham (Oxford, 1988); J. Riley-Smith, *What Were the Crusades?* 4th edition (Basingstoke, 2009).

[58] G. Dickson, *The Children's Crusade: Medieval History, Modern Mythistory* (New York, 2008).

[59] E.-D. Hehl, 'War, Peace and Christian Order', *The New Cambridge Medieval History*, Vol. 4/1, ed. D. Luscombe and J. Riley-Smith (Cambridge, 2004), p. 210.

[60] Hehl, 'Christian Order', pp. 185–228.

opportunity to gain insight into medieval elite society immediately before the innovations of Innocent III.[61] This research extends and tests the conclusions of previous works within the frame of the Third Crusade and contributes to a broader understanding of the crusading movement and its place in certain medieval cultures.

Mapping Patterns of Participation

The ability to carry out this study relied on the successful development of a database of crusaders for the period 1187 to 1192, that is to say, those who took the Cross and/or joined the Third Crusade from north-western Europe after the issue of the papal bull *Audita tremendi* by Gregory VIII on 29 October 1187 through to the departure of the remaining crusaders marked by Richard I leaving the Holy Land on 9 October 1192. Thus, it contains names, titles, relationships, and events drawn from primary sources to identify and locate individuals chronologically and spatially, to establish in whose retinue they travelled or under whose banner they fought, when they were in a given location and why.

From an overall pool of over one thousand persons of potential interest, this data is used to consider the flow of 583 identifiable participants in the Third Crusade from north-western Europe, to detect critical actors, locations and pathways (physical and conceptual), and to track established, emerging, and changing groupings during the course of the expedition. Relevant extracts from the full database are presented in the two appendices including evidence drawn from charters, letters, and narrative sources.

By the twelfth century, written documents had become essential in economic and legal transactions. Indeed, although oral contracts remained binding, it had become accepted that the long-term validity of agreements depended on the survival of their written documentation.[62] The database depends on evidence drawn from such charters, official records, letters, and existing research, the starting point for which was the immensely valuable British Academy 'Acta of the Plantagenets' research project and *Diplomata Belgica: The Diplomatic Sources from the Medieval Southern Low Countries*, as well as the *Revised Regesta Regni Hierosolymitani* (RRRH).[63]

---

[61] For more on Richard's influence on Innocent III see V. Ryan, 'Richard I and the Early Evolution of the Fourth Crusade', *The Fourth Crusade: Event, Aftermath, and Perceptions*, ed. T. Madden (Aldershot, 2008), pp. 3–14.
[62] See, for example, Leah Shopkow's introduction; Lambert of Ardres, *The History of the Counts of Guines and Lords of Ardres*, trans. L. Shopkow (Philadelphia, 2007), pp. 4–5.
[63] The edition of the *acta* of Henry II is in preparation for publication by Oxford University Press: *The Letters and Charters of Henry II, King of England 1154–1189*, ed. N. Vincent. I am very grateful to Professor Nicholas Vincent for making his material on

Giles Constable pioneered the use of charters to investigate crusader finance and attitudes, as well as form the basis of broader prosopographical work.[64] Here, charters have been cross-referenced with data from medieval narratives, primarily chronicles. Data is critically assessed as research indicates that inconsistencies in the naming of individuals and places are to be found even within a single source.[65] Protocols have been established to resolve the standardisation of names and places, as well as the categorisation of crusaders, pilgrims, and those in the Holy Land who seemingly had not taken the Cross.[66]

Social Network Analysis is employed for the methodological consideration of the data. The social network is conceptualised as a graph, that is, a set of nodes (or vertices, units, points) representing social actors or objects and a set of ties (or lines, arcs, links) representing one or more social relations among them, as shown in Figure 1.

These noble elite subjects are treated as individual nodes and the ties between them are based on inter-relations by event, regional background, kinship connections, links to the Holy Land, affiliations to religious orders, membership of higher status households, and other potential influences such as previous familial participation in a crusade. The number of connections increases the relative strength of a tie between two subjects. Table 1 illustrates links between ten actors based on just two such types of connection: religious affiliation[67] and their presence at notable events, such as the cross-taking ceremony near Gisors in 1188.

Henry II and Richard I available, without which this study could not have been written. For *Diplomata Belgica* see http://www.diplomata-belgica.be/colophon_en.html.

[64] G. Constable, 'The Second Crusade as Seen by Contemporaries', *Traditio*, 9 (1953), 213–79; 'The Financing of the Crusades in the Twelfth Century', *Outremer*, ed. B. Kedar et al. (Jerusalem, 1982), pp. 64–88; 'Medieval Charters as a Source for the History of the Crusades', *Crusade and Settlement*, ed. P. Edbury (Cardiff, 1985), pp. 73–89.

[65] A single name without a context is rarely sufficient to identify someone. As the distinguished diplomatic historian, Paul Kehr, wrote, 'the name Leo was as common in medieval Rome as blackberries in England': *Ueber eine römische Papyrusurkunde im Staatsarchiv zu Marburg* (Berlin, 1896), p. 17. For naming traditions in the Latin East see R. Hiestand, 'Der lateinische Klerus in den Kreuzfahrerstaaten: Geographische Herkunft und politische Rolle', *Die Kreuzfahrerstaaten als multikulturelle Gesellschaft: Einwanderer und Minderheiten im 12. und 13. Jahrhundert*, ed. H.E. Mayer (Munich, 1997), pp. 51–2.

[66] When it comes to avoiding identification errors, *cognomina* are very useful. At least seven different types of cognomina can be distinguished, namely an additional first name, a patronym, a family name, a toponym, a personal characteristic, a title pertaining to an office, and a former title retained as a *cognomen*. For a broadly similar approach to *cognomina* see P. Josserand, *Église et pouvoir dans la péninsule ibérique: Les orders militaires dans le royaume de Castille, 1252–1369* (Madrid, 2004), pp. 382–90.

[67] In the study connection by religious affiliation is further filtered by the specific religious house, e.g., a link to the Cistercians of Barbeau is distinguished from an association with their house at Notre-Dame of Ourscamp.

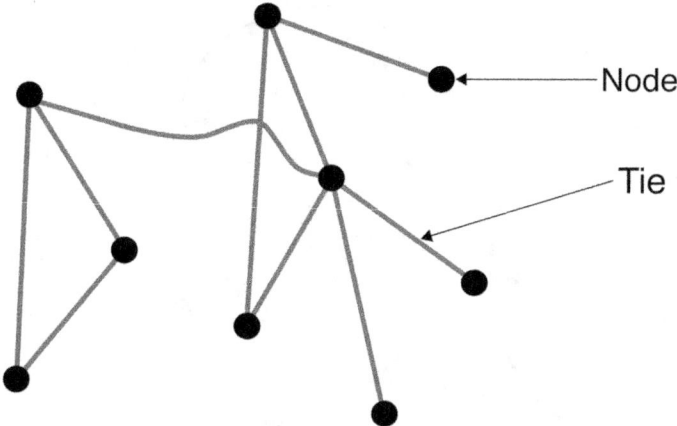

Fig. 1. Nodes and Ties

Table 1. Connections by Religious Affiliation and Notable Events

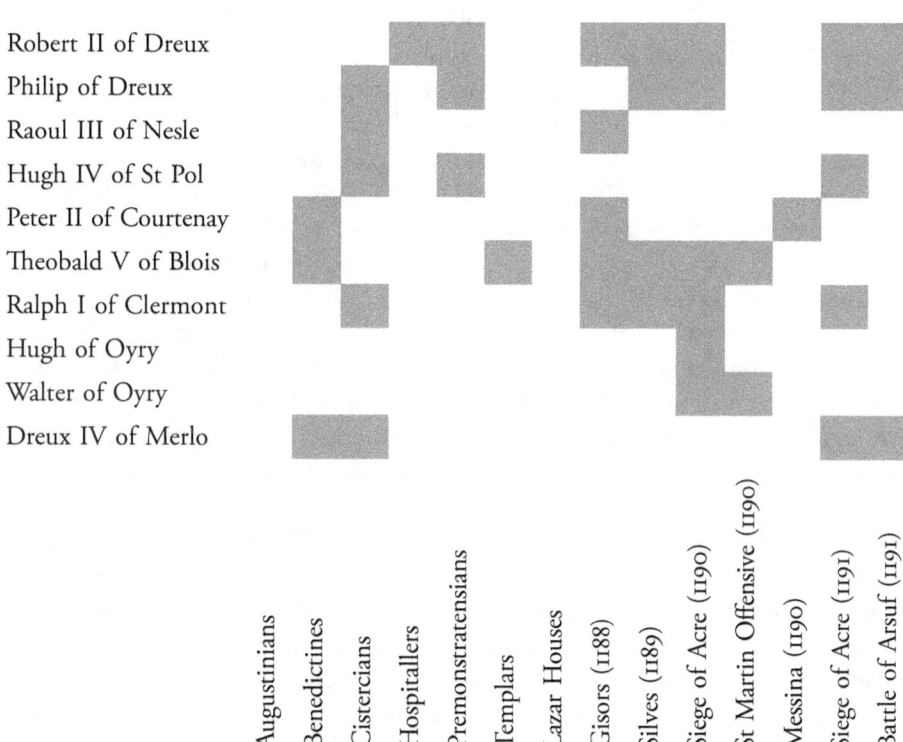

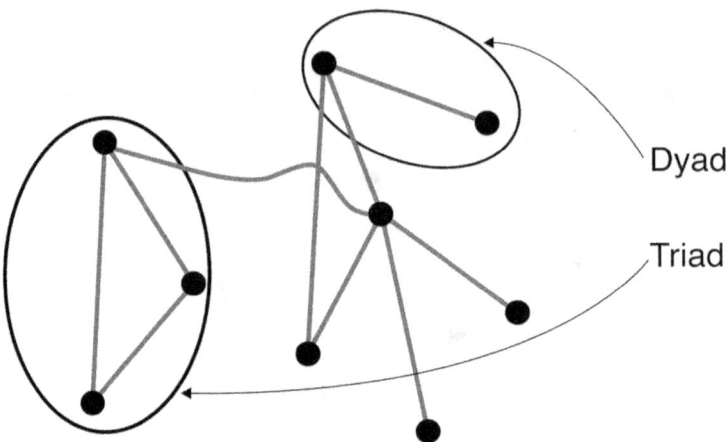

Fig. 2. Dyads and Triads

Analysis of the ties focuses on network topology, the arrangement of the various elements of the structure, and includes connections: the number of content forms in a tie (the number and variety of links between two actors), the extent to which actors form ties with similar versus dissimilar others, the extent to which two actors reciprocate each other's interactions, the completeness of relationship dyads and triads (groups of two and three actors) (Figure 2), and the impact of locality on ties.

In the context of networks, social capital exists where people have an advantage because of their location in a network. Contacts in a network provide information, opportunities, and perspectives that can be beneficial to the central player in the network. Most social structures tend to be characterised by dense clusters of strong connections with opinion and behaviour more homogenous within than between groups, which has implications for the organisation of coalition forces, such as both the Latin and Muslim armies of the Third Crusade. In social networks, tie strength is based on attributing values to ties based on the efficiency, regularity, and robustness of the tie.

The analysis also studies distributions: tie strength, distance, bridges, centrality, density, and structural holes. Distance considers high values to represent closeness and a bridge is a direct tie between nodes that would otherwise be disconnected components of the network (Figure 3). Bridges are used to transmit information from one group to another. Centrality measures the relative importance of an actor within the network and density refers to the relative number of ties in a network or part of that network – both of which are important in analysing an actor's potential ability to influence others, for example, with people connected across groups more familiar with alternative ways of thinking and behaving.

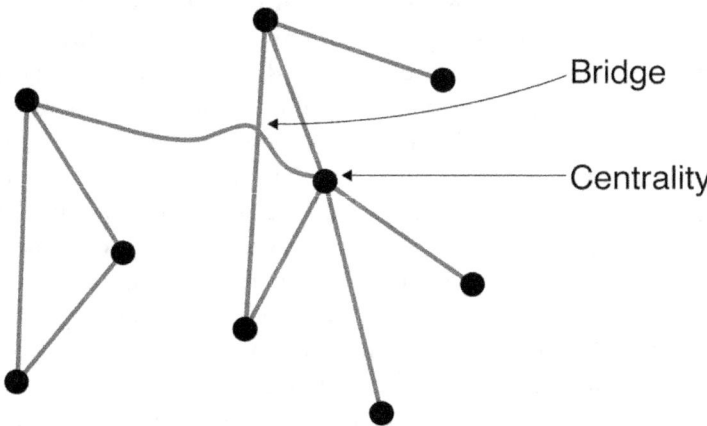

Fig. 3. Bridges and Centrality

The final aspect is segmentation: cliques (where all the nodes are linked to one another), cohesion, and, especially, the identification of clusters (of nodes). Information within these clusters tends to be rather homogeneous and redundant. Non-redundant information is most often obtained through contacts in different clusters, and actors on the periphery or less deeply immersed are well placed to innovate, such as introduce alternative military tactics or adopt different approaches to siege-craft. When two separate clusters possess non-redundant information, there is said to be a structural hole between them. An ideal network structure for a cohesive and adaptive military collation has a vine and cluster structure, providing access to many different clusters and structural holes.[68]

The social network does not ignore non-human actors. Inspired by Bruno Latour's work on Actor-Network Theory, the relationship between traditional actors, such as the European nobles, and non-human actors, such as religious foundations, is an important element in this study.[69] This introduces the key distinction between intermediaries that were responsible for the diffusion of crusade ideology and mediators for participation in crusades, which is used to evaluate ideas and concepts at the heart of the crusader movement.[70]

---

[68] See B. Reynold, *Structural Holes: The Social Structure of Competition* (Cambridge, MA, 1992).
[69] B. Latour, *Reassembling the Social: An Introduction to Actor-Network-Theory* (Oxford, 2005), pp. 10–11.
[70] An intermediary is something that 'transports meaning or force without transformation'. Mediators, on the other hand, 'transform, translate, distort, and modify the meaning or the elements they are supposed to carry', Latour, *Reassembling the Social*, p. 39.

On Chronicles, Letters, Charters, and Other Sources

The availability of data has imposed certain limitations on this study of elite networks. The majority of sources can be divided into three groups. Most important due to the quantity of surviving examples are the ecclesiastical records, and cartularies of the monasteries and priories are included in this category. They provide abundant material on the nobility, even beyond their dealings with the clergy. Incidental references to family structures, property ownership, crusading activity, and the management of estates, found in such collections of charters are essential raw material for the social historian. However, not all cartularies are equally useful. The language of charters tends to follow a formulaic and uniform format, which can obscure the intentions of the donor. Similarly, scribes could frequently omit or delete words and sentences without vitiating the original intent of a document. Such 'unnecessary' phrases would constitute valuable data for a reconstruction of an elite network. Therefore, great caution is necessary in the employment of these documents and the guidance provided by eighteenth- and nineteenth-century editors is not always reliable.

Unfortunately, many such records have been lost to the vagaries of natural and man-made disasters, such as war, civil uprising, and fire. In addition, the relative poverty of a region could limit the surviving sources. While French archives escaped such singular disasters as the Cotton Fire of 1731, many charters were seemingly lost from particular religious houses or in some *départements* during their transfer to state archives after the French Revolution in 1789.[71] Further, the French archival data is heavily weighted towards religious houses, with little material on individual actors surviving the widespread destruction of aristocratic property during the Revolution. Theft and poor maintenance of the charters over the succeeding centuries was compounded by the destruction of material during both World Wars.[72]

Administrative records make up the second group of source materials. These are predominantly of English, Flemish, and French origin, but the realms of north-western Europe were in the process of developing effective systems of maintaining official records and progress was uneven. The survival of exchequer accounts detailing royal logistical preparations for the

---

[71] Sir Robert Cotton (1571–1631) was an antiquary and one of the greatest British collectors of historical manuscripts. His library was vast and of huge national significance, and formed the foundation collection of the British Library. By 1731, the collection was stored at Ashburnham House in London, adjacent to Westminster School, as its previous location had been regarded as a fire hazard. On the night of 23 October 1731, a fire broke out and despite the efforts of the Deputy Librarian and others, a great number of the Cotton manuscripts were badly damaged by the flames or the water used to extinguish the fire, and a few volumes were destroyed in their entirety. Many unique manuscripts were lost for good, such as Asser's biography of King Alfred of Wessex; S.A.P. Murray, *The Library: An Illustrated History* (Chicago, 2009).

[72] For a full review of the survival of Angevin charters, see *Acta*, pp. 26–32.

expedition and recording exemptions from taxation for crusaders, records of juries summoned to determine the lands or heirs of deceased crusaders, and plea rolls recording the claims of widows for their dower lands, as well as trials to determine other land disputes involving a crusader ensure that England, and to a lesser extent Normandy, supply a disproportionate amount of surviving data, which must be taken into account when analysing the results. Moreover, charters and their witness lists can be problematic. While they are legal documents, they do not always survive in the best of condition and some have been identified as forgeries.[73]

Finally, there are the narrative accounts of the period. 'Universal histories', such as those of the English chronicler, Roger of Howden, or biographies like that written on Philip Augustus of France by Rigord, chaplain and physician at Saint-Denis in Paris, often contain local details that were of an immense benefit to this study. However, the distribution of chronicles and vernacular sources is also uneven. The participation of a king of England led to a surge in accounts of the Third Crusade from parts of the Angevin realm.[74] While Poitou, for example, seemingly failed to produce a single one, narratives from England and Normandy have ensured that we are particularly well informed about the identity of crusaders from the northern part of the Angevin realm, as well as their exploits in the Holy Land. Particular attention has been paid to the location, background, and potential motivations of the author, with due heed given to possible literary distortions.[75]

Roger of Howden, for example, was an English royal clerk who arrived in Acre sometime after October 1190 with leading elements of the Angevin fleet and left with King Philip Augustus in August 1191.[76] He wrote the *Chronica* and almost certainly authored the earlier and less polished *Gesta*

---

[73] An infamous example of such forgeries is the Courtois Archive; J. Sayers, 'English Charters from the Third Crusade', *Tradition and Change: Essays in Honour of Marjorie Chibnall Presented by Her Friends on the Occasion of Her Seventieth Birthday*, ed. D. Greenway, C. Holdsworth, and J. Sayers (Cambridge, 1985), p. 197; and R.-H. Bautier, 'La collection des chartes de croisade dite "collection Courtois"', *Comptes-rendus des séances de l'Académie des Inscriptions et Belles Lettres*, 100 (1956), 382–6.

[74] M. Staunton, *The Historians of Angevin England* (Oxford, 2017).

[75] See, for example, *Chronicle of the Third Crusade: The Itinerarium Peregrinorum et Gesta Regis Ricardi*, trans. H.J. Nicholson (Aldershot, 1997), pp. 6–15; R. Bartlett, *Gerald of Wales, 1146–1223* (Oxford, 1982), pp. 58–100; J. Gillingham, 'Historians Without Hindsight: Coggeshall, Diceto and Howden on the Early Years of John's Reign', *King John, New Interpretations*, ed. S.D. Church (Woodbridge, 1999), pp. 1–26; D.A. Carpenter, 'Abbot Ralph of Coggeshall's Account of the Last Years of King Richard and the First Years of King John', *EHR*, 113 (1998), 1210–30.

[76] J. Gillingham, 'Roger of Howden on Crusade', *Medieval Historical Writing in the Christian and Islamic Worlds*, ed. D.O. Morgan (London, 1983), pp. 60–75, and D. Crouch, 'At Home with Roger of Howden', *Military Cultures and Martial Enterprises in the Middle Ages: Essays in Honour of Richard P. Abels*, ed. J.D. Hosler and S. Isaac (Woodbridge, 2020), pp. 156–76.

Regis Henrici Secundi et Gesta Regis Ricardi.[77] Both works share an obvious focus on the Angevin contingent and generally present a favourable impression of both King Richard and Guy of Lusignan, king of Jerusalem.[78] Howden also authored *De viis maris* – an account of his journey from Yorkshire to Acre in 1190.[79]

The accounts of the battle of Acre of 4 October 1189 in both the *Gesta Regis* and *Chronica* also seem to be closely related to a work of prose that William Stubbs included in his edition of the *Chronica*, but first printed by John Basil Herold in 1549. The manuscript identified the author as Monachus, a Florentine who was bishop of Caesarea between 1181 and 1192, and then patriarch of Jerusalem until 1202.[80] Lines 37–48 of the poem indicate that Monachus arrived at Acre in October 1189 as part of the bishop of Verona's contingent and he was not particularly associated with either of the rival claimants to the throne of Jerusalem: Guy of Lusignan or Conrad of Montferrat.[81]

Data from each narrative was assessed, therefore, on the overall consistency of the writer and the ability to cross-reference the material with other sources. Moreover, the reliability of a source was not considered as fixed as it could vary according to the proximity of the author to the particular actor or event being reported, as well as other variables. Returning to Roger of Howden, while one of our most trustworthy sources, he has been treated here as most reliable when describing affiliations with King Richard prior to his departure on the Third Crusade and when he was likely with the king's court in Messina, than when covering the early stages of the siege of Acre and events in the Levant following Howden's probable departure in early August 1191.[82]

Richard of Devizes was a Benedictine monk at St Swithun's Priory, Winchester, but seemingly had access to information from someone who

---

[77] D.M. Stenton, 'Roger of Howden and Benedict', *EHR*, 68 (1953), 574–82; Staunton, *Historians of Angevin England*, pp. 53–4; Roger of Howden, *Gesta Regis Henrici Secundi et Gesta Regis Ricardi Benedicti abbatis*, 2 vols, ed. W. Stubbs (London, 1867); Roger of Howden, *Chronica*, 4 Vols., ed. W. Stubbs (London, 1868–71).

[78] *Gesta Regis*, Vol. 1, pp. 343, 359.

[79] Crouch, 'At Home with Howden', p. 157.

[80] See *De recuperatione Ptolemaidae* (On the Recovery of Ptolemais – Acre), *Chronica*, Vol. 3, pp. cv–cvi, note the discussion on authorship, p. cv. The work is also known as Haymari Monachi, *De expugnata Accone. Liber tetrastichus seu Rithmus de expeditione Ierosolimitana*, ed. P.E. Riant (Paris, 1886). See also, *Der 'Rithmus de expeditione Ierosolimitana' des sogenannten Haymarus Monachus Florentinus*, ed. S. Falk, trans. into Italian A. Placanica and S. Falk (Florence, 2006). I am working on a full translation of Stubbs's edition for future publication.

[81] See also J.D. Hosler, 'The Siege of Acre (1189–1191) in the Historiographical Tradition', *History Compass*, 16/5 (2018), 2.

[82] Gillingham, 'Howden on Crusade', pp. 60–75.

had travelled with the Angevin contingent as far as Sicily, but who then returned with Eleanor of Aquitaine and Walter of Coutances, archbishop of Rouen.[83] Ralph of Diss (Ralph of Diceto), dean of St Paul's Cathedral, was similarly not an eyewitness. His chaplain, however, participated in the Third Crusade and his letters and recollections formed the basis of Ralph's account. In addition, Ralph was closely associated with both Walter of Coutances and King Richard's chancellor, William of Longchamp, giving him access to the highest levels of the Angevin court.[84] Ralph of Coggeshall also based his account on the information gleaned from returning crusaders: in this case, Hugh of Neville and, King Richard's chaplain, Anselm.

The main source written from a Capetian perspective is Rigord's 'enthusiastic' biography of King Philip II, but some of his material can be cross-referenced with Gilbert of Mons, court chaplain and then chancellor to Count Baldwin V of Hainaut. Gilbert provides a wealth of information on crusaders from the Low Countries, especially Hainaut, but also France in his *Chronicon Hanoniense*.[85]

Besides accounts in the chronicles of Richard of Devizes, Ralph of Diss, Gilbert of Mons and others, works like the *Itinerarium Peregrinorum et Gesta Regis Ricardi* (*Itinerarium*) and Ambroise's *Estoire de la Guerre Sainte* provide a preponderance of detail. In 1864 Stubbs published an edition of an anonymously authored eyewitness account of the Third Crusade entitled the *Itinerarium Peregrinorum et Gesta Regis Ricardi*. The first book of the *Itinerarium* provides a summary of events in Palestine before the arrival Philip II and Richard at Acre. Hans Mayer demonstrated that this section was an independent work that followed another eyewitness account written between 1191 and 1192 by an anonymous author, which he called the *Itinerarium Peregrinorum* or IP1.[86] Helen Nicholson initially described this author as a compiler at work in the crusader camp from 1 August 1191 to 2 September 1192 who based their work on oral information and reports permeating the camp.[87] Based on close analysis of the text, she has subsequently revised this timeframe to 19 November 1190 to 2 January 1191 – between the deaths of

---

[83] For a lively description of Richard, see P. Allen, 'Richard of Devizes and the Alleged Martyrdom of a Boy at Winchester', *Transactions & Miscellanies* (Jewish Historical Society of England), 27 (1978–1980), 32–39.
[84] A. Gransden, *Historical Writing in England c.550 to c.1307* (London, 1974), pp. 230–1.
[85] For Gilbert's perspectives on warfare and other contextual information, see, J. France, 'Gilbert of Mons' Chronicle of Hainaut as a Source for Military History in the Twelfth Century', *Military Cultures and Martial Enterprises in the Middle Ages: Essays in Honour of Richard P. Abels*, ed. J.D. Hosler and S. Isaac (Woodbridge, 2020), pp. 136–55.
[86] 89 *Das Itinerarium Peregrinorum, Ein Zeitgenössiche Englische Chronik zum Dritten Kreuzzug in Ursprünglisher Gestalt*, ed. H.E. Mayer (Stuttgart, 1962).
[87] *Chronicle of the Third Crusade*, trans. Nicholson, pp. 6–10.

the Baldwin of Forde, archbishop of Canterbury, and Duke Frederick VI of Swabia.[88]

The authorship of IP1 is problematic: an early version carried the name of Geoffrey of Vinsauf, but Bishop Stubbs attributed the work to Richard of Templo, prior of Holy Trinity (an Augustinian priory in London), who he suggested had been a Templar chaplain serving in the Holy Land during the course of the Third Crusade.[89] However, Hannes Möhring has argued persuasively that, while the author had probably been on the Third Crusade, the evidence does not support his having been a Templar. Möhring also renamed the work *Historia Hierosolimitana*, claiming *Itinerarium Peregrinorum* was a misleading title. Whilst John D. Hosler initially suggested that he may have been a monk based in Tyre, the emphasis the author placed on members of King Richard's contingent at the siege of Acre and the pro-Angevin tone of the narrative indicates that he was most likely an English crusader – a position that is supported by Helen Nicholson – and Hosler remains open to him being the prior of Holy Trinity in London.[90] Nicholson argues that the author was a cleric or clerics in the service of the Archbishop Baldwin, tasked to replace Gerald of Wales in producing a prose history of the crusade to accompany Joseph of Exeter's verse account.[91]

Richard of Templo is generally accepted to be the author of the second section (IP2), written in the period 1217–22.[92] As well as borrowing from Roger of Howden and Ralph of Diss, IP2 seemingly has a relationship with *L'Estoire de la Guerre Sainte*, but Richard of Templo adds invaluable additional material that indicates that he had also most likely been on the Third Crusade, perhaps prior to joining the Augustinian Order.[93] It is probable that he also travelled with the main body of King Richard's contingent, arriving in Acre in 1191.[94]

---

[88] H.J. Nicholson, 'The Construction of a Primary Source. The Creation of *Itinerarium Peregrinorum* 1', *Cahiers de recherches médiévales et humanistes*, 37 (2019), 160.

[89] *Chronicles of the Crusades: Contemporary Narratives of the Crusade of Richard Coeur de Lion by Richard of Devizes and Geoffrey of Vinsauf and of the Crusade of Saint Louis by the Lord John of Joinville*, ed. H. Bohn (London, 1848), pp. iii–v.

[90] Hosler, 'Historiographical Tradition', p. 3 and 'Embedded Reporters? Ambroise, Richard de Templo, and Roger of Howden on the Third Crusade', *Military Cultures and Martial Enterprises in the Middle Ages: Essays in Honour of Richard P. Abels*, ed. J.D. Hosler and S. Isaac (Woodbridge, 2020), p. 184. See also H. Möhring, 'Eine Chronik aus der Zeit des dritten Kreuzzugs: das sogenannte *Itinerarium Peregrinorum* 1', *Innsbrucker Historische Studien*, 5 (1982), 149–62.

[91] Nicholson, 'Construction of a Primary Source', 143–65.

[92] *Itinerarium*, pp. xlvii–iii; Mayer, *Das Itinerarium Peregrinorum*, pp. 94–6.

[93] *Chronicle of the Third Crusade*, trans. Nicholson, pp. 12–14.

[94] J.D. Hosler, *The Siege of Acre, 1189–1191: Saladin, Richard the Lionheart, and the Battle that Decided the Third Crusade* (New Haven and London, 2018), p. 18; for detailed

Gaston Paris published *L'Estoire de la Guerre Sainte* in 1897, from a manuscript dated approximately to the late thirteenth century. Paris conceded that lines 2387–4568, which relate to events in Acre between 1187 and 1191, correspond with IP1. The remainder was an original composition, written in Norman-French prior to 1199, which he attributed to a jongleur called Ambroise.[95] The text indicates that Ambroise was part of Richard's contingent and his poem also presents a distinctly pro-Angevin perspective. Marianne Ailes has suggested that he may have been a Norman cleric who arrived in the Holy Land around the same time as King Richard (June 1191), which is borne out by this study.[96] For the siege of Acre, Ambroise seemingly drew from very similar eyewitness accounts to IP1.[97] Though IP1 is more expansive, both seem to correspond with Monachus' poem and may well have shared a connection to it. Hosler has also highlighted links to Howden's accounts, placing Ambroise, Richard of Templo, and Howden in Acre at the same time.[98]

In addition to the uneven distribution of source material, the limitations are two-fold. Only a handful of local documents are of non-religious origin. We thus lack significant evidence of a lay perspective, and this is difficult to reconstruct. Official records provide some assistance in this area, offering greater insight into the interactions of various members or groups of the nobility. Political motivation and certain social forces must remain somewhat obscure, however. Analogies drawn from the clerical order are not always sound and serve only as unverifiable hypotheses. Secondly, the extant documents reveal very little about the spiritual, ritual, and mental landscape of the nobility. Actual practices remain hidden, as do convictions on allegiance, government, independence, and justice. This can make analysis somewhat impersonal, and only exceptionally active and powerful individuals emerge from the historical fog. However, as will be demon-

---

study on the location of Richard de Templo during the Third Crusade, see, Hosler, 'Embedded Reporters?', pp. 177–91.

[95] *Estoire*, ed. Paris, pp. vi–xii.

[96] She also highlights the frequent presence of Andrew of Chauvigny in Ambroise's account, M.J. Ailes, 'Heroes of War: Ambroise's Heroes of the Third Crusade', *Writing War: Medieval Literary Responses to Warfare*, ed. C. Saunders, F. Le Saux, and N. Thomas (Cambridge, 2004), p. 29; Ambroise, *The History of the Holy War, Ambroise's Estoire de la Guerre Sainte, II. Translation*, trans. M. Ailes (Woodbridge, 2003), pp. 1–3. This has been contested by Françoise Vielliard who, based on a study of the representation of the Norman contingent in the *Itinerarium* and *Estoire*, concluded that Ambroise was more likely to hail from another region of Angevin France; Vielliard, 'Entourage normand', pp. 7–26; See also M. Bennett, 'Stereotype Normans in Old French Vernacular Literature', *ANS*, 19 (1987), 26.

[97] See, M. Bull, *Eyewitness and Crusade Narrative: Perception and Narration in Accounts of the Second, Third, and Fourth Crusades* (Woodbridge, 2018), pp. 219–55.

[98] Hosler, 'Embedded Reporters?', pp. 182–91.

strated, Social Network Analysis allows us a fresh opportunity to consider themes such as motivation and loyalty.

The Noble Crusaders

To present the potential influences on the noble crusaders, the book is organised into three thematic chapters and a case study. The first chapter considers the impact of the concept of *imitatio Christi* on the motivation to join the Third Crusade. After reviewing the content of surviving recruiting sermons, the chapter considers the relationship between religious orders and those who joined the expedition to argue that reformed houses and the Military Orders were closely linked to crusading. By analysing the effect of the Saladin Tithe on financial support to crusaders from religious foundations, gifts made to abbeys, monasteries, commanderies, and so on by those who had taken the Cross after the fall of Jerusalem in 1187 can be better understood, especially in relation to the personal convictions of crusaders and the role of certain institutions as intermediaries for the dissemination of crusade-related concepts. As well as considering the role of prominent ecclesiastical magnates, the chapter studies the consequences of links between crusaders, religious foundations, and senior clerics on royal preparations for the crusade.

Having established familial influences on links to religious houses, the second thematic chapter analyses the degree to which crusading had permeated the fabric of elite society in north-western Europe by identifying specific kinship networks. In addition to considering how crusader preaching also focused on lineage and kinship, this chapter investigates, first, the degree to which participants in the Third Crusade enjoyed a crusader heritage or pedigree (that is to say that their immediate ancestors had joined a previous expedition), and second, those who were joined on the Third Crusade by close relations: fathers, uncles, brothers, cousins, and in-laws. This data is also used to address once more the potential influence of women on inheritance and as mediators for crusading, that is, by persuading, prompting, or inspiring members of their families to join the expedition.

The third theme is the meaning and consequences of locality on the Third Crusade. By focusing on communities – both real and imagined – this chapter considers the diversity of the links between members of the elite network of north-western Europe. In addition to sharing associations to specific religious foundations or orders, and enjoying ties of kinship and a crusading ancestry, this chapter analyses the extent to which participants on the Third Crusade were also trading partners, neighbours, and comrades in arms.

Finally, the role of the noble household or *familia* is analysed by focusing on King Richard's royal household during the course of the Third Crusade and placing it within the broader crusader network to consider how it might be behind the very different results for the Angevin realm and non-Angevin France. Whilst the Anglo-Norman contingent on the Second Crusade was numerous enough to require 150–200 ships to carry it from Dartmouth to Lisbon, only a minority travelled on to the Holy Land.[99] This was not to be the case in regard to the Third Crusade, where the overwhelming majority continued on to Palestine. Unlike other parts of north-western Europe, such as Champagne, this was to be the first crusade to the Holy Land involving significant numbers of noble elites from England, Normandy, and Anjou. While other military households had joined their lords on the crusade, such as that of King Louis VII of France in 1147, Richard was the first king of England to fulfil his crusading vow by fighting in the Holy Land.

The final chapter draws together the principal themes of the book by highlighting the influences of faith, family, locality, and patronage in Richard's household, as well as illustrating the role of complex power relationships and investigating matters of loyalty. It demonstrates the importance of maintaining stability within a crusading household, especially as part of a potentially fractious coalition army. But most important was the need at every level to make careful provision to secure one's lands and maintain status at home while absent on crusade.

The case study also illustrates a medieval military household acting in all its diversity, with members serving as diplomats, councillors, and liaison officers as much as mounted combatants. Although defining themselves by their military function as heavy cavalrymen, the final chapter shows the variety of administrative, political, and diplomatic skills knights (and potential knights) were expected to master if they were to find favour and position in north-western Europe.[100]

Whilst there remains space for a comprehensive history of the Third Crusade, this book offers important insights into why people may have taken the Cross and undertaken the hazardous journey to Palestine in the late 1180s. Data drawn from charters and letters, supports eyewitness accounts that the loss of Jerusalem in 1187 reverberated across Latin Christendom and was a powerful stimulus to participation, but through the employment of Social Network Analysis and prosopographical techniques we can better identify the influence of social factors on motivations, such as heritage and kinship, as well as community – both physical and imagined.

---

[99] Arnulf and Stephen of Mandeville are obvious exceptions, as are William Peverel and Philip, son of Robert, earl of Gloucester; J.D. Hosler, 'Why Didn't King Stephen Crusade?', *Travels and Mobilities in the Middle Ages: From the Atlantic to the Black Sea*, ed. M. O'Doherty and F. Schmieder (Turnhout, 2015), pp. 121–44.

[100] See also D. Simpkin, 'The Organisation of Chivalric Society', *A Companion to Chivalry*, ed. R.W. Jones and P. Coss (Woodbridge, 2019), pp. 46–7.

These approaches also allow us better to understand the influences of faith and spirituality, especially the concept of following in Christ's footsteps in relation to the Third Crusade.

At the core of this book lies the argument that crusading displayed a high degree of social assortativity, a preference for actors to attach to others that are similar in some way. This is balanced, however, by recognition of the dangers of assuming that influences, such as dynastic crusading traditions and ties of lordship, applied equally to all that took the Cross.[101]

---

[101] See Lower, *The Barons' Crusade*.

1

Faith and Finance: Religious Foundations, Ecclesiastical Leaders, and Fraternity

> Therefore indeed the soldiers of Christ sign themselves with the sign of the cross on the body, sign on the heart, sign externally by the image, sign internally by penance; they bear the cross of Christ not with Simon [of Cyrene] as an obligation, but with Christ in patience; with the right-hand robber in penance, not with the left-hand [robber] in violence.[1]
>
> Alan of Lille, 1189

This chapter demonstrates that, along with the recovery of Jerusalem, the concept of following in Christ's footsteps (*imitatio Christi*) was a significant influence on motivation to take the Cross and join the Third Crusade. Whilst it is a topic that has not gone unnoticed by historians, the question of crusader spirituality in relation to participants in this expedition has either received little attention or has been subordinated to emphasis on the roles of the Great Men.[2]

Jean Leclercq introduced the idea that the crusades should be considered as part of the same process that brought about twelfth-century religious reform, including the foundation of the Military Orders and reformed orders, such as the Cistercians and Premonstratensians.[3] The intersection between monastic reform and crusading has been evidenced in a number of studies.[4] It is a theme that is reflected in Jonathan Riley-Smith's argument that the First Crusade was considered by some contemporaries to be

---

[1] 'Eia, ergo, milites Christi signent se signo crucis in corpore, signent in corde, signent exterius per figuram, signent interius per penitentiam; ferant crucem Christi, non cum Symone in angaria, sed cum Christo in patientia, cum dextro latrone in penitentia, non cum sinistro in violentia': *Alain de Lille: Textes inédits, avec une introduction sur sa vie et ses oeuvres*, ed. M.-T. d'Alverney (Paris, 1965), no. 50, p. 281.
[2] Constable, 'Historiography of the Crusades', pp. 1–22.
[3] J. Leclercq, 'The New Orders', *The Spirituality of the Middle Ages*, ed. J. Leclercq, F. Vandenbroucke, and L. Bouyer (London, 1968), pp. 127–61.
[4] See, for example; J. Leclercq, 'Monaschisme et peregrination du XIe au XIIe siècle', *Studia monastica*, 3 (1961), 33–52; B. Hamilton, 'Ideals of Holiness: Crusaders, Contem-

'a military monastery on the move'.[5] Similarly, in his study of the religious practices of members of the military elite, Marcus Bull identified the close relationship between transactions with religious institutions and those beliefs that generated enthusiasm for a crusade.[6]

Giles Constable also placed the devotions of crusaders firmly within the framework of overall medieval religious practice.[7] Rather than focusing purely on the professed religious – monks and canons – he suggested that historians should place religious experience at the centre. He argued that a pilgrimage or a crusade 'might fill as profound a need in some people as a lifetime of reciting psalms or enclosed in a cell did for others'.[8] In his study of crusading spirituality, William Purkis established the crucial importance of the ideal of *imitatio Christi* to crusading spirituality, and he bridged the gap identified by Constable between crusading, pilgrimage, and monasticism.[9] His study stressed that the penitential aspects of a crusade were intimately associated with the ideas of pilgrimage and following in the footsteps of Christ, and that they served to distinguish crusading from other forms of penitential warfare. While Purkis identified attempts to shift the emphasis of Christo-mimesis away from crusaders and towards the Templars from the 1140s onwards, his period of study closes at 1187: a year he presented as a juncture when the aim of recovering Jerusalem became the specific focus of crusading activity in the Holy Land.[10] This is a theme that is analysed in this chapter.

In contrast to the view Riley-Smith expressed in 1986 that 'crusading was becoming markedly less monastic by 1200', this chapter presents the continuing spirituality of participants in the Third Crusade.[11] After a brief review of surviving Third Crusade preaching, links between identifiable crusaders and religious institutions are analysed, as is the role of ecclesiastical magnates in the prosecution of the crusade. The emphasis placed by north-western European princes on support to religious institutions is analysed to show how, in notable cases, reformed houses and their donors were at the forefront of preparations for the expedition to the Holy Land.

---

platives, and Mendicants', *International History Review*, 17 (1995), 693–712; G. Constable, 'The Place of the Crusader in Medieval Society', *Viator*, 29 (1998), 377–403.

[5] J. Riley-Smith, *The First Crusade and the Idea of Crusading* (London, 1986), p. 2. See also, A. Dupont, 'La spiritualité des croisés et des pèlerins d'après les sources de la première croisade', *Pellegrinaggi e culto dei santi in Europa fina alla la crociata* (Todi, 1963), pp. 451–83.

[6] Bull, *Knightly Piety*, p. 280.

[7] G. Constable, *The Reformation of the Twelfth Century* (Cambridge, 1996).

[8] Constable, *Reformation*, pp. 86–7.

[9] W.J. Purkis, *Crusading Spirituality in the Holy Land and Iberia, c.1095–c.1187* (Woodbridge, 2008).

[10] Purkis, *Crusading Spirituality*, pp. 3, 11, 115.

[11] Riley-Smith, *Idea of Crusading*, p. 155.

Through these means, I demonstrate that, immediately following the fall of Jerusalem in 1187 to Saladin, the concept of *imitatio Christi* was inextricably linked to taking the Cross and the recovery of Christ's inheritance: The Holy Land.

Preaching the Third Crusade

William Purkis argued that, notwithstanding a recognition of the impact of the fall of Jerusalem, ancestral obligation had replaced the idea of *imitatio Christi* as 'the most prominent motif used by those who sought to recruit for the crusades to the East' by the end of the twelfth century.[12] Evidence relating to the Third Crusade shows that imitating the life of Christ, especially his sacrifices, as well as individual penance, remained an important element in both crusader motivation and preaching following the fall of Jerusalem.[13] While chroniclers of the First Crusade and preachers of the Second Crusade depicted crusaders as taking up the Cross for individual salvation, Saladin's capture of the True Cross at the battle of Hattin in 1187 led to a greater focus on the Cross itself in recruiting sermons.

The tone for Third Crusade preaching was set by Pope Gregory VIII in his bull, *Audita tremendi*, which called for a crusade to recover the True Cross. As news of the fall of Jerusalem had yet to reach Rome, Gregory's text emphasized the redemptive work of Christ's incarnation and his death on the Cross. The pope encouraged Christendom to imitate Christ by laying down their lives for their brothers and to recover the Holy Land.[14]

The loss of Jerusalem and the majority of the kingdom of Jerusalem to Saladin did not result in a dilution of this emphasis: it saw the integration of the recovery of the Holy City into an established penitential framework. The crusading sermon of the late-twelfth-century French theologian Alan of Lille, for example, focused on crusading as an act of penance for the recovery of the True Cross and the liberation of Christ's inheritance.[15] In

---

[12] W.J. Purkis, 'Elite and Popular Perceptions of *imitatio Christi* in Twelfth-Century Crusade Spirituality', *Elite and Popular Religion*, ed. K. Cooper and J. Gregory (Woodbridge, 2006), pp. 54–64; see also G. Constable, *Three Studies in Medieval Religious and Social Thought: The Interpretation of Mary and Martha, the Ideal of the Imitation of Christ, the Orders of Society* (Cambridge, 1995), pp. 198–228; and Purkis, *Crusading* Spirituality, p. 115.

[13] See also, J. Bird, 'Preaching and Crusading Memory', *Remembering the Crusades and Crusading*, ed. M. Cassidy-Welch (Abingdon, 2017), pp. 22–3.

[14] *Audita Tremendi*, 1187, 'Ansbertus', *Historia de expeditione Friderici imperatoris. Quellen zur Geschichte des Kreuzzuges Kaiser Fredrichs I.*, ed. A. Chroust, Monumenta Germania Historica, scriptores rerum Germanicarum nova series 5 (Berlin, 1928), pp. 6–10. See also, Cole, *Preaching of the Crusades*, pp. 63–5.

[15] Alan of Lille taught in Paris and was part of the mystic reaction against Scholastic

addition to the exhortation to bear Christ's cross heading this chapter, Alan drew upon the concept of *imitatio Christi* when he stated,

> Christians sign themselves with the Cross; crucified they go on pilgrimage in the world, they reach the place; they seek the tomb with the Magdalene; they run with Peter; they discover with John. They weep for the capture of the cross; they labour for its recovery; they avenge the injuries of Christ; they mourn his insults; they free the land of our inheritance, Christ's inheritance, the Virgin's dowry.[16]

It is a message that focused on those wealthy enough to join an expedition to the Holy Land – to retake Jerusalem. As Tyerman has highlighted, Alan preached that 'God's favour was bestowed on the humble not the indigent'.[17] In his article on the 'Thief's Cross', Matthew Phillips argued that the themes of devotion to the Cross and following in Christ's footsteps are combined by Alan to present the true crusader as one that is penitent.[18] Although Alan encouraged crusaders to take up the penitential Cross through love, he insisted that *imitatio Christi* should be a crusader's ultimate goal because Christ had willingly undergone the Passion for their sins.[19] These themes were not uncommon in Cistercian sermons.

The Cistercians and Crusading

Founded in 1098 by a small group of Benedictine monks who sought stricter adherence to the rule of St Benedict of Nursia, the Cistercians had *c.*340 houses across Europe by 1153.[20] The regulations laid down by

---

philosophy, adopting an eclectic Scholastical philosophy composed of rationalism and mysticism. Alan retired to Cîteaux Abbey, the motherhouse of the Cistercian Order, sometime before his death in 1202. For more on Alan's *Sermo de cruce domini* of September 1189; Bysted, *Crusade Indulgence*, pp. 262–3.

[16] 'Signent se cruce christiani, peregrinent in terra crucifixi, accedant ad locum, querant cum Magdalena sepulcrum, currant cum Petro, inueniant cum Iohanne. Fleant crucis raptum, laborent ad recuperandum; vindicent Christi iniurias, doleant contumelias; liberent terram nostre hereditatis, Christi hereditatem, Virginus dotem': *Alain de Lille. Textes inédits*, p. 281.

[17] C. Tyerman, *How to Plan a Crusade: Religious War in the High Middle Ages* (London, 2015), pp. 100–1.

[18] M. Phillips, 'The Thief's Cross: Crusade and Penance in Alan of Lille's *Sermo de cruce domini*', *Crusades*, Vol. 5, ed. B. Kedar, J. Phillips, and J. Riley-Smith (Abingdon, 2006), pp. 143–56. See also, M. Phillips, 'Crucified with Christ: The Imitation of the Crucified Christ and Crusading Spirituality', *Crusades: Medieval Worlds in Conflict. An International Symposium at Saint Louis University, February 2006*, ed. T.F. Madden, J. Naus, and V. Ryan (Abingdon, 2010), pp. 25–33.

[19] 'Sermo de cruce Domini', *Alain de Lille. Textes inédits*, p. 282.

[20] Also known as the Bernardines after St Bernard of Clairvaux, or the 'White Monks' from the colour of their robes, Cistercian derives from *Cistericum*, the Latin name for the village of Cîteaux, near Dijon in eastern France, which was the site of their first abbey. For more on Cistercian foundations, see M. Gervers, 'Donations to the Hospi-

their third abbot, St Stephen Harding, demanded severe asceticism; in a desire to live off their own manual work, in principle they rejected feudal revenues and established physical labour as a principal feature of their monastic life.[21] The Cistercians became identified with crusading through St Bernard of Clairvaux, who wrote a eulogy to the Templars and promoted the cause of the Second Crusade, drafting sermons as well as conducting preaching tours across France and Germany.[22] In addition, Raymond, abbot of Fitero in Navarre, was instrumental in the founding of another Military Order, the Order of Calatrava.[23] As Saladin swept through the Latin East in the summer of 1187, a Cistercian General Assembly voted to incorporate Calatrava fully into the Cistercian Order and affiliated it with the abbey of Morimond.[24]

As will be shown here, the Cistercian Order showed similar support to the Third Crusade. Baldwin of Forde, archbishop of Canterbury and former abbot of the Cistercian abbey of Forde, conducted a preaching tour of Wales and oversaw the Saladin Tithe in England. Similarly, Henry of Marcy, cardinal bishop of Albano and former abbot of Clairvaux, was active in recruiting crusaders in Northern France, the Low Countries, and Germany as a papal legate.[25]

This emphasis on pilgrimage and following in Christ's footsteps seemingly influenced Baldwin of Forde's recruiting sermons. According to Peter of Blois, the archbishop's secretary, Baldwin was initially reluctant, believing that 'He who kills the infidel is a murderer'.[26] In a letter dated to 1188, Peter encouraged him to preach the crusade, arguing that it was his duty to guard

---

tallers in England in the Wake of the Second Crusade', *The Second Crusade and the Cistercians*, ed. M. Gervers (New York, 1992), pp. 153–61.

[21] For insight into what 'being Cistercian' meant in 1153, see C. Hoffman Berman, *The Cistercian Evolution: The Invention of a Religious Order in Twelfth-Century Europe* (Philadelphia, Penn., 2000). The Cistercians were able to develop all branches of farming during the twelfth century, but in the British Isles their focus was on sheep farming and the production of wool and sheepskins; D.H. Williams, *The Cistercians in the Early Middle Ages* (Leominster, 1998), pp. 257–360.

[22] See, for example, C. Tyerman, *God's War: A New History of the Crusades* (London, 2006), p. 422.

[23] P. Linehan, *Spain, 1157–1300: A Partible Inheritance* (Chichester, 2011).

[24] J.F. O'Callaghan, 'The Affiliation of the Order of Calatrava with the Order of Cîteaux', *Analecta Sacri Ordinis Cisterciensis*, 15 (1960), 3–59, 255–92.

[25] On 28 October 1187, for example, Henry of Marcy arrived in Hainault to preach the Cross, Gilbert of Mons, p. 112.

[26] 'Sed dicis: Qui infideles occidit, homicida est': 'Epistola CCXXXII. Exhortatio as eos qui nec accipiunt nec praedicant crucem', *PL*, Vol. 207, col. 532. Peter of Blois had been in Rome when news of the battle of Hattin reached the Curia and, after notifying the Angevin court, he composed a series of exhortatory pamphlets to promote a crusade. It is likely that he was also instrumental in Henry II's decision to take the Cross, Tyerman, *God's War*, p. 381.

'the vineyard of the Lord of Hosts'.[27] Themes employed by Alan of Lille in regard to crusading were notable in Baldwin's earlier treatise *de commendatione fidei* (c.1177). This was written while he was still a Cistercian abbot and was aimed at medieval society in general. It is illustrative of the ease with which Cistercian theology could be turned to preaching the recovery of the True Cross.[28] One of Baldwin's sermons began, for example, by encouraging the congregation to

> Consider diligently Jesus of Nazareth, and him crucified, lovingly for us, desiring us from the depths of His heart, stretching out his arms on the Cross as if to embrace us, prepared to receive anyone who comes to him.[29]

Baldwin then moved on to speak of the two thieves that were crucified alongside Christ. While the thief on the left mocked Christ and was condemned, the thief to his right adored him and was saved.[30] In *Sermo de sancta cruce*, the Cross became the instrument of transformation – to raise up those deserving of crucifixion themselves. In a separate sermon, Baldwin stated that Christ alone ascended His own cross as the sinners had to carry their own. He pointed out that those that focused on a worldly prize for taking up the Cross bore it in vain as only the penitential would enter paradise.[31]

Peter of Blois had composed three pamphlets in 1188–9 to preach the crusade and Christ's martyrdom was a consistent theme, which likely encouraged Archbishop Baldwin to draw upon his earlier work in his recruiting sermons.[32] According to Gerald of Wales, Baldwin's *Sermo de sancta cruce* was drafted by the canons of the Holy Cross at Waltham and it had already

---

[27] 'Si de hac paucitate te subtrahis, negligentiæ aut infidelitatis argui potes, quia quantum in te est, proventum Dominicæ messis imminuis; constituerunt te custodem in vinea. Tua ergo interest ut vinea Domini Saboath latius extendat palmites suos': 'Epistola CCXXXII', *PL*, Vol. 207, col. 532. See also 'De Hierosolymnitana peregrinatione acceleranda', *PL*, Vol. 207, cols. 1057–70.

[28] For more on cross imagery in Third Crusade preaching, see J. Kane, 'The Impact of the Cross on Western Crusade Terminology' (PhD thesis, University of Cambridge, 2016).

[29] 'Intuemini diligeter Iesum Nazarenium, et hunc crucifixum, pro nobis zelantem, cupientem nos in visceribus suis, in cruce brachia tendentem quasi ad amplexus, paratum suscipere omnem hominem venientem ad se': Baldwin of Forde, 'Sermo de sancta cruce', 8.1, *Balduini de Forda Opera: Sermones de Commendatione Fidei*, ed. D.N. Bell, *Corpus Christianorum. Continuatio Mediaevalis*, Vol. 99 (Turnhout, 1991), pp. 128–9.

[30] Baldwin, 'Sermo de sancta cruce', *Sermones*, ed. Bell, p. 133.

[31] Baldwin, 'Sermo de crucifixion veteris hominis', *Sermones*, ed. Bell, p. 47.

[32] '[I]n militia vexillum, in victorie tropheum et triumphi titulum', Baldwin, 'Sermo de sancta cruce', *Sermones*, ed. Bell, p. 127. See also, J.H. Pryor, 'Two *excitationes* for the Third Crusade', *Mediterranean Historical Review*, 25 (2010), 147–68. For Peter's three pamphlets, *De Hierosolymitana peregrinatione*; *Dialogus inter regem Henricum secundum*

described the Cross as akin to a 'military banner, trophy of victory, and a sign of triumph'.[33] While we cannot be certain that Peter also had this example in mind, it is an image that transfers readily across to crusading. Peter eventually accompanied the archbishop to the Holy Land and Baldwin's crusader network, as well as his broader impact on the Third Crusade, is considered later in this chapter.

In reaction to the fall of Jerusalem on 2 October 1187, the former abbot of Clairvaux, Henry of Marcy, completed his crusading manifesto *De peregrinante civitate Dei*. Pope Gregory VIII then appointed him legate in charge of promoting the Third Crusade north of the Alps and this was confirmed on Gregory's death by his successor, Pope Clement III. Henry held a series of recruitment rallies in Hainault, Mons, Nivelles, Louvain, and Liège, culminating with the imperial *diet* in Mainz. Here the Emperor Frederick Barbarossa took the Cross, alongside a swathe of the German nobility, following a sermon by the legate.[34] Given the content of Henry's letter to the leading men of Germany, the sermon likely drew upon the themes in *Audita tremendi*, as well as from St Bernard of Clairvaux's thoughts on crusading. Henry of Marcy died, however, before he could travel to the Holy Land himself.[35]

As can be seen, under Cistercian influence, crusade ideology had increasingly concentrated on sacrificial service, which underpinned emerging ideas of following in Christ's footsteps.[36] This message of penitential discipline was reflected in the ordinances issued by Henry II following his Great Council at Geddington in February 1188, which included restrictions on ostentatious clothing, swearing, and gambling.[37] In 1190 the Cistercians established daily masses for the souls of all crusaders. This arguably aimed to place the expedition at the centre of everyday religious practice in Latin Europe. Their links with crusading, however, were not unique amongst the reformed houses.[38]

---

et abbatem Bonnevallensem; and *Passio Reginaldi*, see *PL*, Vol. 207, cols. 957–75, 976–88, 1058–70.

[33] Gerald of Wales, Vol. 4, pp. 104–5.

[34] Y.M.-J. Congar, 'Henry de Marcy, abbé de Clairvaux, cardinal-évêque d'Albano, et légat pontifical', *Analecta monastica: Textes et études sur la vie des moines au moyen âge*, 5e série, Studia Anselmiana, Vol. 43 (Rome, 1958), pp. 45–54; Tyerman, *Plan a Crusade*, pp. 114–17.

[35] Congar, 'Henry de Marcy', pp. 85–6. For the contents of the letter see, *The History of the Expedition of the Emperor Frederick and Related Texts*, trans. G.A. Loud (New York and London, 2010), pp. 41–2.

[36] See, for example, Purkis, *Crusading Spirituality*, p. 56.

[37] F.M. Powicke and C.R. Cheney, *Councils and Synods, with Other Documents Relating to the English Church* (Oxford, 1964), pp. 1025–9.

[38] *Statuta capitulorum generalium ordinis Cisterciensi*, Vol. 1, ed. J.-M. Canivez, Bibliothèque de la Revue d'histoire ecclésiastique, 9 (1933), 122, no. 16.

The Premonstratensian Order and Crusading

Although inspired by Cistercian ideals, the Order of Canons Regular of Prémontré, also known as the Premonstratensians or the Norbertines, followed the rule of St Augustine. Founded by St Norbert of Xanten in 1120, the Premonstratensians maintained strong links with the crusade movement throughout the twelfth century, playing a prominent role in the conversion of the West Slavs or Wends and sending missionaries to the pagan tribes beyond the Rivers Elbe and Oder.[39] Concepts common with crusading shaped the spirituality of the Premonstratensians with a focus on doing penance for one's sins. The ties were not limited to theology, however; St Norbert, for example, was a relative of Godfrey of Bouillon, hero of the First Crusade and the first Latin ruler of Jerusalem.[40] In 1136, Norbert's successor at Prémontré accepted St Bernard of Clairvaux's offer to establish a house at St Samuel on *Mons Gaudii* overlooking Jerusalem. This was intended to complement missionary work being undertaken across the Levant led by Almaric, prelate of the Premonstratensian monastery at Floreffe.[41] In 1152 Almaric became bishop of Sidon, by which time the Premonstratensians had established the combined abbey of St Habakkuk and St Joseph of Arimathea in Ramla.[42] By this point, the Order had attracted the patronage of King Louis VII of France and Henry of Troyes, as well as other less prominent crusading families, such as the family of Trazegnies from Hainaut.[43]

In 1187 Saladin's troops killed the religious of St Samuel and some of those in Ramla, with the survivors fleeing first to Acre and then on towards Tyre.[44] The new pope, Gregory VIII, was most likely a Premonstratensian,[45] and the letters of the Premonstratensian Gervase of Chichester from the early thirteenth century highlight the order's influence on Innocent III's

---

[39] F. Lotter, 'The Crusading Idea and the Conquest of the Region East of the Elbe', *Medieval Frontier Societies*, ed. R. Bartlett and A. MacKay (Oxford, 1989), p. 281, and K. Guth, 'The Pomeranian Missionary Journeys of Otto I of Bamberg and the Crusade Movement of the Eleventh to Twelfth Centuries', *The Second Crusade and the Cistercians*, ed. M. Gervers (New York, 1992), pp. 13–24.

[40] F. Petit, *La spiritualité des prémontrés au XIIe et XIIIe siècles* (Paris, 1947), p. 81.

[41] Bernard of Clairvaux, *Epistolae*, PL 182, cols. 557–58.

[42] Petit, *La spiritualité*, p. 80.

[43] See, for example, BN, Collection de Picardie, nos. 107, 214, 235, 267.

[44] 'De Expugnatione Terrae Sanctae Libellus', *Radulphi de Coggeshall Chronicon Anglicanum; De expugnatione Terrae Sanctae libellus;...*, ed. J. Stevenson (London, 1875), pp. 229–30.

[45] For example, the necrology of St Martin of Laon identified Pope Gregory as having been a Premonstratensian canon. Guibert of Nogent, *De vita sua*, ed. Dom Luc d'Achery, PL 156, col. 1186, and the *Chronicle of Ninova* (1291) described the pope as having also been a canon of Laon, *Sacrae antiquitatis monumenta*, Vol. 2, ed. C.L. Hugo (Nancy, 1736), p. 171. For more on this see, Petit, *La spiritualité*, pp. 81–2.

preparations for the Fifth Crusade (1217–21), as well as recruitment for the Albigensian Crusade (1209–29).[46]

Richard Mortimer's study of the Premonstratensians illustrates the important role Ranulf of Glanville played in the foundation of four Premonstratensian houses by members of his familial network following his own foundation at Leiston in Suffolk.[47] As is discussed later, Ranulf was affiliated with Baldwin of Forde and travelled with him to the siege of Acre in 1190.

Another member of the Third Crusade, Raoul I of Coucy, had been advocate (protector) and patron of the house of Prémontré. His familial network included Count Robert I of Dreux and his sons, Robert II and Bishop Philip of Beauvais, all of whom were crusaders.[48] Prior to his departure on the Third Crusade, Raoul I had placed the canons at Prémontre in charge of the income he left to his daughter. Although the impending expedition is not emphasised, the only other orders mentioned in the will alongside the Premonstratensians are the Hospitallers and the Templars. This suggests that these donations were linked to his commitment to the crusade. It may not be coincidental that members of Ranulf of Glanville's crusading circle, Robert and Walter of Ros, were associated with Raoul I of Coucy at the siege of Acre.[49] It is also of interest that the fragment of the Holy Cross presented to Richard I in June 1192 was taken from a wall in the Premonstratensian chapel of St Samuel on *Mons Gaudii*.[50]

The focus on the True Cross and *imitatio Christi* in preaching was to have an important influence on the conduct of the Third Crusade. In 1188, Pope Clement III gave remission of sins to those who took part in expeditions against the Muslims in Iberia, as his predecessor Eugenius III had done four decades earlier for the Second Crusade.[51] This effectively placed participation in a military action in Iberia on a par with joining

---

[46] Whilst the future head of the Order was undoubtedly English, his cognomen seems to be based on confusion with another. See C.R. Cheney, 'Gervase, Abbot of Prémontré: A Medieval Letter-Writer', *Bulletin of the John Rylands Library*, 33 (1950), 25–40.

[47] R. Mortimer, 'Religious and Secular Motives for Some English Monastic Foundations', *Studies in Church History*, 15 (1978), 77, 81.

[48] Raoul of Coucy's grandfather, Thomas of Marle, had granted the lands at Prémontré to the order on his return from the First Crusade, and Raoul's grandmother, Melisende, had founded a house of Premonstratensian nuns, as well as the Norbertine house of Thenailles, *Crusade Charters, 1138–1270*, ed. C.K. Slack, trans. H.B. Feiss (Tempe, AZ, 2001), pp. xviii–xxix, 62–3, 70–1.

[49] R.A. Leson, 'A Constellation of Crusade: The Resafa Heraldry Cup and the Aspirations of Raoul I, Lord of Coucy', *The Crusades and Visual Culture*, ed. E. Lapina, A.J. Morris, S.A. Throop, and L.J. Whatley (Farnham, 2015), pp. 75–90.

[50] Coggeshall, pp. 40–1.

[51] J.S. Robinson, 'The Papacy 1122–1198', *The New Cambridge Medieval History*, Vol. 5/2, ed. D. Luscombe and J. Riley-Smith (Cambridge, 2004), p. 347.

the crusade to liberate Jerusalem.[52] However, with the possible exception of William Fitz-Osbert, crusaders from north-western Europe identified in this study all chose to continue on to the Holy Land rather than turn back following the capture of Alvor castle or Silves from the Almohads, or the defence of Santarem in Iberia.[53]

This stands in stark contrast to the behaviour of many participants on the Second Crusade who considered their vow fulfilled with the capture of Lisbon.[54] Jonathan Phillips has established that the involvement of the northern fleet in the siege of Lisbon of 1147 was the result of careful planning. It is likely, he argued, that many took the Cross on the understanding that they were to fulfil their vows in Portugal.[55] There is, however, no surviving evidence that participants in the Third Crusade expected to fulfil their vows in Iberia, even if it is likely that they considered military action there a possibility. Rather, in line with surviving sermons, descriptions of crusaders in official documents, such as the Pipe Rolls, and the actions of the crusaders indicate that they took their crusader vows with the intention of recovering the True Cross and liberating Jerusalem – to follow physically in the footsteps of Christ.[56]

To supplement the impact of reformed houses on crusader theology and the conduct of the Third Crusade, the next section analyses links between the reformed houses, as well as Military Orders, and the noble network in detail. It argues that for members of the noble network, by the time of the Third Crusade, these institutions were considered to be inextricably linked to crusading.

---

[52] J.F. O'Callaghan, *Reconquest and Crusade in Medieval Spain* (Philadelphia, 2003), p. 57.

[53] The only other named crusader to remain was an otherwise unknown, Nicholas the Fleming, who was made bishop of Silves, *De itinere navali. A German Third Crusader's Chronicle of his Voyage to the Siege of Almohad Silves, 1189 AD/Muwahid Xelb, 585 AH*, trans. D. Cushing (Antimony Media, 2013), pp. xc, 102. For William Fitz-Osbert see Appendix 1.

[54] See also, L. Villegas-Aristizábal, 'Norman and Anglo-Norman Participation in the Iberian Reconquista' (PhD thesis, University of Nottingham, 2013), pp. 146–85.

[55] J. Phillips, 'Foreword'. *The Conquest of Lisbon: De Expugnatione Lyxbonensi*, trans. C.W. David (New York, 2001), pp. xviii–xx; See also H. Livermore, 'The "Conquest of Lisbon" and its Author', *Portuguese Studies*, 6 (1990), 1–16.

[56] The Pipe Rolls do not always specify that the individual is a crusader, but routinely described people as going to Jerusalem. For example, whilst Richard Bacon was described as signed by the Cross, 'Ricardo Bacon militibus crucesignati quo abierunt Jrlm' (also as 'militibus qui abierunt Jrlm'), William Stanford was not 'Willelmus de Stanford' qui abiit Jrlm': PR3 RI (1191), pp. 27–8, 44, 152. As they are all cited in relation to the recovery of taxation, it is clear that they were crusaders rather than merely on a pilgrimage.

Links Between 'Crusader' Houses and Elite Participants

Religious institutions, such as the Cistercians and the Military Orders, have been shown to form part of elite social networks. As is considered in more detail in the next chapter, Riley-Smith argued that crusader families often displayed certain features, such as patronage of reformist monastic foundations and an attachment to the reformed papacy.[57] In his study of support to the Order of the Temple in France, Jochen Schenk argued that ties between noble and knightly families and the Order were illustrative of their religious expectations.[58] Whilst mindful of the influence of the clerical scribe in translating the desires of the benefactor through formulaic texts, such investigations into the contents of charters donating or mortgaging lands to religious institutions by crusaders have provided significant insights into their concerns and motivations.[59] In considering such relationships, the mortgaging of property to religious houses to fund participation on crusade cannot be ignored. The success of the Saladin Tithe in England and Normandy in meeting the financial needs of crusaders, however, allows for a clearer picture of donations made to religious foundations for reasons other than fundraising. As will be shown, only fourteen of the 237 crusaders connected to religious orders in this study alienated property to take the Cross. Following consideration of financing participation in the Third Crusade, and the impact of the Saladin Tithe in particular, this chapter situates institutions within the Third Crusade noble network. It argues that religious orders and houses that might be considered to be linked to crusading enjoyed greater support than other establishments.

---

[57] See Riley-Smith, *First Crusaders*.

[58] Schenk, *Templar Families*. See also, J. Schenk, 'Forms of Lay Association with the Order of the Temple', *JMH*, 34 (2008), 79–103.

[59] As well as the pioneering work of Giles Constable, see R. Gossman, 'The Financing of the Crusades' (PhD thesis, University of Chicago, 1965); F.A. Cazel Jr., 'Financing the Crusades', *History of the Crusades: The Impact of the Crusades on Europe*, Vol. 6, ed. M. Setton, H.W. Hazard, and N.P. Zacour (Madison, WI, 1989), pp. 116–49; J. Riley-Smith, 'Early Crusaders to the East and the Costs of Crusading 1095–1130', *Cross Cultural Convergences in the Crusader Period, Essays Presented to Aryeh Grabois on his Sixty-Fifth Birthday*, ed. M. Goodich, S. Menache, and S. Schein (New York, 1995), pp. 237–57; J. Richard, 'Le financement des croisades', *Pouvoir et gestion* (Toulouse, 1997), pp. 63–71; P. Racinet, 'Le départ et le retour du croisé. Arrangements matériels et spirituels avec les moines', *Histoire médiévale et archéologie*, 11 (Amiens, 2000), 11–24; C.B. Bouchard, *Sword, Miter, and Cloister: Nobility and the Church in Burgundy, 980–1198* (London, 1987), and G. Constable, 'The Financing of the Crusades', *Crusaders and Crusading in the Twelfth Century*, ed. G. Constable (Farnham, 2008), pp. 117–42.

Religious Foundations and Crusade Finance

Through the Saladin Tithe, the kings of England and France sought with varying degrees of success to meet the financial needs of potential crusaders in order to facilitate their participation in the Third Crusade.[60] According to Walter Map, Henry II proposed a tithe to be levied on all his subjects, lay and clerical, who did not take the Cross.[61] By allowing those that took the Cross an exemption from the tax and to retain monies levied from their holdings, the kings also sought to reduce the need to mortgage or sell property – most commonly to the Church – to fund participation in the Third Crusade. In addition, Gerald of Wales described that partial indulgences were offered to those unfit or unable to take the Cross.[62] If accurate, this indicates that additional funds might have been raised from non-combatants in advance of Pope Innocent III's introduction of such arrangements. Just as there is insufficient data for meaningful analysis of the impact of donations to religious institutions in response to preaching the Cross, we remain unable to verify Gerald's claim.

The history of religious foundations in the twelfth century is interwoven with crusaders and crusading finance, but it is often challenging to link specific donations to preaching activity. That returning crusaders went on to found religious institutions is well established, as is the selling or mort-

---

[60] In addition to the tens of thousands of pounds netted by the Saladin Tithe, Henry II levied 10,000 *marks* from the Jews of England. On the king's death it was estimated that he had amassed 100,000 *marks*, or three times the Crown's annual income, *Chronica*, Vol. 3, p. 8. King Richard raised a further 2,000 *marks* from the Jewish community, as well as considerable sums from fines relating to public offices, titles, and inheritances; Tyerman, *Plan a Crusade*, pp. 208–9. Gervase of Canterbury set the figure at 60,000*l.*, but recent studies have suggested a much lower figure, perhaps as low as 12,000*l.* paid over two years; R. Chazan, *Medieval Stereotypes and Modern Antisemitism* (Berkeley, CA, 1997), p. 114; Hosler, *Henry II*, p. 169. See also, Tyerman, *England*; S. Lloyd, *English Society and the Crusades, 1216–1307* (New York, 1988); P.W. Edbury, 'Preaching the Crusade in Wales', *England and Germany in the High Middles Ages*, ed. A. Haverkamp and H. Vollrath (Oxford, 1996), pp. 221–33; and, J. Gillingham, *Richard I* (London, 1999).

[61] Walter Map, *Contes pour le gens de cour. De Nugis curialium*, ed. A. Bates (Brussels, 1993), pp. 482–5. The Saladin Tithe was a literal tithe of 10% for one year on revenues and movable properties, excluding the necessities of the taxpayer's profession, such as the arms and horse of a knight. The idea of taking a tenth part was drawn from Leviticus 27:30–32, 10% being the proportion that was supposed to be holy unto the Lord. In the king of England's domain, the tithe was assessed by dioceses, rather than by shires, and the church, including the Military Orders, rather than county sheriffs, oversaw collection. In France, each lord or cleric was to collect the tithes of their tenants. It was inspired, in part, by a desire to avoid the alienation of further land to the Church to finance crusading. See, for example, J.H. Round, 'The Saladin Tithe', *EHR*, 31 (1916), 447–50.

[62] Gerald of Wales, Vol. 6, pp. 73–4.

gaging of property to the Church to fund participation in a crusade. Elphège Vacandard asserted that the cost of the Second Crusade preoccupied participants from the king of France down to peasants and monks, and that their first recourse was to sell or mortgage their possessions.[63] In his chapter on financing the crusades in *Crusaders and Crusading in the Twelfth Century*, Giles Constable also considered levies on the church, like the one issued by Louis VII in 1146–7.[64] His use of charter evidence followed on from Reinhold Röhricht's pioneering research on German pilgrims and crusaders.[65] Röhricht also noted the association of sales or loans with specific groups, 'Jews and priests, who had the most money, received castles, woods, estates, and other property as security for loans, as gifts, and through sale'.[66] In addition to donations made prior to their departure or in order to redeem a crusader vow, crusaders were also known to have made grants based on vows made during times of stress, deprivation, sickness, and danger.[67]

The Saladin Tithe

As news of the crisis in the Holy Land reached Europe, Henry II reacted quickly to secure further financial support to the Latin East. As early as 1187, he ordered the sequestration of monies raised by the shrine to Thomas Becket in Canterbury to help Jerusalem and to redeem Christian captives.[68] After taking the Cross in 1188, he extended this fund-raising with a series of ordinances issued at Le Mans and Geddington to levy for one year a tenth on all revenues and movables, excluding books, clothes, jewels, clerical vestments, and furnishings, as well as essential military equipment, such as horses, arms, and equipment. This became known as the Saladin Tithe and, in England at least, the king established a separate accounting office in Salisbury and made the Church responsible for the assessment and collection of the tax, with defaulters facing excommunication.[69] In addition to enjoying a plenary indulgence of all confessed sins, all those vowing to join the crusade would be exempt from this tax, except those from town and

---

[63] *Vie de saint Bernard, abbé de Clairvaux*, Vol. 2, ed. E. Vacandard (Paris, 1895), p. 274.
[64] Constable, 'Financing of the Crusades', pp. 117–42.
[65] R. Röhricht, *Beiträge zur Geschichte der Kreuzzüge* (Berlin, 1878); and *Die Deutschen in Heiligen Lande* (Innsbruck, 1894).
[66] Röhricht, *Beiträge*, Vol 2, p. 66, see also p. 97, n.29.
[67] J. Choux, *Recherches sur le diocèse de Toul au temps de la Réforme grégorienne. L'épiscopat de Pibon (1069–1107)* (Nancy, 1952), pp. 68, 232. For examples see, A. Castan, *Un episode de la deuxième croisade* (Besançon, 1862), pp. 10–11; G.H. White, 'The Career of Waleran, Count of Meulan and Earl of Worcester (1104–6)', *Transactions of the Royal Historical Society*, 4.17 (1934), 40–1.
[68] Tyerman, *England*, p. 75.
[69] In 1188, Gilbert of Howden, a Templar brother-knight, was caught stealing monies raised in taxation and was punished by the master of the London Temple, *Gesta Regis*, Vol. 2, pp. 47–8.

country who had taken the Cross without permission. Clerics, knights, and serjeants would also receive the tax levied from their lands and vassals to aid in their own preparations.[70] Walter of Dunstanville, for example, was granted 9 *livres* from the Saladin Tithe.[71]

Journeying to the Holy Land, be it as a pilgrim or a crusader, required careful preparation and access to significant funds. Prior to the Saladin Tithe, unless serving within a lord's retinue, crusaders had to finance their own participation.[72] For this reason, Pope Eugenius III had authorised the mortgaging of fiefs to monasteries to finance participation in the Second Crusade.[73] Whilst magnates, moneylenders, and even tenants might provide loans, religious houses acted as the principal institutions of credit in the eleventh and twelfth centuries.[74] For example, Bernard Bligny argued that the large number of grants made to the Cluniac house of Domène was probably attributable to the needs of crusaders.[75] This is supported by Constable's analysis of 149 separate transactions associated with the Second Crusade.[76] Eberhard Pfeiffer has argued that, as well as receiving many endowments from crusaders, the Cistercians seem to have been involved more than other orders in financing crusaders.[77] However, in his chapter on donations made to the Hospitallers following the Second Crusade, Michael Gervers identified a tailing off of support to the Cistercians, as well as the Templars, as the century progressed.[78] Moreover, in his work on the lords of Nesle, William Newman identified that other clerics could be proactive in securing land from those who had taken the Cross.[79]

The Church's success in increasing its land holdings may well have spurred rulers like Henry II to consider alternative methods of financing

---

[70] Those receiving the tax who did not fulfil their vow were subsequently fined; e.g., Osburtus Purchaz in PR5 RI (1194), p. 170.

[71] Details of tax received under the Tithe are rarely available. Walter's revenue only survived as he died before setting out on crusade; 'Assize Roll 1171. The Cornish Eyre (1201) 30225', *Pleas Before the King or His Justices, 1198–1202: Rolls or Fragments of Rolls from the Years 1198, 1201 and 1202*, Vol. 2, ed. D.M. Stenton (London, 1952), p. 49.

[72] Constable, 'Financing of the Crusades', pp. 64–88.

[73] Translated text in J. Riley-Smith, *The Crusades: A History*. 3rd edition (London, 2014). pp. 57–9, no. 5.

[74] In addition to Génestal's work on Normandy, see, for example, G. Salvioli, 'Il monachesimo occidentale e la sua storia economica', *Rivista italiana di sociologia*, 15 (1911), 18.

[75] B. Bligny, *L'Église et les ordres religieux dans le royaume de Bourgogne aux XI et XII siècles* (Paris, 1960), pp. 188–9.

[76] Constable, 'Financing of the Crusades', p. 128.

[77] E. Pfeiffer, 'Die Cistercienser und der zweite Kreuzzug 3. Hilfeleistungen der Cistercienserklöster an Kreuzfahrer', *Cistercienser-Chronik*, 47 (1935), 79.

[78] Gervers, 'Donations to the Hospitallers', pp. 155–61.

[79] W. Newman, *Les seigneurs de Nesle en Picardie*, 2 Vols (Paris, 1871).

crusaders.⁸⁰ The introduction of a crusade tax by rulers in north-western Europe enjoyed a mixed reception, however, and it was widely resisted by the Church in certain areas as establishing a worrying precedent.⁸¹ It is probable that Philip Augustus anticipated their objections as he granted exemptions to the Cistercians, Carthusians, and Fontevraud Abbey.⁸² Notwithstanding these measures, Philip's attempts to implement the Saladin Tithe in France were effectively blocked.⁸³ Similarly, King Richard wrote to John of Anagni, the papal legate, on the lack of activity in Limoges and Poitiers.⁸⁴

According to Gervase of Canterbury, the Saladin Tithe raised 70,000 *livres* in England alone (105,000 *marks*).⁸⁵ While this figure is impossible to verify, the charter evidence suggests that the Saladin Tithe had a significant impact on the requirement for landowners to raise funds to finance participation in the Third Crusade in England. Despite losing a legal case for the right to funds raised from the manors of Groton and Semer, Robert of Cokefield received the tithe from his hereditary manor at Cokefield to fund his participation in the expedition.⁸⁶

While Roger of Mowbray raised 300 *marks* by assigning Nidderdale to Byland Abbey, and another 120 *marks* from Fountains Abbey to fund his journey to Jerusalem *c.*1175, his son Nigel's donations were seemingly unrelated to raising funds for his own journey to the Holy Land.⁸⁷ King Rich-

---

⁸⁰ S.K. Mitchell, *Taxation in Medieval England* (New Haven, 1951), pp. 118–19. See also, W.E. Lunt, *Financial Relations of the Papacy with England to 1327* (Cambridge, MA, 1939).

⁸¹ T. Evergates, *Feudal Society in Medieval France: Documents from the County of Champagne* (Philadelphia, PA, 1993), p.110.

⁸² Rigord, p. 88.

⁸³ J. Bradbury, *Philip Augustus, King of France, 1180–1223* (London and New York, 1998), p. 78.

⁸⁴ *Chronicles and Memorials of the Reign of Richard I, Vol 2: Epistolae Cantuarienses, The Letters of the Prior and Convent of Christ Church Canterbury, From A.D. 1187 to A.D. 1199*, ed. W. Stubbs (London, 1865), no. 325, pp. 310–11. The kings of England and France were also able to tax the Jewish community. As mentioned earlier, in 1188 Henry II raised a *tallage* of 10,000 *marks*, which was followed by an additional 2,000 *marks* imposed by Richard in 1190. At the start of Philip II's reign, Ralph of Diss recorded that Philip Augustus raised 15,000 *marks* from the Jews with a smaller sum raised in 1179, but there is no surviving evidence relating to the Third Crusade; Gervase of Canterbury, *Historical Works*, Vol. 1, ed. W. Stubbs (London, 1880), p. 422; PR1 RI (1189), p. 230; Diss, Vol. 2, p. 4; and, Baldwin, *The Government of Philip Augustus, Foundations of French Royal Power in the Middle Ages* (Berkeley, Los Angeles, CA, and Oxford, 1986), p. 55.

⁸⁵ Gervase of Canterbury, *Historical Works*, Vol. 1, ed. W. Stubbs (London, 1880), p. 422. For a discussion on Richard's crusade finances, see D. Benjamin, 'Support Structures in Crusading Armies, 1095–1241' (PhD thesis, University of Leicester, 2015), pp. 98–101.

⁸⁶ *CRR*, Vol. 1, p. 430.

⁸⁷ Whilst the agreement with Fountains Abbey did not provide terms to recover their

ard's future seneschal of Normandy, Ralph III Tesson, also made a donation for what seem to be purely spiritual reasons. After taking the Cross in 1188, he gave the hermitage of Sainte-Marie-de-la-Colombe and its revenues, as well as the tithe of its provisions of bread, meat, and fish, to the Benedictine abbey of Saint-Sauveur-le-Vicomte for the love of God and the salvation of their souls as long as he or his wife remained at the castle of La Roche-Tesson.[88] Similarly, c.1190, Fulk of Rufford granted 12d. to St Peter's hospital in York, laying the coins on the altar of St Leonard as a seisin of his gift on the approach of 'his journey'.[89] Such a practice was not new, however, indeed it went back to the start of the crusading movement. For example, William Percy had increased his endowment to Whitby Abbey on the eve of the First Crusade without anticipation of a financial return.[90] Similar donations can be noted in France, where collection of the Saladin Tithe was eventually cancelled, such as that of Hagan of Ervy on the eve of his departure on the Third Crusade.[91]

Alternative Methods of Financing Participation in the Third Crusade
From the evidence available, there were but a handful of individuals in England who had to raise funds to finance their journey east. William Fitz-Osbert, joint-leader of a group of London crusaders, mortgaged half a *messuage* in the parish of St Nicholas of Acre in London to his brother, Richard, prior to his departure in 1190.[92] Gilbert of Pecche similarly mortgaged land in Lincolnshire to his brother, Geoffrey; Joscelin of Neville sold his wife's dowry; and William Fitz-Aldelin sold his land in Went and five bovates in Thorpe to his serjeant, Durand Fitz-Drew, for 10 *marks*.[93] Ralph Fitz-Godfrey received a loan from the London financier Henry of Cornhill for 60 *marks*, which was secured by William Marshal – presumably in

---

rights to Nidderdale, that with Byland stipulated a redemption period of up to ten years, *Charters of the Honour of Mowbray, 1107–1191*, ed. D.E. Greenway (London, 1972), no. 54, III.

[88] Ralph's parents, Jordan and Léticie, had founded the nearby priory of La Couperie; L. Delisle, *Histoire du château des sires de Saint-Sauveur-le-Vicomte, suivie de pièces justificatives* (Paris, 1867), p. 81.

[89] *EYC*, Vol. 1, no. 556.

[90] *Cartularium Abbathiae de Whiteby, Ordinis S. Benedicti*, ed. J.C. Atkinson (Durham, 1880), pp. 2–3. Roger of Mowbray made a similar type of donation to the Templars prior to his final crusade, *Honour of Mowbray*, ed. Greenway, no. 276.

[91] Evergates, *Feudal Society: County of Champagne*, pp. 68–9, no. 51 (1190).

[92] *The London Eyre of 1244*, ed. H.A. Chew and M. Weinbaum (London, 1970), p. 120, no. 295.

[93] *Cartularium monasterii de Rameseia*, Vol. 1, ed. W.H. Hart and P.A. Lyons (London, 1884), pp. 123–4; *CCR*, Vol. 4, p. 394; *EYC*, Vol. 3, no. 1641; *Cartulary of Bolton Priory*, f. 162; Bodleian Library, ms. Dodsworth 144, f. 53. For Fitz-Osbert, Chall, and Fitz-Aldelin, see also, Tyerman, *England*, pp. 67, 201, 217.

return for managing Ralph's lands in his absence. Finally, Ralph of Chall demised two bovates of land in Caperby to the Premonstratensian house at Easby for three years to fund his journey to the Holy Land.[94]

As the case of Ralph of Chall demonstrates, religious foundations continued their practice of providing financial aid to crusaders, but such was the success of the Saladin Tithe in England that those occasions were infrequent there in relation to the Third Crusade. The social consequences of religious institutions acting as sources of credit were touched upon by Austin Poole,[95] and considerable work has been done into the financial advantages enjoyed by those that took the Cross.[96] Although pledges by crusaders technically carried no interest, Robert Génestal compared those mortgages that were redeemed with those that remained in clerical hands, arguing that such loans were often highly profitable for the lenders because they enjoyed revenues from the property until repayment was made.[97]

The terms for redemption of such mortgages were usually laid out in the charters, and it was normal that forfeiture would be the consequence of a failure to do so. For example, on the eve of leaving for the Holy Land, Adam of Savoisy pawned to the Cistercians of Fontenay Abbey his share of his father's estate at Planay for 10 *livres*, redeeming it if he returned from crusade.[98] J. Marc and Bernard Bligny have claimed that such mortgages were rarely redeemed, with Constable asserting that the property generally returned to the Church after the crusader died, whether they returned from crusade or not.[99] The terms might also set limitations on the redemption period, method of payment, and who could redeem the mortgage.[100] In

---

[94] *The Acts and Letters of the Marshal Family, Marshals of England and Earls of Pembroke, 1145–1248*, ed. D. Crouch (Cambridge, 2015), no 27, pp. 83–4; *EYC*, Vol. 5, p. 122, no. 215. See also, P. Fergusson, 'The Refectory at Easby Abbey: Form and Iconography', *The Art Bulletin*, 71 (1989), 334–51. A bovate (or oxangang) was a measurement of land based on land fertility and cultivation. It averaged around twenty English acres but could be as low as fifteen.

[95] A.L. Poole, *Obligations of Society in the XII and XIII Centuries* (Oxford, 1946), p. 32. See also P.R. Hyams' study on the transfer of coinage, 'Some Coin Exports from Twelfth Century Yorkshire to the Holy Land', *Coinage in the Latin East: The Fourth Oxford Symposium on Coinage and Monetary History*, ed. P.W. Edbury and D.M. Metcalf (Oxford, 1980), p. 134.

[96] See, for example, E. Bridrey, *La condition juridique des croisés et le privilège de croix* (Paris, 1900), pp. 199–233; J.A. Brundage, *Medieval Canon Law and the Crusader* (Madison, WI, 1969), pp. 175–87.

[97] R. Génestal, *Rôle des monastères comme établissements de crédit étudié en Normandie du XI à la fin du XIII siècle* (Paris, 1901), pp. 2–10.

[98] AD Côte-d'Or, 15H 24–9, no. 3 (1189).

[99] J. Marc, 'Contribution à l'étude du regime féodal sur le domaine de l'abbaye de Saint-Seine', *Revue bourguignonne de l'enseignonne supérieur*, Vol. 6 (1896), p. 72, and Bligny, *L'Église*, p. 86.

[100] Constable, 'Financing of the Crusades', pp. 130–1.

Ralph of Chall's case, if he did not return, the abbey would return his wife her dower and hold the remainder for the maintenance of his only daughter.

Robert the Constable (of Halsham) donated his demesne of Tharlesthorpe to Meaux Abbey and received a loan of 160 *marks* to finance his journey in 1190; pledging the towns of Tharlesthorpe and Halsham to the monks until he had repaid that amount.[101] According to Roger of Howden, Robert died at the siege of Acre in 1190 or 1191, and it seems at least part of the debt had been cleared by 1207 as a legal case was in process over Halsham between Robert Constable the younger and the provost of Beverley.[102] Walter le Nair gained 5 *marks* from St Mary's Swine for two bovates in Skirlington to fund his journey, but the charter does not contain repayment terms and there are no indications that Walter or his heirs ever recovered the property.[103]

Two surviving charters from Champagne indicate that Count Henry II enjoyed some success in taxing the lands of Sens Cathedral, as well as the residents of Chablis.[104] However, the collection of the Saladin Tithe in France by Philip Augustus generally proved problematic, which meant nobles were even more likely to resort to traditional methods of raising funds than in England.[105] King Philip himself drew upon existing fiscal structures, such as rents and tolls, and the *gîte* – the right to demand hospitality for the royal household. In 1189, Philip commuted the three nights' hospitality due from the town of Laon for an annual fee of 200 *livres*.[106] In addition, his treasury was boosted by a payment of 24,000 *marks* from Richard I as his relief for inheriting Henry II's lands in France.[107]

Count Theobald V of Blois was also apparently successful in levying a *taille* (direct tax) upon his subjects in 1190 to finance his crusade.[108] Elsewhere, Hugh of Bourbonne *vifgaged* his pasture rights in Genrupt to the Templars to finance his journey and then endowed them with those rights whilst at the siege of Acre for the 'salvation of his soul and those of his kin'.[109] Alard I of Croisilles and his wife, Eustacia, sold their lands in Flers

---

[101] Bodleian Library, ms. Dodsworth 7, f. 244; *Chronica Monasterii de Melsa*, I, p. 220.
[102] *Chronica*, Vol. 3, p. 89; *Gesta Regis*, Vol. 2, p. 149; See also *EYC*, Vol. 3, pp. 79–80.
[103] *Abstracts of the Charters and Other Documents Contained in the Chartulary of the Priory of Bridlington in the East Riding of the County of York*, ed. W.T. Lancaster (Leeds, 1912), p. 319 (f. 240d); *EYC*, Vol. 3, no. 1409.
[104] Evergates, *Feudal Society: County of Champagne*, pp. 110–11.
[105] In France, each lord was to collect the tithes of his tenants. If he were a crusader, the lord could keep any taxes raised or could pass them on to a crusading heir. Clerical lords were to pass on their taxes to whom they 'ought to give them'. While they were similar threats of excommunication for defaulters as in England, no royal enforcement was in place; Cazel, 'Financing the Crusades', p. 127.
[106] Baldwin, *Government of Philip*, pp. 44–8.
[107] Tyerman, *England*, p. 79.
[108] Cazel, 'Financing the Crusades', p. 125.
[109] To *vifgage* was to make a *vivum vadium* (living pledge), as distinguished from a

(Arras) to Eaucourt Abbey for 20 *marks* to fund a pilgrimage to Jerusalem in 1189 and Gobert and William of Merchin (Cambrai) raised 220 *livres* to fund their journey through the sale of property to Hautmont Abbey.[110] Godfrey of Saint-Vérain in the diocese of Auxerre similarly *vifgaged* property to the Templars prior to going on crusade. Yet an annual rent of three measures of oats and another of grain for the so-called 'bishop's mills' would suggest his focus was on providing for his family in his absence rather than raising finances for his journey to the East.[111]

Even magnates struggled to fund their participation. In early 1189, for example, Count Everard II of Brienne reclaimed a quarter of his right over Sacey that he had given to Saint-Loup Abbey for 20 *sous* of rent and assured them the rents on his revenues from Piney, Rouilly, and Sacey.[112] Similarly, Hugh IV of St Pol sold a third of the tithes from Mortagne to Chateau Abbey prior to departing on the Third Crusade.[113] Count Geoffrey III of Perche returned home from the crusade with significant debts, which prompted a series of confirmation charters and grants to raise funds.[114]

Things appear to have been little better in Angevin France as members of the nobility there also had to raise finance from their holdings. Some were aided, however, by King Philip's long and detailed ordinance on crusaders' debts, which secured their access to the 'crusaders' term'.[115] In spring 1190, John of Sées, count of Ponthieu, and his three sons granted the estate of Robehomme to Troarn Abbey in return for 1200 *livres*, which was confirmed by King Richard on 19 June 1190 at Chinon.[116] Some of these funds were set aside to pay a series of debts laid out in a deed issued by John before he

---

mortgage or dead pledge. A *vifgaged* property served as security for a debt, which could be satisfied out of the rents, issues, or profits. *HdB*, Vol. III, no. 866, pp. 313–14 (1191), no. 1432, p. 476 (1183).

[110] DiBe ID 11344, in *Diplomata Belgica. The Diplomatic Sources from the Medieval Southern Low Countries*, ed. T. de Hemptinne, J. Deploige, J.-L. Kupper and W. Prevenier (Brussels, 2015): www.diplomata-belgica.be (accessed 25 September 2020); *Description analytique de cartulaires et chartriers accompagnés du texte de documents utiles à l'histoire du Hainaut*, Vol. 3, ed. L. DeVilliers (Mons, 1867), no. 29, pp. 133–5.

[111] AN, S5243, dossier 80, no. 1 (1190).

[112] M.-H. d'Arbois Jubainville, 'Catalogue d'actes des Comtes de Brienne 950–1356', *Bibliothèque de l'École des Chartes 33* (Paris, 1872), no. 100; *Cartulaire de l'abbaye de Saint-Loup de Troyes, Collection des principaux cartulaires du diocèse de Troyes*, Vol. 1, ed. C. Lalore (Paris, 1875), no. 103.

[113] *Les chartes des comtes de Saint-Pol, XIe–XIIIe siècles*, ed. J.-F. Nieus (Turnhout, 2008), nos. 54–5, 59, pp.140–3, 145–6.

[114] K. Thompson, *Power and Border Lordship in Medieval France: The County of Perche, 1000–1226* (Woodbridge, 2002), p. 116.

[115] See, for example, E.C. Bramhall, 'The Origin of the Temporal Privileges of Crusaders', *American Journal of Theology*, 5 (1901), 279–92.

[116] *CDF*, nos. 484–5.

left for the Holy Land with his uncle, Guy of Noyelles, but the remainder most likely went to meet his crusade expenses.[117]

The Saladin Tithe was not replicated in imperial lands, so nobles in parts of the Low Countries also had to rely on more traditional methods of raising funds. For example, much as Godfrey of Bouillon had sold his county of Verdun and other lands to Bishop Richer to fund his participation in the First Crusade, according to Gilbert of Mons, Count Conon of Duras sold his advocacy to St Trond and his castle at Duras to Henry, duke of Louvain, for 800 *marks* in 1189.[118] Similarly, as Scotland was also not covered by the Saladin Tithe, Robert Kent, Robert Hunaud, and Ronald, son-in-law to Nicholas of Gôtentin, mortgaged their lands in East Lothian to Kelso Abbey to fund their journey to the Holy Land.[119]

In recognition of the potential fiscal vulnerability of members of military households on crusade, Richard and Philip agreed at Messina in 1190 that upon the death of a crusader part of their wealth should be given to their relations or followers. The remainder was to be held by a council of lords and prelates 'who were to employ the said money towards the relief of the land of Jerusalem, as they should think necessary'.[120]

Through the Saladin Tithe, the kings of England and France looked to meet the financial needs of prospective members of the Third Crusade to encourage greater participation in the expedition. In addition, they aimed to avoid the need for those that took the Cross to mortgage or sell their property to reduce the long-term impact of such participation on land tenure. Data from the Angevin realm, especially England, indicates that the Saladin Tithe was largely successful. Elsewhere, however, crusaders had to resort to more traditional means of securing funds, with accompanying losses to their holdings.

The Saladin Tithe was almost certainly an influence on Pope Innocent III's subsequent attempts to regulate crusader finance. His earlier position in the *Familia Pontificia* as a cardinal-deacon and scribe of papal bulls from 7 December 1190 had placed him at the centre of papal administration.

---

[117] Caen, AD Calvados, 2D54, f. 5047; D. Power, 'The Preparation of Count John I of Sées for the Third Crusade', *Crusading and Warfare in the Middle Ages: Realities and Representations, Essays in Honour of John France*, ed. D. Morton and S. John (Farnham, 2014), pp. 143–166.

[118] J.C. Andressohn, *The Ancestry and Life of Godfrey of Bouillon* (Bloomington, IN, 1947), pp. 51–2; S. John, *Godfrey of Bouillon: Duke of Lower Lotharingia, Ruler of Latin Jerusalem, c. 1060–1100* (London and New York, 2017), pp. 94–115; 'Cono comes de Duras cruce signatus eandem advocatiam sibi abjudicatam et castrum Duras Henrico juniori duci Lovaniensi 800 marchis vendidit', Gilbert of Mons, p. 240.

[119] *Regesta Regum Scottorum*, Vol. 2, *Acts of William I*, ed. G.W.S. Barrow (Edinburgh, 1971), pp. 370, 373–4.

[120] 'qui ad subventionem terrae Jerosolimitanae, ubi viderunt magis necessarium, prædictam pecuniam impendent', *Chronica*, Vol. 3, pp. 58–9.

It is highly likely that he would have noted Baldwin of Forde's success in overseeing the Saladin Tithe in England, as well as its general failure in the face of clerical opposition elsewhere. That he made Baldwin's successor, Hubert Walter, responsible for the collection of his crusader tax in England is unlikely to have been coincidental.

Religious Foundations and Crusader Social Networks

The previous section looked at the network of crusaders that needed to raise funds and the ways in which participation in the Third Crusade was funded. As has been demonstrated, as well as assisting in finance, certain foundations and religious figures were prominent in crusader social networks. This section deals with the crusading elites' relationships with religious houses, usually ascertained through records of their donations to the houses. It looks at identifiable links between known crusaders and religious institutions to discuss the potential influences of such associations – be it through the transmission of ideas or personal relationships – on crusade participation, before considering the role of Baldwin of Forde in greater detail.

The data set for this analysis is based on surviving charters of identifiable crusaders who made donations to religious foundations. It does not include data on parental support to a particular religious house or order, or donations by other family members. Appearance as witness to such a charter is not considered sufficient evidence of having an association with the foundation.[121] Data relating to donations that post-date the Third Crusade, such as Dreux IV de Merlo's co-foundation of the Templar commandery of Sauce-sur-Yonne *c.*1210, are also excluded.[122]

Despite the patchy nature of the surviving data, Table 2 is illustrative of an association or connection to religious institutions, and especially those linked to crusading, amongst participants of the Third Crusade. The quality of such associations could, of course, vary. The relationship between Everard of Aulnay and the Cistercian abbey at Trois-Fontaines, for example, involved a dispute over the alienation of his aunt's grange to the Order.[123] Medieval cartularies also contain charters that record purely business-orientated relationships, such as mortgaging property to fund participation in a crusade, as well as examples of faith and charity.

---

[121] Further information and sources can be found in Appendix 1. It is not possible to assess how complete the data set is.
[122] AN, S5235, dossier I, f. 1r.
[123] T. Evergates, *Henry the Liberal: Count of Champagne, 1127–1181* (Philadelphia, PA, 2016), p. 137.

Table 2. Numbers of Known Crusaders from North-Western Europe Associated with Religious Houses That Participated in the Third Crusade

Religious Order	Angevin Realm	France	Low Countries	Total
Augustinians	12	1	4	17
Benedictines	21	21	17	59
Cistercians *	45	47	8	100
Hospitallers	2	8	2	12
Premonstratensians	10	21	9	40
Templars	12	24	1	37
Lazar Houses	5	5	0	10
Other Houses	30	18	8	56
Total linked to one or more 'crusader' house	60	74	16	150
Total linked to any house	107	97	33	237
Total number of participants	347	147	89	583

* In the case of the Angevin realm, this category includes Sempringham Priory in Lincolnshire.

Significantly, of the 237 crusaders identified in this study as being associated with a religious house, only fourteen examples survive of their funding participation in the expedition by mortgaging or selling property with such a house. As covered in the previous section, Adam of Savoisy, Anselm of Neuvilette, Robert the Constable, and Walter le Nair borrowed money from Cistercian houses; Hugh IV of St Pol and Ralph of Chall dealt with the Premonstratensians; and Hugh of Bourbonne and Godfrey of Saint-Vérain *vifgaged* rights to the Templars to fund their journey eastwards.[124] In three cases, the relationship was with an unreformed religious order, that of Gobert of Werchin and John of Sées with the Benedictine houses at Hautmont and Troarn respectively, and Alard I of Croisilles with the Augustinians of Eaucourt. In addition, Robert Kent, Robert Hunaud, and Ronald, son-in-law to Nicholas of Gôtentin, mortgaged their lands to Kelso Abbey.

Crusading might also encourage a noble to resolve a dispute with a local religious house, of which a single example survives from the Third Crusade. In autumn 1191, Robert of Icklesham issued a charter in Jaffa to settle a

[124] Hugh IV of St Pol was also associated with the Cistercian abbey at Cercamp in northern France.

long-term dispute with Battle Abbey.¹²⁵ The overwhelming majority of the surviving charter evidence relating to participants in the Third Crusade is not, therefore, indicative of hostile or business-related relationships.

Against a backdrop of decreasing support to religious foundations in general, surviving records show that 41 per cent of tracked participants were linked to a religious foundation through a donation or close association, and that 26 per cent were similarly linked to houses associated with crusading, such as those belonging to the orders of Cîteaux, Prémontré, and the Templars.¹²⁶ Notwithstanding a paucity of evidence from non-Angevin France to argue that those links to religious houses were influenced by crusade finance, it is useful to consider how the Saladin Tithe may have affected the data. Within areas covered by the Tithe, the percentages are reduced to 31 per cent and 17 per cent respectively, which is still indicative of substantial crusader support to religious orders.

In terms of support of particular religious foundations, in line with King Richard's *acta*, the data indicates that ties to the Cistercian Order were particularly common amongst the Angevin and French contingents, with 42 per cent and 48 per cent of all those enjoying an association with a religious foundation being linked to a Cistercian house. While Gervers has demonstrated that overall support to the Cistercians tailed off in the latter part of the twelfth century, it remained strong amongst those who took the Cross and joined the Third Crusade from England and France, which is suggestive of a link between Cistercian involvement in crusade recruitment and donations.¹²⁷ Of course, not all of those deprived of part of their inheritance appreciated an ancestor's piety. Baldwin II, lord of Rumes, for example, unsuccessfully contested Baldwin le Carron's donations to the Templars made immediately prior to departing on the Third Crusade and whilst in the Holy Land in 1192.¹²⁸

It is also interesting that this data does not reflect the surge in donations to the Hospitallers and Templars in 1180s England identified by Gervers. A decade that witnessed the visit of Heraclius, the Latin Patriarch of Jeru-

---

¹²⁵ London, Lincoln's Inn, ms. Hale 87 (Battle cartulary), f. 69r. Robert of Icklesham is considered in more detail in Chapter Two. A similar settlement was reached between Guy III of Senlis and Chaalis Abbey in 1171, A. Luchaire, *Études sur les actes de Louis VII* (Paris, 1885), pp. 437–8.

¹²⁶ For a review of the development of religious foundations in England, see D. Knowles and R. Neville Hadcock, *Medieval Religious Houses: England and Wales* (London, 1971), pp. 8–30.

¹²⁷ Gervers, 'Donations to the Hospitallers', pp. 158–61.

¹²⁸ L. Dailliez, *Les Templiers en Flandre, Hainaut, Brabant, Liège et Luxembourg* (Nice, 1978), pp. 333–4, n.61 (fac-similé cartulaire); L. Devillers, *Inventaire commanderies Ordre Saint-Jean* (Mons, 1876), pp. 179–80, 187, 190–1; E. Warlop, *De Vlaamse adel vóór 1300* (Handzame, 1968), pp. 508, 193–9. Baldwin le Carron is considered in some detail in Chapter Four.

salem, to England, defeat at the battle of Hattin, and the fall of Jerusalem saw a 31 per cent increase in donations to the Hospitallers and a 17 per cent increase to the Templars. With the exception of William of Mandeville's pre-crusade donation of the *vill* of Chippenham, however, this increase in donations to the Hospitallers is not reflected amongst those who joined the Third Crusade from the Angevin realm.[129] It is possible that this indicates that donation to the orders was an acceptable alternative to crusading. In common with other religious houses, those of the Military Orders provided a degree of support to travellers, especially pilgrims. It is possible that the success of the Saladin Tithe in securing funds for those who had taken the Cross diminished the immediacy of the Hospitallers' support to crusaders, leading to a decrease in endowments amongst the crusaders themselves.

Whilst fragmentary, the data show considerably higher links between the Templars and crusaders from Capetian France, with 16 per cent of all participants enjoying links to a Templar house. These figures are boosted somewhat by those who made donations on crusade, such as those made by Rainard III of Grancey and by Duke Hugh III of Burgundy to the Templars at the siege of Acre in 1191.[130] The data also indicate that there was a solid core of crusaders linked to the Order centred on Manasses, bishop of Langres, and including members of families with historic links to the Templars, such as the Granceys, Vergys, and Sombernons.[131]

Against the background of links between the Premonstratensians and crusader families described in some detail above, it is worth noting that the Premonstratensian abbey of Floreffe hosted an assembly of crusaders in 1188, which was overseen by Bishop Ralph of Liège.[132] The abbey's patron, Otto II, lord of Trazegnies, had an established crusader lineage and had recently returned from the Holy Land with a fragment of the True Cross, which he gave to the abbey.[133] At the gathering, Duke Godfrey III of Leuven, as well as the counts of Namur and Hainaut, confirmed Otto's donation to Floreffe Abbey of 1184, the so-called Great Tithe of Trazegnies.[134] A number

---

[129] Confirmed by King Richard on 7 December 1190; BL, Cotton ms. Nero C.ix, f. 29v. Henry of Grafton's donation of 1189 to the Hospitallers is suggestive, but there is no evidence that he took the Cross, *Monasticon Anglicanum*, ed. W. Dugdale, Vol. 1 (London, 1655), p. 720.

[130] J. Richard, 'Les Templiers et les Hospitaliers en Bourgogne et en Champagne méridionale (XIIe–XIIIe siécles', *Vorträge und Forschungen: Die Geistlichen Ritterorden Europas*, Vol. 26, ed. J. Fleckenstein and M. Hellmann (1980), pp. 235, 237; *HdB*, Vol. 3, no. 815, 866.

[131] For more on this see, Schenk, *Templar Families*.

[132] *Crusade Charters*, no. 14 and pp. 95–6.

[133] 'Documents concernant Trazegnies, extraits du cartulaire de l'abbaye de Floreffe', ed. J. Barbier, *Analectes pour servir à l'histoire ecclésiastique de la Belgique*, Vol. 7 (1870), no. 3.

[134] In addition to Otto, his seneschal, Amand of Naast, Bishop Rudolf, and Simon of Thiméon, Godfrey of Leuven's son, Henry, took the Cross and travelled at least as far

of witnesses to this charter made their own donations to the house at this time, such as Simon of Thiméon.[135] A number most likely took the Cross at the same time, but record only survives of Godescalc III of Morialmé. Godescalc made a donation to the abbey, as he was 'inspired by a heavenly desire to go to Jerusalem with the gathering of the faithful in order to free the promised land from the hands of the impious'.[136]

Determining the motivation behind every donation to a religious institution can prove elusive. Only fourteen cases from the 237 examples of religious association considered in this section can be attributed to raising funds for the Third Crusade, with a further two charters resolving a long-term dispute between a crusader and a neighbouring religious house. The reduction in support to religious houses in areas covered by the Saladin Tithe is, however, suggestive, as is the prevalence of crusader donations to the Cistercians in England and to the Templars in areas of France. There is significant evidence of forms of association between donors and recipient religious orders that are unrelated to fundraising. Of these, a number can only be explained in terms of individual piety, such as that of Godescalc III of Morialmé.

Baldwin of Forde

There is every indication that piety also drove Baldwin of Forde, archbishop of Canterbury, to take the Cross. As arguably the most influential Cistercian monk in the Britain Isles, he provides a convenient opportunity to consider the impact of ecclesiastical magnates on the Third Crusade elite social network.[137] In addition to undoubtedly promoting Cistercian interests to his new king, which is considered shortly, he can be found in a number

---

as Sicily, but returned on news of his father's death, *Gesta Regis*, Vol. 2, p. 128. Otto also made a donation to the Cistercian abbey at Cambron in northern France whilst at the siege of Acre, *Cartulaire de l'abbaye de Cambron*, Part 1, ed. J.-J. de Smet (Brussels, 1869), p. 351.

[135] *Crusade Charters*, no. 15. Despite his association with the house of Trazegnies, it is likely that Simon of Thiméon joined the Imperial crusading contingent with Bishop Ralph and Henry of Namur.

[136] 'superno afflatus desiderio Iherosolimam proficiscendi cum coetu fidelium ad liberandam terram promissionis de minibus impiorum', *Crusade Charters*, no. 27; see also 'Documents concernant Sautour et Aublin, extraits du cartulaire de l'abbaye de Floreffe', *Analectes pour servir à l'histoire ecclésiastique de la Belgique*, Vol. 8 (1871), 365–6.

[137] Archbishop Baldwin and Bishop Hubert were not the only high-ranking clerics to take the Cross in England. The bishops of Bath, Coventry, Durham, and Norwich, however, were all released from their vows: John of Oxford, bishop of Norwich, for example, was robbed en route to the Holy Land and was given leave to return by the pope; Devizes, pp. 10–11; *Gesta Regis*, Vol. 2, pp. 79, 105–6, 115.

of specific crusader clusters. As was mentioned earlier in this chapter in the section on preaching, according to Peter of Blois, Archbishop Baldwin was initially reluctant to support the crusade. Peter's encouragement was evidently successful, as Baldwin of Forde took the Cross either alongside King Henry II at the ceremony at Gisors, or at Henry's Great Council in Geddington shortly afterwards.[138]

Baldwin preached the crusade with Gilbert of Glanville, bishop of Rochester, at the council, led a preaching tour of Wales that included a Cross-taking ceremony at Usk castle, and oversaw the collection of the Saladin Tithe in England.[139] Thereafter, the archbishop departed for the Holy Land in advance of King Richard following a request for support from King Guy.[140] Having arrived in Tyre on 16 September 1190, Baldwin reached the siege of Acre on 12 October, but died just over a month later, on 19 November 1190.[141]

As joint commander of the army outside Acre, Baldwin is reported in the *Itinerarium* to have had some two hundred knights and three hundred men-at-arms in his contingent, who fought under the banner of St Thomas Becket.[142] After Baldwin's death, however, Ralph of Diss described Hubert Walter's distribution of wages to twenty knights and fifty serjeants to guard the camp in accordance with the archbishop's wishes.[143] As is discussed in greater detail in Chapter Four, below, 'The Size of the Royal Household', the number of troops reported by Ralph of Diss reflects the typical size of an ecclesiastical or lay magnate's military household. This suggests that the remainder of the contingent mentioned in the *Itinerarium* may have been provided by Baldwin of Forde's crusader network. Analysis of his noble network allows us to identify some of them.

As former abbot of Forde Abbey and witness to King Richard's confirmation of the abbey's charter of 1189, Archbishop Baldwin was joined in the Holy Land by a group of crusaders with ties to the abbey, as well as by its

---

[138] Rigord, p. 83; *Annales Cestrienses*, pp. 38–40. It is not clear whether Henry of Marcy, cardinal bishop of Albano and former abbot of Clairvaux, had any influence on Archbishop Baldwin's change of heart.

[139] Gilbert of Glanville had served as a clerk to Baldwin of Forde and was archdeacon of Lisieux prior to being elected to the see of Rochester in 1185.

[140] Devizes, *Chronicon*, p. 19; Diss, Vol. 2, p. 84.

[141] *Gesta Regis*, Vol. 2, pp. 115, 42; *Epistolae Cartuariensis*, pp. 328–9; Wendover, pp. 186, 89.

[142] *Itinerarium*, p. 116. It is unlikely to be coincidental that crusaders from England established an order of regular canons in Acre dedicated to St Thomas. Indeed, there is evidence that the saint was adopted as a special patron by some English crusaders, especially those from London. See, Tyerman, *England*, p. 55.

[143] Diss, Vol. 2, p. 88. In addition, some members of his military household returned to England, such as his seneschal, Sylvester, *Epistolae Cantuarienses*, pp. 8, 25; *Gesta Regis*, Vol. 2, p. 148.

current prior, Robert II.[144] As is considered in more detail in the section on donors, at least two donors to the abbey, Richard Fitz-William of Langford and Henry Pomeroy, joined the crusade. Matthew Oisel, a local knight whose family was linked to the abbey, can also be placed with the expedition. Oisel's daughter married Helias Talbot, son and heir to another Forde donor, Geoffrey Talbot of Heathfield. Geoffrey Talbot was also a neighbour to a Hospitaller manor, through the donation of lands in Heathfield to the order by Hugh of Worcester. It is, however, unclear if that led to Geoffrey Talbot having direct contact with that order.[145] The family's links to the crusader Gerard Talbot are, likewise, unclear. Finally, Baldwin of Forde's clerk and nephew, Joseph of Exeter, travelled to the Holy Land, but returned following the death of his uncle.[146]

At Archbishop Baldwin's side at the siege of Acre was the bishop of Salisbury, Hubert Walter, and his military household.[147] As former dean of York, Bishop Hubert retained links to that diocese and, in addition to major landholders such as Robert Trussebot and Nigel of Mowbray, Yorkshire seems to have provided a significant number of less notable crusaders.[148] Robert of Trussebot's assistance to the bishop in distributing food during Lent at the siege of Acre in 1191 is suggestive that elements of the Yorkshire contingent remained associated with Hubert at the siege of Acre.[149]

Bishop Hubert's mother, Maud of Valoignes, was sister to another member of the Third Crusade, the sometime castellan of Dover, Alan of Valoignes.[150] Perhaps his most important relation amongst participants on the Third Crusade, however, was his uncle, the former chief justiciar, Ranulf of Glanville, elder brother to the bishop of Rochester.[151] The Glanville charters indicate that both Hubert and his brother, Theobald, had served in

---

[144] Baldwin was the third abbot of the abbey and Robert II of Forde was his immediate successor.

[145] *RCR*, Vol. 1, pp. 91, 347.

[146] R. Mortimer, *Angevin England: 1154–1258* (Oxford, 1994), p. 210.

[147] Everard was described as being in the service of the bishop of Salisbury when he lost his hand to an enemy sword during an attack on the march from Acre to Jaffa on 25 August 1191, Ambroise, line 5771; *Itinerarium*, p. 250.

[148] See, for example, Hugh Peitevin, Humphrey of Veilly, John of Penistone, Ralph of Chall, Walter le Noir, and William of Cornebruc. The last of these, however, arrived shortly after King Richard along with his brother and relations, 'et consanguinei cognominati Corneby', Ambroise, lines 4701–3; *Itinerarium*, p. 217.

[149] Ambroise, line 4433; *Itinerarium*, pp. 134–5.

[150] Alan's association with the vicar of Dartford in Kent, described as being on crusade to Jerusalem in 1189, is unclear; Tyerman, *England*, p. 74.

[151] Alan of Valoignes lost custody of Dover castle on the assumption of Richard, but was awarded an heiress in December 1189, TNA C 52/22, *carte antique* roll X, m.2d, no. 27. He was a crusader of the honour of Peverel of London, for which the estate was pardoned 20s. PR2 RI (1190), p. 110. He survived the crusade, but died in 1994, R. Mortimer, 'The Family of Rannulf de Glanville', *Historical Research*, 129 (1981), 1–16,

Ranulf's household.[152] The closeness of their bond is attested by Hubert's calls for prayers for the 'souls of Ranulf Glanvill and Bertha his wife, who nourished us' on founding St Mary's Abbey, West Dereham, in 1188. Interestingly, Dereham was to house Premonstratensian canons, and Bishop Hubert's patronage suggests another dimension to the order's prominence amongst those institutions gaining charters early in King Richard's reign. Ranulf had taken the Cross on the occasion of Patriarch Heraclius of Jerusalem's visit to England in 1185 and renewed his vow in 1188.[153] According to Gerald of Wales, Ranulf accompanied Archbishop Baldwin on the initial stages of his crusade recruitment tour of Wales.[154] Having initially fallen out of favour with the new king, Ranulf was reconciled with King Richard and travelled with him to Marseille. He then most probably jointly led the Angevin advance guard to Acre with Archbishop Baldwin, only to die within a few weeks of arriving at the siege of Acre.[155] He was a prominent landholder in East Anglia and, through him, Baldwin of Forde was linked to crusaders from that region recorded in the Pipe Rolls, including nineteen tenants from the House of Clare.[156] This evidence is revisited in relation to familial networks in the next chapter.

Baldwin of Forde's opposite number in the Capetian contingent was arguably Philip of Dreux, bishop of Beauvais. As nephew and vigorous ally to King Philip II of France, the bishop of Beauvais was at the heart of the Capetian royal social network and, as will be shown, many members of the royal family took the Cross, including the bishop's elder brother, Count Robert II of Dreux.[157] Whilst he was not the only ecclesiastical magnate with links to the royal house or the only one to join the Third Crusade, Bishop Philip was to play a key role in the events that followed and may have been an important influence on Philip Augustus' decision to take the Cross.[158]

---

p. 8. Ranulf had married Maud's sister, Bertha; Stacey, 'Hubert Walter', *Oxford Dictionary of National Biography* (accessed online 30 January 2016).

[152] C.R. Young, *Hubert Walter: Lord of Canterbury and Lord of England* (Durham, 1968), p. 3 and footnote 1.

[153] *Chronica*, Vol. 2, p. 302; Coggeshall, p. 23.

[154] Gerald of Wales, Vol. 4, pp. 104–5.

[155] Devizes, *Chronicon*, p. 19; Diss, Vol. 2, p. 84; *Gesta Regis*, Vol. 2, p. 115; 'CCCXLVI. Conventui Cantuariensi Capellanus Archepiscopi', *Epistolae Cartuarienses*, pp. 328–9.

[156] Ranulf was also a tenant of St Edmund's Abbey, thereby exempting him from 10s. in scutage, along with Henry of Hastings, Ralph of Halsted, Robert of Horningsheath, Richard of St Clare, and William Lovell, PR3 RI (1192), p. 43. Henry of Hastings and Ralph of Halsted were also tenants of the house of Clare, PR3 RI (1192), p. 44. The abbey at Bury St Edmunds was liable for forty knight's fees to the Crown, meaning 15% of its tenant knights went on crusade.

[157] Rigord, pp. 83–4.

[158] Renaud of Monçon, bishop of Chartres and first cousin to King Philip II, took

Bishop Philip was a committed crusader who made personal endowments to both Cistercian and Premonstratensian houses prior to going on the Third Crusade.[159] Indeed, he very much reflected the martial Christianity of some prominent Cistercians, such as Henry of Marcy, and he would go on to found a Cistercian convent at Pentemont in 1217.[160] There is no surviving evidence of his preaching for the crusade, but it would be incongruous for an ecclesiastical magnate who had previously been on crusade and who would take the Cross again to fight the Cathars not to have promoted the Third Crusade in his diocese. However, identifiable crusaders from the Beauvais region are linked to Philip of Dreux's regional rival, Count Ralph I of Clermont-en-Beauvais, constable of France, rather than the bishop.[161]

Late in 1187, news reached France of Saladin's conquest of Jerusalem. Bishop Philip and his brother, Count Robert II, committed themselves to the Third Crusade alongside their king at the ceremony at Gisors on 21 January 1188.[162] They were joined by their brothers-in-law, Raoul III of Nesle, count of Soissons, and Raoul I, lord of Coucy, and their paternal cousins, Peter II of Courtenay, Theobald V of Blois, and Stephen of Sancerre.[163] It is also likely that their maternal second cousin and constable of Champagne, Guy II of Dampierre, and his brothers-in-law, Geoffrey III

---

the Cross alongside his brother, Count Henry I of Bar, and the king of France, at the ceremony between Trie and Gisors on 13 January 1188, Rigord, p. 83.

[159] As a twenty-one-year-old bishop-elect, Philip of Beauvais had accompanied Henry of Troyes, count of Champagne, to Jerusalem in 1179; William of Tyre, *A History of Deeds Done Across the Sea*, Vol. 2, trans. E.A. Babcock and A.C. Krey (New York, 1976), p. 443. See also, T. Evergates, 'Louis VII and the Counts of Champagne', *The Second Crusade and the Cistercians*, ed. M. Gervers (New York, 1992), pp. 109–17. Robert of Torigny, *The Chronicle of Robert of Torigny: Chronicles of the Reigns of Stephen, Henry II, and Richard I*, Vol. 4, ed. R. Howlett (London, 1889), p. 62; BN, ms. latin 11001 (cartulary of Froidmont); *Le chartrier de l'abbaye prémontré de Saint-Yved de Braine: 1134–1250*, ed. élèves de l'École Nationale des Chartes and O. Guyotjeannin (Paris, 2000). In 1184 Bishop Philip also confirmed a donation made by Simon of Fransiriis to the Benedictine abbey of St Vaast, in Arras; L. Ricouart, *Les biens de l'abbaye de Saint-Vaast dans les diocèses de Beauvais, de Noyon, de Soissons et d'Amiens* (Anzin, 1888), pp. 46–7. As mentioned earlier, Philip of Dreux's brother-in-law, Raoul I of Coucy, was advocate of the house of Prémontré; *Crusade Charters*, no. 11.

[160] Abbé Delettre, *Histoire du diocèse de Beauvais, depuis son établissement, au 3me siècle, jusqu'au on 2 septembre 1792*, Vol. 2 (Beauvais, 1843), p. 237.

[161] Count Ralph and his niece's new husband, Hugh of Oyry, died at the siege of Acre, Gilbert of Mons, p. 150. Hugh's brother, Walter of Oyry, was also present at the siege as was his brother-in-law, Baldwin of Dargus. Roger of Howden highlights the role of Walter and Baldwin at the siege, placing them alongside Baldwin le Carron, which may indicate their opposition to the bishop of Beauvais, *Gesta Regis*, Vol. 2, p. 144. See also, Power, 'John I of Sées', pp. 149–50.

[162] *Gesta Regis*, Vol. 2, pp. 58–9.

[163] Rigord, pp. 83–4. Raoul III of Nesle was joined by his brother, John I of Nesle. John's wife, Elizabeth of Cysoing, was descended from Ingelbert IV, a participant in the

of Joinville, seneschal of Champagne, and Narjot II of Toucy, took the crusader vow at the same time.[164]

Like Baldwin of Forde, Bishop Philip formed part of his king's advance guard, sailing for the Holy Land with a party of Flemish and French crusaders as early as August 1189.[165] In addition to his elder brother, his companions included James I of Avesnes, a renowned hero of the tournament circuit, Count Henry I of Bar, and Everard II of Brienne.[166] It is likely that Guy of Dampierre's familial group initially travelled with them as both he and Geoffrey IV of Joinville were recorded by Louis Maimbourg as being in Silves with the Dreux brothers in 1189.[167] Roger of Wavrin, bishop of Cambrai, was in the same party, accompanying his brother, Hellin, seneschal of Flanders, at the head of leading elements of Count Philip of Alsace's contingent.[168] While ecclesiastic magnates routinely participated in military campaigns, it is unlikely to be coincidental that the three main contingents sailing from north-western Europe for the Levant included a senior cleric.

Baldwin of Forde and the bishop of Beauvais took opposing positions in relation to the remarriage of Isabella of Jerusalem, each probably representing the position of their monarch. By late October 1189, the water supply to the crusader camp had been contaminated with human and animal remains. Disease spread and had already carried off Sibylla of Jerusalem and both her daughters. With their deaths, Guy of Lusignan lost his claim to the

---

First Crusade. She seemingly died around the time of the Third Crusade and John then married Aleyde of Dreux.

[164] Henry II, count of Champagne, took the Cross alongside the kings of England and France, and it is likely that his constable and his seneschal joined him. Guy II of Dampierre's sister, Helvis, was married to Geoffrey III of Joinville. Agnes, his youngest sister was married to Narjot III of Toucy; Schenk, *Templar Families*, pp. 194–6.

[165] *Itinerarium*, p. 67. In the interim, according to Howden, Philip of Beauvais commanded a Capetian army that invaded Normandy in 1188. During the campaign, his force burnt the towns of Blangy and Aumale, *Gesta Regis*, Vol. 2, p. 45. According to Ambroise, Andrew of Brienne accompanied his brother, Count Everard II of Brienne, Ambroise, line 2918. However, in her thesis, Dana Celest Asmoui Ismail evidences the two-decade-long hostility between the two brothers. So, it is more likely that Andrew travelled separately, with Geoffrey of Lusignan, D.C. Asmoui Ismail, 'A History of the Counts of Brienne' (PhD thesis, RHUL, 2013), pp. 105–7. Walter II of Brienne was married to Adele of Baudemont, great-aunt to the Dreux brothers, and their daughter had married James I of Chacenay, becoming the parents of the crusader Everard I of Chacenay.

[166] *Gesta Regis*, Vol. 2, pp. 93–4. Although not listed in the sources, it is likely that Bishop Renaud was in the same party as his brother, Henry of Bar.

[167] L. Maimbourg, *Histoire des croisades pour le delivrance de la Terre Sainte*, 3rd edition, Vol. 3 (Paris, 1680), p. 177. Geoffrey III of Joinville was probably in Silves with his son at the same time.

[168] Ambroise, line 2920; Diss, Vol. 2, p. 79; Gilbert of Mons, pp. 136, 167, 180, 274; Wendover, p. 178.

throne of Jerusalem. He had been an unpopular choice, to put it mildly, and remained the subject of intense animosity from the lords of the Latin East, especially Queen Sibylla's stepfather, Balian of Ibelin.[169] Moreover, James of Avesnes and Ludwig III of Thuringia had questioned King Guy's claim to leadership of the crusade.

The rightful heir was now Sibylla's younger sister, Isabella of Jerusalem, and this presented the opportunity to select a new king, someone who would unite the crusade. Unfortunately for Guy of Lusignan's numerous opponents, Isabella was already married, and her husband, Humphrey of Toron, showed neither the ambition to be king nor a willingness to step aside for another candidate, such as Conrad of Montferrat.[170] Cousin to both Frederick Barbarossa and Leopold V of Austria, and second cousin to Philip II of France, Conrad had arrived in the Holy Land in time to lead the defence of Tyre against Saladin. Conrad's father had been captured at the battle of Hattin, but Conrad had refused to surrender Tyre to liberate him. Already an experienced general, Conrad was a popular choice amongst the nobility of the Latin East and crusaders alike, including the bishop of Beauvais, and was well connected.[171]

Once Conrad's men had escorted Isabella of Jerusalem from her husband's quarters in the encampment outside Acre, Bishop Philip annulled her marriage to Humphrey of Toron.[172] The archbishop of Canterbury had strongly opposed this move – seemingly on grounds of piety, but the Lusignans were also Richard I's subjects and active crusaders. Notwithstanding the support of local barons and prominent crusaders, Bishop Philip probably only escaped severe censure due to Baldwin's death on 19 November 1190 and the weakening of Angevin influence in the kingdom of Jerusalem. Following his demise, neither the papal legate nor the archbishop of Pisa was willing to oppose the Capetian-backed Montferrat faction. On 24 November Philip of Dreux oversaw the marriage of his cousin Conrad and Isabella with the support of her mother, Maria Komnenos.[173] Whilst in many cases social networks have to be studiously pieced together, the events of late 1190 provide a rare opportunity to see them in action.

---

[169] The widespread disaffection with his rule is acknowledged even by sympathetic historians. See, for example, B. Hamilton, *The Leper King and His Heirs* (Cambridge, 2000), p. 218.

[170] Ambroise, line 4123; A. Jotischky, *Crusading and the Crusade States*, 2nd edition (Abingdon, 2017), pp. 170–1.

[171] Conrad of Montferrat defeated the Imperial German army at Camerino (1179) and had aided Isaac II Angelus to put down a revolt (1187).

[172] Diss, Vol. 2, p. 86. See also, B.M. Bolton, 'A Matter of Great Confusion: King Richard I and Syria's *Vetus de Monte*', *Diplomatics in the Eastern Mediterranean 1000–1500, Aspects of Cross-Cultural Communication*, ed. A.D. Beihammer, M.G. Parani, and C.D. Schabel (Leiden, 2008), p. 186.

[173] Diss, Vol. 2, p. 86; *Itinerarium*, pp. 119–23.

Notwithstanding potential political aspects, the strength of the archbishop's piety is reflected in the concentration of professed religious in his contingent. In a recent paper, Helen Nicholson drew upon letters to the monks at Canterbury to reflect on the archbishop's consternation with the moral and spiritual state of the crusader host.[174] In a letter dated 21 October 1190, Baldwin's chaplain complains that 'our knights hide in their tents, and those that promised a speedy victory are cowardly and torpid'.[175] This displays a striking similarity to the account in the *Itinerarium* that Baldwin 'saw as he heard that the army had lost all discipline, concentrating on taverns, prostitutes, and games', which Nicholson tentatively suggested might indicate a link between both accounts.[176] However, the language is also reminiscent of Alan of Lille's sermon addressed to knights (*Ad milites*), in which he condemned their felonious and vile behaviour and admonished them for their treatment of the poor.[177]

John Hosler has highlighted the immediate impact of the archbishop and his contingent on the conduct of the campaign.[178] The crusader offensive launched after the feast of St Martin on 12 November was arguably indicative of the renewed vigour his spiritual leadership and the martial strength of his contingent brought to the Latin besiegers. Despite the likelihood that Baldwin of Forde was already suffering from the condition that would lead to his death on 19 November, he first joined the other bishops in absolving the army.[179] Having determined those leaders that would oversee the defence of the siege lines, Henry of Champagne, Conrad of Montferrat, and Geoffrey of Lusignan led the army out from its encampment in a fighting march. Given that English crusaders are described by Ambroise as joining unmounted Templar knights in the rearguard for the withdrawal back to the camp on 13 November, it is likely that Baldwin of Forde was positioned with them.[180] The *Itinerarium* is unequivocal in its description of the aged and infirm archbishop's active participation as he 'fought amongst the rest, but he outstripped them all' in the fighting.[181] Less than a week

---

[174] H. Nicholson, 'The Crusade of Baldwin of Forde, Archbishop of Canterbury', paper given at the 25th International Medieval Congress, University of Leeds (UK), July 2018.

[175] 'Milites nostri infra tentoria sua delitescunt, et qui sibi festinam promittebant victoriam, ignavi et torpidi, et quasi convicti', *Epistolae Cantuarienses*, p. 329.

[176] 'Praeterea archiepiscopus Cantuariensis videns quod ante audiens exercitum omnino dissolutum, tabernis, scortis et ludis talorum insisteret', *Itinerarium*, p. 123.

[177] Alan of Lille, *Ars Praedicandi*, PL, Vol. 210, cols. 185–7.

[178] Hosler, *Siege of Acre*, pp. 89–94.

[179] Ambroise, lines 3961–4; *Itinerarium*, p. 116.

[180] Based on his reading of Ambroise and the *Itinerarium*, Hosler places Baldwin of Forde in the crusader camp, but given the presence of the archbishop's contingent in the army and a description of his being involved in the fighting (see below), it is more likely that he led them; Hosler, *Siege of Acre*, pp. 89–90; Ambroise, lines 4037–9.

[181] 'Sane venerabilis archipraesul Cantuariorum Baldwinus inter caeteros et prae caet-

later, however, the archbishop was dead, leaving Hubert Walter to continue his spiritual mission.

As archbishop of Canterbury, Baldwin of Forde was the senior bishop of the Church in England and one of only a few Cistercian monks to hold high office in the late twelfth century. His continuing support was vital to the viability of King Richard's crusade. Baldwin was instrumental in preparations for the Third Crusade in England, such as through oversight of the Saladin Tithe and his preaching tour of Wales. His influence can be seen amongst members of the noble elite who took the Cross, notably in the West Country and Yorkshire. As spiritual leader of lead elements of King Richard's contingent, he played a prominent role at the siege of Acre before succumbing to illness. Analysis of King Richard's *acta* allows us to consider the degree to which Baldwin of Forde may have influenced the king of England's focus in the early months of his reign.

In stark contrast to the predominantly ecclesiastic nature of Baldwin of Forde's crusader social network, Bishop Philip's prominence lay within the Capetian royal network, but one should not ignore his religious impact on the campaign as the senior cleric in King Philip II's contingent, such as in relation to the struggle for the crown of Jerusalem. Whilst there are no overt signs that Bishop Philip oversaw a preaching campaign, Social Network Analysis places him at the heart of the Capetian crusader contingent and he had considerable influence over the conduct of the subsequent campaign in the Holy Land.

Royal *Acta* and Royal Priorities

Royal *acta* provide a useful basis of analysing a ruler's priorities, as well as the role of patronage, influence, and locality in an itinerant court. This section will consider what surviving *acta* suggest about the priorities of Count Philip of Flanders and the kings of England and France in relation to crusade participation and funding. This section also illustrates how Social Network Analysis can be helpful in identifying institutional affiliations to crusading.

In the central Middle Ages charters were the principal means of recording contracts and grants in northern and western Europe. Most commonly, their stated purpose was to record endowments and they were most often initiated by either the donor or the beneficiary petitioning the king – but access came at a price. King Henry II might have complained that crowds of petitioners constantly harassed him, even during mass,[182] but Nicholas

---

eris insignias militat; quem licet ad segnitiem senilis invitet infirmitas, naturae tamen defectum virtutum perfectione transcendit', *Itinerarium*, p. 116.

[182] Peter of Blois, 'Dialogus inter Regem Henricum Secundem et abbatem Bonevallis', ed. R.B.C. Huygens, *Revue Bénédictine*, 68 (1958), 104–5.

Vincent has demonstrated that the Angevin court controlled access to the king.[183] In addition to royal officers levying bribes, the king might exclude certain individuals from court or isolate them within it.[184] Moreover, securing a charter routinely resulted in a fine, the payment of which might be required immediately or deferred indefinitely. For example, whilst the charter or letter of appointment confirming Michael Belet's retention of the office of royal butler has been lost, evidence of payment of his fee of 100l. survives.[185] Deferred fines served to secure the loyalty of the beneficiaries, and even favoured court officials might be called upon to redeem fines upon retirement.[186] However, as I argue here, there is strong evidence that individuals and institutions enjoyed royal favour based, in part at least, on their relationship with crusading and the Third Crusade in particular.[187]

The *acta* of the veteran crusader Philip of Alsace, count of Flanders, as he prepared to depart on the Third Crusade are illustrative. As Danielle Park has recently demonstrated, Count Philip made the protection of the Church during his absence a priority.[188] From taking the Cross at the assembly at Gisors in January 1188 through to his departure for the Holy Land in 1190, he confirmed the privileges of several religious institutions, as well as the rights of towns, such as Dunkirk, Grammont, and Hulst.[189] For example, the count instructed his officers to respect the Premonstratensians of St

---

[183] N. Vincent, 'The Court of Henry II', *Henry II, New Interpretations*, ed. C. Harper-Bill and N. Vincent (Woodbridge, 2007), pp. 335–61.

[184] See, for example, Gerald of Wales' description of Henry II's dislike of the Baskervilles, *Expugnatio Hibernica: The Conquest of Ireland by Giraldus Cambrensis*, ed. A.B. Scott and F.X. Martin (Dublin, 1978), pp. 128–9.

[185] PR2 RI (1190), p. 102.

[186] See, for example, the fine levied on Reginald of Warenne in 1176, N. Vincent, 'The Foundation of Wormegay Priory', *Norfolk Archaeology*, 43 (1999), 307–12.

[187] The fact that Henry II's charters are not dated makes it difficult to link individual acta to the agreement of 24 June 1184, and the data is ambiguous. Charters to the Cistercian abbeys of Clairvaux, Foucarmont, Rufford, Savigny, and Vaux-de-Cernay, the Premonstratensians of Ile-Dieu, and the Lepers of Le Dézert have been dated to between 1172 and 1189 with a further charter to Foucarmont issued sometime after Henry II took the Cross in 1188, *Letters and Charters of Henry II*, ed. Vincent, nos. 625, 1077, 2299, 2435, 2738, 1344, 758, 1078. However, charters also went to the unreformed Benedictine houses at Jumièges, Lessay, Longues, Sainte-Barbe-en-Auge, Sainte-Foi de Longueville, Saint-Sauveur-le-Vicomte, Troarn, and Valmont between 1172 and 1189, and another to Sainte-Foi after Henry II took the Cross – this last charter is, however, judged by Vincent to be 'either a charter drafted and written by a local, non-chancery scribe, or outright forgery', *Letters and Charters of Henry II*, ed. Vincent, nos. 1400–3, 1483–4, 1657, 2332, 2395, 2685, 2721–3, 1660.

[188] D.E.A. Park, *Papal Protection and the Crusader: Flanders, Champagne, and the Kingdom of France, 1095–1222* (Woodbridge, 2018), pp. 172–7.

[189] *De Oorkonden der Graven van Vlaanderen, (juli 1128–september 1191), Uitgave-Band III, Regering van Filips van de Elzas, Tweede deel: 1178-1191*, ed. T. de Hemptinne, A. Verhurst, and L. de Mey (Brussels, 2009), nos. 789, 808–9.

Michael of Antwerp, as well as the Benedictines of Bergues Abbey, and issued a donation to St Bertin.[190] As Park notes, his charters mentioned the count of Flanders' impending departure on crusade.[191] In addition to a donation to Clairvaux Abbey linked to plans for him to be interred there, Philip donated his chapel and sacred equipment to the Cistercians.[192]

My research reveals that, as King Richard's departure for the Holy Land grew imminent, religious orders traditionally linked to crusading, such as the Military Orders or those associated with crusade preaching, enjoyed priority of access to the king, as did foundations that enjoyed the patronage of influential noble houses. Only once preparations were underway do we see a notable increase in activity in relation to unreformed houses and cathedral chapters, which may indicate a move onto ensuring the security of the realm in the king's absence from October 1189 onwards. Although it is logical that monarchs might favour the petitions of such establishments during periods of particularly intense religious activity, it also raises the question of whether particular houses sought the protection of a royal charter due to an increase in donations brought on by the crusade and if King Richard gave favour to attract the assistance of such donors.

King Richard of England's *Acta*

In the immediate aftermath of his coronation on 3 September 1189, Richard issued thirteen *acta* that survive in some form or another.[193] These serve to illustrate a pattern demonstrating that the king's focus was immediately on setting the pre-conditions for a successful expedition in terms of finance, organisation, and religious motivation. Charters went to religious foundations linked to families that were to provide support to the crusade, as well as those institutions directly linked to crusading, such as the Cistercians. Notwithstanding Walter Map's famous comment on Richard I's criticism of the Cistercians for their wealth and avarice, through their involvement in the wool trade the Cistercians had the ready cash to secure access to the king, which meant that they could also contribute to his campaign chest.[194]

Of King Richard's thirteen charters, eight were to confirm the possessions and liberties of Cistercian houses: one was a confirmation of his

---

[190] *Oorkonden der Graven van Vlaanderen*, nos. 782, 794.

[191] Park, *Papal Protection*, p. 173. See, for example, *Oorkonden der Graven van Vlaanderen*, nos. 778, 797.

[192] *Oorkonden der Graven van Vlaanderen*, no. 830. See also; *Recueil des chartes de l'abbaye de Clairvaux au XIIe siècle*, ed. J. Waquet and J.-M. Roger (Paris, 2004), nos. 844, 846; and N.L. Paul, *To Follow in Their Footsteps: The Crusades and Family Memory in the High Middle Ages* (New York, 2012), p. 118.

[193] From 5 to 9 September 1189.

[194] On Walter Map, see M. Sinex, 'Echoic Irony in Walter Map's Satire against the Cistercians', *Comparative Literature*, 54/4 (2002), 275–90.

parents' gifts to the Templars.[195] The seemingly incongruous inclusion of the unreformed Benedictine priory at Wroxall amongst those *acta* may well be due to the legend surrounding its foundation by a crusader, Hugh of Hatton, to celebrate his release from captivity in the Holy Land.[196] With no obvious crusade links, Malmesbury is an exception to King Richard's tendency to favour houses linked to crusading or crusader families. It was one of the oldest abbeys in England and had, until recently, been under royal stewardship after falling into debt; so it is probable that the charter served to secure Malmesbury's assets prior to the king's departure for the Holy Land. As well as being a Cistercian house, the abbey at Holmcultram in Cumbria had also been under the personal protection of Henry II;[197] it is not clear if it was the demands of stewardship, Cistercian influence, or a combination of the two that led to it receiving a charter so early in Richard's reign. Lastly, Bec-Hellouin Abbey in Normandy was closely associated with the influential Clare family, at least eighteen of whose tenants with lands in East Anglia went on the Third Crusade led by Richard of Clare, lord of Saham and likely brother to Richard of Clare, earl of Hertford.[198] In

---

[195] In addition to Holmcultram Abbey, the Cistercian houses at Flaxley and Waverley received their confirmations on 5 September 1189, and the influential Rievaulx Abbey gained confirmation of lands and pasture in Yorkshire around the same time. See, *The Cartae Antiquae, Rolls 11-20*, ed. J. Conway Davies (1957), pp. 111–12, no. 483; Lincolnshire Archives, Revesby Abbey Box 2, no. 40; *Cartularium Rievallense*, ed. J.C. Atkinson (London, 1889), pp. 127–8, from ms. Cartulary of Rievaulx, fos. 113v–114v.

[196] TNA C 53/114 (Charter Roll 1 Edward III) m.1, in an *inspeximus* dated 7 January 1327; *CCR 1326–41*, pp. 63–4. Exceptions to a pattern of prioritising houses linked to crusading or crusader families include Merton Priory, Newhouse Abbey, and Ramsey Abbey, BL, Harl. ms. 85, f. 413 v.; cf. TNA C 52/31 *carte antique* roll GG, no. 18, partly illegible. *Records of Merton Priory in the County of Surrey*, ed. A. Heales (London, 1898), Appendix, p. xxii, no. XXVIII; *Cal. Charter Rolls*, Vol. 3, p. 388, TNA E 164/28 (Ramsey cartulary) f. 191v. *Cartularium Monasterii de Rameseia*, ed. W.H. Hart (London, 1884-93), Vol. 2, p. 296; and an award to the bishop of Worcester, Worcester Records Office, ms. BA 3814, fos 41v–42r, and TNA C 52/4, *carte antique* roll 4, m. 2d, no. 43. Of the seventy-eight charters issued by King Richard in September 1189, however, only twelve fall outside the pattern of prioritising houses linked to crusading or crusader families.

[197] The abbey of Holmcultram received its confirmation on 6 September, as did the ancient Benedictine house at Malmesbury, Carlisle Record Office, Holm Cultram cartulary, pp. 162–3; TNA C 52/16, *carte antique* roll 16, m. 2; TNA C 52/22, *carta antique* roll 22, m. 1, no. 5; TNA C 52/18, *carte antique* roll 18, m. 1d, no. 20. In 1183 Master Nicholas, a monk of St Albans, succeeded to the abbacy and remained in post until 1186 or possibly 1187. He was deposed after having been accused before the king and archbishop of running into heavy debt and having refused to amend. For most of 1187–9 the abbey was in the king's hands, and Robert of Melun, sub prior of Winchester, must have succeeded in 1187, *Registrum Malmesburiense*, Vol. 1, ed. J.S. Brewer (London, 1879), pp. 259–63.

[198] Bec Abbey received a confirmation of its possessions and liberties, and quittance from tolls and customs, on 5 September 1189, *Stoke by Clare Priory Cartulary*, Vol. I, ed. C. Harper-Bill and R. Mortimer (Woodbridge, 1982), nos. 2, 6. For crusader tenants of

addition, on 1 May 1190, King Richard confirmed a donation by Hugh of Gourney to the abbey.[199] Hugh was a member of Richard's advance guard, arriving in Acre in the autumn of 1190, and camping alongside Otto of Trazegnies during the city's siege. He was appointed to guard Richard's share of Muslim prisoners from Acre and is known to have fought at the battle of Arsuf.[200]

As King Richard headed northwards towards Geddington for his Great Council at nearby Pipewell Abbey on 11 September 1189, he awarded quittance from toll, passage, and all customs to Tiron Abbey in Perche, as well as confirming an annual payment of 20 *marks* to the house.[201] Established by a pre-Cistercian reformer, Bernard of Abbeville, in 1109, the Tironensian Order enjoyed an early saint in Adjutor of Tiron, a Norman knight who had been captured and imprisoned by the Muslims whilst on crusade. His hagiography by Hugh of Amiens, the *Vita Sancti Adjutoris*, relates his miraculous escape and return to France, whereupon he entered the abbey at Tiron as a monk.[202]

On his arrival at Geddington, Richard signed further charters to Cistercian houses, such as Bordesley, Rufford, Swineshead, and Pipewell itself,[203] but in the weeks that followed, a number of confirmations went to other ancient abbeys, including St Albans, and to houses with ties to Richard's own family, such as Reading Abbey, which had been founded by Henry I and became his place of rest.[204] However, Reading Abbey was also tied to

---

the house of Clare in East Anglia see, PR3 RI (1191), p. 44. Engelram of Fiennes, lord of Martock, was also associated with Bec Abbey, his father-in-law having donated lands in his manor of Clapton, Surrey, to the monks, *Monasticon Anglicanum*, ed. Dugdale, Vol. 1, p. 583.

[199] *CCR*, Vol. 4, p. 261.

[200] *Itinerarium*, p. 93, Wendover, p. 178. *Gesta Regis*, Vol. 2, pp. 179–80 (7 September 1191); *Itinerarium*, p. 261; present at the battle with his renowned men, Ambroise, line 6162.

[201] AD Eure-et-Loir, H1374 f. 47v no. 172; Winchester College, Muniments 10628.

[202] For more on Adjutor, see K. Allen Smith, 'Monastic Memories of the Early Crusading Movement', *Remembering the Crusades and Crusading*, ed. M. Cassidy-Welch (London, 2017), pp. 136–40. The order also received benefits from crusaders, such as an annual quantity of wine from Hugh III of Le Puiset, and the gift of a mill from Everard of Villabrum, *Cartulaire de l'abbaye de la Sainte-Trinité de Tiron*, ed. L. Merlet, Vol. 1 (Chartres, 1883), nos. 127–8, 288.

[203] The Cistercian houses at Swineshead, Bordesley, and Pipewell received their confirmations on 11 and 13 September 1189, respectively, *CPR 1494–1509*, pp. 620–1; *CCR*, Vol. 4, pp. 135–6; *Monasticon Anglicanum*, ed. Dugdale, Vol. 5, pp. 490–1; London, College of Arms, Monastic Charters misc. 180. A copy in *CCR*, Vol. 2, p. 66, *inspeximus* of 51 Henry III; *CCR*, Vol. 2, p. 408. The abbeys at Croxton and Rufford received their confirmations on 14 September, *CCR*, Vol. 2, pp. 376–7; Nottinghamshire Record Office ms. DDSR 102/153.

[204] Landon, *Itinerary*, nos. 42, 50; TNA C 52/22, carte antique roll X, no. 12; *Reading*

William of Ferrers, earl of Derby, who would die at the siege of Acre,[205] and William of Mandeville, earl of Essex, who initially took the Cross, but died before completing his vow.[206] Support to Reading Abbey, therefore, presented the opportunity to meet familial obligation and build an association with two crusader magnates.

Of the seventy-seven charters issued in September 1189, four went to either Baldwin of Forde or his cathedral chapter in Canterbury, five to Reading Abbey, three to Sempringham Priory and two to Bec-Hellouin, and forty-one to orders closely associated with crusading, mainly the Cistercians and Premonstratensians, but also the Tironensians, the Hospitallers, and the Order of St Lazarus.[207]

As David Marcombe points out, identifiable crusaders only made up some 7 per cent of the two hundred patrons named in the cartulary of Burton Lazars.[208] When one focuses on donations in advance of the Third Crusade, however, there is sufficient evidence of a potential relationship between participation in the expedition and the Order of St Lazarus to deserve further consideration.[209] Indeed, in comparison to the grants to other houses, only Reading Abbey received more charters than the Lazarite Order in the first month of Richard's reign.

Abbey Cartularies, Vol. 1, ed. B.R. Kemp (London, 1986), pp. 60–3, no. 34.

[205] *Gesta Regis*, Vol. 2, p. 148.

[206] *Gesta Regis*, Vol. 2, p. 92.

[207] Cistercian abbeys at Bruern, Coggeshall, Stratford Langthorne, and Warden received their confirmations on 15 September, TNA C 52/17, *carte antique* roll 17, m. 1, no. 1; *Cartae Antiquae, Rolls 11–20*, ed. R. Conway Davies, no. 503, pp. 120–1; *CCR*, Vol. 5, pp. 221–2, *inspeximus* of 46 Edward III; *CPR 1388–92*, pp. 77–8; TNA C 52/22, *carte antique* roll X, m. 2d, no. 26; *CCR*, Vol. 2, p. 335, *inspeximus* of 14 Edward I, m.2. Forde and Loroux abbeys received their charters on 16 September, TNA C 52/18, *carte antique* roll 18, m. 1d, no. 21; *Cartae Antiquae, Rolls 11–20*, pp. 162–4, no. 561; AN JJ66, f. 8r, no. 18. Fountains and Kirkstall Abbeys received their charters on 17 September 1189, *Memorials of the Abbey of St Mary of Fountains*, ed. J.R. Walbran (Durham, 1863), pp. 11–13, TNA DL 42/7, f. 65r-v. Finally, on 29 September, Merevale Abbey received its confirmation, *CCR*, Vol. 2, p. 431, 21 Edward I, m. 1. Sulby Abbey received its charter sometime in September and was closely associated with the House of Leicester, *CCR*, Vol. 3, p. 311, *inspeximus* of Edward II; *A History of the County of Northampton*, Vol. 2, ed. R.M. Serjeantson and W.R.D. Adkins (London, 1906), p. 138. For the counts of Perche see the award of alms and quittance from tolls, customs etc. to Tiron Abbey, Chartres, AD Eure-et-Loire H1374, f.47v no. 172.

[208] D. Marcombe, *Leper Knights: The Order of St. Lazarus of Jerusalem in England, 1150–1554* (Woodbridge, 2003), pp. 44–6.

[209] This supports John Walker's conclusions on links between the Order and crusading, J. Walker, 'Crusaders and Patrons: The Influence of the Crusades on the Patronage of the Order of St Lazarus in England', *The Military Orders, Vol I: Fighting for the Faith and Caring for the Sick*, ed. M. Barber (Abingdon, 1994), pp. 327–32. See also M. Barber, 'The Order of Saint Lazarus and the Crusade', *The Catholic Historical Review*, 80 (1994), 439–56.

Not only were more charters issued to orders closely associated with crusading, such as the Cistercians and Premonstratensians, but also a significantly greater proportion of their houses received charters compared with those belonging to unreformed Benedictines or Augustinians. Of the ninety-two Cistercian houses in England, eighteen (close to 20%) received a charter in the first month of King Richard's reign, especially during the Great Council at Geddington and at the nearby Cistercian abbey in Pipewell, to which can be added three of the ten Premonstratensian houses in England and those to Tiron Abbey. Whilst it might be argued that King Richard was attracted by their reformed status, of which sympathy for the crusader cause was simply a by-product, the prominent role undertaken by members of the Cistercian Order in the Third Crusade and their strong historical links with crusading suggest that this had an influence on his prioritisation of support to their houses.

The thirty-nine of seventy-seven surviving charters that were issued to the Military Orders, the Cistercians, or the Premonstratensians in the first month of Richard's reign account for 51 per cent of the total *acta*. In comparison, only eight of the *c*.318 unreformed Benedictine houses in England (two of them cathedral priories) and only three of 162 non-Premonstratensian Augustinian foundations received one charter or more, totalling twenty-three charters. That is 30 per cent of the total and just over half the number of the royal charters addressed to the Military Orders, the Cistercians, or the Premonstratensians during the same period.[210]

This trend of favouring crusader institutions carried into early October 1189, with further awards being made to the Templars and the Cistercian foundations at Haliwell and Holme.[211] The data, therefore, indicate that preparations for the Third Crusade coincided with an increase in Angevin donations to Cistercian houses, which stands in contrast to Michael Gervers' assertion that, in contrast to the Military Orders, support to the Cistercians tailed off in the latter part of the twelfth century.[212]

---

[210] The Benedictine houses of Canterbury, Coventry, Crowland, Malmesbury, Ramsey, Reading, St Albans, and Wroxall received fourteen charters in total, and the Augustinian houses of Merton, St Denis, and Thornton upon Humber each received a single charter; Bodleian Library, ms. Ashmole 1527, f. 66r; *CCR*, Vol. 3, pp. 101–2, *inspeximus* of Edward I, 1307; TNA C 52/16, *carte antique* roll 16, m.2; TNA C 52/42 *carte antique* roll SS, m.1, no. 3; TNA E 40/14404; TNA C 52/22, *carte antique* X, m. 2, nos. 12–13; BL, ms. Egerton 3031, f. 28r–v; BL, ms. Additional Charter 19609; Belvoir Castle, Duke of Rutland ms. 'Belvoir cartulary', f. 6v, from *inspeximus* of Henry IV; TNA C 53/114 (Charter Roll 1 Edward III) m.1; BL, Harl. ms. 85, f. 413v; TNA C 52/22, *carte antique* roll X, m. 2d–3d; *CCR*, III, pp. 9–10.
[211] TNA C 52/19 *carte antique* roll 19, m. 4, no. 17–18; BL, ms. Additional Charter 33649; *CCR*, Vol. 4, pp. 372–3; TNA C 52/14 *carte antique* roll 14, m.2, no. 4.
[212] Gervers, 'Donations to the Hospitallers', pp. 155–61.

The presence of a large number of Cistercian abbots at King Richard's coronation on 3 September 1189 and the subsequent use of Pipewell Abbey for his great council may well have influenced the prominence of these houses. Indeed, the abbots of four houses that received a September charter had, according to Roger of Howden, attended the coronation.[213] However, a larger number of abbots were also present whose houses did not enjoy similar favour, which underlines the importance of influence at court.[214]

The Cistercians continued to enjoy Richard's favour in later months. For example, their houses in England received a remission of their debts to the estate of the late Jewish financier, Aaron of Lincoln, on 17 November and one of the last charters signed by Richard as he rode south to meet his fleet at Marseille was a confirmation of the rights of Dalon Abbey on 10 July 1190.[215] With its associated fine of 1,000 *marks*, this charter provides us with solid evidence that the access enjoyed by the Cistercians had come, at least in part, at a price.[216]

On 11 March 1190, King Richard founded the Cistercian abbey of Bonport on the river Seine, near Pont-de-l'Arche. While we lack a foundation charter, two charters relating to particular royal gifts survive from June 1190, and Pope Celestine III confirmed the abbey's possessions in an undated charter that reflects Richard's original endowment.[217] Moreover,

---

[213] Abbots Arnold (Rievaulx), Everard (Holmcultram), Robert of Reading (Crowland), and Warin (St Albans), *Gesta Regis*, Vol. 2, pp. 79–80.

[214] Such as Abbots Benedict (Peterborough), Odo (Battle), John Suthill (Winchester Hyde), Roger le Norreys (St Augustine), and Samson of Totington (St Edmund's). Roger of London was appointed abbot of Selby at Pipewell on 16 September 1189, but his abbey did not gain a charter at that time, however, Walter (Westminster) received three charters once the court had returned to London in October, *Chronica*, Vol. 2, p. 85.

[215] Upon Aaron's death, Henry II had seized his property as the escheat of a Jewish usurer, with the estate eventually being inherited by King Richard, see, R. Chazan, *The Jews of Medieval Western Christendom, 1000–1500* (New York, 2006), p. 159. As well as the Cistercian houses at Ramsey, Haliwell, and Holme, the foundations at Bruern, Savigny, Buildwas, and Le Pin each received a charter in October 1189, as did the Premonstratensian Newhouse Abbey; BL, ms. Additional Charter no. 33649; *CCR*, Vol. 4, pp. 372–3; 5, p. 222; TNA, C 52/14 *carte antique* roll 14, m. 2, no. 4; TNA C 52/17 *carte antique* roll 17, m. 4, no. 20; TNA C 52/19 *carte antique* roll S, m. 1, no. 7; BN ms. latin 1022, pp. 721–2; Cambridge, Pembroke College ms. Soham A2.

[216] Charters confirming inheritances also routinely resulted in a fine, however, such as that of Thomas Fitz-Ralph in October and Robert of Warneford in November 1189. TNA C 52/10, *carte antique* roll 10, m. 1d, no. 29; Gloucestershire Record Office D225, T1; see also Robert of Ameneville, and Simon Wallensi, *CCR*, Vol. 1, p. 27; Vol. 2, p. 431. For Dalon Abbey, see A.W. Lewis, 'Six Charters of Henry II and His Family for the Monastery of Dalon', *EHR*, 110 (1995), 652–65.

[217] Although there is no surviving foundation charter, there is evidence for King Richard's acts in founding and endowing the new abbey. For example, there is an undated charter of William of Champagne, archbishop of Reims, which records that when he had custody of the abbey of Le Val Notre-Dame, the abbey of Bonport was being

Richard later confirmed these donations in a confirmation charter on 23 February 1198 at Château Gaillard.[218] The house quickly attracted gifts from neighbouring barons, such as Matthew II of Montmorency, who went on to participate in the Albigensian Crusade, and Matthew Beaumont, lord of Valois and a relative of Earl Robert III of Leicester, who took the Cross to join the Third Crusade. Another participant in the Third Crusade, Richard of Vernon, made a donation to the abbey for the good of his parents' souls prior to his departure for the Holy Land in 1190 with his son.[219]

In the same month, King Richard confirmed an award by a member of his crusader household, Roger of Saceio, to the Cistercian abbey at Chaloché. Roger arrived in Acre shortly after Richard and joined the relief force to Jaffa. He helped repulse Saladin's counter-attack at the siege and was described as one of only ten knights with a horse, which strongly indicates he was serving with Richard's bodyguard.[220] In May 1190, King Richard also confirmed donations made to the Cistercian abbey at Charron, including one made by William des Roches, who joined Richard on Crusade.[221] William had been a member of Henry II's military household and had served alongside William Marshal as part of the rearguard at Le Mans, where he knocked one of Richard's household knights off his horse. William des Roches had arrived in Acre alongside Roger of Saceio and was a member of the first party of pilgrims to visit Jerusalem in the aftermath of the peace agreement between King Richard and Saladin.[222]

In comparison with similar confirmations to unreformed Benedictine houses, such as that to Chertsey Abbey at made Vézelay on 3 July 1190, or to Augustinian foundations, such as St Botolph's Priory, Colchester, made at Canterbury on 4 December 1189, these Cistercian charters are notable for containing new donations rather than confirming existing holdings, which further underlines continuing support to the Cistercians by nobility across the Angevin realm.[223] Nevertheless, having confirmed new donations to a

---

founded by Richard, AD Eure H193 piece non coté; *Cartulaire de l'abbaye royale de Notre-Dame de Bon-Port*, ed. J. Andrieux (Évreux, 1862), p. 23, no. 22.

[218] BN ms. latin 13906, fos 23r–24v.

[219] *Cartulaire de Bonport*, ed. Andrieux, pp. 5–11, nos. 6, 7, and 9. Richard of Vernon and his son are listed as arriving in Acre, *Itinerarium*, p. 93.

[220] Ambroise, lines 10962, 11396, *Itinerarium*, pp. 218, 405, 415.

[221] *Layettes du Trésor des Chartes*, ed. M.A. Teulet, Vol. 2 (Paris, 1866), no. 367.

[222] Ambroise, line 11869; *CDF*, pp. 94–5, no. 278; *HGM*, line 8817; *Itinerarium*, pp. 218, 432. In Jaffa on 10 January 1192, William des Roches witnessed King Richard's charter to Cato Fitz-Moreheus, AD Eure, G6, p. 17, no. 10.

[223] The award of charters to the Cistercian abbey at Dune and its daughter house at Ter Doest is perhaps indicative of the rewards of support to the king. Cistercian clerics, including Elias, abbot of Dune, played a prominent role in negotiating Richard's release from captivity in 1194. In return for his aid, King Richard confirmed Dune Abbey's mercantile freedoms and, despite being outside the Angevin realm, Ter Doest was taken

number of religious institutions linked to crusading, from October 1189 Richard turned his attention to the older monastic foundations, especially cathedral chapters. Of the fifty-two surviving *acta* dating from October 1189, twenty-nine (56%) went to unreformed Benedictine or Augustinian houses compared with fourteen charters (27%) going to Cistercian or Premonstratensian foundations, or a Military Order.[224] King Richard's sixty-five surviving November *acta* indicate a continuation of this trend with a total of twenty-one charters (32%) being addressed to fifteen Benedictine or Augustinian houses. In comparison, in addition to the remission of debts, only four charters were issued to a Cistercian house, with another three to the Knights Templar, a drop to 11 per cent of the total.[225] Moreover, when it

---

under his protection; *Cronica et Cartularium Monasterii de Dunis*, ed. F. van de Putte (Bruges, 1864), pp. 35, 228, 255, 276–8, 197; *Cronique de l'abbaye de Ter Doest*, ed. F. van de Putte and C. Carton (Bruges, 1845), pp. 38, 40–2.

[224] The Benedictine houses at Boscherville, Bury St Edmunds, Caen, Coventry, Ely, Évreux, Godstow, Peterbrough, Stratford-at-Bow, Séez, Twynham, York, and Westminster received nineteen charters between them, and the Augustinian houses at Canterbury, Merton, Montjoux (Savoy), and Waltham received ten, compared with the eight charters that went to the Cistercians, two to the Templars, three to the Order of St Lazarus, and a single charter to a Premonstratensian house; Angers, AD Maine et Loire, 242H1; BL Additional Charter 33649; BL Additional ms. 14847 (Registrum album), f. 41r; BL Cotton ms. Julius A.i (Chatteris cartulary), f. 77v; Julius D.ii, fos 95v, 97r–v, Vespasian E.xiv, fos 29r–31r; Bodleian Library ms. Ashmole 1527, f. 67r; BN ms. français 18953, p. 228; BN ms. latin 1022, pp. 721–2; *Cal. Charter Rolls*, Vols I, p. 27; II, pp. 105, 176; III, pp. 55–6, 234, 385–7; IV, pp. 372–3; V, pp. 161, 194–5, 222; Cambridge, University Library ms. EDC 1/B/20; Peterborough Dean and Chapter ms. 1, f. 119 (134) r; Cambridge, Pembroke College ms. Soham A2; Évreux, AD Eure G122 f. 7v; Oxford, New College, muniments, Hornchurch charter nos. 85, 151, 164; TNA C 52/3 *carte antique* roll 3, m. 1, no. 6; m. 3d, no. 26; TNA C 52/7, *carte antique* roll 7, m.1, no. 7; TNA C 52/9, *carte antique* roll 9, m. 1 no. 11, 16; TNA C 52/12, *carte antique* roll 12, m. 2d, no. 16; TNA C 52/14 *carte antique* roll 14, m. 2, no. 4; TNA C 52/17, *carte antique* roll 17, m. 1, no. 4; m. 4, no. 20; TNA C 52/19, *carte antique* roll 19, m.4, nos. 17–18; TNA C 52/22, *carte antique* roll X, m.1d, no. 17; TNA C 52/34, *carte antique* roll KK, no. 25; TNA E 164/20 fos 165v–166v; Rouen, Bibl. mun. ms. Y44, f. 108r; BL ms. Harley 391 (Waltham cartulary) fos.44v–46v; Carlisle Record Office, Carlisle Dean and Chapter ms. Register of Wetheral Priory, f. 26v; Westminster Abbey, Westminster Abbey muniments, nos. XLV, XLVI; AD Seine-Maritime, 13 H 8.

[225] The Augustinian houses of Cirencester, Hartland, Oseney, Royston, St Mary de Pré, and Waltham received seven charters, and the Benedictine houses of Buckfast, Bury St Edmunds, Grestain, Lichfield, Selby, Spalding, St Nicholas', St John's, Winchester, and Wix received twelve; Agen, Archives de la ville, ms. DD 14; AN, S5105, liasse 344, no. 2; BL Additional ms. 14847 (Registrum album), f. 40v; BL Harl. Charter 83.c.10; BL ms. Egerton Charter 372; Bodleian Library, ms. Ashmole 1527, f. 67r; C. Bréard, *L'Abbaye de Notre-Dame de Grestain* (Rouen, 1904), pp. 199–209, nos. 1, 2; *Cal. Charter Rolls*, Vols II, pp. 65–6, 431; III, pp. 356, 473–4, 474; V, pp. 212–14, 356–7; Cambridge, University Library, Additional ms. 4220, f.127r; ms. EDR G/3/28 (Liber M), pp. 90–1; Cambridge, Pembroke College, ms. Soham A3; Delisle, 'Examen de treize chartes…', *Mémoires de la Société des Antiquaires de Normandie*, 20 (1853), no. vi, 196–7; Durham

came to unreformed Benedictine houses, a crusading heritage did not always secure favour. Despite being linked to William Percy, who died on the First Crusade, Whitby Abbey had to wait until April 1190 for a confirmation of its liberties and customs. It is not clear, however, how far Whitby Abbey was publicly associated with William Percy, that is, whether crusading was a defining feature of the house in the eyes of King Richard or the public at large.[226] Indeed, the high number of cathedral priories that received a charter suggests the influence of their prelates, and further underlines the importance of patronage at court, and this is explored in greater detail later in this chapter.[227]

Whilst the fine that accompanied his charter to Dalon Abbey is indicative of the financial benefits of prioritising support to a wealthy religious order, such as the Cistercians, Richard's concerns were not wholly with raising funds from religious foundations or supporting those in financial difficulty, such as the Order of St Lazarus.[228] The practical necessities involved in launching a major expedition can also be noted. At an early stage, for example, King Richard issued charters to the men of Exeter and to those of Southampton, two towns that would have an important role in dispatching his fleet to the Holy Land. Entries in the Pipe Rolls indicate that English elements of the royal fleet assembled at Southampton and stopped down

---

Cathedral, Dean and Chapter, Muniments 3.13; Gloucestershire Record Office, D225/T1; C.H. Hartshorne, *Historical Monuments of Northampton* (1848), pp. 24–7; London, Lambeth Palace, ms. 415, f. 84r; Moore (ed.), *Colchester Cartulary*, pp. 42–7; *Monasticon Diocesis Exoniensis*, ed. G. Oliver (Exeter, 1846), pp. 207–8, no. 2; H. Owen and J.B. Blakeway, *A History of Shrewsbury*, Vol. I (London, 1825), plate facing p. 82; AN, JJ66, f. 136 r–v, no. 349; TNA C 52/3, *carte antique* roll 3, m. 1d, no. 21; C 52/10, *carte antique* roll 10, m. 1 d, no. 29; C 52/12, *carte antique* roll 12, m. 2d, no. 14; C 52/15, m. 1d, no. 25; m. 2, nos. 21, 14; C 52/17, *carte antique* roll 17, m. 2, no. 6; m. 3d, no. 31; C 52/18, *carte antique* roll 18, m. 1d, no. 19; m. 3 no. 14; C 52/19, *carte antique* roll 19, m.4, nos. 19, 20; *carte antique* roll S, m. 1, no. 7; C 52/21 *carte antique* roll W, m. 2, nos. 9, 10; C 52/22 *carte antique* roll X, m. 1d, nos. 20, 23; C52/31, *carte antique* roll GG, m. 3d, no. 21; E 40/A5272; E42/310; AD Seine-Maritime G4038; Wells Cathedral Library, ms. DC/CF/2/1 *Liber Albus*, Vol. 1, f. 9r; Ibid. *Liber Fuscus*, fos. 16r, 17r–v; Westminster Abbey Muniments, nos. 657, 659; Dean and Chapter, Westminster Abbey Domesday, f. 317 r–v; Winchester College Muniments, no. 9019; Worcester, Guildhall, City Charters, no. 1.

[226] TNA C 52/28, *carte antique* roll DD, m.2d, no. 28. The lack of surviving commemorative liturgies and the poor state of the few surviving effigies hinder efforts to definitively link religious houses with individual crusaders.

[227] See, for example, the awards to Bath, Canterbury, Coventry, Ely, Évreux, Lichfield, Rouen, Wells, Westminster, and Winchester cathedral priories.

[228] For an idea of how much property and income was lost in the aftermath of the fall of the kingdom of Jerusalem in 1188, see the order's holdings in, A. de Marsy, *Fragment d'un cartulaire de l'ordre de Saint-Lazare en Terre Sainte. Archives de l'Orient latin*, Vol. 2 (Paris, 1883 [reprint New York, 1978]).

the coast from Exeter, at Dartmouth, en route to the planned rendezvous with the king at Marseille.[229]

King Philip II of France's *Acta*

Support to crusade-orientated institutions is less obvious amongst Philip II's *acta*. This is due in part to there being less data to draw upon and his donations being spread over a much longer period of time. Whilst evidence from Capetian France is fragmentary, however, distinct clusters can be found amongst surviving charters to show that Philip II also prioritised such religious foundations at certain times during his reign. For example, twenty charters survive from an unknown number issued at Fontainebleau between 25 March and July 1190. Of these, one each went to the Templars, Hospitallers, and the Lazars of Vitry-aux-Loges, two went to the Cistercian house at Barbeau, and another to the Premonstratensians at Saint-André-au-Bois.[230] A charter to the Cistercians of Vaux-de-Cernay survives from around the same time, but was signed at Dreux.[231] Including this charter, they make up a third of the charters issued, which is not as compelling as the data from the first month of Richard's reign, but is still a significant proportion of the overall total. In France, support predominantly went to leper houses that did not belong to the Order of St Lazarus (the exception being Boigny), and King Philip II's charters reflect this trend.

In June 1190 Philip II set out his arrangements for governing France during his absence. From this time, nine charters survive of which five concerned either the Cistercians or a leper hospital. In a *pancarte*, the king placed the abbots, monks, and brothers of thirteen Cistercian houses under his protection.[232] Two charters went to the Cistercian house of Val-Notre-Dame, another to their foundation at Vauluisant, and a fourth to the leper hospital of the Grand-Beaulieu, which did not belong to the Order of St Lazarus at this time.[233]

---

[229] For details on such preparations see PR2 RI (1190), pp. 8–9, 53, 104, 112, 131.

[230] *Cartulaire de Barbeau*, BN ms. latin 10943, fos. 29, 105; AD Pas-de-Calais, 22 H 1, cartulaire de Saint-André-au-Bois, t. I, f. 48; *Layettes du Trésor des Chartes*, ed. M.A. Teulet, Vol. 1 (Paris, 1863), no. 376; AN, JJ30, no. 340; *Recueil des actes de Philippe Auguste, roi de France*, Vol. 1, ed. M.H.-F. Delaborde (Paris, 1916), pp. 378–82. A charter to the Premonstratensians of Saint-André survives, confirming their privileges, dated to around the same time but issued in Paris – both it and a charter to the Cistercian abbey at Cercanceaux, however, appear to be fakes.

[231] *Cartulaire de l'abbaye de Notre-Dame des Vaux de Cernay*, Vol. 1, ed. L. Merlet and A. Moutié (Paris, 1857), p. 103.

[232] Val-Notre-Dame, Cour-Dieu, Lorroy, Cercanceau, Barbeaux, Chaalis, Longpont, Valloires, Gard, Ourscamp, Lannoy, Beaupré, and Froidmont; AN, JJ30, f. 196v, no. 304.

[233] AN, LL1541, f. 2; BN, ms. latin 9901, f. 38v; and *Cartulaire de la léproserie du Grand-Beaulieu*, ed. R. Merlet (Chartres, 1909), no. 144.

A broader consideration of Philip II's *acta* also indicates that royal favour towards houses linked to crusading might be prompted by external influences. For example, from 24 June 1184, Kings Henry II of England and Philip II of France agreed to raise subsidies for the Holy Land for ten years.[234] In the twelve months that followed, nine of Philip Augustus' thirty-six surviving charters went to Cistercian foundations, two to the Military Orders, four to leper houses (none of which were under the Order of St Lazarus), and six involved members of families linked to crusading, such as Gilbert, lord of Nesle, Eleanor of Beaumont, and Count John of Montgomery.[235] In total, these types of charters make up well over half of the surviving total (58%).[236] Notably, the Cistercians and Carthusians were granted an exemption from the Saladin Tithe in Capetian France by Philip II, but as discussed above in the section dealing with the Saladin Tithe, that may have been an attempt to reduce clerical opposition to the tax.[237]

In comparison with 1184, Philip Augustus' preparations for the Third Crusade seem less focused on protecting the Church than those of either Philip of Alsace or King Richard. Whilst it should not be taken as clear evidence of an intention to spend a minimum amount of time on crusade at the time of taking the Cross, the short time Philip II would eventually spend in the Holy Land, his disregard for the crusading privileges of King Richard demonstrated by his invasion of Normandy, and his tepid support for the Albigensian Crusade later in life, are suggestive of an overall ambivalence to crusading.[238]

From the charter evidence considered in this study, there are strong indications that the protection of the Church was a priority for the king of England and the count of Flanders in the wake of their taking the Cross. Count Philip's support to the Cistercians was linked to arrangements for his eventual burial in Clairvaux, but King Richard and, to a much lesser extent, Philip II of France also prioritised certain religious orders in the months leading up to their joint departure for the Holy Land. Whilst it is possible that this was driven by the financial capacity of individual houses to grease the machinery of government, the influence of their patrons, or royal sympathy for orders in financial need, a common feature to foundations

---

[234] BL, Cotton ms. Claudius D II, f. 74.

[235] *Actes de Philippe Auguste*, Vol. 1, ed. Delaborde (Paris, 1916).

[236] AN JJ81, no. 181; KK945, f. 43v; and AD Eure-et-Loir, G 2980.

[237] Tyerman, *God's War*, p. 381.

[238] Despite having sworn over the gospel not to attack Richard's lands whilst the king of England was away on crusade, Philip Augustus invaded Normandy shortly after his return from crusade even though his efforts to convince Pope Celestine III to release him from his oath had proven unsuccessful. See, for example, T.S. Asbridge, *The Crusades: The War for the Holy Land* (London, 2010), pp. 448–9, 516; Tyerman, *God's War*, pp. 453–5.

that enjoyed royal favour in England, Flanders, and, to a degree, France was a link to crusading and crusaders.

Crusaders and Their Endowments

The argument that King Richard gave priority to foundations linked to crusading in the early months of his reign is reinforced by an examination of the donors listed in these early charters. These charters indicate that such houses enjoyed particular support from those who would join the king on crusade, placing them at the centre of a number of social networks that are considered in the next section. Despite the loss of many of the donations mentioned in the royal confirmation, there is also clear evidence that they received new donations from crusaders and their families, as well as other nobles, which then needed to be secured with a royal charter prior to the king's departure for the Holy Land.

Of the seventy-seven charters granted in September 1189, eight were awards of custody and protection,[239] and lack donor lists, and six were gifts from the king or his immediate family.[240] In total, only twenty-six concerned the possessions of religious foundations and, of these, ten contain lists of donors. However, if one extends the time frame and also considers confirmations granted to the same houses prior to Richard's departure from Marseille on 7 August 1190, a further five donor lists become available.

Religious foundations seemingly linked to crusading, such as the Cistercians and Military Orders, dominate this list of fifteen religious houses. Aside from the Benedictine foundations at Caen and Reading, and the Augustinian abbey at Thornton-upon-Humber, eight donor lists relate to Cistercian houses, to which can be added a list for Sempringham Priory, one each for the Premonstratensian foundations at Newhouse and Croxton, and another for the Order of St Lazarus. Of the fifteen lists, ten contain one or more crusaders, three of these also contain one or more benefactors from a crusader family, and an eleventh donor list has one individual from a crusader family. Of these eleven donor lists, six pertain to a Cistercian charter, two are Benedictine, one is Premonstratensian, one is Lazarite, and the last is from a charter for Sempringham Priory.

Forde Abbey
The donor list appearing on King Richard's confirmation charter to Forde Abbey is illustrative of the king's favour given towards houses enjoying crusader patronage. Undoubtedly assisted by the patronage of its former

---

[239] Bec-Hellouin, Flaxley, Holmcultram, Reading, St Albans, Sulby, and Waverley.
[240] Bec-Hellouin, Malmesbury, Reading, and Waverley.

abbot, Baldwin of Forde, archbishop of Canterbury and future spiritual leader of Richard's advance guard to Acre, the Cistercian abbey at Forde received its confirmation as early as 16 September 1189. It contains sixteen donations, the original charters relating to seven of which have been lost, however, and another three donations predate the fall of Jerusalem to Saladin and fall outside the scope of this analysis.[241]

Of the remaining six donors, Richard Fitz-William of Langford and Henry Pomeroy can be identified as being part of the Third Crusade, to whose number we can add Abbot Robert II of Forde himself. Richard Fitz-William's donation to Forde Abbey was issued on the eve of his departure for Jerusalem prior to September 1189 and Henry Pomeroy died during the course of the Third Crusade. His brother Joscelin made a donation to Forde Abbey for the benefit of Henry's soul c.1194.[242] The Pipe Roll of 1189 describes Robert II, abbot of Forde, as having taken the Cross and Roger of Howden listed him amongst those who died at the siege of Acre.[243] Another donor, Geoffrey Talbot, had a son married to the daughter of a member of the Third Crusade, Matthew Oisel.[244] Geoffrey Talbot may also have been related to Gerard Talbot, but Geoffrey's donation most likely predates the crusade.[245] In addition, Richard of Morville may be linked to Hugh of Moreville, who served with the Templars in the Holy Land in penance for the murder of Thomas Becket.[246]

Forde Abbey also fell within the orbit of a West Country baron, William Brewer, who had taken the Cross sometime before Richard's accession to the throne of England. As sheriff of Devon, William had witnessed eight of the

---

[241] The cartulary of Forde Abbey is missing the charters relating to the donations of Eustace Fitz-Stephen, Henry of Tilly, Henry Pomeroy, Manasser Mauvoisin and his wife, Osbert Dennis, Richard of Raleigh, and Richard Turberville. The donations made prior to the Third Crusade are those of Richard Fitz-Baldwin (c.1137), Henry Fitz-William (1180), and Geoffrey Talbot (1180 x 87), *Cartulary of Forde Abbey*, ed. S. Hobbs (Taunton, 1998).

[242] *Cartulary of Forde Abbey*, ed. Hobbs, p. 56, fols. 88v–89. Henry Pomeroy was married to Alice de Vere, sister to the earl of Oxford, owed the Crown 31.91 knights' fees, T.K. Keefe, *Feudal Assessments and the Political Community under Henry II and His Sons* (Berkeley, Los Angeles, London, 1983), pp. 181, 259 n.121.

[243] Robert II, abbot of Forde, took the Cross and died at the siege of Acre, *Gesta Regis*, Vol. 2, p. 147, *Chronica*, Vol. 3, p. 87.

[244] Also known as John Devonius, Abbot Robert's successor, John of Forde, was less well disposed towards crusaders, intruding on the fief of Matthew Oisel during his absence, *RCR*, Vol. 1, pp. 338–40.

[245] Gerard Talbot had been a member of Henry II's *familia* and arrived at the siege of Acre shortly after King Richard; *Gesta Regis*, Vol. 2, p. 134; *Itinerarium*, p. 217; Landon, *Itinerary*, nos. 226, 260–2, 314, 342. Geoffrey's links to Gilbert Talbot, lord of Linton (Herefordshire) and constable of Ludlow castle, are also unclear; TNA C 52/19, *carte antique* roll 19, m.3, no.12; PR5 RI (1194), p. 86.

[246] *RCR*, Vol. 1, pp. 91, 347.

surviving charter donations to the abbey and he was linked to the Cistercian house at Dunkeswell and the Premonstratensian house at Barlings.[247] Under King Richard, he laid aside the Cross to become one of the *appares* (associate justiciars) appointed to oversee the kingdom whilst Richard travelled to the Holy Land.[248]

Sempringham Priory
Similarly, amongst the nineteen donors to Sempringham Priory listed in King Richard's confirmation charter, Hugh of Neville, William of Reimes, and Maurice of Craon can be identified as participants in the Third Crusade. In addition, Simon of Kyme was probably related to Philip of Kyme, who died at the siege of Acre, and Alice of Gant, a veteran of the Second Crusade, Roger of Mowbray's niece by marriage.[249] Alice was the daughter of the house's initial benefactors, Gilbert and Alice of Gant (Ghent). She was married to Simon III of Senlis whose grandfather Simon I of Senlis had been on crusade sometime between 1103 and 1106.[250]

The importance of patronage is indicated by the likely role of William of Mandeville in championing Sempringham Priory, as he is the sole witness to the charter of 14 September 1189: Alice of Mandeville and William's uncle, Hubert of Rie, were both listed among the donors.[251] Similarly, in addition to Ranulf of Glanville and his nephews, Hubert and Theobald Walter, the Premonstratensians could count amongst their patrons some of the principal servants of the Angevin kings: William Brewer, Geoffrey Fitz-Peter, and Robert of Thornham.[252]

---

[247] Including that of Geoffrey of Furnell, which was linked to the gift of Richard of Morville, *Cartulary of Forde Abbey*, ed. Hobbs, pp. 48–9, f. 76r–v. A Gerard of Furnival is described as participating in the repulse of the counter-attack at Jaffa in August 1191, Ambroise, line 11394; *Itinerarium*, pp. 415. He was also a member of the first party of pilgrims to visit Jerusalem as part of the peace settlement between Richard and Saladin, Ambroise, line 11871; *Itinerarium*, p. 432,

[248] Diss, Vol. 2, pp. 90–1.

[249] *Gesta Regis*, Vol. 2, p. 149.

[250] Simon I was the third son of Landri of Senlis, lord of Chantilly and Ermenonville, and his son, Simon II, founded the Cistercian abbey of Sawtry. Guy III of Senlis, lord of Chantilly, served as butler to King Philip II, supported the Cistercian foundation at Chaalis, and joined the Third Crusade. Sempringham was also linked to the houses of Leicester and Clare through the Alice of Gant, *Monasticon Anglicanum*, ed. Dugdale, Vol. 5, p. 190. For Mowbray's exploits on the Second Crusade, see John of Hexham's account in *Historia Regum: ... per Joannem Hagulstadensem*, Vol. 2, ed. T. Arnold (London, 1885), no. 20.

[251] Unfortunately, few early Sempringham charters survived a fire at Staple Inn in the eighteenth century, but the donations of Alice of Mandeville, Anselm of Walterville, Herbert Fitz-Adelard, Nicholas of Tronwelle, Ranulph of Bathuent, Roger Fitz-Goscelle all predate the fall of Jerusalem.

[252] D. Knowles, *The Monastic Order in England, 943–1216*, 2nd edition (Cambridge, 2002), p. 360.

The link between a number of religious houses and King Richard's preparations for the Third Crusade is less immediately obvious but becomes apparent on further investigation. For example, whilst the confirmation of the Cistercian house of Rievaulx by Richard related solely to the donations of the founder, Walter Espec, who died c.1153 and had no obvious links to crusading, by 1189 his lands in Helmsley, Yorkshire, were held by Robert of Ross.[253] Robert was cousin to Robert of Trussebot, a descendant of Robert Curthose's standard-bearer during the First Crusade and a participant in the Third Crusade.[254] Robert of Ross was also cousin to Walter and Peter of Ross, who died at the siege of Acre in 1190.[255] In addition, Rievaulx was closely tied to the Yorkshire branch of the Stuteville family, as well as to the family of Roger of Mowbray.[256] Osmund of Stuteville and other unidentified members of the family arrived in Acre shortly after King Richard. In addition, William of Stuteville was made sheriff of Northumberland by William of Longchamp and formed part of the social network of nobles that remained in England to secure the realm in their king's absence.[257] It is likely, therefore, that the noble network associated with the abbey and participation in the Third Crusade influenced Richard's decision to prioritise its confirmation charter.[258]

---

[253] The Ross (Roos) arms appear on the Resafa Heraldry Cup; see, Leson, 'Constellation of Crusade', pp 75–90. Robert of Ross entered the Templar order before his death c.1226 and was buried in Temple Church, London.

[254] Robert of Trussebot held a ten-knight fee in Yorkshire with his *caput honoris* at Warter, East Riding, PR2 RI, p. 73. He also had extensive holdings in Normandy, *Magni Rotuli Scaccarii Normanniae*, ed. T. Stapleton (London, 1840), Vol. 2, p. lxxvi. He arrived in Acre, *Itinerarium*, p. 93, and assisted Hubert Walter to distribute food during the siege (Lent 1191), Ambroise, line 4433; *Itinerarium*, p. 135. He also contested his right to be King Richard's standard-bearer, *Chronica*, Vol. 3, p. 129. This was likely based on his descent from Pagan Peverel, Robert Curthose's standard-bearer during the First Crusade; S. Edgington, 'Pagan Peverel: An Anglo-Norman Crusader', *Crusade and Settlement: Papers Read at the First Conference of the SSCLE and Presented to R.C. Smail*, ed. P.W. Edbury (Cardiff, 1985), pp. 90–3. Pagan died c.1130 and his nephew and heir, William, died on the Second Crusade.

[255] Walter de Roos died at the siege of Acre in 1190 alongside his cleric brother, Peter, *Gesta Regis*, Vol. 2, pp. 149, 247; *Chronica*, Vol. 3, p. 89.

[256] On 17 September 1189 King Richard confirmed a donation by Roger of Mowbray, which was also confirmed by his crusader son, Nigel, to the abbey. The same charter lists donations by Edward of Roos and William of Stuteville, BL, Cotton ms. D.1, fos 111r–113v.

[257] William of Longchamp also sent Robert of Stuteville to arrest Hugh of Puiset in April 1190, and in 1191 made Robert sheriff of Lincolnshire, *Chronica*, Vol. 2, pp. 58, 133. Roger of Stuteville had previously held the shrievalty of Northumberland, see for example, PR16 HII, p. 47; For William of Stuteville, see PR2 RI (1190), pp. 8–9; Osmund of Stuteville died at Jaffa c.1192, probably during the battle to recover the city, *Gesta Regis*, Vol. 2, p. 150.

[258] Some confirmations were seemingly unrelated to Richard's planned crusade, but

As an investigation of donor lists has highlighted, despite the odd exception, the correlation between donors linked to crusading with those foundations that received a confirmation charter in the first month of King Richard's reign is compelling. Yet, unlike previous expeditions to the Holy Land, as discussed in relation to the Saladin Tithe, in England such donations were only rarely linked to the need to raise funds to participate in the expedition. What they arguably indicate, therefore, is evidence of King Richard's desire to harness the personal spiritual convictions of potential crusaders.

The Order of St Lazarus

The Order of St Lazarus offers a persuasive example of links between those disposed towards crusading and donations to a religious house in the late twelfth century.[259] In terms of links to crusaders, the founder of the order's headquarters in England, Roger of Mowbray, took the Cross on three occasions and supported a significant number of religious houses, especially those linked to crusading, such as the Cistercians and Military Orders.[260] He participated in the Second Crusade and founded the Templar house at Balsall on his return.[261] He most likely returned to the Holy Land with Philip of Alsace in 1177 and took the Cross again in 1185, following the death of his second wife, Alice of Gant. He survived the battle of Hattin, but was captured by Saladin's army and died in Palestine in 1188.[262] Nigel, his eldest son, died during the Third Crusade and Nigel's brother, William, was recorded with King Richard in 1193 and may well have accompanied him to the Holy Land as well.[263] As we have seen, support to Rievaulx Abbey was common to Roger of Mowbray, the Yorkshire branch of the Stutevilles, and

---

further underline the importance of patronage in the Angevin court. The confirmation of William of Wideville's foundation of a hermitage at Grafton Regis, for example, is remarkable in being witnessed solely by Queen Eleanor. Although undated, this charter was signed at Geddington, which suggests that it was issued in September 1189, TNA E 32/76 (Northampton Forest Eyre 1286) m.5.

[259] For similar links relating to the First Crusade, see Riley-Smith, *First Crusaders*.

[260] Twenty-two religious houses were supported by Roger of Mowbray; E. Jamroziak, *Rievaulx Abbey and its Social Context, 1132–1300* (Turnhout, 2005), pp. 1–2, 63–4.

[261] Roger of Mowbray also donated land at Axholme to the Templars around the same time, *Honour of Mowbray*, ed. Greenway, no. 273.

[262] *Honour of Mowbray*, ed. Greenway, pp. xxxi–ii.

[263] Like his father, Nigel was a patron of the Templars and of the Premonstratensian house at Welford, as well as Burton Lazars, *Honour of Mowbray*, ed. Greenway, no. 29, pp. 274–6, 285–6.

to Baldwin of Forde, as well as to the Ross family and another participant in the Third Crusade, Robert of Trussebot.²⁶⁴

Support to the Order of St Lazarus also dated from Roger's safe return from the Second Crusade and drew in Alice of Gant, the Lacy family, and William of Ferrers, earl of Derby, who also died on the Third Crusade. With access to Roger's noble network and given the link between care for lepers and the concept of *imitatio Christi*, the Order of St Lazarus was well placed to serve as an intermediary for participation in the Third Crusade.²⁶⁵ It has been established that the crusading movement lay within a context of repentance, penance, and pilgrimage – following Christ by being willing to fight in his cause and for the Holy Land, which was seen as his heritage.²⁶⁶ As Anne Lester argued, lepers lived in a state of perpetual penance that the crusader sought to emulate.²⁶⁷

By the latter half of the twelfth century, in contemplation of actually walking in the same land as that of Christ's ministry, some sought to emulate the deeds of Christ, such as helping lepers.²⁶⁸ For example, while gifts to religious houses by the Mowbray family were common, especially to reformist institutions, those given to the Order of St Lazarus by Roger of Mowbray were made 'in pure and perpetual alms [along] with any service'.²⁶⁹ So the primary purpose of these grants was probably not intercessory. This is consistent with Touati and Rawcliffe's argument that lepers represented a branch of the 'new spirituality' of the twelfth century.²⁷⁰ I argue here

---

²⁶⁴ Relations between the Mowbrays and Stutevilles were strained, however, since the grant of Stuteville to Roger of Mowbray's father, Nigel d'Aubigny. Robert I of Stuteville had fought against King Henry I at the battle of Tinchebrai (1106) and after his capture and imprisonment, a large portion of his English lands passed to Aubigny. Some of these lands were restored to Robert's descendant, Robert III of Stuteville, but the dispute was only finally settled in 1201; *Early Yorkshire Families*, ed. C.T. Clay and D.E. Greenway (Cambridge, 1973), p. 85. To complicate matters, in the interim, former Stuteville property had been donated to a number of religious houses. See, for example, Jamroziak, *Rievaulx Abbey*, p. 71.

²⁶⁵ In his thesis, Walker explored the importance of crusading in donations made to the Templars and to the Order of St Lazarus against a background of familial and geographical associations; J. Walker, 'The Patronage of the Templars and the Order of St Lazarus in England in the Twelfth and Thirteenth Centuries' (PhD thesis, University of St Andrews, 1991).

²⁶⁶ See, for example, Hehl, 'Christian Order', p. 210.

²⁶⁷ A.E. Lester, 'A Shared Imitation: Cistercian Convents and Crusader Families in Thirteenth-Century Champagne', *JMH*, 35 (2009), 365.

²⁶⁸ For examples of Christ's interactions with lepers, see Matthew 8:1–4, Mark 1:40–45, and Luke 5:12–16, 17:11–19.

²⁶⁹ Cartulary made for Walter Lynton, master of the hospital of the Virgin Mary and Lazarus, Burton Lazars, Leicestershire, BL, ms. Cotton Nero C.xii, f. 210.

²⁷⁰ F.-O. Touati, *Maladie et société au moyen âge. La lèpre, les lépreux et les léproseries dans la province ecclésiastique de Sens jusqu'au milieu de XIVe siècle* (Paris, 1998), pp. 631–748;

that, along with the Cistercians, Premonstratensians, Templars, and Hospitallers, the Order of St Lazarus served as an intermediary for the diffusion of crusade ideology, which influenced participation in the Third Crusade.

Traditions date the foundation of the Order of St Lazarus to 1115, following on from Pope Paschal II's 1113 bull *Piae postulatio voluntatis*, which had brought the Hospitaller Knights of St John under papal protection.[271] However, it is likely that a Hospitaller community attached to the church of St Lazarus had been established outside the walls of Jerusalem by 1098, that is, before the capture of the city by European crusaders, and King Henry I made a donation to the Lazarites in 1100.[272] Undoubtedly, the two hospitaller orders initially remained close as the second master of the Lazarites, Roger Boyant, had been rector of the Knights of St John.

The Order of St Lazarus attracted early interest from the royal house of Jerusalem. King Fulk of Jerusalem, his wife, Queen Melisende, and his successor, Baldwin III, were all benefactors of the Lazarites' hospital outside Jerusalem, as was King Amalric.[273] Its primary purpose was to care for lepers, and its headquarters remained in the hospital. Grants by the lords of Beirut, Caesarea, Jaffa, Galilee, Nablus, Toron, and Tripoli extended the Order of St Lazarus' holdings to provide a steady income up until the fall of Jerusalem in 1187.[274]

It is hard to determine which of the two characters in the Gospels called Lazarus was the one associated with the order as the two were often conflated.[275] Western traditions provided two alternative burial sites for Lazarus of Bethan: Autun in Burgundy, and nearby Vézelay.[276] The latter was a prominent site in Richard and Philip's crusading itinerary as, during nego-

---

C. Rawcliffe, 'Learning to Love the Leper: Aspects of Institutional Charity in Anglo-Norman England', *ANS*, 23 (2001), 241–2. See also, Marcombe, *Leper Knights*, pp. 8, 37.

[271] J.J. Algrant and J. Beaugourdon, *Armorial of the Military and Hospitaller Order of St Lazarus of Jerusalem* (Delft, 1983), p. 330.

[272] G. de Sibert, *Histoire des Ordres Royaux, Hospitaliers-Militaires de Notre Dame du Mont Carmel et de Saint-Lazare de Jérusalem* (Paris, 1772), pp. ii–iii, lxi–lxii. Henry I's queen, Matilda, founded the leper house in Holborn, London, dedicated to St Giles, the patron saint of sick paupers and lepers.

[273] L. Cibrario, *Précis historique des Ordres réligieux et militaires de S. Lazare et de S. Mauruice avant et après leur réunion*, trans. H. Ferrand (Lyon, 1860), p. 11; also Marsy, *Fragment d'un cartulaire*, Vol. 2, no. 2, pp. 123–57; and, K.P. Jankrift, *Leprose als Streiter Gottes: Institutionalisierung und Organisation des Ordens von Heiligen Lazarus zu Jerusalem von seinen Anfängen bis zum Jahre 1350* (Münster, 1996), pp. 46–56. The degree to which leprosy was central to life in the Latin East is covered in detail by Barber, 'St. Lazarus and the Crusades', pp. 439–56.

[274] Barber, 'St. Lazarus and the Crusade', pp. 439–56.

[275] Marcombe, *Leper Knights*, p. 4.

[276] Saint-Lazare at Autun was not a cathedral until much later; it was the canon's collegiate church at this point.

tiations in November 1189, it was set as the muster point for the Angevin and Capetian contingents.²⁷⁷

The Second Crusade proved highly important for the Lazarites. Louis VII's donation of the castle and barony of Boigny, near Orléans, to the Order of St Lazarus as perpetual fief on his return from crusade was followed by grants of land by David I of Scotland (*c.*1153), Henry II of England (1155), and István III of Hungary (1161).²⁷⁸ After the fall of Jerusalem in 1187, the next mention of the order was in 1191 at Acre (where they had owned property since *c.*1160), but it is not clear where they were based in the interim.²⁷⁹ In the meantime, the order's houses in France and England became vital in the recruitment of brethren and to secure funding, with Boigny acting as the order's magisterial seat. The Order of St Lazarus eventually became militarised, just as the Hospitallers had previously become, but there is no clear evidence when this happened. it is generally supposed, however, that it was a thirteenth-century development, and there is no evidence in this research to support an argument that the Lazarites were militarised at the time of the Third Crusade.²⁸⁰

The headquarters of the Order of St Lazarus in England was at Burton Lazars in Leicestershire. At the time of the Third Crusade, it consisted of a master and eight knights under the protection of the Blessed Virgin and St Lazarus.²⁸¹ It had been founded *c.*1157 by Roger of Mowbray, and was supported by a royal charter granted by Henry II in 1159.²⁸² This charter came shortly after Henry's aunt Sibylla of Anjou entered the convent of SS Mary and Martha near the tomb of their brother, Lazarus, in Bethany.²⁸³ Henry had made his own donation to the Order in 1155, a year after his marriage to another participant in the Second Crusade, Eleanor of Aquitaine.²⁸⁴ King Henry also placed the Lazarites under his personal protection,

---

[277] It was also at Vézelay that King Louis VII of France and Eleanor of Aquitaine took the Cross on Easter Sunday 1146, prior to their joining the Second Crusade; J. Naus, *Constructing Kingship: The Capetian Monarchs of France and the Early Crusades* (Manchester, 2006), pp. 123–4.

[278] Marcombe, *Leper Knights*, pp. 16–20.

[279] Barber, 'St. Lazarus and the Crusade', p. 447.

[280] The first evidence of their active participation in military campaigns is in 1234 when Pope Gregory IX made a general appeal for aid to the Order to clear debts contracted in the defence of the Holy Land, *Les Registres de Grégoire IX* as reported in Barber, 'St. Lazarus and the Crusades', p.448. See also A. Forey, *The Military Orders* (Basingstoke, 1992), p. 19.

[281] W. Toowell, *Leicester Village History: Burton Lazars* (Melton Mowbray, 1882).

[282] *The Burton Lazars Cartulary: A Medieval Leicestershire Estate*, ed. T. Bourne and D. Marcombe (Nottingham, 1987).

[283] Henry II's aunt was also known as Sibylla of Flanders following her marriage to Count Thierry in 1139 during his pilgrimage to the Holy Land.

[284] Robert of Torigny, pp. 193, 205; N. Huyghebaert, 'Une comtesse de Flandre à Béthanie', *Les cahiers de Saint-André*, 21/2 (1964), 5–15.

freed them from all tolls and customary payments to the Exchequer, and granted them the right to hold land free of customary services.²⁸⁵ However, Henry did not restrict his support to the Order of St Lazarus. For example, he also founded the house of Saint-Julien (the Hospitaller) between 1185 and 1188 at the royal manor at Petit-Quevilly near Rouen, specifically to provide for leprous noblewomen. In time, it became known as Salle-aux-Puelles (Maidens' House).²⁸⁶

King Richard issued a confirmation of possessions and liberties to the Order of St Lazarus on 30 September 1189.²⁸⁷ Amongst the donors, Roger of Mowbray's wife, Alice of Gant, appears again; Henry I of Lacy had been on crusade, was the brother of Alice's first husband Ilbert II of Lacy, and was an ancestor of Third Crusade participant, John Fitz-Richard; William Burdet went on crusade some time before 1159; and William Ferrers, earl of Derby (c.1180) joined the Third Crusade only to die at the siege of Acre in 1190.²⁸⁸ Nigel of Mowbray was linked to the order's first benefactor in England, William of Aubigny,²⁸⁹ and Nigel's father had participated in the Second Crusade alongside Louis VII. Nigel died in 1191 whilst on the Third Crusade and William of Mowbray was with King Richard in the German city of Speyer on 20 November 1193.²⁹⁰ However, it is not clear if William had been with his brother, Nigel, in the Holy Land. In addition, the Warin Fitz-Simon who gave one bovate and meadow and pastureland to Burton Lazars may have been the same Warin Fitz-Simon described as being a knight of Clare on crusade to Jerusalem in 1191.²⁹¹

---

²⁸⁵ *Letters and Charters of Henry II*, ed. Vincent, nos. 1390–7.
²⁸⁶ 390 *Letters and Charters of Henry II*, ed. Vincent, no. 2112.
²⁸⁷ TNA C 52/34, *carte antique* roll KK, no. 23. See also TNA C 52/34, *carte antique* roll KK, nos. 21–2, 24–5, and TNA C 52/3 *carte antique* roll 3, m. 1, no. 6.
²⁸⁸ Henry I, lord of Pontefract, died during the course of the crusade of 1177 and both Roger of Mowbray and Henry I were associated with the Templars. Roger of Mowbray founded Temple Balsall and Henry was linked to Temple Hurst, *Monasticon Anglicanum*, ed. Dugdale, Vol. 6, p. 835; J.S. Lee, 'Landowners and Landscapes: The Knights Templar and Their Successors at Temple Hirst, Yorkshire', *The Local Historian*, 41 (2011), 293–307. For William Burdet or Bourdet, see *The Battle Abbey Roll with some Account of the Norman Lineages*, Vol. 2, ed. C. Powlett (London, 1889). For William Ferrers see *Gesta Regis*, Vol. 2, p. 148. However, Wendover places his death in 1191, p. 191. His father, Robert of Ferrers, had founded the Cistercian abbey at Merevale in 1148 and he was distantly linked to Ralph III of Fougères through his grandmother, Hawise of Vitré.
²⁸⁹ R. Bartlett, *England under the Norman and Angevin Kings* (Oxford, 2002), pp. 543–4. Roger of Mowbray supported the revolt against Henry II in 1173–4 along with his sons, Nigel and Robert. He departed for the Levant in 1186 and was present at the Battle of Hattin. He was subsequently ransomed by the Templars and Hospitallers but died in Palestine in 1188. Marcombe, *Leper Knights*, p. 37.
²⁹⁰ TNA C 52/28 *carte antique* roll DD, m.1, n.1.
²⁹¹ BL, ms. Cotton Nero C.xii, f. 28; PR3 RI (1191), p. 44.

The earls of Leicester and Chester sit at the centre of two more crusader clusters and both of them are linked to leper houses. Earl Robert Fitz-Pernel's uncle, Waleran, count of Meulan, had founded and was patron to the leper hospital of St Gilles, on the outskirts of Pont-Audemer, between 1135 and 1166. Waleran's father, Earl Robert I, may have established an earlier leper house on the same site under the auspices of Préaux Abbey.[292] According to Henry of Knighton, the founder of St Leonard's leper hospital in Leicester was William the Leper, son to Robert Blanchemains, earl of Leicester, and a brother to Robert Fitz-Pernel – a prominent participant in the Third Crusade.[293] So whilst Earl Robert III's patronage of the hospital may be in line with Max Satchell's assertion that personal exposure to the condition was an important motive for support to leper houses, ancestral links to leprosariums are notable.[294] With this in mind, it is useful to compare support to the Order to St Lazarus with evidence relating to another Military Order.

Historians have long argued for close ties between Templar commanderies and particular families. Hans Prutz demonstrated that 'personal factors' – ties between Templars and laymen – played an important role in the rapid growth of the Templars in France and Champagne in particular.[295] Marie Luise Bulst-Thiele has also favoured the influence of family and locality on encouraging recruitment to the Templars, suggesting that not all applicants entered entirely of their own volition, but required persuasion by their kith and kin.[296] Alan Forey argued for parental influence on Templar postulants and Anthony Luttrell has identified familial links between many of the first Templars.[297]

In his study of Templar families, Jochen Schenk compared practice in Languedoc with that in northern France, focusing on the duchy of

[292] S.C. Mesmin, 'Waleran, Count of Meulan and the Leper Hospital of S. Giles de Pont-Audemer', *Annales de Normandie*, Vol 32/1 (1982), pp. 3–19.

[293] Henry Knighton, *Chronicon Henrici Knighton; vel. Cnithon, monachi leycestrensis*, Vol. 1, ed. J.R. Lumby (London, 1889–95), pp. 62, 64. The *Wm.* in question is probably William of Breteuil, the earl's son, who died 1189–90. See also N. Orme and M. Webster, *The English Hospital, 1070–1570* (London, 1995), p.112.

[294] A.E.M. Satchell, 'The Emergence of Leper-houses in Medieval England, 1100–1250' (PhD thesis, University of Oxford, 1998), pp. Ix, 221–2.

[295] H. Prutz, *Die geistlichen Ritterorden, ihre Stellung zur kirchlichen, politischen, gesellschaftlichen und wirtschaftlichen Entwicklung des Mittelalters* (Berlin, 1908), p. 352.

[296] M.L. Bulst-Thiele, '*Sacrae domus militiae Templi Hierosolymitani magistri*. Untersuchungen zur Geschichte des Templerordens 1118/9-1314', *Abhandlungen der Akademie der Wissenschaften in Göttingen. Philologisch-Historische Klasse*, Vol. 86 (Göttingen, 1974), p. 171.

[297] A. Forey, 'Recruitment to the Military Orders (Twelfth to Mid-Fourteenth Centuries)', *Viator*, 17 (1986), 139–73; A. Luttrell, 'The Earliest Templars', *Autour de la première croisade. Actes du colloque de la Society for the Study of the Crusades and the Latin East, Clermont-Ferrand, 22–25 juin 1995*, ed. M. Balard (Paris, 1995), pp. 199–200.

Burgundy and the adjoining county of Champagne. He asserted that the Templars received much of their support from noble and knightly families who were deeply influenced by the religious reform movement (principally the Cistercians), were involved in crusading, and were often closely related to one another.[298] Analysis of the diocese of Langres, for example, provides significant support to his argument, with thirty-nine of the forty-nine crusader noblemen identified with the Templars in the diocese joining the Third Crusade.[299] This description of the relationship between the Templars and the noble elite is also entirely suitable for the donors to the Order of St Lazarus listed in Richard's confirmation charter of 30 September 1189.

The Chester cluster indicates a similar familial focus on leprosy. It is linked to that of Mowbray through the constable of Chester, Roger Fitz-John, who assumed the surname of Lacy in 1193 and whose uncle, Richard of Chester, seems to have died of leprosy and was buried at Norton Priory.[300] Roger's father, John Fitz-Richard, handed over the office of constable prior to departing on crusade in March 1190 and died at the siege of Acre seven months later.[301] It has been suggested that Roger also went on the Third Crusade, but he appeared as a witness to the earl of Chester's charters during this period.[302] He is also mentioned in Howden's account of the rebellion of Count John, so it is highly unlikely that he travelled East.[303] Another uncle, Robert Thesaurarius, was prior of the Hospitallers of England, but it is unclear if he joined the Third Crusade.[304]

Just as his father, Hugh II, had founded a leper hospital at Spon, Earl Ranulf III founded St Giles at Boughton, beyond the east gate of Chester, in 1181. Sometime between 1188 and 1192, Ranulf gave an annual rent charge of 10s. to St Werburgh's Abbey, from which the monks were to feed

---

[298] Schenk, *Templar Families*, p. 23.
[299] D. Marie, *Les Templiers dans le diocèse de Langres. Des moines entrepreneurs aux XIIe et XIIIe siècles* (Langres, 2004), pp. 161–2.
[300] G. Ormerod, *History of the County Palatine and City of Chester*, Vol. 1 (London, 1819), p. 510. Norton Priory seems to have been a centre for leper burials and may have had a leprosarium attached. See, P. Green, *Norton Priory, the Archaeology of a Medieval Religious House* (Cambridge, 1989).
[301] *Annales Cestrienses, or the Chronicle of the Abbey of Saint Werburg, Chester*, ed. R. Copley Christie (London, 1887), p. 41.
[302] See, for example, Earl Ranulf III's confirmation of Bordesley Abbey and the liberties of Stanlow Abbey, Oxford, Bodleian Library, Dugdale ms. 17, f. 54; BL, Egerton ms. 3126, f. 33.
[303] *Gesta Regis*, Vol. 2, p. 323
[304] Although he had donated half his property to the Hospitallers, it seems that Adam Dutton, steward to the constable, also stayed at home. His son, Geoffrey, however, joined the earl of Chester on the Fifth Crusade, A. Abram, 'The Augustinian Canons in the Diocese of Coventry and Lichfield and Their Benefactors, 1115–1320' (PhD thesis, University of Wales, 2007), p. 117, no. 4.

one hundred paupers once a year and to give 20*d.* a year to the lepers of Boughton to commemorate his father.³⁰⁵ Ranulf's half-brother, Roger Fitz-Eustace, also gave land for a leper hospital on the banks of the river Ribble near Clitheroe. A leprous knight called William of Anneye was also reportedly a member of their father's household.³⁰⁶ However, there is no evidence that either leprosarium was linked to the Order of St Lazarus.

There is no precise information about what happened to the community of St Lazarus with the fall of Jerusalem to Saladin in 1187. What is certain is that they lost most, if not all, of their possessions in the kingdom of Jerusalem in the wake of the battle of Hattin, but some of those lands may have been recovered after the Peace of Jaffa in 1192.³⁰⁷ The consequences of this situation must have been that the houses of the Order of St Lazarus in Western Europe, chiefly in England and France, became very important after 1187 as a source for recruitment of new brethren and as the principal sources of income. The surviving charters issued by King Richard reflect this.

It was normal for religious houses to seek royal confirmation of their property and privileges at the beginning of a new reign, but compared with the great abbeys of England the Brothers of St Lazarus owned very little; yet they were given priority and additional privileges within weeks of Richard's accession to the throne of England.³⁰⁸ According to Ellul, shortly after his return from captivity, Richard issued another charter to the Lazarites, in which he declared,

> We have recognised that the Holy House and Hospital of Saint Lazarus of Jerusalem is splendid and praiseworthy in the works of mercy, whereof we have sure faith and witness by the experience of our own eyes.³⁰⁹

It seems likely that Richard personally wished to support a small religious order, which was doing good work and whose assets in the Holy Land had almost certainly been lost to Saladin's forces. Baldwin the Leper had only been dead for four years in 1189, and he had been Richard's second cousin. These charters may thus also reflect the king's own charitable impulses, as

---

³⁰⁵ *The Chartulary or Register of the Abbey of St. Werburgh, Chester*, ed. J. Tait (Manchester, 1920), Vol. 1, pp. 96, 211. See also Ormerod, *History of Chester*, Vol. 1. pp. 352–3.

³⁰⁶ See P. Coss, *Lordship, Knighthood and Locality: A Study in English Society c.1180–1280* (Cambridge, 1991), p. 77.

³⁰⁷ In this respect, the Order of St Lazarus would have been in a similar position to the Templars and Hospitallers, both of whom received letters of support from Pope Clement to aid the raising of funds, J. Bronstein, *The Hospitallers and the Holy Land* (Woodbridge, 2005), p. 105.

³⁰⁸ Richard was crowned on 3 September 1189.

³⁰⁹ I have been unable to find any evidence of this charter, said by Ellul to be dated 5 January 1195; M.J. Ellul, *The Sword and the Green Cross: The Saga of the Knights of Saint Lazarus from the Crusades to the 21st Century* (Bloomington IN, 2011), p. 209.

well as familial connections to the condition;[310] however, there was arguably more to it.

In addition to his own family's association with the Order of St Lazarus, Richard may well have wanted to enlist the support of its crusader patrons, which in effect meant the Mowbrays and their wider kin-group, including the Clares, as well as social networks centred on the earls of Leicester and Chester, and Count Rotrou III of Perche.[311] For example, the honour of Mowbray owed the Crown sixty knights' fees in England and another five in Normandy, with a likely normal retinue of over three hundred knights and serjeants, and William of Ferrers was in a similar position.[312] The size of their retinues on crusade is unclear, but the participation of magnates with large and cohesive retinues would have been a significant boost to the military effectiveness of Richard's contingent in the Holy Land, as well as enhancing his status alongside his fellow monarchs.

Patrons of the Lazarites in the Latin East were also notable in Richard's crusading circle. As well as Robert Fitz-Pernel, there was a donation deed dated to 1183 from Humphrey IV of Toron (including property in Acre), and Raymond of Tripoli was named as a *confrater* of the Order of St Lazarus.[313] Indeed, as discussed above, support to the Lazarites was widespread amongst the nobility of Outremer.[314]

As mentioned earlier in this chapter, however, support to leper hospitals in France predominantly went to institutions outside the Order of St Lazarus. For example, in addition to Rotrou III's donation mentioned above, his son

---

[310] Malcolm Barber makes the point that Baldwin's father, Amalric, made a donation to the order in 1171, around the time he would have become aware of his son's condition, Barber, 'St. Lazarus and the Crusades', p. 442.

[311] A leper house dedicated to St Lazarus had been established outside Nogent-le-Rotrou by 1170 and was likely linked to Boigny. The master of the house attested a number of Rotrou III's charters and Rotrou was later to claim that it was founded in memory of his wife. He transferred a tithe to the leper house in May 1190, Barber, 'St. Lazarus and the Crusades', p. 447.

[312] Scutage was charged on about eighty knights' fees when William was a minor in 1159 and 61, but he calculated that he owed sixty on coming of age in 1166, which through new enfeoffments had reached sixty-eight and a half by the time of the Third Crusade, but he only owed a single knight's fee in Normandy, Keefe, *Feudal Assessments*, pp. 146, 170, 253 no. 75. For the Honour of Mowbray see Ibid., p. 179.

[313] Humphrey's grandfather, Humphrey II, had made a donation to the Order in May 1151, Cibrario, *Précis historique des Ordres réligieux et militaires de S. Lazare et de S. Maurice*, pp. 21–2. Hugh of St Pol was master of the order *c.*1155 and the leper house at Nogent-le-Rotrou was probably linked to Louis VII's foundation at Boigny, near Orléans, the centre of the Order of St Lazarus in France; Barber 'St. Lazarus and the Crusades', p. 447ff. On Raymond of Tripoli see Marsy, *Fragment d'un Cartulaire*, no. 29, pp. 146–7; N.P. Zacour and H.W. Hazard, *A History of the Crusades. Vol. 5: The Impact of the Crusades on the Near East* (Madison, WI, 1985), p. 162.

[314] Barber, 'St. Lazarus and the Crusades', pp. 442–4.

and fellow participant in the Third Crusade, Geoffrey, also favoured the leper house at Mauve.[315] Similarly, John of Préaux, a member of the military households of both the Young King Henry and Richard, confirmed his father's donation to the leprosarium of Mont-aux-Malades, which related to an original endowment by John's grandfather, and the marvellously detailed pre-crusade testament of Hagan of Ervy included provision for the lepers of his lordship.[316] It is perhaps illustrative that, amidst the turmoil of the conflict in Normandy in 1193, a group of prominent Anglo-Norman barons attended a ceremony at the Grand-Beaulieu leprosarium, including veterans of the Third Crusade, such as Walkelin of Ferrers, despite it lying outside the Angevin realm.[317] Taken as a whole, this all indicates a strong association between leprosy in general, and in England the Order of St Lazarus in particular, and participation in the Third Crusade.

The link between support of leprosariums as expressions of monastic reform, especially houses belonging to the Order of St Lazarus and its perception as a Military Order, and crusading sits comfortably in the framework laid out by Schenk in his work on Templar families mentioned above. The landowning families in France who began supporting the Order of the Temple in the twelfth century often did so alongside their support to other religious reform institutions – notably the Cistercians – as did the benefactors of the Order of St Lazarus, as well as smaller leper houses. Moreover, some of the same families were also linked to the Templars and the Hospitallers and, just as with Schenk's Templar families, this was indicative of an overall religious and spiritual context that predisposed their participation in the Crusades.

---

[315] 'Querimoniae normannorum', *RHF*, Vol. 14, ed. L. Delisle (Paris, 1904), pp. 28–9, no. 225.

[316] M. Arnoux, 'Les origines et le développement du mouvement canonical en Normandie', *Des clercs au service de la réforme. Études et documents sur les chanoines réguliers de la province de Rouen* (Turnhout, 2000), p. 146. For more on Mont-aux-Malades, see E. Brenner, *Leprosy and Charity in Medieval Rouen* (Woodbridge, 2015). For Hagan of Ervy see Evergates, *Feudal Society: County of Champagne*, pp. 68–9, no. 51 (1190).

[317] Walkelin of Ferrers arrived in Acre in 1190 with Robert Trussebot and Richard of Vernon. He arrived shortly before the death of his relation, William of Ferrers, earl of Derby, at the siege on 21 October 1190. The earl of Derby, however, had travelled separately, arriving at the siege of Acre in 1189. Walkelin assisted Hubert Walter in the distribution of food, and fought at the battle of Arsuf, Ambroise, lines 4431, 6166; *Itinerarium*, pp. 93, 135, 261; Wendover, p. 178; Diss, Vol. 2, p. 79. For William of Ferrers' death, see M. *The Cartulary of the Knights of St John of Jerusalem in England*, Part 2, ed. M. Gervers (Oxford, 1996), p. 51. Fellow crusader Amaury of Montfort made a donation to Grand-Beaulieu in 1199, *Cartulaire de Notre-Dame des Vaux de Cernay*, Vol. 1, p. 71, no. 1, quoting AD d'Eure-et-Loir, fonds du grand séminaire.

Crusading and the Interaction Between the Baronage and the Church

The Saladin Tithe reduced the number of landowners in England who needed to mortgage property to finance their participation in the Third Crusade. This leaves us a much clearer picture of the spiritual intent of crusader endowments made prior to departing for the Holy Land. Donations considered in this chapter, such as to Forde Abbey, Sempringham Priory, and the Order of St Lazarus, indicate that many of those that went on crusade did so within a framework of support to reformist institutions, including the Military Orders, which were closely associated with crusading. The financial and spiritual influence of such foundations on crusaders was reflected in their being prioritised by secular rulers, most notably King Richard of England, with forty-one of the seventy-seven charters he issued in September 1189 going to such orders. A comparison with King John's approach to charters in the first months following his ascension would make for a fascinating study.

To reduce the risk of drawing determinist conclusions, however, this charter evidence must be set against narrative sources of the Third Crusade to contextualise donors with overall crusading activity. Of the 583 participants from north-western Europe on the Third Crusade considered in this study, surviving charters connect 150 crusaders (26%) to the Cistercians, the Premonstratensians, a leprosarium, or a Military Order, which is a considerable proportion given the vulnerability of such evidence to disasters – both man-made and natural. The data indicates that, in the aftermath of the fall of Jerusalem to Saladin, martial elites of north-western Europe that enjoyed an association with these particular religious institutions made up a significant proportion of those who went on the Third Crusade.

Given the wealth of evidence relating to the Third Crusade, it is difficult to doubt the sincerity of the personal spiritual convictions of many crusaders. As the testament of Hagan of Ervy demonstrated, lords might spread their wealth across a number of foundations. Whilst half his estate went to the Cistercians of Pontigny, Hagan also made provision for the lepers of Ervy, four monastic houses in the town, and each of Troyes' hospitals.[318] Such evidence supports Ernst-Dieter Hehl's proposal that crusading integrated the traditional martial life of the warrior elite into a struggle to save one's soul.[319]

The Third Crusade data examined in this chapter demonstrates that many of those inspired to take the Cross did so, at least in part, for spiritual reasons – as a route to individual salvation and to recover Christ's heritage as their superordinate goal. The evidence also suggests that imitating the life

---

[318] Evergates, *Feudal Society: County of Champagne*, pp. 68–9, no. 51 (1190).
[319] Hehl, 'Christian Order', p. 209.

of Christ, especially his sacrifices, as well as individual penance, remained an important element in both motivation and preaching in relation to the Third Crusade. Examination of King Richard's *acta* has also indicated that links between certain religious foundations, crusade recruitment, and crusaders influenced royal policy. In focusing solely on the spiritual dimension to crusader motivation, however, and especially on penitential stimuli, there is a risk of missing other important factors. The next chapter further considers the role of family and personal relationships in participation in the Third Crusade.

2

Family and Heritage: Lineage, Kinship, and Tradition

> Consider therefore, my sons, how you came into this world and how all leave it, how all things pass and thus you will pass on. Use the time for repentance and doing well insofar as it regards you, with thanks. Give yourselves over not to utter destruction, but give for yourselves in service to him, from whom you and everything came because you who cannot make even a gnat upon the land, have nothing of your own.[1]
>
> Pope Gregory VIII, *Audita Tremendi*, 1187

Traditions of familial commitment to the crusading movement were established very quickly.[2] By the time of the Third Crusade some families could draw upon nearly a hundred years of dynastic practice and this chapter shows that significant numbers of participants enjoyed a crusading pedigree. Similarly, from the First Crusade onwards, crusaders often departed for the Holy Land alongside their kith (friends) and kin (family) or as members of military households as part of a collective response. This chapter shows that the Third Crusade was no exception.

In many elite families, crusading took place both across and within generations, and individuals might take the Cross on a number of separate occasions alongside differing members of their family. Based on his comprehensive prosopographical research of the early crusaders, Jonathan Riley-Smith argued that 'the crusading movement itself was as much in the collective consciousness of certain noble and knightly families as in the

---

[1] 'Cogitate itaque, filii, qualiter in hunc mundum venistis et qualiter exituri estis, qualiter transeant universa et pariter transeatis et vos, et penitendi ac bene agendi tempus, quantum spectat ad vos, cum gratiarum actione recipite et date vos ipsos non in exterminium, sed in observationem ei, a quo et vos et vestra omnia accepistis, quia non estis ex vobis nec quidquam ex vobis habetis, qui nec culicem unum potestis facere super terram': *Audita Tremendi*, 1187, 'Ansbertus', *Historia de expeditione Friderici imperatoris.* ed. Chroust , p. 9.

[2] Both Christopher Tyerman and Jonathan Riley-Smith argue that the traditions of familial crusading were laid down early in the twelfth century; Tyerman, *England*, p. 35; and, Riley-Smith, *First Crusaders*, pp. 93–7.

action and the thinking of theoreticians'.[3] Christopher Tyerman came to a similar conclusion in his review of English crusaders, referring to collective consciousness as a 'habit of mind and action to be passed down to succeeding generations'.[4] Current thinking on the Third Crusade is focused predominantly on participants as either part of the contingents of Frederick Barbarossa, the kings of France and England, and the count of Flanders, or listing crusaders from a particular region, such as Normandy.[5] Analysis of the influence of crusading pedigree on participation in the Third Crusade, as well as the degree to which they fought within kinship groups, has yet to have been undertaken.

In this chapter, I analyse the degree to which crusading had permeated the fabric of elite culture in north-western Europe by the time of the Third Crusade. I identify specific kinship networks of crusaders to understand better the role of family (collective) memory or *memoria* in the Third Crusade. Emphasis is placed on the interaction between the baronage and their relations in the Church, including religious orders, and on familial appeals in crusade-related preaching.[6] I use this to demonstrate that crusader pedigree and kinship-based crusader circles formed an important element in the motivation of an influential proportion of those who joined the Third Crusade. I also demonstrate that there were significant geographical variations. For example, the majority of participants in the Third Crusade from the Angevin realm cannot be linked to veterans of earlier expeditions to the Holy Land. This stands in marked contrast to figures from the rest of France, where over half of the participants enjoyed a crusading ancestor.

Surviving evidence also indicates that two-fifths of the overall sample participated as part of a family group and that over two-thirds of crusaders from non-Angevin France had family links to other crusaders on the expedition. Despite all evidence to the contrary, however, the myth of 'The Greedy Younger Son' persists. Based on population increases, the supposed primacy of feudal primogeniture, and a series of poor harvests, there remains a belief in broader medieval scholarship, as well as popular histories, that crusading was the preserve of landless younger sons.[7] In line with research into the First and Fifth Crusades, the evidence from north-western Europe in rela-

---

[3] Riley-Smith, *First Crusaders*, p. 13.
[4] Tyerman, *England*, p. 35.
[5] See, for example, Vielliard, 'Entourage normand', pp. 5–52.
[6] The concept of social memory can be applied to other groups, such as urban settlements or monastic foundations. However, sociologist Maurice Halbwachs proposed the family as the clearest example of a group that identified itself through its own distinct past, M. Halbwachs, *Les cadres sociaux de la mémoire* (Paris, 1925), trans. by L. Coser as, *On Collective Memory* (Chicago, 1992), pp. 54–74. See also, Hehl, 'Christian Order', pp. 185–228.
[7] C. Slack, 'The Quest for Gain: Were the First Crusaders Proto-Colonists?', *Seven Myths of the Crusades*, ed. A.J. Andrea and A. Holt (Indianapolis, 2015), pp. 70–1.

tion to the Third Crusade is that significant numbers of the noble elite participated as part of family groups, which included first-born sons.[8]

Collective Memory and Collective Identity

A better understanding of medieval kinship networks is fundamental to our investigation into collective memory. In relation to the evidence from the Third Crusade, for example, the mutationist view of an evolutionary contraction in family structures (progressive nuclearisation) is deeply problematic. This view argues that younger children were excluded from gaining property via hereditary succession, leading to a narrowing of families, but this is not supported by Third Crusade data. Equally, the traditional depiction of crusading having been the preserve of younger sons does not stand rigorous testing. Here, I demonstrate that patterns of land-holding and inheritance were far more diverse than is commonly presented, with examples of elder brothers acting as stewards of lordships rather than as the sole heir, and of inheritances being divided amongst siblings.[9] This, I argue, had a significant impact on noble identity, family, duty, and, especially, understandings of lineage, which is a form of collective memory.[10]

In retaining influence over familial property, younger brothers maintained a high degree of loyalty to their families and were more likely, it is argued here, to be influenced by a crusading heritage. This also enhanced family solidarity, which was not only accepted by magnates in late twelfth century north-western Europe but was relied upon to enhance the cohesion of their military households. Contemporary accounts highlight the importance of kinship in unit cohesion, with Ambroise describing a Templar force ambushed by Saladin's men during the Third Crusade as fighting as if 'they all sprang from one father'.[11] Indeed, as mentioned in the prologue, Jan-Frans Verbruggen's observation that the *Règle du Temple* was designed to recreate the cohesion formed by kinship in lay military households inspired this book.[12] In stark contrast to Steve Tibble's recent claims that the warrior

---

[8] Riley-Smith, *Idea of Crusading*, pp. 44–7; J.M. Powell, *Anatomy of a Crusade, 1213–1221* (Philadelphia, 1986), p. 82. See also, Jotischky, *Crusading and the Crusader States*, pp. 37–9.

[9] For a comprehensive review of how our understanding of medieval families was structured has fundamentally changed over the last century see Crouch, *Birth of Nobility*, pp. 87–170. For more on stewardship, see Park, *Papal Protection*, for example, pp. 42–62, 118–33, 137–52.

[10] For more on the importance of family memory, see N.L. Paul and J.G. Schenk, 'Family Memory and the Crusades', *Remembering the Crusades and Crusading*, ed. M. Cassidy-Welch (Abingdon, 2017), pp. 173–86.

[11] Ambroise, lines 7261–2.

[12] Verbruggen, *Art of Warfare*, p. 65.

elite were individualists whose virtues were not in alignment with military discipline, this research demonstrates that cohesion lay at the heart of medieval elite military culture.[13] That cohesion, I argue, came from two features: military formations based on family and locality and careful command and control mechanisms, such as the use of members of the commander's retinue to act as subordinate commanders and liaison officers. The latter point will be considered in detail in Chapter Four.

To fight surrounded by one's family was held up as an ideal by chroniclers of the period, such as when James of Avesnes' body was described as lying alongside three of his relatives on the field of Arsuf.[14] Rather than disparate bands of younger sons – of individuals –, the evidence in this chapter points towards north-western European contingents on the Third Crusade being composed of familial knightly retinues or *conroi*.[15] These *conroi* then operated in cohesive squadrons alongside and in close conjunction with both mounted serjeants and infantry through effective command and control measures.

As covered in the introduction, collective memory is the reference to a past that people share and that fundamentally shapes the way these people relate to each other. According to Maurice Halbwachs, collective memory can be shared, passed on, and constructed, by both large and small social groups.[16] Fundamental to the concept is that groups are able to remember more than individuals, because groups can draw on the knowledge and memories of all members.[17] In addition, groups are also able to acquire more information than individuals. Individuals will have differing perceptions based on such things as their experiences, background, and personality, and each will have acquired a unique set of information that can be contributed to a group discussion.[18] Elisabeth van Houts highlighted the inherently social context of the construction of collective memory in the

---

[13] S. Tibble, *Crusader Armies* (New Haven and London, 2018).

[14] 'Jacobus de Avennis cum consanguineis suis': *Itinerarium*, p. 269. James was an Artesian nobleman with lands in southern Flanders who had been enfeoffed by Henry II at the behest of Baldwin V of Hainault in 1172, 'Ibi Jacobus de Avethnis per intercessionem comitas Hanoniensis ab ipso rege triginta marchis infeodatus fuit': Gilbert of Mons, p. 109.

[15] The important role of locality in the retinue composition is analysed in the next chapter.

[16] Halbwachs, *On Collective Memory*, p. 38. See also Paul and Schenk, 'Family Memory and the Crusades', p. 173.

[17] M.F. Stasson and S.D. Bradshaw, 'Explanations of Individual–Group Performance Differences: What Sort of "Bonus" Can Be Gained Through Group Interaction?' *Small Group Research*, 26/2 (1995), 296–308.

[18] D.D. and M.L.M. Henningsen, 'Do Groups Know What They Don't Know? Dealing with Missing Information in Decision-Making Groups', *Communication Research*, 35/5 (2007), 507–25.

Middle Ages, augmenting familial interactions with links to members of the broader household or *familia*, as well as the type of religious communities considered in the previous chapter.[19]

Collective identity construction creates commonness and difference depending on how the past is constructed and reconstructed among people. It can act as a link between actors within a large and diverse elite social network that lacks more intimate connections, but in this chapter the focus is on its place within intimate, familial connections. Karl Schmid and Georges Duby established the role of ancestry within medieval elite identity construction. As a researcher on a larger prosopographical study into German medieval aristocratic society, Schmid presented the growing importance of vertical lineage over horizontal, kin-based groups in the Rhineland. Based on *libri memoriales* and a study of aristocratic naming traditions, Schmid and his colleagues argued for an eleventh-century shift from an elite society made up of broad, yet influential clans containing undifferentiated cousins (*Sippe*) to one focused on lineage (*Geschlecht*).[20] By the twelfth century this process was firmly established, he claimed, as demonstrated by the association of dynasty with title and land in the origins of the Welf 'house' (*Haus*) in *Historia Welforum*.[21]

In contrast to there having been an evolutionary contraction in family structure, such as proposed by Emile Durkheim and Marc Bloch, Duby initially argued that the family expanded or contracted in response to the degree of external threat.[22] In times of relative peace, the nuclear family could look after itself, but if royal or princely authority were perceived as weak, brothers would band together to defend familial lands, and such cohe-

---

[19] E.M.C. van Houts, *Memory and Gender in Medieval Europe, 900–1200* (Basingstoke, 1990); *History and Family Tradition in England and the Continent, 1000–1200* (Aldershot, 1999); and, *Medieval Memories: Men, Women, and the Past* (Harlow, 2001).

[20] K. Schmid, 'Zur Problematik von Familie, Sippe und Geschlecht, Haus und Dynastie beim mittealterlichen Adel: Vortragen zum Thema "Adel und Herrschaft in Mittelalter"', *Zeitschrift für die Geschichte des Oberrheins*, 105 (1957), 1–62. See also, O.G. Oexle, 'Gruppen in der Gesellschaft: Das wissenschaftliche Oeuvre von Karl Schmid', *Frühmittelalterliche Studien*, 28 (1994), 410–23.

[21] K. Schmid, 'Welfisches Selbstverständnis', *Adel und Kirche: Gerd Tellenbach zum 65 Geburtstag dargebracht von Freunden und Schülern*, ed. J. Fleckenstein and K. Schmid (Freiburg, 1968), pp. 390–416. Narrative texts describing the ancestry of a particular noble house flourished through the twelfth century and into the thirteenth. They provide a wealth of detail on aristocratic attitudes towards lineage. See, for example, N. Paul, 'The Chronicle of Fulk le Réchin: A Reassessment', *HSJ*, 18 (2007), 19–35.

[22] For Durkheim's *loi de contraction*, see 'La famile conjugale', *Revue philosophique*, 91 (1901), 1–14. M. Bloch, *Feudal Society*, Vol. 1, 2nd edition, trans. L.A. Manyon (London, 1962), p. 139. The translation of Bloch's theory as 'progressive nuclearisation', comes from D. Herlihy, 'Family Solidarity in Medieval Italian History', *The Social History of Italy and Western Europe, 700–1500. Collected Studies*, trans D. Bird (London, 1978), p. 174.

sion is notable in data relating to the Third Crusade.[23] In time, however, Duby came to adopt the theory of progressive nuclearisation. Drawing from his earlier empirical work, he proposed that Schmid's shift was related to the rise of hereditary titles following the collapse of Carolingian authority in the tenth century. In a process he later called the *mutation féodale* or *mutation de l'an mil*, Duby argued that the passing of titles and associated lands and fortifications down filial lines underpinned the increased importance of ancestry in elite identity.[24] This is evidenced, he argued, in the proliferation of genealogies and the emergence of dynastic historical narratives, such as the *Historia Welforum*.[25] The resulting supposed crisis in family identity for rootless bachelors neatly coincided with the crusades and the emergence of chivalry, which made for a compelling paradigm.[26] Indeed, it was so persuasive an approach to medieval familial structures that it dominated the field for two decades and it took some time for criticism of mutationism to gain ground.

From 1981 onwards, Constance Brittain Bouchard presented a very different model of family structures than that proposed by mutationists. In terms of toponyms, Bouchard challenged the idea that lineages drew their surnames from powerful holdings based on a study of naming patterns in France. Rather than taking the name of a castle as a symbol of power, she argued that during the course of the eleventh century, families began to favour a narrowing selection of first names. With even brothers sharing the same name, additional forms of identification became necessary.[27] John Freed's research into the counts of Falkenstein also highlighted significant inconsistencies in Schmid's argument that leading members of dynasties took their surnames from their principal castle or estate.[28]

In addition, Bouchard demonstrated that patrilineal sensibilities predated the supposed mutation of family structures at the start of the eleventh century. Based on evidence that could be found in Carolingian society, she concluded that there were no significant differences between practice in the ninth and eleventh centuries.[29] She suggested that the mutationists had gained a false impression of regular successions and new lineages being

---

[23] G. Duby, *La société au XIe et XIIe siècles dans la région mâconnaise* (repr. Paris, 1971), pp. 225–6.
[24] G. Duby, 'The Structure of Kinship and Nobility', *Chivalrous Society*, trans. C. Postan (Berkeley, 1977), pp. 134–48.
[25] Duby, 'French Genealogical Literature', *Chivalrous Society*, pp. 149–57.
[26] Crouch, *The Birth of Nobility*, pp. 107–8.
[27] C.B. Bouchard, 'Family Structure and Family Consciousness among the Aristocracy in the Ninth to Eleventh Centuries', *Francia*, 14 (1986), 639–58.
[28] J.B. Freed, 'The Counts of Falkenstein: Noble Self-Consciousness in Twelfth Century Germany', *Transactions of the American Philosophical Society*, 74/6 (1984), 52–7.
[29] C.B. Bouchard, 'The Origins of the French Nobility: A Reassessment', *American Historical Review*, 86 (1981), 501–32.

founded due to the improved survival of documentation in a more peaceful eleventh century.[30] This position was supported by Dominique Barthélemy, who argued for a 'documentary mutation' taking place alongside a realignment of society in 1000.[31] Pauline Stafford took a similar approach to challenge the presumption of the deteriorating social position of women, which lies at the heart of the mutationist view that inheritance began to favour a single male heir from c.1000 onwards.

Part of the mutationist argument rested on grants from dower lands held by the abbey of Cluny, which suggested that women held their lands on less generous terms in the eleventh century than in preceding years.[32] Rather than a change in inheritance customs, Stafford argued that the monks increasingly sought to minimise future challenges to their acquisitions through gaining written assent from potential rivals. Far from there having been a linear progression in land tenure, her data indicated that there remained a variety of different forms in use with none gaining particular dominance.[33] The pattern she identified was far more complex than that presented by the mutationists and undermined the assumption that there were significant numbers of landless bachelors in search of an identity or a purpose.

Stephen White's study of familial relationships in western France during the High Middle Ages, based on analysis of charters and other records, also indicated that far more complex structures existed than argued by Schmid and Duby.[34] The increasing use of *laudatio parentum* in these documents, for example, demonstrated how people clung to formal donations, which were affirmed by their relatives, to remind us of continuing family solidarity. In relation to property, White acknowledged a narrowing of the idea of 'family' but argued that such changes took place within each generation and did not reflect a long-term societal process. Whilst broad at the time of marriage, the legal family narrowed as soon as a couple had children, and rarely extended to first cousins, but broadened again as those children entered wedlock.

---

[30] C.B. Bouchard, *Strong of Body, Brave and Noble: Chivalry and Society in Medieval France* (Ithaca, NY, 1998) and *Those of My Blood: Constructing Noble Families in Medieval Francia* (Philadelphia, 2001).

[31] D. Barthélemy, *La mutation de l'an mil a-t-elle eu lieu? Servage et chevalerie dans la France des Xe et XIe siècles* (Paris, 1997), pp. 13–27.

[32] G. Duby, *Le Chevalier, La Femme et le Prêtre* (Paris, 1981); *The Knight, the Lady, and the Priest: The Making of Modern Marriage in Medieval France*, trans. B. Bray (New York, 1985).

[33] P. Stafford, 'La Mutation Familiale: A Suitable Case for Caution', *Community, the Family and the Saint: Patterns of Power in Early Medieval Europe*, ed. J. Hill and M. Swan (Turnhout, 1998), pp. 103–25.

[34] S.D. White, *Custom, Kinship and Gifts to Saints: the* Laudatio Parentum *in Western France, 1050–1150* (Chapel Hill, NC, 1988).

In her study of the county of Perche, Kathleen Thompson concluded that the lineage of the lords of Perche also did not conform to another aspect of Duby's model. Rather than being a response to declining central control, she argued that castle building, localised warfare, and attacks on Church property were conducted as agents of their overlords and operating within existing power structures and not as independent actors.[35] The relationship between authority and locality is considered in detail in the next chapter.

The mutationist response to these challenges was the introduction of 'progressive nuclearisation', moving the process forward by a century, but retaining the rise of 'dominant local lineages' in which succession of property was based on primogeniture as the family narrowed and younger siblings were excluded.[36] Despite revisions, however, mutationism continues to struggle in the face of empirical data. Based on the evidence related to the Third Crusade, charters marking the transfer of property were witnessed by those that might later challenge such transfers. Wives would witness donations made from their dowry lands and sons affirmed reductions in their potential inheritance, which suggests that the titleholder did not have absolute control over the lordship. For example, Hugh of Vergy confirmed his father's donation to Maizières Abbey and William of Merlo confirmed his father, Dreux IV, lord of Saint-Bris' donation to the Benedictine foundation of Charité-sur-Loire in 1177, as did Ermengarde, Dreux's wife.[37] They also confirmed his donation to the Cistercian house at Pontigny whilst at Vézelay in July 1190, immediately prior to Dreux and William's departure on crusade, as did Dreux's brother, Odo.[38]

In some cases, it was not merely the eldest son that was called upon to certify the transfer, but also their siblings; although this may have been merely a reflection of high mortality rates. What is harder to explain against a backdrop of linear inheritance is the enduring presence of a donor's brothers on such charters, such as Odo of Merlo's appearance on Dreux IV's donation to Pontigny Abbey or the presence of Oger and Guy of Chaisales on a donation by Bartholomew of Chaisales and his son, Raynald, to Maizières Abbey in 1190.[39] I would suggest that their presence is indicative of their

---

[35] Thompson, *Power and Border Lordship*, p. 5.
[36] See, for example, R. Le Jan, *Familie et pouvoir dans le monde franc (VIIe–Xe siècle): Essai d'anthropologie sociale* (Paris, 1995), pp. 414–27.
[37] *Édition des actes originaux de l'abbaye de Maizières, XIIe siècle, Chartes de la Bourgogne du Moyen Âge*, ed. C. Rey (Dijon, 2015), nos. 6 and 7. King Louis VII confirmed Dreux IV of Merlo's donation the same year, *Cartulaire du prieuré de la Charité-sur-Loire (Nièvre), Ordre de Cluni*, ed. R. de Lespinasse (Nevers and Paris, 1887), nos. 73–4.
[38] *Le premier cartulaire de l'abbaye de Pontigny (XII–XIII siècles)*, ed. M. Garrigues (Paris, 1981), no. 342.
[39] *L'Abbaye de Maizières*, ed. Rey, no. 43.

continuing interest in the family estate and that the titleholder was more akin to the steward of the family estate than its outright owner.

Far from being cast adrift, younger sons most often remained part of a cohesive family network and this is reflected in motivations to participate in the Third Crusade. The data demonstrates that a significant number of crusaders from north-western Europe between 1187 and 1192 had a crusading pedigree and that they journeyed to the Holy Land alongside family members.

Female Influence on Inheritance

In his review of the aristocracy of Champagne, Theodore Evergates presented strong evidence that wives retained ownership of dower lands and were paying homage for them in Flanders and Hainaut, as well as Champagne, in the years leading up to the Third Crusade and beyond.[40] A number paid homage while their husbands were still alive, but the majority did so as widows, when they had assumed their dower lands and held custody of their children's inheritances. Many chose to pay homage in person, and this practice continued throughout the thirteenth century.[41] Indeed, women represented 27 per cent of the fiefholders in the balliage of Troyes and 20 per cent in the county of Champagne as a whole in 1250.[42] The successful case brought by Margaret, widow of Robert Sablonières, to recover her dower lands after her husband donated them along with his estate to the Templars during the Third Crusade, highlights that the husband might not enjoy free rein over his wife's dower.[43] This also complicated the matter of inheritance. William IV of Garlande, lord of Livy, gave his wife a provisional dower, until his mother relinquished her lands, prior to departing on the Third Crusade with his son, Anseau, but William died in the Holy Land.[44] Mindful of such problems, a widow might resign her dower, sometimes in return for a rent.[45]

Alternatively, a widow might retain the dower and carry it forward to future marriages. When Andrew, lord of Montmirail and Ferté-Gaucher,

---

[40] T. Evergates, *The Aristocracy in the County of Champagne, 1100–1300* (Philadelphia, PA, 2007), pp. 111–12.

[41] For more on homage-taking see P.R. Hyams, 'Homage and Feudalism: A Judicious Separation', *Die Gegenwart Der Feudalismus*, ed. N. Fryde, P. Monnet, and O.G. Oexle (Göttingen, 2002), pp. 13–50.

[42] In 1190 women made up around 12% of Count Henry II's fiefholders, T. Evergates, *Feudal Society in the Bailliage of Troyes under the Counts of Champagne, 1152–1284* (Baltimore, 1975), p. 71; Evergates, *Aristocracy*, pp. 205, 207.

[43] Schenk, *Templar Families*, p. 178. The Templars eventually paid Margaret 26*l*. for her dower and another 25*l*. for the consent of Robert's daughter, Lucca, and her husband, *Histoire et cartulaire des templiers de Provins. Avec une introduction sur les débuts du Temple en France*, ed. V. Carrière (Paris, 1919; reprint: Marseille, 1978), nos. 73, 87.

[44] Ambroise, lines 4529, 6176; Evergates, *Aristocracy*, p. 114; *Itinerarium*, pp. 92, 213, 261.

[45] Evergates, *Aristocracy*, p. 342, n. 131.

died in 1177, the lordship of Montmirail passed to his son, John of Montmirail, but Andrew's second wife, Alice of Courtenay, gained that of Ferté-Gaucher in Champagne.[46] Sometime afterwards, she married William, count of Joigny, who later joined the Third Crusade, as did her stepson, John of Montmirail, and her brother, Peter II of Courtenay, count of Nevers, Auxerre, and Tonnere.[47] On occasion, a daughter might inherit dower lands in preference to their male siblings. The co-lordship of Coublant, which was shared with Frederick of Bourbonne, seemingly passed from Bartholomew of Vignory's first wife to their daughter, Elizabeth, rather than either of their sons, Guy or Walter of Vignory.[48]

An example from Yorkshire further illustrates the varying forms of inheritance and the role of female members of the family. On the eve of departing on the Third Crusade, Roger Fitz-Richard made a grant of his manor of Overton to his daughter Matilda. As his daughter lacked an heir, the bulk of his estate, however, passed to his contingent heir, his sister Agnes, and her son, Henry of Touke.[49] The retention of inheritance rights potentially changes the way we should look at the influence of women on noble networks. I shall return to the role of women as mediators of crusading later in this chapter.

The Enduring Influence of Siblings on Inheritance

Whilst inheritance of land generally favoured the eldest son, the data shows that it was not exclusive, and that the partition of estates or co-lordship was not unusual. In line with Sir James Holt's findings, the eldest son routinely gained the bulk of the property, as well as received the title, but their siblings also received endowments of land.[50]

Theobold V of Blois, for example, inherited the counties of Blois and Chartres, while his older brother, Henry, became count of Champagne. King Henry II granted the duchy of Aquitaine to his then second son, Richard, which was formally recognised in Poitiers and Limoges in 1172.[51] Whilst it is likely that, by the end of his reign, King Henry II considered primogeniture to be the most desirable system of inheritance for his subjects, the evidence linked to familial participation in the Third Crusade

---

[46] N. Vincent, 'Isabella of Angoulême: John's Jezebel', *King John, New Interpretations*, ed. S.D. Church (Woodbridge, 1999), pp. 176–7.
[47] *Gesta Regis*, Vol. 2, pp. 128, 150, 156, *Cartulaire Général de l'Yonne*, Vol. 2, ed. M. Quantin (Auxerre, 1854–60) no. 407, pp. 413–14. See also *Conquest*, p. 172.
[48] *Cartulaire du prieuré de Saint-Étienne de Vignory*, ed. J. d'Arbaumont (Dangiau, 1882), p. 34.
[49] *EYC*, Vol. 3, no. 1748.
[50] J.C. Holt, 'Politics and Property in Early Medieval England', *Past and Present*, 57 (1972), 3–52.
[51] Vigeois, '*Chronica*', *Novae Bibliothecae Manuscriptorum Librorum*, Vol. 2, ed. P. Labbe (Paris, 1657), Bk 1, ch. 66–7.

indicates that primogeniture was still far from the norm in north-western Europe.⁵² Shortly before Raoul I of Coucy left on crusade, for example, he divided the Coucy barony among his three sons and awarded title and rights to each of them.⁵³ The canons of Prémontré, however, were put in charge of the income he left to his daughter, Agnes.⁵⁴

In addition, having inherited the familial estates after the deaths of his father and three older brothers at Acre in 1190, Daimbert II passed the lordship of Seignelay on to his eldest son, Stephen, less the lordship of Beaumont, which went to Stephen's younger brother, John.⁵⁵ Bouchard highlights that in the years leading up to the Third Crusade, the Seignelay brothers routinely attested documents relating to family property in the name of their elder brother, which supports White's conclusions on familial relationships.⁵⁶ This demonstrates that younger sons were not necessarily excluded from matters relating to the familial estates when the eldest held title and that this reinforced familial loyalty.

Count Walter II of Brienne also split his estate, passing the lordship of Ramerupt to his second son, Andrew. However, it was to take Andrew sixteen years to gain his patrimony due to his elder brother Everard II's attempts to keep him from his inheritance.⁵⁷ On occasion, dowry lands were deemed more prestigious and the father's lordship would pass to a younger son instead. On the death of Third Crusade veteran and constable of Champagne, Guy II of Dampierre in 1216, his wife's inheritance of Bourbon passed their eldest son, Archambaud VIII, leaving the lordship of Dampierre to his younger brother, William.⁵⁸

Similarly, Raynald of Nevers, who participated in the Third Crusade, had received the lordship of Decize from Count William II of Nevers and Auxerre, whilst his elder brothers inherited the county in turn.⁵⁹ Through marriage to Agnes of Nevers, Peter II of Courtenay had inherited Nevers and Auxerre some fifteen years before he joined the Third Crusade, less the lordship of Decize. As is discussed later in this chapter, a crusading heritage seems to have played a role in dynastic marriages. Raynald's sister, for instance, married into the Joigny family who could trace a lineage back

---

⁵² For Henry II, see F. Pollock and F.W. Maitland, *The History of English Law*, Vol. 2 (Cambridge, 1898), pp. 262–78.
⁵³ Leson, 'Constellation of Crusade', pp 75–90.
⁵⁴ *Crusade Charters*, p. xxvii.
⁵⁵ Bouchard, *Those of My Blood*, pp. 162–63.
⁵⁶ Bouchard, *Sword, Miter, and Cloister*, p. 356.
⁵⁷ Asmoui Ismail, 'History of the Counts of Brienne', p. 106.
⁵⁸ Evergates, *Aristocracy*, p. 217; Schenk, *Templar Families*, p. 201.
⁵⁹ Raynald seems to have died on crusade c.1190, Bouchard, *Sword, Miter, and Cloister*, p. 347. For more on the crusading heritage of Raynald of Nevers see E. Siberry, 'The Crusading Counts of Nevers', *Nottingham Medieval Studies*, 34 (1990), 64–70.

to Reynard II of Joigny, who participated in the First Crusade – a lineage shared by Peter II's sister, Alice of Courtenay.[60]

These examples of younger sons inheriting their mother's lands, and the provision of property to siblings, suggest that there remained alternative approaches to inheritance than strict primogeniture. I would argue that such evidence of a more nuanced and inclusive approach to inheritance had an important impact on shared perceptions of the importance of (crusader) lineage, as well as the influence of kinship networks on participation in the Third Crusade. Families were ready to provide support and assistance to aspiring crusaders, especially through membership of the military household of a rich and noble relative. Even quite distant relatives might draw inspiration from a crusading ancestor as part of their motivation to take the Cross.

Kinship and the Third Crusade

In his analysis of the Second Crusade, Jonathan Riley-Smith argued for the concentration of participation in certain kinship groups, such as the counts of Burgundy, conclusions reinforced by the work of Marcus Bull on the Bernards of Bré in the Limousin.[61] These kinship groups, Riley-Smith argued, often demonstrated distinct features: a tradition of pilgrimage to the Holy Land, patronage of reformist monastic foundations, such as Cluny, and an attachment to the reformed papacy. It is a position that is reinforced by the presence of the descendants of the Burgundian counts on the Third Crusade. Duke Hugh III of Burgundy, Robert II of Dreux, his brother, Bishop Philip of Beauvais, and John of Ponthieu were all descendants of the Crusader Duke Odo I and played a prominent role in the Third Crusade. In addition, men like Humbert IV 'the young' of Beaujeu joined the expedition, only to die in the Levant before 1192.[62] Hugh of Issoudun, descended via his mother from Duke Hugh II, survived the siege of Acre.[63]

---

[60] Count William of Joigny participated on the Third Crusade, as did the count's son-in-law, John of Arcis-sur-Aube, *Itinerarium*, p. 93. John also died on crusade, Evergates, *Aristocracy*, p. 232.

[61] J. Riley-Smith, 'Family Traditions and Participation in the Second Crusade', *The Second Crusade and the Cistercians*, ed. M. Gervers (New York, 1992), pp. 101–8. For the Bernards of Bré, see Bull, *Knightly Piety*.

[62] In addition to Duke Odo I, Humbert could also trace his lineage back to the First Crusader Guy II of Rochefort, *Obituaries de la province de Lyon*, II, *Diocèse de Lyon, deuxième partie, dioceses de Mâcon et de Châlon-sur-Saône*, ed. J. Laurent and P. Gras (Paris, 1965), p. 508. On links to Guy II see J. Riley-Smith, 'Family Traditions', p. 104. Similarly, as well as being a descendant of the dukes of Burgundy, Hervé III of Donzy could also trace his lineage back to Geoffrey II, lord of Donzy and count of Chalon, Bouchard, *Sword, Mitre, and Cloister*, p. 327.

[63] Diss, Vol. 2, p. 80; *HdB*, Vol. 3, no, 821; Wendover, p. 178.

Evergates saw similar tendencies amongst the Blois-Champagne circle.[64] Count Thibaut II was a benefactor of the Cistercians and a friend of Bernard of Clairvaux, and his eldest son, Henry, represented the family on the Second Crusade. At fifty-two years old, Henry took the Cross once more and departed from Brindisi in 1179 alongside Peter of Courtenay and Philip, bishop-elect of Beauvais – both of whom were related to crusaders.[65] In 1190, his son, Henry II of Champagne left for the East and participated in the siege of Acre alongside Bishop Philip and the Courtenay grouping mentioned earlier. Jean Longnon's extensive prosopographical study of the Fourth Crusade concluded that many of the participants were related to one another or to veterans of previous expeditions, and that in taking the Cross they were following a dynastic tradition.[66]

Ties of kinship played an influential role in participation in the Third Crusade, both in terms of crusading ancestry and membership of kinship groups.[67] Half (51%) of the crusaders from non-Angevin France had an identifiable crusader heritage and the concentration is particularly high in the military households of Philip II of France and Henry II of Champagne. For example, of the thirteen identifiable members of Philip II's immediate household on the Third Crusade, eleven enjoyed a crusader heritage and ten had relations on the same expedition.[68] The constable of Champagne, Guy II of Dampierre, was closely related to ten identifiable members of the expedition.[69]

The surviving evidence for the Angevin realms and the Low Countries indicates that the percentages there were more modest. In England, where such a heritage existed, it rarely predated the Second Crusade, which reduced the number from the Angevin realm with an identifiable crusading ancestor to just 16 per cent. In all, some 26 per cent of identifiable participants could call upon an identifiable crusader heritage, and these included men of considerable influence. In addition, 41 per cent travelled to the Holy Land

---

[64] Evergates, 'Louis VII and the Counts of Champagne', pp. 109–17.

[65] Peter was the brother of King Louis VII of France. His uncle, Renaud of Burgundy, is thought to have died on the First Crusade.

[66] J. Longnon, 'Sur les croisés de la quatrième croisade', *Journal des savants*, 2/2 (1977), 120. See also, Longnon, *Les compagnons de Villehardouin: Recherches sur les croisés de la quatrième croisade* (Geneva, 1978).

[67] Ancestry here is taken as someone from whom they are descended or a direct ancestor's siblings and their descendants.

[68] Immediate here is taken to mean professional members of the military household rather than magnates, such as Robert II of Dreux, who might only join the household for a particular campaign. In the analysis of King Richard's crusade household undertaken later in this study, temporary, crusader elements of the household are also considered.

[69] See Appendix 1, Guy II of Dampierre.

with another known family member.[70] As will be highlighted, however, a shared crusading pedigree did not guarantee that crusaders would journey to the Holy Land together.

Family Heritage and Participation in the Third Crusade

In comparison, in his research into the Fifth Crusade, James Powell highlighted the importance of a crusader pedigree, citing a charter of Margrave Herman V of Baden, who accompanied Duke Louis of Bavaria on crusade in 1221 after his brother, Frederick, died in 1218 at Damietta.[71] In addition, Graham Loud noted that Margrave Herman IV of Baden and Verona died on the Third Crusade and that his father, Herman the Great, had participated in the Second Crusade.[72] Despite the preponderance of data from the Angevin Realm, as shown in Table 3, approximately a quarter of identifiable participants from north-western Europe on the Third Crusade were found to have a crusader heritage. It should be noted that the large number whose crusader heritage is unknown is not indicative of their not having such a heritage.

Table 3. Family Heritage and Participation in the Third Crusade

Angevin Realm	With crusader heritage	54
	Crusader heritage unknown	294
	Number of cases	348
France	With crusader heritage	75
	Crusader heritage unknown	71
	Number of cases	146
Low Countries	With crusader heritage	19
	Crusader heritage unknown	70
	Number of cases	89
Totals	With crusader heritage	149
	Crusader heritage unknown	434
	Number of cases	583

Examples of Third Crusade participants with ancestral links to previous crusades include Ernald of Mandeville, who arrived in Acre shortly after

---

[70] A family member here includes the immediate family (parents and siblings), but also the broader network of cousins and in-laws.
[71] Powell, *Anatomy of a Crusade*, pp. 82–3.
[72] *Barbarossa*, p. 49.

King Richard, and his second cousin, Roger of Mandeville.[73] Ernald's uncle, William of Mandeville, crusaded in 1177 with Philip of Alsace, count of Flanders and Vermandois, having been raised in the Flemish court and knighted by Count Philip.[74] Like Richard, Count Philip was descended from Fulk V of Anjou and was a cousin to the kings of Jerusalem. However, his taking of the Cross may have resulted from the execution of Walter of Fontaines and subsequent seizure of the familial lands of Elisabeth of Vermandois.[75] Philip of Alsace visited the shrine of Thomas Becket en route to his crusade of 1177 and William of Mandeville was but one of many knights with lands in England who accompanied him on crusade.[76] Others included Henry I of Lacy, Hugh Bigod, Hugh of Valtort, Reginald of St Valery, Robert Pirou, and Walter of Mayenne, along with his brothers, Geoffrey III, lord of Mayenne, Guy, and William.[77]

These in turn seemingly influenced a new generation of crusaders. John Fitz-Richard had married into the Lacy family and departed for the East in March 1190 only to die at the siege of Acre the following October.[78]

---

[73] *Itinerarium*, p. 218.

[74] *Early Yorkshire Families*, ed. Clay and Greenway, p. 56–7. Philip's father, Thierry, was an uncle to the late King Baldwin IV of Jerusalem, and he undertook four expeditions to the Holy Land. Geoffrey Fougères of Brittany, whose son, Ralph II, was to die at the siege of Acre in 1191, had accompanied Thierry on his crusade of 1157, G. Ménage, *Histoire de Sablé* (Paris, 1683), p. 179, Wendover, p. 191. See also, *Gesta Regis*, Vol. 1, p. 159; *The Book of the Foundation of Walden Monastery*, ed. and trans. D. Greenway and L. Watkiss (Oxford, 1999), pp. 52, 58.

[75] Walter had been accused of adultery with Philip of Anjou's wife, Elisabeth of Vermandois. Despite Walter's denials and offers to prove his innocence, Count Philip had him beaten and then drowned in a latrine trench: T.S. Asbridge, *The Greatest Knight: The Remarkable Life of William Marshal, The Power Behind Five English Thrones* (London, 2015), p. 145.

[76] The relationship between Earl William, Count Philip, and William's counterparts in Flanders, the Béthune family, is dealt with in detail in the next chapter. See also, E. Oksanen, *Flanders and the Anglo-Norman World, 1066–1216* (Cambridge, 2012), pp. 86–90.

[77] Henry of Lacy, lord of Pontefract, had previously crusaded in 1158–9. He did not survive the expedition of 1177 and his estates passed to his son, Robert II, *Gesta Regis*, Vol. 2, p. 159, R.W. Eyton, *Court, Household and Itinerary of Henry II* (London, 1878), p. 211, Ménage, *Sablé*, p. 179, Robert of Torigny, *Chronique de Robert de Torigni: Abbé du Mont-Saint-Michel*, Vol. 1, ed. L. Delisle (Rouen, 1872), p. 241.

[78] *Annales Cestrienses, or the Chronicle of the Abbey of Saint Werburg, Chester*, ed. R. Copley Christie (London, 1887), p. 41, or at Tyre, *Gesta Regis*, Vol. 2, p. 148, *Chronica*, p. 80. John Fitz-Richard's brother, Robert Thesaurarius, was prior of the Hospitallers in England, so it is possible that the family sought a wife with crusader credentials. However, the Roger of Lacy listed in the *Itinerarium* as travelling to the Holy Land with Richard is unlikely to be Roger Fitz-John, constable of Chester and great-nephew of Henry I of Lacy. Despite a number of dated secondary works linking him to the Third Crusade, Howden places him in firmly in England in 1191, *Itinerarium*, p. 218; *Gesta Regis*, Vol. 2, pp. 232–4. The Rev. Pratt claimed that Roger Fitz-Eustace was accom-

According to Gilbert of Mons, Bernard of St Valérie also died at Acre, but beyond he and Reginald both holding lands in Oxfordshire, any relationship is unclear.[79] As preceptor of Temple Hurst, near Selby in Yorkshire, Robert Pirou was also linked to the Lacy family.[80] Henry I of Lacy, for example, had confirmed Ralph and William of Hastings' donation of the site to the Templars c.1155.[81] Robert Pirou died after his return from crusade and Henry of Hastings, a significant landowner in East Anglia, represented the family on the Third Crusade.[82]

Freshly released from captivity following his part in the rebellion of 1173, Robert Blanchemains, earl of Leicester, did not take the Cross in 1177 alongside his former comrade in arms, Hugh Bigod. However, both Earl Robert and his son, Robert Fitz-Pernel, owed the return of their remaining lands and castles to King Richard and pledged themselves to the Third Crusade. Moreover, Waleran of Beaumont, Earl Robert's uncle, had joined the Second Crusade. I shall return to this shortly.

In terms of the Third Crusade, Hugh Bigod's successor, Roger, did not take the Cross, but remained in England to secure his newly confirmed earldom of Norfolk. However, he was to play an important role in securing King Richard's release from imprisonment. His interests in the Holy Land may well have been represented by his wife's family, the Tosny, who arrived in Acre shortly after King Richard.[83] Geoffrey III of Mayenne's son, Jocelin III, lord of Mayenne, rescued Roger of Tosny during an attack on an Ayyubid raid in the Levant in June 1192.[84] However, Jocelin had rebelled against Henry II to recover three strategically placed castles in 1189 and his

---

panied on crusade by William of Beaumont of Whitely Hall, C.T. Pratt, *History of Cawthorne* (Barnsley, 1882), p. 17, but it is more likely that he was with Roger's father.

[79] *Itinerarium*, p. 92; Gilbert of Mons, p. 273.

[80] J.E. Burton, 'The Knights Templar in Yorkshire in the Twelfth Century: A Reassessment', *Northern History*, 27 (1991), 28.

[81] Ralph and William were probably related to Richard Hastings, then Master of the Templars in England, in whose presence Henry's charter was issued, Lee, 'Landowners and Landscapes'.

[82] 'The Records of the Templars in England in the Twelfth Century', *British Academy Records of Social and Economic History*, Vol. 9, ed. B.A. Lees (1935), nos. 5, 6; See also E. Lord, *The Knights Templar in Britain* (London and New York, 2002), pp. 82–3, 89. Henry of Hastings was also hereditary steward of the library of St Edmund's Abbey and tenant of the abbot in Norfolk and Suffolk, PR3 RI (1991), p. 43. He was also a tenant of Richard of Clare, PR3 RI (1991), p. 44.

[83] Ambroise, line 4719; *Itinerarium*, p. 217. Ida of Tosny had been a mistress to Henry II and bore him a son, William Longsword, future earl of Salisbury and participant in the Fifth Crusade.

[84] Ambroise, line 10448; *Itinerarium*, p. 389. Jocelin III of Mayenne had become patron of the Cistercian abbey at Fontaine-Daniel immediately prior to departing on crusade. He survived to confirm his uncle, William of Mayenne's, donation to the abbey in 1195, where Jocelin was eventually buried. He also participated in the Albigensian Crusade

participation in the Crusade may have also been influenced by an attempt to gain favour with Richard.[85] Jocelin is considered in more detail in the case study of Richard's *familia regis*.

For crusaders like Geoffrey IV of Rancon, the relationship to the Holy Land was more immediate. Geoffrey's aunt, Bourgogne de Rancon, married Hugh VIII, lord of Lusignan, and was mother to Guy, king of Jerusalem. His father, Geoffrey the Poitevin, had participated in the Second Crusade as part of the contingent from Aquitaine alongside the duchy's seneschal, Saldebreuil of Sanzay, and the magnates Hugh of Lusignan and Guy of Thouars.[86] In the aftermath of Geoffrey III's rebellion against Richard, count of Poitou, of 1187, he took the Cross alongside his cousin and ally, Geoffrey of Lusignan. Through his mother, Isabelle of Angoulême, Geoffrey III was also related to the counts of Angoulême, and Peter of Angoulême, bishop of Tripoli, served as King Guy's treasurer.[87] Given that the dowager queen Eleanor travelled as far as Sicily, one wonders if she held aspirations of remaining with the expedition to the Holy Land with the lords of Aquitaine serving once more within her crusading retinue, or if she influenced their participation in some way. This too is a question to which we will return shortly.

Other members of the Third Crusade drew from a longer pedigree. Walter of Chappes' participation in the First Crusade may well have influenced the decision of Clarembaud IV of Chappes and his brother Guy to join the Third Crusade. Through his mother, Adeline of Chappes, Clarembaud of Noyers, was also descended from Walter and he departed for the siege of Acre, most probably alongside his Templar brother, Guy.[88] Both Hugh VI of Gournay and Raoul I of Coucy could claim descent from First Crusade participants, Thomas of Marle and his father, Enguerrand I of Coucy. Raoul I was descended from Thomas' son and heir, Enguerrand II of Coucy, and Hugh VI from his third daughter, Melisende. Similarly, the Houses of Boves and St Pol could trace their lineage to another of Thomas' sons, Robert, and the House of Amiens to both Thomas' sister, Beatrix of Boves, and his youngest daughter, Mathilde of Coucy.

---

of 1210, BN, ms. français 22450, f. 232; *Cartulaire de l'abbaye cistercienne de Fontaine-Daniel*, ed. A.P.A. Grosse-Duperon and E. Gouvrion (Mayenne, 1896), nos. 4, 7.

[85] The castles of Gorron, Ambrières, and Châtillon lay on the border between Anjou and Normandy and had been secured by Jocelin's father in return for supporting Geoffrey of Anjou's invasion of Normandy. For Jocelin III's revolt see Diss, Vol. 2, pp. 63–4; *Gesta Regis*, Vol. 2, p. 72.

[86] Also known as Sal of Breuil, J. Flori, *Aliénor d'Aquitaine: La Reine insoumise* (Paris, 2004), pp. 69–70, R. Pernoud, *Aliénor d'Aquitaine* (Paris, 1965), p. 67.

[87] Bishop Peter also helped to purify Acre's churches in the aftermath of the siege, *Gesta Regis*, Vol. 2, pp. 180–1.

[88] 'Inventaire de la collection de Chastellux', ed. C. Porée, *Bulletin de la Société des sciences historiques et naturelles de l'Yonne*, 57 (1904), nos. 29, 133, *HdB*, Vol. 3, pp. 43, 61.

Whilst both provide excellent examples of the potential influence of a crusading lineage, they also lead us onto the importance of familial groups on participation in the Third Crusade. For example, Stephen and Guy of Pierre-Perthuis joined their paternal cousins, Clarembaud and Guy of Noyers, in the Levant, as did the Pierre-Perthuis' sororal nephew, Stephen of Brive.[89] It is clear that a significant number of elite participants on the Third Crusade from north-western Europe had a crusading ancestor. Whilst it is impossible to determine the precise effect of that pedigree on a decision to take the Cross in each individual case, the prevalence of a crusader ancestry across the noble network is highly suggestive of an influence on motivation to join the expedition.

Kinship and Participation in the Third Crusade

Of the crusaders identified in this study, 41 per cent had a father, son, brother, cousin, or brother-in-law on the Third Crusade. In relation to the Fifth Crusade, James Powell found that of 132 participants from the 'feudal aristocracy' about 20 per cent had identifiable familial ties to other members of the expedition.[90] Given limitations in surviving genealogical data, Powell presented such ties as a significant factor in crusade participation. This was about half the percentage found in the Third Crusade data for participants from north-western Europe. Moreover, in line with Table 3, the large number for whom familial participation is unknown is not indicative that they did not have family on the expedition.

As with crusader heritage, the surviving data from non-Angevin France is compelling, with 68 per cent having family ties to other members of the expedition – most of whom seemingly travelled east in the company of their kin. Moreover, in line with Powell's work on the Fifth Crusade, such examples demonstrate that younger sons seeking their fortunes in the Levant did not dominate participation in the Third Crusade.[91] Indeed, another cousin of Stephen of Brive, Aswalo II, lord of Seignelay, crusaded with his eldest sons, Rainard, Frederick, and Peter. Aswalo and his sons were also linked to Bernard of Clairvaux through the abbot's mother, Alèthe of Montbard.[92] This familial network was also closely tied to the Knights Templar, as well as regional relationships that are considered in the next chapter.[93] Aswalo II and his three sons all died at the siege of Acre, as did Stephen of Brive,

---

[89] Schenk, *Templar Families*, pp. 243–4.
[90] Powell, *Anatomy of a Crusade*, pp. 82–3.
[91] Powell, *Anatomy of a Crusade*, p. 82.
[92] The second son of Aswalo I of Seignelay, Bochard married Aanor of Montbard, Bouchard, *Those of My Blood*, pp. 156–7. John of Arcis-sur-Aube was uncle to Bernard III of Montbard, lord of Époisses.
[93] On the Templar link, see Schenk, *Templar Families*, pp. 242–4.

leaving Aswalo's infant son to inherit as Daimbert II.[94] This raises important questions as to concern for the preservation of male family members. Whilst it is not clear, I would argue that those taking the Cross and journeying eastwards in 1188–9 anticipated joining a protracted siege with survival rates comparable to that of the siege of Antioch (1097–8). By the time Philip and Richard set sail, the full extent of the commitment was likely well known.[95]

Table 4. Kinship and Participation in the Third Crusade

Angevin realm	With relations on crusade	97
	Familial participation unknown	251
	Number of cases	348
France	With relations on crusade	100
	Familial participation unknown	46
	Number of cases	146
Low Countries	With relations on crusade	42
	Familial participation unknown	47
	Number of cases	89
Totals	With relations on crusade	239
	Familial participation unknown	344
	Number of cases	583

In terms of survival, the lords of Toucy were equally unfortunate. Itier I and his brothers, Hugh and Norgaud, perished on crusade between 1097 and 1110.[96] Itier III of Toucy had fallen in 1147 whilst serving alongside King Louis VII and his eldest son, Narjot, died during the course of the Third Crusade. The next lord of Toucy, Itier IV died at Damietta in 1218, and his son, Jean, perished on John of Brienne's Crusade of 1231.[97] Similarly, Geoffrey III of Joinville had joined Henry I of Champagne on the Second Crusade and returned to the Levant with his son Geoffrey IV, only for both to die at the siege of Acre c.1190.[98] His grandsons Geoffrey V and Robert of Joinville both died on the Fourth Crusade, but Geoffrey V's grandson,

---

[94] Bouchard, *Those of My Blood*, pp. 157–67.
[95] For more on the siege of Antioch see Asbridge, *The First Crusade*.
[96] Phillips, *The Second Crusade*, p. 100.
[97] *Vie de Louis le Gros par Suger, suivie de l'Histoire du roi Louis VII*, Vol. 1, ed. A. Molinier (Paris, 1887), p. 158. See also, Bouchard, *Sword, Miter, and Cloister*, p. 375.
[98] Evergates, *Aristocracy*, pp. 173–4, 257; *Itinerarium*, p. 74.

John of Joinville, survived the Seventh Crusade and left behind an invaluable eyewitness account of the expedition.[99]

These familial networks of crusaders routinely included professed religious members. The Chappes cluster, for example, incorporated the Templar, Brother Guy of Noyers.[100] In addition, as well as lay lords, such as Anselm III of Montréal, Bartholomew of Vignory, Everard I of Chacenay, Geoffrey III of Joinville, Guy II of Dampierre, and Guy's brother-in-law, Narjot II of Toucy, the crusader social network of Count Everard II of Brienne included Archbishop Thierry of Besançon and Bishop Manasses of Langres.[101] Archbishop Thierry may have simply been inspired by his younger brother, Clemence of Montfauçon's participation in the expedition of 1171, but they were both also descended from another member of the First Crusade, Amadeus I, lord of Montfauçon.[102]

Two of every five participants in the Third Crusade identified in this study had a close relation on the same expedition. With only a few exceptions, they travelled to the Holy Land in familial groups and there is evidence that a number of familial groups fought and sometimes died side-by-side, such as James of Avesnes and three of his relatives at the battle of Arsuf. This suggests that there were families more inclined to support crusading, that is, that there were crusading dynasties, as argued by Nicholas Paul and others.

Women as Mediators of Crusading

Jonathon Riley-Smith has also argued that crusading activity was often transmitted down through the female line and that women actively encouraged their male relations to take the Cross in some way.[103] As an exemplar, he presented Isabel of Vermandois, a descendant of First Crusade veteran,

---

[99] Longnon, *Les Compagnons*, pp. 18–20; 'Joinville: The Life of Saint Louis', *Joinville and Villehardouin, Chronicles of the Crusades*, ed. and trans. M.R.B. Shaw (London, 1963), pp. 163–354.

[100] As bishop of Orléans, Manasses of Seignelay later joined the Albigensian Crusade, knighting Amaury of Montfort outside the walls of Castelnaudary on 23 June 1213, Tyerman, *God's War*, p. 563.

[101] Everard II's heritage included a First Crusader, Count Everard I, and Walter II of Brienne, who had participated in the Second Crusade, as had Everard II himself, M.D. Sturdza, *dictionnaire historique et généalogique des grandes familles de Grèce, d'Albanie et de Constantinople*, 2nd edition (Paris, 1999), p. 507. Everard I of Chacenay had crusaded in both 1179 and 1182, before dying at the siege of Acre in 1191.

[102] Thierry journeyed with Count Louis of Ferrette, but at died Acre, *Itinerarium*, pp. 93, 111; Diss, Vol. 2, p. 79; Wendover, p. 178; G. Poull, *La Maison souveraine et ducale de Bar* (Nancy, 1994), p. 78.

[103] Riley-Smith, 'Family Traditions', pp. 101–8. See also Riley-Smith, *First Crusaders*, p. 224, and Paul and Schenk, 'Family Memory and The Crusades', pp. 175–7.

Hugh the Great, within a mid-twelfth-century crusader social network that included her brother, Simon; her sons, William III of Warenne, earl of Surrey, and Waleran of Meulan, earl of Worcester; as well as their cousins, Roger of Mowbray and Dreux II of Mouchy-le-Châtel. Another son, Reginald, managed the Surrey estates whilst his elder brother crusaded and her son-in-law, Roger of Beaumont, joined the expedition after the siege of Lisbon. Dreux II, however, seemingly participated in penance for an incestuous marriage, for which St Bernard absolved him, and Roger of Mowbray enjoyed links to the Templars and had founded the leper hospital at Warwick, which serves to remind us that motivation can be multi-faceted. There could be more than a single influence on someone deciding to take the Cross.[104]

Social networks based on female lineages are notable for the Third Crusade, but they do not appear to have been common. As introduced in Chapter One, the Lacy family were linked to Nigel of Mowbray through his mother, Alice of Gant, and Earl Robert of Leicester and his son, Robert Fitz-Pernel, were both descended from Isabel of Vermandois. Similarly, one wonders about the influence of Alice of Courtenay on her immediate family. Her father had died in Palestine in 1183 and her grandmother, Adélaide of Maurienne, had a crusading pedigree that included Renaud II and Stephen I of Burgundy. Alice's great uncle, Amadeus III of Savoy, had died on the Second Crusade, an expedition that also included two of her paternal uncles, Louis VII of France and Robert I, count of Dreux. Although they divorced c.1184, her second husband, William of Joigny, and her stepson, John of Montmirail, joined the Third Crusade, as did her brother, Peter II of Courtenay – the future Latin Emperor of Constantinople.

Given the close association between the house of Courtenay and Philip Augustus, the womenfolk of the Valoignes family are, however, perhaps a stronger example. Maud of Valoignes had married Hervey of Glanville sometime after his return from the Second Crusade. Their son, Hubert Walter, was bishop of Salisbury and accompanied Baldwin of Forde on crusade. The joint commander of the Angevin advance guard was Ranulf of Glanville, who was married to Maud's sister, Berthe. Ranulf was joined on crusade by Maud's father, Theobald of Valoignes, and her brother, Alan of Valoignes, sheriff of Kent, as well as Durand of Outillé, lord of Valoignes.[105] Ranulf of Glanville died at the siege of Acre in 1190 and Theobald of Valoignes, lord of Parham and butler of Ireland, died in the

---

[104] *De Profectione Ludovici VII in Orientum*, ed. and trans. V.G. Berry (New York, 1948), p. 126; Suger, Abbot of Saint-Denis, 'Epistolae', *RHF*, Vol. 15, ed. M.L. Bouquet (Poitiers, 1878), pp. 485, 500.

[105] PR2 RI (1190), p. 110; PR3 RI (1191), p. 43. After his death, Alan's widow, Hellena of Alvestan, married Hugh of Hastings, another crusader family. Durand died on the Third Crusade and a jury was held to determine his property, *CRR*, Vol. 1, pp. 69, 277–8.

Holy Land a year later.[106] Ralph of Arden, sheriff of Hereford 1185–9, was married to Ranulf of Glanville's daughter, Mabel, and most probably also travelled with him as part of King Richard's advance guard as he is placed at the siege.[107] Ranulf's uncle, Roger of Glanville, was also present at the siege and survived to capture some Muslims whilst scouting the walls of Jerusalem.[108] In addition, Maud of Valoignes' cousin, Everard of Ros, had been a ward of Ranulf of Glanville before marrying Rohese Trussebot. Whilst Everard predeceased the crusade and their son, Robert of Ros, was too young to join the expedition, Walter and Peter of Ros, can be placed at the siege of Acre, as can Robert Trussebot.[109]

Like the Courtenay grouping, however, their motivations are not clear-cut. Ranulf of Glanville, Roger of Glanville, Alan of Valoignes, and Ralph of Arden had all lost position on the ascension of Richard to the throne of England, so their participation may have also been aimed at regaining favour at court.[110] Such evidence of female mediators to crusading stands in stark contrast to contemporary sources that portray women as a hindrance to crusading, bemoaning the departure of their husbands and sons, and describe the reluctance of men to leave their womenfolk.[111] Canon law insisted that those taking the Cross enjoyed the consent of their wives, a rule Pope Innocent III was to relax after the Third Crusade.

As with patterns of inheritance, I would suggest that the reality of feminine influence was no doubt more complex and driven by individual circumstance, as well as character. Marriage could, for example, be used to bind together neighbouring houses on the brink of a great endeavour or challenge, such as crusading, as was seemingly the case in the marriage of Hugh of Oyry to the niece of Count Ralph I of Clermont on the eve of

---

[106] Devizes, *Chronicon*, p. 19; *Gesta Regis*, Vol. 2, p. 149; Wendover, p. 191.
[107] Devizes, *Chronicon*, p. 6.
[108] *Gesta Regis*, Vol. 2, p. 144, *Chronica*, Vol. 3, p. 73; *Itinerarium*, p. 345.
[109] Everard's mother, Sybil of Valoignes was Theobold of Valoignes' younger sister and had married first Robert of Ros. Their grandson, Robert of Ros was fourteen when he paid a relief of 1000 *marks* for his inheritance to King Richard in 1191. For Walter and Peter of Ros, and Robert Trussebot, see *Gesta Regis*, Vol. 2, pp. 147–50; and Leson, 'Constellation of Crusade', pp 75–90.
[110] Ralph of Arden had been sheriff of Hereford and Ranulf of Glanville was displaced as justiciar of England on 16 September 1189, *Gesta Regis*, Vol. 2, pp. 86, 90. Roger of Glanville lost custody of Newcastle-upon-Tyne, R.R. Heiser, 'Castles, Constables, and Politics in Late Twelfth-Century English Governance', *Albion*, 32 (2000), 25. Alan of Valoignes lost custody of Dover castle but retained the position of sheriff of Kent and had received land in Yorkshire from Richard on 4 December 1189, TNA C 52/22, *carte antique* roll X, m.2d, no. 27; Heiser, 'Castles, Constables, and Politics', p. 25.
[111] See, for example, J. Bédier and P. Aubry, *Les chansons de croisade* (Paris, 1909), pp. 32–5, 101–4, 112–14, 126–29, 181–4, 191–4, 202–4, 210–12, 271–3, 283–5, 290. This evidence is literary, however, and may have been a trope that was adopted by crusade preachers. See also, Tyerman, *God's War*, p. 486.

Hugh and Ralph's departure for the Third Crusade.[112] It could also be used to offset a perceived a strategic weakness, such as King Richard's union with Berengaria of Navarre.[113]

Eleanor of Aquitaine and the Third Crusade

Eleanor of Aquitaine's influence on the Third Crusade has long deserved greater consideration. In addition to having participated in the Second Crusade, Queen Eleanor enjoyed close family ties to the Holy Land. Her paternal grandfather, William IX of Poitou, had joined the crusade of 1101 and her uncle, Raymond of Poitiers, was prince of Antioch (1136–49). In addition, her second husband, King Henry II of England, was descended from Fulk the Younger, count of Anjou (1109–29) and king of Jerusalem (1131–43).[114] Her children by Henry II, therefore, were cousins to both Bohemond III of Antioch and Baldwin IV of Jerusalem. The daughter of their eldest child, Matilda, secured an alliance with the House of Perche and both Count Rotrou and Geoffrey III joined the Third Crusade, and Matilda's younger son, Henry V, count palatine of the Rhine, was to join the German Crusade of 1197.[115]

Henry and Eleanor's seventh child, Joanna, was married to William II of Sicily and the Sicilian fleet played a significant role in the earlier stages of the Third Crusade. In July 1188, a sixty-strong Sicilian fleet under Grand Admiral (*ammiratus ammiratorum*) Margarito arrived at Tripoli, relieving Margat, Latakia, and Tyre shortly afterwards. Thereafter, the Sicilians kept the eastern Mediterranean open to Latin vassals until Margarito withdrew the fleet on learning of William's death in November 1189.

The apparent contrast between both lay and clerical sources, and feminine influence on crusading, has been analysed in detail by Nicholas Paul to conclude that women were keepers of a constructed 'family memory'.[116] According to Colette Marie Bowie, foundations chosen for patronage by Matilda, Eleanor, and Joanna, as well as the way in which their families were named and buried, indicate a coherent sense of family consciousness that led to their transplanting Angevin family customs to their marital lands.[117]

---

[112] Power, 'John I of Sées', p. 149. See also Power, *The Norman Frontier in the Twelfth and Early Thirteenth Centuries* (Cambridge, 2004), p. 411.

[113] In marrying Sancho VI of Navarre's daughter, Richard would secure his southern flank, as well as aid relations with neighbouring Castile, whose king had married Richard's elder sister, Eleanor, in 1177.

[114] King Henry II's commitments to crusading activities are summarised in Hosler, *Henry II*, pp. 166–70.

[115] H. Nicholson, *Love, War, and the Grail: Templars, Hospitallers and Teutonic Knights in Medieval Epic and Romance, 1150–1500* (Leiden, 2001), p. 129.

[116] Paul, *Follow in their Footsteps*, p. 64.

[117] C.M. Bowie, 'The Daughters of Henry II and Eleanor of Aquitaine: A Comparative Study of Twelfth-Century Royal Women' (PhD thesis, University of Glasgow, 2011). See

Henry II, Henry the Young King, Richard, and John all took the Cross, and whilst only Richard lived to fulfil his vow through service in the Holy Land, as discussed earlier, the probability of familial influence, and particularly that of Eleanor of Aquitaine, is hard to ignore.[118]

Much as with Joanna and Berengaria, there are no surviving indications of Eleanor taking the Cross nor any firm evidence that she intended to remain with the Third Crusade.[119] It is equally uncertain, however, that she always intended to return to England to secure her eldest son's kingdom, as argued by Ralph Turner.[120] Indeed, her departure from Sicily coincided with that of Walter of Coutances, who gave up the Cross at Richard's behest in order to return to England and join his regency council due to the looming crisis caused by William of Longchamp's management of the realm.[121] It is suggestive that, unlike Adèla of Champagne in France and Matilda of Portugal in Flanders, Eleanor was not appointed as regent or given any formal role in the government of the Angevin Realm. In not taking the Cross, Eleanor also avoided potential conflict with ecclesiastical efforts to improve the military effectiveness of crusading expeditions by reducing the number of non-combatants.[122] It is entirely possible, therefore, that she intended to remain with Richard and his bride to be, and only handed over her familial responsibilities on crusade to Joanna once the seriousness of the situation in England had become clear.

---

also, Bowie, *The Daughters of Henry II and Eleanor of Aquitaine* (Turnhout, 2014); Bowie, 'Matilda, Duchess of Saxony (1169–89) and the Cult of Thomas Becket: A Legacy of Appropriation'; and, J.M. Cerda, 'Leonor Plantagenet and the Cult of Thomas Becket in Castile', *The Cult of St Thomas Becket in the Plantagenet World, c.1170–c.1220*, ed. P. Webster and M.-P. Gelin (Woodbridge, 2016), pp. 113–32, 133–46.

[118] In the Compromise of Avranches (1172), King Henry II undertook to provide monies and soldiers to the Holy Land or Spain if he could not crusade himself. Technically, therefore, one might argue that King Henry II fulfilled his vow, at least in part, but he did not actually join a crusade; Warren, *Henry II*, p. 531.

[119] Henry II's Geddington ordinances specifically excluded all women except laundresses of good character from taking the Cross, *Councils and Synods, A.D.871–1204*, Vol. 1, ed. D. Whitelock, M. Brett, and C.N.L. Brooke (Oxford, 1981), pp. 1025–9.

[120] R.V. Turner, *Eleanor of Aquitaine* (New Haven and London, 2009), pp. 256, 265–9.

[121] *Gesta Regis*, Vol. 2, p. 237.

[122] Eleanor had knelt next to her first husband to take the Cross from Bernard of Clairvaux in Vézelay on Easter Sunday prior to the Second Crusade, but this was highly unusual. Women were not called upon to take a crusade vow or to participate in crusading prior to 1200; S. Lambert, 'Crusading or Spinning', *Gendering the Crusades*, ed. S.B. Edgington and S. Lambert (New York, 2001), pp. 1–15; C.M. Rousseau, 'Home Front and Battlefield: The Gendering of Papal Crusading Policy, 1095–1221', *Gendering the Crusades*, pp. 31–44; and, H.J. Nicholson, 'Women on the Third Crusade', *JMH*, 23 (1997), 335–49. For the regency of Flanders, see Gilbert of Mons, pp. 248–9. For more on the tripartite regency of France under Queen Adèle, Archbishop William of Reims, and Prince Louis during the Third Crusade, see Park, *Papal Protection*, pp. 181–3.

For all these examples of descendants of crusaders taking the Cross and the influence of key women, there are countless others who did not travel to the East, and this was not a new phenomenon.[123] Returning to Isabel of Vermandois and the Second Crusade, for example, her son, Robert II of Beaumont was involved in a private war with Ranulf II of Chester between 1142 and 1149. In addition, Gilbert of Clare, her son-in-law, was in rebellion against King Stephen in 1149. Neither of them, therefore, was inclined to join the Second Crusade. In terms of the Third Crusade, Hugh III of Broyes was a veteran of the Second Crusade, he was related to the counts of Brienne and of Bar, both of whom travelled to the Holy Land, and he was married to Isabelle of Dreux, sister to Third Crusade participants, Count Robert II of Dreux and Philip, bishop of Beauvais. Henry II of Champagne's destruction of Broyes castle prior to departing on crusade may have impeded Hugh III's participation, but it was more likely that his advanced years dissuaded him from taking the Cross.[124] A more notable example is King Richard's younger brother, John, count of Mortain, who showed no inclination to join the Third Crusade.[125] Troublesome though his younger brother proved to be, however, it would arguably have been imprudent for the king to risk losing his brother and heir on crusade.

The decision to take the Cross was one that would have an impact on the wider family. In his description of Third Crusade preaching, Tyerman refers to the use of *exempla* that encouraged would-be crusaders to secure the support of their families prior to taking the Cross.[126] So it is unsurprising that sources indicate that husbands and wives discussed the merits of crusading, and surviving charters demonstrate that participants looked to protect their families during their absence, as well as support the participation of others.[127] What the data indicates is that individual women can be identified at the centre of social networks of crusaders and probably influenced their husbands and relatives in taking the Cross. There is a lack of data, however, on those individual women who may have persuaded their

---

[123] Hosler, 'Why Didn't King Stephen Crusade?', pp. 121–42.

[124] For the destruction of Broyes Castle, see Evergates, *Aristocracy*, p. 218.

[125] John finally took the Cross on Ash Wednesday (4 March) 1215, but contemporary commentators like Wendover acknowledged that his vow was politically motivated. As a crusader, in addition to gaining the usual privileges, King John might call upon papal support in his struggle against his nobles, especially if he could suggest that they were forcing him to delay the fulfilment of his vow. As Tyerman wrote, John's vow was, 'a master stroke of diplomacy', *England*, p. 134.

[126] Tyerman, *God's War*, p. 383.

[127] J. Brundage, 'The Crusader's Wife: A Canonistic Quandary', *Studia Gratiana*, 12 (1967), 425–42; C. Maier, *Crusade Propaganda and Ideology: Model Sermons for the Preaching of the Cross* (Cambridge, 2000), p. 121; Riley-Smith, *First Crusaders*, pp. 93–110, 129–43, 168–90.

relatives not to take the Cross. The efforts the Church undertook to address their influence, however, are compelling.

Stewardship and Substitution

Whilst a large number of crusaders travelled to the East in the company of relatives, there are several examples of their trusting other members of their family to oversee their affairs back home.[128] Recognising such concerns, the papacy had long sought to protect the lands and families of crusaders in their absence.[129] Participants in the Third Crusade were promised the same level of protection afforded to members of earlier crusades and it was a commitment Pope Gregory reiterated in *Audita Tremendi*,

> Their goods, from their reception of the Cross, with their families, remain under the protection of the Holy Roman Church, as well as of the archbishops and bishops and other prelates of the Church of God. They should not face any legal challenge regarding the things they possess legally when they received the Cross until their return or their death is known for certain, but they should also keep all their goods intact and undisturbed. Also, they may not be forced to pay interest if they have a loan, even if they are obligated to anyone, rather they shall be absolved from it in peace and tranquility.[130]

Returning to the lords of Seignelay, Daimbert II was clearly left behind due to his extreme youth, but other families kept siblings at home to manage the lordship. Such examples further challenge the perception that crusading was the preserve of younger sons. Whilst Rotrou III and his heir, Geoffrey, walked the knife-edge between competing Capetian and Angevin interests on crusade, Stephen of Perche, aided by the family's experienced seneschal, Warin of Lonray, remained in France and issued charters in his and the count's joint names.[131] Similarly, James of Durnay tended the estates of his uncle, Everard of Chacenay, John of Penigeston appointed his brother as 'keeper of his lands and heir', and John of Villehardouin stood as guardian for Guy of Dampierre's lands while they were all away on the

---

[128] Phillips, *The Second Crusade*, pp. 110–14; C. Smith, *Crusading in the Age of Joinville* (Aldershot, 2006), p. 175.
[129] Purkis, *Crusading Spirituality*, pp. 73–4.
[130] 'Bona quoque ipsorum, ex quo crucem acceperint, cum suis familiis sub sancte Romane ecclesie necnon et archiepiscoporum et episcoporum et aliorum prelatorum ecclesie dei protectione consistant et nullam de his, que usque ad susceptionem crucis quiete possederint, donec de ipsorum reditu vel obitu certissime cognoscatur, sustineant questionem sed bona eorum integra interim maneant et quieta. Ad dandas quoque usuras, si tenentur alicui, non cogantur sed absolute maneant et quieti': *Audita Tremendi, 1187*, 'Ansbertus', ed. Chroust, p. 10.
[131] Thompson, *Power and Border Lordship*, p. 116.

Third Crusade.[132] John, count of Ponthieu, left detailed guidance for the seneschals of Normandy and Maine, as well as to King Richard's *baillis*, on the extent of the powers he had delegated to his son whilst John was on crusade with Guy of Noyelles, as well as listing the debts his son should pay off.[133]

There is some evidence that family members or loyal retainers represented those who could not fulfil their vow to join the Third Crusade. Just as William Marshal had journeyed to the Levant to complete the crusading vow of Henry the Young King, Bishop William of Exeter later took the Cross and crusaded on behalf of his uncle, William Brewer, and Miles Beauchamp headed a large contingent of Simon II of Beauchamp's tenants.[134] Aside from a single charter that details substitution, the evidence is predominantly suggestive. Robert, constable of Halsham, and Henry Pigot, for example, were both stewards to the late William of Mandeville and most likely accompanied Ernald of Mandeville to redeem their lord's unfulfilled oath.[135] The honour of Mandeville was liable to the Crown for sixty knights' fees in 1166 and it would be reasonable to assume that they were accompanied by a significant retinue that included Roger of Mandeville.[136] Whilst a powerful noble in his own right, it is possible that Ralph of Mauléon crusaded on behalf of his cousin, Guy, viscount of Thouars, or at least represented the House of the Thouars within King Richard's household on crusade.[137]

Such substitution might also carry a physical reward. In return for taking on his oath to journey to Jerusalem, Roger Peitevin granted all his land in Normanton, near Wakefield, to his brother, Hugh.[138] Some prominent lords who had not taken the Cross were also seemingly represented on the expedition. Sven Thorkilsen and the four other Danish nobles listed as setting

---

[132] Evergates, *Aristocracy*, p. 230; 'qui est custos terre et heredis mei', *EYC*, Vol. 3, no. 1787; *Clairvaux*, p. 546, no. 432, p. 303, no. 256.

[133] Caen, AD Calvados, f. 5047. See also, Power, 'John I of Sées', pp. 163–6. Guy's participation is based on his inclusion on the Resafa Heraldry Cup, see Leson, 'Constellation of Crusade', p. 78.

[134] Along with Geoffrey Fitz-Peter, Hugh Bardolf, and Hugh of Puiset, William Brewer had set aside the Cross to act as either a justiciar or *appares* of England, Gillingham, *Richard I*, p. 122. Bishop William joined the Sixth Crusade, sailing from Brindisi in August 1227, Tyerman, *God's War*, p. 744–5. Simon was still in his minority and unable to take the Cross himself. For more on the Beauchamp contingent see Chapter Three.

[135] *EYC*, Vol. 3, pp. 79–80, no. 1364. According to Howden, Robert and Henry both died at the siege of Acre, *Gesta Regis*, Vol. 2, p. 149; *Chronica*, Vol. 3, p. 89.

[136] Keefe, *Feudal Assessments*, pp. 177, 257. Roger of Mandeville died on the Third Crusade, *CRR*, Vol. 1, p. 97. It is unclear if Adam of Mandeville was a close relation; *RCR*, Vol. 1, p. 439.

[137] Ambroise, lines 10965, 11497; *Itinerarium*, pp. 218, 405, 418.

[138] *EYC*, Vol. 3, p. 248, no. 1573.

out for the Holy Land in *Historia de Profectione Danorum in Hierosolymam* were all close associates of King Canute VI and Ulf of Lauvnes stood for King Swarre at the head of a two hundred-strong Norwegian contingent.[139] As well as his former guardian, Bertram of Verdun, Ranulf III of Chester's constable, John Fitz-Richard joined the Third Crusade and may have stood in his lord's stead.[140] Roger of Glanville had married Hugh Bigod's widow, but as has been discussed above, he also formed part of an extensive social network of crusaders.[141]

While Roger le Pole likely represented the teenage Earl William of Salisbury on crusade, there is little to indicate that Robert of Quincy or Osbert Olifard of Arbuthnott took the cross to represent their king, William the Lion.[142] Osbert, then sheriff of Mearns, had taken the Cross from Bishop Hugh of St Andrews, who died in 1188, so it seems likely that he was inspired by the fall of Jerusalem as he had no history of crusading in his family.[143] Like his brother-in-law, Earl Robert Fitz-Pernel of Leicester, Robert of Quincy seemingly joined the Angevin military household for the duration of the crusade. This is revisited in Chapter Four.

---

[139] K. Skovgaard-Petersen, *A Journey to the Promised Land: Crusading Theology in the 'Historia de profectione Danorum in Hierosolymam', c.1200* (Copenhagen, 2001), pp. 7, 75–6.

[140] The *Dieulacres Chronicle* is in error when it claims that Ranulf accompanied Richard on crusade, p. 21, nor is there anything to support the *Annales Cestrienses* in his having taken the Cross, pp. 38–41. John Fitz-Richard was descended from Eustace Fitz-John, a man of middling aristocratic background elevated by Henry I; P. Dalton, 'Eustace Fitz John and the Politics of Anglo-Norman England: The Rise and Survival of a Twelfth-Century Royal Servant', *Speculum*, 71 (1196), 358–83.

[141] Mortimer, 'Family of Rannulf de Glanville', 3–4.

[142] Roger le Pole was a member of Earl William's household, excusing his lord 30s. in scutage for being on crusade, PR3 RI (1191) p. 121. Roger died at the siege of Acre in 1191, *Gesta Regis*, Vol. 2, p. 149. For Robert of Quincy and Osbert Olifard of Arbuthnott, see A. Macquarrie, *Scotland and the Crusades 1095–1560* (Edinburgh, 1985), pp. 27–32. There is no evidence to support the participation of Earl David on the Third Crusade and, unlike Robert, he continued to witness royal charters in Scotland during 1189–92, *Acts of William I*, ed. Barrow. Claims that Alan the Steward joined the expedition seems to be based on confusion with his ancestor, First Crusader Alan Fitz-Flaald, steward of Dol, *Orderic Vitalis*, Vol. 5, p. 58. However, three of his tenants did take the Cross and the Stewards granted lands to St Thomas at Acre, which was founded during the Third Crusade, so Alan's participation is possible.

[143] J. Dowden, *Bishops of Scotland* (Glasgow, 1912), p. 10; *Acts of William I*, ed. Barrow, p. 225. Roger of Beaumont, brother to crusader Earl Robert III of Leicester, succeeded Bishop Hugh in 1189, *Gesta Regis*, Vol. 2, p. 63. Although their father had died in the Holy Land, there are no indications that Bishop Roger took the Cross.

Familial Tradition and Preaching the Third Crusade

Against the backdrop of this analysis of the actual kinship networks of members of the Third Crusade and the evidence of crusader ancestry, it is useful to review how the Church viewed familial tradition. For example, James Naus argues that Pope Gregory's bull to launch the Third Crusade was squarely aimed at European kings, focusing on their sacred responsibilities and the impact on their reputations should they fail to respond.[144] However, Gregory also reminded lay nobles of their obligation to emulate their crusading forebears in defending their Christian brothers.[145] For example, in addition to the opening quote to this chapter, Pope Gregory wrote in his bull,

> Pay attention not to passing profit and glory, but to the will of God who himself taught us to lay down our souls for our brothers ... who sacrifices himself for his brothers; though he may die young, still he accomplishes much. Heed how the Maccabees, afire with the divine zeal experienced extreme dangers for the freedom of their brothers.[146]

In this, the pope was following an established theme. Pope Eugenius III, for example, made crusading traditions the centrepiece of his appeal for the Second Crusade.[147]

As discussed in Chapter One, William Purkis argues that, in this period, ancestral obligation had replaced an earlier focus on the imitation of Christ to become 'the most prominent motif used by those who sought to recruit for the crusades to the East'.[148] The previous chapter demonstrated that *imitatio Christi* remained central to crusader preaching and influenced motivation to take the Cross. In addition, the importance of a familial commitment to the crusading movement dovetailed with the medieval nobility perceiving its legitimacy as being drawn from hereditary privilege, which was underpinned by customary law, and from a duty to protect their patch

---

[144] J. Naus, 'Specter of Failure: The Risk and Reward of Royal Crusading', SSCLE 'Diversity of Crusading' Conference, Odense, 27 June 2016. See also, J. Naus and V. Ryan, 'High Stakes and High Reward: The Memory of Royal Crusading', *Remembering the Crusades and Crusading*, pp. 145–58.

[145] For a thorough examination of this topic, see Bird, 'Preaching and Crusading Memory', pp. 13–33.

[146] 'Et nolite adhuc ad lucrum vel ad gloriam temporalem intendere, sed ad voluntatem dei qui pro fratribus animas in se ipso docuit esse ponendas ... qui oblatum sibi penitentie tempus hilariter amplectatur et animam ponendo pro fratribus consumetur in brevi et compleat tempora multa. Attendite, qualiter Macchabaei zelo divine legis accensi pro fratribus liberandis extrema queque pericula sunt experti': *Audita Tremendi, 1187*, 'Ansbertus', p. 11.

[147] Phillips, 'People, Practicalities and Motivation', *The Second Crusade*, pp. 99–103.

[148] Purkis, *Crusading Spirituality*, p. 115.

of Christendom. Therefore, the Church also focused upon crusader ancestry to motivate potential crusaders. In 1181, for example, Pope Alexander III reminded crusade preachers to tell their audiences that

> they should go quickly to that land, for whose liberation ancestors and fathers shed their blood, and they should fight against the enemies of the Cross with might and strength.[149]

There remained, however, a significant proportion of crusaders without a direct and identifiable crusading pedigree and who cannot be placed within a familial group. As mentioned earlier, Powell found that only about 20 per cent of 132 identifiable 'feudal aristocratic' participants in the Fifth Crusade had known ties to other crusaders. Whilst two-fifths of the 583 subjects analysed in this study had identifiable familial links to other members of the expedition, a significant number were seemingly motivated by other factors.[150]

Lacking similar opportunities to call upon an ancestral participation in crusades to the Holy Land as the preachers in England, France, and the Low Countries, the anonymous author of *Historia de Profectione Danorum in Hierosolymam*, refers to Jesus' exhortation in Luke 14.33 to the disciples to follow him and renounce their homes and families, which harks back to First Crusade texts, such as Albert of Aachen.[151] As the listing of Danish and Norwegian crusade elites in the *Profectione* demonstrates, though, the medieval *familia* encompassed more than blood relations and this is considered in relation to elite participation in the Third Crusade in the next chapter.

Crusading and Family

Data relating to the Third Crusade further challenges argument for 'progressive nuclearisation'. Transfers of property were witnessed by those who might later challenge them and there are sufficient examples of involvement by younger siblings and children other than the donor's eldest son to indicate a broader interest in the family estate. This indicates that, in some cases, the title-holder was viewed more as the principal steward of the family estate

---

[149] 'ut terram illam, pro cujus liberatione patres et genitores eorum sanguinem proprium effuderunt, adeant festinanter, et contra inimicos crucis Christi potentia et virtute decertent': Alexander III, 'Epistolae et privilegia', *PL*, Vol. 188, no. 1505, cols. 1296–7.
[150] Powell, *Anatomy of a Crusade*, pp. 82–3.
[151] Cited in Skovgaard-Petersen, *Journey to the Promised Land*, p. 20. The author also makes considerable use of the fall of Jerusalem through sinfulness, a formula common to other Third Crusade source material and touched upon in the previous chapter, for example, see the speech attributed to Cardinal Henry of Albano in *Historia de expeditione Friderici imperatoris*, pp. 11–13.

than enjoying exclusive rights over it. Whilst inheritance of land generally favoured the eldest son, the data from this study showed that it was not exclusive, and that partition of estates or co-lordship was not unusual. Indeed, far from being forced to seek their fortunes elsewhere, younger sons most often remained part of a cohesive family social network and, as well as retaining a family identity, could be asked to oversee lordships when other family members were absent on crusade. The data also supported Evergates' position that wives customarily retained ownership of their dower lands, which, alongside the continuing inclusion of younger sons in the familial network, was reflected in motivations to participate in the Third Crusade.[152]

Such evidence, I have argued, had an important impact on shared perceptions of the importance of (crusader) lineage, as well as the influence of kinship networks on participation in the Third Crusade. This is supported by the numbers of participants on the Third Crusade from north-western Europe with an identifiable crusader lineage (26%), especially from those regions with an established tradition of crusading, such as from non-Angevin France (51%).

Data on familial participation is equally compelling, with 41 per cent having family links to other crusaders on the expedition – most travelling to the Holy Land in the company of family members. This supports contemporary descriptions of familial groups forming the basis of military formations on the Third Crusade. The noble elite was seemingly organised in the Holy Land in the same way as when they participated in tournaments and when they fought on campaign in north-western Europe. Moreover, rather than acting as a hindrance to crusading, there are threads of evidence that women could positively influence crusader social networks and, on occasion, marriages bound together neighbouring houses whose members would journey eastwards together. This chapter has also highlighted the careful provision made for the stewardship of land and property in the absence of crusading family members and their military households, as well as the perceived requirement to satisfy a relation's unfulfilled crusading vow.

Unsurprisingly the papacy had long recognised the potential for family and ancestry to influence a decision to take the Cross, and these themes were as much a feature of preaching for the Third Crusade as for previous expeditions. Amongst the many influences on crusader motivation, this chapter has demonstrated the crucial importance of both kinship groups and crusader pedigree. In the next chapter, I will move on to consider the potential impact of bonds of friendship and various forms of association on participation in the Third Crusade.

---

[152] Evergates, *Aristocracy*, pp. 111–12.

3

Locality and Fellowship: Territory, Trade, and Tournaments

> There is no truth, there is no mercy in the land: cursing, and lying, and murder, and theft, and adultery have overflowed, and blood has grasped blood.[1]
>
> Pope Gregory VIII, *Audita Tremendi*, 1187

The previous chapters have highlighted how geographical associations underpinned religious and familial influences on participation in the Third Crusade from north-western Europe. Religious houses, such as Forde Abbey and the hospital at Burton Lazars, were often patronised by benefactors who lived in the same locality. Similarly, whilst a crusading heritage or experience on crusade might lead to the joining of families together by marriage, analysis of familial associations with elite social networks has shown that barons routinely married their sons and daughters into the families of their geographical neighbours. This chapter studies the meaning and consequences of locality against the backdrop of the Third Crusade for the noble elite and, where the data permits, non-elite (artisanal) actors.

An assessment of the significance of territorial spaces, such as counties, to those who were associated with them has been an important element in analyses of noble elites. Some historians have approached this through patterns of marriage, friendship, and association – often based on witness lists – while others have concentrated on patterns of office holding and the membership of the retinues of magnates. More recently, localities have been seen as entities whose significance is best explored in cultural and conceptual terms – as imagined communities – rather than in concrete social ones. Coined by Benedict Anderson to address nationalism, imagined communities are socially constructed, imagined by people who perceive that they are part of a group.[2] Unlike physical communities, such as villages or towns,

---

[1] 'Non est veritas, non est scientia dei in terra, furtum mendacium, homicidium et adulterium inundaverunt, sanguis sanguinem tetigit': *Audita Tremendi, 1187*, quoting Hosea 4:1–2, 'Ansbertus', ed. Chroust, p. 8.

[2] B. Anderson, *Imagined Communities: Reflections on the Origin and Spread of Nationalism*, 3rd edition (London, 2006), pp. 6–7.

members of imagined communities accept that they may never know most of their fellow members, yet they share in their mind's eye the image of their communion. However, the question of how imagined communities relate to networks of nobility in pre-nationalist Europe through family, friendship, and commercial or sporting association deserves greater attention.[3] In this chapter, the tournament circuit is considered as a route to a better understanding of the relationship between an imagined noble community and crusading.

The starting point of this chapter is to consider the influence of physical communities, that is, locality or affinity. According to Scott Feld and William Carter, at all levels of analysis, actors are more likely to be connected with one another, other conditions being equal, if they are geographically near to one another. This they call *propinquity* and it was, arguably, even more relevant in the Middle Ages than to Feld and Crater's research into post-modern relationships.[4] While the idea of locality in north-western Europe incorporated a wide range of territorial areas and their associated societies, my starting point is the role of territorial lordships as the core of medieval communities. Wealth and political power were founded in land in the Middle Ages with a landowning (military) elite ruling north-western Europe.[5]

By the late twelfth century, landholdings were often dispersed across a number of districts, counties, and even countries. Through the acquisition of dowry lands and awards of fiefdoms for service, even the minor gentry often held discontinuous estates. A number of lordships might, therefore, hold neighbouring manors within the same political space or community. This would have required a process of negotiation and accommodation between members of the aristocracy, such as over access to resources and positions of local power. This, in turn, influenced the development of a pattern of social life that was tied to locality and commerce, as well as shared values, to create clusters or 'noble neighbourhoods' within the elite social network.

The dispersed nature of landholdings meant that noble neighbourhoods included both close and dispersed geographical associations. Whilst I will provide evidence of groups of Third Crusade participants with close

---

[3] Roger Virgoe's general survey of the county community devoted approximately half its space to 'county-mindedness', but it was not clear how that related to his analysis of participation at the county court; Virgoe, 'Aspects of the County Community in the Fifteenth Century', *Profit, Piety and the Professions in Late Medieval England*, ed. M. Hicks (Gloucester, 1990), pp. 1–13.

[4] S. Feld and W.C. Carter, 'Foci of Activities as Changing Contexts for Friendship', *Placing Friendship in Context*, ed. R.G. Adams and G. Allan (Cambridge, 1998), pp. 136–52.

[5] Military service in north-western Europe depended on the personal bond between lords and their subjects and land tenure, H. Nicholson, *Medieval Warfare* (Basingstoke, 2004), pp. 45–6.

geographical associations, I also argue that, alongside factors such as reformed religious orders and lineage, dispersed associations influenced the development of an imagined community in which crusading played a central role.

As we have seen, the majority of data relating to lordships is to be found in the cartularies of religious houses. In her study of Rievaulx Abbey, Emilia Jamroziak argued that the subtle differences in cartularies are indicative of how each abbey perceived its social and political environment: how it made sense of land acquisitions, grants, conflicts, and lawsuits.[6] Grants to an abbey might also have a familial or tenurial context. As was discussed in Chapter One, religious houses were often tied to a particular powerful family, which encouraged donations from the family's tenants, as well as from members of their retinues. This inevitably leads to a significant overlap between the influence of religious institutions and that of locality on crusader motivation.

Ties are even more common between actors that were *homophilous*, that is to say, they had one or more common attributes, such as kinship, social function, and an activity. Niall Ferguson observed on this phenomenon that 'birds of a feather, flock together' – people with similar attributes are more likely to create ties.[7] As has been discussed, such attributes included an ancestor who had taken the Cross and then participated in a crusade, but participation in tournaments and certain types of trading activity can also be linked to crusader social networks. Whilst individual links may at times seem delicate, when combined with links to religious houses, ecclesiastical magnates, crusading pedigree, familial crusading groups, lordships, and locality, they create stronger bonds. This in turns aids our understanding of the dynamics of the Third Crusade social network and offers insight into why some members of the noble elite took the Cross and travelled to the Holy Land while others did not.

Landholding and Locality

The organisation of land tenure in north-western Europe in the late twelfth century was complex. The English countryside, for example, was divided into the pre-Conquest shires or counties, but also into baronies and honours.[8] With the exception of Chester and Durham, shires belonged to the Crown and were administered by a royal official, the sheriff. The honour was under private jurisdiction. Whilst the shire was fixed, the honour was

---

[6] Jamroziak, *Rievaulx Abbey*, p. 5.
[7] L.M. Verbrugge, 'The Structure of Adult Friendship Choices', *Social Forces*, 56 (1977), 576–97; N. Ferguson, 'The False Prophecy of Hyperconnection: How to Survive the Networked World', *Foreign Affairs* (October 2017).
[8] An honour was the name given to an estate; F. Stenton, *The First Century of English Feudalism, 1066–1166* (Oxford, 1961), pp. 57–9.

built upon grants of lands, marriage alliances, and inheritance. The shire or county was, for the most part, concentrated, while the honour was often dispersed.[9] However, the degree to which an honour could be distributed varied. The property held by actors in the noble network highlights differences in the degree of dispersal between the holdings of established families and of 'new men'.[10]

Robert Fitz-Pernel's inheritance was mainly in or near Leicestershire and in Normandy.[11] In comparison, even before his marriage to the dowager-countess of Aumale on return from the Third Crusade, Baldwin of Béthune's lands were scattered across three English counties: Bedfordshire, Berkshire, and Northamptonshire. This challenges the conclusions of Peter Coss, drawn from his study of the honour and locality of Coventry.[12] The concentration of the large estates of Leicester and Mowbray predate the inflationary pressures of the late twelfth and early thirteenth centuries, which Coss argues stimulated more compact estates and more intense exploitation of resources. This issue deserves further consideration based on analysis of broader patterns of landholding, because it influences the ties between participants on the Third Crusade.

A lack of opportunity or stimulus for consolidation might not be the only reason why a noble might hold land dispersed across various areas. Henry II and Richard both used fiefs to bind influential border lords to them, such as the former seneschal of Brittany, Ralph II de Fougères. In addition to his core inheritance around Fougères, Bazouges, and Antrain, Ralph was granted fiefs near Mont-Saint-Michel in Normandy and in four English counties: Devonshire, Hampshire, Norfolk, and Somerset.[13] Ralph

---

[9] See, for example, Greenway, *Honour of Mowbray*, pp. xviii, xx–xxi, and Coss, *Lordship, Knighthood and Locality*, p. 29.

[10] Twelfth-century English chroniclers complained that monarchs were choosing 'men raised from the dust' for high office and to serve as their councillors instead of members of old noble families. Called *rustici*, *plebes*, and *ignobiles* in their day, they are generally referred to as 'new men'; R.V. Turner, 'Changing Perceptions of the New Administrative Class in Anglo-Norman and Angevin England: The *Curiales* and Their Conservative Critics', *Journal of British Studies*, 29 (1990), 93–177.

[11] However, the honour of Leicester did contain lands or fees in Dorset, Hampshire, Kent, Norfolk, Suffolk and Wiltshire; L. Fox, 'The Administration of the Honor of Leicester in the Fourteenth Century', *Transactions of Leicester Archaeological Society*, 20/2 (1939), 295.

[12] Coss, *Lordship, Knighthood and Locality*, p. 306.

[13] Daniel Power has argued that the granting of dispersed fiefs was a means of limiting a noble's powerbase in the Anglo-Norman realm; D. Power, 'Le régime seigneurial en Normandie (XIIe–XIIIe s.)', *Les seigneuries dans l'espace Plantagenêt (c.1150–c.1250)*, ed. M. Aurell and F. Boutoulle (Bordeaux, 2009), pp. 117–36, and Power, 'Aristocratic Power and Authority in Normandy and England, c. 1150–1250: The Charters of the Du Hommet Constables of Normandy', paper given at the 18th International Medieval Congress, University of Leeds (UK), July 2011.

also provides an excellent illustration of the dangers inherent in failing to meet one's obligations. Whilst King Henry II, King Philip II, and Richard had all taken the Cross by early 1188, the eighteen months that followed saw rivalry slip into war. Initially, Richard sided with his father, but by mid-1189 he had joined Philip II. Ralph II switched loyalty to Richard at the last minute, along with Jocelin III of Mayenne, only a matter of weeks before Henry II died on 6 July 1189. However, once he had gained control of his father's realm, Richard then stripped Ralph of his lands.[14] In contrast, Richard retained loyal members of his father's household and some, such as William Marshal, were rewarded with land and advantageous marriages. John Gillingham has argued that King Richard wished to be viewed as a man with a keen sense of honour, and Heiser stressed the importance of undivided loyalty, but as is discussed in the next chapter, Richard's response appears to have been more nuanced.[15]

As well as manors being held indirectly, nobles held lands from more than one liege lord.[16] Despite holding title from the king of France for Perche, in 1183 Rotrou III regained estates in Wiltshire, which he had inherited through his mother. Even at this first stage, one can begin to consider the challenges to noble elites in being beholden to more than one lord in a complex matrix of obligations. This would have required careful management to avoid a failure to meet one or more obligations and risk losing title. As is considered in more detail in the next chapter, the count of Perche had to walk a particularly careful diplomatic line as the holder of lands placed within both the Capetian and Angevin spheres of interest.[17] This was particularly problematic due to conflicts between the two groups, such as the war between King Henry II and King Philip II in 1188–9.[18]

It was not just great lords like Count Rotrou III who had to navigate their way between competing calls on their loyalty. The lords of Cayeux held lands in England and on the north-eastern Norman frontier. William of Cayeux, lord of Bouillancourt, fought with King Richard's household at Ramla in 1191 and was employed by Richard as his messenger to Conrad of Montferrat in 1192. However, he also held lands from fellow crusader John

---

[14] *Gesta Regis*, Vol. 2, p. 72; Diss, Vol. 2, p. 64.
[15] Gillingham, *Richard I*, pp. 104–5; R.R. Heiser, 'Royal *Familiares* of King Richard I', *Medieval Prosopography*, 10 (1989), 36.
[16] Being beholden to several different lords was neither uncommon nor, seemingly, undesirable in north-western Europe in the High Middle Ages, see for example, H. Boston, 'Change and Continuity: Multiple Lordship in Post-Conquest England', paper given at the Battle Conference on Anglo-Norman Studies 2020: A Virtual Workshop, July 2020.
[17] Thompson, *Power and Border Lordship*, pp. 104–16.
[18] The concept of liege homage was particularly useful in approaching this issue.

I of Sées in Ponthieu, as well as from the count of Eu.[19] His neighbour, Bernard of St Valéry, also held lands outside the Angevin realm, but he had previously crusaded with Count Thierry of Flanders and most likely avoided potential conflict with either King Richard or King Philip II on the Third Crusade by initially serving with Thierry's son, Philip of Alsace.[20]

The complexity of managing one's obligations becomes more evident considering the dispersal of those holdings alongside regional affiliations, which brings us back to Scott Feld and William Carter's assertion that actors are more likely to be connected with one another, other conditions being equal, if they are geographically near to one another. Jonathan Riley-Smith and John France have demonstrated that a lord's commitment to join a crusade could place their vassals under a degree of pressure to follow suit, and this was reflected in levels of regional participation on the First Crusade.[21] The next section looks at how locality influenced membership of military households on the Third Crusade.

Familia and Military Households

The medieval *familia* was the name given to the group of knights and clerics that formed the entourage of a lord or, indeed, a significant lady, such as Eleanor of Aquitaine. Also known as the household or *mesnie privée*, the *familia* was as much a product of feudal ties as those of blood or marriage.[22] Royal households typically comprised three elements. The chancellor would head the clerics, both chaplains and scribes (*scriptores*). Stewards (*dapiferi* or *seneschals*) would oversee the lay staff, both the domestic staff, such as butlers (*pincernæ*), and the military retainers, knights (*milites*), and serjeants (*servientes*), under the marshals, as well as constables and grooms. The chamberlains (*camerarii*) would oversee the royal treasure and deal with the household's operational expenses.[23]

The military retainers of the royal household formed a perennial element in the military organisation of medieval England, France, and the Low

---

[19] Ambroise, lines 7276, 8634; *Itinerarium*, pp. 292, 336; Power, *Norman Frontier*, p. 418.
[20] *Chronicle of the Third Crusade*, trans. Nicholson, p. 8.
[21] J. France, 'Patronage and the Appeal of the First Crusade', *The First Crusade: Origins and Impact*, ed. J. Phillips (Manchester, 1997), pp. 14–17; Riley-Smith, First Crusaders, pp. 81–143.
[22] From the Latin term *mansio* meaning household. A monarch's household is often referred to in primary sources as the *familia regis*.
[23] R.V. Turner, 'Households of the Sons of Henry II', *La cour Plantagenêt, 1154–1204*, ed. M. Aurell (Poitiers, 2000), p. 52. See also the 'Constitutio domus regis', *Dialogus de Scaccario, and Constitutio Domus Regis. The Dialogue of the Exchequer, and The Disposition of the Royal Household. New Edition*, ed. and trans. E. Amt and S.D. Church (Oxford, 2007), pp. 15–17.

Countries.²⁴ The Normans maintained permanent military households capable of independent action, which formed the basis of field armies as well as castle garrisons.²⁵ The history of military households in continental Europe has been traced as far back as the *comitati* of the Roman Tacitus and the *scarae* of the Carolingians.²⁶ Evidence of military elites in royal service has also been found in Anglo-Saxon England.²⁷ Individual members of King Henry I's *familia regis* have been previously identified, and it is clear that he enjoyed a well-trained professional military household.²⁸

The knights of the royal household were credited by Joliffe with making an 'incalculable' contribution to the reigns of King Henry II and his sons, and Hosler describes Henry II's *familia* as being 'omnipresent'.²⁹ Moreover, their households have been identified as being of a similar magnitude to those of the thirteenth and fourteenth centuries, which included a standing professional army of cavalry, infantry, craftsmen, and labourers capable of acting independently towards their master's will.³⁰ Indeed, the royal household was to form the core of royal armies from the twelfth century until at least the mid fourteenth century.³¹

---

²⁴ C.W. Hollister, *The Military Organisation of Norman England* (Oxford, 1965), pp. 174–5.
²⁵ J.O. Prestwich, 'The Military Household of the Norman Kings', *EHR*, 96 (1981), 1–37; see also, S. Harvey, 'The Knight and the Knight's Fee in England', *Past and Present*, 49 (1970), 4–14; M. Chibnall, 'Mercenaries and the Familia Regis under Henry I', *History*, 62 (1977), 15–23.
²⁶ Verbruggen, *Art of Warfare*, pp. 67–9.
²⁷ H.R. Loyn, 'Gesiths and Thegns in Anglo-Saxon England from the Seventh to Tenth Century', *EHR*, 70 (1955), 529–49.
²⁸ Professional is defined here as practitioners of a martial vocation founded on specialised training in warfare in which military service was a way of life. Pinning down the position of military professionals is difficult. Chibnall used the term 'mercenary' to cover any warrior not fulfilling service in return for tenure. It is a very broad definition that she acknowledges fails to distinguish between *stipendarii* and casual soldiers of fortune; Chibnall, 'Mercenaries', pp. 15–23; also J. Green, *The Government of England under Henry I* (Cambridge, 1986). For a typology of military service, see, S. Morillo, 'Mercenaries, Mamluks, Militia, Towards a Cross-Cultural Typology of Military Service', *Mercenaries and Paid Men, The Mercenary Identity in the Middle Ages*, ed. J. France (Leiden, 2008), pp. 243–60.
²⁹ J.E.A. Joliffe, *Angevin Kingship* (London, 1955), p. 211, see also pp. 195, 218–19, and Hosler, *Henry II*, pp. 103–4.
³⁰ On Edward I's household see J.E. Morris, *The Welsh Wars of Edward I* (Oxford, 1901), p. 84; T.F. Tout, *Chapters in the Administrative History of Medieval England*, Vol. 2 (Manchester, 1937), pp. 133, 138; J.O. Prestwich, 'Anglo-Norman Feudalism and the Problem of Continuity', *Past and Present*, 26 (1963), 50–1.
³¹ M. Prestwich, *Armies and Warfare in the Middle Ages, the English Experience* (London, 1996), p. 38; see also J.G. Edwards, 'The Treason of Thomas Turberville, 1295', *Studies in Medieval History Presented to F.M. Powicke*, ed. R.W. Hunt, W.A. Pantin, and R.W. Southern (Oxford, 1948), p. 296.

Lords were typically accompanied on crusade by members of their household, leaving others behind to manage and protect their interests at home, and the influence of locality on membership of military households is well established. In his review of William Marshal's retinue following his marriage to Isabel of Clare, for example, Tom Asbridge identified that William Waleran and Geoffrey Fitz-Robert hailed from the Marshal familial heartland in Wiltshire. Ralph Bloet also held lands in Wiltshire but was most strongly connected via his brother's marriage to Isabel of Clare's aunt. Through his Welsh wife, Nest, Ralph's influence was predominantly in the area of Isabel's inheritance in the Welsh Marches, as was that of Philip of Prendergast, who was married to Isabel's natural sister, Basilia. Roger of Aubernon was son to the lord of Stoke Aubernon, where William and Isabel had spent their honeymoon, and Alan of St Georges can be linked to Marshal family connections to Bosham in Sussex.[32] Eustace of St George was also to join William Marshal's household in due course. In each of these examples, either family or locality is the basis of affinity, that is, the link between lord and retainer. As mentioned earlier, Riley-Smith and France have demonstrated that a lord's commitment to join crusade reverberated through their localities.

Participants on the Third Crusade associated with Robert IV Fitz-Pernel, earl of Leicester, follow a similar pattern of affinity based on family or locality. Headed by his steward, Arnold IV of Bois, those knights placed with Earl Robert at a skirmish in Ramla in 1192 were either linked to him by blood or close geographical association.[33] Apart from Henry Fitz-Nicholas, whose lands neighboured those of the earl in Dorset, and Robert IV's cousin, Robert of Newburgh, all seemingly came from the Leicester geographical sphere of influence in Normandy. Dreux of Fontenil was from Laigle, near Évreux, and Robert Neal came from Saint-Sauveur, Manche, which was less than twelve miles west of Ralph of Saint-Marie's likely familial home in Saint-Mère-Église. Henry of Mailoc was likely from Calvados, as were Saul and William of Bruil. The earl of Leicester's final companion was Warin II Fitz-Gerald, baron of the Exchequer and a fellow member of King Richard's *familia* as a royal chamberlain.[34] Robert of Quincy was Robert IV's brother-in-law and joined the Third Crusade but was not listed as present

---

[32] Asbridge, *Greatest Knight*, pp. 218–22; for further examples of the influence of locality in the Marshal affinity see Crouch, *William Marshal*, 3rd edition, pp. 227–40.

[33] The house of Bois were vassals of the earls of Leicester with lands in both the honour of Breteuil in Normandy and the English Midlands, D. Crouch, *The Beaumont Twins: The Roots and Branches of Power in the Twelfth Century* (Cambridge, 1986), pp. 109–11. The chaplain to the earls of Leicester was another member of the Bois family: Arnold IV's brother, Robert of Bois.

[34] Ambroise, lines 4725, 7496; *Itinerarium*, pp. 217, 300; Landon, *Itinerary*, nos. 131, 175–81, 183–93, 342, 366. See also N. Vincent, 'Warin and Henry Fitz Gerald, the King's Chamberlains: the Origins of the FitzGeralds Revisited', ANS 21 (1999): 233–60.

at this engagement.³⁵ Marianne Ailes and Malcolm Barber have also linked Geoffrey of Bois, who followed King Richard onto the beach at Jaffa in 1192, with the house of Leicester.³⁶

According to information from the Pipe Rolls, nine Beauchamp tenants from the barony of Bedfordshire joined Miles Beauchamp on the Third Crusade.³⁷ These ten tenants make up for just over a fifth of the forty-five and three-quarters knights' fees held by the barony.³⁸ Of these, one only, Guy of St Valery, enjoyed a crusader lineage and was related to Gilbert of Vascoeuil, another member of the expedition. It is likely, therefore, that locality influenced the decision of the remainder to take the Cross, as well as, perhaps, loyalty to their former landlord and veteran of the battle of Hattin, Hugh of Beauchamp. Richard of Clare, lord of Saham, brother to Earl Richard, was presumably the leader of the tenants of Clare of Norfolk and Suffolk.³⁹

Similarly, Robert of Icklesham accompanied Geoffrey of Balliol, his overlord at Barnholme in Sussex, on the Third Crusade. Their participation was recorded in a charter signed in Jaffa, which Jane Sayers dated to September or October 1191.⁴⁰ Robert seemingly died on crusade, but his heir, Ralph of Icklesham, confirmed the charter with the assent of his mother, Sybil, and other relatives.⁴¹ Another example of a crusading cluster based on close geographical association is evident amongst the tenants of Alan the Steward in Scotland. As covered under the section dealing with the Saladin Tithe in Chapter One, Robert Kent, Robert Hunaud, and Ronald, son-in-law to Nicholas of Gôtentin, mortgaged their lands in Innerwick (East Lothian) to fund their journey to the Holy Land.⁴² Just as in the household of William

---

³⁵ Ambroise, lines 7468–7590; *Itinerarium*, pp. 300–3. Robert's absence suggests that he had yet to return from his mission to Antioch. See Chapter Four: Functions within the Royal Household for more details.

³⁶ *The History of the Holy War, Ambroise's Estoire de la Guerre Sainte, II. Translation*, trans. M. Ailes, Notes by M. Ailes and M. Barber (Woodbridge, 2003), p. 179, n. 701.

³⁷ Bernard of Limistre, Gilbert of Passelewe, Guy of Valery, Henry Ruffus, Roger of Salford, Roger Fitz-Bernard, Walter Monk, Osbert of Bray, PR4 RI (1193), p. 200.

³⁸ Keefe, *Feudal Assessments*, p. 249.

³⁹ Robert of la Mare and Robert of Thornham, however, were also associated with King Richard's household, and would have been unlikely to have joined the Clare contingent on crusade. Given his associations with the Glanvilles, Ralph of Arden also most likely did not travel with Richard of Clare.

⁴⁰ The charter is also witnessed by Hugh of Baliol who was likely Geoffrey's brother. This branch of the Balliols was distinct from the Scottish dynasty of the same name; Sayers, 'English Charters from the Third Crusade', p. 208.

⁴¹ Rather than a donation, the award settled a long-running despite between the abbey and Robert of Icklesham, London, Lincoln's Inn, ms. Hale 87 (Battle cartulary), f. 69r.

⁴² *Acts of William I*, ed. Barrow, pp. 370, 373–4.

Marshal, locality can be seen to have influenced membership of military households that joined the Third Crusade.

Noble Neighbourhoods

Not all crusaders can be linked by a familial or feudal relationship. Third Crusade groups were also created from noble neighbourhoods or affinities. Returning to those members of the Third Crusade linked to Forde Abbey introduced in the first chapter, Henry Pomeroy, Matthew Oisel, Richard Morville, and Richard Fitz-William of Langford were all geographical neighbours. Langford also lies next to Little Farandom, home to the lands of Ernard of Mandeville, another member of the expedition to retake Jerusalem. From Shropshire came neighbours Robert Corbet and John le Strange. It is unclear if Corbet's father-in-law, Hugh Pantulf, had intended to join them, but the evidence suggests he remained in the West.[43]

The Resafa Heraldry Cup provides an intriguing insight into the relationship between Ralph I, lord of Coucy, and his neighbours. Unearthed in 1982 by a team led by Thilo Ulbert of the German Archaeological Institute of Damascus and dated to c.1191, the gilt-silver cup is engraved with eleven heraldic shields. Ulbert engaged Hervé de Pinoteau to identify the shields, and Pinoteau associated the central arms with the Coucy family of Picardy. In addition to the arms of Ralph I and his three sons, Enguerrand III, Thomas, and Robert, are those of their neighbours, Eudes III of Ham, Peter of Amiens, the lord of Roye, and, probably, Guy of Noyelles, uncle of another member of the Third Crusade, John I of Sées, count of Ponthieu. Pinoteau hesitantly linked another shield with the house of Sorlieu. As discussed in Chapter Two, the remaining two shields appear to belong to the Kyme and Ros families, both of Lincolnshire.[44] In his review of the Resafa Cup, Richard Leson argued that 'Any medieval viewer of the cup would understand that the relationships alluded to in the basin were informed by this literal geographical proximity'.[45] Leson went on to link the spatial qualities of the cup and its configuration to the circular cartographic representations that placed Jerusalem at the centre of the medieval world. Whilst Peter of Amiens was a close relative, and Eudes III and Ralph I were both descended from the House of Vermandois, the geographical proximity of the majority of those whose shields are displayed is compelling.[46]

---

[43] K. Hurlock, *Wales and the Crusades, c.1095–1291* (Cardiff, 2011), pp. 85, 102–4.

[44] H. de Pinoteau, 'Heraldische Untersuchungen zum Wappenpokal', *Resafa III. Der kreuzfahrerzeitliche Silberschatz aus Resafa–Sergiupolis*, ed. T. Ulbert (Mainz am Rhein: Phillip von Zabern, 1990), pp. 77–86.

[45] Leson, 'Constellation of Crusade', p. 78.

[46] The communal attitude is highlighted by instructions that any money left by a crusader on campaign would be divided amongst the contingent's general fund, alms for the poor, and the crusader's retainers. See, for example, *Chronica*, Vol. 3, p. 264.

The citizens of London present perhaps the most obvious contingent defined by locality. Some eighty to a hundred Londoners led by William Fitz-Osbert and Geoffrey the Goldsmith left port in 1190 aboard their own hired fleet, fought at Silves in Iberia, and established a hospital dedicated to Thomas Becket in Acre.[47] Roger of Howden's chronicles suggest there was also a strong contingent from Yorkshire and Lincolnshire. Howden can be placed at the siege of Acre and he was likely the conveyor of a charter recording John of Hessle's donation of a furlong to the Austin canons of North Ferriby prior to John's death on the Third Crusade.[48] The military head of the Yorkshire contingent may well have been Ralph of Tilly, constable to the archbishop of York. An experienced military commander, Tilly was associated with Ranulf of Glanville from Henry II's 1174 campaign against the king of Scots.[49] In addition to local magnates, like Robert Trussebot and Nigel of Mowbray, and members of important local families, such as Osmund of Stuteville, Walter and Peter of Ross, and Ralph of Aubigny, Howden listed the names of otherwise unremarkable crusaders from the counties who were present at the siege of Acre.[50] Similarly, evidence from the Pipe Rolls indicates that the neighbouring East Anglian families of la Mare and Malet arrived at the siege of Acre c. June 1191.[51]

In relation to Gary Dickson's view that crusading was an eschatological act of the masses, it is perhaps of note that the location of outbreaks of anti-Jewish violence in 1189 and 1190 often coincided with these identifiable regional crusader contingents in England.[52] Royal officials were called upon to suppress anti-Jewish riots in London in the immediate aftermath of the coronation of Richard I in September 1189.[53] In January 1190, the bulk of the Jewish community was massacred at the East Anglian port of Lynn with further attacks at Stamford fair on 7 March and Bury St Edmunds on 18 March. In Lincoln only the intervention of royal officers prevented a similar

---

[47] Tyerman, *England*, pp. 66, 73–4; A. Forey, 'The Military Order of St Thomas of Acre', *EHR*, 92 (1977), 481–503.
[48] Roger's witnessing of this charter substantiates his presence in the Holy Land, *EYC*, Vol. 9, no. 18.
[49] *Gesta Regis*, Vol. 1, pp. 65, 68–9.
[50] In addition to Walter and Peter of Ross, nine named crusaders were from Yorkshire or Lincolnshire: Ralph, parson of Croxby, Richard of Lexby and his brother Berenger, Robert le Venur of Pontefract, Robert Scrop of Barton, Henry Pigot, Walter Scrop, and Walter and Philip of Kyme, *Gesta Regis*, Vol. 2, pp. 147–50.
[51] PR3 RI (1191), p. 44. Robert, lord of la Mare and his brother, Osbert, were seemingly joined in the Holy Land by William and Alan de la Mare, *Itinerarium*, p. 217.
[52] Dickson, *Children's Crusade*, pp. xiii, 78–80, 93.
[53] *Chronica*, Vol. 3, p. 14. According to Ralph of Diss, King Richard's courtiers had prominent Jews that had attended the wedding, stripped, whipped, and expelled from the banquet, Diss, Vol. 2, pp. 68–9.

tragedy by admitting members of the Jewish community into the castle.[54] However, the worst outbreak took place in York in March 1190. Attacked by a mob led by local nobles, surviving members of the Jewish community retreated to York Keep, which was then besieged.[55] In these examples, the perpetrators of the attacks were seemingly dealt with firmly by King Richard, but such outbreaks of violence reflect the emotional depths of the religious enthusiasm that might accompany crusading. There are glimpses of other regional contingents, which provide an insight into non-elite artisans that took the Cross following the fall of Jerusalem, and one concerns the crusaders of Lincolnshire.[56]

Crusading Artisans

In 1196, Pope Celestine II directed that those who had yet to complete their crusader vow should be held to account. This was reinforced by the bulls of his successor, Innocent III, of 1200 and 1201. These stated that, on pain of excommunication, only the poor and feeble might have their vows absolved.[57] Two lists survive in the archives of Canterbury Cathedral that most likely evidence Hubert Walter's response to Innocent III's orders. Although both concern those who took the Cross but were believed to have failed to complete their vow, they are suggestive of the non-elites that did join the expedition. The report covering the rural deanery of Holland in Lincolnshire details twenty-six *crucesignati* and explains why they had not gone on crusade.[58] It also indicates the spread of tradesmen amongst the contingent, a baker, butcher, and vintner, but also a smith, clerk, ditcher, potter, and skinner.

A similar list from the archdeaconry of Cornwall contains forty-four names, divided into the eight rural deaneries of the county. It was presumably compiled by the staff of Henry, bishop of Exeter and brother to William

---

[54] In legal terms, the Jews of England were under the king's protection, but were classed as 'chattel'; D. Cushing, 'Richard I and the Jewish "Servi Camarae" as a Funding Source for the Third Crusade', https://www.academia.edu/983627 downloaded 4 January 2018.
[55] William of Newburgh's account of the siege and subsequent mass suicide of the Jewish community draws heavily from Flavius Josephus' account of the siege of Masada during the First Jewish-Roman war, Newburgh, Vol. 1, p. 312–24. For more on the siege, see R.B. Dobson, *The Jews of Medieval York and the Massacre of 1190* (York, 1974; revised edition 1996).
[56] For discussion on the urban crusaders contained in *De itinere navali*, see *De itinere navali*, trans. Cushing, pp. xlv–xlviii.
[57] Tyerman, *England*, pp. 170–1.
[58] Eight of those listed are described as *pauperrimis* and two more had been reduced to begging. Five more claimed they lacked the funds to make the journey. See also, M.R. Evans, 'Commutation of Crusade Vows: Some Examples from the English Midlands', *From Clermont to Jerusalem: The Crusades and Crusader Societies, 1095–1500*, ed. A.V. Murray (Turnhout, 1998), pp. 219–28

Marshal. However, this report does not include information as to why those named had not fulfilled their vows. In their comprehensive review of the Cornish list, Nicholas Orme and Oliver Padel identified ten individuals whose names were linked to occupations. As well as two chaplains, Turstan and William, there were a smith and two skinners, but also a miller, a cobbler, and a weaver. The list also contains two higher-status individuals, Geoffrey Merchant and Roger Marshal.[59] Moreover, as the Saladin Tithe only excused laundresses of good character who took the cross from paying the tax of one-tenth of the value of their income and moveable goods, the two women listed from Cornwall were presumably so employed.[60]

What emerges from these tantalising glimpses is that hidden behind the elite mounted warriors there were large numbers of specialist artisans and traders who enjoyed close geographical associations.[61] In addition to confirming the impact of preachers on the geographical distribution of those taking the Cross, this also provides yet more evidence that medieval commanders paid proper attention to the question of supply and the needs of their armies.[62] The roots of the sophisticated and efficient supply system established by King Edward I for his campaigns in Wales and Scotland can be found amidst the Pipe Roll entries for victualing King Richard's crusaders.[63] If data relating to horseshoes, crossbow bolts, cheese, and dried beans were the bricks of Richard's logistical system, however, such artisans were its mortar.[64] Hence, one can also encounter evidence of plans for their remittance in the Pipe Rolls.[65] Whilst King Philip II drew the bulk of his

---

[59] N. Orme and O.J. Padel, 'Cornwall and the Third Crusade', *Journal of the Royal Institution of Cornwall* (2005), 71–7. See also, M.R. Evans, '"A Far from Aristocratic Affair": Poor and Non-Combatant Crusaders from the Midlands, c. 1160–1300', *Midland History*, 21 (1996), 72–9.

[60] *Councils and Synods, A.D.871–1204*, Vol. 1, ed. D. Whitelock, M. Brett, and C.N.L. Brooke (Oxford, 1981), pp. 1025–9. Two others in the list have female names, Pilia and Ada, and may have also been women. However, *Pilia* was also a Cornish surname and *Ada* is followed by the masculine form of miller (*molendinarius*), so it was probably intended to be Adam.

[61] Tyerman discusses the communal influence of such groups on crusader social structures and decision-making in, *Plan a Crusade*, pp. 167–70.

[62] See, for example, J.H. Pryor, 'Modelling Bohemond's March to Thessalonike', *Logistics of Warfare in the Ages of the Crusades*, ed. J.H. Pryor (Aldershot, 2006), pp. 1–24.

[63] D. Bachrach, 'Medieval Logistics during the Reign of Edward I of England', *War in History*, 13 (2006), 423–40; see, for example, PR2 RI (1190), pp. 1, 8–9, 53, 104, 112, 131–2, 178; see also, Tyerman, *Plan a Crusade*, p. 263.

[64] The Pipe Rolls record numerous examples, but the return of Henry of Cornhill as sheriff of Hampshire is indicative: nearly 58*l.* for bacon, 20*s.* for beans, over 14*l.* on 10,000 horseshoes, and nearly 20*l.* on a hundredweight of cheese, with additional costs related to carriage and storage, PR2 RI (1190), pp. 8–9, 131–2.

[65] A yearly tariff was set, for example, at 2*d.* a day for soldiers and sailors and 4*d.* for helmsmen in Richard's fleet, PR2 RI (1190), pp. 8–9.

logistical support for a force set at 650 knights and 1,300 serjeants from the Genoese, especially shipping and provisions for eight months, it would not be unreasonable to assume that his contingent also enjoyed a solid artisanal foundation.[66] Given the importance of the south west of England in the international wool trade, the presence of William Fleming in the deanery of *Pydershire* (Pydar) is of interest.

Trade – Wine, Wool, and War

Trade networks are based on a complex combination of underlying factors, both social and natural, such as geology and climate. Social Network Analysis can be applied to medieval trade networks to better understand the nature of those social networks and their relation to participation in the Third Crusade. Whilst it is not suggested that engagement in a particular area of commerce directly influenced someone's decision to take the Cross, relationships formed and strengthened through trade facilitated the spread of ideas, formed the basis for alliances and marriages, and provided the funds to enable participation. In this section, noble networks relating to the trade in wine and wool, as well as military service through money-fiefs are investigated in relation to crusading.

During the twelfth century, the wine trade held an important role in the economies of Europe. In relation to the Third Crusade, it linked crusaders with one another and with religious foundations engaged in viticulture, such as Pontigny Abbey. The revenue from tolls, charges, and taxation on the passage of wine from vineyards to households could also be of great importance to rulers such as Philip II of France.[67] Just as wool formed the foundation of the Cistercian economy in Britain, so their houses in other parts of Europe relied on viticulture.[68] Whilst in some regions wine was a mark of distinction and noble standing, in others it was an unremarkable feature of everyday life. As will be shown, by the time of the Third Crusade, the wine trade linked families that took the Cross and it also necessitated large merchant fleets that were then available to carry crusaders to the Holy Land.

---

[66] *Actes de Philippe Auguste*, Vol. 1, ed. Delaborde, no. 292, see also, Rigord, pp. 99, 107.
[67] The terms of leases for winegrowers in Luxemburg, for example, varied according to the success of the harvest, F. Irsigler, 'Viticulture, vinification et commerce du vin en Allemagne Occidentale des origines au XVI siècle', *Le vigneron, la viticulture et la vinification en Europe occidentale au Moyen Age et à l'époque moderne: onzièmes Journées Internationales d'Histoire, 8–10 septembre 1989* (Bordeaux, 1991), p. 56.
[68] In Burgundy, for example, the vineyards of Meursault, Musigny, and Clos de Vougeot were all established by the Cistercians, G. Garrier, *Histoire sociale et culturelle du vin* (Paris, 2008), pp. 56–7.

Viticulture and the wine trade had been important elements in the social, cultural, and economic life of the Roman Empire and they retained a prominent role in the centuries that followed.[69] Wills and charters continued to list vineyards, and inventories from the Carolingian Empire mention both vineyards and the extent of wine production, such as that of Saint-Germain-des-Prés.[70]

Data relating to the export of wine becomes more available from the eleventh century onwards. Carried in large wooden casks or *tuns*,[71] wine could easily spoil through poor handling and changes in temperature whilst being transported. Unsurprisingly, therefore, vineyards close to navigable rivers or ports emerge in primary sources as those most commonly being marketed. A poem by Henry of Andeli written *c*.1220 described a battle between wines in which the victor would be selected as the favoured wine of Philip II. It provides considerable detail on those vineyards held in highest regard, the types of wine they produced, and the palate of the time.[72] The Norman poet suggested that the most renowned wines came from northern France, and the Loire and Seine-Marne valleys in particular. The ancient vineyards on the shores of the Mediterranean largely produced wines for local consumption, so the wines that reached northern European tables were reserved for those of high social status.

The vineyards of the Cistercian abbey at Longpont, near Soissons in north-eastern France, are a well-studied example of white wine production.[73] A canon in Soissons gave the abbey its first vineyard in 1143, with further donations seeing its holdings spread down the right bank of the river Aisne.[74] John of Montirail joined the community at Longpont as a monk on his return from the Third Crusade, but it is otherwise outside crusader

---

[69] H. Johnson, *The Story of Wine* (London, 2004), p. 36.

[70] For examples of wills, see M. Lachiver, *Vins, vignes et vignerons: histoire du vignoble français* (Paris, 1988), p. 46; on the inventory of Saint-Germain-des-Prés see, J. Durliath, 'La vigne et le vin dans la région parisienne au début du IX siècle d'après le polyptiques d'Irminon', *Le Moyen Age*, 74 (1968), 391–5.

[71] The most widely used terms for quantities of wine in north-western Europe in the twelfth century were hogshead, pipe, and *tun*. A *tun* was the name for the large barrels used to transport wine and their size varied across polities. However, the Bordeaux wine *tun* was the form most commonly used to determine a ship's capacity or 'tonnage'. Under the Bordeaux system, a hogshead was 238.7 litres or 52.5 gallons; two hogsheads made one pipe, and two pipes made one tun. A Bordeaux tun, therefore, was 954.7 litres or 210 gallons.

[72] *Oeuvres de Henri d'Andeli, trouvère du XIIIe siècle*, ed. A. Héron (Paris, 1881), pp. LIII–LXII, 23–30.

[73] It is interesting to consider what influence their association with viticulture may have had on the importance of the theme of the Lord's vineyard in Cistercian rhetoric; B. Mayne Kienzle, *Cistercians, Heresy, and Crusade in Occitania, 1145–1229* (York, 2001), pp. 25–54.

[74] Whilst some of the endowments limited the use of the wine to Mass or to refresh

social networks. Pontigny Abbey, however, was supported by a large number of Third Crusade participants, including Henry II of Champagne, Clarembaud of Noyers, Anselm III of Montréal and his son Anselm IV, their cousin John of Arcis-sur-Aube, Aswalo II, lord of Seignelay, and his brothers, Frederick, Peter, and Rainard, Dreux IV of Merlo and his brother William of Merlo, and Hagan of Ervy.[75] The wine of Pontigny Abbey in Auxerre had gained a good reputation by the mid thirteenth century with the Franciscan friar, Salimbene of Adam, extolling its virtues.[76]

In 1175 Henry II granted the burgesses of Rouen a monopoly on the export of wine to England.[77] It predominantly dealt with white wines from the Ile de France that were floated down the Seine in barges to the city, where they were loaded onto cross-Channel vessels. An idea of the extent of this trade can be gleaned from King Richard's award of 300 *tuns* to St Mary of Rouen to compensate them for losses sustained in the war with Philip II of France.[78] However, wines were also grown in Brittany, Normandy, and England, where forty-two manors with vineyards are listed in the Domesday Book.[79] Despite the monopoly, Rouen suffered from increasing competition from La Rochelle. Duke William X of Aquitaine had granted La Rochelle significant privileges to attract merchants when he founded the new port, and these were confirmed by King Henry II on his marriage to Eleanor of Aquitaine.[80]

Wines from La Rochelle can be traced to Brittany, England, Normandy, and Wales, as well as Scotland, Scandinavia, and the Low Countries.[81] This trade stimulated the growth of merchant fleets, turning the Angevin realm into a maritime polity. These vessels not only made up King Richard's crusading fleet, but also assisted in the carriage of other crusader contingents to the Holy Land. Moreover, the Rôles of Oléron, an island near La

---

travellers, most was available for sale; L. Duval-Arnould, 'Le Vignoble de l'abbaye cistercienne de Longpont', *Le Moyen Age*, 74 (1968), 207–36.

[75] Hagan of Ervy, for example, donated a vineyard at Dannemoine to the abbey for celebrating an anniversary mass in his name, Evergates, *Feudal Society: County of Champagne*, pp. 68–9, no. 51 (1190); *Le Premier cartulaire de l'abbaye de Pontigny (XII–XIII siècles)*, ed. M. Garrigues (Paris, 1981).

[76] Lachiver, *Vins, vignes et vignerons*, p. 62.

[77] Lachiver, *Vins, vignes et vignerons*, pp. 62–5.

[78] A.L. Simon, *The History of the Wine Trade in England*, Vol. 1 (London, 1964), p. 62.

[79] M. Zink, 'Autour de la Bataille des Vins de Henri d'Andeli: le blanc du prince, du pauvre et du poète', *L'Imaginaire du Vin*, ed. M. Milner and M. Chatelain-Courtois (Marseille, 1989), pp. 111–21; K.-U. Jäschke, 'Englands Weinwirtschaft in Antike und Mittelalter', *Weinwirtschaft in Mittelalter*, ed. C. Schrenk and H. Weckbach (Sonderdruck, 1997), p. 308.

[80] Lachiver, *Vins, vignes et vignerons*, pp. 89–91.

[81] S. Rose, *The Wine Trade in Medieval Europe, 1000–1500* (London and New York, 2011), p. 15.

Rochelle, were the first example of maritime law in north-western Europe.[82] It is unlikely to have been coincidental that Richard selected William of Forz from Oléron as one of the justiciars of the crusader fleet.[83]

The identity of individual merchant captains on the Third Crusade is elusive, but their influence can occasionally be identified. In granting rights of trade and passage to the city of Marseille in 1192, Guy of Lusignan and Queen Sibylla identified the city's representatives at Acre, such as Bertrand the Sardinian and Anselm of Marseille, and highlighted their service during the siege of Acre. Interestingly, the list also included Galterius Anglicus – Walter the Englishman.[84] Another example is King Richard's amendment of the law in respect of shipwrecks to protect the cargoes of merchantmen, as well as travellers. Whilst in Sicily on 16 October 1190, he quitclaimed his right of wreck throughout his lands. Rather than be seized by the king's officials or retained by locals in accordance with *jus naufragii* (right of shipwreck), wrecked survivors were to retain ownership of all their goods and possessions that came to land.[85] The heirs of those killed could claim their possessions and only the goods of those who died without children or siblings were to pass to the king.[86] Another example of maritime influence would be the captain of King Richard's royal galley, Alan Trenchemer, who was master of Richard's flagship on the Third Crusade. Alan also carried Richard back from Antwerp in 1194 after the king had been released from captivity.[87] I shall return to Alan in the next chapter, but interestingly, he was seemingly allowed to run a side

---

[82] Issued by Eleanor of Aquitaine c.1160, the rolls were based on the Lex Rhodia, E.T. Fox, 'Piratical Schemes and Contracts: Pirate Articles and their Society, 1660–1730' (PhD thesis, University of Exeter, 2013), pp. 186, 300, 307. See also N.A.M. Rodger, *Safeguard of the Seas, a Naval History of Britain, 660–1649* (London, 1997), p. 141; *Documents Relating to the Law and Custom of the Sea, Vol. 1, A.D. 1205–1648*, ed. R.G. Marsden (London, 1915), p. 2.

[83] The Angevin fleet was seemingly composed of three squadrons. The English squadron sailed from Dartmouth in late March/early April 1190, with another sailing from the Loire in June, and a third from Oléron in July. The fleet mustered at the mouth of the Tagus in late July and reached Marseille in early August; Tyerman, *Plan a Crusade*, p. 237.

[84] Bertrandus Sardus, Anselmus de Marsilia, Stephanus Iohannis, Raymundus de Posqueires, Basac, Raymundus de Saona, Hugo Ferri nepos Anselmi, Petrus Aunda, Giraldus Aldreer, Galterius Anglicus, Willelmus Berardi, Giraldus Catti, Bertrandus Caminali, Willelmus de Posqueres, Pontius de Reuest, Berengerius, Fulco Rostangni and Be. Aunda, RRRH, no. 1279.

[85] Also known as *lex naufragii* (law of shipwreck), *jus naufragii* was a medieval custom that gave local inhabitants or the local lord the right to seize the wreck of a ship and its cargo.

[86] *Chronica*, Vol. 3, p. 68.

[87] *Chronica*, Vol. 3, p. 235.

business as in 1195 he was also listed as jointly owing 8*l.* in Northumberland in customs duty for the sale of Flemish cattle.[88]

The Wool Trade

The landowning classes of north-western Europe also had an established interest in the wool trade. Information contained in the *Little Domesday* summary that covered the counties of Essex, Norfolk, and Suffolk, as well as that of *Exon Domesday* for the south west of England, revealed that sheep rearing was well established by the time of the Norman invasion.[89] John Munro has argued that English wools, particularly from East Anglia, the Welsh Marches, and the West Country, were held in considerable esteem and were exported in large quantities to cloth producers in France, Italy, and the Low Countries.[90]

By the twelfth century, Flanders had come to specialise in luxury cloth making and generated a huge appetite for wool. Flemish merchants dominated the wool trade and, with the conversion of pasture to arable farming in western Flanders and the loss of the pastures of Artois to France, they looked evermore to England for their wool, as well as cattle.[91] This meant that the large flocks reared at religious institutions and major lay farms were influential on pricing.[92] Just as wine played an important role in the Cistercian economy in France and Germany, so wool was a major concern in England and, to a lesser extent, beef cattle.

In his *Economic Geography of England*, Henry Darby credited the Cistercians for transforming northern England from a post-Conquest wilderness to a 'sheep-run'.[93] By 1193 it had become so valuable that a year's clip of wool was considered an appropriate contribution from the Cistercians to King Richard's ransom.[94] In marketing their wool, the Cistercians routinely

---

[88] PR8 RI (1196), p. 20.

[89] These two regions alone accounting for some 300,000 head of sheep in large demesne farms; H. Darby, *Domesday England* (Cambridge, 1977), p. 164.

[90] J.H. Munro, 'Medieval Woollens: Textiles, Textile Technology and Industrial Organisation, c. 800–1500', *The Cambridge History of Western Textiles*, Vol. 1, ed. D.T. Jenkins (Cambridge, 2003), pp. 186–9.

[91] D.M. Nicholas, *Medieval Flanders* (London and New York, 1992), pp. 113–14.

[92] The nuns of Holy Trinity, Caen, had some five hundred head of sheep at their manor of Minchinhampton in Gloucestershire, in 1170, BN, ms. Latin 5650, fols. 27v–28.

[93] H.C. Darby, 'The Economic Geography of England, A.D. 1000–1250', *An Historical Geography of England Before A.D. 1800, Fourteen Studies*, ed. H.C. Darby (Cambridge, 1936), pp. 165–229. See also, R.A. Donkin, 'The Cistercian Order and the Settlement of Northern England', *Geographical Review*, 59 (1969) 409.

[94] In order to help meet the ransom demanded by the Holy Roman Emperor, Henry IV, a year's harvest was also seized from the Premonstratensians and from Sempringham Priory, R.J. Whitwell, 'English Monasteries and the Wool Trade in the 13th Century', *Vierteljahrschrift für Sozial- und Wirtschaftsgeschichte*, 2 (1904), 4.

bypassed local fairs and focused on larger urban markets, especially ports, such as Newcastle and Boston, as well as the large urban market of York.[95] Here they acquired property, including warehouses and wharfs, from which the Cistercians could export their goods directly to continental Europe and secure more favourable returns on their investment.[96] The Cistercian abbey at Les Dunes, some 25 miles west of Bruges, maintained a merchant fleet in the late twelfth century, which was no doubt used in the transport of such goods from England to Flanders.[97] The Order was also not above speculation, receiving payment in advance of the anticipated harvest, which could place them in difficulty. In 1194–5, for example, Martin Fitz-Edric paid the Crown 5*l.* for six sacks of good wool, four sacks of other wool, and 10 *marks* promised him by Swine convent.[98] Hence, in 1181, the General Chapter of the Cistercians had restricted speculation to a single year's harvest and only then in time of great need.[99]

In addition to religious institutions, especially the Cistercians, noble elites also invested heavily in the wool trade and participated in speculation. In his comprehensive review of the English wool trade, for example, Terrence Lloyd identified individual flocks numbering in the hundreds at lay farms and the *Rotuli de Dominabus et Pueris et Puellis* of 1185 listed significant flocks at properties in the king's custody through his wardships.[100] Like the Cistercians, larger landowners developed direct trading links with cloth manufacturers abroad, such as in Arras, Bruges, and Saint-Omer, establishing reciprocal bonds between noble families in England, France, and the Low Countries, and this was replicated amongst other social classes, such as between artisans and merchants.[101] Indeed, Lloyd argued, some of the Flemish nobles that rose in support of the Great Revolt of 1173 may have been influenced by the prospect of obtaining English wool on more favourable terms.

In response, King Henry II seized Flemish goods, including wool from holdings in Essex, Sussex, and Yorkshire.[102] Like the Cistercians, a number of magnates also maintained fleets, which meant that William of Stuteville

---

[95] R.A. Donkin, 'The Urban Property of the Cistercians in Medieval England', *Analecta Sacri Ordinis Cisterciensis*, 15 (1959), 104–31.
[96] Donkin, 'Cistercian Order', pp. 415–16.
[97] R.W. Southern, *Western Society and the Church in the Middle Ages* (New York, 1970), p. 267.
[98] PR7 RI (1196), p. 166.
[99] T.H. Lloyd, *The English Wool Trade in the Middle Ages* (Cambridge, 1977), p. 289.
[100] Lloyd, *English Wool*, p. 298. See also E. Power, *The Wool Trade in English Medieval History: Being the Ford Lectures [for 1939]* (London, 1941); *Rotuli de Dominabus et Pueris et Puellis*, ed. J.H. Round (London, 1913), p. 1.
[101] Lloyd, *English Wool*, pp. 6–7.
[102] King Richard also clamped down on Flemish trade due to the actions of Baldwin VI of Hainaut, count of Flanders, whilst Richard had been incarcerated in Germany. In

was able to rent two fifty-man vessels to King Richard for his crusading fleet. The Marcher lord William III of Braose also supplied a forty-two-man ship, and it is notable that both of these nobles came from prominent wool producing areas, Yorkshire and the Welsh Borders.[103] However, it is unlikely that these vessels were related to ships of the kings' fleet, which were held in fief and distributed about England.[104]

Eileen Power presented evidence of William le Gros, count of Aumale and founder of Meaux, Thornton, and Vaudey abbeys, engaging in bulk sales of wool from his Yorkshire estates to Flemish financier, William Cade, in 1165.[105] Given that wool was a major dimension in the north-eastern European economy, it is arguably incidental that crusaders were involved in the wool trade. Social Network Analysis, however, indicates the potential importance of the wool trade in linking families more disposed to taking the Cross – the type of crusading families identified in the previous chapter. Perhaps the most notable examples in relation to the wool trade are those of the Béthune and the Mandeville families. William of Mandeville was a younger son to Earl Geoffrey II of Essex who had established a power base in East Anglia centred on the castle town of (Saffron) Walden. Sited on a key trading node between London and eastern ports, such as Boston, Yarmouth, and Ipswich, Earl Geoffrey successfully petitioned to establish a market there in 1141.[106] As well as benefiting from trade with the Low Countries, Geoffrey II of Mandeville hired Flemish mercenaries to augment his forces during the uncertainty of the Anarchy.[107] Pre-empting his imprisonment by King Stephen, Geoffrey II sent his younger son, William, to the Low Countries to be raised by Philip of Alsace, count of Flanders. Knighted by Count Philip, William of Mandeville returned to become one of King Henry II's inner circle and was frequently employed as an ambassador.[108]

Money-Fiefs

William of Mandeville was instrumental in re-establishing the Flemish money-fief in 1175 and, as discussed in Chapter Two, he joined Philip of Alsace on crusade in 1177.[109] Overlooked hitherto is the possible relationship

---

1193–4, his officials seized 513*l*. 5*s*. and 9*d*. in Norfolk and Lincolnshire, PR6 RI (1194), pp. 66–7.
[103] PR2 RI (1190), pp. 48, 59, 68.
[104] See, for example, D. Gilmour, 'Bekesbourne and the King's Esnecca, 1110–1445', *Archaeologia Cantiana*, 132 (2012), 315–27.
[105] Power, *Wool Trade*, p. 34.
[106] J.H. Round, *Geoffrey of Mandeville: A Study of the Anarchy* (London, 1892), p. 309.
[107] *The Waltham Chronicle*, ed. and trans. M. Chibnall and L. Watkiss (Oxford, 1994), pp. 80–3.
[108] *The Book of the Foundation of Walden Monastery*, ed. and trans. D. Greenway and L. Watkiss (Oxford, 1999), p. xxvi.
[109] *Gesta Regis*, Vol. 1, pp. 83, 116, 133, 159; *Walden Monastery*, pp. 52, 58.

between the trade in money-fiefs and crusading. Were those who accepted such arrangements more open to participating in expeditionary warfare in the Holy Land, aided by the additional revenue received via such contracts?[110]

While also aimed at providing an income in return for service, the money-fief was distinct from the traditional feudal-vassalic bond. The holder of an ordinary fief received his income from a landed estate or rights, which might take the form of cash (rents) or kind (produce or renders). The holder of a money-fief received an annual payment from the lord's treasury or from a fund put aside for him. Unlike a stipend, grant, or pension, however, the source of the revenue was tied to a specific source, such as an estate or toll.[111] Unlike traditional fiefs, money-fiefs did not require grants of land and were not usually heritable. This provided a degree of flexibility that made them eminently suitable for the employment of knights who owed allegiance to another lord and enabled them to retain overall ownership of the source of revenue.

William of Mandeville had inherited the earldom of Essex following the death of his older brother, Geoffrey the younger, in 1166. Tyerman has argued that William joined the crusade at the behest of Henry II to counter potential moves by Count Philip against Baldwin IV, king of Jerusalem.[112] If so, then this was achieved without souring their relationship. On their return from the Holy Land, William continued to be engaged in arranging money-fief payments to the count of Flanders, as well as overseeing negotiations between King Henry II and Philip of Alsace.[113] Earl William took the Cross alongside King Henry II and the count of Flanders in Gisors in January 1188, but died in November 1189, having laid the groundwork for an agreement between Philip of Alsace and King Henry II's successor, Richard.[114]

Philip of Alsace was not the only recipient of such payments. Money-fiefs were also traded with foreign barons in return for military service. The barons were initially involved as guarantors of a comital agreement in 1101 against a surety of 100 *marks* each. Baronial money-fiefs also accompanied the treaty of 1163 between King Henry II and Count Thierry in which the

---

[110] In 1175, the value of the money-fief paid to Count Philip was increased to an annual payment of 1000 *marks*, Gesta Regis, Vol. 1, pp. 83, 246–7; Vol. 2, pp. 48–9.

[111] They are referred to as fief-rents; B.D. Lyon, 'The Money Fief under the English Kings, 1066–1485', *EHR*, Vol. 66 (1951), pp. 161–93; and, A.V. Murray, 'The Origin of Money-Fiefs in the Latin Kingdom of Jerusalem', *Mercenaries and Paid Men, The Mercenary Identity in the Middle Ages*, ed. J. France (Leiden and Boston, 2008), p. 276. For estates related to the Flanders' money-fief, see, PR21 H2 (1174–5), pp. 11, 29, 144.

[112] Tyerman, *England*, p. 48. See also, Hosler, *Henry II*, p. 167.

[113] *Gesta Regis*, Vol. 1, pp. 321–2, Vol. 2, pp. 4–5.

[114] *Walden Monastery*, pp. 80–1. King Richard's continuation of money-fief payments to Count Philip was recorded in the Pipe Rolls, see, for example, returns in PR1 R1 (1189), pp. 105, 155.

count of Flanders committed one thousand knights in return for a money-fief.[115] In addition to the guarantors of the treaty, individual Flemish barons, such as Robert V, advocate of Béthune, pledged to attend King Henry II, presumably for forty days, along with ten knights, in exchange for 30 *marks* in silver.[116] Interestingly, the treaty between Count Thierry and King Henry II was secured at a lower rate of 500 *marks*, most probably because the count of Flanders was about to embark on crusade and was unlikely to be able to meet his obligations in full.[117] In his absence, however, Philip of Alsace was named to act in his father's stead. William of Mandeville's renewal of this arrangement in 1175 and 1180 secured Henry II one thousand Flemish knights for his defence of the Norman Vexin against King Philip II in 1187. The next section cross-references the trade in money-fiefs with crusading.

The Anglo-Flemish Treaties of 1163

Returning to the two 1163 treaties, the six commanders of the Flemish troops in the first treaty were to be drawn from amongst the twelve guarantors, which is an indication of their position within Flemish noble society. Despite the treaty being signed some twenty-four years before the fall of Jerusalem, five of the twelve (42%) Flemish guarantors either participated in the Third Crusade or, having died prior to the crusade, their heirs took the Cross. Indeed, the treaty stipulated that the count of Flanders must replace any guarantor who died with someone of equal strength at the summons of King Henry II.[118] Based on his relationship to the Mandevilles through the wool trade and familial background in crusading, it is not surprising to see Robert V of Béthune listed.[119] Robert V had served as ambassador to the Angevin court in 1177 and in 1179 had accompanied Count Philip and William of Mandeville's pilgrimage to Thomas Becket's tomb in Canterbury, but his interests in England can be traced back to the reign of King

---

[115] This commitment would be reduced by twenty knights should Henry II require support against the king of France so that Philip of Alsace could also meet his feudal obligations to King Philip II, B. Lyon, *From Fief to Indenture: The Transition from Feudal to Non-Feudal Contract in Western Europe* (Cambridge, MA, 1954), p. 272. For the treaty see, *Diplomatic Documents Preserved in the Public Record Office, Volume I, 1101–1272*, ed. P. Chaplais (London, 1964), pp. 12–14, no. 3.

[116] Eighteen baronial seals were attached to the second treaty, which suggests they were all party to the agreement, *Diplomatic Documents*, no. 4.

[117] Robert of Torigny, *Chronicle*, pp. 193, 205, 220.

[118] If six of the guarantors were not available, then at least two of them would lead, aided by four of Count Thierry's barons of equal strength to those four who were absent; E.M.C. van Houts, 'The Anglo-Flemish Treaty of 1101', *ANS*, 21 (1999), 169–74.

[119] Robert V joined the Third Crusade along with his sons, Baldwin and Conon, but died at the siege of Acre. Baldwin returned to marry Geoffrey of Mandeville's widow, whilst Conon went on to join the Fourth Crusade.

Stephen.[120] His second son, William, held an estate in England[121] and his third son, Baldwin, was a member of first King Henry II's and then Richard I's military households.[122] Baldwin of Béthune had long been a friend to William Marshal and had accompanied Richard on his return from the Third Crusade. In due course, Baldwin would be rewarded with the hand of Geoffrey of Mandeville's widow, Hawisa of Aumale, in marriage and became count of Aumale.[123]

Of the eleven other guarantors, Conon of Nesle, castellan of Bruges, predeceased the Third Crusade, but his son, John I, arrived at the siege of Acre in 1189.[124] As discussed in the previous chapter, John was joined in the Holy Land by his brother, Raoul, count of Soissons.[125] Count Arnold of Guînes died in 1169 and his grandson, Arnold II, took the Cross, but did not travel to the Holy Land.[126] Count Philip's seneschal, Roger III of Wavrin, also died prior to the Third Crusade and his sons, Hellin and Roger, bishop of Cambrai, both died at the siege of Acre. Their younger brother, Robert I of Wavrin, survived the siege, returning early and travelling to Flanders at the behest of King Philip II to secure the county after the death of Philip of Alsace.[127] Baldwin of Bailleul died in 1176 and his son, Baldwin II, also fell at the siege of Acre. Baldwin II was also linked to Thierry of Aalst though marriage to Thierry's niece, Mable of Bourbourg.[128]

Similarly, of the twelve Angevin guarantors, half were linked to participation in the Third Crusade. Richard of Le Hommet's son Jordan, constable of Séez, arrived at the siege of Acre shortly after King Richard.[129] Bernard II of St Valéry died at the siege of Acre in 1190 as did John Fitz-Richard, constable of Chester and heir to the Lucy estates.[130] Henry Fitz-Gerald's heir, Warin II, led a company at the siege of Acre and participated in a skirmish near Ramla in 1192 along with Robert IV of Leicester and his retinue.[131] Both Earl Robert III of Leicester and his son took the Cross,

---

[120] PR8 HII (1161–2), p. 60; PR9 HII (1162–3), p. 9; *Gesta Regis*, Vol. 1, pp. 133, 241.
[121] Rushden in Hampshire, *Rotuli de Oblatis et Finibus in Turri Londinensi*, ed. T.D. Hardy (London, 1835), p. 59; *Rotuli Literarum Patentium in Turri Londinensi Asservati*, Vol. 1, ed. T.D. Hardy (London, 1835), p. 7.
[122] For his service, Baldwin was awarded the three manors of Luton, Wantage, and Norton, TNA, *carte antique* roll EE, no. 27. See also, *HGM*, lines 4543, 7998, 8609, 9374–90, 9396–8; Landon, *Itinerary*, nos. 328, 366; Wendover, p. 218.
[123] Gillingham, *Richard I*, pp. 293–4.
[124] *Itinerarium*, p. 74.
[125] See also E. Warlop, *The Flemish Nobility before 1300* (Kortrijk, 1975), p. 726.
[126] Lambert of Ardres, p. 177.
[127] Ambroise, line 2920; Diss, Vol. 2, p. 79; Wendover, p. 178; Gilbert of Mons, p. 274.
[128] *Gesta Regis*, Vol. 2, p. 149.
[129] Ambroise, lines 4707, 10963; *Itinerarium*, pp. 217, 405.
[130] *Chronica*, Vol. 3, p. 88; *Gesta Regis*, Vol. 2, pp. 80, 148.
[131] *Itinerarium*, p. 300.

but only Robert IV survived the subsequent crusade. Finally, as discussed, Geoffrey of Mandeville's son, William, took the Cross, but died before he could complete his vow. However, William's nephew, Ernald travelled east along with Earl William's former steward, Henry Pigot, and his constable for Halsham, Robert.[132] Of the twenty-four guarantors of the first Treaty of 1163, eleven (46%) were linked either directly or through their close family to the Third Crusade.

In terms of the eighteen Flemish nobles who affixed their seals to the second Treaty of 1163, presumably to commit to supplying their own troops, eight (44%) can be linked to the Third Crusade. It is also unsurprising that Robert V of Béthune appeared again. Conon of Nesle's seal was also attached, as was that of Baldwin of Bailleul, castellan of Ypres, and Roger III of Wavrin.[133] In terms of other signatories linked to the Third Crusade, the castellan of Bourbourg, Arnold I of Guînes' grandson, Arnold II, took the Cross, but did not go on crusade; and William IV, heir to the castellany of Saint-Omer, died on the Third Crusade.[134]

The counts of Flanders had very little domain land south of a line between Saint-Omer and Lille, and it is notable that southern Flemish nobles dominate the list. This may well have been influenced by the difference in financial opportunities available between lords in northern and southern Flanders. The general domanial account of 1187 reflects one of the count's two sources of income: that of the *reneghe* (old domain), which was organised into forty territories, roughly half of which were administered by notaries, that is, clergymen, and the remainder by lay receivers in fief to the count known as castellans.[135] While some money payments were received from the larger centres, most payments were in animal products, dairy goods, or grain, with the castellans deducting any expenses they incurred from the goods they received. These goods were usually then converted into cash at market rates. Hence, whilst all the castellanies had a military function, centred on a comital fortress, those in the *reneghe* were also centres for economic administration and the castles maintained large cellars for

---

[132] *Itinerarium*, p. 218; *EYC*, Vol. 3, pp. 79–80, no. 1364. According to Howden, Robert and Henry both died at the siege of Acre, *Gesta Regis*, Vol. 2, p. 149; *Chronica*, Vol. 3, p. 89.
[133] *Diplomatic Documents*, pp. 12–13, no. 4.
[134] Arnold I's brother, Siger of Guînes, also affixed his seal to the treaty. There is, however, no evidence linking Count Thierry's chamberlain, Eustace of Griminis, his constable and castellan of Cassel, Michael I, or his butler, Razo of Gavere, to the Third Crusade. Similarly, neither Roger, castellan of Courtray, Walter, castellan of Dendermonde, Jordan of Beveren, castellan of Dixmude, the castellan of Berges, nor their descendants can be linked to the expedition. I was unable to trace Roger *de Landasto*, Stephen *de Senningeham*, or Guido *de Steinford*.
[135] B.D. Lyon and A.E. Verhulst, *Medieval Finance: A Comparison of Financial Institutions in Northwestern Europe* (Providence, RI, 1967), pp. 13–14.

the storage of grain, animal products, and dairy goods. The castellans also presided over the courts of justice and retained one-third of any fines.[136] This meant that northern castellans, such as William IV of Saint-Omer, Baldwin II of Bailleul, and John I of Nesle, had access to the financial resources necessary to fund their participation in the Third Crusade.

The other source of the count's income was from the new domain. This was organised on a non-territorial basis and revenues from the exercise of regalian rights, such as tolls and the sale of vacant lands, and taxation went directly to the count. In the south, castellanies were not given central courts until much later, all of which reduced the potential revenue for southern lords, such as Robert V of Béthune and Arnold III of Therouanne, to support their participation in the Third Crusade. In addition to income from other interests in England, such as the wool trade, the money-fief drew the Béthunes ever closer to the Angevin orbit.

This evidence indicates a close link between those involved in the trade of money-fiefs and participation on the Third Crusade, with 46 per cent of the guarantors of the first treaty of 1163 linked to the expedition and 44 per cent of those named in the second treaty.

Anglo-Hainaut Treaty (1172)

A similar treaty signed with Baldwin V of Hainaut in 1172, listed money-fiefs to Eustace of Roeulx, Walter of Ligne, Amand of Prouvy, Henry of Braine, and Robert of Carnières.[137] King Henry II enfeoffed James of Avesnes for 30 *marks* at the same time. Of these, both James and Eustace were to fall on the Third Crusade, and Walter of Ligne was linked to Third Crusade participants Baldwin le Carron and the Fontaine brothers.[138] Amand died at the siege of Enghien in the service of Count Baldwin V in 1191.[139] Unfortunately, due to the vagaries of data survival, we lack evidence on the fates of Henry of Braine and Robert of Carnières. Similarly, as well as recording payments made to Philip of Alsace, the Pipe Roll of 1189 records money-fief payments to a seasoned crusader, Otto II of Trazegnies, worth

---

[136] Nicholas, *Medieval Flanders*, pp. 80–3.

[137] 'Eustacio scilicet de Ruez 15 marche, Waltero de Linea 10 marche, Amando de Provi 10 marche, Henrico de Brania 10 marche, Roberto de Carneriis 10 marche', Gilbert of Mons, p. 109.

[138] According to Gilbert of Mons, Walter of Ligne was married to Mathilda of Mons, sister to Baldwin le Carron's wife, Ida of Jauche. Walter, however, must have died sometime between 1172 and 1183 because Mathilda went on to marry Walter of Fontaine, who joined the Order of Alne and died in 1183. Walter of Ligne's younger brother, Thierry I, inherited the lordship of Ligne and was married to Margaret of Fontaine. Walter of Fontaine's brothers, Alan, Fulk, and Guy, all died on the Third Crusade. Thierry II of Ligne also died in 1190, but he is not listed with those who died in the Holy Land, Gilbert of Mons, pp. 53, 109–10, 139–40, 150, 274.

[139] Gilbert of Mons, pp. 109, 265, 273–4.

40s. from an estate in Sutton, Kent, at the command of King Richard.[140] Nor was the trade in money-fiefs limited to barons outside the realm. In 1180, for example, Robert of Stuteville rendered an account recorded in the Great Rolls of the Norman Exchequer for a money-fief payment to another member of the Third Crusade, William II of Tancarville, hereditary chamberlain of Normandy.[141] King Philip II also utilised money-fiefs, offering James of Avesnes a fief worth 100 *livres* in 1172 in return for support to the Treaty of Boves.[142]

Some Flemish barons were nevertheless retained with traditional fiefs. On 5 July 1190, for example, King Richard confirmed the inheritance of land in England by Hugh IV of St Pol.[143] Traditionally associated with King Philip II of France, according to Angevin sources, Hugh IV was dispatched by King Richard along with the earl of Leicester and members of the Richard's household to rescue a group of Templars that had been ambushed near Ramla on 6 November 1191.[144] The financial aspects of money-fiefs are but part of the story. In addition to financial reward, they also indicate a willingness to serve beyond one's immediate locality, which is suggestive of an expeditionary spirit – a state of mind essential for someone to take the Cross and journey to the Holy Land. A similar attitude was likely required of those who journeyed across Europe to compete in tournaments.

Tournaments

As Eljas Oksanen has pointed out, tournaments were 'many things at the same time'.[145] As well as being competitive military exercises and an opportunity to gain wealth, they were an assembly of social power, an economic and professional opportunity, and an engine of princely politics – they also became a popular spectator sport. I argue here, however, that they were primarily a space for the dissemination of elite secular culture and military practice, and political activity.

---

[140] As introduced in previous chapters, Otto II of Trazegnies had been on crusade to the Holy Land *c.*1186–7, presumably returning prior to Saladin's invasion, PR2 RI (1190), p. 147; PR3 RI (1191), p. 142; PR4 RI (1192), p. 308; see also PR22 HII (1175–6), pp. 28, 77, 90.

[141] William II joined Richard I on crusade along with the late Robert of Stuteville's son, Osmund. Another son, William of Stuteville, supplied King Richard with two fifty-man ships for his crusading fleet. For the money-fiefs, see *Magni Rotuli Scaccarii Normanniae*, ed. Stapleton, Vol. I, pp. 68, 132, 138, 157.

[142] Baldwin, *Government of Philip*, pp. 272–7.

[143] These lands had been awarded to Anselm, his father, by Henry II, BN, ms. Clairambault 5, p. 179, no. 34.

[144] Ambroise, lines 4527, 6046, 7274; *Itinerarium*, pp. 213, 257, 293.

[145] Oksanen, *Flanders*, p. 115.

Within the imagined community of the noble elites of north-western Europe, tournaments bridged the divide between family, society, and association. They underpinned the social networks of the noble military elites of north-western Europe and were the foundation for the effectiveness of coalition armies in the field, such as the forces of the Third Crusade.[146]

Before they evolved into the medieval sporting obsession beloved of modern popular fiction, tournaments were more akin to military manoeuvres: mock battles involving hundreds, sometimes thousands of participants – both on horseback and on foot. They seemingly emerged around the turn of the eleventh century with activities referred to as *militaris ludis* (military game) and *conflictu armorum* (a contest of arms) appearing in primary sources. By the early twelfth century, the name *torneamentum* from the French verb *torner*, meaning to 'revolve' or to 'whirl around', had become established.[147]

David Crouch has argued that tournaments grew out of efforts by local princes to exert a degree of control over endemic violence in northern France and the Low Countries and were linked to the Peace and Truce of God movements.[148] Indeed, the earliest surviving appearance of the term *torneamentum* was in a charter issued by Baldwin III, count of Hainaut, to the town of Valenciennes in 1114 to establish the Peace of God. In this document, Count Baldwin forbade the pursuit of personal vendettas, but permitted officials of the Peace to leave the town for tournaments and similar military activities.[149] The inspiration for the surge in popularity for such exercises, however, may have come from further afield. In a continuation

---

[146] M.A.J. van Duijn, E.P.H. Zeggelink, M. Huisman, F.N. Stokman, and F.W. Wasseur, 'Evolution of Sociology Freshmen into a Friendship Network'. *The Journal of Mathematical Sociology*, 27 (2003), 153–91.

[147] D. Crouch, *Tournament* (London and New York, 2005), p. 3; see also R. Barber and J. Barker, *Tournaments, Jousts, Chivalry and Pageants in the Middle Ages* (Woodbridge, 1989).

[148] For more on the origins of the medieval tournament, see Crouch, *Tournament*, pp. 2–12; Crouch, *William Marshal*, 3rd edition, pp. 53–5, 187–9; and R. Barber, 'Chivalry in the Tournament and Pas d'Armes', *A Companion to Chivalry*, ed. R.W. Jones and P. Coss (Woodbridge, 2019), pp. 119–38.

[149] 'Si in posterum contigat, quod viri pacis villam exeant ad faciendum hastiludia, torneamenta aut consimilia, aut in suis negociis aut mercimoniis processerint, nullus tenetur se conservare de inimico suo mortali et non plus extra quam intra villam. Et caveat sibi, quincunque percusserit aut vulneraverit aut occiderit inimicum suum mortaliem extra villam, reus erit violate pacis aesi in villa comisisset; et hoc intelligendum de hominibus pacis': 'Charta Pacis Valenciennes', ed. G.H. Pertz, Monumenta Germaniae Historica Scriptores Rerum Germanicarum in Usum Scholarum Separatim Editi, Vol. 21 (Hanover, 1869), p. 608. The first evidence of the word *turniamentum* in England was in a charter issued between 1124 and 1139 to Osbert of Arden, *Facsimiles of Royal & Other Charters in the British Museum*, Vol. 1, ed. G. Warner and H. Ellis (London, 1903), no. 12, see also Crouch, *Tournament*, pp. 20, 40–1, 163.

of Late Roman practice, the medieval Byzantine army conducted regular training exercises. It may not be coincidental that tournaments gained in popularity in the Low Countries around the same time as participants from the First Crusade returned home.

Oksanen has suggested a rough but credible chronology, with the emergence of tournaments as distinct military events at around 1100 in the borderlands between France and the Low Countries. From there they spread quickly through north-eastern France, north-western Germany, and the Low Countries in the second and third decades of the twelfth century, including the county of Flanders, as indicated by Galbert of Bruges' commentary on Charles the Good.

> By secular military engagements for the honour of his lands and for the training of his knights in the lands of the counts or princes of Normandy or France, sometimes even held beyond the kingdom of France, he engaged two hundred horsemen in tourneys, thus enhancing his fame and the power and the glory of his county.[150]

By the end of the twelfth century, tournaments were firmly established amongst the elite military classes of Christendom as a significant activity.[151] Just as in war, western knights gained renown through capturing noblemen from opposing teams and amassed booty by ransoming them.[152] Clad in iron helmets, mail chausses (leggings), and tailored hauberks (thigh-length, sleeved shirts of mail), heavily protected knights were virtually invulnerable.[153] Moreover, the financial incentive of gaining a ransom encouraged a reluctance to kill opponents amongst the martial elites.

---

[150] 'sed certamina militia secularis pro honore terrae suae et pro exercitio militum suorum apud aliquem comitum ved principum Normanniae vel Franciae, aliquando vero ultra regnum Franciae, arripuit, illicque cum ducentis equitibus tornationes exercuit. Qua in re famam suam et comitatus sui potentiam ac gloriam sublimavit': on Charles the Good, count of Flanders (1119–27), Galbert of Bruges, *De Multro, Traditione, et Occasione Gloriosi Karoli Comitis Flandriarum*, ed. J. Rider (Turnhout, 1994), p. 13.

[151] Oksanen, *Flanders*, p. 120.

[152] Examples of priority being given to the capture rather than killing of opposing knights include the capture of Robert III, earl of Leicester, at Fordham in 1173 and that of William the Lion, king of Scots, and his household at Alnwick in 1174, William of Newburgh, *The History of English Affairs, Book 2*, ed. and trans. P.G. Walsh and M.J. Kennedy (Oxford, 2007), pp. 143, 153. See also, Prestwich, '*Miles in Armis Strenuus*', 201–20.

[153] That is not to say that fatalities did not occur. According to Roger of Howden, for example, Richard's younger brother, Geoffrey, was unhorsed and trampled to death at a tournament in 1186; *Gesta Regis*, Vol. 1, p. 350. However, such cases were rare enough that even the death of an otherwise unexceptional knight was worthy of comment. See, for example, the death of Walter of Honnecourt at a tournament in 1168, 'Ipse autem Balduinus, secunda feria post octavam pasce, cum multis militibus quibus tunc temporis Hanonia florebat, Trajecti torniavit, ubi probissimus miles Walterus de Hone-

During tournaments, ransoms were seemingly more modest than those which might be gained in war and were generally restricted to a knight's harness (his armour), but more importantly his warhorse.[154] Regular ransom payments would have made tournaments prohibitively expensive, but even the loss of their mount risked financial disaster for a landless knight.[155] As William Marshal was to learn early in his career, when having defeated several opponents he was teased for not securing their ransoms: a knight who failed to secure wealth from military success was deemed foolish.[156] One's reputation for military prowess was based on pragmatic, mercantile foundations.

Tournaments and Collective Identity

Prior to the widespread use of gunpowder in battle and the resulting obscuration, warfare was very much a visual activity. The comprehensive protection worn by the warrior elite described above made the identification of the wearer challenging. This seemingly influenced the development of martial display and the adoption of familial designs (heraldic arms) on shields, as well as on horse coverings (caparisons).[157] In the twelfth century, there is evidence that members of military households were provided with

---

cort, Walteri pater, occisus fuit', Gilbert of Mons, p. 95, and the foundation of Beaulieu Abbey by Eustace 'the Old' of Fiennes in penance for having killed the lord of Ponches-Estruval at a tournament. Eustace's son, Engelram, died on the Third Crusade; *Itinerarium*, p. 74; Lambert of Ardres, p. 84.

[154] King Richard's tournament licences of 1194, however, set the ransoms at 20 *marks* for an earl, 10 *marks* for a baron, 4 *marks* for a landed knight, and 2 *marks* for their landless colleagues, *Feodora*, Vol. 1, ed. T. Rymer (reprint, Farnborough, 1967), p. 65. See also, J.R.V. Barker, *The Tournament in England, 1100–1400* (Woodbridge, 2003), pp. 10–12.

[155] Warhorses were predominantly stallions at no more than 16 hands, which were bred and trained for combat. They were highly prized by knights, and damaging an opponent's mount was to be avoided for both practical (ransom value) and social reasons. Such mounts might easy be worth 30*l*. at a time when agricultural labourers were paid but one or two pennies a day. See, for example, R.H.C. Davis, 'The Warhorses of the Normans', *Anglo-Norman Studies*, 10 (1987), 67–82; M. Bennett, 'The Medieval Warhorse Reconsidered', *Medieval Knighthood*, Vol. 5, ed. S. Church and R. Harvey (Woodbridge, 1995), pp. 19–40; and, A. Hyland, *The Medieval Warhorse: From Byzantium to the Crusades* (Stroud, 1994). It is likely that tournaments forbade the killing of an opponent's horse, M. Strickland, *Henry the Young King, 1155–1183* (New Haven and London, 2016), p. 252. For more on the relationship between military riders and their horses, see J. Flynn, 'Sense and Sentimentality: The Soldier–Horse Relationship in the Great War' (PhD thesis, University of Derby, 2016).

[156] *HGM*, lines 1144–60.

[157] See R.W. Jones, 'Heraldry and Heralds', *A Companion to Chivalry*, ed. R.W. Jones and P. Coss (Woodbridge, 2019), pp. 139–58. Caparisons carrying heraldic designs are evident on seals from the mid twelfth century, such as that of Ralph of Chaynes preserved in Westminster Abbey Muniments, as well as beginning to appear in images of a mounted knights like that in the church at Coincy (Aisne) in northern France.

distinctively coloured items of dress, such as robes to wear over their mail (surcoats) and cloaks, by their lords to distinguish them from other retinues.[158] In time, such items came to be referred to as liveries from the French *livrée* – to hand over. Shields also bore specific designs to reflect their lord's heraldic device.[159]

This approach to collective display was reflected by an agreement made in 1188 that the crusaders of the kings of France and England and of the count of Flanders would each bear a distinct colour of cross: red for France, white for England, and green for Flanders.[160] As well as visibly advertising the wearer's allegiance, such badges and clothing contributed to the development of an *esprit de corps* – a sense of pride and fellowship shared by members of a group, which underpinned martial cohesion.[161]

Whilst individual martial skills, such as swordsmanship and riding, were mastered in knightly households, tournaments provided a legitimate opportunity for cavalrymen to practise unit drills and master military tactics, such as deception, cooperation with other arms, and flank attacks, as well as to gain standing in the noble network.[162] Although the various descriptions in contemporary works of Latin cavalry being so tightly packed that the wind could not blow through their lances or that items could be thrown into their midst and not hit the ground were, no doubt, *topoi*, they highlighted the value of the maintenance of close order (physical cohesion) and discipline in cavalry formations.[163] However, that is not to say that they were incapable of adopting other formations and performing agile manoeuvres.

Recent scholarship has done much to highlight the nuances of medieval tactics, recognising that there was far more to battles than the massed charge

---

[158] See, for example, Strickland, *Henry the Young King*, p. 248.

[159] William Fitz-Empress, for example, bore a lion rampant on his shield, and King Richard's first Great Seal suggests that during the Third Crusade he bore two golden lions rampant combatant, i.e., fighting one another, standing face to face, A. Ailes, 'Heraldry in Twelfth-Century England: The Evidence', *England in the Twelfth Century. Proceedings of the 1988 Harlaxton Symposium*, ed. D. Williams (Woodbridge, 1990), pp. 1–16. See also, Jones, *Bloodied Banners*, pp. 11–12.

[160] *Chronica*, Vol. 2, p. 335.

[161] See, for example, F.J. Manning, 'Morale and Cohesion in Military Psychiatry', *Military Psychiatry: Preparing in Peace and War*, ed. F.D. Jones, L.R. Sparacino, V.L. Wilcox, and J.M. Rothberg (Washington, DC, 1994), p. 5.

[162] Strickland, *Henry the Young King*, pp. 246–7.

[163] 'Qu'entre lor lances ne puet corre le vent', *Chanson d'Aspremont, chanson de geste du XIIe siècle: Texte du manuscrit de Wollaton Hall*, Vol. 2, ed. L. Brandin (Paris, 1921), line 9206; 'De bons chevaliers qu'a grant paine, En peüst l'om le chief veoir, Qui ne se alast en halt seoir, Ne getissiez pas une prune, Fors sor gent fervestue e brune.' Ambroise, lines 3976–80. For more narrative examples, see Verbruggen, *Art of Warfare*, pp. 73–4. The need for closely ordered ranks, in this case for (mounted) serjeants, also appears in *La Regle du Temple*, no. 172, *The Rule of the Templars, The French Text of the Rule of the Order of the Knights Templar*, trans. J.M. Upton-Ward (Woodbridge, 1992), p. 61.

of heavy horse.[164] Donald Bullough and Bernard Bachrach comprehensively demolished Heinrich Brunner's century-old thesis on the supremacy of heavy cavalry in the Carolingian Age.[165] Whilst it is clear that shock action by heavy horse in close formation had become increasingly important by the twelfth century, such charges took place in cooperation with other arms, such as heavy infantry, missile-armed troops, and light cavalry.[166] Rather than as a single, stirrup-to-stirrup mass charge, attacks were often delivered in echelon and a mounted reserve was normally maintained.[167]

In times of combined arms combat, the tournament provided a remarkably effective simulation of medieval warfare.[168] The household of Henry the Young King, for example, suffered a humiliating string of defeats in their first eighteen months on the circuit before they gained the cohesion, tactical skills, and duplicity necessary for success on the simulated battlefield.[169] On one occasion, thereafter, Henry pretended that his household were not going to participate in the battle, before suddenly charging in once the other households were in disarray.[170] Such tricks and stratagems were not considered unchivalrous, and guile was valued. As *L'Histoire de Guillaume le Marechal* described, 'high valour needs to be allied with good sense'.[171]

Unit cohesion developed on the tournament field through practising complex manoeuvres and stratagems, and the *esprit de corps* developed through common emblems and banners was of immense value to

---

[164] For a historiographical review, see J. France, 'Recent Writing on Medieval Warfare: from the Fall of Rome to *c.*1300', *Journal of Military History*, 65 (2001), 441–73.

[165] H. Brunner, 'Der Reiterdienst und die Anfänge des Lehnswesens', *Zeitschrift der Savigny-Stiftung für Rechtsgeschichte, Germanistische Abteilung*, 8 (1887), 1–38; D.A. Bullough, '*Europae Pater*: Charlemagne and his Achievement in the Light of Recent Scholarship', *EHR*, 85 (1970), 84–90; B.S. Bachrach, 'Charles Martel, Shock Combat, the Stirrup, and Feudalism', *Studies in Medieval and Renaissance History*, 7 (1970), 47–75. For a thorough summary of Brunner's thesis, as well as its demolition, see K. DeVries, *Medieval Military Technology* (Ontario, 1992), pp. 95–110.

[166] M. Bennett, 'The Myth of the Military Supremacy of Knightly Cavalry', *Armies, Chivalry, and Warfare in Britain and France: Proceedings of the 1995 Harlaxton Symposium*, ed. M. Strickland (Stamford, 1998), pp. 304–16.

[167] S. Bennett, 'Faith and Authority, Guy of Lusignan at the Battle of Acre (4th October 1189)', *A Military History of the Mediterranean Sea – Aspects of Warfare, Diplomacy and Military Elites*, ed. G. Theotokis and A. Yildiz (Leiden, 2017), pp. 220–34; M. Bennett, '*Le Règle du Temple* as a Military Manual, or How to Deliver a Cavalry Charge', *The Rule of the Templars* (Woodbridge, 1992), pp. 175–88.

[168] See, for example, the description given in Gilbert of Mons, p. 97. The significant exception was the limitation on the use of projectile weapons, such as the crossbow. However, missile-armed troops are mentioned on occasion, normally to protect the *lists*: *HGM*, lines 2816–36.

[169] *HGM*, lines 2563–76. See also, Strickland, *Henry the Young King*, pp. 245–50.

[170] *HGM*, lines 2744–54.

[171] 'A grant proëce a mestier sens': *HGM*, line 2718.

the crusader army in the Levant. It is unsurprising, therefore, that King Richard followed established tournament practice of teams being based on regional affiliation to organise the army for its march on Jaffa and Ascalon in September 1191. Aside from the two Military Orders that held the van and rearguards, as Matthew Bennett has pointed out, the remainder were organised into regional squadrons of 'Bretons and Angevins, Poitevins, English and Normans, Champagnois, and many other unspecified French knights'.[172] Formations and symbols, however, were only part of the influence of tournaments on the Third Crusade. The next section considers the social implications of the tournament circuit on the conduct of the martial elite and their noble networks.

Social Aspects of Tournaments: Power and Opportunity
By the late twelfth century, tournament sites generally benefited from proximity to towns capable of providing suitable accommodation and supplies, as well as being situated close to major thoroughfares.[173] However, the likely economic disruption through damage to crops and livestock by massed formations of infantry and cavalry meant that tournaments tended to be held in sparsely populated borderlands.

Although the 'battles' themselves only lasted a single day, the festivities surrounding them routinely extended to several more. In a continuation of a tradition of single combat, preliminary bouts called *commençailles* or *josts de pladices* (jousts) between individual knights became a feature of tournaments, as did a grand banquet after the main battle, during which prizes were awarded to noteworthy participants. However, the mêlée, the mock battle in which teams charged one another to engage in close combat and capture their opponents, remained the main event. The banquets that followed were, perhaps, one of the most public forums in which a knight could be recognised by high-ranking members of the elite social network as a *preudomme* – a wise and skilful knight and ideal nobleman.[174] As much as on the field, it was at the banquets that reputations were made or lost.

Various attempts by the church to limit tournaments were largely unsuccessful and, despite Henry II's tournament ban in England, such events seemingly continued.[175] However, tournaments were predominantly held in

---

[172] Bennett, 'Why Chivalry?', pp. 61–2.
[173] Crouch, *Tournament*, pp. 39–56.
[174] Asbridge, *Greatest Knight*, pp. 38–40.
[175] The Council of Clermont of 1130 banned all military sports with ecclesiastical burial rights denied to those killed in tournaments, a prohibition repeated at the Third Lateran Council 1179, C-J. Hefele and H. Leclercq, *Histoire de Conciles*, Vol. 5 (Paris, 1912), pt. 1, p. 729, Pt. 2, p. 1102. With regard to England, *HGM* described Henry the Young King and William Marshal returning to England in 1174 where they enjoyed hunting and tourneying, *HGM*, line 2394.

northern France and the Low Countries, especially Flanders and Normandy, with nobles and their military households journeying from far afield. The poems of Bertran of Born, for example, indicate that knights were travelling from Gascony and Aquitaine, but he also described a tournament being held in Toulouse c.1181,

> And they will come to us there,
> the potentates and the barons,
> and the most honourable companions
> in the world, and the most celebrated;
> some for gain, some by command,
> some for praise will be moved.
> And as soon as we arrive,
> the tourney will embroil across the field,
> and the Catalans and the Aragonese
> will fall often and with little effort,
> for their saddle trees cannot hold them up,
> such great blows we will make, us friends! [176]

As Bertran of Born's poem highlights, motivation for participation in a tournament varied. When Baldwin V of Hainaut led a one hundred-strong household around the tournament circuit immediately after inheriting the county in 1172, it was a statement as much of his county's military capability as of individual prowess.[177] Situated in a region that would become known as the cockpit of Europe and surrounded by more powerful neighbours, Hainaut needed to punch above its weight.[178] The tournament field provided a route to building a reputation for military effectiveness without the risk of suffering the widespread devastation of an enemy *chevauchée*.[179]

---

[176] 'E serau I ab nos vengut las poestatz e li baro e li plus honrat compaigno del mon, e li plus mentaugut; qe per aver, que per somo, que per precs s'I serant mogut. E desse que serem vengut mesclar s'a-l torneis pel cambo, e-ll Catalan e-ll d'Arago tombaran soven e emnut, qu no-ls sostenran lor arso, tant grans colps lor ferrem, no drut!': *The Poems of the Troubadour Bertran de Born*, ed. W.D. Paden Jr., T. Sankovitch, and P.H. Stäblein (Berkeley, Los Angeles, London, 1986), p. 109. Silk, sendal, and samite were all are expensive fabrics that attested to the high status of the participants.

[177] Gilbert of Mons, pp. 110–12.

[178] A cockpit was an enclosed space in which cockfighting took place. As the scene of many battles between the powers of Europe, Belgium gained the dubious title of the 'very cockpit of Christendom' c.1642, which evolved into the cockpit of Europe later in the seventeenth century; J. Howell, *Instructions for Foreign Travel* (London, 1642).

[179] The *chevauchée* or mounted raid was endemic to high medieval warfare. Fast moving forces would sweep through enemy territory with the intent of pillaging moveable goods of worth and destroying what remained. As well as gaining booty and causing severe economic hardship, the raid struck at a lord's legitimacy to rule by demonstrating their inability to protect either their people or their lands. See, for example, J. Gillingham, 'Richard I and the Science of War in the Middle Ages', *War and Government in the Middle Ages*, ed. J. Gillingham and J.C. Holt (Woodbridge, 1984), pp. 78–91.

In 1168 the Hennuyers charged down and defeated a French tournament team led by Philip of Alsace, count of Flanders. A tournament at Trazegnies in 1170 turned into a full-scale battle when Duke Godfrey of Brabant came arrayed for war. Heavily outnumbered, by skilful use of the ground, Baldwin V routed his opponents, killing or capturing many Brabanters.[180]

These two victories were important for two very different reasons. So notorious had the mercenary troops of Brabant become, that their name was synonymous with a ruthless and savage approach to war.[181] Defeating them in such a decisive manner secured the Hennuyers' reputation as hardened and canny fighters. In comparison, Philip of Alsace was renowned for his skills at tournament, having led his team to a string of successes across the circuit. He was well known for employing guile to secure a victory. Indeed, Henry the Young King's ruse of not joining the mêlée until the opposing teams were committed had long been employed by Count Philip of Flanders.[182] In defeating Philip of Alsace at a tournament, the count of Hainaut gained prestige and, given his apparent dislike for his cousin, no small measure of personal satisfaction without undue risk to his county.

For Henry the Young King, the tournament circuit provided subtly different opportunities. Crowned co-monarch by his father in 1170, Henry gained title, but lacked both regal power and landed wealth. Deprived of the ability to reward his followers with titles, lands, or fortuitous marriages, Henry the Young King could secure them wealth through victory on the simulated battlefields of Europe.[183] In turn, victory and the opportunity to dispense patronage and *largesse* (generosity) promoted Henry the Young King's status amongst the noble elites of Europe, establishing a reputation as a paragon of knighthood.[184]

Tournaments were also essential to a knight seeking patronage and advancement, such as William Marshal prior to his joining the household of Henry the Young King. If unable to remain within the household in which they were raised or to gain revenues from familial holdings, young knights would be forced to seek employment elsewhere. Analysis of the potential strength of King Richard's household on crusade in the next chapter indicates that the short-term recruitment of individuals and entire households was normal in time of war. Secure employment, however, meant gaining

---

[180] Gilbert of Mons, pp. 180–5.
[181] K. DeVries, 'Medieval Mercenaries, Methodology, Definitions, and Problems', *Mercenaries and Paid Men, The Mercenary Identity in the Middle Ages*, ed. J. France (Leiden and Boston, 2008), pp. 51–2.
[182] *HGM*, lines 2719–29.
[183] For more on potential income from ransoming captive knights, see *HGM*, lines 4489–541; Asbridge, *Greatest Knight*, pp. 124–6.
[184] Strickland, *Henry the Young King*, p. 239–58.

entry into an aristocratic military household, which required connections and a reputation.

As spaces for cultural interaction, unlike mannered courts, feasts, and religious festivals, tournaments were the sole preserve of the martial elites. In this environment, the as yet uncodified rules for noble conduct exemplified by the *preudomme* can be observed stripped of ecclesiastical influence. It was a *habitus*, an environment of behavioural and material expectations,[185] built on the performance of *geste* (a heroic exploit or deed) and pledges of faith. Having pledged to pay a ransom, for example, a knight would be released and could return to the mêlée but was then expected to present himself prior to the banquet to redeem his vow. It was also a highly developed social network that increased the chances of two nobles having a network contact in common, also known as the 'small-world problem'.[186] Having established the crucial role played by tournaments in the elite culture of north-western Europe, the next section considers the extent to which the tournament circuit disseminated crusading as a behavioural and martial expectation.

The Tournament at Lagny-sur-Marne and the Third Crusade

The tourney organised in Lagny-sur-Marne in November 1179 to celebrate the coronation of Philip II of France provides an excellent example of a location where such cultural interactions could take place and the social network can be observed in action. It highlights the intersection between chivalric behaviour and military training. In terms of location, it was situated to the east of Paris, on the border with Champagne.[187] The biography of William Marshal provides us with a rare list of participants by region. Of the three thousand knights said to be present, in addition to Philip II, eighty-seven of the participants are named in *L'Histoire de Guillaume le Marechal*. Despite the absence of members of the French royal family on crusade in the Levant, such as Peter of Courtenay, Henry of Troyes, and Philip of Dreux,[188] at least twenty-one of those listed were to join the Third Crusade just over a decade later.[189]

---

[185] As discussed in the Introduction, *habitus* is a concept developed by French sociologist, Pierre Bourdieu, see *L'Amour de l'art* (Paris, 1966) and, in more detail, *Distinction: A Social Critique of the Judgement of Taste*, trans. R. Nice (London, 1984), pp. 169–225.
[186] The small-world experiment comprised several experiments conducted by Stanley Milgram and other researchers examining the average path length for social networks of people in the United States. These experiments are often associated by the term 'six degrees of separation', but Milgram did not use this phrase himself; S. Milgram, 'The Small World Problem', *Psychology Today*, 2 (1967), 60–7.
[187] Lagny-sur-Marne was an established location for tournaments and part of it is now occupied by Disneyland Paris, Crouch, *Tournament*, p. 51.
[188] Hamilton, *Leper King and His Heirs*, p. 145. The expedition of 1179 also included participant in the Third Crusade, Everard I of Chacenay.
[189] *HGM*, lines 4457–4969.

The listed participants in the Third Crusade came from across the spectrum of the warrior elite. A handful were powerful lords. Hugh III, duke of Burgundy, for example, was a regional magnate and of sufficient stature that Philip Augustus appointed him to be commander of the French crusader contingent when the king departed from Acre in 1191. As seneschal of Flanders, Hellin of Wavrin served alongside Count Philip of Alsace and both were to die on the Third Crusade. As mentioned in Chapter Two, Hellin was joined on crusade by his brothers: Robert I of Wavrin and Roger, bishop of Cambrai, but neither of them were listed as present at Lagny-sur-Marne.

Alexander of Arsic, Baldwin of Béthune, William of Cayeux, Engelram of Fiennes, Roger of Harcourt, Robert of la Mare, and John of Préaux were from the baronage, lords who might be expected to have modest retinues of their own. Baldwin of Béthune, for example, was a knight-banneret in Henry the Young King's retinue, and Alexander of Arsic is described as commanding between fifteen and twenty knights on the Third Crusade.[190] Others, such as Baldwin le Carron, would gain their inheritance sometime between the tournament and the Third Crusade.

Most of those listed were, however, household knights, such as William IV des Barres, Robert of Beaurain, Geoffrey of Brulon, Gerard Talbot, and John of Préaux's brothers: Peter, Roger, and William. Indeed, eighteen of the listed members of the Third Crusade were riding in Henry the Young King's *mesnie*, and the majority would go on to join King Richard's contingent in the Holy Land.[191]

However, some notable figures from the list did not go on the Third Crusade. In 1187 William Marshal had only recently returned from fulfilling Henry the Young King's vow to go to the Holy Land and was, in due course, to be one of the co-justiciars left to administrate England in Richard's absence.[192] Other veterans of the Young King's tournament team also held positions of responsibility during Richard's absence on Crusade. For example, Henry of Longchamp was appointed sheriff of Herefordshire in 1189 and Robert Tresgoz was made castellan of Salisbury Castle in 1190.[193]

---

[190] Asbridge, *Greatest Knight*, p. 133; Ambroise, line 10457; *Itinerarium*, p. 389.

[191] Geoffrey of Brulon, Stephen of Tours, Baldwin of Béthune, William of Cayeux, Alan of Fontaine, Robert of Beaurain, Roger of Harcourt, Baldwin le Carron, Alexander Arsic, Robert of la Mare, John of Préaux and his brothers, Peter, Roger and William, Henry of Hastings, Gerard Talbot, and Engelram of Fiennes, lord of Martock, who went on both the Third and Fourth Crusades. Although with Henry the Young King at Lagny-sur-Marne, William IV des Barres entered the service of King Philip II and formed part of his retinue on the Third Crusade. Those not with the Young King were Hugh, duke of Burgundy, Philip, count of Flanders, and Hellin of Wavrin, seneschal of Flanders. Although there is no evidence he joined the Third Crusade, a Robert Fitz-Walter joined the Fifth Crusade; Powell, *Anatomy of a Crusade*, pp. 77, 115.

[192] Asbridge, *Greatest Knight*, pp. 163–71.

[193] PR2 RI (1190), pp. 45, 117.

Some, perhaps, remained at home for familial interests, such as David of Scotland, who had recently been granted the earldom of Huntington and had made an advantageous marriage.[194] Others were in the service of non-crusaders. Unlike his brothers who served as part of Richard's household, as is covered in more detail in the next chapter, Engelram of Préaux was in the service of the king's brother, John, and remained with his lord in the West.[195]

A number, such as William IV des Barres' father, William the Elder, and Count Robert of Dreux, had died between participating in the tournament at Lagny-sur-Marne in 1179 and the fall of Jerusalem to Saladin in 1187. Much like the descendants of many of those in receipt of money-fiefs, the sons of participants at Lagny-sur-Marne were to join the Third Crusade. In addition to Robert II of Dreux and his brother, the bishop of Beauvais, who were discussed in Chapter One, Alan, Fulk, and Guy of Fontaines served in the Holy Land.[196] Robert III of Stuteville's younger brother; Osmund, was on the expedition; Stephen of Longchamp was linked to the tourney through an elder brother, Henry; and the Third Crusade participant Walter IV of Vienne by his brother, Geoffrey. The reference to the count of Soissons probably relates to Conon of Nesle rather than his crusading younger brother, Raoul III. Raoul went on both the Third Crusade and to Toulouse in 1218. Harduin de Fougères may well have been related to Ralph II de Fougères, as might Odo of Plessis to Philip of Plessis, who would later join the Templars.

Unfortunately, although seemingly well-known names at the time, many of the listed participants cannot, at present, be traced for the period under consideration. Some likely participants are not included in the list preserved in William Marshal's biography. Given Matthew of Walincourt's defeat of William Marshal *c.*1168 and their subsequent disagreement at a tournament at Eu a decade later, it is unsurprising that Matthew was not listed amongst the knights of the Low Countries. However, given the mention of other members of Baldwin V of Hainaut's *mesnie*, such as Baldwin le Carron and William of Cayeux, it is likely that he was also at the tournament.[197]

This is not to suggest that the tournament at Lagny-sur-Marne was directly linked to recruitment to the Third Crusade in the same way as a tournament at the castle of Écry in Champagne at the beginning of Advent in 1199 was related to participation in the Fourth Crusade.[198] Rather, it

---

[194] David was the younger brother of William the Lion, king of Scotland.
[195] TNA C 52/22 *carte antique* roll X, m.2d, no. 28; he was married to the sister of Ranulf, earl of Chester, *Gesta Regis*, Vol. 2, p. 146.
[196] Gilbert of Mons, pp. 139, 274, 328.
[197] Matthew of Walincourt had been a member of Count Baldwin V's tournament team, but died at the siege of Acre, Gilbert of Mons, p. 274; *HGM*, lines 3332–52.
[198] Geoffrey of Villardouin, chronicler of the Fourth Crusade, recounted how Count

served as a point of diffusion for elite military culture, which included crusading. It is clear that the tournament was central to the elite secular cultures of north-western Europe and the social networks of the noble elites themselves. In terms of pragmatic military effectiveness, as highlighted by *L'Histoire de Guillaume le Marechal*, tournaments provided the opportunity for men to fight together as a *conroi* and for the households of bannerets and lords to practise working together in squadrons.[199] In conjunction with the Third Crusade acting as a superordinate goal, the personal relationships, shared military culture, and tactical techniques developed at tournaments were the foundation for knights from across Christendom, but especially from north-western Europe, to fight stirrup-to-stirrup in the Holy Land.

Crusading and Community

This final thematic chapter has highlighted the diversity of the links between members of the noble network of north-western Europe and those who took the Cross and joined the Third Crusade in particular. In addition to sharing associations with specific religious foundations or orders, and enjoying ties of kinship and a crusading ancestry, participants on the Third Crusade were also trading partners, neighbours, and comrades in arms. That is, more than a single tie could be operative at any one time. The data from this chapter demonstrates that the resulting social network has *propinquitious* influences.

The noble actors that constitute our nodes not only made up connectivity-based clusters; they were not only physical neighbours, members of extended families, and linked to the same religious foundations. Through their measure of similarity, many of them were also social network neighbours based on common social values and norms. As highlighted by the influence of the tournament on our noble network, there is evidence of an imagined elite community, a social construct that was not bound by political borders or fealty, but spread across north-western Europe and perhaps beyond. It also demonstrates a high degree of social assortativity, a preference for actors to attach to others who are similar in some way, so that the overall social network is *homophilous*. Acceptance of money-fiefs and participation in tournaments also serve to highlight those members of the noble elite that had the expeditionary mindset required to undertake a crusade.

Thibaud III of Champagne and Brie and his cousin, Louis, count of Blois and Chartres, took the Cross at a tournament at the castle of Écry (just north of Reims) in late November 1199, following a speech by Fulk of Neuilly. See, E.H. McNeal, 'Fulk of Neuilly and the Tournament of Écry', *Speculum*, 28 (1953), 371–5.

[199] These *conroi*, Matthew Bennett argues, 'were made up of the [military] household, local and kin groupings, presumably people who knew each other well'; Bennett, 'Why Chivalry?', p. 58.

4

The Household of King Richard I at the Time of the Third Crusade

For if we do not take the Cross, we shall lose the king; and if we do take the Cross we shall lose God, because we shall not be take the Cross for him, but fear of the king.[1]

John of Joinville, 'La Vie de saint Louis', *c*.1309

In November 1187 Richard, count of Poitou, took the cross at Tours Cathedral.[2] By mid 1190 he had been crowned king of England and had departed on the Third Crusade, only returning some four years later following his release from captivity in Germany. This case study revisits the question of how Richard succeeded in attracting members of the nobility to his crusading contingent whilst ensuring the stability of his realm. In analysing the functions and roles of members of King Richard's military household during the Third Crusade, it offers deeper insights into how medieval armies were commanded in battle, especially crusader armies. It also presents a new perspective on Richard's approach to loyalty, homage, and reciprocity, which is more in line with the pragmatism of *L'Histoire de Guillaume le Marechal* than more romantic depictions of allegiance.

Historians have accused Richard of inept governance of the Angevin realm and lack of interest in English affairs. Norgate portrayed him as 'totally destitute of his father's business capabilities' and Stubbs dismissed him as 'a bad son, a bad husband, a selfish ruler and a vicious man'.[3] In general,

---

[1] 'Car se nous ne nous croisons, nous perdrons le roy; et se nous ne nous croisons, nous perdrons Dieu, que nous ne nous croiserons pas pour li, mais pour paour du roy': John of Joinville, 'La Vie de saint Louis', *RHF*, Vol. 20 (1840), 299. Whilst aimed at Louis IX of France and participation in the Seventh Crusade (1248–52), this quote aptly reflects the potential pressure on a noble subject to follow their king on crusade.

[2] The new cathedral was set atop the one in which Richard's great-grandfather, Fulk V of Anjou, had taken the Cross some sixty years earlier, Gillingham, *Richard*, p. 87. Given that *Audita tremendi*, the bull that launched the Third Crusade, was escorted by papal legates and the cathedral's distance from Rome, it is almost certain that the ceremony pre-empted its arrival in Tours.

[3] K. Norgate, *England under the Angevin Kings*, Vol. 2 (London, 1887), p. 337; *Itinerarium*, pp. xvii. For more unfavourable views on Richard I see; S. Painter, 'The Third

however, this does not match his depiction in contemporary chronicles, and recent research has done much to rehabilitate Richard's reputation.[4]

In many ways, Richard was in a unique situation. He ascended the throne of England having previously taken the Cross and, despite threats to his position – both internal and from beyond the borders of his realm – he remained committed to fulfilling his vow to regain the True Cross and recover Jerusalem.[5] Notwithstanding his father's preparations, that he was able to mount a major expedition to the other side of Europe less than twelve months after becoming king of England was a considerable achievement. Moreover, he sought to establish a robust structure of governance prior to departing on crusade, ensuring that contingencies were in place to deal with potential threats, notably that from his younger brother, John, as well as from King Philip II of France.[6] Despite the many threats, the Third Crusade arguably offered the potential for him to cement his hold over a disparate realm. Many of the measures he undertook can be traced through the use of members of his household – both on crusade and to secure his realm. Nevertheless, limited research has been carried out on the composition of the royal household during the course of the Third Crusade.

For this case study of King Richard household, Richard Heiser's research into Richard's sheriffs and constables, and the households of his justiciars proved invaluable.[7] The importance of local networks is striking in each of

---

Crusade, Richard the Lionhearted and Philip Augustus', *A History of the Crusades*, Vol. 2, ed. K.M. Setton (Madison, WI, 1969), pp. 53–4; and, M. Markowski, 'Richard the Lionheart: Bad King, Bad Crusader', *JMH*, 23 (1997), 352.

[4] See, for example; J. Flori, *Richard Coeur de Lion: le roi-chevalier* (Paris, 1999); trans. into English, *Richard the Lionheart: King and Knight*, trans. J. Birrell (Edinburgh, 2006), pp. 397–412; Gillingham, *Richard I*; M. Aurell (ed.), *Noblesses de l'espace Plantagenêt (1154–1224)* (*Cahiers de Civilisation Médiévale, numéro spécial XI*) (Poitiers, 2001); and, R.V. Turner, 'The Problem of Survival for the Angevin "Empire": Henry II's and His Sons' Visions versus Late Twelfth-Century Realities', *American Historical Review*, 100 (1995), pp. 78–96.

[5] It is almost certain that Richard was unaware of the fall of Jerusalem to Saladin when he took the Cross. *Audita tremendi* was written prior to knowledge of Saladin's capture of the Holy City and, as discussed in note 2, it is unlikely even that the papal bull had reached Tours when Richard took his vow.

[6] Gillingham, *Richard I*, p. 348; J.C. Holt, '*Ricardus Rex Anglorum et Dux Normannorum*', *Magna Carta and Medieval Government* (London, 1985), pp. 67–83; C.W. Hollister and J.W. Baldwin, 'The Rise of Administrative Kingship: Henry I and Philip Augustus', *American Historical Review*, 83 (1978), 867–905. See also, N. Barratt, 'The English Revenue of Richard I', *EHR*, 116 (2001), 635–56; and R.V. Turner, '*Ricardus Dux Aquitanorum et Comes Andegavorum*', *HSJ*, 13 (2004), 151–73.

[7] Heiser, 'Castles, Constables, and Politics', pp. 19–36; 'Richard I and His Appointments to English Shrievalties', *EHR*, 112 (1997), 1–19; 'The Sheriffs of Richard I: Trends of Management as Seen in the Shrieval Appointments from 1189 to 1194', *HSJ*, 4 (1992), 109–122; 'The Households of the Justiciars of Richard I: An Enquiry into the Second Level of Medieval English Government', *HSJ*, 2 (1990), 223–35.

these studies. Where there was an absence of a hereditary claim, Richard's selection of sheriffs, constables, and castellans favoured local men, such as Richard of Engaigne, lord of Bulwick, in Northamptonshire, and William Fitz-Alan, lord of Oswestry and Clun, in Shropshire.[8] By avoiding the imposition of foreign-born royal appointees, I argue here, King Richard drew the local baronage into the royal network rather than excluding them from the management of the Angevin realm.

As with Heiser's review of the *familia regis* based on Richard's *acta*, Landon's major work on the itinerary of the king provides the foundation for this section.[9] However, the work of Holt and Vincent has been vital in extending our knowledge of the *acta* of Kings Henry II and Richard.[10] In addition to revealing many additional charters, their research has identified a few previously accepted charters as forgeries. In addition, on returning to the original texts, it was possible to find an occasional lapse in Landon's data.[11]

The significant departure from previous work on Richard's household undertaken in this study has been the broadening of source material to include data from chronicles, letters, and other official documents, such as the Pipe Rolls. This was inspired by Powell's aforementioned research on the Fifth Crusade and has subsequently been adopted by Heiser.[12] The resulting list was interrogated to consider each actor's likely membership of the *familia regis*, and filtered to distinguish between close family, lay and ecclesiastical magnates, and other actors. A short list of 282 actors formed the basis of further analysis and was then considered in relation to such questions as social and regional background, previous experience, function/role, participation in major events, such as the Third Crusade, and potential rewards for service. This total included twenty-six lay and thirty-four ecclesiastical magnates to provide context, a handful of whom

---

[8] Heiser, 'Castles, Constables, and Politics', p. 19; PR2 RI (1190), pp. 29, 156. For discussion on the impact of royal policy in the Welsh Marches, see B. Holden, *Lords of the Central Marches: English Aristocracy and Frontier Society, 1087–1265* (Oxford, 2008).

[9] Heiser, 'Royal *Familiares* of King Richard I', pp. 25–50; Landon, *Itinerary*. See also, F. Chauvenet, 'L'entourage de Richard Coeur de Lion en Poitou et en Aquitaine', *La cour Plantagenêt*, ed. Aurell (Poitiers, 2000), pp. 138–49; and, Billoré, 'Noblesse normande', pp. 151–66.

[10] *Acta of Henry II and Richard I*, Vol. 2, ed. N. Vincent (Kew, 1996).

[11] For example no. 359 has been found to be a forgery from the Courtois archive and Rog[ero] de Pratell' (Roger of Préaux) is missing from no. 163, Landon, *Itinerary*, pp. 19, 52. For more on the Courtois archive, see Sayers, 'English Charters from the Third Crusade', p. 197; and Bautier, 'La collection des chartes de croisade', pp. 382–6.

[12] This methodology was first laid out in my MA thesis and expanded upon in S. Bennett, 'La mesnie de roi Richard 1er', pp. 70–8; and was adopted by R.R. Heiser, 'The Court of the Lionheart on Crusade, 1190–2', *JMH*, 43 (2017), 505–22.

can be firmly placed in the household, such as William of Mandeville and William of Longchamp.[13]

Using multiple strands of evidence proved beneficial in developing a fuller picture of an individual's relationship with King Richard, as well as their activities between 1189 and 1192. A focus on charter evidence to the exclusion of contemporary chronicles would have left several prominent actors unaccounted for, which risks a partial view of the *familia regis* at this time. As introduced in my article on functions within Richard's crusading household, as a methodology it provides a broad range of actors from which to draw logical deductions on the functions, size, social composition, and background of Richard's military household, as well as to consider the likely composition of King Richard's inner circle, his *familiares*, during the course of the Third Crusade.[14]

Functions Within the Royal Household

Analysis of the composition of the household and the potential domination of certain groups further aids our understanding of King Richard's approach to the management of his realm, diplomacy, and tactical command and control, as well as the influence of his household on the course of the Third Crusade.[15]

Despite previous problems identifying members of the Angevin *familia regis*, significant research by Stephen Church into the royal household of King John, drawing on three surviving lists of his knights from 1209, 1210, and 1215, as well as a further three lists of household knights from the early years of King Henry III's reign, has laid the foundations for renewed attempts to define this group.[16] Belief in the existence of a permanent cadre of professional mounted warriors within the *familia regis* of the Angevins fits within contemporary military practice in north-western Europe. In Turner's review of the households of King Henry II's sons, he concluded that Richard's *mesnie* was almost exclusively Poitevin before 1189, 'except for the occasional Angevin or Norman'.[17] From 1189, I argue that, rather than a Poitevin dominated household supplemented by mercenaries, Richard utilised a strong Anglo-Norman contingent within a substantial retinue of

---

[13] The full list of subjects is contained in Appendix 2.
[14] Bennett, 'La mesnie de roi Richard 1er', pp. 70–8.
[15] For a comparison of the households of Henry the Young King and Richard as count of Poitou see, Turner, 'Households of the Sons', pp. 49–62.
[16] S.D. Church, *The Household Knights of King John* (Cambridge, 1999), pp. 3–4; also, 'The Rewards of Royal Service in the Household of King John: A Dissenting Opinion', *EHR*, 110 (1995), 277–302; and, 'The Knights of John's Household: A Question of Numbers', *Thirteenth Century England: Proceedings of the Newcastle upon Tyne Conference 1991*, Vol. 4 (1992), pp. 151–65.
[17] Turner, 'Households of the Sons', p. 61. See also, Chauvenet, 'L'entourage de Richard', pp. 137–49; and, Billoré, 'Noblesse normande', pp. 151–66.

professional knights, many of whom had previously served Henry the Young King or King Henry II and would remain in the household after King Richard's release from captivity.[18] Heiser suggested that bishops and, to a lesser extent, earls dominated Richard's royal court, but that the royal household became 'increasingly more secular and less distinguished in social rank' as it headed east.[19] However, this study shows that both ecclesiastical and lay magnates continued to be closely associated with the *familia regis* in the Holy Land and that the household was not the sole preserve of low-born knights. The key methodological difference of using a combination of the charter evidence and narrative histories tells us is that King Richard strove to include all ranks of the nobility in his decision-making process.

As discussed earlier, the military *mesnie* formed the foundation of the royal army: it was its permanent, professional cadre.[20] Yet, this was but one of many roles a member of the *familia regis* could fulfil. Knights and clerics appointed to the bureaucracies of the Exchequer and Curia Regis, as well as those who physically remained in the royal household to serve 'the king on a daily, more intimate, basis', had an essential role to perform, not least in overseeing the day-to-day administration of the realm.[21] Henry II's household consisted of three elements: military retainers, a secretariat, and provisioning officials charged with supply of food, drink, and other necessities. In addition to serving as armed retainers, some knights also held provisioning offices as steward, butler, and chamberlain.[22] The knights, sometimes called bachelors, were also employed in military positions such as aides-de-camp and staff officers, bodyguards, escorts, couriers, and liaison officers. Both the knights and the clerics might be used as representatives of their lord, for example, as court officials, castellans, ambassadors, and territorial agents, such as sheriffs.[23] As Church stated,

> [It] followed that it was the household itself which made preparations for, and organised the conduct of the campaign. It was the king's stewards and the king's marshals who were responsible for the administration and discipline of the army, and the clerks of the wardrobe who were responsible for its supplies and wages.[24]

---

[18] See, for example, Strickland, *Henry the Young King*, p. 317.

[19] Heiser, 'Royal *Familiares*', p. 28.

[20] King Henry II's household provided his councillors and judges, sheriffs, governors, and diplomats, as well as his military bodyguard, Hosler, *Henry II*, pp. 103–4.

[21] Heiser, 'Royal *Familiaries*', p. 25; see also, 'English Shrievalties', pp. 25–50; 'Households of the Justiciars', pp. 223–35.

[22] Turner, 'Households of the Sons', p. 52. See also *Constitutio Domus Regis*, ed. and trans. Church, pp. 15–17.

[23] For example, Richard I chose a fellow veteran of the Third Crusade, Saul of Bruil, to deliver a message to King Henry of Jerusalem in 1194, *Chronica*, Vol. 3, p. 233.

[24] Church, *Household Knights*, pp. 1–2; see also Tout, *Chapters*, Vol. 2, pp. 137, 139–40.

Lacking government officials, such as *prévôts* or *baillis*, such knights were the most frequent attestors of Henry the Young King's charters.[25] Similarly, as King Richard moved away from his realm, his *familiares* or *intimates*, supplemented by those barons who enjoyed a particularly close association with the household, replaced territorial agents on the witness lists. Whilst the unique nature of crusading campaigns could distort the nature of the relationship between monarch and household knight, when used in concert with narrative evidence, the *acta* enhance the visibility of these men.

A review of the office holders indicates that the delineation of tasks was not as established in Richard's household as outlined above. The functions of the officers of the court seem to have been in a state of flux during the late twelfth/early thirteenth centuries. The steward had replaced the constable as leader of the household knights under Henry II, and by John's reign, had taken control of most of the functions of the household.[26] However, Jordan of Le Hommet was linked to the office of constable and took an active military role in the crusade until his death in 1192.[27] Similarly, when given command of a force of one hundred knights and five hundred serjeants to protect Antioch, Robert of Quincy is described by Roger of Howden as King Richard's constable.[28] The commitment of this force supports Andrew Buck's argument that Bohemond III lacked the military resources to intervene in the Third Crusade.[29] Saladin was mindful of a threat from Antioch and had deployed troops to monitor the principality. It is likely that Robert of Quincy and his men were dispatched to prevent Saladin redeploying those troops against the Third Crusade. It would follow that Bohemond III's attempts to recover Jabala and Latakia in autumn 1191 were timed to coincide with King Richard's march on Ascalon.

However, the roles of castellan (castle constable) and sheriff in England were well established by the time of Richard's ascension to the throne.[30]

---

[25] Turner, 'Households of the Sons', p. 52.

[26] Jolliffe, *Angevin Kingship*, pp. 210–25; Church, *Household Knights*, pp. 8–10.

[27] For, example, he arrived at the siege of Acre shortly after King Richard I and joined the relief force to Jaffa, *Itinerarium*, pp. 217, 405; Ambroise, lines 4707, 10963. For discussion on his links with the office of constable see, Bennett, 'La mesnie de roi Richard 1er', p. 74, as well as Heiser, 'Court of the Lionheart', p. 513, n. 46.

[28] 802 'Robertum de Quinci constabularium et ducem illorum': *Gesta Regis*, Vol. 2, p. 185. Roger of Howden's experience in Angevin service as a cleric and high-level diplomat, his presence in the royal household in Acre until early August 1191, and the overall reliability of his accounts, make it very highly likely that Robert of Quincy undertook this task. Howden confirms the existence of this force in his more considered later work but refines Robert's appointment to guardian and leader – 'custodem illorum et ducem': *Chronica*, Vol. 3, p. 125.

[29] A.D. Buck, *The Principality of Antioch and its Frontiers in the Twelfth Century* (Woodbridge, 2017), pp. 56–7.

[30] Heiser, 'Castles, Constables, and Politics', pp. 20–2.

There was a degree of overlap, with about half of all royal castles being in the hands of sheriffs, which complicated the daily affairs of the post holder. However, the castellan's primary task was maintaining his fortress in a state of readiness, drawing funds from treasury and shire farms to fund building maintenance, as well as purchasing provisions and military supplies. Unlike in Aquitaine, only a handful of royal castles were held by hereditary castellans,[31] which allowed the king or his justiciar to place loyal members of his household in these positions, especially those with local connections, such as Simon of Pattishall at Northampton castle.[32] In fact, only three castellans appointed by King Richard apparently lacked local influence, such as through existing membership of the respective noble neighbourhood: Hugh of Puiset, Robert of Tresgoz, and Roger Fitz-Reinfrey.[33]

Sheriffs were similarly engaged in the day-to-day security of the realm and were King Richard's most important local officials in England.[34] In addition to managing the collection of taxes and submitting semi-annual accounts to the Exchequer, sheriffs oversaw law enforcement, shire courts, and the militia.[35] In stark contrast to earlier claims that shrievalties were 'sold frivolously to the highest bidder', the data firmly supports Heiser's argument that Richard demonstrated foresight in his selection of sheriffs prior to departing for the Holy Land, as well as on his return in 1194.[36] For example, he placed experienced administrators in locations critical to

---

[31] Such as Beauchamp claims to Bedford and Worcester, H.M. Colvin, R.A. Brown, and A.J. Taylor, *The History of the King's Works*, Vol. 2 (London, 1963), pp. 558, 771–2, 888.

[32] S. Bond, 'The Medieval Constables of Windsor Castle', *EHR*, 82 (1967), 226. For Pattishall, see PR4 RI (1192), pp. 200–1.

[33] Appointed to Windsor, Salisbury, and Wallingford, respectively.

[34] In his examination of Richard I's distribution of patronage in 1189, J.C. Holt saw a 'single unique effort' with the King as the driving force, '*Ricardus Rex*', p. 73.

[35] The noble elite identified themselves with the heavy cavalry, but infantrymen formed an essential part of medieval armies. Whilst Henry II raised funds from scutage to hire mercenaries, infantrymen were also raised through laws and mandates. The Anglo-Danish *fyrd*, for example, required every five hides of land to provide, equip, and maintain, one soldier, and this continued after the Conquest. King Henry II reformed the *fyrd* through the second of two assizes. The first was issued at Le Mans (1180) and pertained to the king of England's continental subjects; the Assize of Arms was issued shortly afterwards. Both specified the arms and equipment each freeman was required to maintain based on their financial situation and which the king could call upon as required. By this means, King Henry II secured access to a body of infantrymen, independent of his nobility. King Philip II of France and Count Philip of Alsace copied the first of these assizes almost immediately, *Chronica*, Vol. 2, pp. 253, 260–3. See also, Hosler, *Henry II*, pp. 113–19.

[36] For example, Morris concluded that Richard I saw shrievalties as saleable commodities; W.A. Morris, *The Medieval English Sheriff to 1300* (Manchester, 1927), p. 138. It is an argument that was comprehensively rebutted by Heiser, 'English Shrievalties', pp. 1–19. See also, R.R. Heiser, 'The Sheriffs of Richard I', pp. 109–222.

the muster of English elements of his crusading fleet: Henry of Cornhill retained the shrievalty of Surrey and gained Kent, whilst Oger Fitz-Oger moved from Bedfordshire to Hampshire, which included the important ports of Southampton and Portchester.

Similar attention was paid to the potentially troublesome Welsh marches with the appointment of Henry of Longchamp, William of Beauchamp, William Fitz-Alan, and William Marshal to neighbouring shrievalties and placing the key castles of Carmarthen, Llawhaden, and Swansea under William of Braose.[37] With Hugh of Puiset set in the north to keep a wary eye on the king of Scots, King Richard was also involved in the selection of territorial agents adjacent to John's new holdings in the West Country, Derbyshire, and Nottingham, as well as those in Yorkshire, site of his natural or half-brother, Geoffrey Fitz-Henry's new archbishopric.[38] It is also of note that four counties that provide some of the strongest Pipe Roll data on crusaders were administered by sheriffs that retained their positions in 1189, whilst another two that provide useful data came under the former sheriff of Sussex, William Rufus.[39]

Richard's unique position of having taken the Cross prior to ascending to the throne of England also required attention to be paid to the matter of the regency.[40] Whilst Turner has highlighted the influence of Eleanor of Aquitaine on the rule of the kingdom whilst its king was away on crusade, as noted earlier, she was not appointed as King Richard's regent and may well have planned to join him on crusade.[41] Instead, in September 1189, Richard selected two justiciars to rule England. Both were powerful magnates: Hugh of Le Puiset, bishop of Durham, and William of Mandeville, earl of Essex.[42] They were aided by an experienced group of *appares* (associate justiciars): Geoffrey Fitz-Peter, Robert of Wheatfield, Roger Fitz-Reinfrey, William Brewer, and William Marshal.

When Earl William died unexpectedly, the king elevated his chancellor, William of Longchamp, to *summus justiciar* and replaced Robert of Wheatfield and Roger Fitz-Reinfrey with Hugh Bardolf.[43] Contrary to Appleby's

---

[37] PR2 RI (1190), pp. 8–9, 48.

[38] Heiser, 'English Shrievalties', p. 11.

[39] William Fitz-Hervey in Norfolk/Suffolk and Otto Fitz-William in Essex/Hertfordshire, and William Rufus replaced Oger Fitz-Oger in Bedfordshire and Buckinghamshire; Heiser, 'Sheriffs of Richard I', pp. 120–1.

[40] B. Wilkinson, 'The Government of England during the Absence of Richard I on Crusade', *Bulletin of John Rylands University*, 28 (1944), 485–509.

[41] Turner, *Eleanor of Aquitaine*, pp. 265–9.

[42] R.V. Turner and R.R. Heiser, *The Reign of Richard the Lionheart, Ruler of the Angevin Empire, 1189–99* (Harlow, 2005), pp. 87–109. See also, F.J. West, *The Justiciarship of England, 1066–1232* (Cambridge, 1966), pp. 65–6.

[43] *Gesta Regis*, 2, pp. 101, 106. Robert of Wheatfield died shortly afterwards, so his replacement may have been due to ill health. Hugh of Puiset, Geoffrey Fitz-Peter, Hugh

claim that Richard's preparations were 'hasty and ill-considered', all the *appares* were former members of Henry II's household and all but William Marshal had previously served as justices.[44] Whilst less familiar with the kingdom of England, William of Longchamp's status as papal legate reflected the potential importance of the curia during the king's absence.[45] As previously discussed, it was a governing structure that would undergo severe trial due to the machinations of first John, count of Mortain, and then Philip Augustus.

Steward

Drawn from the Old English *stīweard* or warden of the household, the steward oversaw the day-to-day running of the *mesnie* whilst their counterparts in Angevin France, seneschals, administered provinces, such as Gascony. The house of Leicester had provided the Lord High Stewards of England from 1154 onwards, which was one of the great hereditary offices of England, the others being the Master Chamberlain and High Marshal.

While the steward did not appear to Jolliffe to have had a leadership function over the knights on campaign under Henry II, during the Third Crusade one of King Richard's stewards was prominent during the assault on Darum in 1191 and helped the earl of Leicester in the rescue of a Christian caravan in 1192.[46] By the time of John's reign, stewards were making an important contribution to logistics and, on occasion, acting as military commanders.[47] Richard II of Le Hommet, Roger of Préaux, and Stephen of Longchamp are named as stewards of Richard's household in 1189 and 1190.[48] Both Roger of Préaux and Stephen of Longchamp accompanied the king to Messina.[49] Stephen of Longchamp continued on to the Holy Land and took an active role in the campaign.[50] In addition, William Fitz-Aldelin is described as the king's steward in a charter granting his land in Went

---

Bardolf, and William Brewer had all taken the Cross under Henry II but put aside their vows at King Richard I's behest.

[44] J.T. Appleby, *England Without Richard, 1189–1199* (London and New York, 1965), pp. 19–20, 36. See also, Gillingham, *Richard I*, pp. 116, 121–2, 222–5.

[45] Park, *Papal Protection*, p. 185.

[46] Stephan of Longchamp, Ambroise, lines 9288, 10459; *Itinerarium*, pp. 355, 376, 389.

[47] Church, *Household Knights*, pp. 9–10.

[48] See, for example, *Acta*, 220; *Gesta Regis*, Vol. 2, p. 190; and Landon, *Itinerary*, nos. 145, 206, 236–9.

[49] Landon, *Itinerary*, nos. 347, 354.

[50] In addition to military service, Stephen served as governor of Acre with Bertram of Verdun following the city's capture by the crusaders, *Gesta Regis*, Vol. 2, p. 190. It is probable that Roger also continued with King Richard to the siege of Acre, but unlike his brothers, he is not specifically named in surviving sources.

(Yorkshire) to Durand Fitz-Drogo, his serjeant, prior to William's journey to Jerusalem in 1190.[51]

Richard II of Le Hommet remained in Europe and became constable of Normandy on 6 May 1190.[52] The constables were the martial equivalent of the seneschals in Angevin France, overseeing the defence of King Richard's provinces. It has been argued that the primary function of the steward was that of paymaster to the king's army.[53] Whilst there is no direct evidence of Richard's stewards fulfilling a similar function, a charter from Jaffa dated 1192 named the former seneschal of Anjou and Henry II's treasurer, Stephen of Tours, as steward of the royal household.[54] According to John Baldwin, seneschals of baronial rank were probably no longer involved in domestic tasks in Philip II's court. Those duties were instead discharged by royal chamberlains, such as Adam of Villebeon, who died at the siege of Acre.[55]

Marshal

Derived from the Old Frankish *marah schalh* (horse servant/groom), marshals were originally subordinate to the constable – the count of the stable (*comes stabularius*).[56] As the title suggests, constables were initially responsible for the maintenance of the military stables, but in due course, as described above, the term came to be employed for senior military commanders. By the time of the Third Crusade, marshals were also evolving from servants in charge of a household's horses, equipment, and materiel into officers with important military functions.[57] A century later, under Edward I, stewards were assisted in their command of household knights by the marshals, who also kept muster rolls.[58] Based on a document describing the organisation of John's army in 1213, Church maintained that Angevin marshals fulfilled a similar role to those of Edward I.[59] In Angevin households, as well as those of Edward I and his successors, he argued that, in addition to maintaining muster lists, the marshals upheld

---

[51] *EYC*, Vol. 3, no. 1641.
[52] As mentioned earlier in this section, Richard II's brother Jordan of Le Hommet served as one of Richard I's constables on crusade, see, for example, Ambroise, lines 4707, 10963.
[53] Jolliffe, *Angevin Kingship*, pp. 218–19.
[54] *Acta*, p. 168, no. 220. Stephen of Tours was later reappointed seneschal of Anjou.
[55] Baldwin, *Government of Philip*, p. 55; *Gesta Regis*, Vol. 2, p. 149.
[56] See R.W. Jones, 'Marshalling the Chivalric Elite for War', *A Companion to Chivalry*, ed. R.W. Jones and P. Coss (Woodbridge, 2019), p. 94.
[57] M. Strickland, *War and Chivalry, The Conduct and Perception of War in England and Normandy, 1066–1215* (Cambridge, 1996), p. 38.
[58] Tout, *Chapters*, Vol. 2, pp. 137, 146.
[59] See 'Constitutions of the Royal Army', *Rotuli Litterarum Clausarum, 1204–27* (Record Commission, 1833–44), Vol. 1, p. 164; and discussion of the office of marshal in Church, *Household Knights*, pp. 11–13.

the constitution of the army, enforced its laws, and punished defaulters. In the field, they controlled deployment of the household and, potentially, the army. Closer consideration of their duties, he continued, indicated that the marshals focused on control and acted as the provosts or disciplinarians of the king's army as early as the 1130s.[60]

Around the time of the Third Crusade, the military functions of marshals are also evident in the two main Military Orders: the Templars and the Hospitallers, reflection on which may prove useful in considering Richard I's royal administration. The Templars' French Rule of c.1165 described the marshal as the leading military official, responsible for the collection and distribution of all military equipment and horses. The marshal is identified as commanding Templar forces in the field, and statutes 164 and 165 detailed when the marshal should carry the banner of the Order and how he should personally lead a charge.[61] The statutes also listed the marshal as a senior officer in the Order, outranked only by the master and the seneschal, who took the place of the master when he was absent. They stipulated that the marshal of the Convent of the Temple (in Jerusalem) commanded the arms of the house, as well as all serjeant brothers and men-at-arms.[62]

The Hospitallers had their origin in a pilgrim hospital founded in Jerusalem around 1070, but following the example of the Templars, in time added military service to its works with the frail and the poor.[63] A marshal is first noted for the Hospitallers c.1165.[64] Papal confirmation of the Rule issued in 1185, and Roger de Moulins' statutes of 1187, both survived the Muslim reconquest of Jerusalem, but neither made any mention of military matters.[65] Accounts of the brothers' involvement in battle indicate that the Hospitallers were just as well organised and disciplined as the Templars, with a broadly similar organisation. For example, in *Tractatus de locis et statu sancte terre ierosolimitane*, written 1168–87, the anonymous author described the two military orders in a list of the peoples of the Levant.[66] They are introduced together and the closing line on the Hospitallers suggests that,

---

[60] *Constitutio Domus Regis*, ed. and trans. Church, p. 134.

[61] M. Barber and K. Bate, *The Templars: Selected Sources* (New York, 2002), p. 72.

[62] *Rule of the Templars*, trans. Upton-Ward, pp. 39–66, statutes 77–197. Analysis of those statutes can be found in Bennett, '*Le Règle du Temple* as a Military Manual', pp. 175–88.

[63] A. Luttrell, 'The Hospitallers' Early Written Records', *The Crusades and their Sources: Essays Presented to Bernard Hamilton*, ed. J. France and W.G. Zajac (Aldershot, 1998), pp. 135–54. See also J.G. Schenk, 'Nomadic Violence in the First Latin Kingdom of Jerusalem and the Military Orders', *Reading Medieval Studies*, 36 (2010), pp. 39–55

[64] J. Riley-Smith, *The Knights of St John in Jerusalem and Cyprus, c.1050–1310* (London, 1967), pp. 313–15.

[65] Luttrell, 'Early Written Records', pp. 137–43.

[66] B.Z. Kedar, 'The *Tractatus de locis et statu sancte terre ierosolimitane*', in *The Crusades and Their Sources: Essays Presented to Bernard Hamilton*, ed. J. France and W.G. Zajac (Aldershot, 1998), pp. 111–31.

in addition to their medical responsibilities, they followed similar military practices,[67] 'The Hospitallers wear a white cross on their cloaks, good knights [as they are]; alongside their service as knights, they manage the care of the poor and sick, with their own strict rule'.[68]

The marshal is described as acting as the Hospitallers' military leader in battle following the military reforms laid out under the direction of Master Alfonso of Portugal, the natural son of King Alfonso Henriques, in the Statutes of Margat of 1204/6. In *The Central Convent of the Hospitallers and Templars*, Jochen Burgtorf argues that these were not new regulations, but a codification of practices introduced in the last quarter of the twelfth century.[69] As Helen Nicholson states, 'the lack of early statutes does not indicate a lack of military organisation'.[70] I would also argue that the resemblance of the statutes of Margat to the legislative texts of the Templars enacted prior to 1187 is highly suggestive that the military function of the Hospitaller marshal largely matched that of their Templar equivalent during the Third Crusade.

This formal organisation does not match the picture that emerges from a review of King Richard's household during the Third Crusade, however, and may have been a later development in England. Alternatively, fluidity of structure may be an indication of the unique circumstances of King Richard's household on crusade. In addition to the hereditary master marshals in England – William Marshal and his brother, John – four men are listed as Richard's marshal. Guy of Dive appears in 1189 and 1190 but cannot be traced outside of the Angevin realm.[71] Hugh Bardolf, sheriff under Henry II, appears as a marshal in 1189.[72] Whilst Hugh took the Cross, he was released from his oath and remained in England as a member of the regency council to oversee that part of the realm in King Richard's absence. Hugh the marshal, a Poitevin knight, can be placed in the Holy Land, but was captured by the Muslims outside Acre in 1191 while fighting alongside Hungarian crusaders – possibly in a similar command and control role to that of John Fitz-Luke and Baldwin le Carron, which will be discussed shortly. The other named marshal was Stephen of Thornham, who is also

---

[67] Statute 167 of the Templar Rule stipulated that if a brother were unable to rally to the Templars' banner, he should seek out the Hospitallers and remain with them until able to re-join his own Order: *Rule of the Templars*, p. 60.

[68] 'Hospitalarii vero albam crucem portant in clamide, milites boni, cum ipsa militia pauperum et infirmorum curam gerentes, suam observantiam et disciplinam habentes': Kedar, '*Tractatus*', p. 126.

[69] J. Burgtorf, *The Central Convent of Hospitallers and Templars: History, Organization, and Personnel (1099/1120–1310)* (Leiden and Boston, 2008).

[70] H.J. Nicholson, *The Knights Hospitaller* (Woodbridge, 2001), p. 22.

[71] Landon, *Itinerary*, nos. 41, 68–71, 80–5, 97–101, 167, 189–93, 227–9.

[72] *Gesta Regis*, Vol. 2, p. 101.

described as the king's treasurer.⁷³ Unlike the royal steward, Stephen of Longchamp, Thornham was not included in descriptions of any of the battles or military encounters. Rather, he seemingly acted as a royal ambassador in the Holy Land and was entrusted with the care of Queens Joanna and Berengaria.⁷⁴

The future Master of the Templars, Robert of Sablé, is described as the treasurer of the Crusade rather than of the royal household. This may indicate that this leading vassal of King Richard with extensive lands in the Sarthe valley might have also acted as royal steward and paymaster.⁷⁵ Despite the delineation of functions presented in analysis of the *domus regis*, tasks given to officers of the court by Richard seem to have been driven by requirement, opportunity, and the relationship between the king and the individual concerned.⁷⁶

After the capture of Hugh the marshal, the sources do not indicate a named marshal fulfilling the sort of military tasks outlined above. This potential deficiency may have contributed to weak cohesion in the early stages in the march from Acre, a deficiency King Richard probably addressed through use of the marshals of the Templars and Hospitallers.

On 22 August 1191 the crusader army left Acre to start a fighting march southwards, along the coast towards Jaffa and Ascalon. Mindful of the potential lure of the fleshpots of Acre, King Richard remained with the rear-guard for the first two days of the march. After resting the army on 24 August, he shifted his attention to the vanguard, placing the French contingent in the rear-guard under Hugh III of Burgundy. With Ayyubid forces shadowing the crusader column, fog or sea-mist seemingly caused Hugh's division to slow down and become separated from the rest of the army.⁷⁷ Saladin's brother, al-Adil, was well placed to exploit the resulting gap and the Muslims sallied out of the sand dunes on the column's left flank. When word of the attack reached the king, he led a swift counter-attack to drive off the attack, narrowly averting disaster.⁷⁸

According to Ambroise, John Fitz-Luke (Johan le fiz Lucas) brought news of the attack to King Richard.⁷⁹ John Horace Round identified John Fitz-

---

⁷³ 'Stephanus etiam de Torneham mareschallus regis et thesauraris', *Itinerarium*, p. 185.
⁷⁴ *Chronica*, Vol. 3, p. 228; Ambroise, *The History of the Holy War, Ambroise's Estoire de la Guerre Sainte, I. Translation*, trans. M. Ailes (Woodbridge, 2003), p. 148, n. 558.
⁷⁵ Alternatively, Robert of Sablé may have entered the Order prior to his departure from France. The link between the Templars and international banking, and the crusading nature of the expedition, might have made him the obvious choice for treasurer.
⁷⁶ *Constitutio Domus Regis*, ed. and trans. Church, pp. 15–17.
⁷⁷ It is worth noting here that the French marshal, Aubrey Clément, died in an assault near the 'Cursed Tower' at Acre on 3 July 1191, *Gesta Regis*, Vol. 2, p. 173. See also, Ambroise, lines 4900–2 and *Itinerarium*, pp. 223–9.
⁷⁸ Ambroise, lines 5744–5815.
⁷⁹ Ambroise, line 5783.

Luke's father as being described as a *pincerna* (butler) holding a knight's fee in Gloucestershire in 1166, which was in John Fitz-Luke's hands by 1187.[80] All of this points to John Fitz-Luke being a member of King Richard's household and that he was posted to keep an eye on the rear-guard, as something akin to liaison officer. So, whilst no mention is made of a marshal, it is highly likely that command and control measures were in place, even if they had failed to prevent the rear division from becoming dislocated from the rest of the column. I shall return to Richard's use of liaison officers again shortly, but his immediate solution was to replace Duke Hugh and his French knights with the Hospitallers under Master Garnier of Nablûs and the Order's marshal.

Elsewhere, as with his regency council, Richard seemingly used the position of justiciar to delegate authority, and five such men commanded the royal fleet en route to the Holy Land. They were drawn from across his domains and included long-term household knights such as William of Forz and Richard of Camville. Stephen of Thornham's brother, Robert, commanded a squadron during the Cyprus campaign and was thereafter made co-justiciar of the island alongside Richard of Camville.[81] King Richard's recruitment of members of the less powerful elite families as his officeholders is paralleled by Capetian practice. Philip II's constable, Dreux IV of Merlo, lord of Saint-Bris, might have been influential in Auxerre and in command of 'not a few men' that included in his brother, William, but he was by no means a powerful magnate.[82]

Chamberlains and Other Officers of the Household

As officers in charge of domestic matters, chamberlains were also intimate members of the household and were responsible for that part of the royal revenue paid directly to the *camera regis* as opposed to the Exchequer via the sheriffs. Of the four named royal chamberlains, only one accompanied Richard on crusade. Ralph Fitz-Godfrey was given charge of Isaac Comnenus in 1191, but died in Tripoli shortly afterwards.[83] Aubrey de Vere, earl of Oxford, had served as Master Chamberlain for forty-eight years by the time Richard ascended to the throne and remained in England.[84] Whilst his eldest son might have been a candidate for the crusading *mesnie*, his presence with King Richard in France from 1194 onwards suggests he may

---

[80] Round also links John Fitz-Lucas' father to two fellow crusaders: John's namesake, the bishop of Évreux, and Robert, earl of Leicester, 'Some Crusaders of Richard I', *EHR*, 18 (1903), 477.

[81] *Gesta Regis*, Vol. 2, pp. 166–7.

[82] Rigord, pp. 83–4; *Gesta Regis*, Vol. 2, pp. 46, 179–80; *Itinerarium*, pp. 199; for his brother see Ambroise, line 6178.

[83] *Gesta Regis*, Vol. 2, pp. 168, 173.

[84] This post is now known as the Lord Great Chamberlain.

have been kept in England to aid with the defence of the realm. However, William II of Tancarville, hereditary chamberlain of Normandy, travelled to the Holy Land as a member of Richard's household and probably fulfilled this function.[85]

Other notable members of the household that travelled to the Levant were the vice-chancellors, John of Alençon and Roger Malchiel; the clerk of the chamber, William of Sainte-Mère-Église; and treasury clerk, Philip of Poitiers.[86] The king's usher, Wigan of Cherbourg, also accompanied him on crusade, as did three royal chaplains: Ralph, who possibly died on crusade, Anselm, who was one of Ralph of Coggeshall's sources on the Third Crusade, and Nicolas, who assisted in the marriage of Richard and Berengaria.[87] Wigan of Cherbourg had previously served King Henry II and, as Henry the Young King's clerk of the kitchens, had held the account of knights taken by the Young King's tournament team.[88] Whilst Michael Belet retained the hereditary office of butler, it is not clear whether he joined King Richard on crusade.[89]

Returning to the military orientation of the household, *acta* and Pipe Rolls offer only rare glimpses of Richard's personal attendants, such as a Ranulf the royal *armiger* in 1189, which makes chronicles essential in providing a fuller picture of his military household.[90] Henry the Teuton was described as Richard's standard-bearer at Jaffa in 1192 and, at the same time, Peter of Préaux was mentioned as carrying the royal standard in place of the Robert Trussebot.[91] King Richard may well have had a personal

---

[85] William Marshal had been raised in the court of his paternal cousin, William II of Tancarville, hereditary chamberlain of Normandy. William of Tancarville was a grandson of Stephen, count of Tréuier, and was also known as the 'father of knights' due to his care for his household. Whilst owing service for ten knights, he held ninety-four and three-quarters knights' fees and would have led a powerful force on crusade, Map, *De Nugis Curialium*, p. 498; *Itinerarium*, p. 217; Ambroise, line 4709; F.M. Powicke, *The Loss of Normandy*, 2nd edition (Manchester, 1961), p. 353.

[86] *Acta*, p. 168, no. 220; *Gesta Regis*, Vol. 2, p. 162; *Itinerarium*, pp. 184, 358; Wendover, p. 218.

[87] Landon, *Itinerary*, no. 342; Anselm was captured alongside his king whilst returning from crusade, Coggeshall, pp. 43–50, 53–6; *Gesta Regis*, Vol. 2, pp. 149, 167.

[88] *HGM*, line 3417; Landon, *Itinerary*, nos. 188, 342; PR28 HII (1182), p. 155.

[89] PR2 RI (1190), p. 102. Belet had been sheriff of Leicestershire, Warwickshire, and Worcestershire under Henry II; R.V. Turner, 'Richard Barre and Michael Belet: Two Angevin Civil Servants', *Judges, Administrators and the Common Law in Angevin England*, ed. R.V. Turner (London, 1994), pp. 180–98.

[90] *Armiger* came from the Latin for someone carrying weapons or armour, in the twelfth century, the term was used alongside *scutarius* (shield-bearer) for a military attendant. These would be amalgamated in time under the term 'squire', PR1 RI (1189), p. 217.

[91] Ambroise, line 4713; *Chronica*, Vol. 3, p. 129; *Itinerarium*, p. 415. Robert Trussebot was a Norman knight from Eure with lands in Yorkshire who had arrived at Acre with Baldwin of Exeter and another possible household knight, Walchelin of Ferrières-Saint

standard displaying two lions rampant combatant, as well as the dragon standard of England. Therefore, more than one standard-bearer may have been required.⁹² Members of the household also carried the king's writ and expressed his will as envoys, ambassadors, and, as highlighted earlier, as liaison officers.⁹³ At the battle of Arsuf, for example, Baldwin le Carron was positioned next to the marshal of the Hospitallers in the rear-guard of the army where, I have argued elsewhere, he acted as Richard's liaison officer.⁹⁴ Baldwin's role at the battle of Arsuf is not only useful in understanding how Richard commanded his army as it marched from Acre to Ascalon in 1191, it also provides a rare glimpse of practical control measures in a medieval army and the degree to which knights could serve within different military units, which is suggestive of commonly known drills and commands.

As mentioned in Chapter Three, 'The Tournament at Lagny-sur-Marne and the Third Crusade', the biography of William Marshal identified Baldwin le Carron as present at the grand tournament at Lagny-sur-Marne in 1179, 'Sir Baldwin le Caron, who was esteemed more than many other man of his rank: there was nobody better than he with lance and sword'.⁹⁵ Already a formidable knight over a decade before the battle of Arsuf, Marshal's biography placed Baldwin with the Flemish contingent, and Gilbert of Mons described him as the son of Roger of Rumes from Hainaut. Gilbert also listed him as a household knight in the service of Baldwin V, count of Hainaut, having previously left the service of Philip of Alsace, count of

---

Hilaire, *Itinerarium*, pp. 93, 135. His claim to be the royal standard-bearer was seemingly based on his ancestor, Pagan Peverel; Edgington, 'Pagan Peverel', pp. 90–3.

⁹² Banners were vital for unit cohesion, for rallying and ethos, as well as for communication. The commander's personal standard was particularly vital, as we see from Guillame the Breton's description of Philip II's banner being raised and lowered to signal his need for help when hard pressed by Imperial knights at the battle of Bouvines. See also, R.W. Jones, '"What Banner Thine?" The Banner as a Symbol of Identification, Status and Authority on the Battlefield', *HSJ*, 15 (2004), 101–9.

⁹³ In addition to formal positions such as marshal, the role of members of the *familia* as councillors is well documented. Henry II held a council of war when faced by the army of Philip II at Gisors in 1188, at which William Marshal advised the king. Emboldened by his success at that council, William returned to Henry II shortly afterwards with advice that led to the successful mid-winter chevauchée of 1188. We can see the council of war at play in discussions in the Holy Land as much as when Richard admitted ignoring his councillors when he marched on Gisors to defeat Philip II; *HGM*, lines 7535–7650, 7784–7802, 7872–8048.

⁹⁴ The section on Baldwin le Carron draws from S. Bennett, 'The Battle of Arsuf/Arsur, A Reappraisal of the Charge of the Hospitallers', *The Military Orders: Culture and Conflict*, Vol. 6.1, ed. M. Carr and J. Schenk (Abingdon and New York, 2017), pp. 44–53. See also, M. Bennett, 'Why Chivalry?', pp. 61–2.

⁹⁵ 'Sire Baudewins de Karon, C'om preisout mielz que tel baron: N'ert nul d'asez par le contree, Mielz fereit de lance e d'espee': *HGM*, lines 4571–4. Note that the knights of Flanders and Hainaut are listed alongside one another here.

Flanders, following a 'disagreement' in 1184. Count Baldwin then gave him a liege fief worth 600 *livres* from Quérénaing, about four miles south of Valenciennes.[96] He acted as a judge in the court of Hainaut and was with the count in Namur in 1185.[97] Count Baldwin gave the wealthy widow, Ida of Jauche, daughter of Goswin III of Mons, to Baldwin le Carron in marriage in 1184.[98] After the death of her brother, Goswin IV, Ida had inherited her father's lands and duties, and her uncle was Nicholas, bishop of Cambrai.[99] Ida's previous husband had died in 1184, but he was survived by their son, Gérard.[100]

In 1187, Alard Fleming conducted a recruiting tour of the Low Countries on behalf of his master, King Henry II. Given Baldwin's earlier disagreement with the count of Flanders, membership of the Angevin contingent would probably have seemed a more attractive proposition than joining Philip of Alsace.[101] In any account, sometime after the king of England's death on 6 July 1189, Baldwin was in the service of Henry's eldest surviving son and successor, Richard. Both Ambroise and the *Itinerarium* described Baldwin as a companion or comrade of King Richard, which is indicative of him being a member of the royal household.[102]

Roger of Howden described Baldwin withstanding a sally by the Muslim garrison of Acre on 11 November 1190 alongside Baldwin of Dargus and Walter of Oyri, and listed him amongst the participants of the St Martin offensive a few days later.[103] It is possible that he only joined the royal household after Richard's arrival at the siege of Acre as one of the knights

---

[96] 'Temporibus illis dominus comes Balduinum Caron, militem magnum, pulchrum et fortem ac probissimum, Rogeri de Ruma filium, qui a comite Flandrie pro quadam discordia recesserat, susceperat commilitonem, et ei 600 libras in feodo ligio dans, ei denarius illos super Karinen, villam prope Valencenas, assignavit': Gilbert of Mons, p. 174. It is possible that Baldwin le Carron was in the service of the count of Flanders during the Great Revolt against King Henry II and participated in the Philip of Alsace's invasion of Normandy in 1173, but there are no indications that he joined him on crusade in 1177.

[97] Gilbert of Mons, pp. 213, 217.

[98] Gilbert of Mons, pp. 53, 180.

[99] Duby, 'The Structure of Kinship and Nobility', *The Chivalrous Society*, p. 136. Ida's mother, Beatrice of Hainaut, a niece of Count Baldwin III, was excommunicated in 1188: C.-G. Roland, *Histoire généalogique de la maison de Rumigny-Florennes* (Brussels, 1891), p. 140.

[100] Gilbert of Mons, *Chronicle of Hainaut by Gilbert of Mons*, trans. L. Napran (Woodbridge, 2005), p. 34, n.138.

[101] *CDF*, pp. 481–505, no. 1361. Baldwin le Carron was not alone in joining King Richard's contingent, Otto II of Trazegnies was another vassal of Count Baldwin V who had taken the Cross *c*. 21 February 1188 following a sermon at Mons by the papal legate, Henry of Albano; Werweke, 'Contribution de la Flandre et de Hainaut', nos. 60, 71, 88.

[102] Ambroise, line 6419; *Itinerarium*, pp. 269.

[103] *Gesta Regis*, Vol. 2, p. 144.

drawn by the king's offer of four bezants.[104] However, given his place in Howden's account and indications from his links to other crusaders, it is more likely that Baldwin le Carron was recruited by Alard and that King Richard initially placed him with his advance guard along with the archbishop of Canterbury, Hubert Walter, and Ranulf of Glanville who had left Marseille on 5 August 1190.[105]

We next find Baldwin at the battle of Arsuf (7 September 1191).[106] As introduced earlier in this section, following the problems with the rear-guard under Duke Hugh III, King Richard had placed the Templars in the vanguard with the Hospitallers holding the rear.[107] Having successfully negotiated their way through the forest of Arsuf, the crusader army came under sustained attack from Saladin's forces. The rear-guard was a particular focus for enemy attention and the Hospitallers sent word that they were under considerable pressure. Shortly afterwards, the master of the Order, Garnier of Nablûs, came personally to seek permission from Richard to launch a counterattack, but the king turned him down.[108] Both Ambroise and the *Itinerarium* then described two knights launching a charge against the wishes of the king:

> All was lost because of two men who could not hold back from charging, They rushed forward first and left two Turks dead. One of these was a knight, the Marshal of the Hospitallers; The other Baldwin le Carron, who was as bold as a lion, a companion of the king of England who had brought him from his land.[109]

Some nine months later, on 17 June 1192, Baldwin jointly commanded the escort to a supply caravan ambushed by Saladin's forces. Indeed, Ambroise described Ferric of Vienne asking Baldwin le Carron and Clarembaud of Châlon to guard the convoy as they 'would not behave foolishly'.[110] Thrown from his horse twice during the attack, Baldwin was provided with fresh mounts by his men each time. On losing his third horse, he was wounded, but was then rescued by Robert, earl of Leicester, at the head of his retinue.[111]

---

[104] Ambroise, lines 4575–99, 4686–90.
[105] C.R. Young, *Hubert Walter: Lord of Canterbury and Lord England* (Durham, 1968), pp. 33–6.
[106] Ambroise, line 6419, *Itinerarium*, p. 269.
[107] Ambroise, lines 5694–5861, *Itinerarium*, pp. 249–51.
[108] Ambroise, lines 6375–6383, *Itinerarium*, p. 267.
[109] 'Mais par deus homes les perdirent, Qui pas de poindre ne se tindrent, Mais tut li premerains eslaisserent, Si que deus Turs morz i laisserent. L'un des deus fud uns chevaliers, Li mareschal Ospitaliers; L'autre iert Baudowins li Carons, Qui iert hardiz com uns leons; Compainz iert le rei d'Engleterre, Qui l'ot amené de sa terre': Ambroise, lines 6413–21.
[110] 'Que les genz folement n'errassent': Ambroise, line 9935.
[111] Ambroise, lines 9920–47, *Itinerarium*, pp. 373–4.

This suggests that trust in Baldwin does not seem to have been diminished by his conduct at the battle of Arsuf. He was asked to hold this command position later in the campaign on account of his reputation as a trustworthy leader. *La chronique de Gislebert de Mons* includes Baldwin in a list of the Third Crusade fallen, and a family charter confirms his death in the Levant sometime before 1212.[112] The same charter indicated that he had become the lord of Rumes sometime before departing for the Holy Land.[113]

If there was a breakdown in discipline in the Hospitaller ranks, as Ambroise and the *Itinerarium* assert, it was led by a senior military commander of the Hospitallers and enjoyed the approval of one of King Richard's subordinate commanders. Of the two, Baldwin was a veteran and it is also very likely the Hospitaller marshal had considerable military experience. It is not beyond the bounds of possibility that both lost control, but neither individual is a natural match for a reckless and disobedient knight.[114] In any event, a potential loss of control does not undermine my argument on the role Baldwin played in the battle – that of Richard's liaison officer to the Order of St John of Jerusalem – a role that has previously gone unnoticed. Moreover, that knights such as Baldwin could move between households – be it on campaign or for a specific tournament – and ride as part of the Hospitaller marshal's *conroi* is suggestive of an established system or systems of tactical commands, signals, and drills, such as to maintain formation, change gait, wheel on a movable pivot, and otherwise manoeuvre as a *conroi* and as part of a larger squadron.

This also has an impact on our understanding of the battle of Arsuf and King Richard's willingness to commit to battle. It is indicative of the measures Richard undertook to maintain the overall cohesion of the crusader army as it marched to secure Ascalon. Whilst it supports the argument that he would only risk battle under the most favourable circumstances, it demonstrates that Richard was anticipating a battle on

---

[112] Gilbert of Mons, p. 274; Dailliez, *Les Templiers en Flandre*, pp. 333–4, no. 61 (facsimilé cartulaire).

[113] Dailliez, *Les Templiers en Flandre*, pp. 333–4, no. 61; L. Devillers, *Inventaire analytique des archives des commanderies belges de l'Ordre de Saint-Jean de Jerusalem ou de Malte* (Brussels, 1876), p. 179–80; Warlop, *De Vlaamse adel vóór 1300*, pp. 193–9, 508.

[114] Cavalry treatises and regulations habitually stress the dangers of individuals breaking ranks and charging forwards. This is because horses in a group tend to act as a herd: if one begins to gallop, others are likely to follow, which breaks up the formation and risks injury through out-of-control horses riding into obstacles, such as ditches, or encountering formed enemy, J. Gassmann, 'Combat Training for Horse and Rider in the Early Middle Ages', *Acta Periodica Duellatorum* (2018), pp. 63–98. For example, the Templar rule only permitted a brother to break ranks without permission to save a 'foolish' Christian under Turkish attack, and a passage in Ambroise relating to Robert of Bruges indicates the Hospitallers also punished brother-knights who broke formation without permission; *Rule of the Templars*, p. 59, statute 163, and Ambroise, lines 9885–9946.

7 September. Indeed, I would argue that he was actively seeking to defeat Saladin in the field that day.

King Richard paid equal attention to those members of the household left to oversee his affairs in the West. Heiser's analysis of the relationship between custodians and the royal household relied heavily on attestations of King Richard's *acta* and he concludes that 'by and large, however, constables [castellans] appointed by the king were unknown to him: he did not fill the castellanies with *familiares regis*, at least at this point in his reign'.[115] As Warren Hollister pointed out, 'the correlation between charter attestations and attendance at court is imperfect'.[116] Non-appearance on charter witness lists does not necessarily indicate non-attendance at court, as several prominent members of the royal household appeared infrequently on witness lists, if at all, as Richard seemingly favoured locals as attestors.[117] Indeed, sheriffs – men who were traditionally closely associated with the court and the king's most important local officials – were also infrequent attestors to charters.

Those castellans presented by Heiser as curial are shown to be local men, so it is not unreasonable to argue that those local men appointed as castellans were part of the household but missing from witness lists. A crucial indication that the castellans and sheriffs were integral members of the royal household is that a number of King Richard's appointees can be firmly placed in his *familia regis*, such as Gerard of Camville, Henry of Cornhill, Robert Tresgoz, Roger Fitz-Reinfrid, William Fitz-Aldelin, and William Marshal.[118]

The Size of the Royal Household

It is difficult to offer a definitive size of King Richard's household due to a dearth of surviving muster rolls. Nevertheless, it is possible to construct an informed picture based on typical royal households of the era, the extent of Angevin wealth at this time, and other surviving data. King Philip II of France, for example, paid the Genoese to ship 650 knights and 1,300 serjeants to the Holy Land in 1190.[119] Many notable members

---

[115] Heiser, 'Castles, Constables, and Politics', p. 24.

[116] C.W. Hollister, *Henry I* (New Haven and London, 2001), p. 499.

[117] This tendency is particularly notable in charters with long witness lists. If one follows Hollister's methodology, however, and focuses on those charters with five or fewer witnesses, then the composition of Richard's day-to-day entourage becomes more apparent. Hollister, *Henry I*, p. 505–6.

[118] *Acta*, p. 168, no. 220; *Gesta Regis*, Vol. 2, pp. 71–2, 223; *HGM*, lines 4525, 8018–19, 8015–24, 9177–9200; Landon, *Itinerary*, nos. 20–2, 41, 146, 164 168–71, 175–82, 184–7, 196–202, 268; PR3/4 RI (1191–2); See also, *List of Sheriffs for England and Wales: From Earliest Times to A.D. 1831* (London, 1898), p. 72.

[119] The fleet was commanded by Simon Doria, former 'consul' of Genoa, who was also

of the French nobility, including his cousins, were already at the siege of Acre with their retainers, so his *mesnie* would have made up a sizeable proportion of this force.

Like his father, King Richard controlled a realm that stretched from the borders of Scotland to the foothills of the Pyrenees, so his household was most probably of a similar scale to that of Henry II. Based on the *servitium debitum* of England in the *Cartae Baronum* commissioned by King Henry II in 1166, theoretically, the king could call upon over 7,500 knights in England alone.[120] However, many were taxed in lieu of service (*scutage*) to fund the recruitment of mercenaries for a particular campaign and, potentially, help maintain the king's military household, so Henry mustered only a third of the knights available to him from his English lands for his 1157 campaign in North Wales.[121] During the rebellion of 1173–4, King Henry II needed thirty-seven ships to transport his household from England to Normandy, a figure that may have excluded his personal escort. In addition to 1846 Norman knights listed in the *Infeudationes Militum* of 1172 as owing service to King Henry II as duke of the duchy, elements of his royal household would have already been in France.[122] To these can be added troops pledged under various Anglo-Flemish treaties. For example, as discussed in Chapter Three, the treaty of 1163 committed one thousand *milites* to Henry, and that of 1180 specified five hundred.[123]

Whilst mindful of potential inaccuracies, we can also draw on narrative sources as a point of comparison and further illustration. The description in *L'Historie de Guillaume Marechal* of the four hundred knights Henry the Young King assembled for the Great Rebellion of 1173 was no doubt swelled by the contingents of allied nobles,[124] but the landless Henry the Young King routinely fielded a company of between eighty and one hundred

---

to command a Genoese fleet at Damietta during the Fifth Crusade; Tyerman, *God's War*, p. 433. For the agreement see *Actes de Philippe Auguste*, Vol. 1, ed. Delaborde, no. 292.

[120] *Cartae Baronum*, ed. N. Stacy, Pipe Roll Society, new series Vol. 62 (Woodbridge, 2019). See also, J. Holt, 'The Introduction of Knight Service in England', *ANS*, 6 (1984), 89–106.

[121] In 1157, some 2,000 knights were called upon to serve on campaign in Wales, Hosler, *Henry II*, p. 109; N.J.C. Smith, '*Servicium Debitum* and Scutage in Twelfth Century England with Comparisons to the *Regno* of Southern Italy' (PhD thesis, Durham University, 2010), pp. 165–85.

[122] Thomas Keefe estimated the figure to be closer to 2,500, Keefe, *Feudal Assessments*, p. 141; I. Heath, *Armies of Feudal Europe, 1066–1300*, 2nd edition (Cambridge, 2016), p. 25.

[123] As well as being a significant boost to Angevin troop numbers, this was a significant commitment from a region that contained some 1,500 knights; Oksanen, *Flanders*, pp. 63–4.

[124] *HGM*, line 2061; see also Turner, 'Households of the Sons', p. 52.

knights drawn by high pay, lavish gifts, and aspirations of advancement.[125] These figures coincide with major tournaments or his attendance at King Philip II of France's coronation and subsequent tournament at Lagny-sur-Marne, which may have inflated his household.[126] However, at the latter event, *L'Historie de Guillaume le Marechal* described that 'there were at least two hundred and more ... who lived off the purse of the young King and were knights of his'.[127]

Earlier royal households are also of interest here; Henry I is said to have had access to a household of some five hundred household knights at Brémule in 1119, and detachments of two hundred and three hundred in 1119 and 1124. Orderic Vitalis estimated the king's household contingent to be two- to three-hundred strong, but Henry I's realm was less extensive than that of both King Henry II and Richard in that it was limited to England and Normandy.[128] So it is unsurprising that Richard could assemble an army containing some 1,500 knights to confront King Philip II at Courcelles-lès-Gisors in September 1198.[129] Only a proportion of this force was drawn from those owing knightly service. King Richard sought baronial support in 1197 to fund a force of three hundred knights to serve for one year in lieu of their military obligations, and Hubert Walter eventually secured one-tenth of the feudal levy from England, which was close to that figure, in time for the subsequent campaign in France.[130] Even accounting for forces drawn from Normandy and other parts of the Angevin realm, the royal household must have made up a significant part of the army.

The sizes of baronial households, as well as those of magnates, are also suggestive. When engaging in a regional struggle against the counts of Boulogne, Flanders, and Ponthieu, according to William Marshal's biography, William II of Tancarville mustered a force of twenty-eight knights, which included the newly knighted William Marshal. Alexander Arsic, lord of Cogges, commanded between fifteen and twenty knights on the

---

[125] *HGM*, lines 3199, 4753, 4775.

[126] The band of eighty knights Henry the Young King took to the coronation was described in *HGM* as 'select' and excludes the forces of the fifteen knights-banneret in his *mesnie*, each of whom would have normally led between ten and twenty knights, lines 4457–4776.

[127] 'Por ce vos plevis en por tant que bien erent deux cenz e plus, si com avez oï desus, qui del giemble rei se vivoient, e qui si chevalier estoient', *HGM*, lines 4772–6.

[128] Orderic Vitalis described Henry I sending his son, Richard, with 200 knights of his household to the relief of Breteuil, *The Ecclesiastical History of Orderic Vitalis*, Vol. 6, ed. and trans. M. Chibnall (Oxford, 1969–), pp. 46–52; for the concentration of 300 knights supported by mounted archers to confront rebel forces at Bourgthéroulde, see *Ecclesiastical History*, pp. 236, 246–50.

[129] Baldwin, *Government of Philip*, p. 280.

[130] Turner and Heiser, *Richard Lionheart*, p. 158.

Third Crusade.[131] David Crouch's biography of William Marshal identified eighteen knights as long-term members in his household after his marriage to Isabel of Clare, with a core of around seven specific knights routinely at his side. A study of Roger of Quincy gives a similar total of about fifteen *familiares*.[132] These examples provide a strong idea of the size of baronial households, as well as tactical formations called *conroi*, which were the building blocks of north-western European medieval armies.

The households of regional magnates do not seem to have been significantly larger. The Count of Pol, for example, led thirty knights to a tournament in 1183 and Baldwin V of Hainaut took a one hundred-strong household around the tournament circuit in 1172.[133] Moreover, numbers might be swelled in anticipation of conflict. Despite leaving trusted members of his *mesnie* to protect his interests in England and Normandy, Earl Patrick of Salisbury joined Henry II's campaign in Poitou at the head of fifty to sixty knights in 1168.[134] In addition, when acting in their official capacity, an officer of the household could expect to augment their own *mesnie* with knights fulfilling feudal obligations. For example, when called upon by King Henry II to support him against the Great Rebellion of 1173, as chamberlain of Normandy, William II of Tancarville headed a contingent of one hundred knights.[135] As mentioned in Chapter One, Archbishop Baldwin's contingent at the siege of Acre included two hundred knights.[136] This figure, however, may have included some of the king's men, such as Robert Trussebot, but it is interesting that it matches the size of Thomas Becket's retinue for his embassy to Paris in 1158.[137]

Whilst medieval estimates of military formations are notoriously unreliable, contemporary accounts of the Third Crusade provide a useful starting point for analysis. Richard of Devizes set the size of the Angevin fleet that sailed for Lisbon during the Third Crusade at one hundred ships, each carrying thirty sailors and forty soldiers, as well as fourteen busses of twice that capacity.[138] Roger of Howden placed one hundred men of London on

---

[131] However, as an example of the potential problems with narrative sources, the size of William II's household seems too small, *HGM*, lines 847–8, 4719–22. For Arsic, see Ambroise, line 10457; and, *Itinerarium*, p. 389.

[132] Crouch, *Court, Career, and Chivalry*, pp. 137–8; Crouch, *William Marshal*, 3rd edition, pp. 231–2. Roger was related to Robert of Quincy, who joined Richard I's household on crusade; G.G. Simpson, 'The *Familia* of Roger de Quincy, Earl of Winchester and Constable of Scotland', *Essays on the Nobility of Medieval Scotland*, ed. K.J. Stringer (Edinburgh, 1985), p. 107.

[133] *HGM*, lines 5995–6146; Gilbert of Mons, pp. 108–9.

[134] Asbridge, *Greatest Knight*, p. 74.

[135] Asbridge, *Greatest Knight*, p. 106.

[136] *Itinerarium*, p. 116.

[137] F. Barlow, *Thomas Becket* (London, 1986), p. 56.

[138] Or 8,750 men – soldiers and crew alike, Richard of Devizes, *The Chronicle of Richard*

board their vessel and, of course, these figures do not include Richard and those who travelled with him down through France to Marseille and on to Messina – a force Christopher Tyerman estimated to be six thousand men.[139]

In line with Graham Loud's work on Emperor Frederick's crusading army, the household was but one element within the crusader contingent from the Angevin territories, so it is useful to consider the force that Richard kept under his personal direction.[140] Even after Baldwin of Forde and Ranulf of Glanville had departed for Acre with the advance force, King Richard had sufficient men to require ten busses and twenty galleys to reach Sicily, a fleet that compares favourably with that employed by his father in 1173.[141] This does not appear to be unduly inflated by the chronicler, but the flotilla also carried crusaders who were probably not part of the *mesnie*, such as Alexander Arsic, Ernald of Mandeville, Osmund of Stuteville, and Roger of Tosny. Richard of Devizes described a fleet of 219 *vasa* (vessels) leaving Sicily in April 1191, made up of 156 *naves* (sailing ships), 24 *busses* (large cargo ships), and 39 *galee* (galleys).[142] Ralph of Diss also detailed the size of the Angevin fleet, claiming there to have been 13 *busses*, 100 other transport ships, and 50 galleys when it left Cyprus in 1191.[143] Thus, Tyerman suggests an overall strength, including sailors, of up to 17,000.[144]

Whilst the breakdown of the force assigned by King Richard to Robert of Quincy to aid the prince of Antioch included a ratio of one hundred knights to five hundred serjeants, it likely that the king was under a degree of pressure from crusader knights to remain with that part of the army that would march on Jerusalem.[145] The mounted component is generally accepted as having accounted for 25 per cent of medieval armies, and so, based on the reported size of the fleet, we can advance the belief that Richard was accompanied by a cavalry force of around three thousand men when he

---

of Devizes of the Time of King Richard the First, ed. and trans. J.T. Appleby (London, 1963), p. 15.

[139] *Gesta Regis*, Vol. 2, p. 117, *Chronica*, Vol. 3, p. 43; Tyerman, *England*, p. 66.

[140] *Barbarossa*, p. 19.

[141] Described as 30 merchant ships in L. Maimbourg, *The History of the Crusade: Or, The Expeditions of the Christian Princes for the Conquest of the Holy Land*, trans. J. Nalson (London, 1864), p. 192. In 1142 Robert of Gloucester used 52 ships to carry a force of 300 knights across the Channel, Oksanen, *Flanders*, p. 159. See also J. Pryor, 'Transportation of Horses by Sea during the Era of the Crusade: Eighth Century to 1285 A.D.', *Medieval Warfare 1000–1300*, ed. J. France (Aldershot, 2006), pp. 523–68.

[142] There were, he wrote, 180 vessels, exclusive of the king's ship and the galleys. According to Devizes, such *naves* carried 40 horses, 40 knights, and 40 foot soldiers, provisions for them all, as well as for the 15-man crew, and the busses carrying twice this amount, Devizes, pp. 15, 28. For more on ship types, see Rodger, *Safeguard of the Sea*.

[143] Diss, Vol. 2, p. 93.

[144] Tyerman, *God's War*, p. 433.

[145] *Gesta Regis*, Vol. 2, p. 185.

arrived at Cyprus.[146] These men would be in addition to those members of the *familia regis* already in Outremer, or who had remained in the West to administer and protect the Angevin realm. Knightly crusaders made up only a part of this force, but on the basis of this data, and a comparison with the households of King Henry II and the crusading contingent shipped by Philip II of France, as well as Baldwin of Forde's overall contingent of two hundred knights and three hundred retainers, it is reasonable to project a conservative estimate of the strength of Richard's crusading household as being at least 1,500 strong, with a further five hundred men left in north-western Europe.[147] Of these, one third would have been knights, that is, around 650 elite cavalrymen, of whom five hundred joined him on crusade – a force comparable to King Henry I's household at the battle of Brémule – with the remainder made up of both mounted serjeants and foot.[148] While these five hundred knights arguably represented a household swollen by the needs of campaigning in the Holy Land alongside Philip II of France and, most probably, Frederick Barbarossa, it is a force of a comparable scale to the likely size of King Richard's household at the battle of Courcelles-lès-Gisors in 1198.[149]

This study's review of King Richard's *acta*, pipe rolls, and letters, as well as contemporary chronicles and eyewitness accounts during the time of the Third Crusade, places 237 individuals in the overall royal household, which included fourteen so closely associated with it on crusade that they were probably members. In addition to the two heads of the Military Orders, thirty-two churchmen were linked to the *mesnie*, but only eight fulfilled roles expected of a member of the *familia regis* – nine if we include Baldwin of Forde. In addition, twenty-six lay magnates were regular members of the itinerant court, of whom five were an integral part of the king's inner circle of *familiares*: Robert Fitz-Pernel, earl of Leicester, William of Mandeville, earl of Essex, Andrew of Chauvigny, count of Châteauroux, William Forz, count of Aumale, and William Marshal.

---

[146] Prestwich, *Armies and Warfare*, pp. 63–8, 71–2. See also Church, 'Question of Numbers', p. 161. Richard of Devizes' observation that each ship carried 40 horses with busses carrying twice as many suggests some 5,000 horses were transported by King Richard to the Holy Land, but this figure would have included spare mounts, Devizes, p. 15.

[147] Tyerman later refined his estimates to set King Richard's army at 2,500–3,000, with his fleet carrying a further 8,000 crusaders; Tyerman, *Plan a Crusade*, p. 189. For Archbishop Baldwin's contingent see *Itinerarium*, p. 116.

[148] The ratio of one knight to two mounted serjeants was common during the late twelfth century, as evidenced by Philip II of France's contract with the Genoese to ship his contingent to the Holy Land in 1190; *Actes de Philippe Auguste*, Vol. 1, ed. Delaborde, no. 292.

[149] Baldwin, *Government of Philip*, p. 280.

Whilst 239 individuals represented only 12 per cent of the estimated overall size of the household, that is unsurprising given the limited availability of reliable data on the members of the household – especially those of non-noble rank. As the 194 subjects of noble rank make up 30 per cent of the likely knightly *mesnie*, it is, I would argue, sufficient to analyse the composition and background of King Richard's *mesnie* and draw some broad conclusions.

The Geographical Circumstances of the Royal Household

Ralph Turner concluded that Richard's household was almost exclusively Poitevin before 1189, 'except for the occasional Angevin or Norman'.[150] Thereafter, Turner went on to argue, very few of the local nobles identified as witnesses were associated with the household.[151] As Turner's analysis was based solely on charter evidence, Richard's preference for empowering local barons rather than imposing outsiders as local officials in the Angevin realm may skew conclusions drawn from such data.[152] The predominance of local names witnessing royal charters at La Réole in February 1190, for example, was an indication of this process in action. Aside from members of the *familia regis*, such as Helias of the Celle, seneschal of Gascony, these local witnesses do not appear on royal *acta* at other locations. In addition, apart from Miles the almoner and the vice-chancellor, Roger Malchiel, of the twenty-eight other people listed on the La Réole charters only Gérard of La Barthe, archbishop of Auch, joined King Richard in the Holy Land after serving as one of his naval justiciars.[153]

The limitation in basing analysis purely on *acta* is reinforced by returning to the Poitevins in Richard's household.[154] Over three-quarters of the Poitevins identified in Table 5 as members of King Richard's household can be

---

[150] Turner, 'Households of the Sons', p. 61. See also, Chauvenet, 'L'entourage de Richard', pp.137–49; Billoré, 'Noblesse normande', pp. 151–66; and Vincent, 'Henry and the Poitevins', pp. 103–35.

[151] 'Local' here meaning someone from the area in which the charter was described as being signed, such as those nobles from La Réole listed as witnesses on charters described as being signed in La Réole.

[152] Turner, 'Households of the Sons', p. 49.

[153] Viscount Peter of Castillon witnessed King Richard's confirmation charter to Grace-Sauve abbey at La Role on 3 February 1190 and went on to die at the siege of Acre, but there are no indications that he formed part of the Angevin contingent, Landon, *Itinerary*, no. 217. It is possible that he marched with the Imperial contingent alongside Gauverand of Aspet, *Itinerarium*, p. 93.

[154] The origin of a significant number of witnesses is simply unknown. Geoffrey Loster, for example, is also referred to in *acta* as Gaufrido Lectoren, which may indicate he was from Lectoire, in southwestern France; Landon, *Itinerary*, nos. 129, 131–2, 283, 321–6.

Table 5. The Geographical Composition of Richard's *Mesnie* 1189–1194

Background	Number	Crusaded
England/Normandy	159	75
Anjou	1	1
Aquitaine	3	3
Brittany	2	1
Maine	7	6
Poitou	11	9
Touraine	1	1
Non-Angevin Realm	16	15
Not Known	38	27
Total	239	138

found with him on the Third Crusade (82%) yet none of them had witnessed his surviving comital charters.[155]

Based on this data, Anglo-Norman knights dominated King Richard's household, forming over half the sample that went on crusade (54%). Nearly half of those Anglo-Normans identified as being in his household joined him in the Levant (48%). However, this does not mean Angevins and Poitevins did not take the Cross.

The low incidence of names from Anjou and Aquitaine within the *mesnie* is tempered by the high proportion of members of the household from those regions that went on crusade with Richard. In comparison with his many years in the southern Angevin realms, the new king was arguably less established in England and Normandy, and a focus on recruiting from these areas may have been a means of cementing political loyalties. However, care must be taken due to a lack of documentary evidence for those knights or churchmen from south of the Loire in general and specifically those who were left to fulfil similar functions to their Anglo-Norman colleagues.

Knights from outside the Angevin realm formed less than a tenth of the identifiable household (7%), but nearly all of them travelled with King Richard on crusade to make up the second largest group with Richard in the Holy Land (11%). Many were professional warriors from the Low Countries who had previously served under Henry the Young King or his father and continued in Richard's service after the Crusade. While a degree

---

[155] Andrew of Chauvigny, for example, can be placed in Richard's comital household, but does not appear on witness lists of surviving *acta* from Poitou. Yet he was a frequent attester to Richard's royal *acta*, Landon, *Itinerary*, nos. 329–30, 342, 358, 366; *HGM*, lines 8662–80.

of local influence was seemingly important in the selection of subordinate commanders such as seneschals and castellans, professional knights from outside the Angevin realm formed another notable group within the military establishment and, as will be seen, were given important roles on campaign.

The Social Composition of the Royal Household

The Anglo-Norman kings are described as having largely recruited their military households from professional warriors of low status: Waleran of Meulan dismissed them as 'peasants and common soldiers'.[156] However, by the time of Henry I, though some were still of humble origin, the household was arguably comprised of mostly landless younger sons recruited from the nobility, and Chibnall's suggested formula of 'feudal vassals, quasi-vassals in receipt of money fiefs, and stipendiaries' resonates with Church's description of King John's household.[157] Meanwhile, the household of Henry the Young King consisted of, 'military retainers, knights of middling Norman or Anglo-Norman families ... supplemented by a clerical element largely chosen by the boy's father and loyal to him'.[158]

Firstborn sons and surviving heirs were prominent members of King Richard's household, however, and served alongside their landless siblings – both on crusade and elsewhere. Indeed, far from being the preserve of landless younger sons, despite the high number of barons that stayed in England as sheriffs, the proportion of titled barons and lay magnates with the crusading household only dropped to 21 per cent from an overall 24 per cent of the full *mesnie*.[159]

---

[156] 'Gregarii et pagenses', *Orderic Vitalis*, Vol. 6, pp. 346–50.
[157] Chibnall, 'Mercenaries and the Familia Regis', pp. 152–5.
[158] Turner, 'Households of the Sons', p. 49; see also, G. Duby, 'Les "jeunes" dans la societé aristocratique dans la France du nord-ouest au XIIe siècle', *Annales*, 27 (1964), 835–46.
[159] Aubrey, a monk of Trois-Fontaines writing between 1227 and 1251, claimed 'cum Rege Ricardo fuit unus Rex de Hibernia unus de Wallia et cum eis Comes de Hollandia'. Whilst there is supporting evidence for the presence of the count of Holland on the Third Crusade and Baldwin's preaching tour of Wales was discussed in Chapter One, I have been unable to find verifiable evidence for participation by Welsh or Irish elites. Moreover, Floris III, count of Holland, journeyed with Frederick Barbarossa rather than King Richard. For Aubrey's account, see 'Chronica Albrici monachi Trium Fontium. A Monachio Novi Monasterii Hoiensis Interpolata', *Monumenta Germaniae Historica, Scriptorium*, Vol. 23, ed. P. Scheffer-Boichorst (Hanover, 1874), p. 867. There is, however, evidence of crusaders with ties to the lordship of Ireland, such as Gilbert Pipard, Bertram III of Verdon, and Theobald of Valoignes, Howden, *Gesta Regis*, Vol. 2, pp. 149–50, Devizes, *Chronicon*, p. 19; Wendover, p. 191. For further information on Irish crusaders see, K. Hurlock, 'The Crusades to 1291 in the Annals of Medieval Ireland', *Irish Historical Studies*, 37 (2011), 517–34. On Pipard and Bertram III see also

Table 6. The Social Composition of Richard's *Mesnie* 1189–1194

Group	Number	Crusaded
Clerical magnate	8	6#
Lay magnate	5	3
Baron	51	26
Knight	146	83
Cleric	19	16
Serjeant	10	4
Total	239	138
Associated clerical magnates*	26	4
Associated lay magnates	23	11
Total	49	15

This figure includes William of Coutances, who cut short his journey to the Holy Land at the behest of King Richard, returning from Messina along with Eleanor the queen mother in 1191.

* The heads of military orders have been included in the 'Clerical magnates' category.

In contrast to Heiser's analysis, Table 6 demonstrates that both clerical and lay magnates remained a feature within the royal court in the Levant, rising from 5 per cent to 7 per cent of the household on crusade. There was, however, a distinct drop in associated magnates with 85 per cent of clerical magnates remaining in north-western Europe, as did roughly half (52%) of their lay equivalents. The clerical magnates that did travel eastwards were predominantly those closely associated with the king's household. Similarly, the high percentage of household clerics that joined the king in the Levant is explained in part by their holding important administrative functions and appearing in official documents, such as charters, but also by a tendency for clerical chroniclers to include them in narrative accounts.

Evidence of non-elite members of the household is scant, with only seven identifiable actors of whom only one can be tracked to the Holy Land: Peter des Barres, a crewman of Richard's flagship, the *Trenchemer*. However, Henry Turpin, the royal arbalester, and Ranulf the armiger most likely remained with the *mesnie* after King Richard left Vézelay in June 1190.[160] Moreover, as

---

B. Smith, *Colonisation and Conquest in Medieval Ireland: The English in Louth, 1170–1330* (Cambridge, 1999), pp. 30–1; M.S. Hagger, *The Fortunes of a Norman Family: The De Verduns in England, Ireland, and Wales, 1066–1316* (Oxford, 1987), pp. 56–7.

[160] *Itinerarium*, p. 205; Landon, *Itinerary*, no. 326. Turpin seemingly died between King Richard's departure from Vézelay and his time in Messina, as Turpin's son travelled to Sicily to petition Richard for his inheritance in Strettington (West Sussex); PR1 RI

Heiser has pointed out, given that Richard went hawking while on crusade, it is also likely that the royal falconer, William of Gatesden, formed part of the crusading household.[161]

In addition to the reasonably diverse backgrounds of the men who were recruited, contemporary accounts indicate the opportunity for advancement based on merit. Henry I, for example, elevated Nigel of Aubigny from carrier of the king's bow to a position on the high council with rewards of land and advantageous marriage.[162] Richard rewarded two of his closest companions, Andrew of Chauvigny and William of Forz, with high position and land soon after his accession.[163] Both men were from the minor noble families and were given positions of responsibility during the crusade. William of Forz's maritime experience was put to good use as a *justiciar* of Richard's fleet and Andrew of Chauvigny led a detachment of fifteen knights, with his standard being the first to be raised above Darum during King Richard's assault of 22 May 1192.[164]

Alard Fleming, whom we encountered earlier in relation to Baldwin le Carron, provides another interesting example. Alard's father, William Fleming, was a royal serjeant of Flemish descent, with lands in Northamptonshire.[165] By 1180, William had been elevated to the office of chamberlain to Richard's mother, Eleanor of Aquitaine.[166] His uncle, Reiner, had been steward to William le Meschine, lord of Copeland and Egremont Castle, in Cumbria. Reiner later founded Kirklees Priory, West Yorkshire, and gave lands to Bolton Abbey. His son, William, was steward of Egremont.[167] This branch of the Flemings was associated with the Lacy family, who were covered in some detail in Chapter Two.[168] An ancestor, also named Alard, was likely a member of the household of William of Aubigny, earl of Lincoln, c.1139.[169]

(1189), p. 217; Turpin had been Henry II's chamberlain, *Itinerarium*, p. 205; Landon, *Itinerary*, no. 326.

[161] Heiser, 'Court of the Lionheart', pp. 517, 519; *The Cartulary of Newnham Priory*, ed. J. Golber (Bedford, 1963), no. 77, p. 43.

[162] Prestwich, 'Military Household', pp. 24–5.

[163] Andrew was married to the heiress of Châteauroux, Denise of Déols, in August 1189, Howden, *Gesta Regis*, Vol. 2, p. 76, and William of Forz married William of Mandeville's widow, Hawisia, before departing on crusade to become count of Aumale, PR2 RI (1190), p. 73.

[164] Ambroise, lines 7262, 9294, *Itinerarium*, pp. 405, 408.

[165] *The Red Book of the Exchequer*, Vol. 1, ed. H. Hall (London, 1896), pp. 24, 458, 696; F.L. Fleming, *A Genealogy of the Ancient Flemings* (Rothersthorpe, 2010), pp. 49–51.

[166] *Recueil des actes de Henri II*, Vol. 2 (Paris, 1920), p. 203.

[167] 'The Coucher Book and Charters of Bolton Priory', ed. K.J. Legg (PhD thesis, University of Sheffield, 2002), pp. 233, 260, 289.

[168] 942 *Gesta Regis*, Vol. 2, p. 148.

[169] *Facsimiles of Royal and Other Charters in the British Museum*, Vol. 1, ed. G.F. Warner

By 1187 Alard Fleming held the manors of Great Rissington, Sapperton, and Frampton Mansell in Gloucestershire, and other manors in Sussex and Kent granted by Henry II.[170] From these lands, he made grants to Belvoir Priory on or before 1187 of all the tithes and lands that his predecessors had given of his fee for the souls of his wife, Idonia, and others.[171] Alard was in Flanders in 1187, recruiting on behalf of King Henry II in the lead-up to Henry taking the Cross in January 1188.[172] We should not be surprised, then, that some crusaders from the Low Countries joined the Angevin contingent rather than Philip of Alsace. A prime example of these is, of course, Baldwin le Carron, lord of Rumes and member of the count of Hainaut's household.[173]

We know that Alard Fleming survived the crusade, as King Richard granted him lands at Fordham in Cambridgeshire in 1194 – indeed, rates of survival in the royal household compare favourably with other crusaders. Despite often being portrayed as being at the centre of the action, Richard could recruit from amongst the finest warriors in his extensive realms – men who could be trusted to act effectively in concert rather than as individuals. They would have been provided with the finest equipment, camped in the best locations, and had first call on rations, all of which made them less vulnerable to injury and disease. Alard seemingly went on to be a royal marshal, as he is described as *Alardo marescalsco* when witnessing a charter of King Richard's younger brother, John, alongside William Marshal and Baldwin of Béthune in 1197.[174] He was temporarily dispossessed of his lands by John in 1216 and died on crusade in 1220.[175] If we now consider the backgrounds of other members of the royal household we can see that Alard fits an overall profile of familial service.

The Background of Members of the Royal Household

Angevin household knights found themselves in a highly competitive environment. Whilst Henry the Young King sought fame on the tournament field, Richard gained his reputation in war. Howden described all the sons of

---

and H.J. Ellis (London, 1903), no. 14.

[170] *The Manuscripts of His Grace the Duke of Rutland, KG, Preserved at Belvoir Castle*, Vol. 4, ed. J.H. Round (London, 1905), p. 150; *Liber Feodorum. Book of Fees Commonly Called Testa de Nevill, Reformed from the Earliest MSS*, Vol. 1 (London, 1920), p. 50.

[171] Identified as 'Alardus le Flamang filius Willelmi' in a charter to Belvoir Priory, dated 1181–7, *Manuscripts of Rutland*, ed. Round, pp. 104, 150.

[172] Fleming, *Genealogy of the Ancient Flemings*, p. 50.

[173] Bennett, 'Battle of Arsuf/Arsur', pp. 44–53.

[174] F.L. Fleming, *The Ancestry of the Earl of Wigton* (London, 2011), pp. 64–5.

[175] *Rotuli Litterarum Clausarum, 1204–27* (Record Commission, 1833–44), 1:129; *Excerpta e Rotulis Finium in Turri Londinensi asservati, Henry III, 1216–72* (Record Commission, 1835–6), 1:54.

King Henry II as professional warriors.[176] The royal *mesnie* generally did not seemingly provide schooling for young squires, or take on untried knights, but recruited experienced professionals.[177] As such, experienced knights were in high demand.[178]

Table 7. The Background of Richard's *Mesnie* 1189–1194

Background	Number	Crusaded
Henry II's *familia regis*	68	34
Richard's comital *mesnie*	8	5
Family ties to members of the household	70	42
Affiliated households	4	3
Foreigners/Crusaders	31	31
Associated barons and clergy	8	7
Mercenaries	3	0
Not known	98	56
Total*	290 (239)	178 (138)

* Note that a number of individuals appear in more than one category, i.e., they might have both been a member of Henry II's household and also have been related to another member of King Richard's *mesnie*. Figures in brackets are the actual total amounts.

King John had several overlapping categories within his household, such as household knights of the previous monarch, members of John's comital *mesnie*, those with kinship ties to existing members or influential patrons, knightly acquisitions from baronial households, and foreign recruits.[179] Analysis of Richard's household on the Third Crusade indicates that his *familia regis* was broadly similar.

Henry II's Household Knights and Retainers
In contrast to Church's observation that Richard was 'ruthless in his clear out of the old king's men', the review of the royal *mesnie* on crusade found thirty-four men, including Richard of Camville and Stephen of Thornham,

---

[176] *Chronica*, Vol. 2, p. 166.
[177] Church, *Household Knights*, p. 37; see also K. Dutton, 'Ad erudiendum tradidir: The Upbringing of Angevin Comital Children', *ANS*, 22 (2009), 24–39.
[178] William Marshal received several offers when Henry the Young King released him from his service, including an income of 500*l*. if he joined the company of Philip of Alsace, *HGM*, Vol. 1, lines 6157–70.
[179] Church, *Household Knights*, pp. 16–38.

who had served Henry II and were known in his lifetime as the *realx* (king's men).[180] During Richard's absence, a further thirty-four remained in England, many in positions of responsibility for the stability of the realm, such as William Fitz-Ralph, seneschal of Normandy, and Henry of Cornhill. Most tellingly, all the *appares* to the regency council were former members of Henry II's household.[181]

This was in line with normal practice. Prestwich identified several members of Henry I's household, for example, whom he had inherited from William Rufus, which undermined Green's assertion that when King Henry I came to the throne he removed the majority of the previous household staff.[182] On the death of Henry the Young King in 1183, several of his knights moved, or perhaps returned, to the old king's service.[183] However, some of these may have only attached themselves to Henry's household for a specific tournament and were not permanent members of his household.

Acceptance by a new monarch, though tempered by pragmatism, appears to have also been somewhat influenced by the degree of loyalty the knight had displayed toward the previous monarch. Whilst William Marshal enjoyed a relatively smooth passage into royal service, three of his contemporaries who had turned coat to join Richard were deprived of their estates by the new king.[184] Ralph II of Fougères, Jocelin III of Mayenne, and Guy of Valle deserted King Henry II for Richard shortly before the burning of Le Mans in 1189 and had their lands seized by Richard on the death of the king a few weeks later.[185]

---

[180] Church, *Household Knights*, p. 17; see also J.C. Holt, *The Northerners: A Study of the Reign of King John* (Oxford, 1961), p. 218. Others include Baldwin of Béthune, Roger Malchiel, Stephen of Tours, Baldwin of Verdun, William des Roches, and Ralph II of Fougères. Experienced Angevin administrator, Gilbert Pipard, left his estates in Ireland to join King Richard on crusade, only to die in Italy, Howden, *Gesta Regis*, Vol. 2, p. 150.

[181] Geoffrey Fitz-Peter, Hugh Bardolf, Robert of Wheatfield, Roger Fitz-Reinfrey, William Brewer, and William Marshal. In addition, Peter Bertin, William Fitz-Ralph, Richard of Le Hommet, William Fitz-Aldelin, Warin II Fitz-Gerald, and Robert Tresgoz had all been Henry II's men.

[182] Green, *Government*, p. 215; Prestwich, 'Military Household', p. 110; Fourteen of Henry the Young King's household eventually found service with King Richard, ten of whom joined him on the Third Crusade.

[183] In addition to William Marshal and Baldwin of Béthune, William of Cayeux, Baldwin le Carron, Ralph Fitz-Godfrey, Roger of Harcourt, Robert of la Mere, Henry of Longchamp, Gerard Talbot, Robert Tresgoz, and the brothers John, Peter, William and Roger of Préaux had been in Henry the Young King's tournament household and were knights of Henry II and/or Richard's after his death, *HGM*, lines 4543, 4662–9, 4691, 4994–5033, 7997–8015.

[184] *HGM*, lines 9304–409.

[185] Both Howden and Diss wrongly identified him as Geoffrey III, Jocelin's dead father, *Gesta Regis*, Vol. 2, p. 72; Diss, Vol. 1, p. 64. See also J.A. Everard, *Brittany and the*

Gillingham argued that Richard wished to be viewed as a man with a keen sense of honour.[186] Heiser stressed the importance of undivided loyalty, but Richard's response may have been more nuanced.[187] Both Ralph II of Fougères and Jocelin III of Mayenne enjoyed close links to Brittany. Indeed, Ralph had previously rebelled against Henry II in 1174, and Jocelin had been a regular attendee at Henry the Young King's court.[188] Even though Jocelin was stepson to the highly regarded Maurice of Craon and Robert III of Sablé's nephew, this was an ideal opportunity for King Richard to set a precedent for disloyal subjects.[189] He was not without mercy, however, as Ralph attested a royal charter in January 1190. Whether the reconciliation was a pragmatic decision based on the needs of the crusade, or intended to be more durable, is impossible to determine as Ralph died at the siege of Acre the following year.[190] As described earlier, Jocelin III of Mayenne also joined the Third Crusade, rescuing Roger of Tosny during an attack on a Muslim raid in June 1192.[191]

Many of the old household had taken the Cross with Henry II in 1187, so it might be argued that they would have gone on crusade in 1189 whether they remained in the household or not. However, the importance of crusading with the king is, perhaps, illustrated by a further example. As covered in Chapter Two, another former knight of King Henry II, Ranulf of Glanville, purchased release from his crusading vow. However, having lost position under King Richard, he went on jointly to lead the Angevin advance party to the Levant along with several family members and the king had favoured his kinsman, Hubert Walter, for the bishopric of Salisbury in 1189.[192] Even after separating the holders of hereditary offices from those positions that had a practical function in the daily running of the household, Richard did not allow useful members of his father's *mesnie* to go to waste.[193] Rather, it can be seen that, although under no obligation to retain

---

Angevins, Province and Empire, 1158–1203 (Cambridge, 2000), pp. 54–5, 147. A Guido De Valle witnessed a donation to the Hospitallers by Girard of Uchey at the siege of Acre in 1191, but it is not clear if this was the same man, *HdB*, Vol. 3, no. 865.

[186] J. Gillingham, *Richard I*, pp. 104–5

[187] Heiser, 'Royal Familiaries', p. 36.

[188] Turner, 'Households of the Sons', 53; see also *Facsimiles of Early Charters from Northamptonshire Collections*, ed. F. Stenton (Northampton, 1930), p. 28, no. 7.

[189] In 1165, Maurice of Craon paid scutage on 30 knights' fees, Keefe, *Feudal Assessments*, pp.168, 252, n.67. He dictated his will and joined the king on crusade, having been replaced as seneschal of Brittany by Alan of Dinan in 1189, B. de la Jacopière, *Chroniques Craonaises* (Le Mans, 1871), p. 596; Everard, *Brittany and the Angevins*, p. 149.

[190] Wendover, Vol. 1, p. 191.

[191] Ambroise, line 10448; *Itinerarium*, p. 389.

[192] Devizes, p. 19; Diss, Vol. 2, p. 84; *Gesta Regis*, Vol. 2, p. 115.

[193] Several members of Henry the Young King's household can also be found amongst King Richard's *familiares*, as well as William Marshal and Baldwin of Béthune, Robert

their service, Richard employed a significant number of them, many of whom joined him on crusade or were entrusted with positions of authority to oversee the Realm in the king's absence.

King Richard also retained less well-born specialists, such as the aforementioned Alard Fleming and clerics like William of Sainte-Mère-Église. Another example would be Alan Trenchemer, the captain of his father's royal galley. Alan first appears in primary sources in 1176 as shipmaster of a vessel also named *Trenchemer* (*The Sea Cleaver*), an *esnecca*, under Henry II, for which he was paid 12*d.* a day.[194] An *esnecca* was a clench or clinker-built galley, a fast and agile longship with the capacity to be propelled by either oars or a square sail.[195] There are references to a 'tilt' or tent, which suggests that they probably lacked cabins.[196] They were commonly built around twenty rowing benches, but *The Sea Cleaver* was large for its class with its crew of sixty and probably displacing some 240 tons. There was also sufficient space for an escort of men-at-arms when carrying valuables.[197]

The Sea Cleaver was maintained by King Henry II as his primary means of travelling between England and his lands in northern France but was capable of longer voyages.[198] The retention of such a vessel was not new; King

---

of Tresgoz, John, Peter and William of Préaux, Gerard Talbot, and Ralph Fitz-Godfrey were all also part of both entourages, Turner, 'Households of the Sons', pp. 57–8. See also Heiser, 'Royal *Familiares*', p. 37.

[194] PR22 HII (1176), pp. 199–200. According to the *Dialogus*, the *nauclerus* or captain received a fixed stipend of 12d. a day, which was paid by the Exchequer, Vol. 1, p. 6. This was not an inconsiderable sum given that the normal rate for a ship's captain in 1207 was half that, at 6d. a day, PR9 J (1207), p. 168. Whether Alan took his name from his ship or vice versa cannot be determined, but it is possible that the eighteenth- and nineteenth-century British Royal Navy practice of naming sailors after their ship stretched back to the twelfth century. Indeed, Alan's fellow shipmaster, Walter Fitz-Batsuein, also seemingly took his name from his profession. He is variously named Batsecarle, probably the naval equivalent of a *huscarle*, and Boatswain. The *butsecarles* are last referred to in the reign of King Henry I when they seemingly merged with the Cinque Ports fleet and Nicholas Rodger suggests that it came to mean men of the Kentish ports; M. Burrows, *The Cinque Ports* (London, 1895), pp. 54–5; Rodger, *Safeguard of the Sea*, p. 38. Boatswain draws from boat and swain (*svein* is Norse for a young man or retainer) and is the root of the modern Bosun/Bos'n. See also, Hollister, *Military Organisation of Norman England*, pp. 248–51 and J. Beeler, *Warfare in England, 1066–1189* (New York, 1966), p. 46.

[195] Clench is an alternative name for clinker-built, and the name *esnacca* was derived from the Old English *snekkja*, which was seemingly linked to *snacca*, meaning 'snake' or 'serpent'. See also, Rodger, *Safeguard of the Sea*, pp. 47, 592–3.

[196] PR17 HII (1171), p. 139.

[197] 'Et in liberation .ij. navium cum hominibus et armis ad conducendum esneccam in predicto passagio thesauri .lxv. s. per breve Ricardo de Luci', PR24 HII (1178), p. 112.

[198] Its ocean-going capabilities had been tested by Alan Trenchemer prior to the Third Crusade by a voyage to Spain, 'Et in emendatione esnecce Regis et pro funibus et aliis necessariis quando transfretavit in Hyspanias pro comitiisa Flandrie .c. et .xliij.

William I had retained Stephen Fitz-Airard to supply an *esnecca* berthed in Southampton. On Stephen's death, the administration of this arrangement passed first to Nicholas of Sceau and then to Alan Trenchemer.[199] It was, one might say, his royal yacht, but other such vessels were stationed at Barfleur, Dieppe, Hastings, and possibly, Chester.[200] When he required greater strategic transport capacity, the king could call into service additional vessels, most commonly from the Cinque Ports: Dover, Hastings, Hythe, New Romney, and Sandwich, in return for tax exemptions.[201]

King Henry II clearly thought the loss of revenue worth the return and the Pipe Rolls show that retaining a royal yacht was not an inexpensive option. In 1184, the king spent nearly 170*d.* on the refitting of *The Sea Cleaver*, while Alan Trenchemer, its captain, required some 80*d.* more for himself, his crew, and for stores.[202] Three years later, Alan received payment of 13*l.* for timber and carpenters' supplies 'in reparando esnecca regis', with a further payment of 36*l.* 11*s.* for repairs following several trips across the Channel.[203]

On ascending to the throne of England, Richard retained the services of Alan and a further 10*l.* was paid for refitting *The Sea Cleaver*. Based on accounts submitted by Henry of Cornhill, sheriff of Kent, the king brought additional ships into royal service. One belonged to the aforementioned Walter Fitz-Batsuein and William of Braose provided a forty-two-man ship, with a further two fifty-man vessels coming from William of

---

l. et .xv. s. et .ix. d. per breve Rannulfi de Glanuill", PR30 HII (1184), p. 80, 'Et Alaano Trenchem' ad procurationem nautarum qui venerunt ad Sudhantonam ad transfretandum in Hyspanias in servitio regis .xl. s. et .iiij. d. per breve Rannulfi de Glanuill.', pp. 86–7; See also PR 34 HII, pp. 14, 179.

[199] A. Lane Poole, *From Domesday to Magna Carta, 1087–1216* (Oxford, 1955), p. 434.

[200] Godwin of Frenes administered an *esnecca* based at Hastings for King Henry I in return for a serjeanty and the manor of Bekesbourne. In 1130 this was inherited by his eldest son, Robert of Hastings, who changed his name to Burnes, derived from the old name for Bekesbourne. His younger brother, Manasser of Hastings, maintained a 20-man vessel in Grange for the fleet of the Cinque Ports. By 1190 the Bekesbourne *esnecca* was in the hands of Eustace of Burnes, Robert's son; Gilmour, 'Bekesbourne and the King's Esnecca', pp. 315, 317–18.

[201] In the mid twelfth century, King Henry II issued a series of charters to these ports granting them special privileges, including a degree of self-government and an exception from royal tax and tolls in return for a yearly provision of 57 ships for fifteen days. Whilst clearly insufficient to support a major expedition, fifteen days would have met the king's need periodically to move troops and supplies across the Channel. Now lost, these charters were confirmed by Edward I in 1278; G.S. McBain, 'The Charters of the Cinque Ports – Are They Still Needed?', *Review of European Studies*, 5 (2013), pp. 90–126. See also, PR7 HII (1161), pp. 56, 59; PR19 HII (1173), p. 43.

[202] PR30 HII (1184), pp. 58, 80, 86–7. See also, PR31 HII (1185), pp. 216.

[203] PR33 HII (1187), pp. 23, 203.

Stuteville.²⁰⁴ In addition, the Cinque Ports provided thirty-three ships, and Southampton and Shoreham another three each, or roughly a third of the crusading fleet.²⁰⁵

Alan Trenchemer, as mentioned, acted as master of King Richard's flagship on the Third Crusade and he carried Richard back from Antwerp in 1194 after the king had been released from captivity.²⁰⁶ He was paid just over 44 *marks* for 'making the king's ship' in 1193 and in 1195 received nearly 12*l*. for providing forty leather head-coverings and forty doublets for the crews of the king's three longships.²⁰⁷ This demonstrates that, as well a commanding the king's flagship, Alan was responsible for the royal squadron. Indeed, he had earlier commanded the three vessels that carried King Henry II and his retinue in 1185 and later took co-charge of the flotilla King Richard assembled in 1196. As discussed in Chapter Three, he was seemingly allowed to run a side business as in 1195 he was also listed as jointly owing 8*l*. in Northumberland in customs duty for the sale of Flemish cattle.²⁰⁸ This no doubt held him in good stead when he fell from royal favour following King John's failed bid to break King Philip II of France's siege of Chateau Gaillard in 1203, after which some of Alan's royal tenancy lands passed to William of Braose.²⁰⁹

Alan's most notable exploit is highlighted by John of Garland in his description of Richard's triumphs. Ambroise and the *Itinerarium* cover King Richard's capture of a large and well-defended Ayyubid ship, near Sidon, on 7 June 1191, and it is also mentioned by Roger of Howden and Kamal al-Din.²¹⁰ However, John of Garland is unique in identifying Alan's role and naming him 'pirata regis' and 'pirata ducis', stating, 'Alan holed the *dromon* for plunder; he was a fierce and tough leader of seamen' and 'Alan, as I

---

²⁰⁴ William III of Braose was made castellan of Carmarthen, Llawhaden, and Swansea by King Richard, and William of Stuteville replaced Hugh of Le Puiset as sheriff of Northumberland. Braose was also granted the wardship of John of Monmouth by Richard for 1,000 *marks*, extending Braose's influence in the Welsh March; PR2 RI (1190), pp. 48, 59, 68.

²⁰⁵ PR2 RI (1190), pp. 8–9.

²⁰⁶ *Chronica*, Vol. 3, p. 235.

²⁰⁷ PR5 RI (1193), p.150; PR7 RI (1195), p. 113.

²⁰⁸ PR8 RI (1196), p. 20.

²⁰⁹ *Rotuli chartarum in Turri Londinensi asservati*, Vol. 1, Pt 1, ed. T.D. Hardy (London, 1837), p. 134b.

²¹⁰ Ambroise, lines 2137–94; *Chronica*, Vol. 3, p. 112; *Gesta Regis*, Vol. 2, pp. 168–9; *Itinerarium*, pp. 204–9; PR2 RI, pp. 8–9, 131. Kamal al-Din claimed, however, that it was scuttled, Kamal al-Din Abu 'l-Qasim, *Zubdat al-h,alab min tar'ih H,alab*, ed. S. Dahan, trans. E. Blochet, 'L'histoire d'Alep de Kamal-al-Din', *Revue de L'Orient Latin*, Vol. 3 (1895), pp. 509–65.

have recounted, the king's sailor, captured a *dromon* of the Saracens which he holed by swimming under water.'[211]

This review of the evidence supports Howden's statement that: 'Richard, count of Poitiers, honourably retained all the servants of his father the king, whom he knew to be loyal and who had faithfully served his father; and gave back to them their own jobs, which they had done for a long time under his father, to each according to his deserts'.[212] This was not a simplistic market where honour or fidelity was paramount; King Richard maintained a pragmatic system where competence was seemingly highly valued. Although long-term membership brought rewards of land and position, associations were not always permanent, and this did not appear to reduce the immediate usefulness of the knight or cleric.

Comital Household

Richard had been engaged in periodic warfare for some eighteen years before becoming king, and it would be of little surprise if he retained trusted followers, some of whom may have entered his household with no expectations of his becoming king.[213] Unfortunately, information relating to membership of his comital household is limited.

Although Poitevins made up an influential group in the household, only eight individuals can be tracked across with any certainty. As discussed, this maybe down to poor survivability of data, but it is likely an indication that Richard wished to avoid disrupting the political dynamics of the region. In his review of the membership of Richard's household as count of Poitou, Turner determined that the majority of witnesses were local barons who remained in situ when Richard moved his household northwards.[214]

Andrew of Chauvigny and William of Forz are the notable exceptions to this and all played a prominent role on crusade, as subordinate commanders,

---

[211] 'Dromonem p[r]o divitiis penetravit Alan[us], Qui pirata ducis trux et ac[er]bus erat' and 'Alanus, ut dixi, pirata regis, dromonem Sarracenorum cepit, quem perforavit sub aqua natando': *John of Garland's De triumphis Ecclesie: a new critical edition with introduction and translation*, ed. M. Hall (Leiden, 2019). Pirate in the twelfth century was seemingly used for professional sea warriors and was a mark of distinction, as opposed to maritime robbers. For a detailed discussion on the use of the term 'pirate' in twelfth-century Danish chronicles, see Thomas K. Heebøll-Holm, 'Between Pagan Pirates and Glorious Sea-Warriors: The Portrayal of the Viking Pirate in Danish Twelfth-Century Latin Historiography', *Viking and Medieval Scandinavia*, 8 (2012), 141–70.

[212] 'Praedictus vero comes Ricardus Pictavensis honorifice retinuit omnes servientes regis patris suis, quos fideles esse noverat, et qui fideliter servierant patri suo; et illis reddidit servitia sua, quae longo tempore fecerant patris sui, unicuiquo secundum meritum suum', *Gesta Regis*, Vol. 2, p. 72.

[213] For detail on Richard's early military career see, Gillingham, 'Richard I and the Science of Warfare', pp. 78–91.

[214] Turner, 'Households of the Sons', p. 59.

or in overseeing the administration of the Angevin realm. In addition, Payn of Rochefort, Peter Bertin, and Helie of la Celle were appointed seneschals of Anjou, Poitou, and Gascony respectively. Philip of Poitiers had served Richard in Aquitaine and as clerk of the chamber he took on the running of the king's crusading chancellery after Roger of Malchiel drowned.[215] Aimery Odart is named as a knight of Count Richard who fought alongside Andrew of Chauvigny at Le Mans in 1189, but, in an illustration of the limitations of surviving data, does not appear thereafter.[216]

Family Ties to Existing Members and Other Forms of Patronage
As introduced at the start of this case study, contemporary accounts highlight the importance of kinship in unit cohesion, with Ambroise describing a Templar force ambushed by Saladin's men during the Third Crusade as fighting as if, 'they all sprang from one father'.[217] Kinship seems to have had a strong influence on entry into King Richard's household.[218] A total of sixty-nine individuals from families with another member either in King Richard's household or that had served in King Henry II's *mesnie* can be placed in the *familia regis* during this period.[219] However, the only members of the royal household who were related to Richard himself were his distant Poitevin cousin, Andrew of Chauvigny, and his constable as count of Poitou, Geoffrey of Chauvigny.[220]

Like William and John Marshal, the Thornham family had been associated with King Henry II's household. Stephen and Robert of Thornham were the sons of Robert of Thornham, a *justiciar* under Henry II. Stephen followed his father into Henry's service and was rewarded with lands in Surrey. King Richard appointed Robert as one of the *justiciars* of the fleet and he was in command of a flotilla during operations against Isaac Comnenus at Cyprus in May 1191. Robert was then given joint custody of the island along with Richard of Camville and quashed an uprising. He became sole custodian of Cyprus following Richard of Camville's death in June 1191 but was in Jaffa with his elder brother Stephen to witness a charter in August 1192, returning home with King Richard's baggage in 1193.[221] While Robert only

---

[215] Wendover, p. 218; see also Sayers, 'English Charters', p. 195.
[216] *HGM*, lines 8703–9.
[217] Ambroise, lines 7261–2.
[218] *Orderic Vitalis*, Vol. 2, pp. 260–2; Ambroise, lines 6187–90. *HGM* sets the size of William's father, John Marshal's retinue at 300 knights, p. 52.
[219] In addition to holders of hereditary posts, such as the Marshals and Harcourts, the families of Camville, Celle, Cornhill, Craon, l'Estable, Le Hommet, Longchamp, Maron, Préaux, and Thornham are notable examples.
[220] Through King Richard's great-aunt, Hawise of Châtellerault.
[221] *Gesta Regis*, Vol. 2, pp. 166–7, 172–3; *Acta*, Vol. 2, p. 168, no. 220; *Chronica*, Vol. 3, p. 233.

appears on a witness list to a single royal charter between 1189 and 1192, Stephen of Thornham appears in twenty-two. He is described as King Richard's marshal and treasurer (an unusual combination), and acted as a royal ambassador, first to al-Adil and then to Saladin himself. Stephen returned from the Levant in 1193 as escort to Queens Joanna and Berengaria.[222]

By the time another of King Henry II's former knights, Roger of Harcourt, had died on the Third Crusade, his elder brother, Robert, lord of Harcourt and Elbeuf, had joined Richard's household and was a regular attester of royal *acta* whilst the king was imprisoned in Germany.[223] Members of the Préaux family from near Rouen in Normandy also appear on witness lists to royal charters during this period and feature strongly in accounts of the royal household on crusade, arriving in Palestine shortly after the king.[224] Indeed, all five of Osbert of Préaux's sons had served Henry the Young King and are associated with at least one other Plantagenet household.[225] John, as the eldest, succeeded his father as lord of Préaux before 1189 and he witnessed eleven of Richard's charters between 1189 and 1192, including at Messina and Jaffa. In 1190, he was one of the knights named as surety for King Richard's peace treaty with King Tancred and, along with his brother Peter, John participated in the relief of Jaffa in July 1192.[226] Peter of Préaux was sent to Tyre to negotiate the release of the Muslim hostages from Conrad of Montferrat and acted as King Richard's standard-bearer during the relief of Jaffa.[227] Their brother, William, acted as an envoy for Richard, but was captured by the Muslims while helping the king escape an ambush. One of King Richard's last acts in the Levant was to negotiate the release of William at the cost of ten notable Muslim prisoners.[228] Their brother, Engelram of Préaux, however, served in John's household, which is suggestive of a familial strategy, such as may also have been employed by the Marshals, with John Marshal also being Count John's man whilst his younger brother served Richard.

The skirmish in which William of Préaux was captured by the Muslims also provides the identities of two other families linked to Richard's household. Reiner of Moron and his nephew, Walter, and Alan and Luke of l'Etable were all killed in this encounter. However, given the lack of other data on these four, they may well have been part of a temporary, crusader element in the *mesnie*.[229] Henry of Longchamp witnessed twenty-six of

---

[222] *Chronica*, Vol. 3, p. 228; Ambroise, p. 148, n. 558.
[223] Heiser, 'Households of the Justiciars', p. 235.
[224] Ambroise, line 4723; *Itinerarium*, p. 217.
[225] Powicke, *Loss of Normandy*, pp. 341, 350.
[226] Ambroise, line 10969; *Itinerarium*, p. 405.
[227] *Itinerarium*, p. 405.
[228] Ambroise, lines 7110, 12228; *Itinerarium*, p. 440.
[229] Ambroise, line 7120; *Itinerarium*, pp. 286–8.

King Richard's *acta* prior to the king's departure for the Holy Land and in 1190 he went north with other members of the household to investigate the reported massacre of York's Jewish community. Henry did not crusade but remained in England as sheriff of Herefordshire until his brother, William of Longchamp, bishop of Ely, was deposed.[230] However, their brother Stephen witnessed an impressive seventy-three of King Richard's *acta*, went on crusade as a royal steward, was appointed joint governor of Acre, and served with distinction during a number of engagements.[231]

Other families of note include the Angevin knights Geoffrey of la Celle and his relation Helia, seneschal of Gascony, William and Anseau IV of Cayeux, and the influential Norman family of Le Hommet, of which Jordan died on crusade while Richard of Le Hommet remained in Normandy as the duchy's constable. Warin II Fitz-Gerald's father had been chamberlain to King Henry II and, as baron of the Exchequer, Warin joined his king on the Third Crusade.[232] In addition, Robert of Quincy's son had married into the Beaumont family, hereditary High Stewards of the royal household. Both Earl Robert and his son, Robert Fitz-Pernel, journeyed to the East and this may account for Robert's service with King Richard for the duration of the Third Crusade rather than with another contingent. However, Quincy was also linked through his mother to the Clare family and his elder brother had married Asceline Peverel, sister to William Peverel who died on the Second Crusade and probable descendant of Pagan Peverel.[233]

In line with the evidence from other Angevin military households, kinship ties with those already in royal service were influential in gaining access to Richard's *familia regis*. However, in stark contrast to Duby's position, it should also be noted that, far from being the preserve of landless younger siblings, first-born sons were also a significant feature within the *mesnie*.[234] While Church suggests that, in the case of John's household, this was perhaps to gain experience and establish their reputations at court prior to inheriting the family patrimony, men such as Henry of Longchamp and John of Préaux remained part of the *familia regis* long after they had come into their inheritance.[235] Arguably, King Richard was capable of meeting

---

[230] Landon, *Itinerary*, nos. 130–2, 135–6, 153, 161–3, 175–82, 196–202, 226; PR 2 R I (1190), p. 8.

[231] Ambroise, lines 9288, 10459, *Gesta Regis*, Vol. 2, p. 190; *Itinerarium*, pp. 355, 376, 389; Landon, nos. 41, 68–76, 80–5, 96–101, 126, 145, 156–60, 167, 175–83, 189–93, 195–202, 206–7, 219, 223, 227–9, 260–2, 292.

[232] Ambroise, lines 4725, 7496; *Itinerarium*, pp. 217, 300; Landon, *Itinerary*, nos. 131, 175–81, 183–93, 342, 366. See also, Vincent, 'Warin and Henry Fitz Gerald', 233–60.

[233] For William Peverel, see *Gesta Stephani, Regis Anglorum et Ducis Normannorum*, Vol. 2, ed. R.C. Sewell (London, 1846), p. 111. For more on Pagan, see Edgington, 'Pagan Peverel', pp. 90–3.

[234] Duby, 'Les "jeunes" dans la societé aristocratique', pp. 835–47.

[235] Church, *Household Knights*, p. 26.

the baron's expectations of power, influence, and reward to retain their service in ways that his younger brother was not.

Affiliated Households

The younger sons of other eminent houses were often placed in the *mesnie* of a powerful ally to be trained as knights. When Raymond of Poitiers was recommended by Fulk V of Anjou, king of Jerusalem, as a potential candidate to marry the heiress of Antioch, he was at the court of King Henry I. He had been knighted by the king of England and, at thirty-four, seems to have been there for many years. Given that permission was requested of Henry, it is very likely that he was a household knight.[236] This is a very rare example of a young noble being raised to knighthood in a royal household rather than that of a noble. As discussed, the overwhelming majority of warriors identified in studies of Angevin households entered service as experienced knights. In comparison, a number of individuals were placed in John's *familia regis* as a demonstration of loyalty or were either promoted or 'poached' from baronial households by the king.[237] Yet the only potential example of such a knight within King Richard's household is Saul of Bruil, who is considered in the next section.

It was seemingly fairly normal for men to be placed by their lord in another household. For example, Henry II attached William Marshal to the household of Henry the Young King and an examination of John's charters shows another son of Osbert of Préaux, Engelram, as a regular witness between 1185 and 1195.[238] It is not possible, however, to determine if Richard lent him to John in the same way as William Marshal joined Henry the Young King, if the family had chosen to protect their position by placing family members in both camps, or if Engelram chose to go his own way and ally himself with John. It is suggestive that his disappearance from John's witness lists coincides with King Richard's return from captivity. Peter of Préaux then seemingly took up position in John's household, witnessing six of John's *acta* between 1197 and 1198.[239] However, Engelram was back within the household in May 1201.[240]

---

[236] William of Tyre, *Historia Rerum in Partibus Transmarinis Gestarum*, xiv, ix, xx; J.P. Phillips, 'A Note on the Origins of Raymond of Poitiers', *EHR*, 106/418 (1991), 66–7.

[237] Church, *Household Knights*, p. 29.

[238] For William Marshal and evidence of other placemen in Henry the Young King's household, see Turner, 'Households of the Sons', pp. 52–5, and Strickland, *Henry the Young King*. Thirty *acta* are witnessed by Engelram between 1185 and 1195, Church, *Household Knights*, p. 21.

[239] M. Preen, 'The Acta of Count John, Lord of Ireland and Count of Mortain, with a Study of his Household', nos. 130, 133, 134, 138, 139, 140, cited in Church, *Household Knights*, p. 21 note.

[240] *Rotuli de Liberate ac de Misis et Praestitis Regnante Johanne*, ed. T.D. Hardy (London, 1844), p. 13.

Once again, while loyalty to the lord was important, it was seemingly understood that knights might have been subject to other considerations such as membership of complex familial and regional networks, as well as the requirement for economic security. This reinforces the view of an acceptance of temporary as well as more permanent membership of the household. This evidence has a significant impact on how we should look upon the relationships between a king and the martial elite. It also indicates why a king demanding unconditional loyalty could provoke a strong response from the nobility.

Associated Powerful Barons and Clergy

Lay magnates also served in military households and some rose to become earls. This had been an accepted route to greater influence under the Norman kings, with William I and II of Warenne, Robert of Beaumont, Ranulf le Meschin, and Robert of Gloucester all being belted earls following membership of the military household.[241] Whilst also a member of King Henry II and then Richard's household, on his marriage to Isabel of Clare, William Marshal joined the select band of great magnates and formed his own *mesnie*.[242] William of Forz and Andrew of Chauvigny were similarly elevated to the high nobility through being given wealthy heiresses in marriage by Richard.[243]

Robert Fitz-Pernel, earl of Leicester, was belted earl by King Richard in Messina following the death of his father on his return from the Holy Land. Whilst it is likely that the bulk of the Leicester retinue was with his father, it would have been surprising for a high-born noble to travel alone. A group of ten knights were named as present with Earl Robert IV at the battle of Ramla in 1192.[244] As discussed in Chapter Three, of these, Arnold IV of Bois was his steward and Dreux of Fontenil was linked to the earldom. Indeed, all were either linked to Earl Robert by blood or close geographical association, which aided the development of unit cohesion. Within the group are

---

[241] Prestwich, 'Military Household', p. 23.

[242] William Marshal was not made an earl until 1199, but quickly adopted the trappings of that position and was even listed as such in a handful of charters prior to being belted, J. Gillingham, 'War and Chivalry in the History of William Marshal', *Thirteenth Century England III: Proceedings of the Newcastle Upon Tyne Conference, 1987*, ed. P.R. Cross and S.D. Lloyd (Bury St Edmunds, 1988), pp. 1–13.

[243] For more on William of Forz, see *Gesta Regis*, Vol. 2, pp. 110, 115–16, 124. For Andrew of Chauvigny, see Ambroise, lines 4990, 7542, 10961, 11378–11620, 11843; *Gesta Regis*, Vol. 2, p. 76; *HGM*, lines 8662–80; *Itinerarium*, pp. 218, 227, 292, 302, 355, 405, 415, 432–3.

[244] *Itinerarium*, p. 301, Ambroise, line 7520. According to the *Infeudationes militum* of 1172, the house of Leicester could draw upon some 140 knights from their estates in Normandy alone with a further 10 owed to the duke of Normandy, Keefe, *Feudal Assessments*, p. 147.

another set of brothers, Saul and William of Bruil, probably of Breuil, near Earl Robert's estate lands in Calvados. However, King Richard employed Saul as a royal messenger to King Henry of Jerusalem in 1194.[245] So the brothers may have been loaned to Earl Robert's household for the duration of the Third Crusade or it is possible that Saul was recruited into King Richard's service sometime later. In any event, the narrative accounts pay particular attention to the young earl and indicate a very close affiliation to King Richard's household on crusade as would befit his hereditary rank of steward of the royal household.

As considered in the last chapter, Rotrou III, count of Perche, is perhaps illustrative of the changeable relationship between magnate and monarch, and the challenges to those that held lands placed within both the Capetian and Plantagenet spheres of interest.[246] In marrying his son, Geoffrey, to Richenza-Matilda of Saxony, Count Rotrou placed his heir at the centre of King Richard's court. Hence, whilst Rotrou travelled with King Philip II's household to the Holy Land, Geoffrey spent much of 1189 with Richard and, after travelling to Sicily with his father and King Philip II, re-joined his uncle-in-law for the Christmas festivities of 1190. Geoffrey then continued on to Palestine with Richard, witnessed the king's wedding settlement with Berengaria at Limassol in May 1191, and, despite the death of his father during the siege of Acre, remained with King Richard until after a skirmish with Muslim forces in June 1192.[247] Other French nobles adjusted their allegiance as the campaign progressed. Whilst the Count of St Pol travelled to the Holy Land with King Philip II, after the French king's departure he appears to have been associated with Richard and was described as fighting alongside the earl of Leicester in 1191.[248]

King Richard enjoyed considerable success in placing his candidates in ecclesiastical posts in England. At the Council of Pipewell in September 1189, in addition to securing the archbishopric of York for his half-brother, Geoffrey, William of Longchamp was elected to the bishopric of Ely, Godfrey of Lucy to Winchester, Richard Fitz-Neal to London, and Hubert Walter to Salisbury. Lucy, Fitz-Neal, and Walter all came from administrative families and Longchamp, of course, had been the new king's chancellor as count of Poitou.

To offset his half-brother's new power base in Yorkshire, King Richard surrounded him with subordinates loyal to the Crown, such as Henry

---

[245] *Chronica*, Vol. 3, p. 233.
[246] Ambroise, line 4537; *Chronica*, Vol. 3, p. 88; *Gesta Regis*, Vol. 2, pp. 73, 92–3, 143; *Itinerarium*, p. 213; Rigord, p. 83; *Gesta Regis*, Vol. 2, pp. 73, 92–3, 143; Wendover, pp. 170, 191. See also, Thompson, *Power and Border Lordship*, pp. 104–16.
[247] *Gesta Regis*, Vol. 2, pp. 73, 128, 150; Devizes, p. 22; *Itinerarium*, p. 372.
[248] Ambroise, line 7274; *Itinerarium*, p. 293.

Marshal as dean of York and Bouchard le Puiset as his treasurer.[249] Most ecclesiastic magnates remained in their sees, indeed, whilst the bishops of Bath, Coventry, Durham, and Norwich had all originally taken the Cross, all but John of Oxford, bishop of Norwich, remained in England and the pope gave him leave to return to England after he was robbed en route to the Holy Land.[250]

There were, however, notable exceptions. In addition to Baldwin of Forde and Hubert Walter, other ecclesiastical magnates from the Angevin realm that joined King Richard in the Levant included Bernard of la Carra, bishop of Bayonne, and Gérard of la Barthe, archbishop of Auch. They both served as two of Richard's naval *justiciars*, acted as surety for the king's treaty with Tancred in Sicily, and continued on to Acre where they participated in the cleansing of its churches on 16 July 1191.[251] Walter of Coutances, archbishop of Rouen, also took the Cross and made it as far as Messina, but was released to join King Richard's regency council once news of William of Longchamp's difficulties reached the king.[252] In addition to performing the coronation of Berengaria and participating in the cleansing of Acre's churches, John Fitz-Luke, bishop of Evreux, played an active role at King Richard's crusading court, but died whilst joint-governor of Jaffa.[253] While Henry II's cleric, Gerald of Wales took the Cross, and was released from his vow, Roger of Howden actually made it to the Holy Land. He then returned with Philip II's party – probably under orders from Richard to accompany the French king.[254]

From this review, it can be seen that the role of lay and ecclesiastical magnates was not set by convention but was balanced by the interplay of needs and desires between the individual and their monarch. Just as

---

[249] William of Chimellé was also made archdeacon of nearby Richmond; Turner and Heiser, *Richard the Lionheart*, p. 95.

[250] Simeon of Durham, *Symeonis Monachi Opera Omnia*, Vol. 1, ed. by T. Arnold (London, 1882), p. lxiii; Devizes, pp. 10–11; *Gesta Regis*, Vol. 2, pp. 79, 105–6, 115.

[251] Bishop Bernard also accompanied King Richard on his visit to Joachim of Fiore, *Gesta Regis*, Vol. 2, pp. 110, 115–16, 134; Wendover, pp. 181, 186, Landon, *Itinerary*, no. 342.

[252] Devizes, pp. 22, 27–8; *Gesta Regis*, Vol. 2, p. 128, 158; *Itinerarium*, p. 176; Rigord, p. 83. For more of Archbishop Walter, see P.A. Poggioli, 'From Politics to Prelate: The Career of Walter of Coutances, Archbishop of Rouen, 1184–1207' (PhD thesis, Johns Hopkins University, 1984).

[253] Ambroise, lines 1006, 4699, 7177; Devizes, p. 22; *Gesta Regis*, Vol. 2, pp. 30–2, 45–6, 75–6, 101, 128, 153, 167; *Itinerarium*, pp. 217, 289; Landon, *Itinerary*, nos. 10–11, 33, 72–6, 97–101, 115, 123, 211–12, 227–9, 231–4, 236–40, 329–30, 344, 347, 358. See also, Heiser, 'Court of the Lionheart', p. 513.

[254] Gerald of Wales, *Giraldi Cambrensis Opera*, 8 Vols, ed. J.S. Brewer, J.F. Dimock and G.F. Warner (London, 1861–91), Vol. 1, pp. 84–5; D. Corner, 'The Earliest Surviving Manuscripts of Roger of Howden's "Cronica"', *EHR*, 98 (1983), 126–40. For his departure see Gillingham, 'Howden on Crusade', pp. 60–75.

William of Longchamp and Robert IV, earl of Leicester, operated as permanent members of the *familia regis*, Bernard of la Carra and Gérard of la Barthe seemingly only joined the household during the initial stages of the Crusade. Despite being one of the few mounted warriors the relief of the siege of Jaffa, Ralph of Mauléon also seems to fit into this second category of being a temporary, crusader attachment, but these are considered in the next section.

Whilst, the Lusignans probably sought Richard's patronage to offset the power of Conrad of Montferrat, William Marshal remained in the West, taking control of his new lands and, perhaps, seeking stability through the extension of his new family.[255] Similarly, with Ranulf III, earl of Chester, only gaining his majority in 1187 and then marrying Constance of Brittany in early 1190, it is likely he also remained in England to secure his own inheritance, as well as the lands of his new wife.[256]

This was a world in which shifting commitments were seemingly more readily accepted than previous research has indicated, and this was likely a feature of the political culture of the Angevin household and governance. Loyalty was not necessarily expected to extend beyond the length of a campaign or mutually convenient accord. As William of Préaux's willingness to sacrifice himself for his king demonstrates, however, there were expectations of the utmost loyalty from the inner circle of household knights.

Foreign-born Knights and Crusader Additions to the Household

Membership of households at all levels was open to knights from outside the polity of its head, be it a baron, a magnate, or a monarch. Knights from the Low Countries, for example, can be routinely found in Angevin *mesnie*. Narrative sources stated that King Richard took men into his service at Marseille and outbid Philip II in hiring knights at Acre, and this is supported by the identification of specific individuals.[257] Men such as the Flemish tournament champion, Baldwin of Béthune, and his compatriots Baldwin le Carron, William of Cayeux, and Otto II of Trazegnies entered Richard's household either in the lead-up to or during the course of the Third Crusade.[258] Whilst some might have been recruited as a result of penury, such as was the case of Joinville in the Seventh Crusade, some enjoyed

---

[255] For more on the Lusignans, see C. de Vasselot de Régné, 'A Crusader Lineage from Spain to the Throne of Jerusalem: The Lusignans', *Crusades*, 16 (2017), 95–114; S. Painter, 'The Lords of Lusignan in the Eleventh and Twelfth Centuries', *Speculum*, 32 (1957), 27–47.

[256] K. Hurlock, 'Cheshire and the Crusades', *Transactions of the Historic Society of Lancashire and Cheshire*, 159 (2010), 1–18.

[257] *Gesta Regis*, Vol. 2, pp. 112, 186; *Itinerarium*, pp. 213–4, 225; Diss, Vol. 2, p. 88.

[258] Ambroise, lines 6421, 7276; *Itinerarium*, pp. 269, 292; Wendover, p. 218. The Low Counties had a strong history of crusading, with contingents in both the First and Second Crusades, see also, J. Phillips, 'The Murder of Charles the Good and the Second

a long association with Richard's family.[259] As we have seen, Baldwin of Béthune's association with the Angevin house stretched back to service with both Henry the Young King and King Henry II, and he had been a knight-banneret long before he joined Richard's *familia regis* in 1189.[260] Baldwin le Carron and William of Cayeux had also served Henry the Young King, and Otto had only recently returned from a pilgrimage to the Holy Land.[261] As has already been highlighted, the apparent ease with which knights could move between households and assimilate into different military formations is indicative of an underlying system or systems of commands, signals, and basic drills.

William of Cayeux saw action near Ramla and, the previous year, he and Otto of Trazegnies were sent by King Richard to support a Templar patrol ambushed by the Muslims.[262] Like Baldwin le Carron, Otto of Trazegnies was a knight of Count Baldwin of Hainaut, but as mentioned in the previous chapter, he also enjoyed revenues in Kent worth 40s. a year.[263] He was said to have camped between Hugh IV of Gournay and Florence of Angest, count of Holland, during the siege of Acre.[264] Given Hugh's close association with Richard during the course of the crusade, it is most likely that Otto, along with Baldwin le Carron and Baldwin of Dargis, joined the Angevin contingent prior to journeying to the Levant, rather than after Richard's arrival.[265]

Crusade: Household, Nobility, and Traditions of Crusading in Medieval Flanders', *Medieval Prosopography* 19 (1998), pp. 55–75.

[259] John of Joinville, 'La Vie de saint Louis', *RHF*, Vol. 20 (1840), 299.

[260] Asbridge, *Greatest Knight*, p. 133. In an undated charter, King Richard awarded the three manors of Luton, Wantage, and Norton to Baldwin of Béthune, TNA, *carte antique* roll EE, no. 27. It was, however, witnessed by William of Forz and must have been sometime before his death in 1195. Pipe Roll returns relating to Norton place the award between 1189 and 1191, see PR3 RI (1191), p. 153 and PR4 RI (1192), p. 258.

[261] Otto II of Trazegnies departed for the kingdom of Jerusalem in 1184, i.e., he was in the Holy Land around the same time as William Marshal. Otto brought back relics, including a fragment of the True Cross, *Crusade Charters*, nos. 14, 88–89. For William Marshal's pilgrimage, see Asbridge, *Greatest Knight*, pp. 165–70.

[262] Ambroise, line 7276; *Itinerarium*, p. 292.

[263] 'et milites strenui comitis Hanoniensis fideles et commilitones, Eustacius scilicet junior de Ruez, Osto de Trasiniis, Walterus de Fontanis...', Gilbert of Mons, p. 132; PR2 RI, p. 147.

[264] Wendover, p. 178. Whilst not a wholly reliable source, Wendover's description is supported in part by Ralph of Diss, who lists Otto between Hugh of Gournay and Count Florence in his description of the Latin camp outside Acre in 1190, Diss, Vol. 2, p. 79.

[265] Richard appointed Hugh IV of Gournay governor of Acre in 1191 and gave him responsibility for the Angevin share of Muslim prisoners, *Gesta Regis*, Vol. 2, pp. 179–80. Baldwin of Dargis was associated with Baldwin le Carron at the siege of Acre, *Gesta Regis*, Vol. 2, p. 144.

Other probable members of Richard's *mesnie* who hailed from outside the Angevin realm include William Bloez and Henry le Teuton, King Richard's standard-bearer at Jaffa in 1192.[266] The standard fulfilled a critical function during a medieval battle, and Henry's selection is another indication of the levels of trust Richard placed in his non-native knights.[267] In addition, the Scottish nobleman Robert of Quincy represented King Richard on the second delegation sent to Tyre to recover the Muslim captives and, as mentioned earlier, was then appointed commander of a six hundred-strong force to assist the principality of Antioch.[268]

Many of the sixteen warriors from outside the Angevin realm were professional warriors, known as *stipendarii*, and, much like William Marshal on the death of Henry the Young King, they would have been in high demand as long as their reputations were intact.[269] Until granted lands and title, their income was dependent on military service. As well as crusaders, King Richard recruited additional manpower from the elite of the Latin East. Humphrey, lord of Toron, the former husband of Isabel of Jerusalem, came to Cyprus with the Poitevins Guy and Geoffrey of Lusignan to pay homage to Richard. Thereafter he can be seen as a member of embassies to Saladin and may well have been used by Richard as a diplomatic translator.[270] These serve as a clear example of a knightly society where loyalty was tempered by pragmatism, and in which an instrumental element in the relationship between lord and household knight was both practical and morally acceptable.

In addition to the non-Angevin knights listed above, a number of Angevin knights entered King Richard's household during the course of the Third Crusade, most likely as a result of their performance in the Holy Land. For example, there is no evidence of William of l'Étang within the *familia regis* until narrative sources mention him in reconnoitring Ascalon by boat with Geoffrey of Lusignan and during the relief of Jaffa in 1192. His first appearance on a witness list was in 1193 and he rose to become an important military commander.[271]

---

[266] Ambroise, line 11402; *Itinerarium*, pp. 218, 415.

[267] R.W. Jones, *Bloodied Banners: Martial Display on the Medieval Battlefield* (Woodbridge, 2010), pp. 33–56.

[268] *Gesta Regis*, Vol. 2, p. 185–7; *Itinerarium*, p. 242.

[269] Baldwin of Béthune, Baldwin le Carron, Henry Teuton, Bertram of Verdun, Geoffrey of Bruillon, William of Cayeux, Renier of Maron, Walter of Moron, Humphrey of Toron, Otto of Trazegnies, Seguin Barrez, William Bloez, Manessier of l'Isle, Alberic of Marines, and Ralph, viscount of Châteaudon.

[270] *Gesta Regis*, Vol. 2, p. 165; *Baha' al-Din*, pp. 194, 231. See also, T.S. Asbridge, 'Talking to the Enemy: The Role and Purpose of Negotiations between Saladin and Richard the Lionheart during the Third Crusade', *JMH*, 39 (2013), 275–96.

[271] Ambroise, lines 6968, 11398; *Itinerarium*, pp. 283, 415; Wendover, p. 220. For William's rise within the court on return from the Crusade see Heiser, 'Royal Familiares', p. 34 and 'Court of the Lionheart', p. 521.

Evidence from the Pipe Rolls and charters places Robert Peverel with the king in Normandy in 1194, 1198, and 1199, but there is no evidence to link Robert to the *mesnie* during the Crusade or, indeed, in the Holy Land alongside his cousin William Peverel, who died in the East, which may have eased Robert's entry into royal service.[272] Whilst owing the Crown but a single knight's fee, Thomas Keefe suggests that the honour of Peverel could call upon one hundred knights in England alone.[273] Despite sharing the fee with Norman of Normanville, William no doubt headed a formidable retinue.[274] After King Richard's death, Church tracks Robert Peverel into the service of John, where he played an 'active part in the defence of Normandy' and eased the passage of his brother Thomas Peverel into the *familia regis*.[275] In comparison, despite Ralph of Mauléon's close association with the household of crusade, he seemingly left the king's service on return from the Holy Land.[276]

Many of the participants listed in the skirmish at Betenoble were probably a temporary, crusader element of the household as they do not appear in accounts or *acta* in the lead-up to the campaign.[277] However, this may be another illustration of the limitations imposed by relying on charter evidence alone as the *Itinerarium* unequivocally described them as 'a few of his household': *rex Ricardus cum paucissimis familiaribus nimis solitarius quadam die egressus*.[278]

Stipendarii and *Mercenarii*

The distinction between the *stipendarii* described above and hired troops/mercenaries can appear very subtle to the modern eye, yet the social division seemed clear to men like William Marshal's biographer.[279] As John

---

[272] With King Richard, Normandy (1194, 1198, 1199), PR6 RI (1194), p. 230, PR9 RI (1197), p. 223, and at Chinon with King Richard (1199), Landon, *Itinerary*, no. 144; as outlined earlier in relation to Robert of Quincy, the Peverels had a crusading pedigree. For William, see PR34 HII (1188), p. 59; PR2 RI (1190), p. 110; *Rotuli de Liberate*, p. 30.

[273] Keefe, *Feudal Assessments*, pp. 181, 259 n.120.

[274] In addition to William, the Pipe Rolls only allow four crusaders of the honour of Peverel to be tracked: Richard of Muntuiron, Brian Fitz-Ralph, Robert Mortimer, Robert of Horningsheath, and Eudes Fitz-Aernisis, PR2 RI (1190), p. 110.

[275] Church, *Household Knights*, p. 19.

[276] Ambroise, lines 10965, 11378–11620, 11497: *Itinerarium*, pp. 218, 405, 418; Landon, *Itinerary*, no. 366.

[277] Philip, Manessier of Lille, and Thierry and Richard of Orcq, as well as Baldwin le Carron and Otto of Trazegnies, Ambroise, lines 9920–47; *Itinerarium*, p. 373. Although not listed in this passage, Gilbert of Mons adds their brothers Ivo and John of Orcq as also having died during the campaign, p. 274.

[278] *Itinerarium*, p. 286.

[279] D. Crouch, 'William Marshal and the Mercenatiat', *Mercenaries and Paid Men, The Mercenary Identity in the Middle Ages*, ed. J. France (Leiden, 2008), pp. 15–32.

France pointed out, by the twelfth century, 'it is apparent that most men serving as soldiers were paid'.[280] Military service was costly and, less those with an income sufficient to finance the long-term expense of arms, horses, grooms, etc., as well as the logistical burdens of a particular campaign, there was a requirement for fighting men to be funded. As considered in relation to money-fiefs in the last chapter, the pension given to a *stipendarius* might serve to distinguish the noble-born paid knight from the lowborn, but sometimes mounted, warrior on a short-term contract.[281] Despite the seemingly low number of household knights on John's muster roll of 1215, for example, a further 375 knights from the Low Countries can be identified on the list, and these may have received money fees.[282] Notwithstanding the obvious distaste in William Marshal's biography towards men like Sancho of Savannac, Mercadier, and Lupescar, the position of mercenary captains was more ambiguous.[283]

Medieval writers adopted generic terms for mercenaries, however, such as *routier*, or linked them to particular regions, like the Brabant and the Basque country, rather than explicitly identifying them as men paid with money to fight.[284] The Third Lateran Council (1179), for example, specified six groups of hired soldiers by region and placed both the mercenaries and those who hired or supported them under anathema.[285] Boussard, in his study of twelfth-century mercenaries, places mercenaries at the core of Angevin armies.[286] In turn, Richard Hosler has highlighted how and why King Henry II used mercenaries on campaign, demonstrating that the king of England recognised their specialist expertise, deployed them in independent and coherent units, and actively sought to recruit mercenaries prior to launching a campaign.[287]

---

[280] France, *Mercenaries and Paid Men*, p. 7.

[281] King Henry I paid his household knights at least 5l. annually and additional moneys when they were in the field. Map, *De Nugis curialium*, p. 314; On King John's reward system see Church, 'Rewards of Royal Service', pp. 287–97.

[282] Church, 'Knights of John's Household', pp. 151–62.

[283] *HGM*, lines 7003, 10933–56, 11117–22, 12595–606. See also H. Geraud, *Mercadier: Les Routiers au treizième siècle*, Bibliothèque de l'École des Chartes, 1st series, t. III. (1842), pp. 417–43

[284] France, *Western Warfare in the Age of the Crusades, 1000–1300* (New York, 1999), pp. 73–4.

[285] Canon 27 of Lateran III excommunicated those that hire, keep, or support Brabanters, Aragonese, Navarese, Basques, Coterelli, and Triavertini who practise cruelty upon Christians, *Decrees of the Ecumenical Councils*, Vol. 1, ed. N.P. Tanner (Washington, D.C., 1990), pp. 224–5.

[286] J. Boussard, 'Les mercenaires au XIIe siècle, Henri II Plantagenêt et les origins de l'armée de métier', *Bibliothèque de l'École de Chartes*, 106 (1945–6), 189–224.

[287] S.D. Hosler, 'Revisiting Mercenaries under Henry Fitz Empress, 1167–1188', *Mercenaries and Paid Men, The Mercenary Identity in the Middle Ages*, ed. J. France (Leiden, 2008), pp. 33–42.

Henry II paid his infantrymen a penny a day, and King Richard raised this to two pence and standardised their equipment.²⁸⁸ Moreover, these men could make their way in society and Contamine contends that mercenaries attempted to integrate themselves into the normal ranks of feudal society, like Philip II's *routier* captain, Cadac, who became castellan of Gaillon, *bailli* of Pont-Audemer, and a knight.²⁸⁹ Similarly, one of Richard's captains, the infamous Mercadier, called himself the king's *famulus* and was eventually made a baron of the Limousin by his king.²⁹⁰ However, the single strand of evidence for any *routier* captains, such as Mercadier, from the Angevin realm being in the Holy Land during the course of the Third Crusade has been found to be a forgery.²⁹¹

As Nicholas Prouteau has pointed out, that is not to say that King Richard did not hire local specialist mercenaries. Ambroise indicated that the king retained military engineers captured onboard the Muslim dromond off the coast of Acre in June 1191 and Baha' al-Din Ibn Shaddad asserted that Richard had succeeded in corrupting miners and sappers from Aleppo into his service.²⁹² Their capture and employment is confirmed by Kamal al-Din, with Ambroise and Ibn Shaddad describing Richard hiring additional fighting troops (*serjanz*) and utilising local expertise at the siege of Darum in May 1192.²⁹³

Despite Wales being a traditional source of recruiting for Angevin kings, there are only subtle indications to substantiate Gerald of Wales' claim that the preaching of Baldwin of Forde successfully produced a sizeable contingent of Welsh crusaders, many of whom were seemingly recruited from outside Angevin territory.²⁹⁴ The period of King Richard's participation

---

²⁸⁸ Boussard, 'Les mercenaires au XIIe siècle', p. 193.

²⁸⁹ P. Contamine, *War in the Middle Ages*, trans. M. Jones (Oxford, 1984), p. 247.

²⁹⁰ Powicke, *Loss of Normandy*, p. 32; S.D.B. Brown, 'The Mercenary and His Master, Military Service and Monetary Reward in the Eleventh and Twelfth Centuries', *History*, 74 (1989), 24–8, 34–5; H. Géraud, 'Les Routiers au XIIe siècle', *Bibliothèque de l'École des Chartes*, 3 (1841–2), 146–7.

²⁹¹ Charter 219, dated Acre, 3 August, forms part of the notorious 'Courtois' archive. It was made out to James de Jhoto requesting credit for Geoffrey de Haia, William de Gorram, Philip Walensi, and Mercadier, described as crusaders returning from the Holy Land. While this charter has been established as a forgery by R.-H. Bautier, it may well be based on a forged original to James of Jhota dated at Acre 21 July 1191, which has since been lost or destroyed, see *Acta*, p. 168.

²⁹² Ambroise, lines 2166–8; Baha' al-Din, p. 203; N. Prouteau, '"Beneath the Battle"? Miners and Engineers as "Mercenaries" in the Holy Land', *Mercenaries and Paid Men, The Mercenary Identity in the Middle Ages*, ed. J. France (Leiden, 2008), pp. 105–17.

²⁹³ *Zubdat al-halab min ta'rih Halab*, 3 Vols, ed. S. Dahan (Damascus, 1951–68), 'L'histoire d'Alep de Kamal-al-Din', 509–65; Ambroise, lines 9136–9243; Baha' al-Din, pp. 203, 210.

²⁹⁴ Gerald of Wales claims 3,000 took the Cross as a result of the preaching tour, but there are only a few references to Welshmen at the siege of Acre and only Marcher lords,

in the Third Crusade and his subsequent captivity marked the only time when there were no significant deployments of Welsh troops on the continent and, in particular, in Normandy between 1187 and 1204.[295] However, numbers were recruited for service closer to home during Richard's absence by Count John, William Marshal, and William of Braose.[296]

In summary, the sources indicate that Richard outbid Philip II for the services of non-aligned warriors at Acre in 1191 and hired additional serjeants for the siege of Darum. In addition, Prouteau's excellent research into locally recruited miners and engineers demonstrates the king's use of indigenous expertise to capture Muslim strongholds. Beyond this, the evidence is too slim to form a firm notion of the role of mercenaries as part of King Richard's household during the Third Crusade. Moreover, what evidence survives is of temporary auxiliaries rather than those who might have been considered members of the household.

The Crusading *Mesnie*

The broadening of a review of Richard's *mesnie* in this work to include evidence other than from charters has led to new information on Richard's household between 1189 and 1192 and adds to our overall understanding of its composition and the manner in which it operated – both within the Angevin realm and on crusade. In contrast to earlier studies, it can now be seen that ecclesiastical magnates, earls, and counts, were closely associated with the *familia regis* in both the Holy Land and in Europe. Whilst archbishops and bishops were represented to a greater degree in *acta* in the West than on crusade, there was an enduring role for the clergy in the crusading household, including in positions of command.

It also has shown that former members of King Henry II's household were a significant element of King Richard's *mesnie*, forming 25 per cent of the identified household on crusade. Not surprisingly, Richard chose to keep some of these experienced warriors close at hand where he could make good use of their skills rather than leave them back in north-western Europe – where they could potentially make mischief. However, they manned his regency council and served as sheriffs in counties of particular concern, such as on the Welsh and Scottish borders and near Count John of Mortain and Geoffrey Fitz-Henry's new power bases in the West Country and Yorkshire.

---

like Bartholomew of Mortimer, can be linked to the *familia regis*, Hurlock, *Wales and the Crusades*, pp. 84, 100–5; Gerald, p. 26; *Chronicle of the Third Crusade*, trans. Nicholson, p. 111, n.1.

[295] See also Edbury, 'Preaching the Crusade in Wales', pp. 221–33.

[296] I.W. Rowlands, 'Warriors Fit for a Prince, Welsh Troops in Angevin Service, 1154–1216', *Mercenaries and Paid Men, The Mercenary Identity in the Middle Ages* (Leiden, 2008), pp. 211–13.

Notwithstanding religious motivations, it was also in their best interests to gain favour with the new king, not least since most had been engaged in combat against Richard's troops in the weeks leading up to his father's death. There was clearly a place in King Richard's household for experienced warriors and clerics, including those lacking a noble heritage. This indicates the continuing potential for social mobility in the late twelfth century. Special favour seems to have been given to those who had displayed loyalty to their sovereign in time of trial and who could provide useful service to the new king.

Kinship or, at least patronage, also appears to be the key to gaining initial access to a position within the *familia regis*. All knights appear to have gained their training elsewhere, such as in baronial households, which may indicate a business-like or mercantile approach to the household, with mature, trained men preferred over the expense of preparing and equipping young nobles whose loyalty might shift once they reached adulthood.[297] Despite the obvious value placed in intimate members of the household, willing to sacrifice themselves for their lord, this was a world in which shifting commitments were seemingly accepted to a degree. It was a world where loyalty was more akin to a bond that might not necessarily be expected to extend beyond the length of a campaign or mutually convenient accord.

This case study reinforces the view that the military household was an instrument matched to the conditions of war prevalent in twelfth-century Europe. It has also shown that the *mesnie* was capable of adapting to meet the demands of expeditionary warfare in the Latin East. Armed conflict focused on the economic reality of medieval society. The seizure or destruction of goods in raids, such as *chevauchée*, or the taking or razing of fortifications through sieges, dominated campaigning. Battles were rare and generally only joined when one side enjoyed a distinct advantage over the other, and amidst inter-realm conflict sat a host of private wars and vendettas. A crusading army in Palestine, however, was a very different affair. It was a loose coalition of conflicting interests and ambitions, operating far from the crusader's home, amidst the turbulent politics of the Latin East.

Within this frame one can observe King Richard's household acting in all its diversity: as liaison officers, diplomats, and envoys seeking to persuade, negotiate, and cajole; as stewards and *justiciars* carefully shepherding royal resources, and controlling newly captured towns and provinces; as well as in the more traditional military roles of leading assaults during sieges, patrolling, overseeing logistics, and fighting in battle. Far from a rigid structure with a strict demarcation of tasks between officers of the household, roles seem to have been fluid, with room for individual talent and circumstance

---

[297] N. Orme, *From Childhood to Chivalry: The Education of the English Kings and Aristocracy*, 1066–1530 (London, 1984), pp. 28–31; Church, *Household Knights*, pp. 37–8.

to influence the tasks a member of the household might be called upon to perform. This presents fresh insight into the mechanics of the royal household and highlights Richard's pragmatism. In addition to his own experience of campaigning and managing potentially fractious coalitions, one does wonder on whom he might have drawn on for counsel particular to fighting in the Levant.

In common with Count Thierry of Flanders' preparations for the Second Crusade, the evidence reaffirms Richard's careful provision for the administration and protection of his realm during his absence, through empowered local nobles backed by experienced and trusted officials. It was a system that secured peace in the Welsh Marches, for example, for the duration of Richard's absence, but that underwent severe trial elsewhere as John flexed his muscles and King Philip II returned early from crusade to pursue his interests in Europe.

Conclusion:

Personal, Spiritual, and Communal Influences on Participation in the Third Crusade

O God, the heathen have come into your inheritance, they have defiled your holy temple; they have laid Jerusalem in heaps.[1]

Pope Gregory VIII, *Audita Tremendi*, 1187

The Third Crusade was one of the largest expeditions to the Holy Land conducted by Latin Christendom. In addition to the royal military households of Frederick Barbarossa, Philip Augustus, and Richard I, the retinues of magnates such as Henry II of Champagne, Hugh III of Burgundy, Philip of Alsace, and Robert Fitz-Pernel, and the military might of the Italian city-states, tens of thousands took the Cross and journeyed eastwards to join the siege of Acre. Failure threatened not only the loss of the kingdom of Jerusalem, but arguably the whole of Outremer.

Despite incurring losses so great that the crusader council decided that, should they take Jerusalem, they lacked the strength to hold it, the Third Crusade recovered sufficient territory that the kingdom of Jerusalem would endure for another century. In addition, the absence of the crusaders from their homes and estates, the raising of funds to cover their participation, and the logistical demands of their journeys to and from the Holy Land meant that the expedition had an impact across Christendom.

Whilst this examination of the official records and narratives from north-western Europe has encountered the leading figures of the Third Crusade – kings, great lords, and ecclesiastical magnates – it has also revealed characters with neither high rank nor substantial influence. Most of the 583 protagonists that have emerged here could be described as important enough to enjoy a degree of independence but were still beholden to a higher secular or clerical authority. That is to say, they were typical of the majority of the noble elite of the late twelfth century. In this way, this research provides

---

[1] 'Deus venerunt gentes in hereditatem tuam, coinquinaverunt templum sanctum tuum, posuerunt Ierusalem in pomorum custodiam': *Audita Tremendi, 1187*, quoting Psalm 78 (79):1, 'Ansbertus', ed. Chroust, p. 6.

a clearer idea of the social norms of the noble elite than might have been possible through a study limited to the great men and women.

Ultimately, as Andrew Jotischky has argued, an individual crusader's motivations for taking the Cross and then journeying to the Holy Land are unknowable.[2] However, the employment of Social Network Analysis to consider elite participants in the Third Crusade highlights a number of characteristics common amongst those who responded to the call to arms that followed the loss of the True Cross in 1187 and the subsequent fall of Jerusalem to Saladin. In particular, it sheds light on religious attitudes and practices, family structures, and patterns of inheritance, and provides an insight into the practical impact of notions of ethical conduct, such as the concepts of the *preudomme* and *imitatio Christi*. Taken as a whole, in addition to adding to our understanding of crusading, this study contributes to our picture of the religious foundations of the nobility of north-western Europe, such as the relationship between martial elites and clerics, and the degree to which nobles internalised the teachings of the Church in the late twelfth century.

Preaching, for example, remained a crucial area of influence by the papacy on ethical conduct in wider society. Surviving sermons and descriptions of preaching tours tell us a great deal about where and how the Church chose to focus its efforts, such as the assembly at the Premonstratensian abbey of Floreffe in 1188. Many aspects of preparations for the Third Crusade reflected established customs and drew upon existing themes – both in regard to crusade recruitment and overall practice in Latin Christendom. From the outset, the idea of just war was at the heart of crusading ideology. The protection of Christian brothers, defending Christendom against threats, and, especially protecting Christ's inheritance – the Holy Land – were also central tenets to the Church's calls for the Third Crusade, as was a desire to reduce intra-Christian violence. This is evidenced not only by the surviving sermons, like those of Alain of Lille, but also through the efforts of papal legates to broker peace between the warring Christian lords, such as Henry II and Philip Augustus. This study has highlighted the role of specific religious institutions in the diffusion of that ideology by the time of the Third Crusade.

In addition, the spiritual and practical benefits offered to those who took the Cross mirrored those of earlier expeditions, as did the presentation of crusading as a spiritual vocation undertaken in imitation of Christ. However, crusading was incorporated into the existing framework of pilgrimage and *imitatio Christi* – it was not presented as a unique activity. It is also indicated in the surviving narratives that, even on crusade, many nobles failed to subscribe to all of the norms prescribed by the Church. As we have seen, Baldwin of Forde was reportedly appalled at the state of the crusaders at the

---

[2] Jotischky, *Crusading and the Crusader States*, pp. 37–9.

siege of Acre. Moreover, despite efforts by the papacy to give the *Reconquista* the same status as the defence of the Holy Land, evidence from the Third Crusade indicates that crusaders did not consider their vows completed through service in Iberia.

Although the kingdom of Portugal benefited from military support of members of the crusader fleets that stopped at Lisbon between 1187 and 1190 in its campaign against the Almohads, the crusaders then elected to continue eastwards. Unlike participants in the planned campaign to capture Lisbon in 1147, the eyes of participants in the Third Crusade were firmly fixed on the Holy City – Jerusalem. Indeed, as Jonathan Phillips has pointed out, such was the popular appeal of the city that Richard was obliged by the crusader army to make two attempts to retake it.[3] Despite its strategic vulnerability, he was only able to turn away on both occasions with great difficulty and he faced criticism on his return for his failure to recover Jerusalem. The primacy of Jerusalem as a destination is unequivocal in the case of the Third Crusade.

The involvement of kings with their extensive military, logistical, and financial resources in the Second Crusade had already changed the dynamic of crusading. While centre-points in social networks can be elusive, the influence of the strong characters stands out in the noble network – and none more so than Philip Augustus and Richard I. The case study highlights Richard's central role, but other characters also emerge through Social Network Analysis as having been highly influential mediators for taking the Cross. Interrogation of the noble network highlights, for example, the importance of individual ecclesiastical magnates to participation in the Third Crusade. Baldwin of Forde, in particular, emerges as crucial to the recruitment and financing of the Angevin contingent and highly influential during his short time in the Holy Land. As well as overseeing the collection of the Saladin Tithe and preaching for the Crusade, he lay at the centre of a network that included the kinship network of Ranulf of Glanville and knights from Baldwin's former abbey in Dorset. It has also revealed less obvious potential mediators for taking the Cross, such as Maud of Valoignes, Alice of Courtenay, and, of course, Eleanor of Aquitaine.

By the time of the Third Crusade the influence of papal legates on the conduct of the campaign is not as readily apparent in contemporary accounts as for earlier expeditions, such as Adhémar, bishop of Le Puy, during the First Crusade. However, despite being much maligned in Angevin sources, the importance of the bishop of Beauvais to the Third Crusade as an enduring representative of both his king and the Church has been shown here to be noteworthy. Yet perceptions of power should not be ignored, and the authority of the Church was arguably further chal-

---

[3] Phillips, *Holy Warriors*, p. 351.

lenged through efforts to finance crusading through secular taxation. The data presented here indicates that the Saladin Tithe was hugely successful in reducing the requirement for landowners in England to mortgage their estates to fund participation in the Third Crusade. It cannot be coincidental that Pope Innocent III would make reform of crusader finance a central feature of preparations for the Fourth Crusade, seeking to bring it under clerical control once more.

The Tithe's success has also left us with a much clearer picture of the spiritual intentions behind donations made by participants in the Third Crusade, which also provides a broader perspective on the piety of the noble elites in north-western Europe. Even in areas where crusader finance was still dependent on mortgaging property to the Church, scrutiny of individual *acta* indicates that the crusaders also made donations to religious foundations based on spiritual conviction. The proximity of death on crusade certainly persuaded some to resign into the hands of the Church disputed property and dues claimed by neighbouring religious foundations. It also inspired crusaders to support particular religious foundations like the Cistercians and Premonstratensians.

The Second Crusade has been acknowledged as having proven highly important to leper hospitals, especially the Order of St Lazarus, and this book shows how the Third Crusade provided further impetus to support for leprosariums, as well as institutions perceived to have been linked to crusading. The survey of religious donations indicates that approximately a quarter of those who went on crusade did so within a framework of support to reformist institutions, such as the Cistercians, but also to the Military Orders and leper hospitals. This demonstrates the continuing importance of the concept of *imitatio Christi* amongst crusaders and its dissemination by particular institutions, which was recognised by those preaching the Cross and reflected in the content of their sermons.

Data relating to the Third Crusade have proven to be yet another nail in the coffin of the 'progressive nuclearisation' paradigm, as well as the idea that crusading was the preserve of landless younger sons. Instead, surviving evidence indicates that two-fifths of the overall sample participated as part of a family group, and that the majority of crusaders from non-Angevin France went on crusade with one or more members of their family, which included first-born sons. The evidence from this study reinforces the argument that patterns of landholding and inheritance were far more diverse than commonly presented, with examples of elder brothers acting as stewards of lordships rather than as the sole heir and of inheritances being divided amongst siblings. Even if the need for land existed, as an expedition to recover the Holy City, lands captured during the Third Crusade were likely to already have a Latin landlord, albeit dispossessed.

Whilst inheritance of land generally favoured the eldest son, the data from this study shows that it was not exclusive, and that partition of estates or co-lordship was not unusual. Indeed, in some notable cases, families showed more than a degree of ambivalence towards giving most of the family estate to the eldest son. No conclusions can be presented, unfortunately, on the treatment of sons and daughters born out of wedlock. The data also supports Evergates' position that wives customarily retained ownership of their dower lands. This had a significant impact on noble identity, family, duty, and, especially, understandings of lineage, which is a form of collective memory, and encouraged younger sons to maintain a high degree of family loyalty.

The prevalence of a crusader heritage amongst a quarter of the participants in the Third Crusade identified here is also suggestive of familial solidarity, which served to enhance the cohesion of crusader contingents built around diverse military households. Such cohesion was further supported by the prevalence of participation in tournaments by members of the noble elite across north-western Europe – many of whom are shown here to have joined the Third Crusade. Based on analysis of *familia*, especially that of King Richard, many nobles undeniably undertook the Third Crusade as members of military households. Notwithstanding potential religious motivations, members of the martial elite journeyed to the Holy Land as constables, stewards, marshals, and bodyguards to crusading magnates, as well as serving as cavalrymen in their *conroi*. Even modest barons, such as Geoffrey of Balliol, can be seen to travel eastwards accompanied by their feudal retainers.

Participation by noble and urban neighbourhoods also aided military cohesion. In addition to contingents from Yorkshire and London, clusters of elite crusaders can be found across north-western Europe: from East Lothian in Scotland through Staffordshire and Dorset to Picardy in northern France. In many cases, in addition to locality, such clusters also enjoyed familial and religious ties. Rather than disparate bands of younger sons – made up of individuals – the evidence from this study points towards north-western European contingents on the Third Crusade being composed of traditional knightly retinues or *conroi*, which were based on family and locality. These then operated in cohesive (regionally organised) squadrons alongside and in close conjunction with both mounted serjeants and infantry through effective command and control measures.

Whilst insufficient to support Dana Cushing's claim that the Third Crusade was 'the townsman's crusade', the data on artisanal crusaders from Cornwall and Lincolnshire also offers a rare glimpse into non-noble crusaders, as well as evidence of the human element within medieval military logistics.[4] Greater attention to trading (social) networks gives an indication of the influence of merchant seafarers on the conduct of the Third

---

[4] 1075 *De itinere navali*, trans. Cushing, pp. xlv–xlviii.

Crusade through changes to Angevin maritime law, as well as their securing trading rights in Acre. It also highlights how enterprises like the wine or wool trade might bind noble houses together and underpin associations with religious foundations, such as Pontigny Abbey.

Ties between money-fiefs and crusading are more mercurial but are arguably indicative of the necessity for expeditionary spirit – a disposition to journey beyond one's immediate locality, beyond even the extent of the tournament circuit. It was also indicative of a willingness to fight an enemy that employed different tactics and stratagems – an enemy that had only recently destroyed the army of the kingdom of Jerusalem in the field.

In addition to confirming King Richard's meticulous preparations for an expedition to the Holy Land and the maintenance of his realm while absent on crusade, detailed analysis of his household over the course of the Third Crusade also reveals aspects of military practice. It provides insights into how medieval generals might use members of their household to aid in their command and control of an army, and especially to coordinate the movement of diverse elements of an international coalition force in the face of an agile enemy force on unfamiliar ground. It also shows that kinship and locality were as important in a royal household as in those of magnates, such as William Marshal and Robert Fitz-Pernel.

The high degree of social cohesion that I have shown to be prevalent in the crusader contingents from north-western Europe and King Richard's ability to effectively command the coalition of various crusader contingents, the forces of the Latin East, and the Military Orders in the field stands in contrast to John France's views on the individualistic nature of medieval armies.[5] Indeed, whilst Ambroise highlights cases of a lack of control by specified knights, these are set against a backdrop of an expectation of high discipline and military professionalism. Although competition for a real or perceived scarcity of resources such as money, political power, military protection, or social status was a basis for conflict, the various social and familial ties identified in this study were reinforced by the superordinate goal that was the Third Crusade to promote cooperate action and strengthen military cohesion.

With such strong religious, familial, and peer group motivation to take the Cross that followed the fall of Jerusalem in 1187, the question should, perhaps, be not why elites from north-western Europe joined the Third Crusade, but why some did not. Aside from local disputes, familial duty, and royal service, the answer may well lie amidst the intangible matter of this expeditionary mindset. However, while survivors of the Third Crusade can be found joining other expeditions, such as the Fourth Crusade or

---

[5] J. France, 'The Three Orders Reconsidered', paper given at the 25th International Medieval Congress, University of Leeds (UK), July 2018.

serving in campaigns against the Cathars, with the exception of merchant communities seeking to secure long-term trading concessions in Acre, few were to remain in the kingdom of Jerusalem. In this, consideration of motivations behind participation in the Third Crusade reveals the inherent tension between crusading as a very personal commitment – to follow in the footsteps of Christ, their crusading forebears, or in the service of a temporal lord; to fight as a form of penance and to seek salvation, and to recover the Holy City – and the long-term, strategic requirements of defending the Holy Land. Once their vow was considered fulfilled, most of the survivors looked to return home.

Appendix 1

The Noble Network: Crusaders from North-Western Europe, 1187–92

Abbreviation	Category*
	Full name
Title/s	Title/s, appointments
Alias/es	Alternative forms of name, nicknames
Notes	Activities relating to the Third Crusade
Ancestor/s	Ancestors that participated in previous crusades
Family	Family members that participated in the Third Crusade
Orders	Associations with religious orders (names of religious houses in brackets)
Region	Regional associations
Sources	Sources relating to information listed in the entry

*Where no information is available categories have been omitted to save space.

Philip II of France

Title/s	King of France
Alias/es	Rex Francie, Phillippo rege Francorum, Felippe, reis Filippes de France, Philippus rex Franciae
Notes	Took the Cross alongside King Henry II (1188). Messina (1190). Siege of Acre (1191). Returned to France after the capture of Acre (1191).
Ancestor/s	Louis VII, Philip of Beauvais
Family	Theobald V of Blois, Robert II of Dreux, Bishop Philip of Beauvais, Henry II of Champagne, Peter II of Courtenay
Orders	Augustinians, Benedictines, Cistercians (Barbeau), Hospitallers, Lazar Houses (Boigny), Premonstratensians (Saint-André-au-Bois), Templars
Region	France
Sources	Ambroise, lines 87–154, 254–60, 4523, 4688, 4809–34, 4835–5032, 5243–97; Baha' al-Din, pp. 145, 147–9, 153, 163; *Chronica*, Vol. 2, p. 335; Devizes, pp. 16, 22, 27, 42, 44; Diss, Vol. 2, pp. 51, 55, 57–8, 62–3, 83–4, 91, 111; Gilbert of Mons, pp. 270–1; *Gesta Regis*, Vol. 2, pp. 29–30, 35–6, 45, 49, 61, 67–8, 7, 147–8, 150–20, 73–4, 104–5, 112–13, 126, 128, 160–1, 170–1, 173–6, 178, 182–3, 185, 192–9, 236–7; Ibn al-Athir, *The Chronicle of Ibn Al-Athir for the Crusading Period from Al-Kamil Fi'l-Ta'rikh. Part 2: The Years 541–589/1146–1193. The Age of Nur al-Din and Saladin*, trans. D.S. Richard (Farnham, 2007), p. 386; *Itinerarium*, pp. 5, 32, 138, 140–1, 155–6, 159–77, 181, 210–23, 229, 231–39, 351; Rigord, pp. 83, 90–1; Wendover, pp. 143, 152, 157–9, 182, 186–7, 195, 197, 208.

Robert II of Dreux

Title/s	Count of Dreux
Alias/es	Robert, count of Dreux, cuens Roberz, coens Robert de Dreues, Drous, Robertus comes Druensis
Notes	Took the Cross alongside King Philip II (1188). Silves (1189). Siege of Acre (1190). Battle of Arsuf (1191). Joined Albigensian Crusade (1210).
Ancestor/s	Robert I of Dreux
Family	Bishop Philip of Beauvais, Philip II of France, Raoul I of Coucy
Orders	Premonstratensians (Saint-Yved of Braine), Templars, and Hospitallers
Region	Dreux
Sources	Ambroise, lines 2926, 6172, 6647; Diss, Vol. 2, pp. 79, 82–3; *Gesta Regis*, Vol. 2, pp. 93–4, 96; *Itinerarium*, pp. 67, 261, 269, 276; Rigord, pp. 83–4; Wendover, pp. 178, 180.

Philip of Dreux

Title/s	Bishop of Beauvais
Alias/es	Philip de Dreux, bishop of Beauvais, l'evesques de Biauveiz, l'evesques de Biavez, Philippus episcopus de Blevez, Belvacensis
Notes	Silves (1189). Siege of Acre (1190). Abduction of Isabel of Jerusalem (1190). Envoy to Cyprus (1191). Purified the churches of Acre. Battle of Arsuf (1191). Dined with Conrad of Montferrat before his assassination (1192). Took command of the French knights on the death of Duke Hugh III and ordered them home. Joined Albigensian Crusade (1210).
Ancestor/s	Robert I of Dreux
Family	Robert II of Dreux, Philip II of France, Raoul I of Coucy
Orders	Cistercians (Hélinand of Froidmont), Premonstratensians (Saint-Yved of Braine)
Region	Picardy, Dreux
Sources	Ambroise, lines 2924, 4123, 6174, 8761; Devizes, pp. 79–80; Diss, Vol. 2, pp. 79, 86; *Gesta Regis*, Vol. 2, pp. 45, 93–4, 96, 178, 180–2; *Itinerarium*, pp. 67, 199, 261, 269, 339; Rigord, p. 83; *RRRH*, no. 1307; Wendover, pp. 178, 180.

Raoul III of Nesle

Title/s	Count of Soissons, castellan of Noyon
Alias/es	Ralph III de Nesle, count of Soissons, comes Suessionensis, Raoul le Bon, Radulfus
Notes	Took the Cross alongside King Philip II (1188). Siege of Acre.
Ancestor/s	Drogo and Yves II of Nesle
Family	Robert II of Dreux, Bishop Philip of Beauvais, John of Nesle
Orders	Cistercians (Notre-Dame of Ourscamp)
Region	Picardy
Sources	*Cartulaire de l'abbaye de Notre-Dame d'Ourscamp de l'ordre de Citeaux*, ed. M. Peigne-Delacourt (Amiens, 1865), p. 169, no. CCLXXXII; Rigord, pp. 83–4; E. Warlop, *The Flemish Nobility before 1300* (Kortrijk, 1975), pp. 726, 1050.

Hugh IV

Title/s	Count of St Pol
Alias/es	Hugh IV, count of St Pol, coens de Saint Pol, conte de seint Pol, Hugo de Kein, Momes de Sancto Paulo
Notes	Sold a third of the tithes of Mortagne to the Premonstratensian house at Château-l'Abbaye prior to departing on crusade (c.1191). Arrived with King Philip II at the siege of Acre. (1191). Skirmish at Ramla (1191).
Ancestor/s	Hugh II, count of St Pol
Family	Ralph I of Clermont, Peter of Amiens, Baldwin of Béthune, Guy of Noyelles, John I of Sées
Orders	Cistercians (Cercamp), Premonstratensians (Château-l'Abbaye)
Region	Picardy
Sources	*Les chartes des comtes de Saint-Pol*, ed. J.-F. Nieus (Turnhout, 2008), nos. 54–5, 59, pp.140–3, 145–6; Ambroise, lines 4527, 6046, 7274; *Itinerarium*, pp. 213, 257, 293.

Peter II of Courtenay

Title/s	Count of Nevers
Alias/es	Peter de Courtenay, count of Nevers, Petrum comitem de Nevers, comes de Neuerso
Notes	Took the Cross alongside King Philip II (1188). Messina (1190).
Ancestor/s	King Louis VII of France, Counts William II and III of Nevers
Family	Philip II of France, Renaud of Nevers, William of Joigny, John of Montmirail, Robert II of Dreux, Bishop Philip of Beauvais
Orders	Benedictines (Saint-Etienne of Nevers)
Region	Burgundy
Sources	*Cartulaire générale de l'Yonne*, Vol. 2, ed. M. Quantin (Auxerre, 1860), no. 409; Devizes, p. 22; *Gesta Regis*, Vol. 2, pp. 128, 150, 156; Rigord, pp. 83–4.

Theobald V of Blois

Title/s	Seneschal of France, count of Blois and Chartres, lord of Châteaurenault
Alias/es	Theobald du Blois, seneschal of France, count of Blois, Thibaut, Tedbald de Bleis, comes Theobuldus, Teobaldus comes de Blays, Tibaldus, Theobaldus comes Blesensis, Theodbaldus comes de Blais
Notes	Philip II's *Familia Regis*. Took the Cross alongside King Philip II (1188). Silves (1189). Participated in the St Martin offensive (1190). Died at the siege of Acre (1190).
Ancestor/s	Stephen II of Blois, King Louis VII of France, Count Henry I of Champagne
Family	Philip II of France, Henry II of Champagne, Richard I of England, Ralph I of Clermont, Stephen of Sancerre
Orders	Benedictines (Saint-Laumer of Blois and Bonneval), Templars (Bonville)

Region	Blois and Chartres
Sources	*Chronica*, Vol. 3, p. 88; Diss, Vol. 2, p. 79; *Les Templiers en Eure-et-Loir: Histoire et Cartulaire*, ed. C. Métais (Chartres, 1902), no. 14; Gilbert of Mons, pp. 132, 153, 191, 203, 206, 242, 270–3, 329; *Gesta Regis*, Vol. 2, pp. 48–9, 148; *Itinerarium*, p. 116; Rigord, pp. 42–3, Wendover, p. 180.

Ralph I of Clermont

Title/s	Constable of France, count of Clermont-en-Beauvais, lord of Breteuil
Alias/es	Raoul de Clermont, constable of France, count of Clermont, coens de Clermon, comes de Claromont, Clarimontis, Raoul 'le Roux'
Notes	Philip II's *Familia Regis*. Constable of France. Took the Cross alongside King Philip II (1188). Silves (1189). Siege of Acre (1190). Supported collection on behalf of the poorest Crusaders at Lent (1191). Died on the Third Crusade (1191).
Ancestor/s	Everard III of Breteuil, Everard III of Le Puiset
Family	Theobald V of Blois and Chartres, Dreux IV and William of Merlo, Theobold of Bar-le-duc, Guy III of Senlis
Orders	Cistercians (Barbeau)
Region	Clermont
Sources	Ambroise, line 3510; Diss, Vol. 2, p. 79; Gilbert of Mons, pp. 117, 120, 128–9, 135, 153, 206, 273; *Itinerarium*, pp. 92, 135; Rigord, pp. 83–4; Wendover, p. 178.

Hugh of Oyry

Alias/es	Hugh d'Oyry, Oyri, Hugh de Hoiry, Hugo de Hoiri, Hugo de Oisi, hugo de Hoyri
Notes	Died at the siege of Acre (1190).
Family	Ralph I of Clermont, Walter of Oyry, Baldwin of Dargus
Region	Oyry (Aumale)
Sources	*Chronica*, Vol. 3, p. 88; Gilbert of Mons, pp. 142, 213; *Gesta Regis*, Vol. 2, p. 148.

Walter of Oyry

Alias/es	Walter of Oyri, Walterus de Oyri
Notes	Siege of Acre (1190). Held off a Muslim sally along with Baldwin le Carron and Baldwin of Dargus (1190). Participated in the St Martin offensive (1190).
Family	Hugh of Oyry
Region	Oyry (Aumale)
Sources	*Chronica*, Vol. 3, p. 73; *Gesta Regis*, Vol. 2, p. 144.

Walter of Moy

Title/s	Lord of Moy
Alias/es	Walter de Moy, Walterus de Moy, Gautier de Moy

Notes	Companion of Hugh of Oyry. Died at the siege of Acre (1190).
Region	Moy (Beauvais)
Sources	*Chronica*, Vol. 3, p. 88; *Gesta Regis*, Vol. 2, p. 148.

Aubrey Clément

Title/s	Royal Marshal (Phillip II), lord of Mez
Alias/es	Aubrey Clément, marshall of France, Auberi Climent, Albéric Clément, Aubrey Clements, Albericus Clement, Aubry, son maréchal, Aubrey de Bullen
Notes	Philip II's *Familia Regis*. Marshal of France. Led assault on breach in city walls (1191). In second assault gained the city walls, but was surrounded, and killed (1191). Died at the siege of Acre (1191).
Orders	Hôtel-Dieu de Paris
Region	Gâtinais
Sources	Ambroise, lines 4900–2; *Gesta Regis*, Vol. 2, p. 173; *Itinerarium*, pp. 223–9.

Adam of Villebeon

Title/s	Royal Chamberlain (Philip II)
Alias/es	Adam, chamberlain to King Philip II, Adam camberlanus regis Franciae
Notes	Philip II's *Familia Regis*. Died at the siege of Acre.
Region	France
Sources	*Chronica*, Vol. 3, p. 89; *Gesta Regis*, Vol. 2, p. 149.

Philip I of Nemours

Title/s	Lord of Nemours and Beaumont-du-Gatinâis, Royal Chamberlain (Philip II)
Alias/es	Philippe de Nemours
Notes	Philip II's *Familia Regis*. Died at the siege of Acre (1191).
Orders	Cistercians (Barbeaux)
Region	Gatinâis
Sources	'Chronica Albrici Monachi Trium Fontium 1204', *MGH SS XXIII*, p. 884; *Chronica*, Vol. 3, p. 89; E.L. Richemond, *Recherches généalogiques sur la famille des Seigneurs de Nemours*, Vol. 1 (Fontainebleau, 1907), p. xxvi.

Dreux IV of Merlo

Title/s	Lord of Saint-Bris, Auxerre, constable of Merlo
Alias/es	Drogo de Merlo, Dreu de Merlo, Drogo de Merlou, Dreux IV de Merlo
Notes	Philip II's *Familia Regis*. Siege of Acre. Envoy to Cyprus (1191). Constable of France (1191). Battle of Arsuf (1191). Brother to William of Merlo. Donations to Templars on return from Crusade. Co-founded the Templar commandery of Sauce-sur-Yonne (c.1210).
Ancestor/s	Everard III of Breteuil, Everard III of Le Puiset

Family	William of Merlo, Theobald V of Blois and Chartres
Orders	Grandmontines, Benedictines (Charité-sur-Loire), Cistercians (Pontigny)
Region	Auxerre
Sources	Ambroise, line 6178; AN S5235, 1, fol. 1r; AN, S5239, 51, no. 3; *Yonne*, Vol. 2, ed. Quantin, no. 226, pp. 242–3; *Gesta Regis*, Vol. 2, pp. 46, 179–80; *Itinerarium*, p. 199; *Le premier cartulaire de l'abbaye de Pontigny (XII-XIII siècles)*, ed. M. Garrigues (Paris, 1981), no. 342, p. 344; Rigord, pp. 83–4.

William I of Merlo

Alias/es	William de Merlo, William of Mello, Williames de Merlo, Guillames de Merlo, Merlou
Notes	Said to be Conrad of Montferrat's man. Brother to Dreux IV. Joined Albigensian Crusade.
Ancestor/s	Everard III of Breteuil, Everard III of Le Puiset
Family	Dreux IV of Merlo, Theobald V of Blois and Chartres
Orders	Benedictines (Charité-sur-Loire), Cistercians (Pontigny)
Region	Auxerre
Sources	Ambroise, lines 4535, 6178; *Gesta Regis*, Vol. 2, pp. 178, 182; *Itinerarium*, p. 213; *Pontigny*, ed. Garrigues, no. 342, p. 344; Rigord, pp. 83–4; *Song of the Cathar Wars. A History of the Albigensian Crusade*, trans. J. Shirley (Aldershot, 1996), pp. 151, 160.

William IV of Garlande

Title/s	Lord of Livry
Alias/es	William de Garlande, Guillames de Garlande, cil de Garlande
Notes	Philip II's *Familia Regis*. Siege of Acre (1191). Battle of Arsuf (1191). Died on the Third Crusade.
Ancestor/s	Guy II the Red of Montlhéry
Family	Anseau of Garlande
Orders	Benedictines (Saint-Martin-des-Champs)
Region	Livry (Ile de France)
Sources	Ambroise, lines 4529, 6176; T. Evergates, *The Aristocracy in the County of Champagne, 1100–1300* (Philadelphia, PA, 2007), p. 114; *Itinerarium*, pp. 213, 261.

Anseau IV of Garlande

Alias/es	Manserius de Garland, Manassier de Garlande
Notes	Silves (1189). Siege of Acre.
Ancestor/s	Guy II the Red of Montlhéry
Family	William IV of Garlande
Sources	*Itinerarium*, p. 92.

William des Barres

Alias/es	le Barrois, Williames des Barres, Guillames de Barres, Cil de Barres, Willelmo de Barres
Notes	Philip II's *Familia Regis*. Messina (1191). Siege of Acre (1191). Battle of Arsuf (1191).
Ancestor/s	Everard of Barres
Family	Robert IV Fitz-Pernel
Orders	Templars, Cistercians (Clairvaux)
Region	Burgundy
Sources	Ambroise, lines 4531, 5794, 6176, 6586; *Gesta Regis*, Vol. 2, p. 45, 46, 155–6; *Itinerarium*, pp. 213, 251, 261, 273; J. Schenk, *Templar Families: Landowning Families and the Order of the Temple in France, c.1120–1307* (Cambridge, 2012), pp. 93, 101.

John of Montmirail

Title/s	Lord of Montmirail
Alias/es	John de Montmirail, Johannes de Monte Mirayl
Notes	Philip II's *Familia Regis*. Siege of Acre. Became a Cistercian monk on return from crusade (Longpont).
Ancestor/s	Peter I of Courtenay
Family	Peter II of Courtenay, Guy II of Dampierre
Region	Champagne
Sources	Evergates, *Aristocracy*, p. 236–7; *Itinerarium*, p. 93.

Guy III of Châtillon-sur-Marne

Title/s	Lord of Châtillon and Montjoy
Alias/es	Guy de Châtillon-sur-Marne, Guido de Castellione, Wido de Castellione, Guido de Castelluno
Notes	Philip II's *Familia Regis*. Silves (1189). Siege of Acre (1191). Died on the Third Crusade.
Ancestor/s	Walter II of Châtillon and Montjoy, Robert I of Dreux
Family	Lovell and Walter III of Châtillon, Robert II of Dreux, bishop of Beauvais
Orders	Longueau Priory
Region	Champagne
Sources	A. Duchesne, *Historie de la Maison de Chastillon-sur-Marne* (Paris, 1621), pp. 27–8; Evergates, *Aristocracy*, p. 222; 'Feoda I', *Documents relatifs au Comté de Champagne et Brie (1172–1361)*, Vol. 1, ed. A. Longnon (Paris, 1901), no. 693; Gilbert of Mons, p. 273; *Itinerarium*, p. 93; *RRRH*, no. 1304.

Lovell of Châtillon-sur-Marne

Alias/es	Lovell de Châtillon-sur-Marne, eius (Guy's) frater, Lovellus frater ejus, cum Lovello fratre suo
Notes	Philip II's *Familia Regis*. Siege of Acre (1191). Died on the Third Crusade.
Ancestor/s	Walter II of Châtillon and Montjoy, Robert I of Dreux
Family	Guy II and Walter III of Châtillon, Robert II of Dreux, Bishop Philip of Beauvais
Orders	Longueau Priory
Region	Champagne
Sources	Duchesne, *Chastillon*, pp. 27–8; Evergates, *Aristocracy*, p. 222; Gilbert of Mons, p. 273; *Itinerarium*, p. 93; *RRRH*, no. 1304.

Walter III of Châtillon-sur-Marne

Title/s	Lord of Châtillon and Montjoy
Alias/es	Gautier de Châtillon, Gaucherus de Castellione eius (Guy's) frater
Notes	Philip II's *Familia Regis*. Silves (1189). Siege of Acre (1191). Inherited title on the death of his older brother, Guy II, on the Third Crusade.
Ancestor/s	Walter II of Châtillon and Montjoy, Robert I of Dreux
Family	Guy II and Lovell of Châtillon, Robert II of Dreux, Bishop Philip of Beauvais
Orders	Longueau Priory
Region	Champagne
Sources	Duchesne, *Chastillon*, pp. 27–8; Evergates, *Aristocracy*, p. 222; *RRRH*, no. 1304.

Raynald of Nevers

Title/s	Lord of Décize
Alias/es	Renaud de Nevers, Reginald
Notes	Philip II's *Familia Regis*. Younger son of Count William III. Denied membership of Henry the Young King's tournament team. Died on the Third Crusade.
Ancestor/s	Counts William II and III of Nevers, Robert of Nevers and Robert of Craon, *alias* Robert Burgundio
Family	Peter II of Courtenay, William of Joigny
Orders	Benedictines (Jully-les-Nonnains, Molesme, Saint-Etienne of Nevers)
Region	Champagne
Sources	Gilbert of Mons, p. 272; *HGM*, lines 3720–63; *Cartulaire du prieuré de Jully-les-Nonnains*, ed. E. Petit (Auxerre, 1881), p. 20; *Cartulaires de l'abbaye de Molesme, ancien diocèse de Langres*, 916–1250, Vol. 2, ed. J. Laurant (Paris, 1911), no. 44, p. 278.

Guy III of Senlis

Title/s	Butler of Senlis, lord of Montépilloy and Chantilly
Alias/es	Guy III of Senlis, butler of Selis, buteillier de Sonlit, Pincerna de Sain Liz, pincerna Silvanectensis, pincerna de Sainzliz, Pincerna de Sancto Licio
Notes	Philip II's *Familia Regis*. Captured on the Third Crusade (1190).
Ancestor/s	William I of Senlis, Rainald II of Clermont
Family	William II of Senlis, Ralph I of Clermont
Orders	Cistercians (Chaalis), Saint-Nicolas d'Acy
Region	Senlis, Clermont
Sources	Ambroise, line 4155; *Chronica*, Vol. 3, p. 88; Diss, Vol. 2, p. 86; *Gallia Christiana*, Vol. 10, Instrumenta ecclesiæ Silvanectensis, XXVIII, col. 219; *Gesta Regis*, Vol. 2, p. 148; *Itinerarium*, pp. 122–3; A. Luchaire, *Études sur les actes de Louis VII* (Paris, 1885), pp. 437–8.

William II of Senlis

Title/s	Lord of Brasseuse
Alias/es	Guillaume II 'le Loup' de Senlis
Notes	Made a donation to Saint-Nicolas d'Acy prior to going on crusade (before 1190).
Ancestor/s	William I of Senlis
Family	Guy III of Senlis
Orders	Cistercians (Chaalis), Saint-Nicolas d'Acy
Region	Senlis, Clermont
Sources	Luchaire, *Actes de Louis VII*, pp. 437–8.

Henry I of Mousson

Title/s	Count of Bar, lord of Mousson
Alias/es	Henry I, count of Bar, cuens de Bar, comes de Baro, Barrensis
Notes	Siege of Acre (1189). Wounded in battle (1189). Died on the Third Crusade (1191).
Ancestor/s	Henry I of Champagne, Archbishop Stephen of Mousson, Stephen of Blois, Thierry and Rainard I of Bar
Family	Stephen of Sancerre, Philip II, Theobold of Bar-le-Duc, Henry II of Champagne, Bishop Renaud of Monçon
Orders	Templars
Region	Lorraine
Sources	Ambroise, line 2928; BN ms. nouv. acq. lat. 53, fol. 255r–v (1191); Diss, Vol. 2, p. 79; Gilbert of Mons, pp. 127, 132, 272, 329; Rigord, pp. 83–4; Wendover, p. 178.

Theobold I of Bar-le-duc

Title/s	Count of Bar
Alias/es	Theobold de Bar-le-duc, Thibaud, Theobaldus de Baro
Notes	Silves (1189). Arrived at the siege of Acre (1189). Became count on the death of his brother, Henry I of Mousson. Joined Albigenisan Crusade (1211).
Ancestor/s	Henry I of Champagne, Stephen of Blois
Family	Henry I of Mousson, Ralph I of Clermont
Orders	Templars
Region	Lorraine
Sources	Gilbert of Mons, p. 272; *Itinerarium*, p. 74; M.G. Pegg, A *Most Holy War: The Albigensian Crusade and the Battle for Christendom* (Oxford, 2008), p. 114; Schenk, *Templar Families*, p. 228.

Renaud of Monçon

Title/s	Bishop of Chartres
Alias/es	Renaud de Monçon, bishop of Chartres, episcopo Carnoti, Carnotensem, Reinaldus, Reginald, de Bar
Notes	Took the Cross alongside Kings Henry II and Philip II (1188). Messina (1190). Siege of Acre (1191).
Ancestor/s	Reginald II, count of Bar
Family	King Philip II, Henry I and Theobald, counts of Bar, Theobald V of Blois and Stephen of Sancerre, Robert II and Philip of Dreux
Orders	Chartres Cathedral
Sources	Devizes, p. 22; *Gesta Regis*, Vol. 2, pp. 128, 56, 80–1; Rigord, p. 83.

Henry II of Salm

Title/s	Count of Salm
Alias/es	Heinrich von Salm, Henricus comes de Salmes, Herman of Luxemburg
Notes	Made a donation to the abbey of Haute-Seille before departing on crusade (1189).
Ancestor/s/s	Henry I of Salm
Family	Floris III
Orders	Cistercians (Haute-Seille)
Region	Lorraine
Sources	*Actes des Princes Lorrains, 1ère série: Princes Laïques, II. Les Comtes, B. Actes des Comtes de Salm*, ed. D. Erpelding (préédition, Nancy, 1979), no. 8, p. 20.

Gobert V of Aspremont

Title/s	Lord of Aspremont and Dun
Alias/es	Gobert d'Aspremont

Notes	Died at the sige of Acre (1190).
Orders	Premonstratensians (Rengéval)
Region	Aspremont
Sources	A. Calmet, *Histoire ecclésiastique et civile de Lorraine*, Vol. 5 (Nancy, 1748), preuves, col. 348.

John of Vendôme

Title/s	Count of Vendôme
Alias/es	Johannes comes Vendomiae
Notes	Died on the Third Crusade (1192).
Ancestor/s	John I and Bartholomew of Vendôme
Family	Hervey of Gien
Orders	Benedictines (Trinity)
Region	Vendôme
Sources	*Chronica*, Vol. 3, p. 89; Gilbert of Mons, p. 273; *Gesta Regis*, Vol. 2, p. 149; *Cartulaire saintongeais de la Trinité de Vendôme*, Vol 2, ed. A. Picard (Vendôme, 1894), no. 625, p. 503.

Hugh III

Title/s	Duke of Burgundy
Alias/es	Hugh III, duke of Burgundy, dux Burgundie, duc de Burgoine, dux de Bugoine, Hugo dux de Burgundiae
Notes	Took the Cross alongside King Philip II (1188). Messina (1190). Siege of Acre (1191). Made a donation to the Templars at the siege of Acre (1191). Part of Crusader council that decided the fate of Muslim prisoners (1191). Oversaw the killing of Muslim captives held by French contingent (1191). Battle of Arsuf (1191). Attack on Muslim caravan (1192). Made a donation to St Stephen's of Dijon whilst gravely ill in Acre (1192). Died on the Third Crusade (1192).
Ancestor/s	Odo I and Renaud II of Burgundy
Family	Count Louis of Ferrette, Simon of Semur
Orders	Cistercians (Maizières)
Region	Burgundy
Sources	Ambroise, lines 277–376, 880, 4747, 5298–321, 5443, 5748, 6197, 7842, 10263, 10625; Baha' al-Din, p. 170; *Chartes et documents concernant l'abbaye de Citeaux*, ed. J. Marilier (Rome, 1961), no. 198, pp. 159–60; *Chronica*, Vol. 3, pp. 79–80; Coggeshall, p. 42; Diceto, p. 95; Devizes, p. 22; *Gesta Regis*, Vol. 2, pp. 69, 128, 130, 150, 156, 178, 189, 192; Gilbert of Mons, pp. 132, 153, 191, 203, 272, 329; *HdB*, Vol. 3, no. 866, 877; *Itinerarium*, pp. 148, 166, 250, 261, 283, 311, 320–2, 326, 349, 365, 384; Rigord, p. 83; Wendover, pp. 157–8, 199, 209, 212.

Simon of Semur

Title/s	Lord of Luzy and Semur-en-Brionnais
Alias/es	Simon de Semur, Symon de Sine Muro
Notes	Made a donation to the Cistercians prior to joining his father-in-law Hugh III on crusade (1190).
Ancestor/s	Hugh-Dalmace of Semur
Family	Hugh III of Burgundy
Orders	Cistercians (Ferté)
Region	Semur (Burgundy)
Sources	*HdB*, Vol. 3, no. 845.

Everard

Title/s	Provost of Dijon
Alias/es	Evvrardus, Divionensis prepositus
Notes	Made a donation to the Cistercians prior to joining the crusade (1190).
Orders	Cistercians (Cîteaux)
Region	Dijon (Burgundy)
Sources	*HdB*, Vol. 3, no. 843, 844.

Anselm III of Montréal

Title/s	Lord of Montréal
Alias/es	Anselm de Montreal, Anselmus de Monte Regali; Anserius
Notes	Grand Seneschal of Burgundy. Silves (1189). Arrived at the siege of Acre (1189). Died at the siege of Acre with his whole household/family (1190).
Ancestor/s	Clemence of Montfauçon, Anselm II of Montréal
Family	Everard II of Brienne, Anseric IV of Montréal, John d'Arcis, Thierry of Montfauçon, Manasses of Langres
Orders	Cistercians (Pontigny)
Region	Burgundy, Champagne
Sources	*Chronica*, Vol. 3, p. 89; *Diss*, pp. 82–3; *Gesta Regis*, Vol. 2, p. 149; *HdB*, Vol. 3, no. 808; *Itinerarium*, p. 74.

Anselm IV of Montréal

Title/s	Lord of Montréal
Alias/es	Anseric, Ancelinus de Monte Regali
Notes	Joined his father on crusade (1189).
Ancestor/s	Clemence of Montfauçon, Anselm II of Montréal
Family	Anselm III, John d'Arcis (both of whom died), Everard II of Brienne, Thierry of Montfauçon, Manasses of Langres

Orders	Cistercians (Pontigny)
Region	Burgundy, Champagne
Sources	*HdB*, Vol. 2, p. 95; Vol. 3, no. 809.

John of Arcis-sur-Aube

Title/s	Lord of Arcis-sur-Aube
Alias/es	John d'Arcis-sur-Aube, Johannes de Arches
Notes	Siege of Acre. Died on the Third Crusade (1190).
Ancestor/s	Anselm II
Family	Anselm III, Anselm IV
Orders	Cistercians (Pontigny)
Region	Burgundy, Champagne
Sources	Evergates, *Aristocracy*, p. 232; *HdB*, Vol. 2, p. 95; Vol. 3, no. 809; *Itinerarium*, p. 93.

Thierry of Montfauçon

Title/s	Archbishop of Besançon
Alias/es	Thierry de Montfauçon, archbishop of Besançon, L'arcevesque de Besençon, archiepiscopus de Besenzun, Besenceuae, archiepiscopus Besezonensis
Notes	Travelled with Count Louis of Ferrette. His battering ram was burnt by Greek fire at the siege of Acre. Died at the siege of Acre (1190).
Ancestor/s	Clemence of Montfauçon
Family	Everard II of Brienne, Guy II of Dampierre, Everard I of Chacenay, Manasses of Langres
Orders	Cistercians (Fontmorigny), Besançon Cathedral
Sources	Ambroise, line 3817; Diss, Vol. 2, p. 79; *Gesta Regis*, Vol. 2, p. 96; *Itinerarium*, pp. 93; 111; G. Poull, *La Maison souveraine et ducale de Bar* (Nancy, 1994), p. 78; *Documents et mémoires pour server à l'histoire du territoire de Belfort*, ed. L. Viellard (Besançon, 1884), no. 192, p. 243; Wendover, p. 178.

Louis of Ferrette

Title/s	Count of Ferrette
Alias/es	Comitis Ludovici
Notes	Travelled with Thierry of Montfauçon. Died at the siege of Acre (1189).
Ancestor/s	Renaud II of Burgundy, Louis of Montbéliard
Family	Hugh III of Burgundy
Orders	Cistercians (Feldbach)
Region	Ferrette
Sources	Poull, *Maison de Bar*, p. 78; *Monuments de l'histoire de l'ancien évêché de Bâle*, Vol. 1, ed. J. Trouillat (Porrentruy, 1852), no. 269, p. 414; *Documents et mémoires*, ed. Viellard, no. 192, p. 243.

Rainard III of Grancey

Title/s	Lord of Grancey
Alias/es	Rainard de Grancey
Notes	Siege of Acre (1189). Made donation to Templars whilst at the siege of Acre. Died at the siege of Acre.
Ancestor/s	Odo I of Grancey (Templars)
Family	Milo of Grancey
Orders	Cistercians (Ligny)
Region	Yonne (Burgundy)
Sources	*Yonne*, Vol. 2, ed. Quantin, no. 405; *HdB*, Vol. 3, no. 815.

Milo of Grancey

Alias/es	Milo de Grancey
Notes	Siege of Acre (1189). Approved his brother's donation to Templars whilst at the siege of Acre.
Ancestor/s	Odo I of Grancey (Templars)
Family	Rainard III of Grancey
Orders	Cistercians (Ligny)
Region	Yonne (Burgundy)
Sources	*Yonne*, Vol. 2, ed. Quantin, no. 405; *HdB*, Vol. 3, no. 815.

Hugh of Grancey

Alias/es	Hugh de Grancey
Notes	Siege of Acre (1189)
Ancestor/s	Odo I of Grancey (Templars)
Family	Calo of Grancey, Amadeus of Arceaux
Orders	Templars (Bure)
Sources	*HdB*, Vol. 3, no. 815.

Calo of Grancey

Alias/es	Calo de Grancey, Galo de Granci, Calo de Ganceio
Notes	Siege of Acre (1191).
Ancestor/s	Odo I of Grancey (Templars)
Family	Hugh of Grancey, Amadeus of Arceaux
Orders	Templars (Bure)
Region	Burgundy
Sources	*HdB*, Vol. 3, no. 815, 867.

Amadeus of Arceaux

Alias/es	Amadeus d'Arceaux
Notes	Siege of Acre (1189).
Family	Hugh and Calo of Grancey
Sources	*HdB*, Vol. 3, no. 815.

Guy of Maizières

Alias/es	Guy de Mezières, Gui de Maciers, Guido de Maceriis
Notes	Siege of Acre.
Orders	Cistercians (Maizières)
Region	Maizières (Burgundy)
Sources	*Itinerarium*, p. 93; AD de Saône-et Loire, H 54/17.

Girard of Uchey

Alias/es	Viard d'Uchay, Viardus de Vulchee
Notes	Siege of Acre (1191). Made a donation to the Hospitallers whilst on crusade.
Family	John of Uchey
Orders	Hospitallers (Dijon, Cromais, Crimolais, and Varanges)
Region	Burgundy
Sources	*Cartulaire général de l'Ordre des Hospitaliers de Saint-Jean de Jérusalem (1100-1310), Tome 1er (1100-1200)*, ed. J. Delaville Le Roulx (Paris, 1894), no. 909; *HdB*, Vol. 3, no. 865.

John of Uchey

Alias/es	Johannes de Vulchoe
Notes	Siege of Acre (1191).
Family	Girard of Uchey
Region	Burgundy
Sources	*HdB*, Vol. 3, no. 865.

Guy of Valle

Alias/es	Guido de Valle
Notes	Siege of Acre (1191).
Sources	*Diss*, Vol. 2, p. 64; *Gesta Regis*, Vol. 2, p. 72; *HdB*, Vol. 3, no. 865.

Guy of Vergy

Title/s	Lord of Vergy
Alias/es	Gui de Vergy

Notes	Siege of Acre (1189). Died at the siege of Acre (1191). Made a donation to the Templars at the siege of Acre.
Ancestor/s	Gerard of Vergy (Templars)
Orders	Templars (Autrey), Cistercians (Maizières)
Region	Burgundy
Sources	*HdB*, Vol. 3, no. 815, 867; J. Richard, 'Les templiers et les Hospitaliers en Bourgogne et en Champagne méridionale (XIIe–XIIIe siécles)', *Vorträge und Forschungen: Die Geistlichen Ritterorden Europas*, Vol. 26, ed. J. Fleckenstein and M. Hellmann (1980), p. 235.

William of Fos

Alias/es	Guillaume du Fossé
Notes	Siege of Acre (1189).
Region	Burgundy
Sources	*HdB*, Vol. 3, no, 815.

Stephen of Fauverney

Alias/es	Etienne de Fauverney, Stephanus de Faverne
Notes	Siege of Acre (1191).
Region	Burgundy
Sources	*HdB*, Vol. 3, no, 865, 867.

Hugh of Champlitte

Alias/es	Eudes de Champlitte, Odo de Chanlite
Notes	Siege of Acre (1191).
Region	Burgundy
Sources	*HdB*, Vol. 3, no. 867.

Garnier of Bruino

Alias/es	Garnier de Bruino, Garnerius de Bruino
Notes	Siege of Acre (1191).
Region	Burgundy
Sources	*HdB*, Vol. 3, no, 867.

Arnold of Dolai

Alias/es	Arnulfus de Dolai
Notes	Siege of Acre (1191).
Region	Burgundy
Sources	*HdB*, Vol. 3, no, 867.

Hugh Levre of Champagne

Alias/es	Ugo Levre de Champagne
Notes	Siege of Acre (1191).
Region	Champagne
Sources	*HdB*, Vol. 3, no. 867.

Godfrey of Saint-Vérain

Alias/es	Godfrey de St Vérain
Notes	Vifgaged a mill to the Templars before going on crusade (1190).
Orders	Templars
Region	Auxerre (Burgundy)
Sources	AN S5243, dossier 80, no. 1.

Hugh of Reynel

Alias/es	Hugues de Reynel, Ugonem de Rinel, Ugo de Rinel
Notes	Siege of Acre (1191).
Sources	*HdB*, Vol. 3, no. 866.

Everard of la Ferté

Alias/es	Arardus de la Ferté
Notes	Siege of Acre (1191).
Region	Burgundy
Sources	*HdB*, Vol. 3, no. 866.

Geoffrey Morell

Alias/es	Gaufridus Morellus
Notes	Siege of Acre (1191).
Family	Everard Morell
Sources	*HdB*, Vol. 3, no. 866.

Everard Morell

Alias/es	Arardus Morellus
Notes	Siege of Acre (1191).
Family	Geoffrey Morell
Sources	*HdB*, Vol. 3, no. 866.

Lord of Camte

Title/s	Lord of Camte
Alias/es	lord of Camte, Burgundy, dominus de Camte in Burgundia
Notes	Siege of Acre.
Region	Burgundy
Sources	*Itinerarium*, p. 93.

Adam of Savoisy

Alias/es	Adam de Savoisy
Notes	Pawned all he had to the Cistercians to fund his participation on the Third Crusade (1189).
Orders	Cistercians (Fortenay)
Region	Savoisy (Burgundy)
Sources	AD de Côte-d'Or, 15H 24–9, no. 3.

Hugh of Bourbonne

Alias/es	Hugh de Bourbonne
Notes	Vifgaged pasture rights to the Templars to finance his participation on the Third Crusade (1191). Siege of Acre.
Ancestor/s	Renier of Bourbonne (T)
Orders	Templars
Region	Genrupt (Burgundy)
Sources	*HdB*, Vol. 3, no. 866, 1432.

Walter of Sombernon

Title/s	Lord of Sombernon
Alias/es	Walter de Sombernon
Notes	Siege of Acre (1191).
Orders	Hospitallers (Sombernon), Templars (Avosne, Uncey)
Region	Avosne (Burgundy)
Sources	*HdB*, Vol. 3, no. 773, 865, 867, 929.

Hugh IV of Berzé

Title/s	Lord of Berzé
Alias/es	Hugh IV de Berzé, Hugh the Poet
Notes	Survived to join the Fourth Crusade.
Ancestor/s	Rollan Bressan

Region	Berzé (Burgundy)
Sources	C. Smith, *Crusading in the Age of Joinville* (Aldershot, 2006), pp. 89–90.

Rotrou III

Title/s	Count of Perche
Alias/es	Rotrou III, count of Perche, comes de Pertico, coens de Perche, Rotrod, comes Perticensis, Rotrodus comes de Pertico, comes Perchensis
Notes	Took the Cross alongside Kings Henry II and Philip II (1188). Siege of Acre (1191). Made donation to Templars and died at the siege of Acre (1191).
Ancestor/s	Rotrou II of Perche
Family	Geoffrey of Perche
Orders	Benedictines (Saint-Laumer of Blois, Bonneval), Carthusians (Val Dieu), Grandmontines (Chêne Galon), St Lazarus (Nogent-le-Rotrou)
Region	Perche
Sources	Ambroise, line 4537; *Chronica*, Vol. 3, p. 88; *Gesta Regis*, Vol. 2, pp. 73, 92–3, 143; *Itinerarium*, p. 213; *Saint-Denis de Nogent-le-Rotrou, 1031–1789: Histoire et Cartulaire*, ed. C. Métais (Vannes, 1899), no. 99; Rigord, p. 83; *RRRH*, no. 1308; Schenk, *Templar Families*, p. 28; Wendover, pp. 170, 191.

Geoffrey III of Perche

Title/s	Count of Perche
Alias/es	Geoffrey, count of Perche, Gaufridum comitem de Pertico
Notes	Married Matilda, Richard I's niece (1189). Messina (1190). Cyprus (1191). Siege of Acre (1191). Skirmish near Betenoble (1192).
Ancestor/s	Rotrou II of Perche
Family	Rotrou III of Perche, King Richard I, Joanna of Sicily
Orders	Grandmontines (Chêne Galon), Benedictines (Nogent-le-Rotrou)
Region	Perche
Sources	Devizes, p. 22; *Gesta Regis*, Vol. 2, pp. 128, 150; *Itinerarium*, p. 372; Landon, *Itinerary*, no. 358; *RRRH*, no. 1308.

Hervey III of Gien

Title/s	Lord of Donzy and Gien
Alias/es	Hervey de Gien, Hervé, Henry of Danzy, Henricus de Danziaco, Herveiis de Gienis, Herveus de Donziaco
Notes	Assisted in the landing of William of Sicily's fleet. Arrived at the siege of Acre (1189).
Ancestor/s	Itier I and II, Hugh, and Norgaud of Toucy
Family	Narjot II of Toucy, Ralph of Vendôme, Stephen of Sancerre
Orders	Benedictines (Charité-sur-Loire)

Region	Donzy
Sources	Abbé Lebeuf, *Mémoires concernant l'histoire civil et ecclésiastique d'Auxerre et de son ancien diocèse*, ed. M. Challe and M. Quantin, Vol. 4 (Auxerre, 1855), pp. 28–9; *Cartulaire du prieuré de la Charité-sur-Loire (Nièvre), Ordre de Cluni*, ed. R. de Lespinasse (Nevers and Paris, 1887), no. 76; *Itinerarium*, pp. 28, 74; *Recueil des chartes de l'abbaye de Saint-Benoît-sur-Loire*, ed. M. Prou and A. Vidier (Paris, 1900), no. 264.

Robert of Sablonières

Alias/es	Robert de Sablonières
Notes	Died on the Third Crusade.
Region	Nemours
Sources	*Histoire et cartulaire des Templiers de Provins. Avec une introduction sur le débuts du Temple en France*, ed. V. Carrière (Paris, 1919; reprint: Marseille, 1978), no. 87.

Guy III of Chevreuse

Title/s	Lord of Chevreuse
Alias/es	Guido de Caprosia
Notes	On his crusade with his neighbour Philip of Lévis.
Region	Chevreuse
Sources	N. Civel, *La fleur de France. Les seigneurs d'Île-de-France au XIIe siècle* (Turnhout, 2006), pp. 185–6; *Cartulaire de l'abbaye de Notre-Dame de la Roche, de l'ordre de Saint-Augustine, au diocèse de Paris*, ed. A. Moutié (Paris, 1863), p. 431.

Philip of Lévis

Title/s	Lord of Lévis-Saint-Nom
Alias/es	Philippe de Levis
Notes	On his crusade with his neighbour Guy III of Chevreuse.
Region	Chevreuse
Sources	*Cartulaire de Notre-Dame de Prouille*, Vol. 1, ed. J. Guiraud (Paris, 1907), no. 2; *Notre-Dame de la Roche*, ed. Moutié, pp. x, xxix–xxx, no. 1, 431; Civel, *La fleur de France*, pp. 185–6.

Raoul I of Coucy

Title/s	Lord of Coucy-le-Château and Marle
Alias/es	Raoul de Coucy, Ralph, Radulphus de Cochi
Notes	Confirmed and augmented the donation made by his father to Ribemont Abbey prior to leaving on crusade (1190). Arrived before the death of Walter Ross and Walter of Kyme (1190). Died on the Third Crusade (1191).

Ancestor/s	Enguerrand I and II of Coucy, Thomas of Marle
Family	Dreux IV and Peter of Amiens, Robert II of Dreux, Bishop Philip of Beauvais, Hugh VI of Gournay, and Robert of Boves
Orders	Benedictines (Nogent-sous-Coucy and Ribemont), Premonstratensians (Mont-Saint-Martin), Templars
Region	Picardy
Sources	*Crusade Charters*, nos. 9, 10; J. Folda, *Crusader Art in the Holy Land, from the Third Crusade to the Fall of Acre, 1187–1291* (New York, 2005), p. 45; Gilbert of Mons, pp. 117–18, 128, 131–5, 140, 165, 273.

Dreux IV of Amiens

Title/s	Lord of Flexicourt, Vignacourt, la Broye, and Etoile
Alias/es	Drogo d'Amiens, Dreus d'Amiens, Droon d'Amïens, Drogo de Amiens
Notes	Arrived at the siege of Acre with Philip II (1191). Sent by Richard I to Tyre (1191).
Ancestor/s	Enguerrand I and II of Coucy, Thomas of Marle
Family	Peter of Amiens, Hugh IV of St Pol, Raoul I of Coucy, Hugh VI of Gournay, and Robert of Boves
Orders	Premonstratensians (Flexicourt)
Region	Amiens
Sources	Ambroise, lines 4533, 5444; *Gesta Regis*, Vol. 2, p. 182; *Itinerarium*, pp. 213, 242; H. and A. Passier, *Trésor généalogique de Dom Villevieille*, Vol. 1 (Paris, 1877), p. 354; *Nécrologe de l'église d'Amiens*, ed. J.B.M. Roze (Amiens, 1885), pp. 181–2.

Peter of Amiens

Alias/es	Pierre de Amiens
Notes	Siege of Acre. Participated in the Fourth Crusade.
Ancestor/s	Enguerrand I and II of Coucy, Thomas of Marle
Family	Dreux IV of Amiens, Hugh IV of St Pol, Raoul I of Coucy, Hugh VI of Gournay, and Robert of Boves
Region	Amiens
Sources	H. de Pinoteau, 'Heraldische Untersuchungen zum Wappenpokal,' ed. T. Ulbert, *Resafa III. Der kreuzfahrerzeitliche Silberschatz aus Resafa-Sergiupolis* (Mainz am Rhein, 1990), pp. 77–86.

Gérard II of Picquigny

Title/s	Vidame of Amiens
Alias/es	vidame of Picquigny, vice-dominus de Pinkinio
Notes	Died at the siege of Acre (1191).
Ancestor/s	Guermond III of Picquigny

Orders	Cistercians (Lannoy), Lepers of Picquigny
Region	Amiens
Sources	Gilbert of Mons, p. 273; 'Histoire de l'abbaye de Lannoy, ordre de Cîteaux [reconstitution de 80 actes]', ed. L.E. Deladreue, *Mémoires de la Société académique d'archéologie, sciences et arts du département de l'Oise*, Vol. 10 (1877), no. LXXXII, p. 693; *Documents inédits, Extraits du Cartulaire de Picquigny*, ed. L.-E. de la Gorgue-Rosny (Boulogne-sur-Mer, 1877), p. 30.

Walter of Wargnies

Alias/es	Walterus de Warini, Walter de Wargnies
Notes	Made a donation to Saint-Amand Abbey prior to departing on crusade (1189).
Orders	Benedictines (Saint-Amand)
Region	Amiens, Amfroipret
Sources	AD du Nord 12H 3, Cartulaire de Saint-Amand, f.208 r–v, no, 264; Gilbert of Mons, pp. 141–2, 155, 165, 175, 213, 217, 274, 328.

Gerald

Alias/es	le miles Gérard
Notes	Donated an annual rent to Vaucelles Abbey prior to departing on crusade (1190).
Orders	Cistercians (Vaucelles)
Region	Picardy
Sources	*Les chartes de l'abbaye cistercienne de Vaucelles au XIIe siècle*, ed. B.-M. Tock (Turnhout, 2010), no. 123.

Gerard of Hamel

Alias/es	Gérard de Hamel
Notes	Yielded his right to a mill at Fons to Arrouaise Abbey prior to departing on crusade (1190).
Orders	Arrouasians (Arrouaise)
Region	Picardy
Sources	Amiens, Bibliothèque centrale Louis Aragon, ms. 1077 inséré entre fos. 74–75.

Florence III of Angest

Title/s	Lord of Hangest
Alias/es	Florence III de Angest, Florentius de Angest, de Hangi, Florentius de Hangest
Notes	Died at the siege of Acre.
Region	Hangest
Sources	*Chronica*, Vol. 3, p. 89; Diss, p. 79; Gilbert of Mons, p. 273; Wendover, p. 178.

Manasses of Villegruis

Alias/es	Manasses de Villegruis
Notes	Siege of Acre (1191).
Orders	Benedictines (Paraclete)
Region	Villegruis
Sources	Provins, Bibliothèque Municipale, ms. 85, no. 19; '*Feoda I*', ed. Longnon, no. 1523; *Cartulaire de l'abbaye du Paraclet*, ed. C. Lalore (Paris, 1878), no. 71; *RRRH*, no. 1305.

Robert of Boves

Title/s	Count of Amiens, lord of Boves
Alias/es	Robert de Boves, Robertus de Boves, Boives, Robert de Coucy, Robert of Coucy
Notes	Died at the siege of Acre (1191).
Ancestor/s	Enguerrand I and II of Coucy, Thomas of Marle
Family	Hugh IV of St Pol, Raoul I of Coucy, Dreux IV and Peter of Amiens, Hugh VI of Gournay
Orders	Premonstratensians (Amiens)
Region	Boves
Sources	Amiens, Bibliothèque centrale Louis Aragon, ms. 781, no. 23; *Chronica Albrici Monachi Trium Fontium* 1119, MGH SS XXIII, p. 824; *Chronica*, Vol. 3, p. 89; *Crusade Charters*, no. 4.

Jocelin of Montoire

Title/s	Count of Montoire
Alias/es	Jocelinus de Montoire, count of Montoire, Jocelinus de Munmorenc, comes Jocelinus
Notes	Supported collection on behalf of poorest Crusaders at Lent (1191). Died at the siege of Acre (1190).
Region	Montoire (Loire)
Sources	*Itinerarium*, pp. 73, 135.

Henry II of Champagne

Title/s	Count of Troyes, king of Jerusalem
Alias/es	Henry de Champagne, count of Troyes, Henricum comitem Campanie, dux Iudee, coens Henris, sires de Champaigne, conte Henri
Notes	Siege of Acre, military commander (1190). Repulsed Muslim sally (1190). Led St Martin offensive (1190). Supported collection on behalf of poorest Crusaders (1191). Battle of Arsuf (1191). Relief of Jaffa (1192).
Ancestor/s	Louis VII of France, Henry I of Champagne, Stephen of Blois

Family	Richard I, Joanna of Sicily, Philip II of France, Henry I of Mousson, Stephen of Sancerre
Orders	Cistercians (Pontigny), Hospitallers (Bar-sur-Aube), Lepers of Deux-eaux, Premonstratensians, Templars
Region	Troyes
Sources	Ambroise, lines 3505, 3827, 5298–321, 6184, 7848, 8630, 8906 9349, 11288, 11378–620, 11675; Baha' al-Din, pp. 120–1, 138, 143, 208, 212, 231; BN ms. nouv. acq. lat. 51, fol. 103r; *Chronica*, Vol. 3, p. 182; Diss, Vol. 2, pp. 79, 95; Devizes, pp. 19, 81, 84; *Gesta Regis*, Vol. 2, p. 144; Ibn al-Athir, Vol. 2, p. 377–8; *Itinerarium*, pp. 92, 112–13, 135, 238, 261, 269, 326, 336, 344–5, 349, 356, 373, 413, 415, 425; *Pontigny*, ed. Garrigues, no. 200; Rigord, pp. 83–4; *RRRH*, no. 1297; *Yonne*, Vol. 2, ed. Quantin, no. 412; Wendover, pp. 178, 199.

Stephen of Sancerre

Title/s	Count of Sancerre
Alias/es	Stephen, count of Sancerre, cuens Estiefnes, Stephanus comes de Sauneis, Stephanus comes de Saunais, comes Stephanus
Notes	Silves. Died at the siege of Acre (1190).
Ancestor/s	Louis VII of France, Henry I of Champagne, Stephen of Blois
Family	Count of Bar, Duke of Burgundy, Rotrou III of Perche, Theobald V of Blois, Henry II of Champagne, Hervey of Gien
Orders	Benedictines (Saint-Evroul)
Region	Sancerre
Sources	AD de l'Orne, H 708; Ambroise, line 3508; *Chronica*, Vol. 3, p. 88; Gilbert of Mons, pp. 132, 153, 191, 206, 273, 329; *Itinerarium*, p. 92; Wendover, p. 191.

Guy II of Dampierre

Title/s	Constable of Champagne, lord of Dampierre
Alias/es	Guy de Dampierre, Guiz de Dampierre, Guido de Dunnipetra, Guide de Danpiera
Notes	Constable of Champagne. Silves (1189). Arrived at the siege of Acre (1189). Witness of the abduction of Isabel of Jerusalem, her marriage to Conrad of Montferrat, and later union with Henry II of Champagne (1189–92). Siege of Acre (1190, 1191).
Ancestor/s	Clemence of Montfauçon
Family	Everard II of Brienne, Everard I of Chacenay, Anseric II of Montréal, Thierry of Montfauçon, Manasses of Langres, John of Montmirail, Narjot of Toucy, Geoffrey IV of Joinville, Robert II of Dreux, and Philip, bishop of Beauvais
Region	Dampierre, Saint-Dizier, Saint-Just (Champagne)
Sources	Ambroise, line 3124; Diss, Vol. 2, pp. 79, 82–3; *The Conquest of Jerusalem and the Third Crusade*, ed. P.W. Edbury (Aldershot, 1998), 6e, p. 172; *Gesta Regis*, Vol. 2, p. 178; *Itinerarium*, p. 74; *RRRH*, nos. 1297, 1304; Wendover, p. 180.

Manasses of Bar

Title/s	Bishop of Langres
Alias/es	Manasser bishop of Langres
Notes	Messina (1190). Siege of Acre (1191).
Ancestor/s	Clemence of Montfauçon
Family	Everard II of Brienne, Guy II of Dampierre, Everard I of Chacenay, Thierry of Montfauçon
Orders	Cistercians (Mores), Templars (Avalleur), Langres Cathedral
Region	Bar-sur-Seine
Sources	*Gesta Regis*, Vol. 2, pp. 128, 130; *HdB*, Vol. 3, no, 867.

Everard II

Title/s	Count of Brienne
Alias/es	Everard II, count of Brienne, comes de Brenes, comes Brenes, comes Brenensis
Notes	Silves (1189). Battle of Acre (1189). Died at the siege of Acre (1190).
Ancestor/s	Everard I and Walter of Brienne
Family	Andrew of Brienne, Everard I and James of Chacenay, Bartholomew of Vignory, James of Avesnes
Orders	Premonstratensians (Basse-Fontaine), Saint-Marie-de-Ramerupt
Region	Brienne
Sources	Ambroise, lines 2917, 2966; Asmoui Ismail, 'Counts of Brienne', p. 106; *Cartulaire de l'abbaye de Basse-Fontaine et Chartres de la commanderie de Beauvoir de l'ordre Teutonique*, ed. C. Lalore (Paris, 1878), nos. 5–7; *Chronica*, Vol. 3, p. 88; Diss, Vol. 2, p. 79; *Gesta Regis*, Vol. 2, pp. 93–4, 148; *Itinerarium*, p. 67; Wendover, p. 178.

Andrew of Brienne

Title/s	Lord of Ramerupt
Alias/es	Andrew de Brienne, Andreu de Braine, Andreas de Briena, Andreas frater ejus, Andreas de Breno
Notes	Silves (1189). Accompanied Geoffrey of Lusignan to the Holy Land (1189). Siege of Acre (1189). Died at the battle of Acre as part of the mounted reserve (1189).
Ancestor/s	Everard I, Walter, and Everard II of Brienne
Family	Everard III of Brienne, James and Everard I of Chacenay, Bartholomew of Vignory, James of Avesnes
Orders	Premonstratensians (Basse-Fontaine)
Region	Brienne
Sources	Ambroise, lines 2917, 2966, 2952–3071; Basse-Fontaine, ed. Lalore, nos. 5, 6, 7; *Chronica*, Vol. 3, p. 88; Diss, Vol. 2, p. 79; *Gesta Regis*, Vol. 2, pp. 96, 148; Gilbert of Mons, p. 273; *Itinerarium*, p. 71; Wendover, p. 178.

Simon of Bishop's Ville

Alias/es	Simon, miles de Villa Episcopi
Notes	Gave the land of Busus to Premonstratensians prior to embarking on crusade (1189).
Orders	Premonstratensians (Basse-Fontaine)
Region	Brienne
Sources	*Crusade Charters*, no. 16.

Narjot II of Toucy

Title/s	Lord of Toucy
Alias/es	Narjot de Toucy, Nargevot de Toci, Narjod
Notes	Arrived at the siege of Acre (1189). Died in the Holy Land (1192).
Ancestor/s	Itier I and II, Hugh, and Norgaud of Toucy
Family	Guy II of Dampierre, Hervey of Gien
Orders	Templars (Sauce-sur-Yonne)
Region	Burgundy, Champagne
Sources	BN, ms. latin 9885; *Itinerarium*, p. 74; Molinier, *Vie de Louis le Gros*, p. 158; Lebeuf, *Mémoires*, ed. Challe and Quantin, p. 45; *Saint-Benoît-sur-Loire*, ed. Prou and Vidier, nos. 173, 177, 189, 207; *Yonne*, Vol. 2, ed. Quantin, no. 429.

Everard II of Aulnay

Alias/es	Erard d'Aulnay, Erardus de Alneto, Odardus de Alneto
Notes	Siege of Acre (1190, 1191). Witness of the abduction of Isabel of Jerusalem, her marriage to Conrad of Montferrat, and later union with Henry II of Champagne (1189–92). Marshal of Champagne (1213).
Ancestor/s	Urs of Aulnay (T)
Family	Oger of Saint-Chéron, Godfrey of Villehardouin
Orders	Cistercians (Trois-Fontaines)
Region	Troyes
Sources	*Conquest*, ed. Edbury, no. 6e, p. 173; '*Feoda I*', ed. Longnon, p. 13; T. Evergates, *Henry the Liberal: Count of Champagne, 1127–1181* (Philadelphia, PA, 2016), p. 137; *RRRH*, no. 1304.

William of Aulnay

Alias/es	William d'Aulnay, Guillaume d'Aulnay, Guillaume d'Aunoy
Notes	Travelled to the Holy Land with Henry II of Champagne (1190).
Region	Troyes
Sources	AN S5188/A, dossier 25, no. 4; Schenk, *Templar Families*, p. 173.

Milo II Breban of Provins

Alias/es	Milo II le Bréban, Milo Brabancius
Notes	Chamberlain. Siege of Acre (1191). Accompanied Count Henry II on crusade and remained with him in the Holy Land until Henry's death (1190–7).
Ancestor/s	William le Roi, Milo I
Orders	Benedictines (Paraclete)
Region	Provins
Sources	BM Provins, ms. 85, no. 19 (1191); '*Feoda I*', ed. Longnon, no. 1523; *Paraclet*, ed. Lalore, no. 71; *RRRH*, no. 1305.

Roger of Saint-Chéron

Alias/es	Ogier of Saint-Chéron, Rogerius de Sancto Karauno
Notes	Witness of the abduction of Isabel of Jerusalem, her marriage to Conrad of Montferrat, and later union with Henry II of Champagne (1189–92).
Ancestor/s	Urs of Aulnay (T)
Family	Everard II of Aulnay, Godfrey of Villehardouin
Orders	Cistercians (Trois-Fontaines)
Region	Arzillières
Sources	AN S 4956, dossier 15, no. 3; *Diocèse ancien de Châlons-sur-Marne. Histoire et monuments*, ed. E. de Barthélemy (Paris, 1861), no. 10, pp. 336–7; *Conquest*, ed. Edbury, no. 6e, p. 173.

Vilain of Nully

Title/s	Lord of Nully
Alias/es	Vilain de Nully
Notes	Travelled to the Holy Land with Henry II of Champagne (1190). Siege of Acre (1191). Survived to join the Fourth Crusade.
Family	Geoffreys of Joinville
Orders	Cistercians (Boulancourt)
Region	Nully
Sources	AN S4956, dossier 15, no. 3; *RRRH*, no. 1304; Schenk, *Templar Families*, pp. 171–3.

Geoffrey of Villehardouin

Title/s	Lord of Villehardouin, marshal of Champagne
Alias/es	Geoffrey de Villahardouin, Geoffroi, Gaufridus Campanie marescalcus
Notes	Marshal of Champagne (1185). Siege of Acre. Chronicler of Fourth Crusade.
Family	Godfrey and Geoffrey of Villehardouin, Everard II of Aulnay, Oger of Saint-Chéron

Orders	Troyes Cathedral
Region	Troyes
Sources	Evergates, *Aristocracy*, p. 245; '*Feoda I*', ed. Longnon, no. 1999; [M. Roserot, Note on genealogy of Villehardouin], *Revue de Champagne et de Brie*, 18 (1885), 392; *Chronique*, p. 392, citing Archives de l'Aube.

Villain of Villehardouin

Title/s	Marshal of Champagne
Alias/es	Villain de Villehardouin, Villain of Arzillières, marescallus comitis Henrici
Notes	Marshal of Champagne. Captured at the siege of Acre (1190).
Family	Godfrey and Geoffrey of Villehardouin, Everard II of Aulnay, Oger of Saint-Chéron
Region	Troyes
Sources	*Chronica*, Vol. 3, p. 89.

Godfrey of Villehardouin

Alias/es	Godfrey de Villehardouin, Godfridus de Ville Hardoin
Notes	Siege of Acre. Participated in the Fourth Crusade.
Family	William and Geoffrey of Villehardouin, Everard II of Aulnay, Oger of Saint-Chéron
Region	Troyes
Sources	AN S4956, dossier 15, no. 3; Evergates, *Aristocracy*, p. 263; *Joinville and Villehardouin, Chronicles of the Crusades*, ed. and trans. M.R.B. Shaw (London, 1963), pp. 6–7, 31; Schenk, *Templar Families*, p. 172.

Geoffrey IV of Joinville

Title/s	Seneschal of Champagne, lord of Joinville
Alias/es	Godfrey IV of Joinville, Gaufridos de Gienvilla
Notes	Seneschal of Champagne (1188–90). Silves (1189). Arrived at the siege of Acre (1189). Died at the siege of Acre (1190).
Ancestor/s	Geoffrey III of Joinville
Family	Geoffrey III of Joinville, Guy II of Dampierre, Everard II of Brienne
Orders	Templars (Ruetz)
Region	Joinville
Sources	Evergates, *Aristocracy*, p. 235; H.-F. Delaborde, *Jean de Joinville et les seigneurs de Joinville, suivi d'un catalogue de leurs actes* (Paris, 1894), no. 82; *Itinerarium*, p. 74.

Geoffrey III of Joinville

Title/s	Seneschal of Champagne, lord of Joinville
Alias/es	Gaufridos de Gienvilla

Notes	Seneschal of Champagne. Died at the siege of Acre (*c.*1190).
Family	Geoffrey IV of Joinville, Villain of Nully, Everard II of Brienne
Orders	Vaux-en-Ornois convent
Region	Joinville
Sources	Evergates, *Aristocracy*, p. 173; Delaborde, *Seigneurs de Joinville*, no. 28; *Itinerarium*, p. 74.

Henry of Arzillières

Alias/es	Henry d'Arzillières
Notes	Siege of Acre (1190). Made a donation to the Templars during the siege of Acre (1191). Participated in the Fourth Crusade.
Ancestor/s	Urs of Aulnay (T)
Family	William of Arzillières; Geoffrey, William, and Godfrey of Villehardouin
Region	Arzillières
Sources	Schenk, *Templar Families*, p. 173; *Die Kanzlei der lateinischen Könige von Jerusalem*, ed. H.E. Mayer Vol. 2 (Hanover, 1996), no. 14; *Joinville and Villehardouin*, pp. 2, 12; *RRRH*, no. 1304.

William of Arzillières

Alias/es	William d'Arzillières, Walterus de Arzilleriis
Notes	Siege of Acre (1189, 1191). Later became Marshal of the Templars (1201).
Ancestor/s	Urs of Aulnay (T)
Family	Henry of Arzillières, Geoffrey, William, and Godfrey of Villehardouin
Region	Arzillières
Sources	AN S4956, dossier 15, no. 3; *Itinerarium*, p. 93; *Könige von Jerusalem*, Vol. 2, ed. Mayer, no. 14; *RRRH*, no. 1304.

Clarembaud of Montchâblon

Alias/es	[C]larenbaldus de Montcaulon, Clarembaud de Montchâblon
Notes	Knight of Henry I of Champagne (*c.*1178). Siege of Acre (1191). Jointly commanded the escort to a convoy ambushed by Saladin's forces (1192).
Region	Aisne
Sources	Ambroise, lines 9931–5; '*Feoda* I', ed. Longnon, p. 29; *RRRH*, no. 1304.

Hugh of Coiffy-le-Haut

Alias/es	Hugo de Coy
Notes	Siege of Acre (1191).
Sources	*RRRH*, no. 1304.

Ado Puntiel

Notes	Siege of Acre (1191).
Sources	*RRRH*, no. 1304.

Hugh of Landricourt

Alias/es	Hugo de Landricurt
Notes	Siege of Acre (1191).
Region	Marne
Sources	*RRRH*, no. 1304.

Guy of Chouilly

Alias/es	Guido de Choili
Notes	Siege of Acre (1190)..
Family	Hugh of Chouilly
Orders	Templars
Sources	*RRRH*, no. 1297.

Hugh of Chouilly

Alias/es	Odo de Choili
Notes	Siege of Acre (1190)
Family	Guy of Chouilly
Orders	Templars
Sources	*RRRH*, no. 1297.

Clarembaud IV of Chappes

Alias/es	William de Chappes
Notes	Siege of Acre (1190). Died en route to either the Fourth Crusade or Compostela.
Ancestor/s	Walter de Chappes, Everard I of Brienne
Family	Guy of Chappes
Orders	Benedictines (Montiéramey)
Region	Aube
Sources	*Cartulaire de l'abbaye de Montiéramey*, ed. C. Lalore (Paris, 1890), no. 83; Schenk, *Templar Families*, pp. 243–4, n. 189.

Guy of Chappes

Title/s	Lord of Jully
Alias/es	Guy de Chappes

Notes	Witness of the abduction of Isabel of Jerusalem, her marriage to Conrad of Montferrat, and later union with Henry II of Champagne (1189–92).
Ancestor/s	Walter de Chappes, Everard I of Brienne
Family	Clarembaud of Chappes, Clarembaud of Noyers
Orders	Benedictines (Montiéramey)
Region	Aube
Sources	AN S4956, dossier 17, no. 1; *Montiéramey*, ed. Lalore, no. 83; *Conquest*, ed. Edbury, no. 6e, p. 173; Schenk, *Templar Families*, p. 173.

Philip of Plancy

Alias/es	Philip de Planceio
Notes	Asked his wife to found an anniversary mass for his mother immediately prior to his departing on the Third Crusade.
Family	Giles of Plancy, Guy of Chappes
Orders	Saint-Pierre Chapel
Region	Aube
Sources	*Cartulaire de Saint-Pierre de Troyes*, ed. C. Lalore (Paris, 1880), no. 144.

Giles of Plancy

Alias/es	Giles de Placy, de Planceio, Gilon
Notes	Asked his wife to found an anniversary mass immediately prior to his departing on the Third Crusade. Died on the Third Crusade (1190).
Family	Philip of Plancy
Orders	Benedictines (Montiéramey)
Region	Aube
Sources	*Montiéramey*, ed. Lalore, no. 88; *Paraclet*, ed. Lalore, no. 77.

Everard I of Chacenay

Alias/es	Erard de Châtiney, de Chacennaio, Erardus de Castiniaco
Notes	Crusaded in 1179 and 1182. Died at the siege of Acre (1191).
Ancestor/s	James and Anseric of Chacenay, Everard I of Brienne
Family	Everard III and Andrew of Brienne, James of Chacenay
Orders	Cistercians (Mores, Clairvaux), Premonstratensians (Basse-Fontaine)
Region	Aube
Sources	A. de Barthélemy, 'Pèlerins champenois en Palestine (1097-1249)', *Revue de l'Orient Latin*, Vol. 1 (1893), p. 358; *Crusade Charters*, p. 113; *Itinerarium*, p. 92.

James of Chacenay

Alias/es	Jacques de Châtiney
Notes	Died in the Holy Land shortly after his father, Everard I (1191).
Ancestor/s	James, Anseric, and Everard I of Chacenay, Everard I of Brienne
Family	Everard III and Andrew of Brienne, Everard I of Chacenay
Orders	Premonstratensians (Basse-Fontaine)
Region	Aube
Sources	*Crusade Charters*, p. 113; *Montiéramey*, ed. Lalore, no. 90.

John I of Sées

Title/s	Count of Ponthieu
Alias/es	John, count of Pontigny, Pontif, John of Seis, Johannes comes Ponciaci, comes Pantif, Johannes de Seis
Notes	Died at the siege of Acre (1191).
Ancestor/s	Guy II and William of Ponthieu
Family	Guy of Noyelles, Hugh IV of St Pol
Orders	Premonstratensians (Saint-Josse-au-Bois), Cistercians (Perseigne, Valloires), Benedictines (Troarn)
Region	Ponthieu
Sources	*Chronica*, Vol. 3, p. 88; Gilbert of Mons, p. 273; *Itinerarium*, p. 74; D. Power, 'The Preparation of Count John I of Sées for the Third Crusade', *Crusading and Warfare in the Middle Ages*, ed. D. Morton and S. John (Farnham, 2014), pp. 163–6.

Guy of Noyelles

Title/s	Lord of Noyelles
Alias/es	Guido
Notes	Siege of Acre (1191).
Ancestor/s	Guy II and William of Ponthieu
Family	John I of Sées, Hugh IV of St Pol
Region	Ponthieu
Sources	AD Calvados, F 5047; Leson, 'Resafa Heraldry Cup', p. 78; Power, 'John I of Sées', pp. 163–6.

Clarembaud of Noyers

Title/s	Lord of Noyers
Alias/es	Clarembold de Noyers, Clarembaldus de Nuheriis
Notes	Siege of Acre (1189, 1190). Died at the siege of Acre (1190).

Ancestor/s	Walter de Chappes,
Family	Guy of Noyers, Godfrey of Argenteuil, Guy and Stephen of Pierre-Perthuis
Orders	Hospitallers (Arbonne), Benedictine (Jully-les-Nonnains), Cistercians (Pontigny), Templars (Yonne)
Region	Yonne
Sources	*Recueil des Chartes de l'Abbaye de Cluny*, Vol. 5, ed. A. Bernard, revised A. Bruel (Paris, 1894), no. 3804; *HdB*, Vol. 3, no. 852; *Itinerarium*, p. 93; *Jully-les-Nonnains*, ed. Petit, p. 26; *Pontigny*, ed. Garrigues, nos. 47, 55; *RRRH*, No. 1288; *Yonne*, Vol. 2, ed. Quantin, no. 406.

Guy of Noyers

Alias/es	Gui de Noyers, Gui de Noyelles
Notes	Made a donation prior to his journey to Jerusalem (1190). Joined the Templars around the time of the Third Crusade.
Ancestor/s	Walter de Chappes,
Family	Clarembaud of Noyers, Godfrey of Argenteuil, Guy and Stephen of Pierre-Perthuis
Orders	Cistercians (Reigny)
Region	Yonne
Sources	BN, ms. nouv. acq. lat. 55, fol. 555r; *HdB*, Vol. 3, pp. 43, 61; 'Inventaire de la collection de Chastellux', ed. C. Porée, *Bulletin de la Société des sciences historiques et naturelles de l'Yonne*, Vol. 57 (1904), no. 29; *Jully-les-Nonnains*, ed. Petit, p. 26; *Pontigny*, ed. Garrigues, nos. 46, 55; Schenk, *Templar Families*, pp. 242–3.

William of Stables

Alias/es	Willelmus de Stables
Notes	Siege of Acre (1190–1).
Sources	*HdB*, Vol. 3, no. 852, 865.

Godfrey of Argenteuil

Alias/es	Godfrey d'Argenteuil, Humbertus d'Argentoil
Notes	Went on Crusade (1189). Siege of Acre (1190).
Ancestor/s	Walter de Chappes
Family	Clarembaud, Guy and Stephen of Pierre-Perthuis
Region	Yonne
Sources	*HdB*, Vol. 3, no. 852; *RRRH*, no. 1288; *Yonne*, Vol. 2, ed. Quantin, no. 406.

Guy of Pierre-Perthuis

Alias/es	Guy de Pierre-Perthuis
Notes	Went on Crusade (1189), Siege of Acre (1190).

Family	Stephen of Pierre-Perthuis, Stephen of Brive, Aswalo II, Rainard, Frederick, and Peter of Seignelay, Clarembold of Chappes
Region	Yonne
Sources	*HdB*, Vol. 3, no. 852; Schenk, *Templar Families*, p. 243; *Yonne*, Vol. 2, ed. Quantin, no. 429.

Stephen of Pierre-Perthuis

Alias/es	Stephen de Pierre-Perthuis, Stephanus li Bories de Petra Pertuis
Notes	Went on Crusade (1189), Siege of Acre (1190)
Family	Guy de Pierre-Perthuis, Stephen of Brive, Aswalo II, Rainard, Frederick, and Peter of Seignelay
Orders	Templars (Yonne)
Region	Yonne
Sources	*HdB*, Vol. 3, no. 852; Schenk, *Templar Families*, p. 243; *RRRH*, no. 1288; *Yonne*, Vol. 2, ed. Quantin, no. 406.

Stephen of Brive

Alias/es	Stephan de Brive
Notes	Granted his sister, a nun at Crisenon, an annual revenue on the eve of departing on crusade (1189). Siege of Acre (1191). Died on the Third Crusade.
Family	Reinard, Peter, and Frederick of Seignelay (all of whom died on crusade), Guy and Stephen or Pierre-Perthuis
Orders	Premonstratensians (Basse-Fontaine); Crisenon Convent
Region	Yonne
Sources	BN, ms. latin 9885, fol. 78v. no. 161; *Yonne*, Vol. 2, ed. Quantin, no. 429.

Aswalo II

Title/s	Lord of Seignelay
Alias/es	Aswalo de Seignelay
Notes	Went on Crusade (1190). Died on the Third Crusade.
Family	Reinard, Peter, and Frederick of Seignelay (all of whom died on crusade), Guy and Stephen or Pierre-Perthuis
Orders	Premonstratensians (Basse-Fontaine), Cistercians (Pontigny)
Region	Auxerre
Sources	C.B. Bouchard, *Those of my Blood: Constructing Noble Families in Medieval Francia* (Philadelphia, 2001), pp. 157–8, 161, 167; *Yonne*, Vol. 2, ed. Quantin, no. 410.

Frederick of Seignelay

Alias/es	Frederick de Seignelay
Notes	Went on Crusade (1190). Died on the Third Crusade.

Family	Reinard and Peter of Seignelay, Stephen of Brive (all of whom died on crusade), Guy and Stephen or Pierre-Perthuis
Orders	Premonstratensians (Basse-Fontaine), Cistercians (Pontigny)
Region	Auxerre
Sources	Bouchard, *Those of my Blood*, p. 167; *Pontigny*, ed. Garrigues, no. 110, 138, *Yonne*, Vol. 2, ed. Quantin, no. 410.

Peter of Seignelay

Alias/es	Peter de Seignelay
Notes	Went on Crusade (1190). Died on the Third Crusade.
Family	Reinard and Frederick of Seignelay, Stephen of Brive (all of whom died on crusade), Guy and Stephen or Pierre-Perthuis
Orders	Premonstratensians (Basse-Fontaine), Cistercians (Pontigny)
Region	Auxerre
Sources	Bouchard, *Those of my Blood*, p. 167; *Pontigny*, ed. Garrigues, no. 110, 138, *Yonne*, Vol. 2, ed. Quantin, no. 410.

Rainard of Seignelay

Alias/es	Rainard de Seignelay
Notes	Went on Crusade (1190). Died on the Third Crusade.
Family	Frederick and Peter of Seignelay, Stephen of Brive (all of whom died on crusade), Guy and Stephen or Pierre-Perthuis
Orders	Premonstratensians (Basse-Fontaine), Cistercians (Pontigny)
Region	Auxerre
Sources	Bouchard, *Those of my Blood*, p. 167; *Pontigny*, ed. Garrigues, no. 110, 138, *Yonne*, Vol. 2, ed. Quantin, no. 410.

William

Title/s	Count of Joigny
Alias/es	William, count of Joigny, Willelmus comes de Juvenni
Notes	Siege of Acre (1190). Witness of the abduction of Isabel of Jerusalem, her marriage to Conrad of Montferrat, and later union with Henry II of Champagne (1189–92).
Ancestor/s	Counts William II and III of Nevers, Reynard II of Joigny
Family	John I of Arcis-sur-Aube, Raynald of Nevers
Orders	Premonstratensians (Dilo), Hospitallers (Joigny), Templars (Sauce-sur-Yonne)
Region	Joigny
Sources	AN, S5242, dossier 75, no. 1; *Conquest*, ed. Edbury, no. 6e, p. 173; Evergates, *Aristocracy*, pp. 226, 232; *Gesta Regis*, Vol. 2, p. 150; *Yonne*, Vol. 2, ed. Quantin, no. 407.

Simon III of Chefmont

Title/s	Lord of Chefmont
Alias/es	Simon de Chefmont
Notes	Made gifts to Clairvaux on eve of his departure on crusade (1188). Died on the Third Crusade.
Ancestor/s	Anselme II of Ribemont
Family	Robert Wicard III, Bartholomew, Guy, and Walter of Vignory
Orders	Cistercians (Clairvaux), Hospitallers (Esnouveaux)
Region	Chefmont (Aube)
Sources	AD d'Aube, 3H9, no. 73; Evergates, *Aristocracy*, pp. 220, 225.

Robert Wicard III

Alias/es	Robert Wicard of Chefmont
Notes	Died on the Third Crusade.
Ancestor/s	Anselme II of Ribemont
Family	Simon III of Chefmont, Bartholomew, Guy, and Walter of Vignory
Region	Chefmont
Sources	Evergates, *Aristocracy*, p. 220.

Bartholomew of Vignory

Title/s	Lord of Vignory
Alias/es	Bartholomew de Vignory
Notes	Died at the siege of Acre (1191).
Family	Guy and Walter of Vignory, Simon III of Chefmont, Robert Wicard III, Everard II and Andrew of Brienne
Orders	Cistercians (Auberive)
Region	Vignory
Sources	AD Marne, G 1063, nos. 2, 3; AD d'Aube, 3H9, no. 8; *Chartres en langue française antérieures à 1271 conservées dans le département de la Haute-Marne*, ed. J.-G. Gigot (Paris, 1966), nos. 83, 246, 302–3; *Cartulaire du prieuré de Saint-Etienne de Vignory*, Vol. 2, ed. J. d'Arbaumont (Langres, 1882), nos. 46, 60.

Guy of Vignory

Alias/es	Gui de Vignory
Notes	Died at the siege of Acre (1191).
Family	Bartholomew and Walter of Vignory, Simon III of Chefmont, Robert Wicard III
Orders	Cistercians (Auberive)

Region	Vignory
Sources	AD Marne, G 1063, nos. 2, 3; AD d'Aube, 3H9, no. 8; *Haute-Marne*, ed. Gigot, nos. 83, 246, 302, 303; *Saint-Etienne de Vignory*, ed. Arbaumont, nos. 46, 60.

Walter of Vignory

Alias/es	Walter de Vignory
Notes	Joined his father and elder brother on crusade (1191). Survived to inherit the lordship of Vignory.
Family	Bartholomew and Guy of Vignory, Simon III of Chefmont, Robert Wicard III
Region	Vignory
Sources	AD Marne, G 1063, nos. 2, 3; AD d'Aube, 3H9, no. 8; *Haute-Marne*, ed. Gigot, nos. 83, 246, 302, 303; *Saint-Etienne de Vignory*, ed. Arbaumont, nos. 46, 60.

Robert of Milly

Title/s	Chamberlain of Champagne
Alias/es	Robert of Milly, Milliaco
Notes	Chamberlain of Champagne. Made a donation to the Templars prior to departing on crusade (c.1190). Witness of the abduction of Isabel of Jerusalem, her marriage to Conrad of Montferrat, and later union with Henry II of Champagne (1189–92).
Orders	Templars (Moissy)
Region	Trilbardou (Ile of France), Orgeval (Aisne)
Sources	AN, S5009, dossier 40, no, 1; *Regesta regni Hierosolymitani 1097–1291*, Vol. 1, ed. R. Röhricht (Innsbrusk, 1893), no. 867; *RRRH*, no. 1291.

Hugh of Saint-Maurice

Alias/es	Hugh de Saint-Maurice
Notes	Siege of Acre (1190). Witness of the abduction of Isabel of Jerusalem, her marriage to Conrad of Montferrat, and later union with Henry II of Champagne (1189–92).
Region	Saint-Maurice
Sources	*Conquest*, ed. Edbury, no. 6e, p. 173.

Geoffrey of la Bruyere

Alias/es	Geoffrey de la Bruyere, Gaufridus la Bruiere, Geoffroi de la Briere
Notes	Died at the siege of Acre.
Region	Briel-sur-Barse (Champagne)
Sources	*Chronica*, Vol. 3, p. 89; *Gesta Regis*, Vol. 2, p. 149.

Guy of Bazoches

Title/s	Canon of Châlons-sur-Marne
Alias/es	Guy of Bazoches
Notes	Travelled to the Holy Land with Henry II of Champagne (1190).
Ancestor/s	Baldwin II of Hainaut
Region	Châlons-sur-Marne
Sources	Guy of Bazoches, *Liber epistularum Guidonis de Basochis*, ed. H. Adolfsson (Stockholm, 1969), no. 34.

Matthew of Montmorency

Title/s	Lord of Marly, Marshal of France
Alias/es	Matthieu de Montmorency
Notes	Siege of Acre. Became Philip II's marshal on the death of Aubrey Clément (1191).
Family	Bouchard IV, Thibaut, and Joscelin of Montmorency, Guy of Coucy
Orders	Cistercians (Notre-Dame de Val)
Region	Marly
Sources	A. Duchesne, *Histoire génealogique de la Maison de Montmorency et de Laval* (Paris, 1624), pp. 52, 58, *Gesta Regis*, Vol. 2, p. 149.'

Bouchard IV

Title/s	Lord of Montmorency
Alias/es	Bouchard de Montmorency
Notes	Died at the siege of Acre (1190).
Family	Thibaut of Montmorency, Guy of Coucy
Orders	Cistercians (Notre-Dame de Val)
Region	Montmorency
Sources	Duchesne, *Montmorency*, pp. 52, 58; *Obituaires de la province de Sens*, Vol. 1/1, ed. A. Molinier (Paris, 1902), p. 630.

Thibaut of Montmorency

Alias/es	Thibaud de Montmorency
Notes	Died at the siege of Acre (1190).
Family	Joscelin of Montmorency, Guy of Coucy
Orders	Cistercians (Notre-Dame de Val)
Region	Montmorency
Sources	Duchesne, *Montmorency*, pp. 52, 58; *Obituaires*, ed. Molinier, p. 630.

Guy IV of Coucy

Alias/es	Châtelain of Couci, Guy de Thourotte
Notes	Trouvère.
Family	Bouchard IV, Matthew, Thibaut, and Joscelin of Montmorency
Sources	*Lyrics of the Troubadours and Trouvères: An Anthology and a History*, ed. and trans. F. Goldin (New York, 1973).

Aubrey of Reims

Alias/es	Aubrey de Reims, Aubri de Rains, Albericus de Remis
Notes	Commander of Jaffa garrison (1192). Taken as captive to Damascus (1192). Beaten and tortured to death in captivity.
Region	Reims
Sources	Ambroise, line 10846; Baha' al-Din, pp. 218–21; *Itinerarium*, p. 402.

Theobald of Troyes

Alias/es	Theobold de Troyes, Tiebauz de Treis, Theobaldus de Treies
Notes	Taken as captive to Damascus (1192).
Region	Troyes
Sources	Ambroise, line 10899; *Itinerarium*, p. 403.

Hagan of Ervy

Title/s	Lord of Ervy
Alias/es	Hagan d'Ervy
Notes	Drew up his testament prior to departing on crusade (c.1190).
Ancestor/s	Milo of Ervy
Orders	Templars (Troyes), Cistercians (Pontigny), Lepers of Ervy, church of Saint-Pierre of Auxerre
Region	Troyes
Sources	T. Evergates, *Feudal Society in Medieval France: Documents from the County of Champagne (Philadelphia, 1993)*, no. 51.

Raoul of Thour

Alias/es	Raoul de Thour, Raoul de Thaon, Radulphus de Tur
Notes	Bound to the count of Champagne (1188). Died on the Third Crusade.
Orders	Premonstratensians (Notre-Dame of Ardennes)
Region	Ardennes
Sources	Gilbert of Mons, pp. 142, 168, 224, 273.

Otto of Guelders

Title/s	Count of Guelders
Alias/es	Otto, count of Guelders, comes de Galres, Otton I de Gueldre
Notes	Made a donation to Val-Dieu Abbey before departing on crusade (1189). Marched with Frederick Barbarossa and joined the siege of Acre with duke of Swabia (1190).
Orders	Cistercians (Val-Dieu)
Region	Guelders
Sources	J. Riley-Smith, *The Crusades - A Short History* (London, 1990), pp. 112–13; *Cartulaire de l'abbaye cistercienne du Val-Dieu (XIIe-XIVe siècle)*, ed. J. Ruwet (Brussels, 1955), no. 2.

Robert V

Title/s	Lord of Béthune
Alias/es	Robert V, lord of Béthune, Roberto Betuniensus advocatus, Robertus Betuniæ advocatus, Roberti advocate Bethunie, Robertus advocatus Betunensis
Notes	Died at the siege of Acre (1191). Married to Adelisa of St Pol.
Ancestor/s	William II of Béthune
Family	Baldwin and Conon of Béthune, William of Cayeux, St Pol
Orders	Saint-Pry chapel, Augustinians (Choques, Warneton, and Gossuin), Benedictines (Bourbourg, Corvey)
Region	Béthune
Sources	A. Duchesne, *Histoire génealogique de la Maison de Béthune* (Paris, 1639), pp. 42–3; Gilbert of Mons, p. 273.

Conon of Béthune

Alias/es	Conon de Béthune, Cononis, Cono de, Bethunia, Conrado
Notes	Famed troubadour who wrote recruiting verse prior to joining the Third Crusade. Participated in the Fourth Crusade.
Ancestor/s	Robert V and William II of Béthune
Family	Robert V and Baldwin of Béthune, William of Cayeux
Orders	Saint-Pry chapel, Augustinians (Choques)
Region	Béthune
Sources	H. van Werveke, 'La contribution de la Flandre et de Hainaut à la troisième croisade', *Le Moyen Age*, 78 (1972), p. 80; *Lyrics of the Troubadours*, ed. and trans. Goldin.

Arnold III of Thérouanne

Title/s	Advocate of Thérouanne
Alias/es	Arnold de Thérouanne, Arnulf

Notes	Siege of Acre (1191).
Orders	Ardres chapel
Region	Thérouanne
Sources	*Cartulaires de l'église de Thérouanne*, ed. T. Duchet and A. Giry (Fleury-Lemaire, 1881), nos. 89–91, 98–9; Warlop, *Flemish Nobility*, p. 1149.

William IV

Title/s	Advocate of Saint-Omer, lord of Fauquembergues
Alias/es	William castellan of Saint-Omer, Willelmus castellanus Sancti Audomari
Notes	Died on the Third Crusade. Married to Ida of Avesnes.
Ancestor/s	Gauthier and Hosto (T) of Fauquemberghes
Family	James I of Avesnes
Orders	Benedictines (Watten)
Region	Saint-Omer
Sources	Duchesne, *Béthune*, pp. 50–1; Gilbert of Mons, pp. 75, 273; Warlop, *Flemish Nobility*, 1112.

Baldwin II of Heuchin

Title/s	Lord of Heuchin
Alias/es	Chamberlain to Countess of Flanders
Notes	On crusade (1191).
Family	Philip of Aire
Region	Heuchin
Sources	Warlop, *Flemish Nobility*, p. 604.

Philip of Aire

Notes	On crusade (1191).
Family	Baldwin II of Heuchin
Sources	Warlop, *Flemish Nobility*, p. 604.

John I of Nesle

Title/s	Constable of Bruges
Alias/es	John de Neele, castellan of Bruges, Johanne de Neele, Jean de Neele, castellanus de Bruges
Notes	Arrived at the siege of Acre (1189).
Ancestor/s	Drogo and Ives II of Nesle
Family	Raoul III of Nesle
Region	Bruges
Sources	*Itinerarium*, p. 74; W. Newman, *Les seigneurs de Nesle en Picardie*, 2 Vols (Paris, 1871), Vol. 1, p. 36.

William

Title/s	Dean of Bruges
Notes	Made donations to Saint-Amand Abbey prior to departing on crusade (1189).
Orders	Benedictines (Saint-Amand), Bruges Cathedral
Region	Bruges
Sources	*Cartulaire de Saint-Amand*, AD du Nord, 12H 3, fols.42v–43r, no. 47.

Henry I

Title/s	Count of Leuven
Alias/es	Henry III, count of Leuven, comitem de Luvein, Louvain
Notes	Sicily (1190). Returned to take up the duchy of Brabant (1191). Later joined the German Crusade.
Ancestor/s	Godfrey III of Leuven
Region	Leuven
Sources	*Gesta Regis*, Vol. 2, p. 128.

Godfrey of Aarschot

Title/s	Count of Aarschot
Alias/es	Godried von Aarschot, Godefroy grave von Arscot, Godefroid d'Arscot
Notes	Sold the county of Aarschot to Henry of Brabant (1172) to fund his participation on crusade. Captured in 'Damiolen'.
Ancestor/s	Arnold I and IV, counts of Aarschot
Orders	Benedictines (Brogne)
Region	Aarschot
Sources	L. Liekens, *Geschiedenis van het oude Graafschap van de Stad en de Parochie den Lande en hertogdomme van Aarschot*, Vol. 1 (Goed, 1925), p. 74; A. Miraeus, *Donationes Belgicæ*, Vol. 1 (Antwerp, 1723), p. 689.

Floris III

Title/s	Count of Holland
Alias/es	Floris de Holland, Florence III of Angest
Notes	Took the cross at Mainz and accompanied Barbarossa. Died at Antioch (1190). Father to William of Holland and brother to Otto of Bentheim.
Ancestor/s	Theodoric II of Lorraine
Family	William of Holland, Count Otto of Bentheim, Henry II of Salm
Orders	Benedictines (Rijnsburg)
Region	Holland
Sources	Diss, Vol. 2, p. 79; *Gesta Regis*, Vol. 2, p. 149; Gilbert of Mons, p. 150; *Barbarossa*, p. 49; Wendover, p. 178.

William of Holland

Alias/es	Willem van Holland
Notes	Accompanied his father, Count Floris III, and uncle, Count Otto of Bentheim. Joined Fifth Crusade.
Ancestor/s	Theodoric II of Lorraine
Family	Counts Floris II of Holland and Otto of Benthiem
Region	Holland
Sources	*Barbarossa*, p. 49.

Otto of Bentheim

Alias/es	Otto de Holland
Notes	Visited Jerusalem (1173). Accompanied his brother, Count Floris III and nephew, William, on crusade.
Ancestor/s	Theodoric II of Lorraine
Family	Count Floris III, William of Holland
Region	Holland
Sources	'Annales Egmundani 1173', *Monumenta Germaniae Historica Scriptores*, Vol. 17, ed. G.H. Pertz (Hanover, 1861), p. 468; *Barbarossa*, p. 49.

Henry of Kuick

Title/s	Count of Kuick
Notes	Siege of Alexandria (1174). Accompanied Frederick Barbarossa.
Region	Brabant
Sources	*Barbarossa*, p. 50.

Conon of Montaigu

Title/s	Count of Montaigu and Duras
Alias/es	Cono
Notes	Sold advocacy of St Trond and castle of Duras to Henry, duke of Louvain for 800 *marks* to fund his participation on the Third Crusade. Made a donation to the religious of Ferté prior to departing on crusade (1190).
Ancestor/s	Lambert and Gozelo of Montaigu
Family	Count Gerald II of Looz
Orders	Cistercians (Ferté), Hospitallers
Region	Montaigu (Ardennes)
Sources	*HdB*, Vol. 3, no. 847.

Gerald II of Looz

Title/s	Count of Looz
Alias/es	Gérard of Loon

Notes	Died at the siege of Acre (1191).
Ancestor/s	Lambert and Gozelo of Montaigu
Family	Count Conon of Montaigu
Orders	Cistercians (Herkenrode)
Region	Loon (Limburg)
Sources	*Barbarossa*, p. 56.

Rutger II of Meerheim

Title/s	Lord of Meerheim
Alias/es	Rutger van Mereheim, Mereheym, Rutgerus de Merheim
Notes	Donated property to Kamp Abbey before departing on crusade (1189).
Orders	Cistercians (Kamp)
Region	Linn, Bemmel
Sources	*Oorkondenboek van Holland-Zeeland tot 1299. I: eind van de zevende eeuw tot 1222*, Vol. 1 ed. A.C.F. Koch (S-Gravenhage, 1970), no. 219, pp. 375–6.

Gerard I of Schelderode

Title/s	Lord of Schelderode
Alias/es	Gerard van Rodes
Notes	Siege of Acre (1189).
Region	Schelderode
Sources	Warlop, *Flemish Nobility*, p. 1121.

Philip of Alsace

Title/s	Count of Flanders and Vermandois
Alias/es	Philip d'Alsace, count of Flanders, cuens de Flandres, Philippus comes Flandriae
Notes	Led a crusade and participated in King Baldwin IV's defeat of Saladin (1177). Died at the siege of Acre (1191).
Ancestor/s	Thierry, count of Flanders; Fulk, king of Jerusalem
Family	Richard I of England, Joanna of Sicily
Orders	Benedictines (Bruge), Cistercians (Clairvaux), Premonstratensians (Laon and Thérouanne)
Region	Flanders, Vermandois
Sources	Ambroise, lines 277–376; Baha' al-Din, p. 146; Diss, Vol. 2, p. 51; *Gesta Regis*, Vol. 2, pp. 48–9, 69, 101, 149, 157, 168; Gilbert of Mons, pp. 86, 97, 112–13, 126, 130–41, 145–7, 153, 180–5, 193, 206, 248, 273; *Itinerarium*, pp. 147, 213, 217, 219; Rigord, p. 83; Wendover, pp. 157–8.

Engelram of Fiennes

Title/s	Lord of Martock
Alias/es	Engelram de Fiennes, Enguerrand, Ingelram, Ingeram de Fenes, Ingelramnus de Vienis
Notes	Arrived at the siege of Acre (1189). Served with the count of Flanders at the siege of Acre. Died at the siege of Acre (1190).
Ancestor/s	Godfrey of Bouillon
Region	Buckinghamshire
Sources	*Chronica*, Vol. 3, p. 88; *Itinerarium*, p. 74; Lambert of Ardres, *The History of the Counts of Guines and Lords of Ardres*, trans. L. Shopkow (Philadelphia, 2007), p. 84.

Manessier of Lille

Alias/es	Manessier de L'Isle, Manessier de L'Isle, Manessiers de Lille, Manesulus de Insula, Manesserius de Insula
Notes	Escort to caravan ambushed by Saladin's troops (1192). Participated in the Fourth Crusade.
Ancestor/s	Roger I and Robert II of Lille
Region	Flanders
Sources	Ambroise, lines 9920–47; *Itinerarium*, p. 373; Warlop, *Flemish Nobility*, pp. 940–2.

Eudes III of Ham

Alias/es	Eudes de Ham
Notes	Siege of Acre (1189). Participated in the Fourth Crusade.
Region	Flanders
Sources	Pinoteau, 'Heraldische', pp. 77–86.

Odo Hame

Alias/es	Ode of Hame, Odone de Hame
Notes	Siege of Acre (1190).
Family	Godescalc III of Morialmé
Region	Flanders
Sources	Wendover, p. 178.

Baldwin III of Comines

Title/s	Lord of Comines
Alias/es	Baldwin of Comines

Notes	Crusaded with count of Flanders (1177). Married Mathilda of Bethune on return from Third Crusade.
Region	Comines
Sources	Th. Leuridan, *Recherches sur les Sires de Commines* (Danel, 1880), p. 10; Warlop, *Flemish Nobility*, p. 737.

Oliver of Machelen

Alias/es	Oliver of Machelen, Olicarus de Maskelinis
Notes	Died on the Third Crusade (1191).
Family	James I of Avesnes
Region	Machelen
Sources	Gilbert of Mons, p. 273; Warlop, *Flemish Nobility*, p. 958.

Alard I of Croisilles

Alias/es	Adalhardus de Croisilles
Notes	Sold his and his wife's property at Flers for 20 *marks* to finance his pilgrimage to Jerusalem (1189).
Orders	Augustinians (Eaucourt)
Region	Croisilles (Arras)
Sources	BN, ms. Moreau, Vol. 91, fols. 111–12.

Walter of Hondschoote

Alias/es	Gauthier de Hondschotte, Flandre
Notes	Joined Third Crusade.
Region	Hondschoote
Sources	D. Schwennicke, *Europaische Stammtafeln*, New Series, Vol. 29 (Frankfurt, 2013), table 110.

Bernard of Saint-Valéry-sur-Somme

Alias/es	Bernard de Saint-Valéry-sur-Somme, Bernard de S. Valerie, Bernardum de Sancto Walerio, Bernardus de Walerico
Notes	Participated on Thierry of Flanders' Crusade (1164). Died at the siege of Acre (1190).
Region	Saint-Valéry-sur-Somme
Sources	*Recueil des actes de Henri II, roi d'Angleterre et duc de Normandie, concernant les provinces françaises et les affaires de France*, ed. L. Delisle (Paris, 1916), pp. 357–8; *The Red Book of the Exchequer*, ed. H. Hall (RS, 1896), Vol. 2, pp. 189–90; Gilbert of Mons, pp. 142, 273; *Itinerarium*, p. 92; Landon, *Itinerary*, nos. 231–3; Rigord, pp. 83–4; Robert of Torigny, Vol. 1, p. 316.

Joscelin of Montmorency

Title/s	Châtelain of Ypres
Alias/es	Castelan of Ypres, castellanus de Ypre
Notes	Died at the siege of Acre (1190).
Region	Montmorency
Sources	*Chronica*, Vol. 3, p. 89; *Gesta Regis*, Vol. 2, p. 149.

Anselm of Pas

Alias/es	Anseau de Pas, Ansellus de Passo
Notes	Sold lands to Clairmarais Abbey to fund participation on the crusade (1189).
Orders	Cistercians (Clairmarais)
Region	Neuvilette
Sources	AN, S1423, no. 34.

Frederick

Title/s	Canon of St Paul's
Alias/es	Fredericus
Notes	Canon of St Paul's Cathedral, Liège. The abbot of Liège notified that he would be entitled to half the income from Roclenge-sur-Geer should he return from crusade (1189).
Orders	Benedictines (Liège)
Region	Roclenge-sur-Geer (Liège)
Sources	Liège, State Archives, Saint-Jacques, no. 33.

Robert III

Title/s	Count of Nassau
Alias/es	Count Robert of Nassau, Ruprecht der Streitbare, Rupertus comes de Nassowe
Notes	Proceeded the Imperial army as an envoy. Served as standard bearer in the Emperor's division. Died on the Third Crusade (1191).
Family	Walram of Nassau
Region	Nassau
Sources	Gilbert of Mons, pp. 232, 273.

Walram I of Nassau

Title/s	Count of Nassau
Alias/es	Count Walram I of Nassau, Valéran de Nassau, Walram von Laurenburg
Notes	Siege of Acre (1189).
Family	Robert of Nassau

Region	Nassau
Sources	*Barbarossa*, pp. 44, 76.

Radulf of Zähringen

Title/s	Bishop of Liège
Alias/es	Rudolph, Raoul
Notes	Joined Emperor Frederick I on crusade. Siege of Acre (1188). Died at Herdern, en route back from the crusade.
Ancestor/s	Herman III of Baden
Family	Margrave Herman IV of Baden and Verona
Orders	Benedictines (Liège), Liège Cathedral
Region	Liège, Herdern
Sources	*Barbarossa*, pp. 12, 28, 48, 65.

Herbrand

Title/s	Castellan of Bouillon
Alias/es	Herbrand of Bouillon, Herbrandus Buloniensis castellanus, Heribrandus
Notes	Made donation to Bouillon Abbey prior to departing on crusade (1189).
Orders	Benedictines (Saint-Hubert)
Region	Bouillon (Liège), Noyers-Pont-Maugis (Ardennes)
Sources	*Les chartes de l'abbaye de Saint-Hubert en Ardenne*, Vol. 1, ed. G. Kurth (Brussels, 1903), no.123, pp. 158–60.

Simon of Thiméon

Title/s	Knight
Alias/es	Symon de Tymiun miles, Simon de Timion
Notes	Promised a quarter of his tithe in Thiméon to Floreffe Abbey should he die whilst on crusade (1188).
Family	Hugh of Rumigny
Orders	Premonstratensians (Floreffe)
Region	Thiméon (Liège)
Sources	*Crusade Charters*, no. 15.

Godescalc III of Morialmé

Title/s	Lord of Morialmé
Alias/es	Godescalc III of Morialmeis, Gottschalk III de Morialmé
Notes	Promised the church of Sautour to Floreffe Abbey (1188). Joined the Hospitallers sometime after the Third Crusade. Crusaded with Hugh of Florennes.

Family	Odo of Ham
Orders	Premonstratensians (Floreffe)
Region	Morialmé (Namur, Liège)
Sources	*Crusade Charters*, no. 27.

Hugh of Rumigny

Title/s	Lord of Florennes
Alias/es	Hugues de Rumigny
Notes	Crusaded with Godescalc of Morialmé.
Family	James I of Avesnes, Simon of Thiméon
Region	Liège
Sources	*Crusade Charters*, p. 175.

Otto II of Trazegnies

Title/s	Lord of Trazegnies
Alias/es	Otto de Trasinges, Otes de Transigees, Trezegnies, Otho de Tresoni, Otoni de Traseigni, Osto de Traziegnies, Osto de Trasiniis, Othonem de Trasynges, Otho de Transinges
Notes	Knight of Baldwin V of Hainaut, dubbed (1181). Richard I's *Familia Regis*. On crusade to the Holy Land (1186–7). Made a donation to Floreffe abbey, which was confirmed prior to his departure on crusade again (1188). Siege of Acre (1190). Skirmish at Ramla (1191). Royal envoy to Conrad of Montferrat (1192). Died in the Holy Land (1192). Recipient of money-fief from Richard I worth 40*s*. in Kent.
Ancestor/s	Egidius of Trazegnies
Orders	Cistercians (Cambron), Premonstratensians (Floreffe), Soignies Cathedral chapter
Region	Trazegnies (Liège)
Sources	Ambroise, lines 7278, 8632, 9920–48; Diss, Vol. 2, p. 79; Gilbert of Mons, pp. 132, 196, 274, 328; *Itinerarium*, pp. 292, 336–7, 373; PR2 RI (1190), p. 147; PR3 R (1191), p. 142; PR4 RI (1192), p. 308; Wendover, p. 178.

Amand of Naast

Alias/es	Amand de Naast, Amandus de Nasta
Notes	Otto of Trazegnies confirmed Amand's donation to Le Roeulx prior to their departing on crusade (1189). Died on the Third Crusade.
Orders	Premonstratensians (Saint-Feuillien)
Region	Naast (Cambrai)
Sources	Gilbert of Mons, p. 274; E. Matthieu, 'Les seigneurs de Naast', *Annales du Cercle archéologique du canton de Soignies*, 4 (1909), p. 30.

Baldwin of Dargus

Alias/es	Baldwin de Dargis, Baldewinus de Dargus
Notes	Siege of Acre (1190). Held off a Muslim sally along with Baldwin le Carron and Walter of Oyri (1190). Participated in the St Martin offensive (1190).
Family	Hugh and Walter of Oyry
Region	Dargis (Hainaut)
Sources	*Chronica*, Vol. 3, p. 73; *Gesta Regis*, Vol. 2, p. 144.

Baldwin le Carron

Title/s	Lord of Rumes
Alias/es	Baldwin de Carron, Baudowins li Carons, Baldwin of Carew, Baudouïn le Caron, Baldewinus de Carun, Baldwin li Charnus, Balduinus Caron, Baldewinum Carron, Baldewinus de Carro
Notes	Former knight of Philip of Alsace. Enfeoffed by Baldwin V of Hainaut (1184). Knight of Baldwin V of Hainaut. Made a donation to the Templars (Rumes) prior to departing on crusade. Joined Richard I's *Familia Regis* whilst on crusade. Siege of Acre (1190). Held off a Muslim sally along with Baldwin of Dargus and Walter of Oyri (1190). Participated in the St Martin offensive (1190). Battle of Arsuf (1191). Subcommander of a crusader supply convoy (1192). Made another donation to the Templars whilst on crusade (1192). Died in the Holy Land (1192).
Orders	Templars (Rumes)
Region	Rumes
Sources	Ambroise, lines 6419, 6421, 9920–47; *Chronica*, Vol. 3, p. 73; L. Dailliez, *Les Templiers en Flandre, Hainaut, Brabant, Liège et Luxembourg* (Nice, 1978), pp. 333–4, no. 61 (facsimilé cartulaire); L. Devillers, *Inventaire analytique des archives des commanderies belges de l'Ordre Saint-Jean de Jérusalem ou de Malte* (Mons, 1876), pp. 179–80, 187, 190–1; *Gesta Regis*, Vol. 2, p. 144; Gilbert of Mons, pp. 174, 180, 213, 217, 274, 328; *Itinerarium*, pp. 269, 373–4; Warlop, *De Vlaamse adel vóór 1300*, pp. 508, 193–9.

Philip

Alias/es	Philip, Fellippes, Philippus
Notes	Richard I's *Familia Regis*. Comrade to Baldwin le Carron. Member of a crusader supply convoy (1192).
Sources	Ambroise, lines 9920–47, 10004; *Itinerarium*, p. 373.

Thierry of Orcq

Alias/es	Thierry d'Orcq, Terri, Theodericus de Orca, Orques
Notes	Attack on crusader caravan (1192). Died on the Third Crusade. Associated with Baldwin le Carron.
Family	John, Richard, and Ivo of Orcq
Sources	Ambroise, lines 9920–47; Gilbert of Mons, p. 274; *Itinerarium*, p. 373.

Ivo of Orcq

Alias/es	Ivo d'Orcq, Ivo de Orca
Notes	Died on the Third Crusade.
Family	John, Richard, Thierry of Orcq
Sources	Gilbert of Mons, p. 274.

Richard of Orcq

Alias/es	Richard d'Orcq, Ricard d'Orques, Richardus de Orca, Ricardus de Orques
Notes	Attack on crusader caravan (1192). Died on the Third Crusade. Associated with Baldwin le Carron.
Family	John, Ivo, Thierry of Orcq
Sources	Ambroise, lines 9920–47; Gilbert of Mons, p. 274; *Itinerarium* p. 373.

John of Orcq

Alias/es	John d'Orcq, Johannes de Orca
Notes	Died on the Third Crusade.
Family	Richard, Ivo, Thierry of Orcq
Sources	Gilbert of Mons, p. 274.

Hellin of Wavrin

Title/s	Seneschal of Flanders
Alias/es	seneschal of Flanders, seneschal de Flandres, dapifer Flandiae, Hellinus de Waurin, Hellinus, Hellinus de Wavrin Flandrie senescalus
Notes	Accompanied James I of Avesnes. Siege of Acre (1189). Died on the Third Crusade. Brother of Roger of Wavrin.
Ancestor/s	Hellin of Wavrin
Family	Robert Wavrin, Bishop Roger of Cambrai, Eustace I of Le Roeulx
Region	Wavrin
Sources	Ambroise, line 2920; Diss, Vol. 2, p. 79; Gilbert of Mons, pp. 136, 167, 180, 274; Warlop, *Flemish Nobility*, p. 1196; Wendover, p. 178.

Robert I of Wavrin

Alias/es	Robert of Waurin, seneschal of Flanders
Notes	Returned to secure Flanders on behalf of Philip II (1191).
Ancestor/s	Hellin of Wavrin
Family	Hellin Wavrin, Bishop Roger of Cambrai, Eustace I of Le Roeulx
Region	Wavrin
Sources	Ambroise, line 2920; Diss, Vol. 2, p. 79; Gilbert of Mons, pp. 258, 294–5; Warlop, *Flemish Nobility*, p. 1197; Wendover, p. 178.

Roger of Wavrin

Title/s	Bishop of Cambrai
Alias/es	bishop of Cambrai, Roger of Waurin, episcopus Cambraiensis, Rogerus Cameracensis episcopus
Notes	Made a donation to Oevel abbey and to the Augustinian canons of his diocese prior to departing on crusade (1189). Died on the Third Crusade. Brother of Hellin of Wavrin.
Ancestor/s	Hellin of Wavrin
Family	Hellin and Robert Wavrin, Eustace I of Le Roeulx
Orders	Benedictines (Tournai), Premonstratensians (Oevel), Augustinians (Cambrai), Cambrai Cathedral
Region	Cambrai, Brabant
Sources	Ambroise, line 2920; Diss, Vol. 2, p. 79; Gilbert of Mons, pp. 158, 274; Wendover, p. 178.

Hugh III of Oisy-le-Verger

Title/s	Castellan of Cambrai
Alias/es	Hugo, Cameracensis castellanus
Notes	Trouvére and mentor to Conon of Béthune. Pledged the revenue of his ovens in Oisy-le-Verger and tithes from Sauchy-Cauchy to Anchin Abbey should he die on crusade (1189). Died in the Holy Land (1190).
Orders	Benedictines (Anchin), Hospitallers (Dijon), Premonstratensians (Mont-Saint-Martin)
Region	Oisy-le-Verger (Cambrai)
Sources	*Annales d'Anchin dans le recueil des Histoires de la France*, ed. A. Le Mire (Paris, 1608), pp. 412–541; Duchesne, *Béthune*, p. 106.

Hugh

Title/s	Castellan of Beaumetz
Alias/es	Hugo, castillanus de Bellomanso
Notes	His donation to Anchin Abbey made prior to departing on crusade was confirmed by his son (1190).
Orders	Benedictines (Anchin)
Region	Beaumetz (Cambrai)
Sources	Lille, AD du Nord, 1 H 43/486.

Gobert of Werchin

Alias/es	Gobertus de Wercin, Godebertus de Verchain-Maugré
Notes	Sold lands to Hautmont Abbey for 220 livres to finance his and his brother's participation on crusade (1189).

Family	William of Werchin
Orders	Benedictines (Hautmont)
Region	Werchin (Cambrai)
Sources	BN, ms. nouv. acq. lat. 1386.

William of Werchin

Alias/es	Willelmus de Wercin, Guillaume de Verchain-Maugré
Notes	Sold lands to Hautmont Abbey for 220 livres to finance his and his brother's participation on crusade (1189).
Family	Godbert of Werchin
Orders	Benedictines (Hautmont)
Region	Werchin (Cambrai)
Sources	BN, ms. nouv. acq. lat. 1386.

Guy of Villers

Alias/es	Gui de Villers-Outréaux
Notes	Donated lands in Tilleroi to Vaucelles Abbey prior to departing on crusade (1190).
Orders	Cistercians (Vaucelles)
Region	Villers (Cambrai)
Sources	Lille, AD du Nord, 37H 30/108.

James I of Avesnes

Title/s	Lord of Avesnes, advocate of Hautmont Abbey, lord of Conde and Guise
Alias/es	James de Avenses, Jackes d'Avernes, Jakes D'Averne, Avennes, Jacobus de Avethnis
Notes	Made donations to the abbeys of Brogne, Bucilly, and Le Roeulx prior to departing on crusade (1189). Mortgaged all his properties to fund his contingent. Siege of Acre, acting as joint military commander (1189). Died at the battle of Arsuf (1191).
Family	Oliver of Machelen, William IV of Saint-Omer, Hugh of Rumigny, Everard II and Andrew of Brienne
Orders	Benedictines (Brogne and Hautmont), Premonstratensians (Bucilly, Le Roeulx)
Region	Avesnes (Hainaut)
Sources	Ambroise, lines 2848–51; BN ms. latin 10121; BN ms. nouv. acq. lat. 1386; Gilbert of Mons, pp. 273–4; *Itinerarium*, pp. 65, 71, 94, 261, 269, 275–7.

Eustace I of Le Roeulx

Title/s	Lord of Le Roeulx
Alias/es	Eustace de Le Roeulx, Eustace the elder

Notes	Baldwin V of Hainaut's *Familia Regis*. Donated lands to Aulne Abbey prior to departing on crusade (1189). Died on the Third Crusade.
Family	Robert and Hellin Wavrin, Bishop Roger of Cambrai
Orders	Aulne Abbey
Region	Le Roeulx
Sources	Gilbert of Mons, p. 141, 274; Mons, State Archives, *Fonds Cartulaires*, no. 1.

Yves

Alias/es	Yves, noble croisé
Notes	Promised a quarter of his tithe in Ghislenghien should he die whilst on crusade (1189).
Orders	Benedictines (Ghislenghien)
Region	Ghislenghien (Cambrai)
Sources	*Inventaire des archives de l'abbaye de Ghislenghien*, ed. D. van Overstraeten (Brussels, 1976), no. 26, p. 215.

Hellin of Maisnil

Alias/es	Hellin de Maisnil, Hellinus de Maisnil
Notes	Died on the Third Crusade.
Family	Peter of Maisnil
Region	Maisnil (Flanders)
Sources	Gilbert of Mons, p. 274.

Peter of Maisnil

Alias/es	Pierre de Maisnil, Petrum de Maisnil
Notes	Siege of Acre (1190). Returned to secure Flanders on behalf of Philip II.
Family	Hellin of Maisnil
Region	Maisnil (Flanders)
Sources	*Recueil des Actes de Philippe Auguste, roi de France*, Vol. 1, ed. M.H.-F. Delaborde (Paris, 1916), pp. 473–4, no. 383; Gilbert of Mons, p. 274.

Renaud Agulius

Alias/es	Renaud Agulius
Notes	Died on the Third Crusade.
Sources	Gilbert of Mons, p. 258.

Nivel Pauper

Alias/es	Nivelo agnomine Pauper
Notes	Died on the Third Crusade.
Sources	Gilbert of Mons, p. 273.

Raoul of Vendegies

Alias/es	Raoul de Vendegies, Radulphus de Vendegiis
Notes	Died on the Third Crusade.
Region	Vendegies (Cambrai)
Sources	Gilbert of Mons, p. 274.

Walter of Aunoit

Alias/es	Walter d'Aunoit, Walterus de Aunoit
Notes	Died on the Third Crusade.
Region	Aunoit (Hainaut)
Sources	Gilbert of Mons, p. 274.

Ivo of Thumaide

Alias/es	Ivo de Thumaide, Ivo de Thumaidis
Notes	Died on the Third Crusade.
Region	Thumaide (Hainaut)
Sources	Gilbert of Mons, p. 274.

Walter of Quesnoy

Alias/es	Walter de le Quesnoy, Walterus de Casnoit
Notes	Died on the Third Crusade.
Region	Le Quesnoy (Hainaut)
Sources	Gilbert of Mons, p. 274.

Guy of Herlincourt

Alias/es	Guy de Herlincourt, Wido de Erbelaincort
Notes	Died on the Third Crusade.
Region	Herlincourt (Flanders)
Sources	Gilbert of Mons, p. 274.

Raoul of Anvaing

Alias/es	Raoul d'Anvaing, Radulphus de Anvin
Notes	Died on the Third Crusade.
Region	Anvaing (Hainaut)
Sources	Gilbert of Mons, p. 274.

Raoul of Maini

Alias/es	Raoul de Maini, Radulphus de Maini
Notes	Died on the Third Crusade.
Sources	Gilbert of Mons, p. 274.

John of Housset

Alias/es	John de Housset, Johannes de Hossel
Notes	Died on the Third Crusade.
Region	Housset (Aisne)
Sources	Gilbert of Mons, p. 274.

John of Housset

Alias/es	John de Housset, Johannes de Hossel
Notes	Died on the Third Crusade.
Region	Housset (Aisne)
Sources	Gilbert of Mons, p. 274.

Iwan of Valenciennes

Alias/es	Iwan de Valenciennes, Ywanus de Valencenis
Notes	Died on the Third Crusade.
Region	Valenciennes (Hainaut)
Sources	Gilbert of Mons, p. 274.

Nicholas of Péruwelz

Alias/es	Nicholas de Péruwelz, Nicholaus de Pereweis, de Peruwez
Notes	Baldwin V of Hainaut's *Familia Regis*. Died on the Third Crusade.
Family	Baldwin and Nicholas II of Péruwelz
Region	Péruwelz
Sources	Gilbert of Mons, pp. 139, 141, 213, 274.

Baldwin of Péruwelz

Alias/es	Baldwin de Péruwelz, Balduinus de Pereweis, de Peruwez
Notes	Baldwin V of Hainaut's *Familia Regis*. Died on the Third Crusade.
Family	Nicholas and Nicholas II of Péruwelz
Region	Péruwelz
Sources	Gilbert of Mons, pp. 139, 141, 274.

Nicholas II of Péruwelz

Alias/es	Nicholas de Péruwelz, Nicholaus de Pereweis
Notes	Died on the Third Crusade.
Family	Baldwin and Nicholas I of Péruwelz
Region	Péruwelz
Sources	Gilbert of Mons, p. 274.

Henry

Title/s	Castellan of Binche
Alias/es	Henry castellan of Binche, Henricus Bincensis castellanus
Notes	Baldwin V of Hainaut's *Familia Regis*. Died on the Third Crusade.
Region	Binche
Sources	Gilbert of Mons, pp. 213, 274.

Guy of Fontaine

Alias/es	Guy des Fontaines, Wido de Fontanis
Notes	Baldwin V of Hainaut's *Familia Regis*. Died on the Third Crusade.
Family	Alan and Fulk of Fontaine
Region	Fontaines
Sources	Gilbert of Mons, pp. 139, 274, 328.

Fulk of Fontaine

Alias/es	Fulk des Fontaines, Fulco de Fontanis
Notes	Baldwin V of Hainaut's *Familia Regis*. Died on the Third Crusade.
Family	Alan and Guy of Fontaine
Region	Fontaines
Sources	Gilbert of Mons, pp. 139, 274, 328.

Alan of Fontaine

Alias/es	Alan des Fontaines, Alelmus de Fontanis, Alanus de Fontanis
Notes	Arrived at the siege of Acre (1190). Died on the Third Crusade.
Region	Fontaines
Sources	*Itinerarium*, pp. 92–3; Gilbert of Mons, p. 274.

Walter of Gouy

Alias/es	Walter de Gouy, Walterus de Goi
Notes	Baldwin V of Hainaut's *Familia Regis*. Died on the Third Crusade.

Family	Arnoul of Gouy
Region	Courcelles
Sources	Gilbert of Mons, pp. 139, 274.

Arnoul of Gouy

Alias/es	Arnoul de Gouy, Arnulphus de Goi
Notes	Baldwin V of Hainaut's *Familia Regis*. Died on the Third Crusade.
Family	Walter of Gouy
Region	Courcelles
Sources	Gilbert of Mons, pp. 139, 274, 328.

Godfrey of Tuin

Alias/es	Godefroid miles de Tuin
Notes	Made a donation to Bonne-Espérance Abbey prior to departing on crusade (1188).
Orders	Premonstratensians (Bonne-Espérance)
Region	Courcelles
Sources	*Actes et documents anciens intéressant la Belgique*, Vol. 2, ed. C.H. Duvivier (Brussels, 1903), no. 68, pp.139–40.

Humbert IV

Title/s	Lord of Beaujeu
Alias/es	Humbert the Young
Notes	Died on the Third Crusade.
Region	Beaujeu
Sources	*Cartulaire de l'église collégiale Notre-Dame de Beaujeu, suivi d'un appendice et d'un tableau généalogique de la maison de Beaujeu*, ed. M.-C. Guigue (Lyon, 1864), p. 50; *Obituaires de la province de Lyon*, Vol. 2, ed. J. Laurent and P. Gras (Paris, 1965), p. 508.

William of Pierrepont

Alias/es	William de Pierrepont, Willelmum de Pentraponte
Notes	Enfeoffed by Baldwin of Hainaut (1184). Died on the Third Crusade.
Region	Hainaut
Sources	Gilbert of Mons, pp. 175, 273.

Robert of Beaurain

Alias/es	Robert de Beaurain, Robertus de Belren
Notes	Knight of Baldwin V of Hainaut. Died on the Third Crusade.

Region	Hainaut
Sources	Gilbert of Mons, pp. 175, 210, 212, 274, 328.

Matthew of Walincourt

Alias/es	Matthew de Walincourt, Matheus de Wallaincort,
Notes	Knight of Baldwin V of Hainaut and member of his tournament team. Died on the Third Crusade.
Region	Hainaut
Sources	Gilbert of Mons, p. 274; *HGM*, lines 3332–52.

Hugh of Arbre

Alias/es	Hugh d'Arbre, Hugo filius ejus
Notes	Died on the Third Crusade.
Family	Matthew of Arbre
Sources	Gilbert of Mons, p. 274.

Matthew of Arbre

Alias/es	Matthew d'Arbre, Matheus de Arbro
Notes	Died on the Third Crusade.
Family	Hugh of Arbre
Orders	Benedictines (Ghislenghien)
Sources	C. Duvivier, *Recherches sur le Hainaut ancien* (Brussels, 1865), no. 619; Gilbert of Mons, p. 274.

Richard I of England

Title/s	King of England, duke of Normandy, Aquitaine, and Gascony, count of Anjou, Maine, Nantes, and Poitiers
Alias/es	Ricardus comes Pictavensis, Richarz, rex Anglie, rei Richard, comes Pictaviae
Notes	One of the first nobles to take the Cross (1187). Messina (1190). Cyprus (1191). Siege of Acre (1191). Battle of Arsuf (1191). Skirmish near Ramla (1191). Siege of Darum (1192). Attacked Muslim caravan (1192). Relief of Jaffa (1192). Held captive in Germany on return from the crusade (1192–4).
Ancestor/s	Fulk V of Anjou, Eleanor of Aquitaine
Family	Joanna of Sicily, Philip II of France, Berengaria of Navarre
Orders	Cistericans (Bonport), Benedictines (Reading), Augustinians, St Lazarus, Templars
Region	Angevin Realm

Sources   Ambroise, lines 244–56, 581, 1187, 1260, 1282, 1436, 2006, 2115, 2139–2294, 4603, 4739, 4764–93, 4921–81, 5298–321, 6114–931, 6597, 6978, 7080, 7204, 7724, 8086, 9127–407, 9484, 9722, 9761, 9776, 9787, 9824, 10239–610, 12244; Baha' al-Din, pp. 150–1, 153, 170, 181, 183–8, 204, 206–7, 217, 222–3; A.W. Lewis, 'Six Charters of Henry II and His Family for the Monastery of Dalon', *EHR*, 110 (1995), 652–65, no. 6; *Chronica*, Vol. 3, pp. 143–4; Devizes, pp. 3, 17, 23–4, 28, 36, 38, 44, 79, 84; Diss, Vol. 2, pp. 50, 54, 57–8, 63–4, 66–7, 69, 83–6, 91–5, 104–7, 112; *Gesta Regis*, Vol. 2, pp. 29–32, 34–5, 45–6, 49–50, 61, 67–8, 71–8, 92–3, 98, 101, 106, 110, 112, 125, 128, 133–5, 146, 150, 153, 155–6, 158–62, 164, 168–70, 174–6, 178, 182–3, 189–92, 235; *Itinerarium*, pp. 32, 138, 142–5, 147, 149–57, 169–175, 187–201, 206, 211–15, 220–1, 224–5, 229, 234–5, 238, 240–45, 247–51, 253, 255, 265–74, 281, 283–90, 292–4, 295–8, 307, 310–11, 315–20, 322–26, 329–30, 333–5, 341–7, 351–3, 356–7, 359–66, 369–70, 376–7, 379–80, 382, 384–9, 392–3, 395, 398–9, 403–11, 415–25, 427–31, 439–44; Rigord, pp. 83, 90, 92–3; Wendover, pp. 143–5, 152, 155, 157–8, 161–7, 170, 172–3, 175, 182, 186–7, 195, 197, 199, 208–9, 212–17.

Berengaria of Navarre

Title/s   Queen of England
Alias/es   Berengiere, regina Angliae
Notes   Messina (1190). Cyprus (1191). Siege of Acre (1191).
Family   Richard I of England, Joanna of Sicily
Sources   Ambroise, lines 1141, 1728, 7062; Devizes, p. 35; *Gesta Regis*, Vol. 2, pp. 157, 163, 167–8, 182, 235; *Itinerarium*, pp. 175–6, 182, 187, 191, 195, 204, 441; Wendover, p. 217.

Joanna of England

Title/s   Queen of Sicily
Alias/es   Joan, Iohannam, reginam reginam quondam Sicilie
Notes   Dowager queen of Sicily. Cyprus (1191). Siege of Acre (1191). Relief of Jaffa (1192).
Ancestor/s   Fulk V of Anjou, Eleanor of Aquitaine
Family   Richard I of England, Berengaria of Navarre
Sources   Ambroise, lines 523, 7062; Diss, Vol. 2, p. 85; Devizes, pp. 8, 28, 35; *Gesta Regis*, Vol. 2, pp. 126–7, 163–4, 167–8, 182, 235; *Itinerarium*, pp. 154, 165, 169, 176, 405, 441; Wendover, pp. 187, 217.

William of Forz

Title/s   Royal Justiciar (Richard I)
Alias/es   William de Forz, William de Fors of Oleron, Willelmum de Forz, Fortis de Uelerun, de Foret, Willelmus de Fortibus
Notes   Justiciar of Richard I's fleet, *Familia Regis*. Dartmouth (1190). Marseille (1190). Messina (1190).

Region	Niort (Poitou)
Sources	*Chronica*, Vol. 3, p. 306; *Gesta Regis*, Vol. 2, pp. 110. 115–16, 124; Landon, *Itinerary*, nos. 153, 225, 236–9, 242–5, 290, 306, 308, 312, 315–18, 321–6; PR4 RI (1192), p. 308; Wendover, pp. 181, 186.

Stephen of Longchamp

Title/s	Royal Steward (Richard I), Steward of Normandy
Alias/es	Stephen Longchamp, Estiene de Longchamp, Loingchamp Estienes, Stephen de Longchamps, Longo Campo
Notes	Richard I's steward, *Familia Regis*. Joint Governor of Acre (1191). Siege of Darum (1192). Attack on Muslim caravan (1192).
Ancestor/s	Gilbert of Lacy (T)
Region	Herefordshire, Suffolk
Sources	Ambroise, lines 9288, 10459; *Gesta Regis*, Vol. 2, p. 190; *Itinerarium*, pp. 355, 376, 389; Landon, *Itinerary*, no. 68–76, 80–5, 96–101, 126, 145, 156–60, 167, 175–83, 189–93, 195–202, 206–7, 219, 223, 227–9, 260–2, 292.

Ançon of Faï

Alias/es	Anscon, Ançons, Ansconus, Achus de Fay
Notes	Attack on Muslim caravan (1192). Relief of Jaffa (1192). Comrade to Stephen Longchamp.
Sources	Ambroise, lines 10047, 10967; *Itinerarium*, pp. 376, 405.

Stephen of Tours

Alias/es	Stephen de Tours, Staphanum de Turonis (Tours), Stephen de Marsai, Stephen de Marçay; Stephanus de Turnham
Notes	Richard I's *Familia Regis*. Henry II's seneschal of Anjou and initially imprisoned by Richard I. Reappointed seneschal (*c.*1192). Lucon (1190). Jaffa (1192).
Orders	Maison-Dieu (Angers)
Region	Anjou
Sources	*Acta*, no. 220; Devizes, pp. 4–5; *Gesta Regis*, Vol. 2, pp. 71–2; *HGM*, lines 8015–24; Landon, *Itinerary*, no. 286.

Robert of Thornham

Title/s	Royal Justiciar (Richard I)
Alias/es	Robert de Thornham, Roberto de Turnham, Tornham, Roberto de Torneham
Notes	Richard I's *Familia Regis*. Naval squadron commander. Joint governor of Cyprus (1191). Jaffa (1192).
Family	Stephen of Thornham

Orders	Premonstratensians (Newhouse)
Region	East Anglia (Clare), Kent, Yorkshire
Sources	*Acta*, no. 220; *Chronica*, Vol. 3, pp. 109, 116; *Gesta Regis*, Vol. 2, pp. 166–7, 172–3; *Itinerarium*, p. 176; PR2 RI (1191), p. 44; *Red Book*, ed. Hall, Vol. 1, pp. 79, 130, 164,194; Vol. 2, p. 490.

Stephen of Thornham

Title/s	Royal Marshal and Treasurer (Richard I)
Alias/es	Stephen of Thornham, Estiennes de Thornan, Stephen of Turnham, Stephano de Torneham, Stepam de Turnham
Notes	Richard I's marshal and treasurer, *Familia Regis*. Escorted Queens Berengaria and Joanna back from the Holy Land. With Queen Berengaria in Rome (1193).
Family	Robert of Thornham
Orders	Augustinians (Combwell)
Sources	*Acta*, no. 220; Ambroise, line 8684; *Chronica*, Vol. 3, p. 228; *Itinerarium*, pp. 185 296, 299, 337; Landon, *Itinerary*, nos. 175–81, 207, 277–7B, 283, 288, 292, 301, 321–6, 336; PR1 RI (1189), p. 213.

Geoffrey of la Celle

Alias/es	Geoffrey de la Celle, Geoffrey Lascelles, Gaufridus de Lacellis
Notes	Richard I's *Familia Regis*. Vézelay (1190). Arrived at the siege of Acre with Angevin contingent (1191). Jaffa (1192).
Sources	*Itinerarium*, p. 218; Landon, *Itinerary*, nos. 319, 321–6, 366; *Documents*, Vol. 1, ed. Round, pp. 94–5.

William of Reimes

Alias/es	William de Reimes
Notes	Richard I's *Familia Regis*. On crusade to Jerusalem in the king's service (1191).
Orders	Sempringham
Region	East Anglia (Clare)
Sources	PR3 RI (1191), p. 44; PR8 RI (1196), p. 118.

William of Sirenton

Alias/es	William de Sirenton
Notes	Richard I's *Familia Regis*. Described as being in the king's service on crusade (1191). Lost his claim to a knight's fee in Surrey to a rival whilst on crusade.
Region	Surrey
Sources	PR3 R1 (1191), p. 152; *RCR*, Vol. 1, pp. 54–5.

Walter Fitz-Batsuein

Alias/es	Walteri f. Batsuein
Notes	Richard I's *Familia Regis*. Committed his vessel to the king's crusader fleet.
Sources	PR2 R1 (1190), pp. 8–9.

Alan Trenchemer

Alias/es	Alano Trenchemer, Alanus Trench'
Notes	Richard I's shipmaster, *Familia Regis*. Participated in defeat of Muslim great ship off Acre (1191). Sailed Richard back to England from Antwerp (1194).
Sources	Ambroise, lines 2137–94; *Chronica*, Vol. 3, p. 112; *Gesta Regis*, Vol. 2, pp. 168–9; *Itinerarium*, pp. 204–9; PR2 RI (1190), pp. 8–9, 131.

Ranalf

Title/s	Royal armiger
Notes	Vézelay (1190)
Sources	PR1 RI (1189), p. 217.

Dreux of Trubleville

Title/s	Canon of Rouen
Alias/es	Drogo de Fréville, Trouville
Notes	Moved with Walter of Coutances from Lincoln on his being appointed archbishop and received a prebend. Part of Walter of Coutances contingent but remained with the crusade.
Orders	Rouen Cathedral
Region	Rouen
Sources	K. Hurlock and P. Oldfield, *Crusading and Pilgrimage in the Norman World* (Woodbridge, 2015), p. 96; J. Peltzer, *Canon Law, Careers, and Conquest: Episcopal Elections in Normandy and Greater Anjou, c.1140–c.1230* (Cambridge, 2007), p. 222; D.S. Spear, *The Personnel of the Norman Cathedrals During the Ducal Period, 911–1204* (London, 2006), pp. 237–8.

Gilbert of Gascuil

Title/s	Castellan of Gisors
Alias/es	Gilbert de Gascuil, Gilebuertus de Gascuil, castellan of Gisors, Gilbert de Vascueil, Gilebertde Wascoil, castri constabularius
Notes	Richard I's *Familia Regis*. Returned to Normandy from Sicily with Queen Eleanor and Archbishop Walter of Rouen (1190).
Ancestor/s	Walter of St Valery
Family	Guy of St Valerie, de Danmartin

Orders	Premonstratensians (Notre-Dame of l'Ile-Dieu)
Region	Gisors
Sources	Ambroise, line 1163; Devizes, p. 57; *Itinerarium*, p. 176; Landon, *Itinerary*, nos. 236–9, 342; PR24 H2, p. 54.

Gerard Talbot

Alias/es	Gerard Talbot, Gerard de Talbot, Girardum, Girardus de Talebus
Notes	Henry II's *Familia Regis*. Assigned to Young Henry's household. Messina (1190). Arrived at the siege of Acre with Angevin contingent (1191).
Orders	La Madeleine Hospital, Rouen
Region	Herefordshire, Rouen
Sources	*Gesta Regis*, Vol. 2, p. 134; *Itinerarium*, p. 217; Landon, *Itinerary*, nos. 226, 260–2, 314, 342.

Roger of Harcourt

Title/s	Lord of Renneville
Alias/es	Roger de Harcourt, de Hardecourt, Rogiers Hardincort, Roges de Hardencourt, Rogerus de Hardencort, Rogerus de Harecurt
Notes	Richard I's *Familia Regis*. Conquest of Cyprus (1191). Arrived at the siege of Acre with Angevin contingent (1191). Died on the Third Crusade.
Ancestor/s	Pagan Peverel, William Peverel
Family	Robert II of Harcourt, Ralph II Tesson, Robert Trussebot
Region	Brionne (Eure)
Sources	Ambroise, line 4721; Gilbert of Mons, p. 273; *Itinerarium*, pp.186, 217; Landon, *Itinerary*, nos. 131, 189–93, 236–9.

Robert II of Harcourt

Title/s	Lord of Harcourt and Elbeuf
Alias/es	Robert de Harcourt, Hardencourt
Notes	Richard I's *Familia Regis*. Captured alongside King Richard I whilst returning from the Holy Land (1192).
Ancestor/s	Pagan Peverel, William Peverel
Family	Roger of Harcourt, Ralph II Tesson, Richard of Camville, Robert Trussebot
Orders	Benedictines (Crestain)
Region	Elbeuf (Vexin)
Sources	Landon, *Itinerary*, nos. 1, 34–40, 61, 107–10, 208–10, 227–9, 234, 240, 251–8, 292, 295, 298, 300–02, 310–11.

Bernard of la Carra

Title/s	Bishop of Bayonne
Alias/es	Bernard de la Carra, bishop of Bayonne, episcopo Bairnoci, Bernardum episcorum de Baonia, Baionensis, episcopis de Baneria
Notes	Justiciar of Richard I's fleet. Sailed from Dartmouth (1190). Messina (1190). Present at Richard and Berengaria's wedding on Cyprus (1191). Purified the churches of Acre (1191).
Orders	Bayonne Cathedral
Region	Bayonne (Gascony)
Sources	Devizes, p. 22; *Gesta Regis*, Vol. 2, pp. 110, 115–16, 134, 153, 180–1; *Itinerarium*, p. 196; Landon, *Itinerary*, nos. 342, 344; Wendover, p. 181.

Roger of Tosny

Alias/es	Roger de Tosni, Toony, Thoeni Rogiers, Teoni Rogiers, Roger de Töenie, Tosny, Rogerus de Toony
Notes	Richard I's *Familia Regis*. Arrived at the siege of Acre with Angevin contingent (1191). Battle of Arsuf (1191). Jaffa (1192). Attack on Muslim caravan (1192).
Ancestor/s	Godechilde of Tosny
Family	Jokelin of Maine
Orders	Benedictines (Saint-Evroul), Fontevraud
Region	Louviers (Eure), Norfolk
Sources	Ambroise, lines 4701–3, 6168, 10444; BN, ms. latin 11055, fol.28, no. 25; *Itinerarium*, pp. 217, 261, 389; Landon, *Itinerary*, nos. 146, 189–93, 366.

Jordan of Le Hommet

Title/s	Lord of Cléville, Constable of Séez
Alias/es	Jordan du Hommet, constable of Séez, Jordanz de Homez, Jordan de Hommet, Omes Jordan, Jordanus de Homez
Notes	Richard I's *Familia Regis*. Arrived at the siege of Acre with Angevin contingent (1191). Jaffa (1192). Died on the Third Crusade (1192).
Family	Ralph II of Fougères
Region	Cléville (Calvados)

William II of Tancarville

Title/s	Chamberlain of Normandy
Alias/es	William III de Tancarville, chamberlain of Normandy, chamberlins de Tancarvile, Camberarius de Tancarville
Notes	Richard I's *Familia Regis*. Messina (1190). Arrived at the siege of Acre with Angevin contingent (1191). Died on the Third Crusade.
Family	Ralph II of Tancarville, Richard of Vernon and his son

Orders	Benedictines (Saint-Georges de Boscherville)
Region	Tancarville (Normandy)
Sources	Ambroise, line 4709; *Itinerarium*, p. 217; Landon, *Itinerary*, no. 342

Ralph II of Tancarville

Alias/es	Raoul II de Tancarville
Notes	Crusaded with his father, William II.
Family	William II of Tancarville, Richard of Vernon and his son
Region	Tancarville
Sources	AD Calvados, 2D 54, no. 10.

Henry Teuton

Alias/es	Henri le Tyois, Henricus Teutonicus, regis signifer
Notes	King Richard I's standard bearer. Relief of Jaffa (1192).
Sources	Ambroise, line 111402; *Itinerarium*, p. 415.

Ralph III Tesson

Title/s	Lord of Thury and Saint-Saveur-le-Vicomte
Alias/es	Ralph Taisson, lord of St-Saveur-le-Vicomte, Raof Teissons, Raols Tessons, Ralf Teisso, Raoul Tesson, Radulfo Taissun
Notes	Took the Cross (1188). Arrived at the siege of Acre with Angevin contingent (1191). Lead second group of pilgrims to Jerusalem (1192).
Ancestor/s	Ralph Tesson
Family	Roger and Robert II of Harcourt
Orders	Benedictines (Saint-Saveur-le-Vicomte)
Region	Thury (Calvados), Saint-Saveur-le-Vicomte (Manche)
Sources	Ambroise, lines 4715, 11845; *Itinerarium*, pp. 217, 432; Landon, *Itinerary*, no. 1.

Hugh V

Title/s	Vicount of Châteaudun
Alias/es	Hugues V, vicomte de Châteaudun, vescuens de Chasteldon, vicecomes de Castello Dun
Notes	Arrived at the siege of Acre with Angevin contingent (1191). Died in 1191.
Ancestor/s	Hugh IV of Châteaudun
Orders	Templars (Arville), Tironensians
Region	Châteaudun
Sources	Ambroise, line 4717; Diss, Vol. 2, p. 55; *Itinerarium*, p. 217.

Bertram III of Verdun

Alias/es	Bertram de Verdun, Bertrand de Verdun, Bertrans de Verdon, Bertrum de Verdun, Bertramno de Verdun, Bertramnus de Verdun
Notes	Messina (1190). Arrived at the siege of Acre with Angevin contingent (1191). Joint Governor of Acre. Died at Jaffa (1192).
Ancestor/s	Roland of Verdun
Orders	Cistercians (Aunay and Croxton)
Region	Alton (Staffordshire)
Sources	Ambroise, line 4718; *Gesta Regis*, Vol. 2, pp. 149–50, 190; *Itinerarium*, p. 217; Landon, *Itinerary*, nos. 34–40, 143, 164, 172–4, 186–7, 227–9, 248, 335, 340, 347.

John of Préaux

Title/s	Lord of Préaux
Alias/es	John de Préaux, Johans de Praeals, Jean
Notes	Richard I's *Familia Regis*. Member of Young Henry's household. Messina (1190). Jaffa (1192). Relief of Jaffa (1192).
Family	Peter, William, and Roger of Préaux
Orders	Lepers of Mont-aux-Malades, Cistercians (Beaulieu)
Region	Préaux (Rouen)
Sources	Ambroise, line 11442, 11872; *Itinerarium*, pp. 405; Landon, *Itinerary*, nos. 104, 153, 236–39, 329–30, 342, 354, 366.

Roger of Préaux

Title/s	Royal Steward
Alias/es	Roger de Préaux, de Pratell
Notes	Arrived at the siege of Acre with Angevin contingent (1191).
Family	John, Peter, and William of Préaux
Orders	Cistercians (Beaulieu)
Region	Préaux (Rouen)
Sources	*Acta*, no. 220; *Itinerarium*, p. 217, 405; Landon, *Itinerary*, nos. 41, 68–76, 80–5, 96–101, 104, 114, 120, 125–6, 130, 134, 146, 153, 156–9, 160–3, 167, 175–81, 196–202, 206–7, 223, 227–9, 231–4, 236–9, 242–5, 260–2, 277–8, 283, 289, 329–30, 331, 347, 354, 356–7.

William of Préaux

Alias/es	William des Préaux, cil de Preals, Guillames de Preals, de Préaux, Willelmum de Pratellis
Notes	Richard I's *Familia Regis*. Member of Young Henry's household. Arrived at the siege of Acre with Angevin contingent (1191). Saved king from capture, by was captured himself near Acre (1191). Exchanged by Richard I for ten Muslim nobles.

Family	John, Peter, and Roger Préaux
Orders	Cistercians (Beaulieu)
Region	Préaux (Rouen)
Sources	Ambroise, line 4723–4, 7111, 12228; Baha' al-Din, p. 181; Ibn al-Athir, Vol. 2, p. 392; *Itinerarium*, pp. 217, 287–8, 440; Landon, *Itinerary*, nos. 146, 175–82.

Peter of Préaux

Alias/es	Pieres de Preials
Notes	Richard I's *Familia Regis*. Arrived at the siege of Acre with Angevin contingent (1191). Battle of Arsuf (1191). Relief of Jaffa as royal standard bearer (1192). Envoy to Jerusalem (1192).
Family	John, Roger, and William of Préaux
Orders	Cistercians (Beaulieu)
Region	Préaux (Rouen)
Sources	Ambroise, line 4723, 5416, 7544, 10969, 11102, 11872; *Itinerarium* pp. 217, 242, 302, 405, 408, 432; Landon, *Itinerary*, nos. 286, 331.

Roger of Saceio

Alias/es	Roger de Saty, Sathy, Sacu, Sacié, Rogerus de Satya, Rogerus de Sacy
Notes	Richard I's *Familia Regis*. Arrived at the siege of Acre with Angevin contingent (1191). Relief of Jaffa (1192). With Queen Berengaria in Rome (1193).
Orders	Cistercians (Chaloché)
Region	Sassy (Calvados)
Sources	Ambroise, lines 10962, 11396; *Itinerarium*, pp. 218, 405, 415; *Documents*, Vol. 1, ed. Round, pp. 94–5.

Andrew of Chauvigny

Title/s	Count of Châteauroux
Alias/es	Andrew de Chavigny, Andui de Chavingni, Andriu de Chavigni, Andrew de Chauveny, Andreas de Chavengny
Notes	Richard I's *Familia Regis*. Arrived at the siege of Acre with Angevin contingent (1191). Skirmish at Ramla (1191). Siege of Darum (1192). Relief of Jaffa (1192).
Ancestor/s	Eleanor of Aquitaine
Family	King Richard I, Queen Joanna
Region	Châteauroux, Déols (Berry)
Sources	Ambroise, lines 4990, 7542, 10961, 11378–620, 11843; *Gesta Regis*, Vol. 2, p. 76; *HGM*, lines 8662–80; *Itinerarium*, pp. 218, 227, 292, 302, 355, 405, 415, 432–3; Landon, *Itinerary*, nos. 329–30, 342, 358, 366.

Hugh

Title/s	Royal Marshal (Richard I)
Alias/es	Hugh the marshal, Hugelot, Hugh, Hugo nominee, regis Ricardi marescallus
Notes	Richard I's marshal. Captured at the siege of Acre (1191).
Sources	Ambroise, line 5638; *Itinerarium*, p. 246.

William l'Etang

Alias/es	William l'Etang, Williame de L'Estanc, Guillames, de Stagno (Estain), Willelmum de Stagno
Notes	Richard I's *Familia Regis*. Relief of Jaffa (1192). Returned from Holy Land with Richard I and present at his capture (1192).
Sources	Ambroise, line 6968, 11398; *Itinerarium*, pp. 283, 415; Wendover, p. 220.

Renier of Marun

Alias/es	Renier de Marun, Reinier de Maron, Reignerius de Marun
Notes	Killed in skirmish outside Jaffa (1191). Uncle of Walter.
Family	Walter of Marun
Sources	Ambroise, line 7116; *Itinerarium*, p. 287.

Walter

Alias/es	Walter, Gautier, Walterus
Notes	Killed in skirmish outside Jaffa (1191). Nephew of Renier of Marun.
Family	Renier of Marum
Sources	Ambroise, line 7116; *Itinerarium*, p. 287.

Alan of l'Estable

Alias/es	Alan de l'Estable, Alain de l'Estable, Alanus de Stabulo
Notes	Killed in skirmish outside Jaffa (1191).
Sources	Ambroise, line 7120; *Itinerarium*, p. 287.

Luke of l'Estable

Alias/es	Luke de l'Estable, Lucas, Lucas de Stabulo
Notes	Killed in skirmish outside Jaffa (1191).
Sources	Ambroise, line 7120; *Itinerarium*, p. 287.

Hugh Ribol

Alias/es	Hugh Ribol, Hugh Ribole, Hue Ribole, Hugo Ribole
Notes	Placed in joint-command of Jaffa whilst King Richard rebuilt the castles of the Plains and Maen.
Sources	Ambroise, line 7180; *Itinerarium*, p. 289.

Philip

Title/s	Royal Herald (Richard I)
Alias/es	Philip, herald to Richard I, Felippe, Philippo, praecone suo
Notes	Richard I's herald. Ascalon (1192).
Sources	Ambroise, line 9685; *Itinerarium*, pp. 365.

William of Cayeux

Title/s	Lord of Bouillancourt
Alias/es	William de Caieux, William of Cageu, Guillames de Caieu, Willelmum de Cageu
Notes	Richard I's *Familia Regis*. Skirmish near Ramla (1191). King's messenger to Conrad of Montferrat (1192).
Family	Anseau IV of Cayeux, Robert V, Baldwin, and Conon of Béthune
Region	Bouillancourt (Somme)
Sources	Ambroise, lines 7276, 8634; *Itinerarium*, pp. 292, 336.

Anseau IV of Cayeux

Alias/es	Anseau de Cayeux, Ansil de Kaeu
Notes	Richard I's *Familia Regis*. Participated in the Fourth Crusade with Hugh IV, count of St Pol.
Family	William of Cayeux
Orders	Cistercians (Beaulieu)
Region	Cayeux-sur-Mer (Somme)
Sources	*Eustache Le Moine: pirate boulonnais du XIIIe siècle*, trans. E. Mousseigne (Lille, 1996), pp. 112–13, 158, 178, 231.

Ralph Fitz-Godfrey

Title/s	Royal Chamberlain (Richard I)
Alias/es	Ralf fitz Godfrey, Radulfo filio Godefridi
Notes	Richard I's *Familia Regis* and chamberlain. Messina (1191). Given custody of Isaac Comnenus (1191). Died in Tripoli (1191).
Sources	*Chronica*, Vol. 3, pp. 111, 116; *Gesta Regis*, Vol. 2, pp. 167–8, 173; Landon, *Itinerary*, nos. 41, 68–71, 80–5, 97–101, 125–6, 150–3, 159–60, 167, 196–202, 204, 207, 215, 227–9, 276, 283, 286, 288–9, 298, 300–2, 310–11, 313–18, 328, 336, 347.

Wigan of Cherbourg

Title/s	Royal Usher (Richard I)
Alias/es	Wigan de Cherbourg
Notes	Richard I's *Familia Regis* and porter. Member of Henry II's household as usher. As Henry the Young King's kitchen clerk, he kept a tally of tournament victories. Received a quarter knight's fee in Melksham (1189). Messina (1190).

Region	Melksham (Wiltshire)
Sources	*HGM*, line 3417; Landon, *Itinerary*, nos. 188, 342; PR28 HII (1182), p. 155.

Geoffrey Hose

Alias/es	Galfridus Hose
Notes	Paid the exchequer 100*l.* prior to going on crusade. Died in the Holy Land.
Region	Wiltshire
Sources	PR34 HII, p. 141; PR5 RI, p. 80.

Nigel of Mowbray

Alias/es	Nigellus de Mumbray
Notes	Drowned on crusade (1191).
Ancestor/s	Roger of Mowbray
Orders	Cistercians (Byland, Rievaulx), Premonstratensians (Welford), St Lazarus
Region	Yorkshire
Sources	BL, Cotton ms. D.i, fos. 111r–113v.; *Charters of the Honour of Mowbray, 1107–1191*, ed. D.E. Greenway (London, 1972), no. 29, pp. 274–6, 285–6; *Gesta Regis*, Vol. 2, pp. 80, 149; TNA, C 52/28 *carte antique* roll DD, m. 1, no. 1.

Ralph of Hauterive

Title/s	Archdeacon of Colchester
Alias/es	Ralph d'Hautrey, archdeacon of Colchester, Ralf, Ralph of Hauterive, Radulfus, Radulfi de Halterive, Radulfus archidiaconus Colecestriae, Altaripa, Alta Ripa, Rad Archid Colecr
Notes	Died at the siege of Acre, fighting to rescue his men (1189).
Orders	Colchester Cathedral
Sources	Ambroise, lines 3480–5; *Chronica*, Vol. 3, p. 70; *Itinerarium*, p. 93.

William Bloez

Alias/es	William Bloez, Willelmus Bloez
Notes	Arrived at the siege of Acre with Angevin contingent (1191).
Orders	Templars (Lincolnshire)
Region	Newton and Ormsby (Lincolnshire)
Sources	*Itinerarium*, p. 218.

Geoffrey of Brulon

Alias/es	Geoffrey de Bruillon, Gaufridus de Bruilun, [Geoffrey de Bruslone?]
Notes	Richard I's *Familia Regis*. Fought at le Mans for Henry II (1189). Jaffa (1192).
Sources	*Gesta Regis*, Vol. 2, p. 67; Landon, *Itinerary*, no. 366; Wendover, p. 155.

Gilbert Pipard

Title/s	Lord of Ardee, Sheriff of Lincolnshire
Alias/es	Gilbert Pipard, Gilbertus Pipard
Notes	Richard I's *Familia Regis*. Died on crusade at Brindisi (1191).
Orders	Cistercians (Fountains)
Region	Papcastle (Cumbria)
Sources	*Gesta Regis*, Vol. 2, p. 150; Landon, *Itinerary*, nos. 164, 186–7, 335, 337, 340.

Richard of Camville

Alias/es	Richard de Camville, Richard de Canvill, Richardus de Camvilla, Chamvill, de Kamvil
Notes	Justiciar of Richard I's fleet, *Familar Regis*. Lisbon (1190). Messina (1190–1). Cyprus (1191). Governor of Cyprus. Died at the siege of Acre (1191).
Ancestor/s	Godfrey III, Count of Louvain
Family	Peter and Walter of Ross, Robert II of Harcourt
Orders	Cistercians (Combe)
Region	Avington (Berkshire), Stanton Harcourt (Oxfordshire), Blackland (Wiltshire)
Sources	*Chronica*, Vol. 3, pp. 62, 111; *Gesta Regis*, Vol. 2, pp. 80, 110, 115–16, 119–20, 124, 134, 149, 167, 172; Landon, *Itinerary*, nos. 342, 347, 354, 356–7; PR4 RI (1192), p. 252; Wendover, pp. 181, 186.

Randulf

Title/s	Royal Clerk (Richard I)
Alias/es	Randulf cleric, Randulfus clericus
Notes	Died on the Third Crusade.
Sources	*Gesta Regis*, Vol. 2, p. 149.

Henry Turpin

Title/s	Royal Arblaster (Richard I)
Alias/es	Turpin, chamberlain to King Henry II
Notes	Arblaster to King Richard I. Richard I's *Familia Regis*. Vézelay (1190), died prior to King Richard's arrival at Messina as his son journeyed there to petition for his inheritance (1191).
Region	Strettington (West Sussex)
Sources	Landon, *Itinerary*, no. 326; *CRR*, Vol. 1, p. 285.

William of Gatesden

Title/s	Royal Falconer
Alias/es	Willelmo de Gatesdene

Notes	Falconer to Richard I.
Region	Stanbridge (Bedfordshire)
Sources	*The Cartulary of Newnham Priory*, ed. J. Godber (Bedford, 1963), no. 77; *Itinerarium*, p. 286.

Baldwin of Béthune

Alias/es	Baldwin de Béthune, Bethûne, Bethsan
Notes	Richard I's *Familia Regis*. Relief of Jaffa (1192). Travelled with Richard I back from the Holy Land (1192).
Ancestor/s	Robert V and William II of Béthune
Family	Robert V and Conon of Béthune, Hugh IV, count of St Pol, William of Cayeux
Region	Béthune
Sources	*HGM*, lines 4543, 7998, 8609, 9374–90, 9396–8; Landon, *Itinerary*, nos. 328, 366; Wendover, p. 218.

Hugh VI of Gournay

Title/s	Lord of Gournay
Alias/es	Hugh de Gourney, Gornai Hues, Hugh de Gournai, Hugo de Gorniaco
Notes	Richard I's *Familia Regis*. Member of Angevin advance guard. Siege of Acre (1190). Joint governor of Acre (1191). Guarded prisoners taken at Acre. Battle of Arsuf (1191).
Ancestor/s	Gerald and Hugh II of Gournay, Thomas of Marle, Enguerrand I of Coucy
Family	Robert of Boves, Ralph I of Coucy, Dreux IV and Peter of Amiens
Orders	Benedictines (Bec-Hellouin)
Region	Gournay-en-Bray
Sources	Ambroise, line 6162; Diss, Vol. 2, p. 79; *Gesta Regis*, Vol. 2, pp. 179–80; *Itinerarium*, pp. 93, 261; Landon, *Itinerary*, nos. 1, 236–9, 262; Wendover, p. 178.

Roger of Howden

Title/s	Royal Clerk (Richard I)
Alias/es	Roger of Howden, Roger of Hoveden
Notes	Richard I's *Familia Regis*. Former member of Henry II's household. Marseille (1190). Departed the Holy Land with Philip II (1191).
Region	Howden (Yorkshire)
Sources	Author: *Chronica*; *Gesta Regis*; *De viis maris*; D. Crouch, 'At Home with Roger of Howden', *Military Cultures and Martial Enterprises in the Middle Ages: Essays in Honour of Richard P. Abels*, ed. J.D. Hosler and S. Isaac (Woodbridge, 2020), pp. 156–76; Gillingham, 'Howden on Crusade', pp. 60–75.

Anselm

Title/s	Royal Chaplain
Alias/es	Anselm
Notes	Richard I's *Familia Regis*. Captured alongside Richard I.
Sources	Coggeshall, p. 54; Wendover, p. 218.

Ralph

Title/s	Royal Chaplain (Richard I)
Alias/es	Ralph royal chaplain
Notes	Richard I's *Familia Regis*. Died on the Third Crusade.
Sources	*Gesta Regis*, Vol. 2, p. 149; Landon, *Itinerary*, no. 286.

Nicholas

Title/s	Chaplain
Alias/es	Nicholas chaplain, Nicholao capellano
Notes	Richard I's *Familia Regis*. Cyprus (1191).
Sources	*Gesta Regis*, Vol. 2, p. 167; Landon, *Itinerary*, no. 276.

Philip of Poitiers

Title/s	Royal Clerk (Richard I), Archdeacon of Canterbury (1194–5), bishop of Durham (1195)
Alias/es	Philip of Poitiers, clerk to Richard I
Notes	Richard I's *Familia Regis*.
Orders	Canterbury Cathedral
Sources	Coggeshall, p. 54; Landon, *Itinerary*, no. 366; R.V. Turner, 'Richard Lionheart and English Episcopal Elections', *Albion*, Vol. 29 (1997), p. 9; Wendover, p. 218.

Henry of Yllega

Alias/es	Henry de Yllega
Notes	On crusade to Jerusalem with King Richard (1190).
Region	Essex/Hertfordshire
Sources	PR 2 RI (1190), p. 109.

R. Warin Fitz-Henry

Alias/es	R. Warino f. Henrico camerario
Notes	On crusade to Jerusalem with King Richard (1190).
Region	Essex/Hertfordshire
Sources	PR 2 RI (1190), p. 109.

William

Title/s	Viscount of Pecquigny
Alias/es	William viscount of Pecquigny, Willelmus de Pinkenni
Notes	Richard I's *Familia Regis*. Died at the siege of Acre.
Region	Gloucestershire
Sources	*Gesta Regis*, Vol. 2, p. 149; *Chronica*, Vol. 3, pp. 89, 184; PR4 R1 (1192), p. 285; PR5 R1 (1193), p. 113.

Alard Fleming

Alias/es	Ayllardo Flandr'
Notes	Richard I's *Familia Regis*. Recruiting tour of the Low Countries (1187).
Region	Gloucestershire, Kent, Sussex
Sources	*Documents*, Vol. 1, ed. Round, pp. 481–505, no. 1361; TNA C53/43; *CCR*, Vol. 1, p. 355.

Simon

Alias/es	Simoni Pincerne nostro
Notes	Richard I's *Familia Regis*. Received royal manor of St Kew (1194).
Region	St Kew (Cornwall)
Sources	TNA C 52/18, *carte antique* roll 18, m.2d, no. 26.

Eudes Fitz-Aernisi

Alias/es	Eudus filius Ernisi
Notes	Richard I's *Familia Regis*. Member of Henry II's household. Held land of the king in Maldon. Crusader of the honour of Peverel of London (1190).
Region	Maldon (Essex), Hertfordshire
Sources	PR 33 H2, p. 121; PR 34 H2, p. 30; PR1 R1 (1189), p. 20, PR2 R1 (1190), pp. 104, 110.

Bartholomew of Mortimer

Alias/es	Bartholomew de Mortimer, Bertelmeü de Mortemer, Bartholomaeus de Mortuo Mari
Notes	Richard I's *Familia Regis*. Relief of Jaffa (1192).
Sources	Ambroise, lines 11378–620; *Itinerarium*, p. 415.

Gerard of Furnival

Alias/es	Gerard de Furnival, Gerard de Fornival, Girard de Fornival, Girardus de Furnival, Gerardus de Fornivallis
Notes	Richard I's *Familia Regis*. Relief of Jaffa (1192). Envoy to Jerusalem (1192).
Sources	Ambroise, lines 11394, 11871; *Itinerarium*, pp. 415, 432.

William des Roches

Title/s	Lord of Sablé
Alias/es	Roches Guillames, Willelmus de Rupibus
Notes	Richard I's *Familia Regis*. Former member of Henry II's household. Arrived at the siege of Acre with Angevin contingent (1191). Battle of Arsuf (1191). Siege of Jaffa (1192). Envoy to Jerusalem (1192). With Queen Berengaria in Rome (1193). It is not clear if he married Marguerite of Sablé prior to the crusade or after his return.
Ancestor/s	Robert of Rupibus
Family	Robert III of Sablé
Orders	Benedictines (Marmoutier), Cistercians (Charron, La Boissiére), Premonstratensians (Le Perray-Neuf)
Region	Touraine
Sources	Ambroise, line 11869; *CDF*, pp. 94–5; *Documents*, Vol. 1, ed. Round, pp. 94–5; *HGM*, line 8817; *Itinerarium*, pp. 218, 432; Landon, *Itinerary*, no. 366.

Hugh of Neville

Alias/es	Hugh de Neville, Hue de Noefvile, Hugo de Nova Villa
Notes	Richard I's *Familia Regis*. Relief of Jaffa (1192). Eyewitness for Ralph of Coggeshall's entries on the Third Crusade.
Orders	Sempringham, Templars
Region	Hallingbury (Essex)
Sources	*Itinerarium*, p. 415; Landon, *Itinerary*, no. 171; *Monasticon*, Vol. 6, p. 833; PR6 RI, p. 80.

Hugh of la Fierte

Alias/es	Hugh de la Fierte, Hugo Fierte
Notes	Conquest of Cyprus (1191). Arrived at the siege of Acre with Angevin contingent (1191).
Sources	*Itinerarium*, p. 218.

Peter Tirepreie

Alias/es	Peter Tireproie, Pieres Tireproie, Petrum de Tirepreie
Notes	Killed in Sicily (1190).
Sources	Ambroise, line 761; *Itinerarium*, p. 162.

Matthew of Sauley

Alias/es	Matthew de Sauley, Mahau of Sauçoi, Maher de Sauçoi, Matthaeum de Saliceto
Notes	Killed in Sicily (1190).
Sources	Ambroise, line 763; *Itinerarium*, p. 162.

William of Poitiers

Title/s	Chaplain
Alias/es	William, Guillames de Peitiers, Willelmus
Notes	Sent as messenger to Richard I in the Holy Land (1192).
Region	Poitou
Sources	Ambroise, line 9532; *Itinerarium*, pp. 361; Landon, *Itinerary*, no. 219.

William Fitz-Richard

Alias/es	William filius Richardi, William fitz Richard
Notes	With Richard I in Marseille en route to the Holy Land (1190).
Sources	Landon, *Itinerary*, nos. 276, 335, 337, 340.

Henry of Gray

Alias/es	Henry de Gray, Henris de Graié, Henrico de Gray, Henrico de Grue
Notes	Skirmish near Ramla (1192). Jaffa (1192).
Orders	Benedictines (Longues-sur-Mer)
Region	Graye-sur-Mer (Calvados)
Sources	Ambroise, line 7543; *Itinerarium*, p. 302; Landon, *Itinerary*, no. 366.

Ambroise

Alias/es	Amboise
Notes	Chronicler: author of *Le Guerre Sainte*;
Sources	Ambroise, lines 1194–1351.

Warin II Fitz-Gerald

Title/s	Baron of the Exchequer, royal chamberlain
Alias/es	Warin Fitz-Gerald, Garin, Guarins le fitz Gerod, Garinus filius Geroldi
Notes	Messina (1190). Arrived at the siege of Acre with Angevin contingent (1191). Led his company at siege of Acre (1191). Skirmish near Ramla (1192). Jaffa (1192).
Family	Hugh de Grancey, Amadeus d'Arceaux
Region	Normandy
Sources	Ambroise, lines 4725, 7496; *Itinerarium*, pp. 217, 300; Landon, *Itinerary*, nos. 131, 175–81, 183–93, 342, 366; N. Vincent, 'Warin and Henry Fitz Gerald, the King's Chamberlains: the Origins of the FitzGeralds Revisited', *ANS* 21 (1999): 233–60.

John of Alençon

Title/s	Vice Chancellor, Archdeacon of Lisieux
Alias/es	John d'Alençon, vice chancellor, archdeacon of Lisieu, Johans d'Alençon, John de Alençon, John d'Alenconx, Johannes de Alenzun
Notes	Richard I's *Familia Regis* and vice chancellor. Travelled to Holy Land in 1192 to update King Richard I on events in his realm.
Orders	Lisieux Cathedral
Sources	Ambroise, line 9414; *Itinerarium*, pp. 358; Landon, *Itinerary*, nos. 6–8, 147, 156, 207–10, 214–17, 219–20, 222–3, 225–34, 236–8, 263, 268, 272–8, 283–4, 286, 288–90, 292, 295, 298–304, 306, 308, 310, 312–18, 321, 324, 326, 328–9, 331.

Roger of Malchiel

Title/s	Vice Chancellor, Keeper of the King's Seal
Alias/es	Roger Malchael, Rogerus Malus Catulus
Notes	Messina (1190). Drowned off Cyprus (1191).
Sources	*Gesta Regis*, Vol. 2, p. 162; *Itinerarium*, p. 184; Landon, *Itinerary*, nos. 292, 344, 346–7, 354, 356–7.

William of Sainte-Mère-Église

Title/s	Royal clerk of the chamber, Dean of St Martin le Grand, London
Alias/es	Willelmo de Sancte Marie Ecclesia, dean of Mortain
Notes	Member of Henry II's household. Vézelay (1190). Jaffa (1192).
Orders	St Martin le Grand (London)
Region	Normandy
Sources	*Acta*, no. 220; *Chronica*, Vol. 2, p. 85; Landon, *Itinerary*, nos. 6–8, 27–32, 128, 195, 225–6, 246, 256–8, 268, 292, 299, 313–18, 321–6.

John Fitz-Luke

Title/s	Bishop of Évreux
Alias/es	episcopo Ebroici, Johan, l'evesque d'Evreues, Johannis Ebroycensis episcopi, Johannem Ebroicensem episcopum
Notes	Former royal chaplain. Helped formulate Saladin Tithe at Le Mans (1188). Geddington (1189). Rouen (1190). Lyon (1190). Messina (1190). Cyprus (1191). Siege of Acre (1191). Joint-commander of Jaffa (1192). Died in Jaffa (1192).
Orders	Évreux Cathedral
Sources	Ambroise, lines 1006, 4699, 7177; Devizes, p. 22; *Gesta Regis*, Vol. 2, pp. 30–2, 45–6, 75–6, 101, 128, 153, 167; *Itinerarium*, pp. 217, 289; Landon, *Itinerary*, nos. 10–11, 33, 72–6, 97–101, 115, 123, 211–2, 227–9, 231–4, 236–40, 329–30, 344, 347, 358.

Robert
Title/s	Prior of Hereford
Alias/es	Robert, prior of Hereford, Robertus prior Herefordensis
Notes	Sent by William of Longchamp as messenger to Richard I, Acre (1192).
Orders	Benedictines (Hereford)
Sources	Ambroise, line 8502; Devizes, p. 40; *Itinerarium*, pp. 333.

John Fitz-Luke
Alias/es	Johan le fils Lucas
Notes	March to Jaffa (1191).
Region	Gloucestershire
Sources	Ambroise, line 5783.

Oliver of Rochefort
Alias/es	Oliver de Rochefort
Notes	Jaffa (1192).
Sources	Landon, *Itinerary*, no. 366.

William of Miners
Alias/es	William de Miners
Notes	Jaffa (1192).
Sources	Landon, *Itinerary*, no. 366.

William Fitz-Nigel
Alias/es	Willelmo filio Nigelli
Notes	Jaffa (1192).
Sources	*Acta*, no. 220.

Alexander Fitz-Hugh
Alias/es	Alexandro filio Hulte
Notes	Jaffa (1192).
Sources	*Acta*, no. 220.

Matthew of Harengod'
Alias/es	Matthew de Harengod'
Notes	Jaffa (1192).
Sources	*Acta*, no. 220.

John of Montes
Alias/es	John de Montes, Iohanne de Montes
Notes	Jaffa (1192).
Sources	*Acta*, no. 220.

William Rifford
Alias/es	Willelmo de Rifford
Notes	Jaffa (1192).
Sources	*Acta*, no. 220.

John Branton
Alias/es	Iohanne de Brantun'
Notes	Jaffa (1192).
Sources	*Acta*, no. 220.

William Quatregarbes
Alias/es	Guillaume Quartregarbes
Notes	Jaffa (1192).
Sources	*Acta*, no. 220.

William of Bruil
Alias/es	William de Bruil, Willelmus de Bruil
Notes	Attached to earl of Leicester. Skirmish at Ramla (1192).
Family	Saul of Bruil
Region	Bruile (Calvados) – possible
Sources	Ambroise, line 7120; *Itinerarium*, p. 301.

Saul of Bruil
Alias/es	Saul de Bruil, Saol del Bruel, Saut, Salt de Bruil, Saulus de Bruil
Notes	Attached to earl of Leicester. Skirmish at Ramla (1192). Royal messenger to king of Jerusalem (1194).
Family	William of Bruil
Region	Bruile (Calvados) – possible
Sources	Ambroise, line 7120; *Chronica*, Vol. 3, p. 233; *Itinerarium*, p. 301.

Peter of Barres

Alias/es	Peter des Barres, Petrum de Barris
Notes	Crewman of the Trenchemer. Participated in defeat of Muslim great ship off Acre (1191).
Sources	*Itinerarium*, p. 205.

Guy of Berniers

Alias/es	Guy de Bernez'
Notes	Companion of King Richard who borrowed 150 *marks* on behalf of Queen Berengaria whilst in Rome (1193).
Family	Ralph of Berniers
Sources	*Documents*, Vol. 1, ed. Round, pp. 94–5.

Geoffrey of Vendôme

Alias/es	Geoffrey de Vendosm'
Notes	Companion of King Richard who borrowed 150 *marks* on behalf of Queen Berengaria whilst in Rome (1193).
Sources	*Documents*, Vol. 1, ed. Round, pp. 94–5.

John of Subligny

Alias/es	John de Suloeitum
Notes	Favourite of Henry II and member of Young Henry's household. Held as surety for the loan to Queen Berengaria (1193).
Ancestor/s	Guy of Subligny
Orders	Augustinians (Mont-Morel)
Region	Avranchin, Bessin (Normandy)
Sources	*Documents*, Vol. 1, ed. Round, pp. 94–5; Torigni, 1, pp. 360–2; *HGM*, p. 65

Guichard Leidett

Alias/es	Guichard Leidett'
Notes	Held as surety for the loan to Queen Berengaria (1193).
Sources	*Documents*, Vol. 1, ed. Round, pp. 94–5.

Roger of St Germain

Alias/es	Roger de Sancto Germano
Notes	Held as surety for the loan to Queen Berengaria (1193).
Region	Cavendish (Suffolk)
Sources	*Documents*, Vol. 1, ed. Round, pp. 94–5.

Alan Fitz-Alan of Shoreham

Alias/es	Alan fis de Alan de Sorham
Notes	Held as surety for the loan to Queen Berengaria (1193).
Sources	*Documents*, Vol. 1, ed. Round, pp. 94–5.

Gérard of la Barthe

Title/s	Archbishop of Auch (1170–91)
Alias/es	Gérard de la Barthe, archbishop of Auch, archiepiscopus Anxie, Anxiensis, Girardum, Gérault de Labarthe
Notes	Justiciar of Richard I's fleet, Messina (1190), Cyprus (1191). Purified churches of Acre (1191). Died in the East (1191).
Region	Auch (Gascony)
Sources	Devizes, p. 22; *Gesta Regis*, Vol. 2, pp. 110, 115–16, 128, 134, 153, 180–1; Landon, *Itinerary*, nos. 216–17, 342; Wendover, pp. 181, 186.

Miles Beauchamp

Alias/es	Miles of Beauchamp
Notes	On crusade to Jerusalem (1192).
Ancestor/s	Hugh of Beauchamp
Orders	Cistercians (Warden)
Region	Bedfordshire
Sources	PR4 RI (1192), p. 200.

Bernard of Liminstre

Alias/es	Bernard de Liminstre
Notes	On crusade to Jerusalem (1192).
Region	Bedfordshire
Sources	PR4 RI (1192), p. 200.

Gilbert of Passelewe

Alias/es	Gilbert Passelewe
Notes	On crusade to Jerusalem (1192).
Region	Bedfordshire
Sources	PR4 RI (1192), p. 200.

Guy of St Valery

Alias/es	Guy de St Valerie, Valary
Notes	On crusade to Jerusalem (1192).

Ancestor/s	Walter of St Valery
Family	Gilbert of Vascoeuil
Region	Bedfordshire
Sources	PR4 RI (1192), p. 200.

Henry Ruffus

Alias/es	Henry Ros
Notes	On crusade to Jerusalem (1192).
Region	Bedfordshire
Sources	PR4 RI (1192), p. 200.

Roger of Salford

Alias/es	Roger de Salford
Notes	On crusade to Jerusalem (1192).
Region	Bedfordshire
Sources	PR4 RI (1192), p. 200.

Robert Fitz-Bernard

Alias/es	Robert filius Bernardi
Notes	On crusade to Jerusalem (1192).
Region	Bedfordshire
Sources	PR4 RI (1192), p. 200.

Walter Monk

Alias/es	Walter Monk
Notes	On crusade to Jerusalem (1192).
Region	Bedfordshire
Sources	PR4 RI (1192), p. 200.

Osbert of Bray

Alias/es	Osbert de Bray
Notes	On crusade to Jerusalem (1192).
Region	Bedfordshire
Sources	PR4 RI (1192), p. 200.

Baldwin of Forde

Title/s	Archbishop of Canterbury

Alias/es	Baldwin of Exeter, archbishop of Canterbury, Baldewino, Baldewinum archiepiscopum Cantuarie, de Canturbirie l'arcevesques, Baldewini Cantuariensis archiepiscopi
Notes	Took the Cross alongside Henry II (1188). Oversaw collection of the Saladin Tithe (1188). Preaching tour of Wales (1188). Commanded 200 knights and 300 men-at-arms at siege of Acre (1190). Participated in the St Martin offensive (1190). Died at the siege of Acre (1190).
Family	Joseph of Exeter
Orders	Benedictines (Canterbury), Cistercians (Forde)
Region	Forde (Dorset), Swindon (Wiltshire)
Sources	Ambroise, lines 3963, 4122; *Chronica*, Vol. 3, p. 87; Diss, Vol. 2, pp. 61–2, 84, 88; Devizes, pp. 3, 15, 19; *Gesta Regis*, Vol. 2, pp. 30–3, 40, 68–70, 75, 105–6, 115, 118–19, 142, 147; *Itinerarium*, pp. 93, 115–17, 121–2, 123–4, 142; Landon, *Itinerary*, nos. 2–9, 16–22, 27–32, 34, 40–55, 58, 61, 113, 123, 128, 147, 150–2, 155, 164–5, 168–81, 183, 186–93, 196–202, 231–3, 240, 263–4, 335, 337–8, 340; Rigord, p. 83; Wendover, pp. 152, 162, 164–7, 170, 186, 189.

Joseph of Exeter

Title/s	Clerk (Baldwin of Ford)
Alias/es	Joseph of Exeter
Notes	Joined his uncle on crusade but returned to England after Baldwin's death (1190).
Family	Baldwin of Forde
Orders	Canterbury Cathedral
Sources	R. Mortimer, *Angevin England: 1154–1258* (Oxford, 1994), p. 210.

Sylvester

Title/s	Seneschal of the Archbishop of Canterbury
Alias/es	Sylvester seneschal of the archbishop of Canterbury
Notes	Clerk and steward to the archbishop of Canterbury. Died at the siege of Acre (1190).
Orders	Canterbury Cathedral
Region	Canterbury
Sources	*Epistolae Cantuarienses*, pp. 8, 25; *Gesta Regis*, Vol. 2, p. 148.

William Fitz-Neal

Title/s	Steward of St Thomas of Canterbury
Alias/es	William Fitz-Neal
Notes	Died at the siege of Acre (1191).
Orders	St Thomas of Canterbury
Sources	*Gesta Regis*, Vol. 2, p. 150.

Peter of Blois

Title/s	Chancellor of Canterbury Archdiocese, Archdeacon of Bath
Alias/es	Peter of Blois
Notes	Journeyed with Baldwin of Forde and returned to England via Sicily after the archbishop's death (1190). Travelled with Eleanor of Aquitaine from Sicily to France.
Orders	Canterbury Cathedral
Sources	*Petrus Blesensis Bathoniensis in Anglia Archidiaconus. Patrologiae cursus completus. Series Secunda*, Vol. 207, ed. J.P. Migne (Paris, 1855), col. 532; Tyerman, *God's War*, p. 381.

Robert II

Title/s	Abbot of Forde
Alias/es	Robert, abbot of Ford, abbas de Forde
Notes	Died at the siege of Acre (1190).
Orders	Cistercians (Forde)
Region	Forde (Dorset)
Sources	*Chronica*, Vol. 3, p. 87; *Gesta Regis*, Vol. 2, p. 147.

Richard Fitz-William of Langford

Title/s	Lord of Little Windsor
Alias/es	Ricardo de Langeford, cil de Parve Windesorie
Orders	Cistercians (Forde)
Region	Forde (Dorset)
Sources	*Cartulary of Forde Abbey*, fos. 93v–94.

Henry Pomeroy

Alias/es	Henry de la Pomeray
Notes	Died on the Third Crusade.
Orders	Cistercians (Forde)
Region	Forde (Dorset)
Sources	*Cartulary of Forde Abbey*, ed. S. Hobbs (Taunton, 1998), fos. 88v–89.

Matthew Oisel

Notes	Redeemed his prospective son-in-law's fief from his creditors before departing on crusade.
Orders	Cistercians (Forde)
Region	Street, Forde (Dorset), Heathfield (Somerset)
Sources	*RCR*, Vol. 1, pp. 338–40.

Robert of Tracy

Alias/es	Roberti de Traci
Notes	On crusade to Jerusalem (1191).
Region	Barnstaple (Devon)
Sources	PR1 RI (1189), p. 133.

William Marcel

Alias/es	Willelmus Marcel, Guillelmus Martel
Notes	Arrived at the siege of Acre with Angevin contingent (1191).
Orders	Templars
Region	West Country
Sources	'The Records of the Templars in England in the Twelfth Century', *British Academy Records of Social and Economic History*, Vol. 9, ed. B.A. Lees (1935). pp. 15, 75; *Itinerarium*, p. 218.

Ranulf of Glanville

Title/s	Justiciar (England)
Alias/es	Ranulf de Glanville, Rannulfus de Glanuilla, Rannulf Glandvill, Ranulfus de Glanvilla
Notes	Member of Henry II's household. Took the Cross during Heraclius' visit (1185), renewed his vow (1188). Richard I's coronation (1189). Marseille (1190). Joint commander of Angevin advance guard, arriving at siege of Acre (1190) via Tyre. Died at the siege of Acre (1190).
Ancestor/s	Hervey of Glanville
Family	Alan of Valoignes, Hubert Walter
Orders	Augustinians (Butley), Premonstratensians (Leiston), leprosarium (Somerton)
Region	Suffolk, Glanvill (Calvados)
Sources	Coggeshall, p. 23; Diss, Vol. 2, p. 84; Devizes, pp. 4–5, 19; *Gesta Regis*, Vol. 2, pp. 40, 80, 86, 90, 149; Landon, *Itinerary*, nos. 2–8, 18–19, 20–33, 41–54, 250, 263, 274; Wendover, p. 191.

Roger of Glanville

Alias/es	Roger de Glanville, Roger Glanvill, Rogerus de Glanvil, Rogerus de Glanvilla
Notes	Siege of Acre (1190). Participated on an assault on the city walls with Humphrey of Veilly, Robert of Lanlande, and Ralph of Tilly (1190). Captured some of Saladin's men whilst scouting Jerusalem (1192).
Ancestor/s	Hervey of Glanville
Family	Ranulf of Glanville, Alan of Valoignes
Orders	Benedictines (Bungay), Premonstratensians (Leiston)
Region	Glanvill (Calvados), Montfichet (Essex)

Sources	*Gesta Regis*, Vol. 2, p. 144; R.R. Heiser, 'Castles, Constables, and Politics in Late Twelfth-Century English Governance', *Albion*, 32 (2000), 25; *Itinerarium*, p. 345; Landon, *Itinerary*, no. 127.

Alan of Valoignes

Title/s	Sheriff of Kent
Alias/es	Alan de Valognes, Alan de Valoignes, de Valeines
Notes	Member of Henry II's household as sheriff of Kent. Received royal charter for lands in Yorkshire (1189). Crusader of the honour of Peverel. Died on return from crusade (1194).
Family	Theobald of Valoignes, Ranulf of Glanville, Roger of Glanville
Region	Kent, London, (Allerton, Ebberson, and Thorphin) North Yorkshire
Sources	Landon, *Itinerary*, nos. 175–82; Mortimer, 'Family of Ranulf de Glanville', p. 8; PR2 RI (1190), p. 110.

Theobald of Valoignes

Title/s	Lord of Parham, Butler of Ireland,
Notes	Died on the Third Crusade (1191).
Family	Alan of Valoignes
Orders	Augustinians (Hickling)
Region	Parham (Suffolk)
Sources	Young, *Hubert Walter*, p. 3 and footnote 1; PR2 R1 (1190), p. 110; 3 R1 (1191), p. 43.

Durand of Outillé

Title/s	Lord of Valoignes
Alias/es	Durand d'Outillé
Notes	Jury held to determine his property after he died on the Third Crusade.
Family	Theobald and Alan of Valoignes
Region	Ashwell (Hertfordshire)
Sources	*CRR*, Vol. 1, pp. 69, 277–8.

Reiner of Waxham

Title/s	Steward and Dapifer (Ranulf de Galnville)
Alias/es	Reiner of Waxham, viscount Reiner of York, Reiner vicecomes Eboraci
Notes	Died on Cyprus (1191).
Sources	Gesta Regis, Vol. 2, p. 150; Mortimer, 'Family of Ranulf de Glanville', pp. 11–12.

Ralph of Arden

Alias/es	Ralph of Arden, Radulfus de Ardenna
Notes	On crusade to Jerusalem (1191).
Family	Ranulf of Glanville, Roger of Glanville
Region	Suffolk (Clare)
Sources	PR2 RI (1190), pp. 110, 130; 3 RI (1191), p. 44.

Hubert Walter

Title/s	Bishop of Salisbury (1189–93), archibishop of Canterbury (1193–1205)
Alias/es	Hubert Walter, bishop of Salisbury, Hubertus Walteri, Hubertum episcopum Saresberie, evesques de Salesberes, Salesbires, Hubert Fitz-W
Notes	Joint commander of Angevin advance guard, arriving at the siege of Acre (1190). Organised poor relief at the siege (1190). Participated in the St Martin offensive (1190). Attack on Cursed Tower repulsed (1191). Purified churches at Acre (1191). March to Jaffa (1191). Skirmish at Betenoble (1192). Pilgrimage to Jerusalem (1192).
Ancestor/s	Hervey of Glanville
Family	Ranulf of Glanville, Theobald and Alan of Valoignes
Orders	Premonstratensians (West Dereham), Salisbury Cathedral
Region	West Dereham (Norfolk)
Sources	*Acta*, no. 220; Ambroise, lines 4411, 4590, 4994, 5414, 11847; Baha' al-Din, p. 228; Diss, Vol. 2, pp. 79, 84, 88, 108–9; Devizes, pp. 15, 82, 84; *Gesta Regis*, Vol. 2, pp. 77, 85, 96, 98–100, 115, 145, 180–1, 186; *Itinerarium*, pp. 93, 116, 134–5, 137, 242, 372, 432, 437–8; Landon, *Itinerary*, nos. 33, 42–54, 92–101, 110–12, 114, 116, 118–20, 123, 125, 127, 130, 134, 140–42a, 143, 146–7, 153–7, 160–5, 168–202, 240. 256–8, 263–4, 268, 274, 276, 321–6, 336–8, 340; Wendover, pp. 161, 167, 178, 186, 189, 204.

Everard

Alias/es	Everard, Evradz, Evrart, Everardo homini episcopi Saresberiensis
Notes	Member of Hubert Walter's household. Wounded on the march to Jaffa (1191).
Region	Salisbury
Sources	Ambroise, line 5771; *Itinerarium*, p. 250.

Warreis of Pillesdon

Alias/es	Werreheis de Pillesdon'
Notes	Knight of Bishop Hubert, on crusade to Jerusalem. Died on crusade.
Region	Salisbury
Sources	*Abbreviato Placitorum, Richard I – Edward II*, ed. G. Rose and W. Illingworth (London, 1811), p. 121b; PR 3 RI (1191), p. 121.

Robert III Beaumont

Title/s	Earl of Leicester, Lord High Steward (up to 1190)
Alias/es	Robert III Beaumont, earl of Leicester, comes de Leicestriae, comes Belmontis, Robert ès Blanchmains, Robert the Whitehanded, Robert de Breteuil
Notes	Richard I's Lord High Steward. Took the Cross alongside Henry II (1188). Died en route to the siege of Acre (1190).
Ancestor/s	Aubrey, Odo, and William of Grandmesnil, Hugh the Great, Waleran of Meulan
Family	Amaury of Montfort, Robert Fitz-Pernel, Robert of Quincy, Raymond II of Turenne
Orders	Augustinians (Leicester), Cistercians (Bordesley), Templars
Region	Leicester
Sources	*Chronica*, Vol. 3, pp. 5, 88; *Gesta Regis*, Vol. 2, pp. 75, 80–1, 148; Landon, *Itinerary*, nos. 9, 33, 41–55, 80–9, 97–101, 104, 126–7, 148–53, 161–64, 166–7, 183, 186, 196–202, 211–12, 227–9, 265; Rigord, pp. 83–4; Wendover, p. 191.

Robert IV Fitz-Pernel of Breteuil

Title/s	Earl of Leicester, Lord High Steward (from February 1191)
Alias/es	Robert IV de Breteuil, earl of Leicester, Robert de Leicestre, conte de Leicestre, coens de Leicestre, Fitz-Pernel, robertus de Bretuil
Notes	Richard I's Lord High Steward. Belted earl of Leicester by Richard I at Messina (1191). Siege of Acre (1191). Arrived at the siege of Acre with Angevin contingent (1191). Skirmish near Ramla (1192). Siege of Darum (1192). Attack on Muslim caravan (1192). Relief of Jaffa (1192).
Ancestor/s	Hugh the Great, Waleran of Meulan
Family	Amaury of Montfort, Robert III Beaumont, Robert of Quincy, Raymond II of Turenne, Robert of Newburgh
Orders	Benedictines (Lire)
Region	Leicester
Sources	*Acta*, no. 220; Ambroise, lines 4711, 4988, 5415, 6160, 7274, 7470, 9292, 10040, 10454, 10960, 11378–620, 11491; *Gesta Regis*, Vol. 2, p. 156; *Itinerarium*, pp. 217, 227, 242, 261, 269, 292–3, 300, 355, 375–6, 389, 405, 415, 418; Landon, *Itinerary*, nos. 24, 366.

Robert II of Newburgh

Title/s	Deputy chamberlain
Alias/es	Robert de Neuborg, Robert de Newburgh, Robert de Noefbroc, Novo Burgo
Notes	Messina (1190). Arrived at the siege of Acre with Angevin contingent (1191). Skirmish near Ramla (1192).
Ancestor/s	Hugh the Great, Waleran of Meulan
Family	Robert Fitz-Pernel

Orders	Cistercians (Bindon)
Region	Winfrith (Dorset), Neubourg, Basildon (Berks)
Sources	Ambroise, lines 4705, 7520; *Chronica*, Vol. 3, p. 62; *Itinerarium*, p. 301; Landon, *Itinerary*, no. 342.

Arnold IV of Bois

Title/s	Lord of Thorpe
Alias/es	Arnald du Bois, Ernaus del Bois, Arnold of Bois, Arnold de Bosco, Ernald de Bosco, Ernauld de Bois, Arnaldus de Bosco
Notes	Steward to Earl Robert III of Leicester. Accompanied Earl Robert IV on crusade. Skirmish near Ramla (1192).
Family	Robert of Bois
Orders	Cistercians (Biddlesden)
Region	Leicester
Sources	Ambroise, line 7520; *Itinerarium*, p. 301.

Robert of Bois

Title/s	Rector of Claybrooke
Alias/es	Robert du Bois
Notes	Household chaplain to earls of Leicester.
Family	Arnold IV of Bois
Orders	Claybrooke Church
Region	Leicester
Sources	AD Eure, G 105 (i).

Henry of Mailoc

Alias/es	Henry de Mailoc, Henri de Malloc, Henricus de Mailoc
Notes	Skirmish near Ramla (1192). Wounded on the Third Crusade (1192).
Family	William of Mailoc
Region	Calvados
Sources	Ambroise, line 7501; *Itinerarium*, p. 301.

Dreux of Fontenil

Alias/es	Drogo de Fontenil, Dreu de Fontenil, Dreux, Drogo de Fontenillo
Notes	Skirmish near Ramla (1192).
Region	L'Aigle (Evreux) possible
Sources	Ambroise, line 7501; *Itinerarium*, p. 300.

Ralph of Sainte Marie

Alias/es	Ralph de Sainte Marie, Raols de Sainte Marie, Radulphus de Sancta Maria
Notes	Skirmish near Ramla (1192).
Region	Sainte-Mère-Église (Manche)
Sources	Ambroise, line 7501; *Itinerarium*, p. 301.

Robert Neal

Alias/es	Robert Neal, Robert Neel, Robertus Nigelli
Notes	Skirmish near Ramla (1192).
Region	Saint-Saveur (Manche)
Sources	Ambroise, line 7501; *Itinerarium*, p. 300.

Henry Fitz-Nicholas

Alias/es	Henry Fitz-Nicholas, Henris le filz Nicole, Henricus filius Nicholai
Notes	Arrived at the siege of Acre with Angevin contingent (1191). Saved by earl of Leicester near Ramla (1192).
Region	Dorset and Somerset
Sources	Ambroise, line 7508; *Itinerarium*, pp. 218, 301.

Robert of Laund

Alias/es	Robert de la Landa, Robertus Lalande
Notes	Siege of Acre (1190).
Sources	*Chronica*, Vol. 3, p. 73; *Gesta Regis*, Vol. 2, p. 144.

Ernald of Mandeville

Alias/es	Ernald de Grandeville, Arnulf de Mandeville, Ernaldis de Magna Villa
Notes	Arrived at the siege of Acre with Angevin contingent (1191).
Ancestor/s	Geoffrey of Mandeville
Region	Little Farendon (Berkshire)
Sources	*Itinerarium*, p. 218.

Roger of Mandeville

Alias/es	Roger de Mandeville
Notes	Jury held to determine his property after he died on the Third Crusade.
Ancestor/s	Geoffrey of Mandeville
Family	Ernald of Mandeville
Region	Erlestoke (Wiltshire)
Sources	*CRR*, Vol. 1, p. 97.

Adam of Mandeville

Alias/es	Adam de Mandeville
Notes	His widow claim dower on lands after he died on crusade. Relationship to Earl William and Ernald of Mandeville unknown.
Region	'Lole' (in Hertfordshire)
Sources	*RCR*, Vol. 1, p. 439.

Henry Pigot

Title/s	Seneschal to Earl of Essex (Warenne)
Alias/es	Henricus Pigot senescallus comitis de Warenna, Henricus Pikot, senescallus comitis Willelmi de Mandevilla
Notes	Died at the siege of Acre (1190).
Region	Huntingdon
Sources	*Chronica*, Vol. 3, p. 89; *Gesta Regis*, Vol. 2, p. 149.

Robert

Title/s	Constable of Halsham
Alias/es	Robertus constabularius
Notes	Steward to William Mandeville, earl of Essex. Died at the siege of Acre.
Orders	Cistercians (Meaux)
Region	Halsham (Yorkshire)
Sources	*Chronica*, Vol. 3, p. 89.

William I of Ferrers

Title/s	Earl of Derby
Alias/es	William I de Ferrers, earl of Derby, cuens de Ferieres, earl Ferrers, Willelmus comes de Ferrers, Willelmus comes de Ferreres, comes de Ferrariis
Notes	Arrived at the siege of Acre (1189). Died at the siege of Acre (1190).
Ancestor/s	Pagan Peverel, William Peverel
Family	Walkelin, Ralph II of Fougères, William Peverel
Orders	Benedictines (Reading, Tutbury), Cistercians (Dore, Merevale), St Lazarus
Region	Derbyshire
Sources	*Chronica*, Vol. 3, p. 88; *Gesta Regis*, Vol. 2, p. 148; *Itinerarium*, pp. 73–4.

Walkelin of Ferrers

Alias/es	Walkelin de Ferrers, Walchelin of Ferrières, Wakelins de Ferieres, Guaquelins de Ferieres, Walcherin of Ferrieres-St Hilary
Notes	Sicily (1191). Siege of Acre (1190). Supported collection on behalf of poorest Crusaders at Lent (1191). Battle of Arsuf (1191).

Family	William and Henry of Ferrers
Orders	Cistercians (Barbery)
Region	Ferrières-Saint-Hilaire (Normandy), Oakham (Rutland)
Sources	Ambroise, lines 4431, 6166; Diss, Vol. 2, p. 79; *Itinerarium*, pp. 93, 135, 261; Landon, *Itinerary*, nos. 1, 10–11, 329–31; Wendover, p. 178.

Amaury of Montfort

Title/s	Count of Évreux, lord of Montfort
Alias/es	Aimery de Montfort
Notes	In Holy Land (1187). Messina (1190).
Ancestor/s	Robert of Montfort
Family	Robert Fitz-Pernel
Sources	AD d'Eure, H703, fol. 75r–v, no. 69; Landon, *Itinerary*, no. 342.

William of la Mare

Alias/es	William de la Mare, illi de Mara
Notes	Arrived at the siege of Acre with Angevin contingent (1191).
Family	Robert, Osbert, Alan of la Mere
Orders	Cistercians (Bruern)
Sources	*Itinerarium*, p. 217.

Osbert of la Mare

Alias/es	Osbert de la Mare, illi de Mara
Notes	On crusade to Jerusalem. Arrived at the siege of Acre with Angevin contingent (1191).
Family	Robert, William, Alan of la Mere
Region	Essex and Hertfordshire
Sources	*Itinerarium*, p. 217; PR3 RI (1191), pp. 44.

Robert of la Mare

Title/s	Lord of Mare
Alias/es	Robert de la Mare, cil de la Mare, Robertus de Mara, illi de Mara
Notes	Henry II's *Familia Regis*. On crusade to Jerusalem. Arrived at the siege of Acre with Angevin contingent (1191). Benevento (1192).
Family	Osbert, William, Alan of la Mere
Orders	Cistercians (Bruern), Augustinian (Haughmond)
Region	Tenant of Clare (Norfolk/Suffolk), Normandy
Sources	*Itinerarium*, p. 217; PR2 RI, pp. 103, 111; PR3 RI (1191), p. 44.

Alan of la Mare

Alias/es	Alan de la Mere, illi de Mara
Notes	Arrived at the siege of Acre with Angevin contingent (1191). Benevento (1192).
Family	Osbert, William, Robert of la Mere
Sources	*Itinerarium*, p. 217.

Hugh of la Mare

Title/s	Cleric
Alias/es	Hugh de la Mare, Huge de la Mare, Hugo nomine de Mara
Notes	Conquest of Cyprus (1191). Died on the Third Crusade (1190).
Sources	Ambroise, line 1605; *Itinerarium*, p. 192.

William Peverel

Alias/es	Guillaume Peverel
Notes	On crusade to Jerusalem (1190). Died in the East.
Ancestor/s	Pagan Peverel, William Peverel
Family	William of Ferrers
Orders	Hospitallers (Hogshaw)
Region	Peverel (London), Norfolk
Sources	PR34 H2, p. 59; PR2 R1 (1190), p. 110; *Rotuli de Liberate*, ed. Hardy, p. 30.

Richard of Muntuiron

Alias/es	Richard de Muntuiron
Notes	On crusade to Jerusalem (1190).
Family	Robert II of Dreux and Bishop of Beauvais
Region	Norfolk
Sources	PR2 RI (1190), p. 110.

Brian Fitz-Ralph

Alias/es	Brian filius Ralph
Notes	On crusade to Jerusalem (1190). Died at the siege of Acre (1190).
Region	Norfolk, Essex/Hertfordshire
Sources	W. Farrer, *Honors and Knights' Fees*, 3 Vols (Manchester, 1923–5), Vol. 3, pp. 21–2; PR2 RI (1190), p. 110.

Robert Mortimer

Alias/es	Robert de Mortimer
Notes	On crusade to Jerusalem (1190).

Region	Norfolk, Lincolnshire, and Normandy
Sources	PR2 RI (1190), p. 110, 4 RI (1192), p. 194; *Magni Rotuli Normanniae*, Vol. 1, ed. T. Stapleton (London, 1840), p. 67.

Vivian

Alias/es	Uncle of Baldwin of l'Angevin
Notes	Jury held to determine his property after he died on the Third Crusade.
Region	Pedwardine (Lincolnshire)
Sources	*CRR*, Vol. 1, p. 133.

Robert of Cokefield

Title/s	Warden of St Edmund's Abbey
Alias/es	Robert de Cokefield
Notes	Died on the Third Crusade (1191).
Orders	St Edmund's Abbey
Region	Suffolk
Sources	*CRR*, Vol. 1, p. 133.

William Lovel

Title/s	Lord of Dorking
Alias/es	William Lovell, Guillaume Louvel d'Ivry
Notes	On crusade to Jerusalem (1191).
Region	Dorking (Norfolk)
Sources	PR3 RI (1191), p. 43.

Robert of Horningsheath

Alias/es	Roberto de Horningserda
Notes	On crusade to Jerusalem (1191).
Region	Norfolk and Suffolk
Sources	PR3 RI (1191), p. 43.

Richard of St Clare

Alias/es	Richard de St Clare
Notes	Holder of the manor of Dorking for which he paid 140 *marks* (c.1190). On crusade to Jerusalem (1191).
Region	Norfolk and Suffolk
Sources	PR3 RI (1191), p. 43.

Henry of Hastings

Alias/es	Henry de Hastings, Count Henry II of Eu
Notes	Hereditary steward of St Edmund's library. On crusade to Jerusalem (1191).
Ancestor/s	Godechilde of Tosny
Family	Roger of Tosny
Orders	Benedictines (St Edmund's)
Region	Norfolk and Suffolk
Sources	PR3 RI (1191), pp. 43, 44.

Richard of Clare

Title/s	Lord of Saham
Alias/es	Richard of Clare, Ricardus de Clare
Notes	Died at the siege of Acre (1190). Likely brother to Earl Richard of Clare.
Ancestor/s	Walter of Clare
Region	Saham, Norfolk
Sources	Landon, *Itinerary*, no. 146; PR3 RI (1191), p. 33; PR4 RI (1192), p. 179.

Stephen of Cameis

Alias/es	Stephen de Cameis
Notes	Son to Robert Fitz-Humphrey, constable of the earls of Clare. On crusade to Jerusalem (1191).
Region	Norfolk and Suffolk
Sources	PR3 RI (1191), p. 44.

John of Walton

Alias/es	John de Walton
Notes	On crusade to Jerusalem (1191).
Region	Norfolk and Suffolk
Sources	PR3 RI (1191), p. 44.

Robert Fitz-Herbert

Alias/es	Robert f. Herbert
Notes	On crusade to Jerusalem (1191).
Region	Norfolk and Suffolk
Sources	PR3 RI (1191), p. 44.

Warin Fitz-Simon

Alias/es	Warin filius Simon
Notes	On crusade to Jerusalem (1191).
Orders	Lazarus (Burton)
Region	Norfolk and Suffolk
Sources	PR3 RI (1191), p. 44.

William Fitz-Walter

Alias/es	William filius Walter
Notes	On crusade to Jerusalem (1191).
Region	Norfolk and Suffolk
Sources	PR3 RI (1191), p. 44.

Adam Fitz-Robert

Alias/es	Adam filius Roberti
Notes	On crusade to Jerusalem (1191).
Region	Norfolk and Suffolk
Sources	PR3 RI (1191), p. 44.

Adam of Talworth

Alias/es	Adam de Talworth, Talewurde
Notes	On crusade to Jerusalem (1191). Borrowed 150 *marks* on behalf of Queen Berengaria whilst in Rome (1193).
Region	Norfolk and Suffolk
Sources	PR3 RI (1191), p. 44; *Documents*, Vol. 1, ed. Round, pp. 94–5.

Lambert of Carleville

Alias/es	Lambert de Carleville
Notes	On crusade to Jerusalem (1191).
Region	Norfolk and Suffolk
Sources	·PR3 RI (1191), p. 44.

Manasser Aguillun

Alias/es	Manasser d'Aguillun
Notes	On crusade to Jerusalem (1191).
Region	Norfolk and Suffolk
Sources	PR3 RI (1191), p. 44.

Richard of Valhadun

Alias/es	Richard de Valhadun
Notes	On crusade to Jerusalem (1191).
Region	Norfolk and Suffolk
Sources	PR3 RI (1191), p. 44.

Peter of Clopton

Alias/es	Peter de Clopton
Notes	On crusade to Jerusalem (1191).
Region	Norfolk and Suffolk
Sources	PR3 RI (1191), p. 44.

Ralph of Berniers

Alias/es	Ralph de Berniers, Bernui
Notes	With Richard I in Lyon (1190). On crusade to Jerusalem (1191).
Region	Norfolk and Suffolk
Sources	'Dalon Charters', ed. Lewis, no. 6; PR3 RI (1191), p. 44.

Gilbert Malet

Alias/es	Gilbert Malez
Notes	On crusade to Jerusalem (1191).
Family	William Malet
Orders	Templars
Region	Somerset
Sources	'Templars in England', ed. Lees, p. 61; PR3 RI (1191), pp. 44, 141.

William Malet

Title/s	Lord of Curry Mallet
Alias/es	Willelmus Malez
Notes	On crusade to Jerusalem (1190). Arrived at the siege of Acre with Angevin contingent (1191). Survived to become sheriff of Dorset and Somerset under King John.
Family	Gilbert Malet
Region	Curry Mallet, Shepton Mallet (Somerset), Essex and Hertfordshire
Sources	*Itinerarium*, p. 218; PR 2 RI (1190), p. 110.

Geoffrey Malet

Notes	His grand-nephews attested that their lord had died in the Holy Land before King John lost Normandy (1214). Relationship with William Malet unknown.
Region	Lilley, Willian (Hertfordshire)
Sources	*CRR*, Vol. 16, no. 1758.

John le Poer

Alias/es	Joannes le Poh, Poher
Notes	Conceded his lands in Pirton to his son Drogo prior to travelling to the Holy Land.
Region	Pirton (Worcestershire)
Sources	College of Arms, Charter Collection Box 19, no. 688/2.

Ralph of Halstead

Alias/es	Ralph d'Alstead
Notes	On crusade to Jerusalem (1191).
Region	Suffolk
Sources	PR3 RI (1191), p. 44.

Roger of St Denis

Alias/es	Roger de St Denis
Notes	On crusade to Jerusalem (1191). Returned safely.
Region	Suffolk or Norfolk
Sources	PR3 RI (1191), p. 43; *Red Book*, ed. Hall, Vol. 1, p. 142, Vol. 2, pp. 476–7.

Baldwin of Rosei

Alias/es	Walkelinus de Rosei, Baldewinus
Notes	Set out on crusade.
Region	Hougton, Creale, Gooderstone (Norfolk)
Sources	PR6 RI (1194), p. 64, 7 RI (1195), p. 72.

John of St Helens

Alias/es	Johanni de Sancta Helena
Notes	On crusade to Jerusalem (1191).
Region	Berkshire
Sources	PR2 RI (1190), p. 35.

William of Docland

Alias/es	Willelmus de Doclanda
Notes	On crusade to Jerusalem (1191).
Region	Berkshire
Sources	PR2 RI (1190), p. 35.

Miles of Fretewell

Alias/es	Miles de Fretewell
Notes	On crusade to Jerusalem (1191).
Region	Berkshire
Sources	PR2 RI (1190), p. 35.

William Bockland

Alias/es	William Bocland
Notes	Took the Cross before September 1190 whilst sheriff of Cornwall. Candidate for Ambroise's 'chastelain de Cornewaille'. Died in the East sometime before 1200.
Region	Bedfordshire
Sources	*CRR*, Vol. 1, p. 219; PR2 RI (1190), p. 35, 3 RI (1191), p. 109.

Simon of Odell

Alias/es	Simon d'Odell
Notes	Died at the siege of Acre.
Region	Bedfordshire
Sources	PR4 RI (1192), p. 285.

Robert of Courtenay

Alias/es	Robert de Curtenay
Notes	On crusade to Jerusalem (1192).
Region	Sutton (Berkshire), Northamptonshire
Sources	PR3 RI (1191), p. 160, 162, 4 RI (1192), pp. 261, 276.

Roland Malet

Notes	On crusade to Jerusalem (1192).
Region	Berkshire
Sources	PR32 HII, p. 46, 33 HII, p. 191, 4 RI (1192), p. 316.

William Monk
Notes	On crusade to Jerusalem (1192).
Region	Northamptonshire (Basset)
Sources	PR3 RI (1192), p. 261.

William of Curzon
Alias/es	William de Curzon, de Curtun'
Notes	Listed as on crusade to Jerusalem (1191) but fined for not completing his vow (1192). Travelled to Jaffa (1192).
Region	Mildenhall (Cambridgeshire)
Sources	*Acta*, no. 220; PR3 RI (1192), p. 115, 4 RI (1192), p. 188.

Geoffrey of Capell
Alias/es	Geoffrey de Capell
Notes	Died on the Third Crusade.
Region	Cambridgeshire
Sources	*Fines, sive Pedes finium: sive Finales concordiae in Curia Domini regis: ab anno septimo regni regis Ricardi I. ad annum decimum sextum regis Johannis, A.D. 1195–A.D. 1214*, Vol. 1, ed. J. Hunter (London, 1831), p. 259.

William Brereton
Title/s	Lord of Malpas
Notes	Made a promise to build a church dedicated to St Oswald whilst on crusade.
Region	Brereton (Cheshire)
Sources	J.C. Sladden, *Beside the Bright Stream: The Background and History of St. Oswald's Church Lower Peover*, 4th edition (Altrincham, 1994).

John Fitz-Richard
Title/s	Constable of Chester
Alias/es	Johannes constabularius Cestrae
Notes	Constable of Cheshire. Died at the siege of Acre or whilst convalescing at Tyre (1190).
Ancestor/s	Henry I of Lacy
Family	Robert Fitz-Richard
Orders	Cistercians (Stanlaw, Fountains), Templars
Region	Chester (Cheshire)
Sources	*Annales Cestrienses*, p. 41; *Chronica*, Vol. 3, p. 88; *Gesta Regis*, Vol. 2, pp. 80, 148; 'Templars in England', ed. Lees, pp. 79–80; TNA, DL 41/1.

Hugh

Title/s	Cleric
Notes	On crusade to Jerusalem (1190).
Region	Essex or Hertfordshire
Sources	PR1 RI (1189), p. 20.

William Hellemus

Alias/es	Willelmi Hillem'
Notes	His wife received royal support whilst he was away on crusade (1193).
Region	Gloucester
Sources	PR4 RI (1192), p. 285.

Robert

Notes	His wife received royal support whilst he was away on crusade (1193).
Region	Gloucester
Sources	PR4 RI (1192), p. 285.

Adam of Bristol

Notes	Wounded at Messina and returned to England (1191).
Region	Gloucester
Sources	PR3 RI (1191), p. 92.

Geoffrey of Bois

Alias/es	Geoffrey du Bois, Giefroi del Bois, de Bosco, Godefri de Bosco, Galfridus de Bosco
Notes	Jaffa (1192). Relief of Jaffa (1192).
Region	Hampshire
Sources	Ambroise, line 11103; *Itinerarium*, p. 408; Landon, *Itinerary*, no. 366; PR34 HII, p. 176; PR2 RI (1190), p. 134.

Richard of Luvetot

Alias/es	Richard de Luvetot
Notes	On crusade to Jerusalem (1190).
Region	Huntington
Sources	PR 1 RI (1189), p. 190, 2 RI (1190), p. 117; *Red Book*, Vol. 1, ed. Hall, p. 75.

Gilbert Pecche

Notes	Mortgaged much of his property to finance his participation.
Ancestor/s	Pagan Peverel, William Peverel

Region	Lincolnshire
Sources	*Cartularium Monasterii de Rameseia*, 3 Vols., ed. W.H. Hart (London, 1884–93), Vol. 1, pp. 123–4.

Walter of Kyme

Alias/es	Walter de Kyma, Walterus de Kyma, Walter Fitz-Philip of Kime
Notes	Died at the siege of Acre, after the arrival of Ralph I of Coucy (1190).
Family	Philip of Kyme
Region	Lincolnshire
Sources	*Chronica*, Vol. 3, p. 89; *Gesta Regis*, Vol. 2, p. 149

Philip of Kyme

Alias/es	Philip de Kyma, Philippi de Kyma
Notes	Died at the siege of Acre (1190).
Family	Walter of Kyme
Orders	Templars (Lincolnshire)
Region	Lincolnshire
Sources	*Chronica*, Vol. 3, p. 89; *Gesta Regis*, Vol. 2, p. 149; 'Templars in England', ed. Lees, p. 84

Walter of Braitoft

Alias/es	Waltero de Braitoft
Notes	Richard I's *Familia Regis*.
Region	Surfleet (Lincolnshire)
Sources	BL ms. Harley. 742, f. 172v

Drogo Fitz-Randulf

Alias/es	Drogo filius Radulfi
Notes	Died at the siege of Acre (1191).
Region	Lincolnshire
Sources	*Gesta Regis*, Vol. 2, p. 150

Reginald of Suffield

Alias/es	Reginaldus de Suffeld
Notes	Died on Cyprus (1191).
Region	Lincolnshire
Sources	*Gesta Regis*, Vol. 2, p. 150

William Fitz-Osbert
Alias/es	Willelmus filius Osberti, William cum barba
Notes	Joint leader of the London contingent. Lisbon (1190). Silves (1190). Returned to England (*c.*1190).
Orders	St Nicholas of Acre
Region	London
Sources	*Chronica*, Vol. 3, pp. 42–3; *Gesta Regis*, Vol. 2, pp. 116–17; Wendover, pp. 185–6.

Geoffrey Goldsmith
Alias/es	Gaufridus Aurifaber
Notes	Joint leader of the London contingent. Lisbon (1190). Silves (1190).
Region	London
Sources	*Gesta Regis*, Vol. 2, pp. 116–17; Wendover, p. 185.

Augustine of London
Alias/es	Augustine de London, Augustinus de Londoniis
Notes	Captured on the Third Crusade (1192).
Region	London
Sources	*Itinerarium*, p. 403.

William Beard
Alias/es	Willelmus cum Barba
Notes	London contingent (1190).
Region	London
Sources	Wendover, p. 185.

Richard of Verley
Alias/es	Richard de Verli
Notes	On crusade to Jerusalem (1191).
Region	Essex and Hertfordshire
Sources	PR3 RI (1191), pp. 27–8.

Richard Bacon
Notes	On crusade to Jerusalem (1191).
Region	Essex and Hertfordshire
Sources	PR3 RI (1191), pp. 27–8; *Rotuli Littterarum Clausarum*, Vol. 1, 18b.

Robert of Creverquer

Alias/es	Robert de Crevecuer
Notes	Delayed departure until 1191. Travelled with his cook, a chaplain, and a retainer.
Region	Kent
Sources	PR3 RI (1191), p. 147, 4 RI (1192), p. 313, 5 RI (1193), p. 170.

Alfred of Tottenham

Alias/es	Amfrido
Notes	Robert of Creverquer's retainer.
Sources	PR3 RI (1191), p. 147, 4 RI (1192), p. 313, 5 RI (1193), p. 170.

Benjamin

Title/s	Chaplain
Notes	Robert of Creverquer's chaplain.
Sources	PR3 RI (1191), p. 147, 4 RI (1192), p. 313, 5 RI (1193), p. 170.

William Trussel

Notes	Went on Crusade after the manslaughter of his wife (1189).
Sources	*CRR*, Vol. 10, pp. 292–3.

Thomas Bardolph

Notes	Crusader of the honour of Peverel (1190). Died on return from the Holy Land (1194).
Orders	Benedictines (Holy Trinity, Caen)
Region	Northamptonshire, Hertfordshire, London (Peverel)
Sources	Delisle, *Henry II*, Vol. 2, no. 147; PR1 RI (1189), p. 159; PR2 RI (1190), p.110.

Alexander Arsic

Title/s	Lord of Cogges
Alias/es	Alixandre Arsis
Notes	Commanded between fifteen and twenty knights on crusade. Attack on Muslim caravan (1192).
Region	Cogges (Oxfordshire)
Sources	Ambroise, line 10457; *HGM*, lines 4919–22; *Itinerarium*, p. 389; PR2 RI (1190), p. 14.

Bernard II of St Valéry

Alias/es	Bernard II de St Valérie, Bernardus de Sancto Valerico junior, Valery, Valary
Notes	Arrived at the siege of Acre (1189). Died at the siege of Acre (1190).
Ancestor/s	Walter of St Valery, Reginald of St Valery
Region	Oxford
Sources	*Epistolae Cantuarienses*, p. 329; *Itinerarium*, p. 74; Landon, *Itinerary*, nos. 231–3.

Roger le Pole

Notes	Earl William of Salisbury's household. On crusade (1191). Died at the siege of Acre and his wife, Alice Brewer, claimed dower on lands at Plymptree and Depeworth.
Region	Plymptree (Devon), Depeworth (Dorset)
Sources	*Gesta Regis*, Vol. 2, p. 149; PR3 R1, p. 121; *CRR*, Vol. 1, p. 85.

Robert

Alias/es	father of William of Buckland
Notes	Jury held to determine his property after he died on the Third Crusade.
Region	Upcott (Devon)
Sources	*CRR*, Vol. 1, p. 219.

John II le Strange

Title/s	Lord of Ruyton
Notes	Crusaded with his neighbour, Robert Corbet (1191). Returned with a reliquary, until recently held by Rowley's House.
Orders	Augustinians (Haughmond)
Region	Ruyton (Shropshire)
Sources	Bodleian, ms. Ashmole 1120, fo. 174r.

Robert Corbet

Title/s	Lord of Caus
Notes	Richard I restored the forest of Tenefrestanes to him (1190). Crusaded with his neighbour, John le Strange (1191).
Ancestor/s	Thomas Corbet
Region	Caus (Shropshire)
Sources	Bodleian, ms. Ashmole 1120, fo. 174r.

William of Courcy

Alias/es	William de Courcy, William de Curci, Willelmum de Curci
Notes	Brother-in-law to Henry of Cornhill. Messina (1190).
Region	Somerset
Sources	*Chronica*, Vol. 3, p. 62; *Gesta Regis*, Vol. 2, p, 134; Landon, *Itinerary*, no. 33.

William Fitz-Peter

Notes	On crusade to Jerusalem with the king (1191).
Region	Staffordshire
Sources	PR3 RI (1191), p. 152.

William of Stanford

Alias/es	William de Stamford, Willelmo de Stanford'
Notes	On crusade to Jerusalem with the king (1191).
Region	Staffordshire
Sources	PR3 RI (1191), p. 152.

Robert III of Stafford

Alias/es	Robert de Stafford
Notes	On crusade to Jerusalem (1190).
Orders	Benedictines (Evesham), Cistercians (Bordesley), Templars
Region	Staffordshire
Sources	'Templars in England', ed. Lees, pp. 28, 86, 92.

Richard of Gulafre

Alias/es	Richard Gulaffre
Notes	His wife recovered 6s.3d. scutage on account of his being a crusader (1192).
Region	Sussex
Sources	PR3 RI (1191), p. 56.

Richard Fitz-William

Alias/es	Ricardo f. Willelmi
Notes	On crusade to Jerusalem (1192).
Region	Sussex
Sources	PR3 RI (1191), p. 58.

Robert of Icklesham

Alias/es	Roberti de Iclesham
Notes	Donated a virgate in Bernore to Battle Abbey whilst on crusade (1191).
Orders	Battle Abbey
Region	Barnholme (Sussex)
Sources	Lincoln's Inn, ms. Hale 87, Battle cartulary, fo. 69r.

Geoffrey Balliol

Alias/es	Galfrido de Baillol
Notes	Witnessed Robert of Icklesham's charter in Jaffa (1191).
Family	Hugh Balliol
Region	Barnholme (Sussex)
Sources	Lincoln's Inn, ms. Hale 87, Battle cartulary, fo. 69r.

Hugh Balliol

Alias/es	H. De Baillol
Notes	Witnessed Robert of Icklesham's charter in Jaffa (1191).
Family	Geoffrey Balliol
Region	Barnholme (Sussex)
Sources	Lincoln's Inn, ms. Hale 87, Battle cartulary, fo. 69r.

Ralph of Chall

Alias/es	Ralph de Chall
Notes	Demised two bovates of land to the Premonstratensians to fund his journey to the Holy Land.
Orders	Premonstratensians (Easby)
Region	Caperby (Yorkshire)
Sources	*EYC*, Vol. 5, no. 215.

William Fitz-Aldelin

Title/s	Sheriff of Cumberland and castellan of Carlisle castle
Alias/es	Willelmus filius Aldlini, seneschaldus domini regis
Notes	Sold his land in Went and five bovates in Thorpe to fund his journey. Survived the crusade to witness a charter by Eleanor of Aquitaine (1194).
Region	Thorpe (Yorkshire)
Sources	*EYC*, Vol. 3, no. 1641, TNA C 52/6, *carte antique* roll 6, m. 1d, no. 14.

Fulk of Rufford

Alias/es — Fulk de Rufford, Fulco de Ruhford
Notes — Grant to St Peter's hospital York of 12*d.* prior to his journey to Jerusalem (1190).
Orders — St Peter's hospital, York
Region — Yorkshire
Sources — *EYC*, Vol. 1, no. 556.

Ralph of Tilly

Title/s — Constable to archbishop of York
Alias/es — Ralph de Tilly, Radulfus de Tilly
Notes — Siege of Acre (1190). Participated on an assault on the city walls with Humphrey of Veilly, Robert of Lanlande, and Roger of Glanville (1190).
Orders — York Cathedral, Cistercians (Hampole)
Region — Yorkshire
Sources — *Chronica*, Vol. 3, p. 73; *Gesta Regis*, Vol. 1, p. 65, Vol. 2, p. 144.

John of Morwic

Title/s — Canon of York
Alias/es — Johannes de Morwic canonicus Eboracensis
Notes — Died at the siege of Acre (1190).
Orders — York Cathedral
Region — Pickwell, Leesthorpe (Yorkshire)
Sources — *Gesta Regis*, Vol. 2, p. 148.

Robert Scrop

Alias/es — Robertus Scrop de Bartun, Escrop
Notes — Died at the siege of Acre (1190).
Family — Walter Scrop
Region — Barton, Flotmanby (Yorkshire)
Sources — *Gesta Regis*, Vol. 2, p. 149.

Walter Scrop

Alias/es — Walterus Scrop
Notes — Died at the siege of Acre (1190).
Family — Robert Scrop
Sources — *Gesta Regis*, Vol. 2, p. 149.

Hugh Peitevin

Notes	Crusaded in place of his brother, Roger.
Region	Normanton (Yorkshire)
Sources	*EYC*, Vol. 3, no. 1573.

John of Penigeston

Alias/es	John of Penistone, Johannes de Pen
Notes	Gave notice he was about to depart for Jerusalem and appointed his brother as 'keeper of his land and heir'.
Orders	Augustinians (Nostell)
Region	Penistone (Yorkshire)
Sources	*EYC*, Vol. 3, no. 1787.

Walter le Nair

Alias/es	Walter le Noir
Notes	Sold two bovates of land to Swine Priory to fund his journey to the Holy Land.
Orders	Cistercians (Swine)
Region	Yorkshire
Sources	*EYC*, Vol. 3, no. 1409.

Osmund of Stuteville

Alias/es	Osmund de Stuteville, Osmundus de Stutevil, Stutevillenses
Notes	Arrived at the siege of Acre with Angevin contingent (1191). Died at Jaffa (1192).
Orders	Cistercians (Rievaulx)
Region	Yorkshire
Sources	*Gesta Regis*, Vol. 2, p. 150; Itinerarium, p. 218.

Robert Trussebot

Alias/es	Robertus Trossebot, Robert Trussebut
Notes	Siege of Acre (1191). Assisted Hubert Walter distribute food at Lent (1191). Contested the right to be King Richard's standard bearer.
Ancestor/s	Pagan and William Peverel
Family	Walter and Peter of Ross, Roger and Robert Harcourt
Orders	Cistercians (Rievaulx)
Region	Warter (Yorkshire) and Normandy
Sources	Ambroise, line 4433; *Chronica*, Vol. 3, p. 129; *Itinerarium*, pp. 93, 135; *Magni Rotuli Scaccarii Normanniae,* Vol. 2, p. lxxvi.

Roger Fitz-Richard Touche

Alias/es	Roger, son of Richard Touche, knight, Rogerus filius Ricardi Touche militis
Notes	Grant of Overton to his daughter, Matilda, on her marriage to Roger of Birkin on the day Roger joined King Richard on crusade.
Region	Overton (West Yorkshire)
Sources	*EYC*, Vol. 3, no. 1748.

John of Hessle

Alias/es	John de Hessle
Notes	Siege of Acre.
Orders	Augustinians (North Ferriby)
Region	North Ferriby (Yorkshire)
Sources	BL. ms. Add. C.51, fo. 5v.

Humphrey of Veilly

Alias/es	Humphrey de Veilly, Humfridus de Veili, Humfrey de Villeio
Notes	Siege of Acre (1190). Participated on an assault on the city walls with Robert of Tilly, Robert of Lanlande, and Roger of Glanville (1190).
Region	Yorkshire
Sources	*Chronica*, Vol. 3, p. 73; *Gesta Regis*, Vol. 2, p. 144; *EYC*, Vol. 3, no. 1585.

Ralph of Croxby

Title/s	Parson of Croxby
Alias/es	Radulfus persona de Croxebi
Notes	Died at the siege of Acre (1190).
Orders	Croxby church
Region	Croxby (Yorkshire)
Sources	*Gesta Regis*, Vol. 2, p. 149.

Richard of Lexby

Alias/es	Ricardus de Lexebi, Richard de Lesebi, Ric de Lesebi
Notes	Died at the siege of Acre (1190).
Family	Berenger of Lexby
Region	Yorkshire, Lincolnshire
Sources	*Gesta Regis*, Vol. 2, p. 149; PR1 RI (1189), p. 62.

Berenger of Lexby

Alias/es	Berenger de Lexebi
Notes	Died at the siege of Acre (1190).
Family	Richard of Lexby
Region	Yorkshire
Sources	*Gesta Regis*, Vol. 2, p. 149.

Joscelin of Neville

Alias/es	Jocelin de Nevill, Jollan
Notes	Sold his wife's dowry to fund his journey to the Holy Land.
Region	Yorkshire
Sources	Tyerman, *England and the Crusades*, p. 210; *Gesta Regis*, Vol. 2, p. 80.

Robert Venator of Pontefract

Alias/es	Robert le Venur de la Pumfrait, Robertus le Venur de la Pumfrait, Robert Hunter
Notes	Died at the siege of Acre (1190).
Region	Pontefract (Yorkshire)
Sources	*Gesta Regis*, Vol. 2, p. 149.

Walter of Ross

Alias/es	Walterus de Ros
Notes	Died at the siege of Acre, after the arrival of Ralph I of Coucy (1190).
Family	Peter of Ross, Richard of Camville
Region	Yorkshire
Sources	*Chronica*, Vol. 3, p. 89; *Gesta Regis*, Vol. 2, p. 149.

Peter of Ross

Title/s	Archdeacon of Carlisle
Alias/es	Petri de Ros
Notes	Died at the siege of Acre (1190).
Family	Walter of Ross, Richard of Camville
Region	Yorkshire
Sources	*Chronica*, Vol. 3, p. 89; *Gesta Regis*, Vol. 2, pp. 247–8.

Ralph of Aubigny

Alias/es	R. de Aubigny
Notes	Died on the Third Crusade.

Family	Peter and Walter of Ross
Orders	Premonstratensians (Orford), Templars
Region	Arundel (Yorkshire)
Sources	Farrer, *Honors*, Vol. 3, p. 142; *Gesta Regis*, Vol. 2, p. 149; Landon, *Itinerary*, no. 33.

William of Corneburg

Alias/es	William de Cornebruc, Cornborough
Notes	It has been argued that he is 'cil de Cornebu' who arrived in Acre with his brothers (1190). Skirmish (1191).
Region	Yorkshire
Sources	Ambroise, lines 4701–2; *Chronica*, Vol. 3, p. 133; *Facsimiles of Early Charters from Northamptonshire*, ed. F. Stenton (Northampton, 1930), p. 44; PR32 HII, p. 93, 33 HII, p. 87.

William of Tournebu

Title/s	Bishop of Coutances
Alias/es	Cornebu, Guillaume de Tournebu
Notes	Rouen (1190). Acre (1190).
Family	Thomas, Richard and John of Tournebu
Sources	Ambroise, line 4703; Landon, *Itinerary*, nos. 231–3, 235–9.

Roger le Abbé

Alias/es	Rogerus le Habe
Notes	Died at the siege of Acre (1190).
Sources	*Gesta Regis*, Vol. 2, p. 147.

Guy of Dancy

Alias/es	Guy de Dancy, Guido de Danci, Guy de Dane
Notes	Died at the siege of Acre (1190).
Sources	*Gesta Regis*, Vol. 2, p. 148.

Odo of Gunes

Alias/es	Odo de Gunesse, Odo de Gunes
Notes	Died at the siege of Acre (1190).
Sources	*Chronica*, Vol. 3, p. 88; *Gesta Regis*, Vol. 2, p. 148.

Reginald of Magny
Alias/es	Reginald de Magny, Reginaldus de Magni
Notes	Died at the siege of Acre (1190).
Sources	*Chronica*, Vol. 3, p. 89; *Gesta Regis*, Vol. 2, p. 148.

Adam of Leun
Alias/es	Adam de Leun, Adam de Loum
Notes	Died at the siege of Acre.
Sources	*Chronica*, Vol. 3, p. 89; *Gesta Regis*, Vol. 2, p. 149.

Henry of Brailey
Alias/es	Henricus de Braeley
Notes	Fell at Catania, Italy (1190).
Sources	*Gesta Regis*, Vol. 2, p. 149.

John of Malepalu
Alias/es	Johannes de Malepalu
Notes	Fell at Catania, Italy (1190).
Sources	*Gesta Regis*, Vol. 2, p. 149.

Ranulph of Tange
Alias/es	Ranulph de Tange, Ranulfus de Tange
Notes	Died at the siege of Acre (1190)
Sources	*Gesta Regis*, Vol. 2, p. 149.

John of Lambourne
Alias/es	Johannes de Lamburne
Notes	Died at the siege of Acre (1190).
Sources	*Chronica*, Vol. 3, p. 89; *Gesta Regis*, Vol. 2, p. 149.

Randulf of Albany
Alias/es	Randulfus de Aubeni
Notes	Died at the siege of Acre.
Sources	*Gesta Regis*, Vol. 2, p. 149.

Simon of Wale

Alias/es	Simon de Wale
Notes	Excused scutage for five of his knights that served with the army in Wales whilst he was on crusade. Drowned on the Third Crusade.
Region	Yorkshire?
Sources	*Gesta Regis*, Vol. 2, p. 149; PR4 RI (1192), pp. 200–1.

William Fitz-Philip

Alias/es	Willelmus filius Philippis Baro
Notes	Died at the siege of Acre (1191).
Sources	*Epistolae Cantuarienses*, pp. 134, 143; *Gesta Regis*, Vol. 2, p. 150

William Gifford

Alias/es	Willelmus Gifford'
Notes	Messina (1191).
Sources	Landon, *Itinerary*, nos. 356–7.

William of Bois

Alias/es	William du Bois, Willelmus etiam de Bosco Normannus
Notes	Cyprus (1191).
Region	Normandy
Sources	*Itinerarium*, p. 186.

Hugh of Brémontier

Alias/es	Hugh de Brémontier
Notes	Granted lands to his son before departing for the Holy Land. Died on crusade (before1192).
Sources	*The Thane Cartulary*, Vol. 1, ed. H.E. Salter (Oxford, 1947), no. 60.

Ralph of Rouvray

Alias/es	Ralph de Rouvray, Raols de Rovroi, Ralph de Roverei, Radulfum de Roverei
Notes	Killed in Sicily (1190).
Region	Normandy
Sources	Ambroise, line 765; *Itinerarium*, p. 162.

Gilbert Crespin of Tillières

Title/s	Lord of Tillières-sur-Avre
Alias/es	Gilbert, lord of Tillieres-sur-Avre, Gillebertus de Tillers, Gilbert de Trillieres, Gilbertus de Tileres
Notes	Siege of Acre with a 'strong force of warriors' (1190). Died at the siege of Acre.
Orders	Benedictines (Saint-Evroul)
Region	Tillières (Normandy)
Sources	BN, ms. latin 11055, fol. 28, no. 25; *Chronica*, Vol. 3, p. 89; *Itinerarium*, p. 93.

Ivo of Vipont

Title/s	Lord of Alston Moor
Alias/es	Ivo de Vipont, Ivo de Veteri Ponte, Vieuxpoint, Yves III de Courville
Notes	Siege of Acre (1190, 1191). Naval skirmish off Tyre, where he captured a Muslim galley. Yves III of Courville accompanied Count Louis of Chartres on crusade (1202).
Family	Robert of Vipont
Orders	Templars
Region	Courville
Sources	AN, S4977, no. 9; *Itinerarium*, pp. 93, 104; *RRRH*, no. 1307.

Robert of Vipont

Alias/es	Robertus de Veteri Ponte, Vieuxpoint, Robert de Courville
Notes	Siege of Acre (1191).
Family	Ivo of Vipont
Region	Courville
Sources	AN, S4977, no. 9; *RRRH*, no. 1307.

Robert Mordens

Alias/es	Robertus Mordenz
Notes	Siege of Acre (1191).
Family	Hubert Mordens
Sources	AN, S4977, no. 9; *RRRH*, no. 1307.

Hubert Mordens

Alias/es	Ubertus Mordenz
Notes	Siege of Acre (1191).
Family	Robert Mordens
Sources	AN, S4977, no. 9; *RRRH*, no. 1307.

William of Corsera
Alias/es   Willelmus de Corseraus
Notes   Siege of Acre (1191).
Sources   AN, S4977, no. 9; *RRRH*, no. 1307.

Ralph of la Rucoira
Alias/es   Radulfus de la Rucoira
Notes   Siege of Acre (1191).
Sources   AN, S4977, no. 9; *RRRH*, no. 1307.

Escorfauz
Alias/es   Escorfaz
Notes   Siege of Acre (1191).
Sources   AN, S4977, no. 9; *RRRH*, no. 1307.

'Episcopus de Foreste'
Alias/es   Episcopi de Foret
Notes   Siege of Acre (1191).
Sources   AN, S4977, no. 9; *RRRH*, no. 1307.

Gilbert of Malmain
Alias/es   Gilbert de Malmain, Gileberz Malesmains, Gilebertus Malemanus
Notes   Siege of Acre (1190). Jaffa (1192). Attack on Muslim caravan (1192).
Region   Normandy
Sources   Ambroise, line 10455; *Itinerarium*, p. 389; Landon, *Itinerary*, no. 366.

Richard of Vernon
Alias/es   Richard II de Vernon, Ricardus de Vernone
Notes   Siege of Acre (1191).
Family   His son, and William II and Ralph II of Tancarville
Orders   Cistercians (Bonport)
Region   Normandy
Sources   *Itinerarium*, p. 93.

Morel le Diveis

Alias/es	Moreheus Le Diueis
Notes	Jaffa (1192).
Region	Yllees (Normandy)
Sources	Landon, *Itinerary*, no. 366.

Thorel of Mesnil

Alias/es	Thorel de Menil
Notes	Died at the siege of Acre (1190).
Region	Mesnil (Calvados)
Sources	Ambroise, line 3486.

Ralph II of Fougères

Title/s	Lord of Fougères, Seneschal of Brittany
Alias/es	Ralph II de Fougères, seneschal of Brittany, Radulfus de Fulgeriis, Ralf, Randulphus
Notes	Angers (1190). Died at the siege of Acre (1191).
Ancestor/s	Geoffrey of Fougères
Family	William of Ferrers
Orders	Cistercians (Savigny)
Region	Brittany
Sources	Diss, Vol. 2, p. 64; *Gesta Regis*, Vol. 1, pp. 56–8; 2, p. 72; Landon, *Itinerary*, no. 215; Wendover, p. 191.

Maurice II of Craon

Alias/es	Constable of Ancenis, Maurice de Craon
Notes	Former member of Henry II's household. Dictated his will prior to departing on crusade.
Family	Guy of Craon, Jocelin III of Mayenne
Orders	Sempringham, Augustinians (La Roë)
Region	Brittany
Sources	*Gesta Regis*, Vol. 1, p. 71; *HGM*, lines 9304–409, *Chroniques Craonaises*, ed. B de la Jacopière (Le Mans, 1871), p. 596.

Guy of Craon

Alias/es	Guy de Craon
Notes	Surety for Richard I's treaty with Tancred (1190).
Family	Maurice of Craon

Region	Brittany
Sources	Landon, *Itinerary*, no. 342.

Jocelin III of Mayenne

Alias/es	Jokelin of Maine, Juhil III, Juques del Maine, Jocelin of Mayenne, Juhellus de Meduanà, Jokelinus Cenomannensis
Notes	Made a donation to the Cistercians of Fontaine-Daniel and the Benedictines of Mont-Saint-Michel on eve of departing on crusade (1189). Attack on Muslim caravan (1192). Survived to confirm his uncle's donation to Fontaine-Daniel (1195). Participated in the Abligensian crusade (1210).
Ancestor/s	Geoffrey III of Mayenne, Walter of Mayenne
Family	Roger of Tosny, Maurice II of Craon, Robert V of Sablé
Orders	Benedictines (Mont-Saint-Michel), Cistercians (Fontaine-Daniel, Montguyon)
Region	Maine
Sources	Ambroise, line 10448; *Cartulaire de l'abbaye cistercienne de Fontaine-Daniel*, ed. A.P.A. Grosse-Duperon and E. Gouvrion (Mayenne, 1896), no. 4, 7; *Cartulaire de Saint-Michel de l'Abbayette, prieuré de l'abbaye du Mont-Saint-Michel (997–1421)*, ed. P. de Farcy (Paris, 1894), no. 17; *Itinerarium*, p. 389.

Hugh III of Issoudun

Title/s	Lord of Issoudun
Alias/es	Odo III, Eudes
Notes	Confirmed the rights of the people of Issoudun prior to departing on crusade (1190). Siege of Acre (1190).
Ancestor/s	Geoffrey of Déols, Odo I of Burgundy
Family	Hugh III of Burgundy
Region	Issoudun
Sources	Diss, Vol. 2, p. 80; *HdB*, Vol. 3, no, 821; Wendover, p. 178.

William II

Title/s	Count of Châlons-sur-Saône
Alias/es	William II, count of Châlons-sur-Saône, cuens de Chaalons, comes de Chalunsis, comes de Scaloniis, comes Chalonensis
Notes	Ratified his donations to the Cistercians prior to departing on crusade (1189). Silves (1189). Siege of Acre (1190). Placed in joint command of Jaffa (1192).
Orders	Cistercians (Ferté)
Region	Châlons-sur-Saône
Sources	Ambroise, lines 3512, 7179; Diss, Vol. 2, p. 79; *HdB*, Vol.3, no. 799; *Itinerarium*, pp. 92, 289, 324; Wendover, p. 178.

Walter IV of Vienne

Title/s	Count of Salins, lord of Bourbon
Alias/es	Gaucher IV de Vienne
Notes	His wife divorced him for maltreatment on his return from crusade (1195).
Ancestor/s	Reginald II, count of Burgundy
Region	Vienne
Sources	Evergates, *Aristocracy*, pp. 117, 217, 343; *Gallia Christiana in provincias ecclesiasticas distributa*, Vol. 4 (Paris, 1725), no. 61.

Ferric of Vienne

Title/s	Lord of Gerbéviller and Ormes
Alias/es	Ferric de Vienne, Ferri, Ferricus de Viana, Ferry of Lorraine
Notes	Son of the Duke of Lorraine. Linked to Henry II and Countess Marie (1186–7). Commanded a crusader supply convoy (1191).
Ancestor/s	Henry III of Baden
Family	Hugh III of Burgundy, Henry IV of Baden
Orders	Premonstratensians (Sainte-Marie-aux-Bois)
Region	Gerbéviller and Ormes
Sources	Ambroise, lines 9920–47; H. d'Arbois de Jubainville, *Histoire des Ducs et des Comtes de Champagne, depuis le VIe s. jusqu'a la fin du XIe*, Vol. 3 (Paris, 1861), no. 153; *Itinerarium*, p. 373.

Hugh IX le Brun

Title/s	Count of La Marche
Alias/es	Hugon le Brun, Hugo Brunus, Hugh the Brown, Hugonis le Brun
Notes	Messina (1190). Arrived at the siege of Acre with Angevin contingent (1191). Jaffa (1192).
Ancestor/s	Hughs VI, VII, and VIII of Lusignan, Raymond of St Giles, Herbert and Geoffrey of Thouars
Family	Geoffrey of Lusignan, Geoffrey IV of Rancon, Ralph of Exoudun
Region	Poitou
Sources	Ambroise, lines 719, 4992; Diss, Vol. 2, p. 85; Devizes, p. 23; *Gesta Regis*, Vol. 2, pp. 128–9; *Chronica*, Vol. 3, p. 57; *Itinerarium*, pp. 161, 219, 227; Landon, *Itinerary*, nos. 342, 366; Wendover, p. 187.

Geoffrey of Lusignan

Title/s	Lord of Jaffa and Caesaria
Alias/es	Geoffrey de Lusignan, Jiefrei de Leuzengnan; Giefré de Luizeignan, Lenzeignan Jefreis, Guifridus de Lezinnan, Gaufridus de Lesinan, de Lexinant, de Luziniaco, Galfrido

Notes	Siege of Acre (1189). Commanded the rearguard at the Battle of Acre (1190). Participated in the St Martin offensive (1190). Battle of Acre (1189). Cyprus (1191). Jaffa (1192).
Ancestor/s	Hughs VI, VII, and VIII, and Guy of Lusignan, Raymond of St Giles, Herbert and Geoffrey of Thouars
Family	Hugh IX le Brun, Geoffrey IV of Rancon, Ralph of Exoudun (Eu)
Orders	Cistercians (Absie)
Region	Poitou
Sources	Ambroise, lines 2810–79, 3042, 4073, 4651, 6964; Chronica, Vol. 1, p. 274; Diss, Vol. 2, pp. 54, 70, 80; *Gesta Regis*, Vol. 2, pp. 95, 144, 166, 170, 184; *Itinerarium*, pp. 26, 60, 72, 119, 216, 235, 283, 307; Landon, *Itinerary*, nos. 365–6; Wendover, pp. 144–5.

Ralph of Exoudun

Title/s	Lord of Exoudun, count of Eu (1191)
Alias/es	Radulfum de Esselduno, Raoul I of Luisgnan, Ralph of Issoudun, Ysoldone
Notes	Tours (1190). Siege of Acre (1190). Hugh IX's brother.
Ancestor/s	Hughs VI, VII, and VIII, and Guy of Lusignan, Raymond of St Giles.
Family	Hugh IX le Brun, Geoffrey of Lusignnan, Geoffrey IV of Rancon.
Region	Issoudun (Poitou)
Sources	Diss, Vol. 2, p. 80; Landon, *Itinerary*, no. 306.

Joscelin of Lezay

Alias/es	Joscelinus de Munmorenc
Notes	Died at siege of Acre (1190). Cadet branch of the Lusignans
Ancestor/s	Hughs VI, VII and VIII.
Family	Hugh IX le Brun, Ralph of Exoudun
Region	Lezay (Poitou)
Sources	*Chronica*, Vol. 3, p. 89; Gesta *Regis*, Vol. 2, p. 149.

Ralph of Mauleon

Alias/es	Ralph de Mauleon, Raols de Maillion, Mallion, Rad de Mallion, Radulphus de Maloleone
Notes	Richard I's crusader household. Arrived at the siege of Acre with Angevin contingent (1191). Jaffa (1192). Relief of Jaffa (1191).
Ancestor/s	Herbert II, Geoffrey, and Guy of Thouars
Family	Hugh IX le Brun
Region	Thouars (Poitou)
Sources	Ambroise, lines 10965, 11378–620, 11497: *Itinerarium*, pp. 218, 405, 418; Landon, *Itinerary*, no. 366.

Bernard of Durfort

Alias/es	Bernard du Durfort
Notes	Survived the Third Crusade to make a donation to the Templars.
Region	Durfort
Sources	L. Macé, *Les comtes de Toulouse et leur entourage (XIIe-XIIIe siècles). Rivalités, alliances et jeux de pouvoir* (Toulouse, 1999), p. 274; Schenk, *Templar Families*, p. 233.

Geoffrey IV of Rancon

Title/s	Lord of Taillebourg
Alias/es	Geoffrey de Rancona, Gaufr' de Raboin, Gaufridus de Rancona
Notes	Messina (1190). Arrived at the siege of Acre with Angevin contingent (1191).
Ancestor/s	Geoffrey the Poitevin
Family	Hugh X le Brun and Geoffrey of Lusignan, Peter of Angoulême
Orders	Cistercians (Absie)
Region	Taillebourg
Sources	*Gesta Regis*, Vol. 1, pp. 46–7; *Itinerarium*, p. 218; Landon, *Itinerary*, no. 342.

Raymond II

Title/s	Viscount of Turenne
Alias/es	Vicecomes de Turonia, de Turoniae, vicecomes de Turena
Notes	Arrived at the siege of Acre (1189). Died at siege of Acre (1190).
Ancestor/s	Raymond I of Turenne
Family	Rotrou III and Geoffrey of Persche, Robert III and IV of Leicester
Orders	Cistercians (Dalon)
Region	Turenne
Sources	*Cartulaire de l'abbaye de Beaulieu (en Limousin)*, ed. M. Delouche (Paris, 1859), no. 194; *Chronica*, Vol. 3, p. 89; *Diss*, Vol. 2, p. 80; *Gesta Regis*, Vol. 2, p. 148; *Itinerarium*, p. 74; Wendover, p. 178.

Peter

Title/s	Viscount of Castillon
Notes	La Réole (1190). Died at the siege of Acre.
Ancestor/s	Peter of Castillon
Region	Gascony
Sources	*Gesta Regis*, Vol. 2, p. 149; Landon, *Itinerary*, no. 217.

Gaucerand of Aspet

Alias/es	Gaubert d'Aspremont, Gaucerand d'Aspet, Gaubertus de Monte Aspero
Notes	Marched with the Imperial army. Arrived at the siege of Acre. Made endowments to the Templars on his return from the Third Crusade.
Ancestor/s	Raymond Ato
Family	Arnold Raymond of Aspet
Orders	Cistercians (Bonnefont)
Region	Aspet
Sources	'Cartulaire des Templiers de Montsaunès', ed. C. Higounet, *Bulletin philologique et historique du comité des travaux historiques* (1957), no. 40; *Itinerarium*, p. 93.

Arnold Raymond of Aspet

Alias/es	Arnold Raymond d'Aspet
Notes	Most likely died on crusade.
Ancestor/s	Raymond Ato
Family	Gaucerand of Aspet
Region	Aspet
Sources	Schenk, *Templar Families*, p. 239.

Peter of Gascony

Alias/es	Pieres li Gascoinz, Petras de Gastonia
Notes	Siege of Darum (1192).
Region	Gascony
Sources	Ambroise, line 9283; *Itinerarium* p. 355.

William of Rochefoucauld

Title/s	Viscount of Châtel Herault
Alias/es	William de Rochefoucauld, viscount of Châtel Herault, vicecomes de Castello Heraldi, Castel Heraud, Catello Eraud
Notes	Died at the siege of Acre (1190).
Sources	*Chronica*, Vol. 3, p. 89; *Gesta Regis*, Vol. 2, p. 149; *Itinerarium*, p. 74; Wendover, p. 178.

John Rudd

Title/s	Castellan of Ystrad Meurig
Notes	Died on the Third Crusade.
Region	Deheubarth (Wales)
Sources	K. Hurlock, *Wales and the Crusades, c.1095–1291* (Cardiff, 2011), pp. 85, 102, 120, 153, 200.

Robert of Quincy

Title/s	Lord of Buckley (Northamptonshire)
Alias/es	Robert de Quency, Robert de Quincy, Robert de Quinci, Robertum de Quinci, Robertus de Quenci
Notes	Richard I's crusader household. Siege of Acre (1191). Envoy to Tyre (1191). Commander of force sent to aid Antioch by Richard I (1191).
Ancestor/s	Pagan Peverel, William Peverel
Family	Robert IV Fitz-Pernel
Region	East Lothian
Sources	Ambroise, line 5446; Chronica, Vol. 3, p. 125: *Gesta Regis*, Vol. 2, p. 187; *Itinerarium*, p. 242.

Osbert Olifard of Arbuthnott

Title/s	Sheriff of Mearns
Alias/es	Osbert Olifard of Arbuthnott
Notes	Took the Cross (1188).
Region	Arbuthnott
Sources	K. Hurlock, *Britain, Ireland and the Crusades, c.1000–1300* (New York, 2013), p. 71.

Robert Kent

Notes	Mortgaged his lands in Innerwick to Kelso Abbey to fund his journey to the Holy Land.
Orders	Tironensians (Kelso)
Region	Innerwick (East Lothian)
Sources	*Regesta Regum Scottorum*, Vol. 2, *Acts of William I*, ed. G.W.S. Barrow (Edinburgh, 1971), pp. 370, 373–4.

Robert Hunaud

Notes	Mortgaged his lands in Innerwick to Kelso Abbey to fund his journey to the Holy Land.
Orders	Tironensians (Kelso)
Region	Innerwick (East Lothian)
Sources	*Regesta Regum Scottorum*, Vol. 2, ed. Barrow, pp. 370, 373–4.

Ronald, son-in-law to Nicholas of Gôtentin

Notes	Mortgaged his lands in Innerwick to Kelso abbey to fund his journey to the Holy Land.
Orders	Tironensians (Kelso)

Region	Innerwick (East Lothian)
Sources	*Regesta Regum Scottorum*, Vol. 2, ed. Barrow, pp. 370, 373–4.

Aimery of Torel

Alias/es	Aimery Torel
Notes	Messina (1190).
Sources	Landon, *Itinerary*, no. 342.

Robert of Lanlande

Alias/es	Robert de Lanlande, Robertus de la Lande
Notes	Siege of Acre (1190). Participated in an assault on the city walls with Humphrey of Veilly, Ralph of Tilly, and Roger of Glanville (1190).
Sources	*Gesta Regis*, Vol. 2, p. 144.

Otto of la Fosse

Alias/es	Otto de la Fosse, Otho de Fossa
Notes	Arrived at the siege of Acre (1189).
Sources	*Itinerarium*, p. 74.

William Goeth

Alias/es	William Goeth, Willelmus de Goez
Notes	Arrived at the siege of Acre (1189).
Sources	*Itinerarium*, p. 74.

Louis of Assela

Alias/es	Louis d'Assela, Lodowicus de Arceles, Ludovicus de Assela
Notes	Arrived at the siege of Acre (1190). Died at the siege of Acre (1190).
Sources	*Chronica*, Vol. 3, p. 88; *Gesta Regis*, Vol. 2, p. 149; *Itinerarium*, p. 93.

Ferrand

Alias/es	Ferrand, Ferrandus (*miles*)
Notes	Siege of Acre (1189).
Sources	*Itinerarium*, p. 72.

Chotard of Loreora

Alias/es	Chotard de Loreora, Chotardus de Loreora
Notes	Arrived at the siege of Acre with Angevin contingent (1191).

Region	Poitiers?
Sources	*Itinerarium*, p. 218.

William of Borris

Alias/es	William de Borris, Guillames de Borriz, Willelmus de Borriz
Notes	Battle of Arsuf (1191).
Sources	Ambroise, line 6164; *Itineraium*, p. 261.

Osbert Waldin

Alias/es	Osbertus Waldinus
Notes	Taken captive at the siege of Jaffa (1192).
Sources	*Itinerarium*, p. 403.

Henry of St John

Alias/es	Henry de St John, Henricus de Sancto Johanne
Notes	Taken captive at the siege of Jaffa (1192).
Sources	*Itinerarium*, p. 403.

John I of Seningham

Alias/es	John de Seningham
Notes	On crusade to the Holy Land (1191).
Orders	Benedictines (Saint-Bertin)
Sources	*Cartulaire de l'Abbaye de Saint-Bertin*, ed. B.E.C. Guérard (Paris, 1841), no. 389.

Robert III of Sablé

Title/s	Master of the Templars
Alias/es	Robert de Sablé, Robert de Sabloil, de Sable, Sablul, Salburis
Notes	Former lord of Sablé, justiciar of Richard I's fleet (1190). Dartmouth (1190). Lisbon (1190). Marseille (1190). Messina (1190) Cyprus (1191). Siege of Acre (1191). Elected Master of the Templars during the course of the Third Crusade.
Ancestor/s	Robert of Nevers, Robert I of Burgundio
Family	William des Roches, Jocelin III of Mayenne
Orders	Premonstratensians (Le Perray-Neuf), Cistercians (Savigny)
Region	Sablé (Anjou)
Sources	Ambroise, line 883; *Gesta Regis*, Vol. 2, pp. 110, 115–16, 119. 120, 124; *Itinerarium*, p. 166; Landon, *Itinerary*, nos. 222–3, 270–2, 284, 358, 365; Wendover, pp. 181, 186.

Philip of Plessis

Alias/es	Phillipe de Plessis
Notes	Joined the Templars during the course of the Third Crusade or shortly afterwards.
Sources	BN ms. latin 15054; E. de Barthélemy, 'Obituarie de la Commanderie du Temple de Reims', *Mélanges historiques. Collection des Documents inédits*, Vol. 4 (Paris, 1882), pp. 313–32.

Robert Fitz-Richard

Title/s	Prior of the Hospitallers in England
Alias/es	Robert Thesaurarius, fratre Roberto filio Ricardi
Notes	Prior of the Hospitallers in England. Likely accompanied Garnier of Nablûs to the Holy Land. Acre (1192).
Ancestor/s	Henry I of Lacy
Family	John Fitz-Richard
Orders	Cistercians (Fountains), Hospitallers
Sources	G. Barraclough, *The Charters of the Anglo-Norman Earls of Chester, c.1071–1237* (Gloucester, 1988), no. 313.

Desiderius

Title/s	Bishop of Toulon
Alias/es	Episcopus Tolensis
Notes	Siege of Acre (1190).
Orders	Toulon cathedral
Sources	*Itinerarium*, p. 93.

Bishop of Thérouanne

Title/s	Bishop of Thérouanne
Alias/es	bishop of Therouanne, episcupus Mordrensis
Notes	Siege of Acre (1190).
Orders	Thérouanne Cathedral
Sources	*Itinerarium*, p. 93.

Hélie of Malemort

Title/s	Archbishop of Bordeaux
Alias/es	archbishop of Bordeaux, archiepiscopus Burdellis
Notes	Cyprus (1191).
Orders	Bordeaux cathedral
Sources	*Itinerarium*, p. 196.

Archbishop of Arles-le-Blanc

Title/s	Archbishop of Arles-le-Blanc
Alias/es	archbishop of Arles-le-Blanc, archiepiscopus de Arle la Blanche
Notes	Died at the siege of Acre (1190).
Orders	Arles-le-Blanc Cathedral
Sources	*Gesta Regis*, Vol. 2, p. 96.

Abbot of St Pierre de Lesterps

Title/s	Abbot of St Pierre de Lesterps
Alias/es	abbot of St Pierre de Lesterps, abbas Esterpensis
Notes	Siege of Acre (1190).
Orders	Augustinians (St Pierre de Lesterps)
Sources	*Itinerarium*, p. 93.

Abbot of Châlons

Title/s	Abbot of Châlons
Alias/es	abbot of Châlons, abbas de Scaloniis
Notes	Siege of Acre (1190).
Orders	Benedictines (St Peter of Châlons)
Sources	*Itinerarium*, p. 93.

Robert

Title/s	Deacon of Salford
Alias/es	Robert deacon of Salford, Roberto decano de Saldeford
Notes	Jaffa (1192).
Sources	*Acta*, no. 220.

William of Camville

Title/s	Archdeacon of Richmond
Alias/es	William de Camville, Archdeacon of Richmond
Notes	Drowned on the Third Crusade.
Family	Richard of Camville
Sources	*Gesta Regis*, Vol. 2, pp. 85, 149.

William

Title/s	Chaplain to dean of London
Alias/es	Gwilellmus, Willelmus

Orders	St Paul's Cathedral, London
Sources	Diss, Vol. 2, pp. 80–1; Wendover, pp. 178–9.

Vicar of Dartford

Title/s	Vicar of Dartford
Alias/es	vicar of Dartford
Notes	On crusade to Jerusalem (1189).
Sources	Tyerman, *England and the Crusades*, p. 74.

Robert of Wacelin

Title/s	Cleric
Alias/es	Robert de Wacelin, Robertus Wacelin clericus
Notes	Died at the siege of Acre (1191).
Sources	*Gesta Regis*, Vol. 2, p. 150.

Seguin Barrez

Alias/es	Seguins Barrez, Seguinus Barrez
Notes	Siege of Darum (1192).
Sources	Ambroise, line 9280; *Itinerarium*, p. 355.

Ospiard

Title/s	Squire (Segiun Barrez)
Alias/es	Espiard, Ospiardo
Notes	Siege of Darum (1192).
Sources	Ambroise, line 9281; *Itinerarium*, p. 355.

Took the Cross but did not travel to the Holy Land

Henry II of England

Title/s	King of England, duke of Normandy, Aquitaine, and Gascony, count of Anjou, Maine, Nantes, and Poitiers
Alias/es	Henry II Plantagenet, king of England, Henri, Henricus rex Angliae
Notes	Took the cross alongside King Philip II (1188). Died before departing (1189).
Ancestor/s	Fulk V of Anjou
Family	Richard I of England, Joanna of Sicily
Orders	Cistericans (Holmcultram), Benedictines (Reading), Augustinians, St Lazarus, Templars, Malmesbury

Sources	*Chronica*, Vol. 2, pp. 335; Diss, Vol. 2, pp. 55, 57–8, 62–4; *Gesta Regis*, Vol. 2, pp. 29–33, 40, 46, 49–50, 68–9; Gilbert of Mons, pp. 206; *Itinerarium*, pp. 26; Rigord, pp. 83, 92; Wendover, pp. 152, 157–9.

Eleanor of Aquitaine

Title/s	Queen of England, duchess of Acquitaine
Alias/es	Queen Eleanor, duchess of Aquitaine, Regina Alienor, mater regis Angliae
Notes	Escorted Berengaria of Navarre to Sicily (1191). Returned from Sicily (1191). It is uncertain if she took the cross.
Ancestor/s	Fulk V of Anjou
Family	Richard I of England, Joanna of Sicily, Berengaria of Navarre
Orders	Templars
Sources	'Dalon Charters', ed. Lewis, no. 5; Diss, Vol. 2, p. 81; Devizes, pp. 28, 58; *Gesta Regis*, Vol. 2, pp. 76, 98–100, 105–6, 157, 161, 235–7, 247–8; *Itinerarium*, pp. 142, 174–6; Landon, *Itinerary*, no. 268; Wendover, pp. 161.

Geoffrey Fitz-Peter

Alias/es	Geoffrey Fitz-Peter, Gaufrido filio Petri
Notes	Richard I's *Familia Regis*. Took the cross but remained as a member of Richard I's regency council.
Orders	Benedictines (Walden)
Region	Essex
Sources	Diss, Vol. 2, pp. 90–1; Devizes, p. 6; *Gesta Regis*, Vol. 2, pp. 213, 223, 225, 247–8; Landon, *Itinerary*, nos. 10–11, 27–32, 57–8, 63, 72–6, 86–9, 94–5, 104, 117, 131–2, 140–2a, 143, 147–52, 155–64, 167–71, 175–82, 184–94, 196–202, 256–8, 273; Wendover, pp. 203–4.

William Brewer

Alias/es	William Briwere, Willelmo Briwere, Briwerre, Bruer, Bruere, Briwere
Notes	Richard I's *Familia Regis*. Took the cross but remained as a member of Richard I's regency council.
Orders	Cistercians (Dunkeswell), Premonstratensians (Torre)
Region	Devon
Sources	Devizes, p. 6; Diss, Vol. 2, pp. 90–1; *Gesta Regis*, Vol. 2, pp. 101, 213, 225, 237, 247–8; Landon, *Itinerary*, nos. 298, 300–2, 351; Wendover, pp. 203–4.

Hugh Bardolf

Title/s	Royal Marshal (Richard I)
Alias/es	Hugone Bardulfi, Bardolph

Notes	Richard I's *Familia Regis*. Took the cross but remained as a member of Richard I's regency council. Royal Marshal.
Orders	Premonstratensians (Barlings)
Sources	Diss, Vol. 2, pp. 90–1; Devizes, p. 6; *Gesta Regis*, Vol. 2, pp. 224–5, 237, 247–8; Landon, *Itinerary*, nos. 1, 57, 63, 72–6, 86–9, 94–5, 104, 114, 117, 125, 130–2, 134, 148–53, 160, 168–81, 183, 186–202, 256–8, 260–2, 276, 306, 313, 315–8, 321–6; PR1 R1 (1189), pp. 15, 37, 44, 177; Wendover, pp. 202–3.

Walter of Coutances

Title/s	Archbishop of Rouen
Alias/es	Walter de Coustances, archbishop of Rouen, Walterus archiepiscopus Rothomagi, Walteri Rothomagensis archiepiscopi, Galterus, Walter of Rouen
Notes	Helped formulate Saladin Tithe at Le Mans (1188). Invested Richard I as Duke of Normandy. Geddington (1189). Rouen (1190). Vézelay (1190). Lyon-sur-Rhône (1190). Messina (1190). Laid aside the Cross to return to England at Richard I's behest (1191).
Orders	Rouen Cathedral
Region	Cornwall, Rouen
Sources	'Dalon Charters', ed. Lewis, no. 6; Devizes, pp. 22, 27–8, 32; Diss, Vol. 2, pp. 68, 90, 663; *Gesta Regis*, Vol. 2, pp. 30–2, 45–6, 68–70, 73, 79, 101, 128, 153, 158, 212–13, 223, 225–6, 237, 247–8; *Itinerarium*, pp. 170, 176; Landon, *Itinerary*, nos. 2–8, 10–11, 33–55, 61, 72–6, 104, 115, 129, 132, 135–6, 148–52, 164–5, 183, 186–93, 196–202, 208–10, 226–48, 251–9, 264–5, 284, 321–6, 328–30, 344, 347; Rigord, p. 83; Wendover, pp. 152, 164–6, 204.

Hugh of le Puiset

Title/s	Bishop of Durham
Alias/es	Hugonem de Pusat, Hugonem Dunelmensem episcopum, de Piuset, de Pusaz
Notes	Geddington (1189). Gave up the Cross (1189). Rouen (1190). Marseille (1190).
Ancestor/s	Hughs II and III of le Puiset
Sources	Devizes, pp. 6, 10; *Gesta Regis*, Vol. 2, pp. 44, 76–7, 79, 87, 90–1, 101, 105–6, 109–10, 209, 212, 225–6, 235–8, 247–50; Landon, *Itinerary*, nos. 2–8, 16–17, 20–2, 27–54, 61–106, 109–14, 116–20, 123–8, 130–7, 139–144, 146–204, 227–9, 231–3, 235–9, 241–7, 249, 256–8, 263, 265, 268, 274–6, 340; PR2 RI (1190), pp. 2, 18; PR3/4 RI (1191–2), pp. 61, 275; Wendover, p. 168.

Savaric Fitz-Geldwin

Title/s	Bishop of Bath
Alias/es	Savaric, archdeacon of Northampton, bishop of Bath, Sauaricus
Notes	Took the cross, but there is no evidence that he went on crusade.
Sources	Devizes, p. 29; Diss, Vol. 2, pp. 105–6; Landon, *Itinerary*, no. 353; Wendover, p. 106.

Hugh of Nonant

Title/s	Bishop of Coventry
Alias/es	Hugh de Nonant, bishop of Coventry, Hugo de Nonante, Hugo de Nunaunt, Hugo Cestrensis episcopus, Hugoni Cestrensi episcopi
Notes	Geddington (1189). Rouen (1190). Tours (1190). Montrichard (1190). Took the cross but did not go on crusade.
Sources	Diss, Vol. 2, p. 111; Devizes, p. 8; *Gesta Regis*, Vol. 2, pp. 30–2, 68–70, 75, 105–6, 215–20, 223; Landon, *Itinerary*, nos. 10–11, 15–22, 34–54, 58, 63–67, 97–101, 126–7, 131–2, 135–7, 139, 148–54, 161–5, 168–81, 186, 194, 196–205, 227–9, 231–9, 246, 249, 263, 265, 268, 274–6, 298, 300–2, 306, 308, 313.

John of Oxford

Title/s	Bishop of Norwich
Alias/es	Iohannes, Johanne Norwicensi epsicopo
Notes	Geddington (1189). Took the cross but was robbed en route to the Holy Land and given leave by the pope to return home.
Sources	Devizes, pp. 10–11; *Gesta Regis*, Vol. 2, pp. 79, 105–6, 115; Landon, *Itinerary*, nos. 2–5, 9, 20–2, 41–55, 61, 114, 125, 134, 140–3, 147, 155–7.

William of Mandeville

Title/s	Earl of Essex
Alias/es	William de Mandeville, earl of Essex, Willelmo de Mandavilla, Willelmus comes Albemarliae et Eessessae, de Magnavilla
Notes	Joined Philip of Alsace on earlier crusade (1177). Took the cross but died before departing (1189).
Ancestor/s	Geoffrey of Mandeville
Orders	Benedictines (Reading), Hospitallers, Sempringham
Region	Essex and Hertfordshire
Sources	Coggeshall, p. 26; Diss, Vol. 2, p. 73; *Gesta Regis*, Vol. 2, pp. 87, 92; Landon, *Itinerary*, nos. 2–11, 14–55, 57–67, 80–5, 91, 97–101, 105–6, 115, 118–19, 126; Wendover, p. 169.

Arnold II of Guines

Notes	Took the cross but did not go to the Holy Land.
Ancestor/s	Arnold II of Ardres, Baldwin of Ardres
Region	Guines
Sources	Lambert of Ardres, p. 177.

Gerald of Wales

Alias/es	Gerald of Barri
Notes	Took the cross but did not go to the Holy Land. Chronicler.

Region	Wales
Sources	Angevin chronicler.

Rhys ap Gruffydd

Title/s	Prince of Deheubarth
Alias/es	Rhys ap Gruffydd
Notes	Took the cross (1188).
Region	Wales
Sources	Gerald of Wales, Vol. 4, p. 179; *Gesta Regis*, Vol. 2, pp. 87, 97.

Appendix 2

King Richard I's Household, 1189–92

Abbreviation	Category*
	Full name
Title/s	Title/s, appointments
Notes	Activities relating to the Third Crusade
Sources	Sources relating to information listed in the entry

*Where no information is available categories have been omitted to save space.

Royal Household

    William of Longchamp

Title/s   Royal chancellor, regency council, royal justiciar, papal legate, bishop of Ely, castellan of Cambridge castle

Notes   Richard I's chancellor when count of Poitou, made chancellor of England (1189). Great Council at Pipewell (1189). Papal legate (1190). Related to Stephen, Osbert, and Henry of Longchamp.

Sources   Devizes, pp. 4, 7, 13; Diss, Vol. 2, pp. 96, 100–1; *Gesta Regis*, Vol. 2, pp. 35, 105–6, 108, 207, 210–15, 225, 239–40, 243–4; *Itinerarium*, pp. 145, 333; Landon, *Itinerary*, nos. 1–3, 5–12, 15–16, 19–22 etc.; PR2 RI (1190), p. 26; Wendover, pp. 167, 172, 175, 194.

    Walter of Coutances

Title/s   Archbishop of Rouen, regency council

Notes   Brother to Roger Fitz-Reinfrid and uncle to Gilbert Fitz-Reinfrid. Former member of Young Henry's household. Helped formulate Saladin Tithe at Le Mans (1188). Invested Richard I as Duke of Normandy. Geddington (1189). Rouen (1190). Vézelay (1190). Lyon-sur-Rhône (1190). Messina (1190). Laid aside his crusading vow to return to England at Richard I's behest (1191).

Sources   A.W. Lewis, 'Six Charters of Henry II and his Family for the Monastery of Dalon', *EHR*, 110 (1995), no. 6; Devizes, pp. 22, 27–8, 32; Diss, Vol. 2, pp. 68, 90, 663; *Gesta Regis*, Vol. 2, pp. 30–2, 45–6, 68–70, 73, 79, 101, 128, 153, 158, 212–13, 223, 225–6, 237, 247–8; *Itinerarium*, pp. 170, 176; Landon, *Itinerary*, nos. 2–8, 10–11, 33–55, 61, 72–6, 104, 115, 129, 132, 135–6, 148–52, 164–5, 183, 186–93, 196–202, 208–10, 226–48, 251–9, 264–5, 284, 321–6, 328–30, 344, 347; Rigord, p. 83; *RHF*, XXIII, pp. 359, 362; Wendover, pp. 152, 164–6, 204.

John of Alençon

Title/s   Vice chancellor, archdeacon of Lisieux

Notes   Vézelay (1190). Arrived in Holy Land with news of the grave situation in England.

Sources   Ambroise, line 9414; *Itinerarium*, pp. 358; Landon, *Itinerary*, nos. 6–8, 147, 156, 207–10, 214–16, 219–20, 217, 219–20, 222–3, 225–34, 236–8, 263, 268, 272–8, 283–4, 286, 288–90, 292, 295, 298–304, 306, 308, 310, 312–18, 321, 324, 326, 328–9, 331.

Roger of Malchiel

Title/s   Vice chancellor, keeper of the Great Seal

Notes   Member of Henry II's household. Messina (1190). Drowned off Cyprus (1191).

Sources   *Gesta Regis*, Vol. 2, p. 162; *Itinerarium*, p. 184; Landon, *Itinerary*, nos. 292, 344, 346–7, 354, 356–7.

Amaury the Dispenser

Title/s   Royal dispenser

Notes   Member of Henry II's household as sheriff of Rutland. Dispenser through the serjeanty tenure of Great Rollright. Inherited lands at King's Worthy (Hampshire) and Stanley Regis (Gloucester) on the death of his brother Walter, Henry II's usher

Sources   Landon, *Itinerary*, no. 189–93; J.H. Round, *The King's Serjeants and Officers of State* (London, 1911), pp. 187–96.

Thurstan

Title/s   Royal butler

Notes   Holder of the butler-serjeanty of Cropwell (Nottinghamshire). Brother to Amaury the dispenser.

Sources   Round, *The King's Serjeants*, pp. 187–96.

Miles the Almoner

Title/s   Royal almoner

Notes   Marseille (1190).

Sources   Landon, *Itinerary*, nos. 6–8, 214, 216, 276, 286–7, 290, 338.

Philip of Poitiers

Title/s   Royal treasury clerk

Notes   Richard I's clerk when count of Poitou. Jaffa (1192). Accompanied Richard I back from the Holy Land.

Sources   Coggeshall, p. 54; Landon, *Itinerary*, no. 366; R.V. Turner, 'Richard Lionheart and English Episcopal Elections', *Albion*, 29 (1997), p. 9; Wendover, p. 218.

John of Walton
Title/s	Royal treasury clerk
Notes	Treasury clerk (1191). On crusade to Jerusalem as tenant of earl of Clare.
Sources	PR3 RI (1191), p. 44.

William of Sainte-Mère-Église
Title/s	Royal clerk of the chambers, dean of St Martin le Grand, London
Notes	Member of Henry II's household. Vézelay (1190). Jaffa (1192).
Sources	*Acta*, no. 220; *Chronica*, Vol. 2, p. 85; Landon, *Itinerary*, nos. 6–8, 27–32, 128, 195, 225–6, 246, 256–8, 268, 292, 299, 313–18, 321–6;

William of la Mare
Title/s	Royal clerk to the Exchequer
Notes	Arrived at the siege of Acre with Angevin contingent (1191).
Sources	Ambroise, p. 53, n. 127; *Itinerarium*, p. 217.

Randulf
Title/s	Royal clerk
Notes	Died on the Third Crusade.
Sources	*Gesta Regis*, Vol. 2, p. 149.

Roger of Howden
Title/s	Royal clerk
Notes	Member of Henry II's household. Marseille (1190). Departed the Holy Land with Philip II (1191).
Sources	Author: *Chronica*; *Gesta Regis*; J. Gillingham, 'Roger of Howden on Crusade', *Medieval Historical Writing in the Christian and Islamic Worlds*, ed. D.O. Morgan (London, 1983), pp. 60–75.

Roger of St Edmund
Title/s	Royal clerk
Notes	Received charter for the soke of Lothingland for the duration of the crusade (1190). Marseille (1190).
Sources	Landon, *Itinerary*, no. 336.

Damien
Title/s	Royal clerk
Notes	Received royal charter in Speyer (1194).
Sources	Landon, *Itinerary*, no. 388.

Anselm

Title/s	Royal chaplain
Notes	Captured alongside Richard I whilst returning from the Holy Land. Eyewitness for Ralph of Coggeshall's entries on the Third Crusade.
Sources	Coggeshall, p. 54; Wendover, p. 218.

Nicholas

Title/s	Royal chaplain
Notes	Cyprus (1191).
Sources	*Gesta Regis*, Vol. 2, p. 167; Landon, *Itinerary*, no. 276.

Ralph

Title/s	Royal chaplain
Notes	Died on the Third Crusade.
Sources	*Gesta Regis*, Vol. 2, p. 149; Landon, *Itinerary*, no. 286.

Richard

Title/s	Royal chaplain
Sources	Landon, *Itinerary*, no. 57.

Segwin

Title/s	Royal chaplain
Sources	Landon, *Itinerary*, no. 286.

William of Poitiers

Title/s	Royal chaplain
Notes	Sent as messenger to Richard I in the Holy Land (1192).
Sources	Ambroise, line 9532; *Itinerarium*, pp. 361; Landon, *Itinerary*, no. 219.

Warin II Fitz-Gerald

Title/s	Baron of the Exchequer, royal chamberlain
Notes	Messina (1190). Arrived at the siege of Acre with Angevin contingent (1191). Led his company at siege of Acre (1191). Skirmish near Ramla (1192). Jaffa (1192).
Sources	Ambroise, lines 4725, 7496; *Itinerarium*, pp. 217, 300; Landon, *Itinerary*, nos. 131, 175–81, 183–93, 342, 366; N. Vincent, 'Warin and Henry Fitz Gerald, the King's Chamberlains: the Origins of the FitzGeralds Revisited', *ANS* 21 (1999), 233–60.

William of Mandeville

Title/s   Earl of Essex, justiciar of England

Notes   Member of Henry II's household. Joined Philip of Alsace on earlier crusade (1177). Took the cross but died in Rouen before departing (1189).

Sources   Coggeshall, p. 26; Diss, Vol. 2, p. 73; *Gesta Regis*, Vol. 2, pp. 87, 92; Landon, *Itinerary*, nos. 2–11, 14–55, 57–67, 80–5, 91, 97–101, 105–6, 115, 118–19, 126; Wendover, p. 169.

Hugh of Puiset

Title/s   Bishop of Durham, justiciar of the North, castellan of Pickering, Windsor, and Newcastle-upon-Tyne castles

Notes   Geddington (1189). Gave up the Cross (1189). Rouen (1190). Marseille (1190).

Sources   Devizes, pp. 6, 10; *Gesta Regis*, Vol. 2, pp. 44, 76–7, 79, 87, 90–1, 101, 105–6, 109–10, 209, 212, 225–6, 235–8, 247–50; Landon, *Itinerary*, nos. 2–8, 16–17, 20–2, 27–54, 61–106, 109–14, 116–20, 123–8, 130–7, 139–144, 146–204, 227–9, 231–3, 235–9, 241–7, 249, 256–8, 263, 265, 268, 274–6, 340; PR2 RI (1190), pp. 2, 18; PR3/4 RI (1191–2), pp. 61, 275; Wendover, p. 168.

Robert IV Fitz-Pernel of Breteuil

Title/s   Earl of Leicester, Lord High Steward (February 1191–)

Notes   Richard I's lord high steward. Belted earl of Leicester by Richard I at Messina (1191). Siege of Acre (1191). Arrived at the siege of Acre with Angevin contingent (1191). Jaffa (1192). Skirmish near Ramla (1192). Siege of Darum (1192). Attack on Muslim caravan (1192). Relief of Jaffa (1192).

Sources   *Acta*, no. 220; Ambroise, lines 4711, 4988, 5415, 6160, 7274, 7470, 9292, 10040, 10454, 10960, 11378–620, 11491; *Gesta Regis*, Vol. 2, pp. 156; *Itinerarium*, pp. 217, 227, 242, 261, 269, 292–3, 300, 355, 375–6, 389, 405, 415, 418; Landon, *Itinerary*, nos. 24, 366.

William Marshal

Title/s   Appares to the Regency Council, lord of Strigoil, High Marshal, sheriff of Gloucestershire, castellan of Gloucester castle

Notes   Former member of Young Henry's household. Member of Henry II's household. Brother to John and Henry Marshal. Received heiress of Strigoil from Richard I (1189). Carried Richard I's sceptre at coronation (1189). Founded religious foundation of Augustinian canons at Cartmel, Lancashire (1189). Vézelay (1190). Marseille (1190). Possibly brought news of problems in England to Richard, Messina (1191).

Sources   Diss, Vol. 2, pp. 90–1; *Gesta Regis*, Vol. 2, pp. 45–6, 73, 80–1, 109, 158, 223, 225, 237, 247–8; Landon, *Itinerary*, nos. 2–8, 10–11, 15, 214, 216, 276, 286–7, 290, 338; PR2 RI (1190), p. 58; Wendover, pp. 170, 203–4.

Geoffrey Fitz-Peter

Title/s	Appares to the Regency Council, castellan of Hertford castle
Notes	Member of Henry II's household. Took the Cross but remained in England as a member of Richard I's regency council.
Sources	Diss, Vol. 2, pp. 90–1; Devizes, p. 6; *Gesta Regis*, Vol. 2, pp. 101, 213, 223, 225, 237, 247–8; Landon, *Itinerary*, nos. 10–11, 27–32, 57–8, 63, 72–6, 86–9, 94–5, 104, 117, 131–2, 140–4, 147–53, 155–64, 166–71, 175–8, 180–2, 184–202, 256–8, 273, 347, 351; PR3/4 RI (1191–2), p. 24; Wendover, pp. 203–4.

William Brewer

Title/s	Appares to the Regency Council, forester of Bere, castellan of Southampton
Notes	Member of Henry II's household. Took the Cross but remained in England as a member of Richard I's regency council. Made sheriff of Oxford by William of Longchamp (1190).
Sources	Devizes, p. 6; Diss, Vol. 2, pp. 90–1; *Gesta Regis*, Vol. 2, pp. 101, 213, 223, 225, 237, 247–8; Landon, *Itinerary*, nos. 298, 300–2, 351; PR3/4 RI (1191–2), p. 92.

Hugh Bardolf

Title/s	Appares to the Regency Council, royal marshal, castellan of Kenilworth, Montsorrel, Newcastle-under-Lyme, and Tamworth
Notes	Member of Henry II's household. Took the Cross but remained in England as a member of Richard I's regency council. Made sheriff of Staffordshire by William of Longchamp (1190).
Sources	Devizes, p. 6; *Gesta Regis*, Vol. 2, pp. 101, 213, 203–4, 223–5, 237, 247–8; Landon, *Itinerary*, nos. 1, 57, 63, 72–6, 86–9, 94–5, 104, 114, 117, 125, 130–2, 134, 148–52, 160, 168–9, 172–81, 183, 186–202, 256–8, 260–2, 276, 306, 313, 315–18, 321–6, 342, 351; PR2 RI (1190), pp. 15, 37, 44.

Robert of Wheatfield

Title/s	Appares to the Regency Council
Notes	Member of Henry II's household as an itinerant justice since 1180. He died early in Richard I's reign.
Sources	Landon, *Itinerary*, nos. 18–19, 20–2, 27–40, 55, 61, 64, 86–9, 96–101, 113–14, 125, 134, 146, 153–4, 156–7, 161–4, 168–81, 184–6, 189–93, 195–204; PR26 HII (1180), p. 40–1, 109–11, 120–1; PR33 HII (1187), pp. 45, 114, 209; PR34 HII (1188), pp. 61, 115, 125, 132, 153, 206.

Ranulf of Glanville

Title/s	Joint-commander of Richard's vanguard
Notes	Member of Henry II's household. Took the Cross during Heraclius' visit (1185), renewed his vow (1188). Richard I's coronation (1189). Marseille (1190). Joint commander of Angevin advance guard, arriving at siege of Acre (1190) via Tyre. Died at the siege of Acre (1190). Nephew to Roger of Glanville.

Sources	Coggeshall, p. 23; Diss, Vol. 2, p. 84; Devizes, pp. 4–5, 19; *Gesta Regis*, Vol. 2, pp. 40, 80, 86, 90, 149; Landon, *Itinerary*, nos. 2–8, 18–19, 20–33, 41–54, 250, 263, 274; Wendover, p. 191.

William of Forz

Title/s	Count of Aumale, justiciar of Richard I's fleet
Notes	Justiciar of Richard I's fleet. Dartmouth (1190). Vézelay (1190). Marseille (1190). Messina (1190).
Sources	*Chronica*, Vol. 3, p. 306; *Gesta Regis*, Vol. 2, pp. 110 115–16, 124; Landon, *Itinerary*, nos. 153, 225, 236–9, 242–5, 290, 306, 308, 312, 315–18, 321–6; PR4 RI (1192), p. 308; Wendover, pp. 181, 186.

Richard of Camville

Title/s	Justiciar of Richard I's fleet
Notes	Member of Henry II's household. Justiciar of Richard I's fleet. Led the fleet from Dartmouth to Messina. Given joint custody of Cyprus. Died at the siege of Acre (1191). Brother to Gerard of Camville.
Sources	*Chronica*, Vol. 3, pp. 62, 111; *Gesta Regis*, Vol. 2, pp. 80, 110, 115–16, 119–20, 124, 134, 149, 167, 172; Landon, *Itinerary*, nos. 342, 347, 354, 356–7; PR4 RI (1192), p. 252; Wendover, pp. 181, 186.

Stephen of Longchamp

Title/s	Royal steward, joint-governor of Acre
Notes	Joint governor of Acre (1191). Siege of Darum (1192). Defence of Latin caravan (1192). Attack on Muslim caravan (1192). Related to William, Osbert, and Henry of Longchamp.
Sources	Ambroise, lines 9288, 10459; *Gesta Regis*, Vol. 2, p. 190; *Itinerarium*, pp. 355, 376, 389; Landon, *Itinerary*, no. 68–76, 80–5, 96–101, 126, 145, 156–60, 167, 175–83, 189–93, 195–202, 206–7, 219, 223, 227–9, 260–2, 292.

Roger of Préaux

Title/s	Royal steward
Notes	Lyon (1190). Messina (1191). Arrived at the siege of Acre with Angevin contingent (1191). Brother to William, Peter, and John of Préaux.
Sources	Acta, no. 220; *Itinerarium*, p. 217, 405; Landon, *Itinerary*, nos. 41, 68–76, 80–5, 96–101, 104, 114, 120, 125–6, 130, 134, 146, 153, 156–9, 160–3, 167, 175–81, 196–202, 206–7, 223, 227–9, 231–4, 236–9, 242–5, 260–2, 277–8, 283, 289, 329–30, 331, 347, 354, 356–7.

Richard of Le Hommet

Title/s	Royal steward, constable of Normandy
Notes	Member of Henry II's household. Received lands in Popeville and Warrville, Chinon (1190).
Sources	Landon, *Itinerary*, nos. 107, 206, 236–9, 288, 292, 295, 299, 312.

Stephen of Thornham

Title/s
: Royal marshal and treasurer

Notes
: Member of Henry II's household. Received royal charter for lands in Chinon (1190). Marseille (1190). Envoy to al-Adil (1191). Acre (1191). Jaffa (1192). Brother to Richard of Thornham. Escorted Queens Berengaria and Joanna back from the Holy Land. Companion of King Richard who borrowed 150 *marks* on behalf of Queen Berengaria whilst in Rome (1193).

Sources
: *Acta*, no. 220; Ambroise, line 8684; *Chronica*, Vol. 3, p. 228; *Itinerarium*, pp. 185 296, 299, 337; Landon, *Itinerary*, nos. 175–81, 207, 277–7B, 283, 288, 292, 301, 321–6, 336; PR1 RI (1189), p. 213.

John Marshal

Title/s
: Hereditary high marshal, escheator general, sheriff of Yorkshire, seneschal to Count John

Notes
: Member of Henry II's household. Carried King Richard's spurs at coronation (1189), which followed the ritual used for King Stephen's recrowning, but moved into John's affinity thereafter as seneschal. Received perpetual grants of Wexcombe and Bedwyn (Wiltshire), and Bosham (Sussex) from Richard I (1189).

Sources
: *Gesta Regis*, Vol. 2, pp. 81, 91, 223; Landon, *Itinerary*, nos. 16–17, 20–2, 27–32, 41, 63–4, 97–101, 104, 125, 130–2, 134, 137, 145–6, 148–54 etc.; PR2 RI (1190), p. 52.

Hugh

Title/s
: Royal marshal

Notes
: Captured at the siege of Acre (1191)

Sources
: Ambroise, line 5638; *Itinerarium*, p. 246.

Guy of Dive

Title/s
: Royal marshal

Notes
: Linked to William of Dive, a member of Young Henry's household.

Sources
: Landon, *Itinerary*, nos. 41, 68–71, 80–5, 97–101, 126, 167, 189–93, 227–9.

William Manduit

Title/s
: Lord of Hanslope, hereditary chamberlain of the exchequer, sheriff of Rutland, castellan of Rockingham castle

Sources
: Landon, *Itinerary*, no. 137; PR2 RI (1190), p. 36.

Geoffrey of Chauvigny

Title/s
: Royal chamberlain

Notes
: Richard's chamberlain when count of Poitou. Related to Andrew of Chauvigny.

Sources
: Landon, *Itinerary*, nos. 41, 68–71, 80, 97–101, 126, 167, 227–9; R.V. Turner, 'The Households of the Sons of Henry II', *La cour Plantagenêt, 1154–1204*, ed. M. Aurell (Poitiers, 2000), p. 58.

Ralph Fitz-Godfrey

Title/s	Royal chamberlain
Notes	Young Henry's chamberlain. Received loan from Henry of Cornhill for 60 *marks*, which was secured by William Marshal (1190). Messina (1190). Given charge of Emperor Isaac. Died in Tripoli (1191).
Sources	*Chronica*, Vol. 3, pp. 111, 116; *Gesta Regis*, Vol. 2, pp. 167–8, 173; Landon, *Itinerary*, nos. 41, 68–71, 80–5, 97–101, 125–6, 150–3, 159–60, 167, 196–202, 204, 207, 215, 227–9, 276, 283, 286, 288–9, 298, 300–2, 310–11, 313–18, 328, 336, 347.

Richard Rufus

Title/s	Royal chamberlain
Notes	Received royal charter for wood and houses at Devizes (1190).
Sources	Landon, *Itinerary*, no. 256.

Robert II of Newburgh

Title/s	Royal deputy chamberlain
Notes	Messina (1190). Arrived at the siege of Acre (1191). Skirmish near Ramla (1191)
Sources	Ambroise, lines 4705, 7520; *Chronica*, Vol. 3, p. 62; *Itinerarium*, pp. 301; Landon, *Itinerary*, no. 342.

Michael Belet

Title/s	Royal butler
Notes	Member of Henry II's household as sheriff of Worcestershire and then butler.
Sources	PR2 RI (1190), p. 102.

Philip

Title/s	Royal herald
Notes	Ascalon (1192).
Sources	Ambroise, line 9685; *Itinerarium*, pp. 365.

Alan Trenchemer

Title/s	Royal shipmaster
Notes	Member of Henry II's household. Off the coast of Acre (1191). Sailed Richard I back to England from Antwerp (1194).
Sources	Ambroise, lines 2137–94; *Chronica*, Vol. 3, p. 112; *Gesta Regis*, Vol. 2, pp. 168–9; *Itinerarium*, pp. 204–9; PR2 RI (1190), pp. 8–9, 131.

Alard Fleming

Notes	Member of Henry II's household. Recruiting tour of the Low Countries (1187).
Sources	*CDF*, pp. 481–505, no. 1361; TNA C 53/43; *CCR*, Vol. 1, p. 355.

Henry Teuton

Title/s   Royal standard bearer
Notes   Relief of Jaffa (1192).
Sources   Ambroise, line 11402; *Itinerarium*, p. 415.

Robert Trussebot

Title/s   Royal standard bearer
Notes   Siege of Acre (1191). Assisted Hubert Walter distribute food at Lent (1191). Contested the right to be King Richard's standard bearer.
Sources   Ambroise, line 4433; *Chronica*, Vol. 3, p. 129; *Itinerarium*, pp. 93, 135; *Magni Rotuli Scaccarii Normanniae*, Vol. 2, ed. T. Stapleton (London, 1844), p. lxxvi.

Peter of Préaux

Title/s   Royal standard bearer
Notes   Arrived at the siege of Acre with Angevin contingent (1191). Sent as envoy to Tyre (1191). Battle of Arsuf (1191). Relief of Jaffa as royal standard bearer (1192). Envoy to Jerusalem (1192). Member of first party of pilgrims to Jerusalem (1192). Brother to William, Roger, and John of Préaux.
Sources   Ambroise, lines 4723, 5416, 7544, 10969, 11102, 11872; *Itinerarium* pp. 217, 242, 302, 405, 408, 432; Landon, *Itinerary*, nos. 286, 331.

Vassal

Title/s   King's singer
Sources   Landon, *Itinerary*, no. 193.

Wigan of Cherbourg

Title/s   Royal usher
Notes   Member of Henry II's household as usher. As Henry the Young King's kitchen clerk, he kept a tally of tournament victories. Received a quarter knight's fee in Melksham (1189). Messina (1190).
Sources   *HGM*, line 3417; Landon, *Itinerary*, nos. 188, 342; PR28 HII (1182), p. 155.

Henry Turpin

Title/s   Royal arblaster
Notes   Member of Henry II's household as dispenser and chamberlain. Vézelay (1190), died prior to King Richard's arrival at Messina as his son journeyed there to petition for his inheritance.
Sources   Landon, *Itinerary*, no. 326.

John of Palerna

Title/s	Royal serjeant, holder of Pevensey gatehouse
Notes	Lyon (1190).
Sources	Landon, *Itinerary*, nos. 189, 333.

Robert of Warneford

Title/s	Royal serjeant
Notes	Received royal charter for lands at Esceleston and Alton (1189).
Sources	Landon, *Itinerary*, no. 159.

William of Gatesden

Title/s	Royal falconer
Sources	*The Cartulary of Newnham Priory*, ed. J. Golber (Bedford, 1963), no. 77; *Itinerarium*, p. 286.

John Fitz-Luke

Title/s	Bishop of Evreux
Notes	Helped formulate Saladin Tithe at Le Mans (1188). Geddington (1189). Rouen (1190). Lyon (1190). Messina (1190). Crowned Berengaria on Cyprus (1191). Siege of Acre (1191). Joint-commander of Jaffa (1192). Died in Jaffa (1192).
Sources	Ambroise, lines 1006, 4699, 7177; Devizes, p. 22; *Gesta Regis*, Vol. 2, pp. 30–2, 45–6, 75–6, 101, 128, 153, 167; *Itinerarium*, pp. 217, 289; Landon, *Itinerary*, nos. 10–11, 33, 72–6, 97–101, 115, 123, 211–12, 227–9, 231–4, 236–40, 329–30, 344, 347, 358.

Robert of Thornham

Title/s	Naval squadron commander, joint-governor of Cyprus
Notes	Cyprus (1191). Jaffa (1192). Brother to Stephen of Thornham.
Sources	*Acta*, no. 220; *Chronica*, Vol. 3, pp. 109, 116; *Gesta Regis*, Vol. 2, pp. 166–7, 172–3; *Itinerarium*, p. 176; PR2 RI (1191), p. 44; *The Red Book of the Exchequer*, ed. H. Hall (London, 1896), Vol. 1, pp. 79, 130, 164, 194; Vol. 2, p. 490.

Bertram III of Verdun

Title/s	Joint-governor of Acre
Notes	Member of Henry II's household. Marseille (1190). Messina (1191). Siege of Acre (1191). Joint-governor of Acre (1191). Died at Jaffa (1192).
Sources	Ambroise, line 4718; *Gesta Regis*, Vol. 2, pp. 149–50, 190; *Itinerarium*, p. 217; Landon, *Itinerary*, nos. 34–40, 143, 164, 172–4, 186–7, 227–9, 248, 335, 340, 347.

Payne of Rochefort

Title/s	Lord of Rochefort-sur-Loire. Seneschal of Anjou
Sources	Landon, *Itinerary*, nos. 223, 225, 242–5, 270–2, 299–304, 308.

Peter Bertin

Title/s	Seneschal of Poitou
Notes	Member of Henry II's household as *balli* of Benon and then seneschal of Poitou.
Sources	Landon, *Itinerary*, nos. 219–20, 286, 289–90; Turner, 'Households of the Sons', p. 58.

Helias of la Celle

Title/s	Seneschal of Gascony
Notes	Related to Geoffrey of la Celle.
Sources	Landon, *Itinerary*, nos. 216–18, 278.

William Fitz-Ralph

Title/s	Seneschal of Normandy
Notes	Member of Henry II's household. Met with King Philip II of France who demanded the return of his sister, Gisors, Aumale, and Eu (1192). Turned papal legates away from Normandy due to King Richard I's 'special privilege', excommunicated. Hugh le Puiset travelled to Paris and persuaded the legates to lift the interdict if the seneschal came to Rouen, but the seneschal refused, and the Pope lifted the interdict (1192).
Sources	*Gesta Regis*, Vol. 2, pp. 236, 246, 249–50; Landon, *Itinerary*, nos. 34–40, 207–12, 227–9, 231–4, 236–47, 249, 251–8, 292, 295, 298–9, 300–4, 306, 308, 310–12.

Alan of Dinan

Title/s	Lord of Becherel, seneschal of Brittany
Notes	Replaced Maurice II of Craon as seneschal (1189).
Sources	J.A. Everard, *Brittany and the Angevins: Province and Empire 1158–1203* (Cambridge, 2000), p. 149.

William of Le Hommet

Title/s	Lord of Brix and Beaumont, constable of Normandy
Notes	Inherited position from his father, Richard of Le Hommet, and received lands in Stamford, Ketton, Duddington, Princes Risborough, Sheringham, Whaddon, Nether Winchendon, Maisy, the hay of La Luthumière and Auppegard (1190).
Sources	Landon, *Itinerary*, nos. 1, 208–10, 222, 231–4, 236–9, 241–7, 251–5, 263, 271, 273, 275–77b, 284, 292, 298, 306, 308, 310–12.

William Rufus

Title/s	Sheriff of Bedfordshire/Buckinghamshire
Notes	Member of Henry II's household as sheriff of Sussex.
Sources	PR2 RI (1190), p. 116.

Robert of la Mare

Title/s	Lord of Mare, sheriff of Berkshire and Oxford
Notes	Member of Henry II's household as sheriff of Oxford. Fined 100 *marks* to retain his offices and gain Berkshire. On crusade to Jerusalem. Arrived at the siege of Acre with Angevin contingent (1191). Benevento (1192).
Sources	*Itinerarium*, p. 217; PR2 RI, pp. 103, 111; PR3 RI, p. 44.

William Muschet

Title/s	Sheriff of Cambridge/Huntington
Sources	R.R. Heiser, 'The Sheriffs of Richard I: Trends of Management as Seen in the Shrieval Appointments from 1189 to 1194', *HSJ*, 4 (1992), pp. 120–1.

William Fitz-Aldelin

Title/s	Sheriff of Cumberland and castellan of Carlisle castle
Notes	Held royal manor of Maplederwell. Sold his land in Went and five bovates in Thorpe to fund his journey. Survived the crusade to witness a charter by Eleanor of Aquitaine (1194).
Sources	*EYC*, Vol. 3, no. 1641; TNA C 52/6, *Carte antique* roll 6, m. 1d, no. 14; Landon, *Itinerary*, nos. 20–2, 41, 146, 164, 168–71, 175–82, 184–6, 187, 196–202, 268; PR2 RI (1190), p. 10.

Otto Fitz-William

Title/s	Sheriff of Essex/Hertfordshire
Notes	Member of Henry II's household as sheriff of Essex/Hertfordshire. Fined 100 *marks* to retain his office.
Sources	PR2 RI (1190), pp. 14, 91.

Oger Fitz-Oger

Title/s	Sheriff of Hampshire
Notes	Member of Henry II's household as sheriff of Bedfordshire/Buckinghamshire.
Sources	PR2 RI (1190), p. 138.

Henry of Longchamp

Title/s	Sheriff of Herefordshire (1190)
Notes	Sent to York by Richard I after the massacre of the Jewish community (1190). Related to William, Osbert, and Stephen of Longchamp.

Sources	Landon, *Itinerary*, nos. 124, 130–3, 135–6, 153, 161–3, 175–82, 196–202, 226; PR2 RI (1190), p. 8.

Henry of Cornhill

Title/s	Sheriff of Kent and Surrey, Warden of the Mint (1191)
Notes	Member of Henry II's household as sheriff of Surrey. Taken into Richard's service (1189) and awarded lands in East Horndon. Fined 100 *marks* for the shrievalty of Kent. Brother to Reginald of Cornhill.
Sources	*Acta*, no. 331; Landon, *Itinerary*, nos. 91, 147, 175–6, 177–82, 337; PR2 RI (1190), pp. 152, 155.

Gerard of Camville

Title/s	Sheriff of Lincolnshire, castellan of Lincoln castle
Notes	Shifted allegiance to Prince John (1191). Brother to Richard of Camville.
Sources	*Gesta Regis*, Vol. 2, pp. 80, 207, 223; Landon, *Itinerary*, no. 182, 260–2; PR2 RI (1190), pp. 84, 89.

William Fitz-Hervey

Title/s	Sheriff of Norfolk/Suffolk
Notes	Member of Henry II's household as sheriff of Norfolk/Suffolk.
Sources	PR2 RI (1190), p. 49.

Richard Engaigne

Title/s	Lord of Bulwick, sheriff of Northamptonshire
Notes	Engaigne fined 300 *marks* to hold the shrievalty for three years (1189).
Sources	PR2 RI (1190), p. 29; PR2 RI, p. 156.

William of Stuteville

Title/s	Sheriff of Northumberland
Notes	Hired two fifty-man ships to Richard I for his crusading fleet (1189). Replaced Hugh of le Puiset in Northumberland (1190).
Sources	PR2 RI (1190), pp. 8–9.

William Fitz-Alan

Title/s	Lord of Oswestry and Clun, sheriff of Shropshire
Sources	PR2 RI (1190), p. 124.

Thomas Cresswell

Title/s	Sheriff of Staffordshire
Notes	Replaced by Hugh Bardolf by William of Longchamp (1190).
Sources	PR2 RI (1190), p. 24.

Urse of Lincis

Title/s	Sheriff of Sussex
Sources	Heiser, 'Sheriffs of Richard I', pp. 120–1.

Hugh of Nonant

Title/s	Bishop of Coventry, sheriff of Warwick/Leicestershire, castellan of Kenilworth, Montsorrel, and Newcastle-under-Lyme castles
Notes	Resigned as castellan due to the pressures of his clerical office, i.e. Archbishop Baldwin judged holding such posts to be in violation of canon law. Geddington (1189). Rouen (1190). Tours (1190). Montrichard (1190).
Sources	Diss, Vol. 2, p. 111; Devizes, p. 8; *Gesta Regis*, Vol. 2, pp. 30–2, 68–70, 75, 105–6, 215–20, 223; Landon, *Itinerary*, nos. 10–11, 15–22, 34–54, 58, 63–67, 97–101, 126–7, 131–2, 135–7, 139, 148–54, 161–5, 168–81, 186, 194, 196–205, 227–9, 231–9, 246, 249, 263, 265, 268, 274–6, 298, 300–02, 306, 308, 313; PR2 RI (1190), pp. 15, 37, 44.

William II of Beauchamp

Title/s	Sheriff and castellan of Worcester, forester of Feckenham
Sources	R.R. Heiser, 'Castles, Constables, and Politics in Late Twelfth-Century English Governance', *Albion*, 32 (2000), p. 21.

Jordan of Le Hommet

Title/s	Lord of Cleville, constable of Séez
Notes	Messina (1190). Siege of Acre (1191). Relief of Jaffa (1192). Died on the Third Crusade (1192).
Sources	Ambroise, line 4707; *Gesta Regis*, Vol. 2, p. 134; *Itinerarium*, pp. 217, 405; Landon, *Itinerary*, nos. 312, 342.

Simon of Beauchamp

Title/s	Castellan of Bedford castle
Sources	PR2 RI (1190), p. 144.

Richard of the Peak

Title/s	Castellan of Bolsover castle
Sources	PR3/4 RI (1191–2), p. 29.

William III of Braose

Title/s	Lord of Bramber, Radnor, Brecon, and Abergavenny, castellan of Carmathen, Llawhaden, and Swansea castles, sheriff of Herefordshire (1191)
Notes	Received 500*l*. for his work as custodian of Welsh castles. Hired his 42-man ship to King Richard. Was granted the wardship of John of Monmouth for 1,000 *marks*.
Sources	PR2 RI (1190), pp. 8–9, 48.

John Fitz-Richard

Title/s	Lord of Halton, castellan of Chester castle
Notes	Member of households of Henry II and earl of Chester. Constable of Cheshire. Died at the siege of Acre or whilst convalescing at Tyre (1190).
Sources	*Annales Cestrienses, or the Chronicle of the Abbey of Saint Werburg, Chester*, ed. R. Copley Christie (London, 1887), p. 41; *Chronica*, Vol. 3, p. 88; *Gesta Regis*, Vol. 2, pp. 80, 148; 'The Records of the Templars in England in the Twelfth Century', *British Academy Records of Social and Economic History*, Vol. 9, ed. B.A. Lees (1935), pp. 79–80; TNA, DL 41/1.

Roger Fitz-John

Title/s	Castellan of Chester castle
Notes	Also, a member of earl of Chester's household. Son of John Fitz-Richard.
Sources	*Gesta Regis*, Vol. 2, pp. 232–4.

Ralph Fitz-Guy Extraneus

Title/s	Castellan of Church Stretton
Notes	Young Henry's steward.
Sources	PR2 RI (1190), p. 124; Turner, 'Households of the Sons', p. 53.

John Fitz-Godfrey

Title/s	Castellan of Colchester
Sources	PR3/4 RI (1191–2), p. 24.

Matthew of Clares

Title/s	Castellan of Dover castle
Notes	Arrested Geoffrey, archbishop of York, at Dover Priory with the help of Richeut. Restored as castellan of Dover on Richard I's return from captivity.
Sources	PR1 RI (1189), pp. 75, 156; PR6 RI, p. 242; Wendover, p. 193.

Robert Fitz-Roger

Title/s	Joint-castellan of Eye and Orford castles
Notes	Made sheriff of Norfolk/Suffolk by William of Longchamp.
Sources	PR3/4 RI (1191–2), pp. 29, 34.

Walter Fitz-Robert

Title/s	Joint-castellan of Eye and Orford castles
Sources	Landon, *Itinerary*, nos. 140–142a, 143, 147; PR3/4 RI (1191–2), pp. 29, 34.

Gilbert of Gascuil

Title/s	Castellan of Gisors
Notes	Returned to Normandy from Sicily with Queen Eleanor and archbishop Walter of Rouen (1190).
Sources	Ambroise, line 1163; Devizes, p. 57; *Itinerarium*, p. 176; Landon, *Itinerary*, nos. 236–9, 342; PR24 H2, p. 54.

Hugh Bardolf

Title/s	Castellan of Kenilworth, Montsorrel, and Newcastle-under-Lyme castles
Sources	PR2 RI (1190), pp. 15, 37, 44.

Walter of Clifford

Title/s	Lord of Clifford and Cantref Selyf
Notes	Member of Henry II's household, Rosamund Clifford was the king's mistress. Died in 1190 whereupon his brother Richard was granted his manors in Shropshire for a 300-*mark* fine.
Sources	*Liber Feodorum. Book of Fees Commonly Called Testa de Nevill*, ed. H.C. Maxwell Lyte (London, 1920–31), Vol. 1, pp. 146, Vol. 2, pp. 798–9, 802, 808, 810–12; PR2 RI (1190), p. 126.

Walter II of Clifford

Title/s	Lord of Clifford, castellan of Knighton castle
Notes	Inherited the lordship in 1190. Appointed castellan of Knighton castle of William of Longchamp.
Sources	PR3/4 RI (1191–2), p. 81.

Gilbert Talbot

Title/s	Lord of Linton, castellan of Ludlow castle
Notes	Received royal charter for manor of Linton (1190).
Sources	Landon, *Itinerary*, no. 286; PR2 RI (1190), pp. 45, 124, PR5 RI (1193), p. 86.

Gilbert of Essart
Title/s	Castellan of Ludlow castle
Sources	PR2 RI (1190), pp. 45, 124

Turstin Fitz-Simon
Title/s	Castellan of Ludlow castle
Sources	PR2 RI (1190), p. 45.

Oillard of Hull
Title/s	Castellan of Newcastle-upon-Tyne castle
Sources	PR2 RI (1190), p. 2.

Simon of Pattishall
Title/s	Castellan of Northampton castle
Notes	Served in Wales (1193).
Sources	PR4 RI (1192), pp. 200–1.

Hugh of Say
Title/s	Castellan of Norton castle
Sources	PR3/4 RI (1191–2), p. 141.

Robert of Crocstune
Title/s	Castellan of Nottingham
Notes	Threatened with being hanged by Roger of Lacy, constable of Chester, for handing Nottingham castle over to Count John (1191).
Sources	*Gesta Regis*, Vol. 2, p. 232.

Henry of Oilli
Title/s	Castellan of Oxford castle
Sources	*The History of the King's Works*, ed. H. M. Colvin, R. A. Brown, and A. J. Taylor (London, 1963), Vol. 2, pp. 771–2.

Joscelin Fitz-Reinfrid
Title/s	Castellan of Pevensey castle
Notes	William of Longchamp wrote to Hugh, bishop of Lincoln, ordering his excommunication along with a long list of other opponents (1191).
Sources	*Gesta Regis*, Vol. 2, p. 223; PR3/4 RI, (1191–2) p. 58.

Alan Fitz-Ruald
Title/s	Castellan of Richmond castle
Notes	Purchased custodianship for 200 *marks*.
Sources	PR2 RI (1190), pp. 66, 144.

Hugh of Bosco
Title/s	Castellan of Rochester castle
Sources	PR3/4 RI (1191–2), p. 141.

Robert Tresgoz
Title/s	Castellan of Salisbury castle
Notes	Steward to Young Henry. Member of Henry II's household as *balli* of Cotentin.
Sources	Landon, *Itinerary*, nos. 189–93; PR2 RI, p. 117; Turner, 'Households of the Sons', pp. 53, 57.

Gilbert of Lacy
Title/s	Castellan of Scarborough castle
Sources	PR2 RI (1190), p. 112.

Reginald of Wasseville
Title/s	Castellan of Tickhill castle
Sources	Devizes, p. 34.

Roger Fitz-Reinfrid
Title/s	Castellan of the Tower of London and Wallingford castle, appares to the Regency Council
Notes	Member of Henry II's household and royal justice. Brother to Walter of Coutances, archbishop of Rouen, and father to Gilbert Fitz-Reinfrid. William of Longchamp wrote to Hugh, bishop of Lincoln, ordering his excommunication along with a long list of other opponents (1191).
Sources	*Gesta Regis*, Vol. 2, p. 223; Landon, *Itinerary*, no. 64, 164, 175–87, 196–202; PR1 RI, p. 159; PR2 RI (1190), p. 149; *Recueil des historiens de la France*, XXIII, pp. 359, 362.

Philip of Puintel
Title/s	Castellan of York castle
Sources	PR1 RI, pp. 58–9, 75.

Osbert of Longchamp

Title/s — Steward of Westminster and London gaol

Notes — Received custody of the king's houses in Westminster and the gaol of London (1189). Made sheriff of Westmorland and Yorkshire, and castellan of Newcastle-upon-Tyne by William of Longchamp (1190). Related to Henry, Stephen, and William of Longchamp.

Sources — *Gesta Regis*, Vol. 2, p. 109; Landon, *Itinerary*, no. 162; PR2 RI (1190), pp. 18, 45, 58–9, 75.

Maurice II of Craon

Title/s — Constable of Ancenis

Notes — Member of Henry II's household. Dictated his will prior to departing on crusade. Father to Guy of Craon.

Sources — *Gesta Regis*, Vol. 1, p. 71; *HGM*, lines 9304–409, *Chroniques Craonaises*, ed. B. de la Jacopière (Le Mans, 1871), p. 596.

Andrew of Chauvigny

Title/s — Count of Châteauroux.

Notes — Member of Richard's comital household. Siege of Acre (1191). Skirmish near Ramla (1191). Jaffa (1192). Relief of Jaffa (1192). Led first party of pilgrims into Jerusalem (1192). Related to Geoffrey of Chauvigny.

Sources — Ambroise, lines 4990, 7542, 10961, 11378–620, 11843; *Gesta Regis*, Vol. 2, p. 76; *HGM*, lines 8662–80; *Itinerarium*, pp. 218, 227, 292, 302, 355, 405, 415, 432–3; Landon, *Itinerary*, nos. 329–30, 342, 358, 366.

Geoffrey of la Celle

Notes — Vézelay (1190). Arrived at the siege of Acre with Angevin contingent (1191). Jaffa (1192). Related to Helia of la Celle.

Sources — *Itinerarium*, p. 218; Landon, *Itinerary*, nos. 319, 321–6, 366; *CDF*, pp. 94–5, no. 278.

John of Préaux

Title/s — Lord of Préaux

Notes — Member of Young Henry's household. Messina (1190). Jaffa (1192). Relief of Jaffa (1192). Brother to William, Roger, and Peter of Préaux.

Sources — Ambroise, line 11442, 11872; *Itinerarium*, pp. 405; Landon, *Itinerary*, nos. 104, 153, 236–9, 329–30, 342, 354, 366.

William of Préaux

Notes	Member of Young Henry's household. Arrived at the siege of Acre with Angevin contingent (1191). Saved king from capture, by was captured himself near Acre (1191). Exchanged by Richard I for ten Muslim nobles. Brother to John, Roger, and Peter of Préaux.
Sources	Ambroise, line 4723–4, 7111, 12228; Baha' al-Din, p. 181; Ibn al-Athir, Vol. 2, p. 392; *Itinerarium*, pp. 217, 287–8, 440; Landon, *Itinerary*, nos. 146, 175–82.

Roger of Harcourt

Title/s	Lord of Renneville
Notes	Cyprus (1191). Siege of Acre (1191). Died on the Third Crusade. Related to Robert II of Harcourt.
Sources	Ambroise, line 4721; Gilbert of Mons, p. 273; *Itinerarium*, pp.186, 217; Landon, *Itinerary*, nos. 131, 189–93, 236–9.

Robert II of Harcourt

Title/s	Lord of Harcourt and Elbeuf
Notes	Tours (1190). Captured alongside King Richard I whilst returning from the Holy Land. Related to Roger of Harcourt.
Sources	Landon, *Itinerary*, nos. 1, 34–40, 61, 107–10, 208–10, 227–9, 234, 240, 251–8, 292, 295, 298, 300–2, 310–11.

Hugh Ribol

Notes	Placed in joint-command of Jaffa whilst King Richard rebuilt the castles of the Plains and Maen.
Sources	Ambroise, line 7180; *Itinerarium*, p. 289.

Baldwin of Béthune

Notes	Member of Young Henry's household. Member of Henry II's household. Led the vanguard to relieve the siege of Jaffa (1192). Travelled as a companion to Richard I on his return from crusade.
Sources	*HGM*, lines 4543, 7998, 8609, 9374–90, 9396–8; Landon, *Itinerary*, nos. 328, 366; Wendover, p. 218.

William of Cayeux

Title/s	Lord of Bouillancourt
Notes	Skirmish near Ramla (1191). Richard I's messenger to Conrad of Montferrat (1192).
Sources	Ambroise, lines 7276, 8634; *Itinerarium*, pp. 292, 336.

Anseau IV of Cayeux

Notes   Served King Richard I in the Holy Land, returned to join Fourth Crusade.

Sources   *Eustache Le Moine: pirate boulonnais du XIIIe siècle*, trans. E. Mousseigne (Lille, 1996), pp. 112–13, 158, 178, 23.

Gilbert of Malmain

Notes   Siege of Acre (1190). Jaffa (1192). Attack on Muslim caravan (1192).

Sources   Ambroise, line 10455; *Itinerarium*, p. 389; Landon, *Itinerary*, no. 366.

William Cook

Notes   Received a royal charter (1190) for the meadow, oven, and old market at Beauchamp.

Sources   Landon, *Itinerary*, no. 310.

Gerard Talbot

Notes   Member of Henry II's household. Assigned to Young Henry's household. Messina (1190). Arrived at the siege of Acre with Angevin contingent (1191).

Sources   *Gesta Regis*, Vol. 2, p. 134; *Itinerarium*, p. 217; Landon, *Itinerary*, nos. 226, 260–2, 314, 342.

Gilbert Pipard

Title/s   Lord of Ardee

Notes   Member of Henry II's household as sheriff of Lancaster. Died on the Third Crusade.

Sources   *Gesta Regis*, Vol. 2, p. 150; Landon, *Itinerary*, nos. 164, 186, 335, 337, 340.

Peter of Barres

Notes   Crewman of the Trenchemer.

Sources   *Itinerarium*, p. 205.

Saul of Bruil

Notes   Attached to earl of Leicester. Skirmish at Ramla (1192). Royal messenger to king of Jerusalem (1194).

Sources   Ambroise, line 7120; *Chronica*, Vol. 3, p. 233; *Itinerarium*, p. 301.

William of Bruil

Notes   Attached to earl of Leicester. Skirmish at Ramla (1192).

Sources   Ambroise, line 7120; *Itinerarium*, p. 301.

Philip II of Columbiers

Title/s	Lord of Nether Stowey
Notes	Member of Henry II's household. Vézelay (1190). Regular attestor of King Richard's *acta*.
Sources	*HGM*, line 8817; Landon, *Itinerary*, nos. 143, 292, 299, 300–04, 306, 308, 310–12, 315–19, 321–6, 328.

William of Courcy

Notes	Messina (1190). Brother-in-law to Henry of Cornhill.
Sources	*Chronica*, Vol. 3, p. 62; *Gesta Regis*, Vol. 2, p, 134; Landon, *Itinerary*, no. 33.

Guy of Craon

Notes	Messina (1190). Son of Maurice II of Craon.
Sources	Landon, *Itinerary*, no. 342.

Alan of l'Estable

Notes	Killed in skirmish outside Jaffa (1191).
Sources	Ambroise, line 7120; *Itinerarium*, p. 287.

Luke of l'Estable

Notes	Killed in skirmish outside Jaffa (1191).
Sources	Ambroise, line 7120; *Itinerarium*, p. 287.

Ançon of Faï

Notes	Attack on Muslim caravan (1192). Relief of Jaffa (1192). Comrade to Stephen of Longchamp.
Sources	Ambroise, lines 10047, 10967; *Itinerarium*, pp. 376, 405.

Hugh of la Fierte

Notes	Conquest of Cyprus (1191). Arrived at the siege of Acre with Angevin contingent (1191).
Sources	*Itinerarium*, p. 218.

William Fitz-Richard

Notes	Marseille (1190).
Sources	Landon, *Itinerary*, nos. 276, 335, 337, 340.

Gerard of Furnival
Notes | Relief of Jaffa (1192). Envoy to Jerusalem (1192).
Sources | Ambroise, lines 11394, 11871; *Itinerarium*, pp. 415, 432.

Peter of Gascony
Notes | Siege of Darum (1192).
Sources | Ambroise, line 9283; *Itinerarium* p. 355.

Hugh VI of Gourney
Title/s | Lord of Gurnay
Notes | Member of Angevin advance guard. Siege of Acre (1190). Joint governor of Acre (1191). Guarded prisoners taken at Acre. Battle of Arsuf (1191).
Sources | Ambroise, line 6162; Diss, Vol. 2, p. 79; *Gesta Regis*, Vol. 2, pp. 179–80; *Itinerarium*, pp. 93, 261; Landon, *Itinerary*, nos. 1, 236–9, 262; Wendover, p. 178.

Henry of Gray
Notes | Skirmish near Ramla (1192). Jaffa (1192).
Sources | Ambroise, line 7543; *Itinerarium*, p. 302; Landon, *Itinerary*, no. 366.

Renier of Marun
Notes | Killed in skirmish outside Jaffa (1191). Uncle of Walter.
Sources | Ambroise, line 7116; *Itinerarium*, p. 287.

Walter
Notes | Killed in skirmish outside Jaffa (1191). Nephew of Renier of Marun.
Sources | Ambroise, line 7116; *Itinerarium*, p. 287.

Bartholomew of Mortimer
Notes | Relief of Jaffa (1192).
Sources | Ambroise, lines 11378–620; *Itinerarium*, p. 415.

Hugh of Neville
Notes | Relief of Jaffa (1192). Eyewitness for Ralph of Coggeshall's entries on the Third Crusade.
Sources | *Itinerarium*, p. 415; Landon, *Itinerary*, no. 171; *Monasticon*, Vol. 6, p. 833; PR6 RI (1194), p. 80.

Eustace of Neville

Notes — Received royal manors whilst with King Richard in Lyon (1190).
Sources — Landon, *Itinerary*, no. 331.

Jollan of Neville

Notes — Confirmed in the royal manor of Shorne (Kent) 1199.
Sources — *RCR*, p. 12b.

William des Roches

Title/s — Lord of Sablé
Notes — Member of Henry II's household. Arrived at the siege of Acre with Angevin contingent (1191). Battle of Arsuf (1191). Siege of Jaffa (1192). Envoy to Jerusalem (1192). Companion of King Richard who borrowed 150 *marks* on behalf of Queen Berengaria whilst in Rome (1193). It is not clear if he married Marguerite of Sablé prior to the crusade or after his return.
Sources — Ambroise, line 11869; *CDF*, pp. 94–5 no. 278; *HGM*, line 8817; *Itinerarium*, pp. 218, 432; Landon, *Itinerary*, no. 366.

Roger of Saceio

Notes — Arrived at the siege of Acre with Angevin contingent (1191). Relief of Jaffa (1192). Companion of King Richard who borrowed 150 *marks* on behalf of Queen Berengaria whilst in Rome (1193).
Sources — Ambroise, lines 10962, 11396; *Itinerarium*, pp. 218, 405, 415; *CDF*, pp. 94–5 no. 278.

Matthew of Sauley

Notes — Killed in Sicily (1190).
Sources — Ambroise, line 763; *Itinerarium*, p. 162.

Ralph III Tesson

Title/s — Lord of Saint-Saveur-le-Vicomte
Notes — Took the Cross (1188). Arrived at the siege of Acre with Angevin contingent (1191). Led second group of pilgrims to Jerusalem (1192).
Sources — Ambroise, lines 4715, 11845; *Itinerarium*, pp. 217, 432; Landon, *Itinerary*, no. 1.

Ambroise

Notes — With fleet from Sicily to Cyprus (1190).
Sources — Ambroise, lines 1194–1351.

Seguin Barrez
Notes   Siege of Darum (1192).
Sources   Ambroise, line 9280; *Itinerarium*, p. 355.

William Bloez
Notes   Arrived at the siege of Acre with Angevin contingent (1191).
Sources   *Itinerarium*, p. 218.

Geoffrey of Bois
Notes   Jaffa (1192). Relief of Jaffa (1192).
Sources   Ambroise, line 11103; *Itinerarium*, p. 408; Landon, *Itinerary*, no. 366; PR34 (1188), p. 176; PR2 RI (1190), p. 134.

Chotard of Loreora
Notes   Arrived at the siege of Acre with Angevin contingent (1191).
Sources   *Itinerarium*, p. 218.

Geoffrey Loster
Notes   Vézelay (1190).
Sources   Landon, *Itinerary*, nos. 129, 131–2, 283, 321–6.

William Malet
Title/s   Lord of Curry Mallet
Notes   On crusade to Jerusalem (1190). Arrived at the siege of Acre with Angevin contingent (1191). Survived to become sheriff of Dorset and Somerset und King John.
Sources   *Itinerarium*, p. 218; PR2 RI (1190), p. 110.

William Marcel
Notes   Arrived at the siege of Acre with Angevin contingent (1191).
Sources   'Records of the Templars', ed. Lees, pp. 15, 75; *Itinerarium*, p. 218.

Alan of la Mare
Notes   Arrived at the siege of Acre with Angevin contingent (1191). Benevento (11
Sources   *Itinerarium*, p. 217.

Hugh of la Mare

Title/s	Cleric
Notes	Conquest of Cyprus (1191). Died on the Third Crusade (1191).
Sources	Ambroise, line 1605; *Itinerarium*, p. 192.

Stephen of Tours

Title/s	Seneschal of Anjou
Notes	Henry II's seneschal of Anjou and initially imprisoned by Richard I, but reappointed (*c.*1192). Lucon (1190). Jaffa (Aug 1192).
Sources	Acta, no. 220; Devizes, pp. 4–5; *Gesta Regis*, Vol. 2, pp. 71–2; *HGM*, lines 8015–24; Landon, *Itinerary*, no. 286.

Maurice of Berkeley

Title/s	Lord of Berkeley
Notes	Appointed to the barony by Queen Eleanor on behalf of her son (1189).
Sources	Landon, *Itinerary*, p. 13.

William l'Etang

Notes	Relief of Jaffa (1192). Returned from Holy Land with Richard I and present at his capture.
Sources	Ambroise, line 6968, 11398; *Itinerarium*, pp. 283, 415; Wendover, p. 220.

Alan of Valoignes

Notes	Member of Henry II's household as sheriff of Kent. Received royal charter for lands in Yorkshire (1189). Crusader of the honour of Peverel. Died on return from crusade (1194).
Sources	Landon, *Itinerary*, nos. 175–82; R. Mortimer, 'The Family of Rannulf de Glanville', *Historical Research*, 129 (1981), p. 8; PR2 RI (1190), p. 110.

Gilbert Fitz-Reinfrid

Title/s	Royal Steward, lord of Kendal
Notes	Member of Henry II's household. Son to Roger Fitz-Reinfrid and nephew to Walter of Coutances, archbishop of Rouen. Received wardship of Kendal and its lady from William Marshal (1189). Received hand of Helewisia from Richard I (1189).
Sources	*Gesta Regis*, Vol. 2, p. 73; *Lancashire Pipe Rolls*, p. 395; *RHFrance*, XXIII, pp. 359, 362.

William Pipart
Notes — Received royal lands in Hintlesham (Suffolk) for one hawk per year (1190).
Sources — Landon, *Itinerary*, no. 251

Richard Revel
Notes — Received royal manors of Lamport and Curry Rivel (Somerset) whilst with King Richard in Rouen (1190).
Sources — Landon, *Itinerary*, no. 248.

John Fitz-William of Writtle
Notes — Received confirmation of the royal tenancy held by his father (1190).
Sources — Landon, *Itinerary*, no. 260.

Richard Fitz-Aucher
Notes — Received confirmation of the royal tenancy held by his father for one knight's fee (1189).
Sources — TNA ,C 52/17, *carte antique* roll 17, m. 3d, no. 31.

Peter Tirepreie
Notes — Killed in Sicily (1190).
Sources — Ambroise, line 761; *Itinerarium*, p. 162.

William of St John
Notes — Dover (1189). Domfort (1190).
Sources — Landon, *Itinerary*, nos. 1–5, 72–90, 94–6, 104, 118–20, 123, 132, 135–6, 145, 153–4, 156–65, 168–82, 186–94, 269.

Renier of Marun
Notes — Killed in skirmish outside Jaffa (1191). Uncle of Walter.
Sources — Ambroise, line 7116; *Itinerarium*, p. 287.

Walter
Notes — Killed in skirmish outside Jaffa (1191). Nephew of Renier of Marun.
Sources — Ambroise, line 7116; *Itinerarium*, p. 287.

Ralph of Rouvray
Notes — Killed in Sicily (1190).
Sources — Ambroise, line 765; *Itinerarium*, p. 162.

Walkelin of Ferrers
Notes   Lyon (1190). Sicily (1191). Siege of Acre (1190). Battle of Arsuf (1191).
Sources   Ambroise, lines 4431, 6166; Diss, Vol. 2, p. 79; *Itinerarium*, pp. 93, 135, 261; Landon, *Itinerary*, nos. 1, 10–11, 329–31; Wendover, p. 178.

John Fitz-Luke
Notes   March to Jaffa (1191).
Sources   Ambroise, line 5783.

Philip Fitz-Helgot
Notes   Received royal vill of Kinver (1189).
Sources   Landon, *Itinerary*, no. 190.

Everard of Beuvrière
Notes   Held royal manor of Saham (Norfolk).
Sources   *Liber Feodorum, Part 1*, p. 324.

Robert Fitz-Hugh of Northampton
Notes   Received king's award and land in Northampton.
Sources   Landon, *Itinerary*, no. 229.

Robert of Ameneville
Notes   Received king's award of Bitton, held by his father for one knight's fee.
Sources   Landon, *Itinerary*, no. 115.

Simon of Wellensi
Notes   Received king's award of land in Writtle, as held by his father, Roger of Writtle.
Sources   *CCR*, Vol. 2, p. 431.

Eudes Fitz-Aernisi
Notes   Member of Henry II's household. Held land of the king in Maldon. Crusader of the honour of Peverel of London (1190).
Sources   PR33 H2 (1187), p. 121; PR34 H2 (1188), p. 30; PR1 R1 (1189), p. 20, PR2 R1 (1190), pp. 104, 110.

William of Reimes
Notes   On crusade to Jerusalem in the king's service (1191).
Sources   PR 3 RI (1191), p. 44; PR8 RI (1196), p. 118.

William of Sirenton
Notes   On crusade to Jerusalem in the king's service (1191).
Sources   PR3 R1 (1191), p. 152; RCR, Vol. 1, pp. 54–5.

Henry of Yllega
Notes   On crusade to Jerusalem with King Richard (1190).
Sources   PR2 RI (1190), p. 109.

Warin Fitz-Henry
Notes   On crusade to Jerusalem with King Richard (1190).
Sources   PR2 RI (1190), p. 109.

Geoffrey of Brulon
Notes   Member of Henry II's household. Fought at Le Mans for Henry II (1189). Jaffa (1192).
Sources   *Gesta Regis*, Vol. 2, p. 67; Landon, *Itinerary*, no. 366; Wendover, p. 155.

Geoffrey of Haya
Notes   Member of Henry II's household as itinerant justice and envoy to Constantinople. Forged charter placed him in Jaffa (1192).
Sources   *Acta*, no. 219; *Gesta Regis*, Vol. 2, p. 147; PR23 HII (1177), p. 166; PR33 HII (1187), p. 17.

Adam of Talworth
Notes   On crusade to Jerusalem (1191). Companion of King Richard who borrowed 150 *marks* on behalf of Queen Berengaria whilst in Rome (1193).
Sources   CDF, pp. 94–5 no. 278; PR3 RI (1191), p. 44.

Guy of Berniers
Notes   Companion of Richard I who borrowed 150 *marks* on behalf of Queen Berengaria whilst in Rome (1193).
Sources   CDF, pp. 94–5 no. 278.

Geoffrey of Vendôme
Notes   Companion of Richard I who borrowed 150 *marks* on behalf of Queen Berengaria whilst in Rome (1193).
Sources   CDF, pp. 94–5 no. 278.

John of Subligny
Notes   Held as surety for the loan to Queen Berengaria (1193).
Sources   *CDF*, pp. 94–5 no. 278.

Guichard Leidett
Notes   Held as surety for the loan to Queen Berengaria (1193).
Sources   *CDF*, pp. 94–5 no. 278.

Roger of St Germain
Notes   Held as surety for the loan to Queen Berengaria (1193).
Sources   *CDF*, pp. 94–5 no. 278.

Alan Fitz-Alan of Sorham
Notes   Held as surety for the loan to Queen Berengaria (1193). William Fitz-Alan was sheriff of Shropshire.
Sources   *CDF*, pp. 94–5 no. 278.

Walter of Braitoft
Sources   BL ms. Harley 742, f. 172v.

Ranalf
Title/s   Royal armiger
Notes   Vézelay (1190)
Sources   PR1 RI (1189), p. 217.

Orry
Title/s   Royal engineer/master of siege engines
Notes   Held lands in Wickford (1190).
Sources   *CCR*, Vol. 2, pp. 100–1; Landon, *Itinerary*, p. 145; PR2 RI (1190), p. 147; PR4 RI (1192), p. 308; PR 6 RI (1194), p. 244

Mercadier
Title/s   Mercenary Captain
Notes   Charter placing him in Jaffa identified as a forgery (1192).
Sources   *Acta*, no. 219.

Philip of Wales

Title/s	Mercenary Captain
Notes	Charter placing him in Jaffa identified as a forgery (1192).
Sources	*Acta*, no. 219.

William of Goram

Title/s	Mercenary Captain
Notes	Charter placing him in Jaffa identified as a forgery (1192).
Sources	*Acta*, no. 219.

Crusader Attachments

Bernard of la Carra

Title/s	Bishop of Bayonne, justiciar of Richard I's fleet
Notes	Sailed from Dartmouth (1190). Messina (1190). Present at Richard and Berengaria's wedding on Cyprus (1191). Purified the churches of Acre (1191).
Sources	Devizes, p. 22; *Gesta Regis*, Vol. 2, pp. 110, 115–16, 134, 153, 180–1; *Itinerarium*, p. 196; Landon, *Itinerary*, nos. 342, 344; Wendover, p. 181.

Gérard de la Barthe

Title/s	Archbishop of Auch, justiciar of Richard I's fleet
Notes	La Réole (1190). Dartmouth (1190). Marseille (1190). Messina (1190), Cyprus (1191). Purified churches of Acre (1191). Died in the East (1191).
Sources	Devizes, p. 22; *Gesta Regis*, Vol. 2, pp. 110, 115–16, 128, 134, 153, 180–1; Landon, *Itinerary*, nos. 216–17, 342; Wendover, pp. 181, 186.

Robert of Sablé

Title/s	Master of the Templars, justiciar of Richard I's fleet
Notes	Former lord of Sablé, justiciar of Richard I's fleet (1190). Dartmouth (1190). Lisbon (1190). Marseille (1190). Messina (1190) Cyprus (1191). Siege of Acre (1191). Elected master of the Templars during the course of the Third Crusade.
Sources	Ambroise, line 883; *Gesta Regis*, Vol. 2, pp. 110, 115–16, 119. 120, 124; *Itinerarium*, p. 166; Landon, *Itinerary*, nos. 222–3, 270–2, 284, 358, 365; Wendover, pp. 181, 186.

Ralph II of Fougères

Title/s	Lord of Fougères
Notes	Member of Henry II's household as seneschal of Brittany. Angers (1190). Died at the siege of Acre (1191).
Sources	Diss, Vol. 2, p. 64; *Gesta Regis*, Vol. 1, pp. 56–8; 2, p. 72; Landon, *Itinerary*, no. 215; Wendover, p. 191.

Baldwin le Carron

Title/s — Lord of Rumes

Notes — Knight of Baldwin V of Hainaut. Siege of Acre (1190). Battle of Arsuf (1191). Jointly commanded the escort to a convoy ambushed by Saladin's forces (1192).

Sources — Ambroise, lines 6419, 6421, 9920–47; *Chronica*, Vol. 3, p. 73; L. Dailliez, *Les templiers en Flandre, Hainaut, Brabant, Liège et Luxembourg* (Nice, 1978), p. 333–4, no. 61 (facsimilé cartulaire); L. Devillers, *Inventaire analytique des archives des commanderies belges de l'Ordre Saint-Jean de Jérusalem ou de Malte* (Mons, 1876), pp. 179–80, 187, 190–1; *Gesta Regis*, Vol. 2, p. 144; Gilbert of Mons, pp. 174, 180, 213, 217, 274, 328; *Itinerarium*, pp. 269, 373–4; E. Warlop, *De Vlaamse adel vóór 1300* (Handzame, 1968), pp. 508, 193–9.

Baldwin of Dargus

Notes — Siege of Acre (1190). Associated with Baldwin le Carron.

Sources — *Chronica*, Vol. 3, p. 73; *Gesta Regis*, Vol. 2, p. 144.

Manessier of Lille

Notes — Escort to caravan ambushed by Saladin's troops (1192). Associated with Baldwin le Carron.

Sources — Ambroise, lines 9920–47; *Itinerarium*, p. 373; E. Warlop, *The Flemish Nobility before 1300*, 4 Vols (Kortrijk, 1975), pp. 940–2.

Philip

Notes — Escort to caravan ambushed by Saladin's troops (1192). Associated with Baldwin le Carron.

Sources — Ambroise, lines 9920–47, 10004; *Itinerarium*, p. 373.

Thierry of Orcq

Notes — Attack on crusader caravan (1192). Died on the Third Crusade. Associated with Baldwin le Carron. Brother to Ivo, Richard, and John.

Sources — Ambroise, lines 9920–47; Gilbert of Mons, p. 274; *Itinerarium*, p. 373.

Ivo of Orcq

Notes — Attack on crusader caravan (1192). Died on the Third Crusade. Associated with Baldwin le Carron. Brother to Thierry, Richard, and John.

Sources — Gilbert of Mons, p. 274.

Richard of Orcq

Notes — Attack on crusader caravan (1192). Died on the Third Crusade. Associated with Baldwin le Carron. Brother to Thierry, Ivo, and John.

Sources — Ambroise, lines 9920–47; Gilbert of Mons, p. 274; *Itinerarium* p. 373.

John of Orcq

Notes — Attack on crusader caravan (1192). Died on the Third Crusade. Associated with Baldwin le Carron. Brother to Thierry, Ivo, and Richard.

Sources — Gilbert of Mons, p. 274.

Humphrey IV of Toron

Title/s — Lord of Toron

Notes — Constable of the king of Jerusalem (1190). Siege of Acre (1190). Cyprus (1191). Richard I's interpreter and envoy (1191–2).

Sources — Ambroise, line 4123; Baha' al-Din, pp. 173, 179, 231; Diss, Vol. 2, p. 80; *Gesta Regis*, Vol. 2, p. 165; *RRRH*, no. 1291; Wendover, p. 178.

Otto II of Trazegnies

Title/s — Lord of Trazegnies

Notes — Knight of Baldwin V of Hainaut, dubbed (1181). On crusade to the Holy Land (1186–7). Made a donation to Floreffe Abbey, which was confirmed prior to his departure on crusade again (1188). Siege of Acre (1190). Skirmish at Ramla (1191). Royal envoy to Conrad of Montferrat (1192). Died in the Holy Land (1192). Recipient of money-fief from Richard I worth 40s. in Kent.

Sources — Ambroise, lines 7278, 8632, 9920–48; Diss, Vol. 2, p. 79; Gilbert of Mons, pp. 132, 196, 274, 328; *Itinerarium*, pp. 292, 336–7, 373; PR2 RI (1190), p. 147; PR3 R (1191), p. 142; PR4 RI (1192), p. 308; Wendover, p. 178.

Walter Fitz-Batsuein

Title/s — Shipmaster

Notes — Committed his vessel to the king's crusader fleet.

Sources — PR2 R1 (1190), pp. 8–9.

Robert of Quincy

Title/s — Lord of Buckley (Northamptonshire)

Notes — Siege of Acre (1191). Envoy to Tyre (1191). Commander of force sent to aid Antioch by Richard I.

Sources — Ambroise, line 5446; Chronica, Vol. 3, p. 125: *Gesta Regis*, Vol. 2, p. 187; *Itinerarium*, p. 242.

Ralph of Mauleon

Notes — Arrived at the siege of Acre with Angevin contingent (1191). Jaffa (1192). Relief of Jaffa (1191).

Sources — Ambroise, lines 10965, 11378–620, 11497: *Itinerarium*, pp. 218, 405, 418; Landon, *Itinerary*, no. 366.

Members of Allied Households on Crusade

Alexander Arsic
Title/s	Lord of Cogges
Notes	Commanded between fifteen and twenty knights on crusade. Attack on Muslim caravan (1192).
Sources	Ambroise, line 10457; *HGM*, lines 4919–22; *Itinerarium*, p. 389; PR2 RI (1190), p. 14.

William II of Tancarville
Title/s	Lord of Tancarville, chamberlain of Normandy
Notes	Messina (1190). Arrived at the siege of Acre with Angevin contingent (1191). Died on the Third Crusade.
Sources	Ambroise, line 4709; *Itinerarium*, p. 217; Landon, *Itinerary*, no. 342.

Ernald of Mandeville
Notes	Arrived at the siege of Acre with Angevin contingent (1191). Nephew to Earl of Essex.
Sources	*Itinerarium*, p. 218.

Robert
Title/s	Constable of Halsham
Notes	Steward to William Mandeville, earl of Essex, Died at the siege of Acre. Steward to William Mandeville.
Sources	*Chronica*, Vol. 3, p. 89; *Gesta Regis*, Vol. 2, p. 149.

Henry Pigot
Notes	Died at the siege of Acre (1190). Seneschal to William Mandeville.
Sources	*Gesta Regis*, Vol. 2, p. 149; *Chronica*, Vol. 3, p. 89.

Osmund of Stuteville
Notes	Arrived at the siege of Acre with Angevin contingent (1191). Died at Jaffa (1192).
Sources	*Itinerarium*, p. 218.

Roger of Tosny
Notes	Arrived at the siege of Acre with Angevin contingent (1191). Battle of Arsuf (1191). Jaffa (1192). Attack on Muslim caravan (1192).
Sources	Ambroise, lines 4701–3, 6168, 10444; BN, ms. latin 11055, f. 28, no. 25; *Itinerarium*, pp. 217, 261, 389; Landon, *Itinerary*, nos. 146, 189–93, 366.

Jocelin III of Mayenne

Notes	Attack on Muslim caravan (1192).
Sources	Ambroise, line 10448; *Itinerarium*, p. 389.

Roger of Glanville

Notes	Member of Henry II's household as sheriff. Siege of Acre (1190). Outside Jerusalem (1192). Uncle to Ranulf of Glanville.
Sources	*Gesta Regis*, Vol. 2, p. 144; Heiser, 'English Governance', p. 25; *Itinerarium*, p. 345; Landon, *Itinerary*, no. 127.

Durand of Outillé

Title/s	Lord of Valoignes
Notes	Jury held to determine his property after he died on the Third Crusade.
Sources	*CRR*, Vol. 1, pp. 69, 277–8.

Theobald of Valoignes

Title/s	Lord of Parham, Butler of Ireland
Notes	Died on the Third Crusade (1191). Father to Alan of Valoignes
Sources	Young, *Hubert Walter*, p. 3 and footnote 1; PR2 R1 (1190), p. 110; 3 R1 (1191), p. 43.

Ralph of Arden

Notes	Member of Henry II's household as sheriff of Hereford. On crusade to Jerusalem (1191). Son-in-law to Ranulf of Glanville.
Sources	PR2 RI (1190), pp. 110, 130; 3 RI (1191), p. 44.

Ivo of Vipont

Title/s	Lord of Alston Moor
Notes	Siege of Acre (1190, 1191). Naval skirmish off Tyre.
Sources	AN, S4977, no. 9; *Itinerarium*, pp. 93, 104; *RRRH*, no. 1307.

Robert of Vipont

Notes	Siege of Acre (1191).
Sources	AN, S4977, no. 9; *RRRH*, no. 1307.

Associates Magnates

William of Aubigny

Title/s	Earl of Sussex, Castellan of Peak (Castleton) castle
Sources	PR2 R1 (1190), p. 75.

William III of Aubigny

Title/s — Earl of Arundel

Notes — Regular attestor of King Richard's *acta*.

Sources — Devizes, p. 34; Landon, *Itinerary*, nos. 2–5, 55, 72–6, 80–5, 90, 94–101, 104, 118–19, 126, 140–3, 146, 148–52, 160, 227–9, 241–5, 247, 256–8, 260–4, 277–7B, 306, 308, 312–13.

Robert III Beaumont

Title/s — Earl of Leicester, Lord High Steward (<1190)

Notes — Richard I's Lord High Steward. Took the Cross alongside Henry II (1188). Died en route to the siege of Acre (1190).

Sources — *Chronica*, Vol. 3, p. 5; *Gesta Regis*, Vol. 2, pp. 75, 80–1, 148; Landon, *Itinerary*, nos. 9, 33, 41–55, 80–9, 97–101, 104, 126–7, 148–53, 161–4, 166–7, 183, 186, 196–202, 211–12, 227–9, 265; Rigord, pp. 83–4; Wendover, p. 191.

Roger Bigot

Title/s — Earl of Norfolk

Sources — *Gesta Regis*, Vol. 2, p. 80; Landon, *Itinerary*, nos. 55, 127, 140–3, 145, 260–2.

Richard of Clare

Title/s — Earl of Hereford

Sources — Landon, *Itinerary*, nos. 146–146a.

William I of Ferrers

Title/s — Earl of Derby

Notes — Arrived at the siege of Acre (1189). Died at the siege of Acre (1190).

Sources — *Chronica*, Vol. 3, p. 88; *Gesta Regis*, Vol. 2, p. 148; *Itinerarium*, pp. 73–4.

Rotrou III of Perche

Title/s — Count of Perche

Notes — Took the Cross alongside Kings Henry II and Philip II (1188). Siege of Acre (1191). Made donation to Templars and died at the siege (1191).

Sources — Ambroise, line 4537; *Chronica*, Vol. 3, p. 88; Gesta *Regis*, Vol. 2, pp. 73, 92–3, 143; *Itinerarium*, p. 213; *Saint-Denis de Nogent-le-Rotrou, 1031-1789: Histoire et Cartulaire*, ed. C. Métais (Vannes, 1899), no. 99; Rigord, p. 83; *RRRH*, no. 1308; J. Schenk, *Templar Families: Landowning Families and the Order of the Temple in France, c.1120–1307* (Cambridge, 2012), p. 28; Wendover, pp. 170, 191.

Geoffrey III of Perche

Title/s	Count of Perche
Notes	Married Matilda, Richard I's niece (1189). Messina (1190). Cyprus (1191). Siege of Acre (1191). Skirmish near Betenoble (1192).
Sources	Devizes, p. 22; *Gesta Regis*, Vol. 2, pp. 128, 150; *Itinerarium*, p. 372; Landon, *Itinerary*, no. 358; *RRRH*, no. 1308.

Hugh IV of St Pol

Title/s	Count of St Pol
Notes	Sold a third of the tithes of Mortagne to the Premonstratensian house at Château-l'Abbaye prior to departing on crusade (c.1191). Siege of Acre (1191). Skirmish at Ramla (1191).
Sources	*Les chartes des comtes de Saint-Pol, XIe-XIIIe siècles*, ed. J.-F. Nieus (Turnhout, 2008), pp. 140–3, 145–6, nos. 54–5, 59; Ambroise, lines 4527, 6046, 7274; *Itinerarium*, pp. 213, 257, 293.

Hugh IX le Brun

Title/s	Count of La Marche
Notes	Messina (1190). Arrived at the siege of Acre with Angevin contingent (1191). Jaffa (1192).
Sources	Ambroise, lines 719, 4992; Diss, Vol. 2, p. 85; Devizes, p. 23; *Gesta Regis*, Vol. 2, pp. 128–9; *Chronica*, Vol. 3, p. 57; *Itinerarium*, pp. 161, 219, 227; Landon, *Itinerary*, nos. 342, 366; Wendover, p. 187.

Ralph of Exoudun

Title/s	Lord of Exoudun, count of Eu (1191)
Notes	Tours (1190). Siege of Acre (1190). Hugh IX's brother.
Sources	Diss, Vol. 2, p. 80; Landon, *Itinerary*, no. 306.

Geoffrey of Lusignan

Title/s	Lord of Jaffa and Caesaria
Notes	Siege of Acre (1189). Battle of Acre (1189). Cyprus (1191). Jaffa (1192).
Sources	Ambroise, lines 2810–79, 3042, 4073, 4651, 6964; Diss, Vol. 2, pp. 54, 70, 80; *Gesta Regis*, Vol. 2, pp. 95, 144, 166, 170, 184; *Itinerarium*, pp. 26, 60, 72, 119, 216, 235, 283, 307; Landon, *Itinerary*, nos. 365–6; Wendover, pp. 144–5.

Geoffrey IV of Rancon

Title/s	Lord of Taillebourg
Notes	Messina (1190). Arrived at the siege of Acre with Angevin contingent (1191).
Sources	*Gesta Regis*, Vol. 1, pp. 46–7; *Itinerarium*, p. 218; Landon, *Itinerary*, no. 342.

William II
Title/s   Count of Châlons-sur-Saône
Notes   Siege of Acre (1190). Placed in joint command of Jaffa (1192).
Sources   Ambroise, lines 3512, 7179; Diss, Vol. 2, p. 79; *HdB*, Vol.3, no. 799; *Itinerarium*, pp. 92, 289, 324; Wendover, p. 178.

Hugh V
Title/s   Viscount of Châteaudun
Notes   Arrived at the siege of Acre with Angevin contingent (1191). Died in 1191.
Sources   Ambroise, line 4717; Diss, Vol. 2, p. 55; *Itinerarium*, p. 217.

William
Title/s   Viscount of Pecquigny
Notes   Died on the Third Crusade.
Sources   *Chronica*, Vol. 3, *Gesta Regis*, Vol. 2, p. 149; *Chronica*, Vol. 3, pp. 89, 184; PR4 R1 (1192), p. 285; PR5 R1 (1193), p. 113.

Hamelin
Title/s   Earl of Warenne
Sources   Devizes, p. 34; *Gesta Regis*, Vol. 2, p. 80; Landon, *Itinerary*, nos. 41–55, 140–3, 153, 164–5, 183, 186, 236–9, 242–5, 247, 312.

William
Title/s   Earl of Salisbury
Sources   *Gesta Regis*, Vol. 2, pp. 80–1, 223; Landon, *Itinerary*, nos. 55, 118–19, 150–2, 164, 186–7.

Ranulf
Title/s   Earl of Chester
Sources   Landon, *Itinerary*, no. 264.

Richard of Clare
Title/s   Earl of Clare
Sources   *Gesta Regis*, Vol. 2, p. 80.

Robert
Title/s   Count of Meulan
Sources   *Gesta Regis*, Vol. 2, p. 223; Landon, *Itinerary*, nos. 235, 283.

David of Scotland

Title/s   Earl of Huntington

Notes   Brother to William the Lion, king of Scotland

Sources   *Gesta Regis*, Vol. 2, pp. 80–1, 98–100; Landon, *Itinerary*, nos. 20–2, 33, 41, 186–7, 306.

Aubrey of Vere

Title/s   Earl of Oxford, Lord High Chamberlain

Sources   *Gesta Regis*, Vol. 2, p. 80; Landon, *Itinerary*, nos. 140–142a, 146–7, 263.

Waleran of Warenne

Title/s   Earl of Warwick

Sources   *Gesta Regis*, Vol. 2, p. 80; Landon, *Itinerary*, nos. 41, 55.

Associated Religious Magnates

Baldwin of Forde

Title/s   Archbishop of Canterbury, joint commander of Richard I's advance guard

Notes   Took the Cross alongside Henry II (1188). Oversaw collection of the Saladin Tithe (1188). Preaching tour of Wales (1188). Geddington (1189). Pipewell (1189). Rouen (1190). Marseille (1190). Commanded 200 knights and 300 men-at-arms at siege of Acre (1190). Died at the siege of Acre (1190).

Sources   Ambroise, lines 3963, 4122; *Chronica*, Vol. 3, p. 87; Diss, Vol. 2, pp. 61–2, 84, 88; Devizes, pp. 3, 15, 19; *Gesta Regis*, Vol. 2, pp. 30–3, 40, 68–70, 75, 105–6, 115, 118–19, 142, 147; *Itinerarium*, pp. 93, 115–17, 121–2, 123–4, 142; Landon, *Itinerary*, nos. 2–9, 16–22, 27–32, 34, 40–55, 58, 61, 113, 123, 128, 147, 150–2, 155, 164–5, 168–81, 183, 186–93, 196–202, 231–3, 240, 263–4, 335, 337–8, 340; Rigord, p. 83; Wendover, pp. 152, 162, 164–7, 170, 186, 189.

Bartholomew

Title/s   Archbishop of Tours

Notes   Gave the Cross to Richard I (1187). Helped formulate Saladin Tithe at Le Mans (1188). Signed agreement with Richard I at Gisors (1190). Vézelay (1190). Consecrated Geoffrey, archbishop-elect of York at Tours (1191).

Sources   Diss, Vol. 2, pp. 50, 96; *Gesta Regis*, Vol. 2, pp. 30–2; Landon, *Itinerary*, nos. 214–15, 222, 259, 268, 319; Wendover, pp. 143, 193.

Bertrand

Title/s   Bishop of Agen

Notes   La Réole (1190).

Sources   Landon, *Itinerary*, nos. 216–17; Lewis, 'Dalon Charters', no. 5.

Gaillard of la Mothe
Title/s	Bishop of Bazas
Notes	La Réole (1190).
Sources	Landon, *Itinerary*, no. 217.

Garnier of Nablûs
Title/s	Master of the Hospitallers
Notes	Messina (1190). Cyprus (1191). Battle of Arsuf (1191). Skirmish near Betenoble (1192).
Sources	Ambroise, lines 6375, 9905; *Chronica*, Vol. 3, p. 210; *Gesta Regis*, Vol. 2, pp. 130, 173; *Itinerarium*, pp. 197, 267–8, 371–2; Landon, *Itinerary*, nos. 42–54, 346, 358.

Gilbert of Glanville
Title/s	Bishop of Rochester
Notes	Geddington (1189). Linked to Roger and Ranulf of Glanville.
Sources	*Gesta Regis*, Vol. 2, pp. 33; 68–7; 75–6; 79; Landon, *Itinerary*, nos. 18–19, 33–40, 42–55, 61, 92, 97–101, 123, 126–7, 155, 165, 168–71.

Godfrey of Lucy
Title/s	Bishop of Winchester
Notes	Geddington (1189). Rouen (1190). Tours (1190). Prominent attestor of King Richard's *acta*.
Sources	Devizes, pp. 7–8, 33; *Gesta Regis*, Vol. 2, pp. 81, 96, 105–6, 223; *Itinerarium*, p. 145; Landon, *Itinerary*, nos. 33, 42–54, 68–76, 80–90, 92–101, 104, 110–12, 114, 116, 118–20, 123, 125–7, 130, 132, 134, 137, 139, 150–4, 160, 164–5, 168–71, 175–93, 195–202, 227–9, 231–3, 235, 241–7, 249. 298–302, 308; Wendover, pp. 167, 170.

Hélie of Malemort
Title/s	Archbishop of Bordeaux
Notes	Cyprus (1191).
Sources	*Itinerarium*, p. 196.

Henry II
Title/s	Bishop of Bayeux
Notes	Geddington (1189). Rouen (1190). Consecrated Geoffrey, archbishop-elect of York in Tours (1191).
Sources	Diss, Vol. 2, p. 96; *Gesta Regis*, Vol. 2, p. 75; Landon, *Itinerary*, nos. 10–11, 33, 40, 231–3, 235–40.

Herbert

Title/s	Bishop of Rennes
Notes	Angers (1190). Domfront (1190).
Sources	Landon, *Itinerary*, nos. 214–15, 270–2.

Hubert Walter

Title/s	Bishop of Salisbury
Notes	Geddington (1189). Rouen (1190). Vézelay (1190). Marseille (1190). Siege of Acre (1190). Organised poor relief at the siege (1190). Attack on Cursed Tower repulsed (1191). Purified churches at Acre (1191). March to Jaffa (1191). Skirmish at Betenoble (1192). Pilgrimage to Jerusalem (1192).
Sources	*Acta*, 2, no. 220; Ambroise, lines 4411, 4590, 4994, 5414, 11847; Baha' al-Din, p. 228; Diss, Vol. 2, pp. 79, 84, 88, 108–9; Devizes, pp. 15, 82, 84; *Gesta Regis*, Vol. 2, pp. 77, 85, 96, 98–100, 115, 145, 180–1, 186; *Itinerarium*, pp. 93, 116, 134–5, 137, 242, 372, 432, 437–8; Landon, *Itinerary*, nos. 33, 42–54, 92–101, 110–12, 114, 116, 118–20, 123, 125, 127, 130, 134, 140–142a, 143, 146–7, 153–7, 160–5, 168–202, 240. 256–8, 263–4, 268, 274, 276, 321–6, 336–8, 340; Wendover, pp. 161, 167, 178, 186, 189, 204.

Hugh of Avalon

Title/s	Bishop of Lincoln
Notes	Geddington (1189).
Sources	Diss, Vol. 2, p. 72; *Gesta Regis*, Vol. 2, p. 40, 68–70, 75, 79, 223–4; Landon, *Itinerary*, nos. 18–32, 41–55, 58, 164, 183, 186–7, 196–202.

John of Oxford

Title/s	Bishop of Norwich
Notes	Geddington (1189). Took the Cross but was robbed en route to the Holy Land and given leave by the pope to return home.
Sources	Devizes, pp. 10–11; *Gesta Regis*, Vol. 2, pp. 79, 105–6, 115; Landon, *Itinerary*, nos. 2–5, 9, 20–2, 41–55, 61, 114, 125, 134, 140–3, 147, 155–7.

John Cummin

Title/s	Archbishop of Dublin
Notes	Geddington (1189). Pipewell (1189).
Sources	Diss, Vol. 2, p. 68; *Gesta Regis*, Vol. 2, pp. 40, 79; Landon, *Itinerary*, nos. 20–2, 41–55, 164, 183, 186–93; Wendover, pp. 164–6.

John

Title/s	Bishop of Exeter
Notes	Geddington (1189).
Sources	*Gesta Regis*, Vol. 2, p. 79; Landon, *Itinerary*, no. 55.

John

Title/s	Archbishop of Lyon
Notes	Lyon-sur-Rhône (1190).
Sources	Landon, *Itinerary*, nos. 329–30.

Lisiard

Title/s	Bishop of Sées
Notes	Helped formulate Saladin Tithe at Le Mans (1188). Rouen (1190).
Sources	*Gesta Regis*, Vol. 2, pp. 30–2; Landon, *Itinerary*, nos. 231–5, 268.

Maurice of Blazon

Title/s	Bishop of Nantes
Notes	Helped formulate Saladin Tithe at Le Mans (1188). Angers (1190). Domfront (1190).
Sources	*Gesta Regis*, Vol. 2, pp. 30–2; Landon, *Itinerary*, nos. 214–15, 270–2.

Ralph

Title/s	Bishop of Angers
Notes	Domfront (1190).
Sources	Landon, *Itinerary*, no. 208–10, 222, 270–2, 283–4.

Ralph of Verneville

Title/s	Bishop of Lisieux
Notes	Rouen (1190).
Sources	Landon, *Itinerary*, no. 236–9.

Reginald Fitz-Jocelin

Title/s	Bishop of Bath
Notes	Geddington (1189). Rouen (1190). Regular attestor of King Richard's *acta*.
Sources	Diss, Vol. 2, p. 103; Devizes, p. 33; *Gesta Regis*, Vol. 2, pp. 79, 105–6, 226–7; Landon, *Itinerary*, nos. 10–11, 16–17, 20–2, 27–32, 34–55, 57–8, 64–7, 126, 135–6, 153–4, 156–7, 164, 183, 186–7, 196–202, 204, 227–9, 231–3, 235–9, 249, 263–4, 321–6, 328–30; Wendover, p. 208.

Richard Fitz-Neal

Title/s	Bishop of London
Notes	Geddington (1189). Pipewell (1189).
Sources	Diss, Vol. 2, pp. 75, 97–8; *Gesta Regis*, Vol. 2, pp. 96, 238; Landon, *Itinerary*, nos. 42–54, 68–76, 80–9, 91–101, 104, 118–20, 137–9, 160; Wendover, pp. 167, 173, 194.

Sefrid

Title/s	Bishop of Colchester
Notes	Geddington (1189). Rouen (1190).
Sources	*Gesta Regis*, Vol. 2, p. 79; Landon, *Itinerary*, nos. 42–54, 97–101, 235, 242–5.

William Northall

Title/s	Bishop of Worcester
Notes	Geddington (1189).
Sources	*Gesta Regis*, Vol. 2, pp. 76, 79; Landon, *Itinerary*, nos. 55, 165.

William le Tempier

Title/s	Bishop of Poitiers
Notes	Angers (1190).
Sources	Landon, *Itinerary*, no. 214.

William of Tournebu

Title/s	Bishop of Coutances
Notes	Rouen (1190). Acre (1190). Linked to Roger of Tosny.
Sources	Ambroise, line 4703; Landon, *Itinerary*, nos. 231–3, 235–9.

William of Vere

Title/s	Bishop of Hereford
Notes	Geddington (1189). Brother to Aubrey, earl of Oxford.
Sources	Landon, *Itinerary*, nos. 41–54.

Bibliography

Manuscripts

AD de Calvados, 2 D 54, f. 5047.
AD de Côte-d'Or, 15 H 24–9.
AD d'Eure, G122, G6, H703.
AD d'Eure-et-Loir, G 2980, H 1374.
AD de Maine-et-Loire, 242 H 1.
AD du Nord, 1 H 43/486, 12 H 3, 37 H 30/108.
AD de Pas-de-Calais, 22 H 1.
AD de Saône-et-Loire, H 54/17.
AD de la Seine-Maritime, G 4038, 8 H 13H, 8 H 83, 9 H 26.
AD de la Somme, 1 MI 5.
Agen, Archives de la ville, ms. DD 14.
Amiens, Bibliothèque centrale Louis Aragon, mss. 781, no. 23; 1077 inséré entre fos. 74–75.
AN, JJ30, JJ66, JJ81; LL1541; S5105, S5235, S5243; liasse 344.
Belvoir Castle, Duke of Rutland ms. Belvoir cartulary.
BN, *Collection de Picardie*, nos. 107, 214, 235, 267; mss. latin 1022, 5650, 9901, 9885, 10121, 10943, 11055; ms. Moreau, Vol. 91, fols 111–12; ms. français 18953; ms. nouvelles acquisitions latines 53.
Cambridge, Pembroke College ms. Soham A2 and A3.
Cambridge, University Library, Additional ms. 4220; ms. EDC; ms. EDR G/3/28 (Liber M).
Carlisle Record Office, Carlisle Dean and Chapter ms. Register of Wetheral Priory; ms. Holm Cultram cartulary.
Durham Cathedral, Dean and Chapter, Muniments 3.
Gloucestershire Record Office, D225/T1.
Liège, State Archives, Saint-Jacques, no. 33.
Lincolnshire Archives, Revesby Abbey Box 2.
London, British Library (BL), Additional Charters 14847, 19609, 33649; mss. Egerton 327, 3031, 3126; Cotton mss. Julius A.i (Chatteris cartulary), Julius D.ii, Nero C.xii, Vespasian E.xiv; Harley mss. 83, 85, 742.
London, College of Arms, Charter Collection Box 19, no. 688/2, Monastic Charters misc 180.
London, Guildhall, City Charters.
London, Lambeth Palace, ms. 415.
London, Lincoln's Inn, ms. Hale 87 (Battle cartulary).
Mons, State Archives, *Fonds Cartulaires*, no. 1.
Nottinghamshire Record Office, Savile Charters, ms. DDSR 102/153.

Oxford, Bodleian Library, Ashmole ms. 1527; Dodsworth mss. 7, 144; Dugdale ms. 17.
Oxford, New College muniments, Hornchurch charter.
Peterborough Cathedral, Dean and Chapter ms. 1.
Provins, Bibliothèque Municipale, ms. 85, no. 19.
Rouen, Bibliothèque Municipale ms. Y44.
TNA, C 52, *carte antique* rolls 3–4, 7, 9–10, 12, 14–19, 21–2, 28, 31, 34, 42, EE, DD, KK; C 53/114; DL 42/7; E 32 rolls 40, 76, rolls A 5272 and 14404; E 164 rolls 20 and 28.
Wells Cathedral Library, ms. DC/CF/2/1.
Westminster Abbey, Muniments, ms. XLV, 657, 659, Dean and Chapter, Westminster Abbey Domesday.
Winchester College Muniments, 9019, 10628.
Worcestershire Record Office, ms. BA 3814.

Printed Sources

L'Abbaye de Notre-Dame de Grestain, ed. C. Bréard (Rouen, 1904).
Abbé Lebeuf, *Mémoires concernant l'histoire civil et ecclésiastique d'Auxerre et de son ancien diocèse*, Vol. 4, ed. M. Challe and M. Quantin (Auxerre, 1855).
Abbreviatio Placitorum, Richard I–Edward II, ed. G. Rose and W. Illingworth (London, 1811).
Abstracts of the Charters and Other Documents Contained in the Chartulary of the Priory of Bridlington in the East Riding of the County of York, ed. W.T. Lancaster (Leeds, 1912).
Acta of Henry II and Richard I of England, 1154–1199, ed. J.C. Holt and R. Mortimer (Kew, 1986).
Acta of Henry II and Richard I, Vol. 2, ed. N. Vincent (Kew, 1996).
Actes des Princes Lorrains, 1ère série: princes laïques, II. Les Comtes, B. Actes des Comtes de Salm, ed. D. Erpelding (préédition, Nancy, 1979).
Actes et documents anciens intéressant la Belgique, Vol. 2, ed. C.H. Duvivier (Brussels, 1903).
The Acts and Letters of the Marshal Family, Marshals of England and Earls of Pembroke, 1145–1248, ed. D. Crouch (Cambridge, 2015).
Alain de Lille. Textes inédits, avec une introduction sur sa vie et ses oeuvres, ed. M.-T. d'Alverney (Paris, 1965).
Alan of Lille, 'Ars Praedicandi', *PL*, Vol. 210.
Alexander III, 'Epistolae et privilegia', *PL*, Vol. 188.
Ambroise, *Estoire de la Guerre Saint, Histoire en vers de la Troisième Croisade*, ed. G. Paris (Paris, 1897).
Ambroise, *The History of the Holy War, Ambroise's Estoire de la Guerre Sainte*, 2 Vols, ed. M. Barber, trans. M. Ailes (Woodbridge, 2003).
Annales d'Anchin dans le recueil des Histoires de la France, ed. A. Le Mire (Paris, 1608).
Annales Cestrienses, or the Chronicle of the Abbey of Saint Werburg, Chester, ed. R. Copley Christie (London, 1887).

'Annales Egmundani 1173', *Monumenta Germaniae Historica Scriptores*, Vol. 17, ed. G.H. Pertz (Hanover, 1861), 442–79.

'Assize Roll 1171. The Cornish Eyre (1201) 30225', *Pleas Before the King or His Justices, 1198–1202: Rolls or Fragments of Rolls from the Years 1198, 1201 and 1202*, Vol. 2, ed. D.M. Stenton (London, 1952), pp. 30–225.

Audita Tremendi, 1187, 'Ansbertus', *Historia de expeditione Friderici imperatoris. Quellen zur Geschichte des Kreuzzuges Kaiser Fredrichs I.*, ed. A. Chroust (Berlin, 1928), pp. 6–10.

Baha' al-Din ibn Shaddad, *The Rare and Excellent History of Saladin*, trans. D.S. Richards (Aldershot, 2002).

Baldwin of Forde, 'Sermo de sancta cruce', 8.1, *Balduini de Forda Opera: Sermones de Commendatione Fidei*, ed. D.N. Bell, *Corpus Christianorum. Continuatio Mediaevalis*, Vol. 99 (Turnhout, 1991), pp. 128–9.

The Battle Abbey Roll with some Account of the Norman Lineages, Vol. 2, ed. C. Powlett (London, 1889).

Benoît de Sainte-Maure, *La Chronique des ducs de Normandie*, 4 Vols, ed. C. Fahlin (Uppsala, 1951–79).

Bernard of Clairvaux, *Epistolae*, in *RHF*, Vol. 15, ed. M.L. Bouquet (Poitiers, 1878).

The Book of the Foundation of Walden Monastery, ed. and trans. D. Greenway and L. Watkiss (Oxford, 1999).

The Burton Lazars Cartulary: A Medieval Leicestershire Estate, ed. T. Bourne and D. Marcombe (Nottingham, 1987).

Calendar of Charter Rolls Preserved in the Public Record Office, Vols. 1–5 (London, 1903–27).

Calendar of Close Rolls of the Reign of Henry III Preserved in the Public Record Office (London, 1902–37).

Calendar of Patent Rolls Preserved in the Public Record Office, 1388–92 (London, 1891–1982).

Calendar of Documents Preserved in France, Illustrative of the History of Great Britain and Ireland, Vol. I, A.D. 918–1206, ed. J.H. Round (London, 1899).

The Cartae Antiquae Rolls 1–10, ed. L. Landon (Pipe Roll Society, new series, 17, 1939).

The Cartae Antiquae Rolls 11–20, ed. J. Conway Davies (Pipe Roll Society, new series, 33, 1957).

Cartae Baronum, ed. N. Stacy, Pipe Roll Society, new series Vol. 62 (Woodbridge, 2019).

Cartulaire de l'abbaye de Basse-Fontaine et chartes de la commanderie de Beauvoir de l'ordre Teutonique, ed. C. Lalore (Paris, 1878).

Cartulaire de l'abbaye de Beaulieu (en Limousin), ed. M. Delouche (Paris, 1859).

Cartulaire de l'abbaye de Cambron, Part 1, ed. J.-J. de Smet (Brussels, 1869).

Cartulaire de l'abbaye cistercienne de Fontaine-Daniel, ed. A.P.A. Grosse-Duperon and E. Gouvrion (Mayenne, 1896).

Cartulaire de l'abbaye cistercienne du Val-Dieu (XIIe-XIVe siècle), ed. J. Ruwet (Brussels, 1955).

Cartulaire de l'abbaye de Montiéramey, ed. C. Lalore (Paris, 1890).

Cartulaire de l'abbaye de Notre-Dame d'Ourscamp de l'ordre de Citeaux, fondée en 1129 au diocèse de Noyon, ed. M. Peigne-Delacourt (Amiens, 1865).

Cartulaire de l'abbaye de Notre-Dame de la Roche, de l'ordre de Saint-Augustine, au diocèse de Paris, ed. A. Moutié (Paris, 1863).
Cartulaire de l'abbaye de Notre-Dame des Vaux de Cernay, ed. L. Merlet and A. Moutié (Paris, 1857).
Cartulaire de l'abbaye d'Orbestier, ed. L. de la Boutetiere (Poitou, 1877).
Cartulaire de l'abbaye du Paraclet, ed. C. Lalore (Paris, 1878).
Le premier cartulaire de l'abbaye de Pontigny (XII-XIII siècles), ed. M. Garrigues (Paris, 1981).
Cartulaire de l'abbaye royale de Notre-Dame de Bon-Port de l'ordre cîteaux au diocèse d'Évreux, ed. J. Andrieux (Évreux, 1862).
Cartulaire de l'abbaye de Saint-Bertin, ed. B.E.C. Guérard (Paris, 1841).
Cartulaire de l'abbaye de Saint-Michel de Tréport, ed. P.L. de Kermaingant (Paris, 1880).
Cartulaire de l'abbaye de la Sainte-Trinité de Tiron, ed. L. Merlet, Vol. 1 (Chartres, 1883).
Cartulaire de l'église collégiale Notre-Dame de Beaujeu, suivi d'un appendice et d'un tableau généalogique de la maison de Beaujeu, ed. M.-C. Guigue (Lyon, 1864).
Cartulaire général de l'Ordre des Hospitaliers de Saint-Jean de Jérusalem (1100-1310), Tome 1er (1100-1200), ed. J. Delaville Le Roulx (Paris, 1894).
Cartulaire général de l'Yonne, Vol. 2, ed. M. Quantin (Auxerre, 1860).
Cartulaire de la léproserie du Grand-Beaulieu, ed. R. Merlet (Chartres, 1909).
Cartulaire de Notre-Dame de Prouille, Vol. 1, ed. J. Guiraud (Paris, 1907).
Cartulaire du prieuré de la Charité-sur-Loire (Nièvre), Ordre de Cluni, ed. R. de Lespinasse (Nevers and Paris, 1887).
Cartulaire du prieuré de Jully-les-Nonnains, ed. E. Petit (Auxerre, 1881).
Cartulaire du prieuré de Saint-Étienne de Vignory, ed. J. d'Arbaumont (Langres, 1882).
Cartulaire de Saint-Michel de l'Abbayette, prieuré de l'abbaye du Mont-Saint-Michel (997-1421), ed. P. de Farcy (Paris, 1894).
Cartulaire de Saint-Pierre de Troyes, ed. C. Lalore (Paris, 1880).
Cartulaire saintongeais de la Trinité de Vendôme, Vol. 2, ed. A. Picard (Vendôme, 1894).
'Cartulaire des templiers de Montsaunès', ed. C. Higounet, *Bulletin philologique et historique du comité des travaux historiques* (Paris, 1957), 225–93.
Cartulaires de l'abbaye de Molesme, ancien diocèse de Langres, 916-1250, Vol. 2, ed. J. Laurant (Paris, 1911).
Cartulaires de l'église de Thérouanne, ed. T. Duchet and A. Giry (Fleury-Lemaire, 1881).
Cartularium Abbathiae de Whiteby, Ordinis S. Benedicti, ed. J.C. Atkinson (Durham, 1880).
Cartularium Monasterii de Rameseia, 3 Vols, ed. W.H. Hart (London, 1884–93).
Cartularium Monasterii Sancti Johannis Baptiste de Colecestria, 2 Vols, ed. S.A. Moore (London, 1897).
Cartularium Rievallense, ed. J.C. Atkinson (London, 1889).
Cartulary of Forde Abbey, ed. S. Hobbs (Taunton, 1998).
The Cartulary of the Knights of St John of Jerusalem in England, Part 2, ed. M. Gervers (Oxford, 1996).

The Cartulary of Newnham Priory, ed. J. Golber (Bedford, 1963).
Chanson d'Aspremont, Chanson de geste du XIIe siècle: Texte du manuscrit de Wollaton Hall, Vol. 2, ed. L. Brandin (Paris, 1921).
'Charta Pacis Valenciennes', ed. G.H. Pertz, *Monumenta Germaniae Historica Scriptores Rerum Germanicarum in Usum Scholarum Separatim Editi*, Vol. 21 (Hanover, 1869), pp. 605–10.
The Charters of the Anglo-Norman Earls of Cheshire, c.1071–1237, ed. G. Barraclough, Record Society of Lancashire and Cheshire, 126 (1988).
Charters of the Honour of Mowbray, 1107–1191, ed. D.E. Greenway (London, 1972).
Les chartes de l'abbaye cistercienne de Vaucelles au XIIe siècle, ed. B.-M. Tock (Turnhout, 2010).
Les chartes de l'abbaye de Saint-Hubert en Ardenne, Vol. 1, ed. G. Kurth (Brussels, 1903).
Les chartes des comtes de Saint-Pol, XIe-XIIIe siècles, ed. J.-F. Nieus (Turnhout, 2008).
Chartes et documents concernant l'abbaye de Cîteaux, ed. J. Marilier (Rome, 1961).
Chartes en langue française antérieures à 1271 conservées dans le département de la Haute-Marne, ed. J.-G. Gigot (Paris, 1966).
Le chartrier de l'abbaye prémontrée de Saint-Yved de Braine: 1134-1250, ed. *les élèves de l'École Nationale des Chartes*, under the direction of O. Guyotjeannin (Paris, 2000).
The Chartulary or Register of the Abbey of St. Werburgh, Chester, Part 1, ed. J. Tait (Manchester, 1920).
'Chronica Albrici monachi Trium Fontium. A Monachio Novi Monasterii Hoiensis Interpolata', *Monumenta Germaniae Historica, Scriptorium*, 23, ed. P. Scheffer-Boichorst (Hanover, 1874), pp. 631–950.
Chronica Monasterii de Melsa, a fundatione usque ad annum 1396, Vol. 1, ed. E.A. Bond, Rolls Series (London, 1866).
The Chronicle of Ernoul and the Continuations of William of Tyre, ed. M.R. Morgan (Oxford, 1973).
Chronicle of the Third Crusade: The Itinerarium Peregrinorum et Gesta Regis Ricardi, trans. H.J. Nicholson (Aldershot, 1997).
Chronicles and Memorials of the Reign of Richard I, Vol. 1: Itinerarium peregrinorum et gesta regis Ricardi, auctore, ut videtur, Ricardo, canonico Sanctæ Trinitatis Londoniensis, ed. W. Stubbs (London, 1864).
Chronicles and Memorials of the Reign of Richard I, Vol 2: Epistolae Cantuarienses, The Letters of the Prior and Convent of Christ Church Canterbury, From A.D. 1187 to A.D. 1199, ed. W. Stubbs (London, 1865).
Chronicles of the Crusades: Contemporary Narratives of the Crusade of Richard Coeur de Lion by Richard of Devizes and Geoffrey of Vinsauf and of the Crusade of Saint Louis by the Lord John of Joinville, ed. H. Bohn (London, 1848).
Chroniques Craonaises, ed. B. de la Jacopière (Le Mans, 1871).
The Conquest of Jerusalem and the Third Crusade, ed. P.W. Edbury (Aldershot, 1998).
Constitutio Domus Regis, ed. and trans. S.D. Church (Oxford, 2007).
Councils and Synods with Other Documents Relating to the English Church, ed. F.M. Powicke, and C.R. Cheney (Oxford, 1964).
Councils and Synods with Other Documents Relating to the English Church, A.D.871–

1204, Vol. 1 part 2, ed. D. Whitelock, M. Brett, and C.N.L. Brooke (Oxford, 1981).
Cronica et Cartularium Monasterii de Dunis, ed. F. van de Putte (Bruges, 1864).
Cronique de l'abbaye de Ter Doest, ed. F. van de Putte and C. Carton (Bruges, 1845).
Crusade Charters, 1138–1270, ed. C.K. Slack, trans. H.B. Feiss (Tempe, AZ, 2001).
The Crusade of Frederick Barbarossa, The History of the Expedition of the Emperor Frederick and Related Texts, trans. G.A. Loud (New York and London, 2010).
Delisle, L., 'Examen de treize chartes de l'ordre de Grammont', *Memoires de la Société des Antiquaires de Normandie*, 20 (1853), 171–221.
Description analytique de cartulaires et chartriers accompagnés du texte de documents utiles à l'histoire du Hainaut, Vol. 3, ed. L. DeVilliers (Mons, 1867).
Dialogus de Scaccario, ed. C. Johnson (Edinburgh, London, and New York, 1950).
Diocèse ancien de Châlons-sur-Marne. Histoire et monuments, ed. E. de Barthélemy (Paris, 1861).
Diplomatic Documents Preserved in the Public Record Office, Volume I, 1101–1272, ed. P. Chaplais (London, 1964).
Diplomata Belgica. The Diplomatic Sources from the Medieval Southern Low Countries, ed. T. de Hemptinne, J. Deploige, J-L. Kupper, and W. Prevenier (Brussels, 2015–).
'Documents concernant Sautour et Aublin, extraits du cartulaire de l'abbaye de Floreffe', *Analectes pour servir à l'histoire ecclésiastique de la Belgique*, Vol. 8 (1871), 364–9.
'Documents concernant Trazegnies, extraits du cartulaire de l'abbaye de Floreffe', ed. J. Barbier, *Analectes pour servir à l'histoire ecclésiastique de la Belgique*, Vol. 7 (1870), no. 3.
Documents et mémoires pour servir à l'histoire du territoire de Belfort, ed. L. Viellard (Besançon, 1884).
Documents inédits, Extraits du Cartulaire de Picquigny, ed. L.-E. de la Gorgue-Rosny (Boulogne-sur-Mer, 1877).
Documents Relating to the Law and Custom of the Sea, Vol. 1, A.D. 1205–1648, ed. R.G. Marsden (London, 1915).
Early Yorkshire Charters, Vols. 1–3, ed. W. Farrer (Edinburgh, 1914–16), and Vols. 4–12, ed. C.T. Clay (Leeds, 1935–64).
Early Yorkshire Families, ed. C.T. Clay and D.E. Greenway (Cambridge, 1973).
Édition des actes originaux de l'abbaye de Maizières, XIIe siècle, Chartes de la Bourgogne du Moyen Âge, ed. C. Rey (Dijon, 2015).
Eustache Le Moine: pirate boulonnais du XIIIe siècle, trans. E. Mousseigne (Lille, 1996).
Excerta e Rotulis Finium in Turri Londinense Asservatis, AD 1216-72, Vol. 1 (London, 1835).
'De Expugnatione Terrae Sanctae Libellus', *Radulphi de Coggeshall Chronicon Anglicanum; De expugnatione Terrae Sanctae libellus;...*, ed. J. Stevenson, Rolls Series, Vol. 66 (London, 1875), pp. 209–62.
Facsimiles of Early Charters from Northamptonshire Collections, ed. F. Stenton (Northampton, 1930).
Facsimiles of Royal and Other Charters in the British Museum, Vol. 1, ed. G.F. Warner and H.J. Ellis (London, 1903).

'Feoda I', *Documents relatifs au Comté de Champagne et Brie (1172-1361)*, Vol. 1, ed. A. Longnon (Paris, 1901).
Fines, sive Pedes finium: sive Finales concordiae in Curia Domini regis: ab anno septimo regni regis Ricardi I. ad annum decimum sextum regis Johannis, A.D. 1195-A.D. 1214, ed. J. Hunter (London, 1831).
Foedora, Vol. 1, ed. T. Rymer (reprint, Farnborough, 1967).
Galbert of Bruges, *De Multro, Traditione, et Occasione Gloriosi Karoli Comitis Flandriarum*, ed. J. Rider (Turnhout, 1994).
Guy of Bazoches, *Liber epistularum Guidonis de Basochis*, ed. H. Adolfsson (Stockholm, 1969).
Fulcheri Carnotensis Historia Hierosolymitana (1095-1127), ed. H. Hagenmeyer (Heidelberg, 1913).
Gerald of Wales, *Giraldi Cambrensis opera*, 8 Vols, ed. J.S. Brewer, J.F. Dimock and G.F. Warner (London, 1861–91).
Gerald of Wales, *Journey Through Wales*, ed. B. Radice and trans. L. Thorpe (London, 1978).
Gerald of Wales, *Expugnatio Hibernica: The Conquest of Ireland by Giraldus Cambrensis*, ed. A.B. Scott and F.X. Martin (Dublin, 1978).
Gervase of Canterbury, *The Historical Works of Gervase of Canterbury*, Vol. 1, ed. W. Stubbs (London, 1880).
Gilbert of Mons, *Chronicle of Hainaut by Gilbert of Mons*, trans. L. Napran (Woodbridge, 2005).
Gilbert of Mons, *La chronique de Gislebert de Mons*, ed. L. Vanderkindere (Brussels, 1904).
Glanville, *The Treatise on the Law and Customs of the Realm of England commonly called Glanvill*, ed. G.D.G. Hall (London, 1965).
The Great Roll of the Pipe for the Sixth Year of the Reign of King Richard the First, Michaelmas 1194, ed. D.M. Stenton (London, 1928).
Guibert of Nogent, *De vita sua*, ed. Dom Luc d'Achery (1651), *PL*, Vol. 156.
Haymar Monaschus, *Der 'Rithmus de expeditione Ierosolimitana' des sogenannten Haymarus Monachus Florentinus*, ed. S. Falk, Italian trans. A. Placanica and S. Falk (Florence, 2006).
Haymari Monachi, *De expugnata Accone. Liber tetrastichus seu Rithmus de expeditione Ierosolimitana*, ed. P.E.D. Riant (Paris, 1866).
'Histoire de l'abbaye de Lannoy, ordre de Cîteaux [reconstitution de 80 actes]', ed. L.E. Deladreue, *Mémoires de la Société académique d'archéologie, sciences et arts du département de l'Oise*, 10 (1877), 405–84, 569–696.
Histoire et cartulaire des Templiers de Provins. Avec une introduction sur les débuts du Temple en France, ed. V. Carrière (Paris, 1919; reprint: Marseille, 1978).
Histoire de Guillaume le Maréchal History of William Marshal, Vol. 1 – Text and Translation (ll. 1–20031), ed. A.J. Holden, trans. S. Gregory, historical notes D. Crouch (London, 2002).
Historia de Profectione Danorum in Hierosolymam, Scriptores minors, Vol. 2, ed. M. Cl. Gertz (Copenhagen, 1922), pp. 457–92.
Historia Regum: Eadem Historia ad quantum et vicesimum Annum Continuata, per Joannem Hagulstadensem, Vol. 2, ed. T. Arnold (London, 1885).
Ibn al-'Adim, *Zubdat al-h,alab min tar'ih H,alab*, 3 Vols, ed. S. Dahan (Damascus,

1951–68), 'L'histoire d'Alep de Kamal-al-Din', partially trans. E. Blochet, *Revue de L'Orient Latin*, Vol. 3 (1895), pp. 509-65.

Ibn al-Athir, *The Chronicle of Ibn Al-Athir for the Crusading Period from Al-Kamil Fi'l-Ta'rikh. Part 2: The Years 541–589/1146–1193. The Age of Nur al-Din and Saladin*, trans. D.S. Richard (Farnham, 2007).

Inventaire des archives de l'abbaye de Ghislenghien, ed. D. van Overstraeten (Brussels, 1976).

'Inventaire de la collection de Chastellux', ed. C. Porée, *Bulletin de la Société des sciences historiques et naturelles de l'Yonne*, 57 (1904), 117–292.

De Itinere Navali. A German Third Crusader's Chronicle of his Voyage to the Siege of Almohad Silves, 1189 AD/Muwahid Xelb, 585 AH, trans. D. Cushing (Antimony Media, 2013).

Das Itinerarium Peregrinorum, Ein Zeitgenössiche Englische Chronik zum Dritten Kreuzzug in Ursprünglisher Gestalt, ed. H.E. Mayer (Stuttgart, 1962).

Jean de Joinville et les seigneurs de Joinville, suivi d'un catalogue de leurs actes, ed. H.-F. Delaborde (Paris, 1894).

John of Garland's De triumphis Ecclesie: A New Critical Edition with Introduction and Translation, ed. and trans. M. Hall (Leiden, 2019).

'Joinville: The Life of Saint Louis', *Joinville and Villehardouin, Chronicles of the Crusades*, ed. and trans. M.R.B. Shaw (London, 1963), pp. 163-354.

Kamal al-Din Abu 'l-Qasim, *Zubdat al-h,alab min tar'ih H,alab*, ed. S. Dahan, trans. E. Blochet, 'L'histoire d'Alep de Kamal-al-Din', *Revue de L'Orient Latin*, Vol. 3 (1895), pp. 509-65.

Die Kanzlei der lateinischen Könige von Jerusalem, Vol. 2, ed. H.E. Mayer (Hanover, 1996).

Knighton, Henry, *Chronicon Henrici Knighton; vel Cnithon, monachi Leycestrensis*, Vol. 1, ed. J.R. Lumby (London, 1889-95).

Lambert of Ardres, *The History of the Counts of Guines and Lords of Ardres*, trans. L. Shopkow (Philadelphia, 2007).

Layettes du Trésor des Chartes, ed. M.A. Teulet, Vols 1 and 2 (Paris, 1863–66).

The Letters and Charters of Henry II, King of England 1154–1189, ed. N. Vincent (Oxford, forthcoming).

Liber Feodorum. Book of Fees Commonly Called Testa de Nevill, Reformed from the Earliest MSS, ed. H.C. Maxwell Lyte, 3 Vols. (London, 1920–31).

List of Sheriffs for England and Wales: From Earliest Times to A.D. 1831. Lists and Indexes no. IX (London, 1898).

The London Eyre of 1244, ed. H.A. Chew and M. Weinbaum (London, 1970).

Lyrics of the Troubadours and Trouvères: An Anthology and a History, ed. and trans. F. Goldin (New York, 1973).

Magni Rotuli Scaccarii Normanniae, 2 Vols, ed. T. Stapleton (London, 1840–4).

The Manuscripts of His Grace the Duke of Rutland, KG, Preserved at Belvoir Castle, IV, ed. J.H. Round (London, 1905).

Marsy, A. de, *Fragment d'un cartulaire de l'ordre de Saint-Lazare en Terre Sainte. Archives de l'Orient latin*, 2 (Paris, 1883 [reprint New York, 1978]).

Memorials of the Abbey of St Mary of Fountains, ed. J.R. Walbran (Durham, 1863).

Monasticon Anglicanum, or, The history of the ancient abbies, and other monasteries, hospitals, cathedral and collegiate churches in England and Wales. With divers

French, Irish, and Scotch monasteries formerly relating to England, ed. W. Dugdale, Vols 1, 5 and 6 (London, 1655, 1693).
Monasticon Diocesis Exoniensis, ed. G. Oliver (Exeter, 1846).
Monuments de l'histoire de l'ancien évêché de Bâle, Vol. 1, ed. J. Trouillat (Porrentruy, 1852).
Nécrologe de l'église d'Amiens, ed. J.B.M. Roze (Amiens, 1885).
'Nithard's Histories', *Carolingian Chronicles, Royal Frankish Annals and Nithard's Histories*, trans. B.W. Scholz and B. Rogers (Ann Arbor, MI, 1970), pp. 127–74.
'Obituaire de la Commanderie du Temple de Reims', *Mélanges historiques. Collection des Documents inédits*, Vol. 4 (Paris, 1882).
Obituaires de la province de Lyon, II, *Diocèse de Lyon, deuxième partie, dioceses de Mâcon et de Châlon-sur-Saône*, ed. J. Laurent and P. Gras (Paris, 1965).
Obituaires de la province de Sens, 1.1, ed. A. Molinier (Paris, 1902).
Oeuvres de Henri d'Andeli, trouvère du XIIIe siècle, ed. A. Héron (Paris, 1881).
Oeuvres de Rigord et de Guillaume de Breton, historiens de Philippe-Auguste, Vol. 1, ed. H.F. Delaborde (Paris, 1882).
De Oorkonden der Graven van Vlaanderen, (juli 1128-september 1191), Uitgave-Band III, Regering van Filips van de Elzas, Tweede deel: 1178-1191, ed. T. de Hemptinne, A. Verhurst, and L. de Mey (Brussels, 2009).
Orderic Vitalis, *The Ecclesiastical History of Orderic Vitalis*, Vol. 2, ed. and trans. M. Chibnall (Oxford, 1978).
Ottonis et Rahewini Gesta Friderici primi imperatoris, ed. G. Waitz, *Monumenta Germaniae Historica Scriptores Rerum Germanicarum in Usum Scholarum Separatim Editi*, Vol. 10 (Hanover, 1912), pp. 1–161.
Peter of Blois, 'Dialogus inter Regem Henricum Secundem et abbatem Bonevallis', ed. R.B.C. Huygens, *Revue Bénédictine*, 68 (1958), 104–5.
Peter of Blois, *Petrus Blesensis Bathoniensis in Anglia Archidiaconus. PL*, Vol. 207.
The Poems of the Troubadour Bertran de Born, ed. W.D. Paden Jr., T. Sankovitch, and P.H. Stäblein (Berkeley, CA, and London, 1986).
De Profectione Ludovici VII in Orientum, ed. and trans. V.G. Berry (New York, 1948).
'Querimoniae normannorum', *RHF*, Vol. 14, ed. L. Delisle (Paris, 1904).
Ralph of Coggeshall, *Radulphi de Coggeshall Chronicon Anglicanum, De expugnatione Terrae Sanctae libellus;...*, ed. J. Stevenson, Rolls Series, Vol. 66 (London, 1875).
Ralph of Diss, *Ymagines Historiarum, Opera Historica*, ed. W. Stubbs, 2 Vols (London, 1876).
Raoul de Houdenc, *Songe d'Enfer*, ed. M.T. Mihm (Tübingen, 1984).
Reading Abbey Cartularies, Vol. 1, ed. B.R. Kemp (London, 1986).
'The Records of the Templars in England in the Twelfth Century', *British Academy Records of Social and Economic History*, Vol. 9, ed. B.A. Lees (1935).
Records of Merton Priory in the County of Surrey, Chiefly from Early and Unpublished Documents, ed. A. Heales (London, 1898).
Recueil des actes de Henri II, roi d'Angleterre et duc de Normandie, concernant les provinces françaises et les affaires de France, 2 Vols, ed. L. Delisle (Paris, 1916–20).
Recueil des Actes de Henri II roi d'Angleterre et duc de Normandie concernant les provinces françaises et les affaires de France: Introduction, ed. L. Delisle and E. Berger (Paris, 1909).

Recueil des Actes de Philippe Auguste, roi de France, Vol. 1, ed. M.H.-F. Delaborde (Paris, 1916).
Recueil des chartes de l'abbaye de Clairvaux au XIIe siècle, ed. J. Waquet and J.-M. Roger (Paris, 2004).
Recueil des chartes de l'abbaye de Cluny, Vol. 5, ed. A. Bernard, revised A. Bruel (Paris, 1894).
Recueil des chartes de l'abbaye de Saint-Benoît-sur-Loire, ed. M. Prou and A. Vidier (Paris, 1900).
The Red Book of the Exchequer, Vols. 1 and 2, ed. H. Hall (London, 1896).
Regesta Regni Hierosolymitani, 1097-1291, ed. R. Röhricht (Innsbruck, 1893).
Regesta Regum Scottorum, Vol. 2, *Acts of William I*, ed. G.W.S. Barrow (Edinburgh, 1971).
Rhabanus Maurus, 'De procinctu Romanae miliciae', ed. E. Dümmler, *Zeitschrift für deutsches Alterthum*, 15 (1872), 443–51.
Richard of Devizes, 'The Chronicle of Richard of Devizes', *Chronicles of the Reigns of Stephen, Henry II and Richard I*, Vol. 2 ed. R.G. Howlett (London, 1886).
Robert of Torigny, *Chronique de Robert de Torigni: Abbé du Mont-Saint-Michel*, 2 Vols, ed. L. Delisle (Rouen, 1872–3).
Robert of Torigny, *The Chronicle of Robert of Torigny: Chronicles of the Reigns of Stephen, Henry II, and Richard I*, Vol. 4, ed. R. Howlett (London, 1889).
Roger of Howden, *Chronica magistri Rogeri de Houedone*, 4 vols. ed. W. Stubbs (London, 1868–71).
Roger of Howden, *Gesta Regis Henrici Secundi Benedicti Abbatis: The Chronicle of the Reigns of Henry II and Richard I A.D. 1169–1192, Known Commonly under the Name of Benedict of Peterborough*, 2 Vols, ed. W. Stubbs (London, 1867).
Roger of Wendover, *Flores Historiarum*, Vol. 1, ed. H.G. Howlett (London, 1886).
Rotuli Chartarum in Turri Londinensi Asservati, Vol. 1, Pt 1, ed. T.D. Hardy (London, 1837).
Rotuli Curia Regis, Vol. 1, ed. F. Palgrave (London, 1835).
Rotuli de Dominabus et Pueris et Puellis, ed. J.H. Round (London, 1913).
Rotuli de Liberate ac de Misis et Praestitis Regnante Johanne, ed. T.D. Hardy (London, 1844).
Rotuli Literarum Patentium in Turri Londinensi Asservati, Vol. 1, ed. T.D. Hardy (London, 1835).
Rotuli Litterarum Clausarum in Turri Londinensi Asservati, Vol. 1 (London, 1833).
Rotuli de Oblatis et Finibus in Turri Londinensi, ed. T.D. Hardy (London, 1835).
The Rule of the Templars, The French Text of the Rule of the Order of the Knights Templar, trans. J.M. Upton-Ward (Woodbridge, 1992).
Sacrae antiquitatis monumenta, Vol. 2, ed. C.L. Hugo (Nancy, 1736).
Saint-Denis de Nogent-le-Rotrou, 1031-1789: Histoire et Cartulaire, ed. C. Métais (Vannes, 1899).
Statuta capitulorum generalium ordinis Cisterciensis, Vol. 1, ed. J.-M. Canivez, Bibliothèque de la Revue d'histoire ecclésiastique, Vol. 9 (1933).
Simeon of Durham, *Symeonis Monachi Opera Omnia*, Vol. 1, ed. by T. Arnold (London, 1882).
Song of the Cathar Wars. A History of the Albigensian Crusade, trans. J. Shirley (Aldershot, 1996).

Stoke by Clare Priory Cartulary, Vol. I, ed. C. Harper-Bill and R. Mortimer (Woodbridge, 1982).
Suger, Abbot of Saint-Denis, 'Epistolae', *RHF*, Vol. 15, ed. M.L. Bouquet (Poitiers, 1878), pp. 483–532.
The Thame Cartulary, Vol. 1, ed. H.E. Salter (Oxford, 1947).
Les Templiers en Eure-et-Loir: Histoire et Cartulaire, ed. C. Métais (Chartres, 1902).
Vie de Louis le Gros par Suger, suivie de l'Histoire du roi Louis VII, ed. A. Molinier (Paris, 1887).
Vie de saint Bernard, abbé de Clairvaux, Vol. 2, ed. E. Vacandard (Paris, 1895).
Vigeois, Geoffrey de, '*Chronica*', *Novae Bibliothecae Manuscriptorum Librorum*, Vol. 2, ed. P. Labbe (Paris, 1657).
Walter Map, *Contes pour le gens de cour. De Nugis curialium*, ed. A. Bates (Brussels, 1993).
The Waltham Chronicle, ed. and trans. M. Chibnall and L. Watkiss (Oxford, 1994).
William of Newburgh, 'Historia Rerum Anglicarum', *Chronicles of the Reigns of Stephen, Henry II and Richard I*, 2 Vols, ed. R.G. Howlett (London, 1884–9).
William of Newburgh, *The History of English Affairs, Book 2*, ed. and trans. P.G. Walsh and M.J. Kennedy (Oxford, 2007).
William of Tyre, *A History of Deeds Done Across the Sea*, Vol. 2, trans. E.A. Babcock and A.C. Krey (New York, 1976).
William of Tyre, *Historia Rerum in Partibus Transmarinis Gestarum*, *PL*, Vol. 201.

Secondary Sources

Abels, R., *Lordship and Military Obligation in Anglo-Saxon England* (Berkeley, CA, 1988).
Ailes, A., 'Heraldry in Twelfth-Century England: The Evidence', *England in the Twelfth Century. Proceedings of the 1988 Harlaxton Symposium*, ed. D. Williams (Woodbridge, 1990), pp. 1–16.
Ailes, M.J., 'Heroes of War: Ambroise's Heroes of the Third Crusade', *Writing War: Medieval Literary Responses to Warfare*, ed. C. Saunders, F. Le Saux, and N. Thomas (Cambridge, 2004), pp. 29–48.
Algrant, J.J., and Beaugourdon, J., *Armorial of the Military and Hospitaller Order of St Lazarus of Jerusalem* (Delft, 1983).
Allen, P., 'Richard of Devizes and the Alleged Martyrdom of a Boy at Winchester', *Transactions & Miscellanies* (Jewish Historical Society of England), 27 (1978–1980), 32–9.
Anderson, B., *Imagined Communities: Reflections on the Origin and Spread of Nationalism*, 3rd edition (London, 2006).
Andressohn, J.C., *The Ancestry and Life of Godfrey of Bouillon* (Bloomington, IN, 1947).
Appleby, J.T., *England Without Richard* (London and New York, 1965).
Arbois de Jubainville, H. d', *Histoire des Ducs et des Comtes de Champagne, depuis le VIe siècle jusqu'à la fin du XIe*, Vol. 3 (Paris, 1861).
Arnoux, M., 'Les origins et le developpement du mouvement canonical en

Normandie', *Des clercs au service de la réforme. Etudes et documents sur les chanoines réguliers de la province de Rouen* (Turnhout, 2000).

Asbridge, T.S., *The First Crusade, A New History* (Oxford, 2004).

——, *The Crusades, The War for the Holy Land* (London, 2010).

——, 'Talking to the Enemy: The Role and Purpose of Negotiations between Saladin and Richard the Lionheart during the Third Crusade', *JMH*, 39 (2013), 275–96.

——, *The Greatest Knight, The Remarkable Life of William Marshal, the Power Behind Five English Thrones* (London, 2015).

Aurell, M. (ed.), *Noblesses de l'espace Plantagenêt (1154-1224)* (*Cahiers de Civilisation Médiévale, numéro spécial XI*) (Poitiers, 2001).

——, *The Plantagenet Empire, 1154–1224*, trans. D. Crouch (Harlow, 2007).

Aurell, M., and Tonnerre, N.-Y. (eds.), *Plantagenêts et Capétiens: Confrontations et Héritages* (Turnhout, 2006).

Bachrach, B.S., 'Charles Martel, Shock Combat, the Stirrup, and Feudalism', *Studies in Medieval and Renaissance History*, 7 (1970), 47–75.

——, 'The Idea of the Angevin Empire', *Albion*, 10 (1978), 293–9.

——, *Early Carolingian Warfare: Prelude to Empire* (Philadelphia, 2001).

——, *Religion and the Conduct of War c. 300–1215* (Woodbridge, 2003).

Bachrach, D., 'Medieval Logistics during the Reign of Edward I of England', *War in History*, 13 (2006), 423–40.

Baldwin, J.W., *The Government of Philip Augustus: Foundations of French Royal Power in the Middle Ages* (Berkeley, Los Angeles, CA, and Oxford, 1986).

Balfour, D., 'The Origins of the Longchamp Family', *Medieval Prosopography*, 18 (1997), 73–92.

Barber, M., 'The Order of Saint Lazarus and the Crusade', *The Catholic Historical Review*, 80 (1994), 439–56.

Barber, M., and Bate, K., *The Templars: Selected Sources* (New York, 2002).

Barber, R., and Barker, J., *Tournaments, Jousts, Chivalry and Pageants in the Middle Ages* (Woodbridge, 1989).

Barber, R., 'Chivalry in the Tournament and *Pas d'Armes*', *A Companion to Chivalry*, ed. R.W. Jones and P. Coss (Woodbridge, 2019), pp. 119–38.

Barker, J.R.V., *The Tournament in England, 1100–1400* (Woodbridge, 2003).

Barlow, F., *Thomas Becket* (London, 1986).

Barnes, J.A. and Harary, F., 'Graph Theory in Network Analysis', *Social Networks*, 5 (1983), 235–44.

Barratt, N., 'The Revenues of John and Philip Augustus revisited', *King John: New Interpretations*, ed. S.D. Church (Woodbridge, 1999), pp. 75–99.

——, 'The English Revenue of Richard I', *EHR*, 116 (2001), 635–56.

——, 'Counting the Cost: the Financial Implications of the Loss of Normandy', *Thirteenth Century England X: Proceedings of the Durham Conference 2003*, eds. M. Prestwich, R. Frame and R. H. Britnell (Woodbridge, 2005), pp. 31–40.

Barthélemy, A. de, 'Pèlerins champenois en Palestine (1097-1249)', *Revue de l'Orient Latin*, 1 (1893), 354–78.

Barthélemy, D., *La mutation de l'an mil a-t-elle eu lieu? Servage et chevalerie dans la France des Xe et XIe siècles* (Paris, 1997).

Bartlett, R., *Gerald of Wales, 1146–1223* (Oxford, 1982).

——, *England under the Norman and Angevin Kings* (Oxford, 2002).
Bates, D., and Curry, A. (eds.), *England and Normandy in the Middle Ages* (London, 1994).
Bates, D., 'The Prosopographical Study of Anglo-Norman Charters', *Family Trees and the Roots of Politics: The Prosopography of Britain and France from the Tenth to the Twelfth Century*, ed. K.S.B. Keats-Rohan (Woodbridge, 1997), pp. 89–102.
Bautier, R.-H., 'La collection des chartes de croisade dite "collection Courtois"', *Comptes-rendus des séances de l'Académie des Inscriptions et Belles Lettres*, 100 (1956), 382–6.
——, (ed.), *La France de Philippe Auguste: le temps des mutations* (Paris, 1982).
——, '"Empire Plantagenêt" ou "espace Plantagenêt": Y eut-il une civilisation du monde Plantagenêt?', *Cahiers de Civilisation Médiévale*, 24 (1986), 139–47.
Beaune, C., *Naissance de la nation de France* (Paris, 1986).
Bédier, J., and Aubry, P., *Les chansons de croisade* (Paris, 1909).
Beech, G., 'The Scope of Medieval Prosopography', *Medieval Prosopography*, 1, no. 1 (1980), 3–7.
Beeler, J., *Warfare in England, 1066–1189* (New York, 1966).
Bell, A.R., Curry, A., Chapman, A., King, A. and Simpkin D., eds., *The Soldier Experience in the Fourteenth Century* (Woodbridge, 2017).
Bennett, M., *Community, Class and Careerism: Cheshire and Lancashire Society in the Age of Sir Gawain and the Green Knight* (Cambridge, 1983).
——, 'Stereotype Normans in Old French Vernacular Literature', *ANS*, 19 (1987), 25–42.
——, '*Le Règle du Temple* as a Military Manual, or How to Deliver a Cavalry Charge', *The Rule of the Templars* (Woodbridge, 1992), pp. 175–88.
——, 'The Medieval Warhorse Reconsidered', *Medieval Knighthood*, 5, ed. S. Church and R. Harvey (Woodbridge, 1995), pp. 19–40.
——, 'The Myth of the Military Supremacy of Knightly Cavalry', *Armies, Chivalry, and Warfare in Britain and France: Proceedings of the 1995 Harlaxton Symposium*, ed. M. Strickland (Stamford, 1998), pp. 304–16.
——, 'Why Chivalry? Military "Professionalism" in the Twelfth Century: the Origins and Expressions of a Socio-Military Ethos', *The Chivalric Ethos and the Development of Military Professionalism*, ed. D.J. Trim (Leiden, 2003), pp. 41–64.
——, 'Remembering Chivalry', paper given at the 25th International Medieval Congress, University of Leeds (UK), July 2018.
——,, 'Manuals of Warfare and Chivalry', *A Companion to Chivalry*, ed. R.W. Jones and P. Coss (Woodbridge, 2019), pp. 263–79.
Bennett, S., 'La mesnie de roi Richard 1er lors la troisième croisade', *Richard Cœur de Lion, Entre Mythe et Réalités*, ed. M. Aurell and C. Vital (Gent, 2016), pp. 70–8.
——, 'The Battle of Arsuf/Arsur, A Reappraisal of the Charge of the Hospitallers', *The Military Orders: Culture and Conflict*, 6/1, ed. M. Carr and J. Schenk (Abingdon and New York, 2017), pp. 44–53.
——, 'Faith and Authority, Guy of Lusignan at the Battle of Acre (4th October 1189)', *A Military History of the Mediterranean Sea – Aspects of Warfare, Diplomacy and Military Elites*, ed. G. Theotokis and A. Yildiz (Leiden, 2017), pp. 220–34.

Berger, É., 'Les préparatifs d'une invasion anglaise et la descente de Henri III en Bretagne', *Bibliothéque de l'École des Chartes*, 54 (1893), 5–44.

Billoré, M., 'La noblesse normande dans l'entourage de Richard 1er', *La cour Plantagenêt (1154-1204): Actes du Colloque tenu á Thouars du 30 avril au 2 mai 1999*, ed. M. Aurell (Poitiers, 2000), pp. 151–68.

———, 'Le château, enjeu de pouvoir en Normandie, du règne d'Henri II à la conquête de Philippe Auguste', *Cinquante années d'études médiévales à la confluence de nos disciplines. Actes du Colloque organisé à l'occasion du Cinquantenaire du CESCM, Poitiers, 1-4 septembre 2003*, ed. C. Arrignon, M.-H. Debiès, C. Galderisi, and É. Palazzo (Turnhout, 2005), pp. 165–87.

———, 'Y a-t-il une "oppression" des Plantagenêt sur l'aristocratie en Normandie à la veille de 1204?', *Plantagenêts et Capétiens: confrontations et héritages*, ed. M. Aurell and N.-Y. Tonnerre (Turnhout, 2006), pp. 145–61.

Bird, J., 'Preaching and Crusading Memory', *Remembering the Crusades and Crusading*, ed. M. Cassidy-Welch (Abingdon, 2017), pp. 13–33.

Blair, A., *History of the Waldenses*, Vol. 1 (Edinburgh, 1832).

Bligny, B., *L'Église et les ordres religieux dans le royaume de Bourgogne aux XI et XII siècles* (Paris, 1960).

Bloch, M., *Feudal Society*, Vol. 1, 2nd edition, trans. L.A. Manyon (London, 1962).

Boas, A., *Archaeology of the Military Orders. A Survey of the Urban Centres, Rural Settlements and Castles of the Military Orders in the Latin East, c.1120–1291* (London, 2006).

Bolton, B.M., *Innocent III: Studies on Papal Authority and Pastoral Care* (Aldershot, 1995).

———, 'A Matter of Great Confusion: King Richard I and Syria's *Vetus de Monte*', *Diplomatics in the Eastern Mediterranean 1000–1500, Aspects of Cross-Cultural Communication*, ed. A.D. Beihammer, M.G. Parani and C.D. Schabel (Leiden, 2008), pp. 171–99.

Bolton, D'A.J.D., 'Classic Knighthood as Nobiliary Dignity: The Knighting of Counts and Kings' Sons in England, 1066–1272', *Medieval Knighthood V, Papers from the Sixth Strawberry Hill Conference 1994*, ed. S. Church and R. Harvey (Woodbridge, 1995), pp. 41–100.

Bond, S., 'The Medieval Constables of Windsor Castle', *EHR*, 82 (1967), 225–49.

Borderie, A. de la, *Histoire de Bretagne* (Rennes and Paris, 1899).

Boston, H., 'Change and Continuity: Multiple Lordship in Post-Conquest England', paper given at the Battle Conference on Anglo-Norman Studies 2020: A Virtual Workshop, July 2020.

Bouchard, C.B., 'The Origins of the French Nobility: A Reassessment', *American Historical Review*, 86 (1981), 501–32.

———, 'Family Structure and Family Consciousness among the Aristocracy in the Ninth to Eleventh Centuries', *Francia*, 14 (1986), 639–58.

———, *Sword, Miter, and Cloister: Nobility and the Church in Burgundy, 980–1198* (London, 1987).

———, *Strong of Body, Brave and Noble: Chivalry and Society in Medieval France* (Ithaca, 1998).

———, *Those of My Blood: Constructing Noble Families in Medieval Francia* (Philadelphia, 2001).

Bourdieu, P., *L'Amour de l'art* (Paris, 1966).
——, *Distinction: A Social Critique of the Judgement of Taste*, trans. R. Nice (London, 1984).
Boussard, J., *Le comté d'Anjou sous Henri Plantagenêt et ses fils, 1151-1204* (Paris, 1938).
——, 'Les mercenaires au XIIe siècle, Henri II Plantagenêt et les origins de l'armée de métier', *Bibliothéque de l'École de Chartes*, 106 (1945–6), 189–224.
——, *Le Gouvernement d'Henri II Plantagenêt* (Paris, 1956).
Bowie, C.M., *The Daughters of Henry II and Eleanor of Aquitaine* (Turnhout, 2014).
——, 'Matilda, Duchess of Saxony (1169–89) and the Cult of Thomas Becket: A Legacy of Appropriation', *The Cult of St Thomas Becket in the Plantagenet World, c.1170–c.1220*, ed. P. Webster and M.-P. Gelin (Woodbridge, 2016), pp. 113–32.
Bradbury, J., *Philip Augustus, King of France 1180–1223* (London and New York, 1998).
Bramhall, E.C., 'The Origin of the Temporal Privileges of Crusaders', *American Journal of Theology*, 5 (1901), 279–92.
Brenner, E., *Leprosy and Charity in Medieval Rouen* (Woodbridge, 2015).
Bridrey, E., *La condition juridique des croisés et le privilège de croix* (Paris, 1900).
Bronstein, J., *The Hospitallers and the Holy Land* (Woodbridge, 2005).
Brown, S.D.B., 'The Mercenary and His Master, Military Service and Monetary Reward in the Eleventh and Twelfth Centuries', *History*, 74 (1989), 20–38.
Brundage, J., 'The Crusader's Wife: A Canonistic Quandary', *Studia Gratiana*, 12 (1967), 425–42.
——, *Medieval Canon Law and the Crusader* (Madison, WI, 1969).
Brunner, H., 'Der Reiterdienst und die Anflänge des Lehnswesens', *Zeitschrift der Savigny-Stiftung für Rechtsgeschichte, Germanistische Abteilung*, 8 (1887), pp. 1–38.
Brühl, C., *Naissance de deux peuples: Français et Allemands, IX-XI siècle* (Paris, 1994).
Buck, A.D., 'Settlement, Identity, and Memory in the Latin East: An Examination of the Term "Crusader States"', *EHR*, 135 (2020), 271–302.
——, *The Principality of Antioch and its Frontiers in the Twelfth Century* (Woodbridge, 2017).
Bull, M.G., *Knightly Piety and the Lay Response to the First Crusade: The Limousin and Gascony c.970–c.1130* (Oxford, 1993).
——, 'Views of Muslims and of Jerusalem in Miracle Stories, c.1000–c.1200: Reflections on the Study of First Crusaders' Motivations', *The Experience of Crusading: Western Approaches*, ed. M.G. Bull and N.J. Housley (Cambridge, 2003), pp. 13–38.
——, *Eyewitness and Crusade Narrative: Perception and Narration in Accounts of the Second, Third, and Fourth Crusades* (Woodbridge, 2018).
Bullough, D.A., '*Europae Pater*: Charlemagne and his Achievement in the Light of Recent Scholarship', *EHR*, 85 (1970), 84–90.
Bulst-Thiele, M.L., '*Sacrae domus militiae Templi Hierosolymitani magistri*. Untersuchungen zur Geschichte des Templerordens 1118/9-1314', *Abhandlungen der Akademie der Wissenschaften in Göttingen. Philologisch-Historisch Klasse*, 86 (Göttingen, 1974).
Burgtorf, J., *The Central Convent of Hospitallers and Templars: History, Organization, and Personnel (1099/1120–1310)* (Leiden and Boston, 2008).

Burt, R., *Toward a Structural Theory of Action: Network Models of Social Structure, Perception and Action* (New York, 1982).
——, *Structural Holes: The Social Structure of Competition* (Cambridge, MA, 1992).
Burton, J.E., 'The Knights Templar in Yorkshire in the Twelfth Century: A Reassessment', *Northern History*, 27 (1991), 26–40.
Bysted, A.L., *The Crusade Indulgence: Spiritual Rewards and the Theology of the Crusades* (Leiden, 2015).
Calmet, A., *Histoire ecclésiastique et civile de Lorraine*, 5 (Nancy, 1748).
Campbell, D.T., *Ethnocentric and Other Altruistic Motives*. (Lincoln, NE, 1965).
Carpenter, C., *Locality and Polity: A Study of Warwickshire Landed Society, 1401–99* (Cambridge, 1992).
Carpenter, D., *The Minority of Henry III* (London, 1990).
——, *The Struggle for Mastery: Britain, 1066–1284* (Oxford and New York, 2003).
Carpenter, D.A., 'Abbot Ralph of Coggeshall's Account of the Last Years of King Richard and the First Years of King John', *EHR*, 113 (1998), 1210–30.
Castan, A., *Un episode de la deuxième croisade* (Besançon, 1862).
Cazel Jr., F.A., 'Financing the Crusades', *History of the Crusades: The Impact of the Crusades on Europe*, Vol. 6, ed. M. Setton, H.W. Hazard, and N.P. Zacour (Madison, WI, 1989), pp. 116–49.
Cerda, J.M., 'Leonor Plantagenet and the Cult of Thomas Becket in Castile', *The Cult of St Thomas Becket in the Plantagenet World, c.1170–c.1220*, ed. P. Webster and M.-P. Gelin (Woodbridge, 2016), pp. 133–46.
Chauvenet, F., 'L'entourage de Richard Cœur de Lion en Poitou et en Aquitaine', *La cour Plantagenêt (1154-1204): Actes du Colloque tenu á Thouars du 30 avril au 2 mai 1999*, ed. M. Aurell (Poitiers, 2000), pp. 137–49.
Chazan, R., *Medieval Stereotypes and Modern Antisemitism* (Berkeley, CA, 1997).
——, *The Jews of Medieval Western Christendom, 1000–1500* (New York, 2006).
Cheney, C.R., 'Gervase, Abbot of Prémontré: A Medieval Letter-Writer', *Bulletin of the John Rylands Library*, 33 (1950), 25–40.
Cheng-Ti, L., Shou-De, L., and Man-Kwan, S., 'Finding Influential Mediators in Social Networks', *Proceedings of the 20th International Conference Companion on World Wide Web* (New York, 2011), pp. 75–6.
Chibnall, M., 'Mercenaries and the Familia Regis under Henry I', *History*, 62 (1977), 15–23.
Choux, J., *Recherches sur le diocèse de Toul au temps de la Réforme grégorienne. L'épiscopat de Pibon (1069-1107)* (Nancy, 1952).
Church, S.D., 'The Knights of John's Household: A Question of Numbers', *Thirteenth Century England: Proceedings of the Newcastle upon Tyne Conference 1991*, 4 (1992), 151–65.
——, 'The Rewards of Royal Service in the Household of King John: A Dissenting Opinion', *EHR*, 110 (1995), 277–302.
——, *The Household Knights of King John* (Cambridge, 1999).
——, (ed.), *King John: New Interpretations* (Woodbridge, 1999).
——, 'Some Aspects of the Royal Itinerary in the Twelfth Century', *Thirteenth Century England*, 11 (2007), 31–45.
Cibrario, L., *Précis historique des Ordres réligieux et militaires de S. Lazare et de S. Maurice avant et après leur reunion*, trans. H. Ferrand (Lyon, 1860).

Civel, N., *La fleur de France. Les seigneurs d'Île-de-France au XIIe siècle* (Turnhout, 2006).
Clanchy, M.T., *England and its Rulers*, 3rd edition (Oxford, 2006).
Cohen, A.P., *The Symbolic Construction of Community* (Chichester, 1985).
Cole, P., *The Preaching of the Crusades to the Holy Land, 1095–1270* (Cambridge, MA, 1991).
Colvin, H.M., R.A. Brown, and A.J. Taylor, *The History of the King's Works*, Vol. 2 (London, 1963).
Congar, Y.M.-J., 'Henry de Marcy, abbé de Clairvaux, cardinal-évêque d'Albano, et légat pontifical', *Analecta monastica: Textes et etudes sur la vie des moines au moyen âge, 5e série, Studia Anselmiana*, 43 (Rome, 1958), 1–90.
Constable, G., 'The Second Crusade as Seen by Contemporaries', *Traditio*, 9 (1953), 213–79.
——, 'The Financing of the Crusades in the Twelfth Century', *Outremer*, ed. B. Kedar et al. (Jerusalem, 1982), pp. 64–88.
——, 'Medieval Charters as a Source for the History of the Crusades', *Crusade and Settlement*, ed. P. Edbury (Cardiff, 1985), pp. 73–89.
——, *Three Studies in Medieval Religious and Social Thought: The Interpretation of Mary and Martha, the Ideal of the Imitation of Christ, the Orders of Society* (Cambridge, 1995), pp. 198–228.
——, *The Reformation of the Twelfth Century* (Cambridge, 1996).
——, 'The Place of the Crusader in Medieval Society', *Viator*, 29 (1998), 377–403.
——, 'The Historiography of the Crusades', *The Crusades from the Perspective of Byzantium and the Muslim World*, ed. A.E. Laiou and R.P. Mottahedeh (Washington, DC, 2001), pp. 1–22.
——, 'The Financing of the Crusades', *Crusaders and Crusading in the Twelfth Century*, ed. G. Constable (Farnham, 2008), pp.117–42.
Contamine, P., *War in the Middle Ages*, trans. M. Jones (Oxford, 1984).
Corner, D., and Roger of Howden, 'The Earliest Surviving Manuscripts of Roger of Howden's "Cronica"', *EHR*, 98 (1983), 126–40.
Coss, P., *Lordship, Knighthood and Locality: A Study in English Society c.1180–1280* (Cambridge, 1991).
——, 'The Origins and Diffusion of Chivalry', *A Companion to Chivalry*, ed. R.W. Jones and P. Coss (Woodbridge, 2019), pp. 7–38.
Coulson, C.L.H., 'Fortress-Policy in Capetian Tradition and Angevin Practice: Aspects of the Conquest of Normandy by Philip Augustus', *ANS*, 6 (1984), 13–38.
——, 'The Impact of Bouvines on the Fortress-Policy of Philip Augustus', *Studies in Medieval History presented to R. Allen Brown*, ed. C. Harper-Bill, C.J. Holdsworth, and J.L. Nelson (Woodbridge, 1989), pp. 71–80.
Crook, D., 'The "Lands of the Normans" in Thirteenth Century Nottinghamshire: Bingham and Wheatley', *Transactions of the Thoroton Society of Nottinghamshire*, 108 (2004), pp. 101–7.
Crouch, D., *The Beaumont Twins: The Roots and Branches of Power in the Twelfth Century* (Cambridge, 1986).
——, *William Marshal: Court, Career and Chivalry in the Angevin Empire, 1147–1219* (London, 1990).

——, 'Normans and Anglo-Normans: a Divided Aristocracy?', *England and Normandy in the Middle Ages*, ed. D. Bates and A. Curry (London, 1994), pp. 51–67.
——, *William Marshal: Knighthood, War and Chivalry, 1147–1219*, 2nd edition (Harlow, 2002).
——, *The Normans: The History of a Dynasty* (London, 2002).
——, *The Birth of Nobility: Constructing Aristocracy in England and France, 900–1300* (Harlow, 2005).
——, *Tournament* (London and New York, 2005).
——, 'William Marshal and the Mercenatiat', *Mercenaries and Paid Men, The Mercenary Identity in the Middle Ages*, ed. J. France (Leiden, 2008), pp. 15–32.
——, *William Marshal*, 3rd edition (Abingdon, 2016).
——, 'At Home with Roger of Howden', *Military Cultures and Martial Enterprises in the Middle Ages: Essays in Honour of Richard P. Abels*, ed. J.D. Hosler and S. Isaac (Woodbridge, 2020), pp. 156–76.
Dailliez, L., *Les Templiers en Flandre, Hainaut, Brabant, Liège et Luxembourg* (Nice, 1978).
Dajani-Shakeel, H., 'Some Medieval Accounts of Salah al-Din's Recovery of Jerusalem (Al-Quds)', *Studia Palaestina. Studies in honour of Constantine K. Zurayk*, ed. H. Nashabe (Beirut, 1988).
Dalton, P., 'Eustace Fitz John and the Politics of Anglo-Norman England: The Rise and Survival of a Twelfth-Century Royal Servant', *Speculum*, 71 (1196), 358–83.
Darby, H.C., 'The Economic Geography of England, A.D. 1000-1250', *An Historical Geography of England Before A.D. 1800, Fourteen Studies*, ed. H.C. Darby (Cambridge, 1936), pp. 165–229.
Darby, H., *Domesday England* (Cambridge, 1977).
Davies, R.R., *The Revolt of Owain Glyn Dwr* (Oxford and New York, 1995).
Davis, G.R.C., *Medieval Cartularies of Great Britain and Ireland*, revised by C. Breay, J. Harrison and D.M. Smith (London, 2010).
Davis, R.H.D., 'The Warhorses of the Normans', *ANS*, 10 (1987), 67–82.
Dawes, G. (ed.), *Commise 1204. Studies in the History and Law of Continental and Insular Normandy* (St Peter Port, Guernsey, 2004).
Débord, A., *La Société laïque dans les pays de la Charente Xe-XIIe siècles* (Paris, 1984).
Delettre, C., *Histoire du diocèse de Beauvais, depuis son établissement, au 3me siècle, jusqu'au 2 septembre 1792*, Vol. 2 (Beauvais, 1843).
Delisle, L., *Historie du château des sires de Saint-Sauveur-le-Vicomte, suivie de pièces justificatives* (Paris, 1867).
Devillers, L., *Inventaire analytique des archives des commanderies belges de l'Ordre Saint-Jean de Jérusalem ou de Malte* (Mons, 1876).
DeVries, K., *Medieval Military Technology* (Ontario, 1992), pp. 95–110.
——, 'Medieval Mercenaries, Methodology, Definitions, and Problems', *Mercenaries and Paid Men, The Mercenary Identity in the Middle Ages*, ed. J. France (Leiden and Boston, 2008), pp. 43–60.
Dickson, G., *The Children's Crusade: Medieval History, Modern Mythistory* (New York, 2008).
Diggelmann, L., 'Hewing the Ancient Elm: Anger, Arboricide, and Medieval Kingship', *Journal of Medieval and Early Modern Studies*, 40/2 (2010), 249–72.

Dobson, R.B., *The Jews of Medieval York and the Massacre of 1190* (York, 1974; revised edition 1996).

Donkin, R.A., 'The Urban Property of the Cistercians in Medieval England', *Analecta Sacri Ordinis Cisterciensis*, 15 (1959), pp. 104–31.

——, 'The Cistercian Order and the Settlement of Northern England', *Geographical Review*, 59 (1969), 403–16.

Dowden, J., *Bishops of Scotland* (Glasgow, 1912).

Duby, G., 'Les "jeunes" dans la societé aristocratique dans la France du Nord-Ouest au XIIe siècle', *Annales*, 27 (1964), 835–46.

——, 'Structure de parenté et noblesse, France du nord, XIe-XIIe siècles', *Miscellanea mediaevalia in memoriam Jan Frederik Niermeyer*, ed. J.B. Wolters (Groningen, 1967), pp. 149–65.

——, *La société au XIe et XIIe siècles dans las région mâconnaise* (repr. Paris, 1971).

——, 'The Structure of Kinship and Nobility', *Chivalrous Society*, trans. C. Postan (Berkeley, CA, 1977), pp. 134–48.

——, 'French Genealogical Literature', *Chivalrous Society*, trans. C. Postan (Berkeley, CA, 1977). pp. 149–57.

——, *The Chivalrous Society*, trans. C. Postan (London/Berkeley, 1977).

——, *Le Chevalier, la femme et le prêtre* (Paris, 1981).

——, *The Knight, the Lady, and the Priest: The Making of Modern Marriage in Medieval France*, trans. B. Bray (New York, 1985).

Duchesne, A., *Histoire de la Maison de Chastillon-sur-Marne* (Paris, 1621).

——, *Histoire généalogique de la Maison de Montmorency et de Laval* (Paris, 1624).

——, *Histoire généalogique de la Maison de Béthune* (Paris, 1639).

Duijn, M.A.J. van, Zeggelink, E.P.H., Huisman, M.. Stokman, F.N., and Wasseur, F.W., 'Evolution of Sociology Freshmen into a Friendship Network', *The Journal of Mathematical Sociology*, 27 (2003), 153–91.

Dupont, A., 'La spiritualité des croisés et des pèlerins d'après les sources de la première croisade', *Pellegrinaggi e culto dei santi in Europa fina alla la crociata* (Todi, 1963), pp. 451–83.

Durkheim, E., 'La famile conjugale', *Revue philosophique*, 91 (1901), 1–14.

Durlauf, S.N., and Blume, L.E., *New Palgrave Dictionary of Economics*, 2nd edition (London, 2008).

Durliath, J., 'La vigne et le vin dans la région parisienne au début du IX siècle d'après le polyptiques d'Irminon', *Le Moyen Age*, 74 (1968), 391–5.

Dutton, K., 'Ad erudiendum tradidir: The Upbringing of Angevin Comital Children', *ANS*, 22 (2009), 24–39.

Duval-Arnould, L., 'Le Vignoble de l'abbaye cistercienne de Longpont', *Le Moyen Age*, 74 (1968), 207–36.

Duvivier, C.H., *Recherches sur le Hainaut ancien* (Brussels, 1865).

Edbury, P.W., *The Kingdom of Cyprus and the Crusades, 1191–1374*, (Cambridge, 1991).

——, 'Preaching the Crusade in Wales', A. Haverkamp and H. Vollrath (eds), *England and Germany in the High Middle Ages* (Oxford, 1996), pp. 221–33.

Eder, K., 'Remembering National Memories Together: The Formation of a Transnational Identity in Europe', *Collective Memory and European Identity: The Effects of Integration and Enlargement*, ed. W. Spohn and K. Eder (Aldershot, 2005), pp. 197–220.

Edgington, S., 'Pagan Peverel: An Anglo-Norman Crusader', *Crusade and Settlement: Papers Read at the First Conference of the SSCLE and Presented to R.C. Smail*, ed. P.W. Edbury (Cardiff, 1985), pp. 90–3.

Edwards, J.G., 'The Treason of Thomas Turberville, 1295', *Studies in Medieval History Presented to F.M. Powicke*, ed. R.W. Hunt, W.A. Pantin and R.W. Southern (Oxford, 1948).

Eisenstadt S.N. and Giesen, B., 'The Construction of Collective Identity', *European Journal of Sociology*, 36/1 (1995), pp. 72–102.

Ellul, M.J., *The Sword and the Green Cross: The Saga of the Knights of Saint Lazarus from the Crusades to the 21st Century* (Bloomington, IN, 2011).

Epps, G. van, 'Relooking Military Cohesion: A Sensemaking Approach', *Military Review* (November/December, 2008), 102–10.

Evans, M.R., '"A far from Aristocratic Affair": Poor and Non-Combatant Crusaders from the Midlands, c. 1160–1300', *Midland History*, 21 (1996), 72–9.

——, 'Commutation of Crusade Vows: Some Examples from the English Midlands', *From Clermont to Jerusalem: The Crusades and Crusader Societies, 1095–1500*, ed. A.V. Murray (Turnhout, 1998), pp. 219–28.

Everard, J.A., *Brittany and the Angevins: Province and Empire 1158–1203* (Cambridge, 2000).

——, 'Lay Charters and the *Acta* of Henry II', *ANS*, 30 (2008), 100–16.

Everard, J.A., and Holt, J.C., *Jersey 1204: the Forging of an Island Community* (London, 2004).

Evergates, T., *Feudal Society in the Bailliage of Troyes under the Counts of Champagne, 1152–1284* (Baltimore, MD, 1975).

——, 'Louis VII and the Counts of Champagne', *The Second Crusade and the Cistercians*, ed. M. Gervers (New York, 1992), pp. 109–17.

——, *Feudal Society in Medieval France: Documents from the County of Champagne* (Philadelphia, PA, 1993).

——, *The Aristocracy in the County of Champagne, 1100–1300* (Philadelphia, PA, 2007).

——, *Henry the Liberal: Count of Champagne, 1127–1181* (Philadelphia, PA, 2016).

Eyton, R.W., *Court, Household and Itinerary of Henry II* (London, 1878).

Farrer, W., *Honors and Knights' Fees: An Attempt to Identify the Component Parts of Certain Honors and to Trace the Descent of the Tenants of the Same Who Held by Knight's Service or Serjeanty from the Eleventh to the Fourteenth Century*, 3 Vols (Manchester, 1923–5).

Feld, S., and Carter, W.C., 'Foci of Activities as Changing Contexts for Friendship', *Placing Friendship in Context*, ed. R.G. Adams and G. Allan (Cambridge, 1998), pp. 136–52.

Fergusson, P., 'The Refectory at Easby Abbey: Form and Iconography', *The Art Bulletin*, 71 (1989), 334–51.

Fiske, A.P. and S.T., 'Social Relationships in Our Species and Cultures', *Handbook of Cultural Psychology*, ed. S. Kitayama and D. Cohen (New York, 2007).

Flambard-Héricher, A., and Gazeau, V. (eds.), *1204: La Normandie entre Plantagenêts et Capétiens* (Caen, 2007).

Fleming, F.L., *A Genealogy of the Ancient Flemings* (Rothersthorpe, 2010).
——, *The Ancestry of the Earl of Wigton* (Rothersthorpe, 2011).
Flori, J., *Richard the Lionheart: Knight and King* (Edinburgh, 1999).
——, *Aliénor d'Aquitaine: La Reine insoumise* (Paris, 2004).
——, *Richard Coeur de Lion: le roi-chevalier* (Paris, 1999); *Richard the Lionheart: King and Knight*, trans. J. Birrell (Edinburgh, 2006).
Folda, J., *Crusader Art in the Holy Land, from the Third Crusade to the Fall of Acre, 1187–1291* (New York, 2005).
Forey, A., 'Recruitment to the Military Orders (Twelfth to mid-Fourteenth Centuries)', *Viator*, 17 (1986), 139–73.
——, *The Military Orders* (Basingstoke, 1992).
——, 'The Military Order of St Thomas of Acre', *EHR*, 92 (1977), 481–503.
Fox, L., 'The Administration of the Honor of Leicester in the Fourteenth Century', *Transactions of Leicestershire Archaeological Society*, 20/2 (1939), 289–374.
France, J., *Western Warfare in the Age of the Crusades, 1000-1300* (New York, 1999).
——, 'Patronage and the Appeal of the First Crusade', *The First Crusade: Origins and Impact*, ed. J. Phillips (Manchester, 1997), pp. 5–20.
——, 'Recent Writing on Medieval Warfare: from the Fall of Rome to *c*.1300', *Journal of Military History*, 65 (2001), 441–73.
——, *Mercenaries and Paid Men, The Mercenary Identity in the Middle Ages*, ed. J. France (Leiden, 2008).
——, 'The Three Orders Reconsidered', paper given at the 25th International Medieval Congress, University of Leeds (UK), July 2018.
——, 'Gilbert of Mons' Chronicle of Hainaut as a Source for Military History in the Twelfth Century', *Military Cultures and Martial Enterprises in the Middle Ages: Essays in Honour of Richard P. Abels*, ed. J.D. Hosler and S. Isaac (Woodbridge, 2020), pp. 136–55.
Freed, J.B., 'The Counts of Falkenstein: Noble Self-Consciousness in Twelfth Century Germany', *Transactions of the American Philosophical Society*, 74/6 (1984), 52–7.
Garaud, M., *Les châtelains de Poitou et l'avenement du régime féodale, XIe et XIIe siècles* (Poitiers, 1967).
Garrier, G., *Histoire sociale et culturalle du vin* (Paris, 2008).
Gassmann, J., 'Combat Training for Horse and Rider in the Early Middle Ages', *Acta Periodica Duellatorum* (2018), 63–98.
Gazeau, V. and Bouet, M. (eds.), *La Normandie et l'Angleterre au Moyen Âge* (Turnhout and Paris, 2003).
Génestal, R., *Rôle des monastères comme établissements de credit étudié en Normandie du XI à la fin du XIII siècle* (Paris, 1901).
Géraud, H., 'Les Routiers au XIIe siècle', *Bibliothèque de l'École des Chartes*, 3 (1841-2), 146–7.
Gervers, M., 'Donations to the Hospitallers in the Wake of the Second Crusade', *The Second Crusade and the Cistercians*, ed. M. Gervers (New York, 1992), pp. 153–61.
Gillingham, J., 'Roger of Howden on Crusade', *Medieval Historical Writing in the Christian and Islamic Worlds*, ed. D.O. Morgan (London, 1983), pp. 60–75.

——, 'Richard I and the Science of Warfare', *War and Government: Essays in Honour of J.O. Prestwich* (1984), pp. 78–91.

——, 'War and Chivalry in the History of William Marshal', *Thirteenth Century England III: Proceedings of the Newcastle upon Tyne Conference, 1987*, ed. P.R. Cross and S.D. Lloyd (Bury St Edmunds, 1988), pp. 1–13.

——, *Richard I* (New York and London, 1999).

——, 'Historians Without Hindsight: Coggeshall, Diceto and Howden on the Early Years of John's Reign', *King John, New Interpretations*, ed. S.D. Church (Woodbridge, 1999), pp. 1–26.

——, *The Angevin Empire*, 2nd edition (London, 2001).

Gilmour, D., 'Bekesbourne and the King's Esnecca, 1110–1445', *Archaeologia Cantiana*, 132 (2012), pp. 315–27.

Gransden, A., *Historical Writing in England c.550 to c.1307* (London, 1974).

Green, J.A., 'Lords of the Norman Vexin', *War and Government in the Middle Ages*, ed. J. Gillingham and J.C. Holt (Woodbridge, 1984), pp. 47–61.

Green, J., *The Government of England under Henry I* (Cambridge, 1986).

Green, P., *Norton Priory, the Archaeology of a Medieval Religious House* (Cambridge, 1989).

Guerreau, A., *L'avenir d'un passé incertain* (Paris, 2001).

Guth, K., 'The Pomeranian Missionary Journeys of Otto I of Bamberg and the Crusade Movement of the Eleventh to Twelfth Centuries', *The Second Crusade and the Cistercians*, ed. M. Gervers (New York, 1992), pp. 13–24.

Hagger, M.S., *The Fortunes of a Norman Family: The De Verduns in England, Ireland, and Wales, 1066–1316* (Dublin, 2001).

Hajdu, R., 'Castle, Castellans and the Structure of Politics in Poitou, 1152–1271', *JMH*, 4 (1978), 27–53.

Halbwachs, M., *Les cadres sociaux de la mémoire* (Paris, 1925), trans. L. Coser, *On Collective Memory* (Chicago, 1992).

Haldon, *Byzantium at War: AD 600–1453* (Stroud, 2008).

Hallam, E.M., 'Henry II, Richard I and the Order of Grandmont', *JMH*, 1 (1975), 183–5.

Hallam, E.M., and J. Everard, *Capetian France 937–1328*, 2nd edition (Harlow, 2001).

Hamilton, B., 'Ideals of Holiness: Crusaders, Contemplatives, and Mendicants', *International History Review*, 17 (1995), 693–712.

——, *The Leper King and His Heirs: Baldwin IV and the Crusader Kingdom of Jerusalem* (Cambridge, 2000).

Harary, F. and Norman, R.Z., *Graph Theory as a Mathematical Model in Social Science* (Ann Arbor, MI, 1953).

Hare, A.P., *Handbook of Small Group Research* (New York, 1962).

Harper-Bill, C., and Van Houts, E. (eds.), *A Companion to the Anglo-Norman World* (Woodbridge, 2003).

Harvey, S., 'The Knight and the Knight's Fee in England', *Past and Present*, 49 (1970), 4–14.

Heath, I., *Armies of Feudal Europe, 1066–1300*, 2nd edition (Cambridge, 2016).

Heebøll-Holm, T.K., 'Between Pagan Pirates and Glorious Sea-Warriors: The

Portrayal of the Viking Pirate in Danish Twelfth-Century Latin Historiography', *Viking and Medieval Scandinavia*, 8 (2012), 141–70.
Hefele, C.-J., and Leclercq, H., *Histoire de conciles d'après les documents originaux*, Vol. 5 (Paris, 1912).
Hehl, E.-D., 'War, Peace and Christian Order', *The New Cambridge Medieval History*, 4/1, ed. D. Luscombe and J. Riley-Smith (Cambridge, 2004), pp. 185–228.
Heiser, R.R., 'The Royal *Familiares* of King Richard I', *Medieval Prosopography*, 10 (1989), 25–50.
——, 'The Households of the Justiciars of Richard I: An Enquiry into the Second Level of Medieval English Government', *HSJ*, 2 (1990), 223–35.
——, 'The Sheriffs of Richard I: Trends of Management as Seen in the Shrieval Appointments from 1189 to 1194', *HSJ*, 4 (1992), pp. 109–22.
——, 'Richard I and His Appointments to English Shrievalties', *EHR*, 112/445 (1997), 1–19.
——, 'Castles, Constables, and Politics in Late Twelfth-Century English Governance', *Albion*, 32 (2000), 19–36.
——, 'The Court of the Lionheart on Crusade, 1190-2', *JMH*, 43 (2017), 505–22.
Henningsen, D.D. and M.L.M., 'Do Groups Know What They Don't Know? Dealing with Missing Information in Decision-Making Groups', *Communication Research*, 35/5 (2007), 507–25.
Herlihy, D., 'Family Solidarity in Medieval Italian History', *The Social History of Italy and Western Europe, 700–1500. Collected Studies*, trans. D. Bird (London, 1978).
Hiestand, R., 'Der lateinische Klerus in den Kreuzfahrerstaaten: Geographische Herkunft und politische Rolle', *Die Kreuzfahrerstaaten als multikulturelle Gesellschaft: Einwanderer und Minderheiten im 12. und 13. Jahrhundert*, ed. H.E. Mayer (Munich, 1997), pp. 43–68.
Hilton, R.H., *A Medieval Society: The West Midlands at the End of the Thirteenth Century* (London, 1966).
Hivergneaux, M. 'Autour d'Aliénor d'Aquitaine', *Plantagenêts et Capétiens: confrontations et heritages*, ed. M. Aurell and N.-Y. Tonnerre (Turnhout, 2006), pp. 61–94.
——, 'Queen Eleanor and Aquitaine, 1137–1189', *Eleanor of Aquitaine: Lord and Lady*, ed. B. Wheeler and J.C. Parsons (Basingstoke, 2002), p. 55–76.
Hoffman Berman, C., *The Cistercian Evolution: The Invention of a Religious Order in Twelfth-Century Europe* (Philadelphia, 2000).
Holden, B., *Lords of the Central Marches: English Aristocracy and Frontier Society, 1087–1265* (Oxford, 2008).
Hollister, C.W., *The Military Organisation of Norman England* (Oxford, 1965).
——, *Henry I* (New Haven and London, 2001).
Hollister C.W. and T.K. Keefe, 'The Making of the Angevin Empire', *Journal of British Studies*, 12 (1973), 1–25.
Hollister, C.W., and Baldwin, J.W., 'The Rise of Administrative Kingship: Henry I and Philip Augustus', *American Historical Review*, 83 (1978), 867–905.
Holt, J.C., *The Northerners: A Study of the Reign of King John* (Oxford, 1961).
——, 'Politics and Property in Early Medieval England', *Past and Present*, 57 (1972), 3–52.

——, 'The End of the Anglo-Norman Realm', *Proceedings of the British Academy*, 61 (1975), 223–65.
——, 'The Loss of Normandy and Royal Finance', *War and Government in the Middle Ages*, ed. J. Gillingham and J.C. Holt (Woodbridge, 1984), pp. 92–105.
——, 'The Introduction of Knight Service in England', *ANS*, 6 (1984), 89–106.
——, '*Ricardus Rex Anglorum et Dux Normannorum*', *Magna Carta and Medieval Government* (London, 1985), 67–83.
——, 'Aliénor d'Aquitaine, Jean sans Terre et la succession de 1199', *Cahiers de Civilisation Médiévale*, 34 (1986), 95–100.
——, *Colonial England, 1066–1215* (London, 1997).
Hosler, J.D., *Henry II: A Medieval Soldier at War, 1147–1189* (Leiden, 2007).
——, 'Revisiting Mercenaries under Henry Fitz Empress, 1167–1188', *Mercenaries and Paid Men, The Mercenary Identity in the Middle Ages*, ed. J. France (Leiden, 2008), pp. 33–42.
——, *John of Salisbury, Military Authority of the Twelfth-Century Renaissance* (Leiden and Boston, 2013).
——, 'Why Didn't King Stephen Crusade?', *Travels and Mobilities in the Middle Ages: From the Atlantic to the Black Sea*, ed. M. O'Doherty and F. Schmieder (Turnhout, 2015), pp. 121–42.
——, *The Siege of Acre, 1189–1191: Saladin, Richard the Lionheart, and the Battle that Decided the Third Crusade* (New Haven and London, 2018).
——, 'The Siege of Acre (1189–1191) in the Historiographical Tradition', *History Compass*, 16/5 (2018), 1–11.
——, 'Embedded Reporters? Ambroise, Richard de Templo, and Roger of Howden on the Third Crusade', *Military Cultures and Martial Enterprises in the Middle Ages: Essays in Honour of Richard P. Abels*, ed. J.D. Hosler and S. Isaac (Woodbridge, 2020), pp. 177–91.
Houts, E.M.C. van, *Memory and Gender in Medieval Europe, 900–1200* (Basingstoke, 1990).
——, *History and Family Tradition in England and the Continent, 1000–1200* (Aldershot, 1999).
——, 'The Anglo-Flemish Treaty of 1101', *ANS*, 21 (1999), 169–74.
——, *Medieval Memories: Men, Women, and the Past* (Harlow, 2001).
Howell, J., *Instructions for Foreign Travel* (London, 1642).
Hurlock, K., 'Cheshire and the Crusades', *Transactions of the Historic Society of Lancashire and Cheshire*, 159 (2010), 1–18.
——, 'The Crusades to 1291 in the Annals of Medieval Ireland', *Irish Historical Studies*, 37 (2011), 517–34.
——, *Wales and the Crusades, c.1095–1291* (Cardiff, 2011).
——, *Britain, Ireland and the Crusades, c.1000–1300* (New York, 2013).
Hurlock, K., and Oldfield, P., *Crusading and Pilgrimage in the Norman World* (Woodbridge, 2015).
Huyghebaert, N., 'Une comtesse de Flandre à Béthanie', *Les cahiers de Saint-André*, 21/2 (1964), 5–15.
Hyams, P.R., 'Some Coin Exports from Twelfth Century Yorkshire to the Holy Land', *Coinage in the Latin East: The Fourth Oxford Symposium on Coinage and Monetary History*, ed. P.W. Edbury and D.M. Metcalf (Oxford, 1980), pp. 133–5.

——, 'Homage and Feudalism: A Judicious Separation', *Die Gegenwart Der Feudalismus*, ed. N. Fryde, P. Monnet, and O.G. Oexle (Göttingen, 2002), pp. 13–50.
Hyland, A., *The Medieval Warhorse: From Byzantium to the Crusades* (Stroud, 1994).
Irsigler, F., 'Viticulture, vinification et commerce du vin en Allemagne Occidentale des origines au XVI siècle', *Le Vigneron, la viticulture et la vinification en Europe occidentale au Moyen Age et à l'époque moderne: onzièmes Journées Internationales d'Histoire, 8-10 septembre 1989* (Bordeaux, 1991), pp. 49–65.
Jacoby, D., 'Montmusard, Suburb of Crusader Acre: The First Stage of Development', *Outremer, Studies in the History of the Crusading Kingdom of Jerusalem Presented to Joshua Prawer* (Jerusalem, 1982), pp. 205–17.
Jamroziak, E., *Rievaulx Abbey and its Social Context, 1132–1300* (Turnhout, 2005).
Jankrift, K.P., *Leprose als Streiter Gottes: Institutionalisierung und organisation des ordens von Heiligen Lazarus zu Jerusalem von seinen anfängen bis zum jahre 1350* (Münster, 1996).
Jäschke, K.-U., 'Englands Weinwirtschaft in Antike und Mittelalter', *Weinwirtschaft in Mittelalter*, ed. C. Schrenk and H. Weckbach (Sonderdruck, 1997), pp. 256–388.
Jenkins, R., *Social Identity* (London, 1996).
John, S., *Godfrey of Bouillon: Duke of Lower Lotharingia, Ruler of Latin Jerusalem, c. 1060–1100* (London and New York, 2017).
Johnson, H., *The Story of Wine* (London, 2004).
Joliffe, J.E.A., *Angevin Kingship* (London, 1955).
Jones, R.W., '"What Banner Thine?" The Banner as a Symbol of Identification, Status and Authority on the Battlefield', *HSJ*, 15 (2004), 101–9.
——, *Bloodied Banners: Martial Display on the Medieval Battlefield* (Woodbridge, 2010).
——, 'Marshalling the Chivalric Elite for War', *A Companion to Chivalry*, ed. R.W. Jones and P. Coss (Woodbridge, 2019), pp. 85–98.
——, 'Heraldry and Heralds', *A Companion to Chivalry*, ed. R.W. Jones and P. Coss (Woodbridge, 2019), pp. 139–58.
Josserand, P., *Église et pouvoir dans la péninsule ibérique: Les orders militaires dans le royaume de Castille, 1252-1369* (Madrid, 2004).
Jotischky, A., *Crusading and the Crusader States*, 2nd edition (Abingdon, 2017).
Jouet, R., *Et la Normandie devint française* (Paris, 1983).
Keats-Rohan, K.S.B., 'Two Studies in North French Prosopography', *JMH*, 20 (1994), 3–37.
Kedar, B.Z., 'The *Tractatus de locis et statu sancte terre ierosolimitane*', in *The Crusades and Their Sources: Essays Presented to Bernard Hamilton*, ed. J. France and W.G. Zajac (Aldershot, 1998), pp. 111–31.
Keefe, T.K., *Feudal Assessments and the Political Community under Henry II and His Sons* (Berkeley, Los Angeles, London, 1983).
Kehr, P., *Ueber eine römische Papyrusurkunde im Staatsarchiv zu Marburg* (Berlin, 1896).
King, A., 'The Word of Command: Communication and Cohesion in the Military', *Armed Forces and Society*, 32/4 (2006), 493–512.
——, 'The Existence of Group Cohesion in the Armed Forces: A Response to Guy Siebold', *Armed Forces and Society*, 33/4 (2007), 638–45.

Knowles, D. and Neville Hadcock, R., *Medieval Religious Houses: England and Wales* (London, 1971).
Knowles, D., *The Monastic Order in England, 943–1216*, 2nd edition (Cambridge, 2002).
Koch, A.C.F., *Oorkondenboek van Holland-Zeeland tot 1299. I: eind van de zevende eeuw tot 1222*, Vol. 1 (S-Gravenhage, 1970).
Konvitz, J.W., 'The Nation-State, Paris, and Cartography in 18th and 19th Century France', *Journal of Historical Geography*, 16 (1990), 3–16.
Lachiver, H., *Vins, vignes et vignerons: histoire du vignoble français* (Paris, 1988).
Lambert, S., 'Crusading or Spinning', *Gendering the Crusades*, ed. S.B. Edgington and S. Lambert (New York, 2001), pp. 1–15.
Lambert, T.B., 'Some Approaches to Peace and Protection', *Peace and Protection in the Middle Ages*, ed. T.B. Lambert and D. Rollason (Durham, 2009), pp.1–18.
Lane Poole, A., *From Domesday to Magna Carta, 1087–1216* (Oxford, 1955).
Landon, L., *The Itinerary of King Richard I: with Studies on Certain Matters of Interest Connected with his Reign* (London, 1935).
Latour, B., *Reassembling the Social: An Introduction to Actor-Network-Theory* (Oxford, 2005).
Leclercq, J., 'Monachisme et peregrination du XIe au XIIe siècle, *Studia monastica*, 3 (1961), 33–52.
——, 'The New Orders', *The Spirituality of the Middle Ages*, ed. J. Leclercq, F. Vandenbroucke, and L. Bouyer (London, 1968), pp. 127–61.
Lee, J.S., 'Landowners and Landscapes: The Knights Templar and Their Successors at Temple Hirst, Yorkshire', *The Local Historian*, 41 (2011), 293–307.
Le Jan, R., *Familie et pouvoir dans le monde franc (VIIe.Xe siècle): Essai d'anthropologie sociale* (Paris, 1995).
Leson, R.A. 'A Constellation of Crusade: The Resafa Heraldry Cup and the Aspirations of Raoul I, Lord of Coucy', *The Crusades and Visual Culture*, ed. E. Lapina, A.J. Morris, S.A. Throop, and L.J. Whatley (Farnham, 2015), pp 75–90.
Lester, A.E., 'A Shared Imitation: Cistercian Convents and Crusader Families in Thirteenth-Century Champagne', *JMH*, 35 (2009), 353–70.
Leuridan, Th., *Recherches sur les Sires de Commines* (Danel, 1880).
Lewis, A.W., 'Six Charters of Henry II and His Family for the Monastery of Dalon', *EHR*, 110 (1995), 652–65.
Leyser, K., 'Ottonian Government', *EHR*, 56 (1981), 721–53.
Lieberman, M., 'Knightings in the Twelfth and Thirteenth Centuries: A New Approach', paper given at the Battle Conference on Anglo-Norman Studies 2020: A Virtual Workshop, July 2020.
Liekens, L., *Geschiedenis van het oude Graafschap van de Stad en de Parochie den Lande en hertogdomme van Aarschot*, Vol. 1 (Goed, 1925).
Linehan, P., *Spain, 1157-1300: A Partible Inheritance* (Chichester, 2011).
Livermore, H., 'The "Conquest of Lisbon" and its Author', *Portuguese Studies*, 6 (1990), 1–16.
Lloyd, S., *English Society and the Crusades, 1216–1307* (New York, 1988).
Lloyd, T.H., *The English Wool Trade in the Middle Ages* (Cambridge, 1977).
Longnon, J., 'Sur les croisés de la quatrième croisade', *Journal des savants*, 2/2 (1977), 119–27.

——, *Les compagnons de Villehardouin: Recherches sur les croisés de la quatrième croisade* (Geneva, 1978).
Lord, E., *The Knights Templar in Britain* (London and New York, 2002).
Lotter, F., 'The Crusading Idea and the Conquest of the Region East of the Elbe', *Medieval Frontier Societies*, ed. R. Bartlett and A. MacKay (Oxford, 1989), pp. 267–306.
Lovell, N., ed., *Locality and Belonging* (London, 1998).
Lower, M., *The Barons' Crusade: A Call to Arms and Its Consequences* (Philadelphia, PA, 2005).
Loyd, L.C., *Origins of some Anglo-Norman families*, ed. C.T. Clay and D.C. Douglas (Leeds, 1951).
Loyn, H.R., 'Gesiths and Thegns in Anglo-Saxon England from the Seventh to Tenth Century', *EHR*, 70 (1955), 529–49.
Luchaire, A., *Études sur les actes de Louis VII* (Paris, 1885).
Lunt, W.E., *Financial Relations of the Papacy with England to 1327* (Cambridge, MA, 1939).
Luttrell, A., 'The Hospitallers' Early Written Records', *The Crusades and Their Sources: Essays Presented to Bernard Hamilton*, ed. J. France and W.G. Zajac (Aldershot, 1998), pp. 135–54.
——, 'The Earliest Templars', *Autour de la première croisade. Actes du colloque de la Society for the Study of the Crusades and the Latin East, Clermont-Ferrand, 22–25 juin 1995*, ed. M. Balard (Paris, 1995), pp. 193–202.
Luttwak, E., *The Grand Strategy of the Byzantine Empire* (Cambridge, MA, 2009).
Lyon, B.D., 'The Money Fief under the English Kings, 1066–1485', *EHR*, 66 (1951), 161–93.
——, *From Fief to Indenture: The Transition from Feudal to Non-Feudal Contract in Western Europe* (Cambridge, MA, 1954).
Lyon, B.D. and Verhulst, A.E., *Medieval Finance: A Comparison of Financial Institutions in Northwestern Europe* (Providence, RI, 1967).
Macauley, T.B., *History of England* (London, 1849).
Macé, L., *Les comtes de Toulouse et leur entourage (XIIe-XIIIe siècles). Rivalités, alliances et jeux de pouvoir* (Toulouse, 1999).
Macquarrie, A., *Scotland and the Crusades 1095–1560* (Edinburgh, 1985).
Madeline, F., 'L'empire des Plantagenêts: Espace feudal et construction territoriale', *Hypothèsis 2007, Travaux de l'École Doctorale d'Histoire* (Paris, 2008), pp. 239–252.
Maier, C., *Crusade Propaganda and Ideology: Model Sermons for the Preaching of the Cross* (Cambridge, 2000).
Maimbourg, L., *Histoire des croisades pour le delivrance de la Terre Sainte*, 3rd edition, Vol. 3 (Paris, 1680).
Manning, F.J., 'Morale and Cohesion in Military Psychiatry', *Military Psychiatry: Preparing in Peace and War*, ed. F.D. Jones, L.R. Sparacino, V.L. Wilcox, and J.M. Rothberg (Washington, DC, 1994), pp. 1–18.
Marc, J., 'Contribution à l'étude du regime féodal sur le domaine de l'abbaye de Saint-Seine', *Revue bourguignonne de l'enseignment supérieur*, 6 (1896), 55–123, 295–340.
Marcombe, D., *Leper Knights: the Order of St Lazarus of Jerusalem in England, 1150–1554* (Woodbridge, 2003).

Marie, D., *Les Templiers dans le diocèse de Langres, des moines entrepreneurs aux XIIe et XIIIe siècles* (Langres, 2004).
Markowski, M., 'Richard the Lionheart: Bad King, Bad Crusader', *JMH*, 23 (1997), 351–65.
Matthew, D.J.A., *The Norman Monasteries and their English Possessions* (Oxford, 1962).
Matthieu, E., 'Les seigneurs de Naast', *Annales du Cercle archéologique du canton de Soignies*, 4 (1909), 43–72.
Mayer, H.E., *The Crusades*, 2nd edition, trans. J Gillingham (Oxford, 1988).
Mayne Kienzle, B., *Cistercians, Heresy, and Crusade in Occitania, 1145–1229* (York, 2001).
McBain, G.S., 'The Charters of the Cinque Ports – Are They Still Needed?', *Review of European Studies*, 5 (2013), 90–126.
McGeer, E., *Sowing the Dragon's Teeth: Byzantine Warfare in the Tenth Century*. Dumbarton Oaks Studies 33 (Cambridge, MA, 1995).
McGlynn, S., 'The Myths of Medieval Warfare', *History Today*, 44 (1994), 28–34.
McNeal, E.H., 'Fulk of Neuilly and the Tournament of Écry', *Speculum*, 28 (1953), 371–5.
McPherson, M., Smith-Lovin, L., and Cook, J., 'Birds of a Feather: Homophily in Social Networks', *Annual Review of Sociology*, 27 (2001), 415–44.
Ménage, G., *Histoire de Sablé* (Paris, 1883).
Mesmin, S.C., 'Waleran, Count of Meulan and the Leper Hospital of St Giles de Pont-Audemer', *Annales de Normandie*, 32/1 (1982), 3–19.
Milgram, S., 'The Small World Problem', *Psychology Today*, 2 (1967), 60–7.
Miraeus, A., *Donationes Belgicæ*, 1 (Antwerp, 1723).
Mitchell, S. K., *Taxation in Medieval England* (New Haven, CT, 1951).
Möhring, J., 'Eine Chronik aus der Zeit des dritten Kreuzzugs: das sogenannte *Itinerarium Peregrinorum* 1', *Innsbrucker Historische Studien*, 5 (1982), 149–62.
Morillo, S., 'The "Age of Cavalry" Revisited', *The Circle of War in the Middle Ages: Essays on Medieval Military and Naval History*, ed. D.J. Kagay and L.J.A. Villalon (Woodbridge, 1999), pp. 46–56.
——, 'Mercenaries, Mamluks, Militia, Towards a Cross-Cultural Typology of Military Service', *Mercenaries and Paid Men, The Mercenary Identity in the Middle Ages*, ed. J. France (Leiden, 2008), pp. 243–60.
Morris, J.E., *The Welsh Wars of Edward I* (Oxford, 1901).
Morris, W.A. *The Medieval English Sheriff to 1300* (Manchester, 1927).
Mortimer, R., 'Religious and Secular Motives for Some English Monastic Foundations', *Studies in Church History*, 15 (1978), 77–85.
——, 'The Family of Rannulf de Glanville', *Historical Research*, 129 (1981), 1–16.
——, *Angevin England: 1154–1258* (Oxford, 1994).
Moss, V.D., 'The Norman Exchequer Rolls of King John', *King John: New Interpretations*, ed. S.D. Church (1999), 101–16.
——, 'The Defence of Normandy 1193–8', *ANS*, 24 (2002), 145–61.
Munro, J.H., 'Medieval Woollens: Textiles, Textile Technology and Industrial Organisation, c. 800–1500', *The Cambridge History of Western Textiles*, Vol. 1, ed. D.T. Jenkins (Cambridge, 2003), pp. 181–227.
Murray, A., *Crusader Kingdom of Jerusalem: A Dynastic Study* (Oxford, 2000).

——, 'The Origin of Money-Fiefs in the Latin Kingdom of Jerusalem', *Mercenaries and Paid Men, The Mercenary Identity in the Middle Ages*, ed. J. France (Leiden and Boston, 2008), pp. 275–88.
Murray, S.A.P., *The Library: An Illustrated History* (Chicago, 2009).
Musset, L., 'Quelques problèmes de l'annexation de la Normandie au domaine royal français', *La France de Philippe Auguste: le temps des mutations*, ed. R.-H. Bautier (Paris, 1982), 291–307.
Naus, J., *Constructing Kingship: The Capetian Monarchs of France and the Early Crusades* (Manchester, 2006).
——, 'Specter of Failure: The Risk and Reward of Royal Crusading', SSCLE 'Diversity of Crusading' Conference, Odense, 27 June 2016.
Naus, J. and Ryan, V., 'High Stakes and High Reward: The Memory of Royal Crusading', *Remembering the Crusades and Crusading*, ed. M. Cassidy-Welch (Abingdon, 2017), pp. 145–58.
Newman, W., *Les seigneurs de Nesle en Picardie*, 2 Vols (Paris, 1871).
Nicholas, D.N., *Medieval Flanders* (London and New York, 1992).
Nicholson, H.J., 'Women on the Third Crusade', *JMH*, 23 (1997), 335–49.
——, *Love, War, and the Grail: Templars, Hospitallers and Teutonic Knights in Medieval Epic and Romance, 1150–1500* (Leiden, 2001).
——, *The Knights Hospitaller* (Woodbridge, 2001).
——, *Medieval Warfare* (Basingstoke, 2004).
——, 'The Crusade of Baldwin of Forde, Archbishop of Canterbury', paper given at the 25th International Medieval Congress, University of Leeds (UK), July 2018.
——, 'The Construction of a Primary Source. The Creation of *Itinerarium Peregrinorum* I', *Cahiers de recherches médiévales et humanistes*, 37 (2019), 143–65.
Nooy, W.D., Mrvar, A. and Batagelj, V., *Exploratory Social Network Analysis with Pajek* (Cambridge, 2005).
Nora, P., *Les Lieux de memoire: La Republique* (Paris, 1984); *La Nation*, 3 Vols. (Paris, 1986).
Nordman, D., 'Des limites d'État aux frontières nationales', *Les Lieux de memoire, La Nation*, 2 (Paris, 1986), 35–61.
Nordman, D. and J. Revel, 'La Formation de l'espace français', *Histoire de la France*, 1 (Paris, 1989), 29–169.
Norgate, K., *England under the Angevin Kings*, Vol. 2 (London, 1887).
——, *The Minority of Henry III* (London, 1912).
Nortier, M., 'Un rôle des biens tombés en la main du roi en la baillie de Lisieux après la conquête de la Normandie par Philippe Auguste', *Annales de Normandie*, 45 (1995), 55–68.
O'Callaghan, J.F., 'The Affiliation of the Order of Calatrava with the Order of Cîteaux', *Analecta Sacri Ordinis Cisterciensis*, 15 (1960), 3–59, 255–92.
——, *Reconquest and Crusade in Medieval Spain* (Philadelphia, 2003).
Oexle, O.G., 'Gruppen in der Gesellschaft: Das wissenschaftliche Oeuvre von Karl Schmid', *Frühmittelalterliche Studien*, 28 (1994), 410–23.
Oksanen, E., *Flanders and the Anglo-Norman World, 1066–1216* (Cambridge, 2012).
Pacaut, M., *Louis VII et son royaume* (Paris, 1964).
Orme, N., *From Childhood to Chivalry: The Education of the English Kings and Aristocracy, 1066–1530* (London, 1984).

Orme, N.I. and Padel, O.J., 'Cornwall and the Third Crusade', *Journal of the Royal Institution of Cornwall* (2005), 71–7.
Orme, N., and Webster, M., *The English Hospital, 1070–1570* (London, 1995).
Ormerod, G., *History of the County Palatine and City of Chester*, Vol. 1 (London, 1819).
Owen, H. and Blakeway, J.B., *A History of Shrewsbury*, 2 Vols (London, 1825).
Painter, S., 'The Lords of Lusignan in the Eleventh and Twelfth Centuries', *Speculum*, 32 (1957), 27–47.
———, 'The Third Crusade, Richard the Lionhearted and Philip Augustus', *A History of the Crusades*, Vol. 2, ed. K.M. Setton (Madison, WI, 1969).
Parisse, M., 'Le tournoi en France, des origines à la fin du XIIIe siècle', *Das ritterliche Turnier in Mittelalter: Beitrage zu einer vergleichenden Formenund verhallengeschinchte des Rittertum*, ed J. Fleckenstein (Göttingen, 1985), pp. 175–211.
Park, D.E.A., *Papal Protection and the Crusader: Flanders, Champagne, and the Kingdom of France, 1095–1222* (Woodbridge, 2018).
Passier, H. and A., *Trésor généalogique de Dom Villevieille*, Vol. 1 (Paris, 1877).
Patourel, J. Le, 'The Plantagenet Dominions', *History*, 50 (1965), 289–308.
Paul, N., 'The Chronicle of Fulk le Réchin: A Reassessment', *HSJ*, 18 (2007), 19–35.
———, *To Follow in their Footsteps: The Crusades and Family Memory in the High Middle Ages* (New York, 2012).
Paul, N.L. and Schenk, J.G., 'Family Memory and The Crusades', *Remembering the Crusades and Crusading*, ed. M. Cassidy-Welch (Abingdon, 2017), pp. 173–86.
Pegg, M.G., *A Most Holy War: The Albigensian Crusade and the Battle for Christendom* (Oxford, 2008).
Peltzer, J., *Canon Law, Careers, and Conquest: Episcopal Elections in Normandy and Greater Anjou, c.1140–c.1230* (Cambridge, 2007).
Penent, J., *Occitanie: L'épopée des origines* (Paris, 2009).
Pernoud, R., *Aliénor d'Aquitaine* (Paris, 1965).
Petit, E., ed., *Histoire des ducs de Bourgogne de la race capétienne*, 9 Vols (Paris, 1885–1905).
Petit, F., *La spiritualité des prémontrés au XIIe et XIIIe siècles* (Paris, 1947).
Petit-Dutaillis, C., *Étude sur la vie et le règne de Louis VIII* (Paris, 1984).
———, 'Le déshéritement de Jean sans Terre et le meurtre d'Arthur de Bretagne', *Revue historique*, 147 (1924–5), 161–203; 148 (1925), 1–62.
———, 'Querimoniæ Normannorum', *Essays in Medieval History presented to T.F. Tout*, ed. A.G. Little and F.M. Powicke (Manchester, 1925), pp. 99–118.
Pfeiffer, E., 'Die Cistercienser und der zweite Kreuzzug 3. Hilfeleistungen der Cistercienserklöster an Kreuzfahrer', *Cistercienser-Chronik*, 47 (1935), 78–81.
Phillips, J.P., 'A Note on the Origins of Raymond of Poitiers', *EHR*, Vol. 106/418 (1991), 66–7.
———, 'The Murder of Charles the Good and the Second Crusade: Household, Nobility, and Traditions of Crusading in Medieval Flanders', *Medieval Prosopography*, 19 (1998), 55–75.
———, 'Foreword', *The Conquest of Lisbon: De Expugnatione Lyxbonensi*, trans. C.W. David (New York, 2001).
———, *The Second Crusade: Extending the Frontiers of Christendom* (New Haven and London, 2007).

——, *Holy Warriors, A Modern History of the Crusades* (London, 2009).
Phillips, M., 'The Thief's Cross: Crusade and Penance in Alan of Lille's *Sermo de cruce domini*', *Crusades*, Vol. 5, ed. B. Kedar, J. Phillips, and J. Riley-Smith (Abingdon, 2006), pp. 143–56.
——, 'Crucified with Christ: The Imitation of the Crucified Christ and Crusading Spirituality', *Crusades: Medieval Worlds in Conflict. An International Symposium at Saint Louis University, February 2006*, ed. T.F. Madden, J. Naus, and V. Ryan (Abingdon, 2010), pp. 25–33.
Phythian-Adams, C., 'Introduction: An Agenda for English Local History', *Societies, Cultures and Kinship 1580–1850: Cultural Provinces and English Local History* (Leicester and London, 1993), pp. 1–23.
Pinoteau, H. de, 'Heraldische Untersuchungen zum Wappenpokal,' *Resafa III. Der kreuzfahrerzeitliche Silberschatz aus Resafa-Sergiupolis*, ed. T. Ulbert (Mainz am Rhein, 1990), pp. 77–86.
Pollock, F., and Maitland, F.W., *The History of English Law*, Vol. 2 (Cambridge, 1898).
Poole, A.L., *Obligations of Society in the XII and XIII Centuries* (Oxford, 1946).
Poull, G., *La Maison souveraine et ducale de Bar* (Nancy, 1994).
Pouzet, P., *L'Anglais Jean dit Bellemains (1122-1204?)* (Lyon, 1927).
Powell, J., *Anatomy of a Crusade, 1213–1221* (Philadelphia, 1986).
Power, D., 'Angevin Normandy', *Companion to the Anglo-Norman World*, ed. C. Harper-Bill and E.M.C. van Houts (Woodbridge, 2003), pp. 63–85.
——, 'The French Interests of the Marshal Earls of Striguil and Pembroke, 1189–1234', *ANS*, 25 (2003), 199–224.
——, '*Terra regis Anglie et terra Normannorum sibi invicem adversantur*: les héritages anglo-normands entre 1204 et 1244', *La Normandie et l'Angleterre au Moyen Âge*, ed. V. Gazeau and M. Bouet (Caen, 2003), pp. 123–41.
——, *The Norman Frontier in the Twelfth and Early Thirteenth Centuries* (Cambridge, 2004).
——, 'The Norman Church and the Angevin and Capetian Kings', *Journal of Ecclesiastical History*, 56 (2005), 205–34.
——, 'Les dernières années du régime angevin en Normandie', *Plantagenêts et Capétiens: Confrontations et Héritages*, ed. M. Aurell and N.-Y. Tonnerre (Turnhout, 2006), pp. 163–92.
——, 'L'établissement du régime capétien en Normandie', *1204: La Normandie entre Plantagenêts et Capétiens*, ed. A. Flambard-Héricher and V. Gazeau (Caen, 2007), pp. 319–43.
——, 'Le régime seigneurial en Normandie (XIIe-XIIIe s.)', *Les seigneuries dans l'espace Plantagenêt (c.1150-c.1250)*, ed. M. Aurell and F. Boutoulle (Bordeaux, 2009), pp. 117–36.
——, 'Aristocratic Power and Authority in Normandy and England, c. 1150–1250: The Charters of the Du Hommet Constables of Normandy', paper given at the 18th International Medieval Congress, University of Leeds (UK), July 2011.
——, 'The Preparation of Count John I of Sées for the Third Crusade', *Crusading and Warfare in the Middle Ages: Realities and Representations, Essays in Honour of John France*, ed. D. Morton and S. John (Farnham, 2014), pp. 143–66.

Power, E., *The Wool Trade in English Medieval History: Being the Ford Lectures [for 1939]* (Oxford, 1941).
Powicke, F.M., *The Loss of Normandy, 1189–1204: Studies in the History of the Angevin Empire*, 2nd edition (Manchester, 1961).
Pratt, C.T., *History of Cawthorne* (Barnsley, 1882).
Prestwich, J.O., 'Anglo-Norman Feudalism and the Problem of Continuity', *Past and Present*, 26 (1963), 39–57.
——, 'The Military Household of the Norman Kings', *EHR*, 96 (1981), 1–37.
Prestwich, M., '*Miles in Armis Strenuus*: The Knight at War', *Transactions of the Royal Historical Society*, 6th series, Vol. 5 (1995), 201–20.
——, *Armies and Warfare in the Middle Ages, the English Experience* (London, 1996).
Prouteau, N., '"Beneath the Battle"? Miners and Engineers as "Mercenaries" in the Holy Land', *Mercenaries and Paid Men, The Mercenary Identity in the Middle Ages*, ed. J. France (Leiden, 2008), pp. 105–17.
Prutz, H., *Die geistlichen Ritterorden, ihre Stellung zur kirchlichen, politischen, gesellschaftlichen und wirtschaftlichen Entwicklung des Mittelalters* (Berlin, 1908).
Pryor, J.H., 'Modelling Bohemond's March to Thessalonike', *Logistics of Warfare in the Ages of the Crusades*, ed. J.H. Pryor (Aldershot, 2006), pp. 1–24.
——, 'Transportation of Horses by Sea During the Era of the Crusade: Eighth Century to 1285 A.D.', *Medieval Warfare 1000–1300*, ed. J. France (Aldershot, 2006), pp. 523–68.
——, 'Two *excitationes* for the Third Crusade', *Mediterranean Historical Review*, 25 (2010), 147–68.
Purkis, W.J., 'Elite and Popular Perceptions of *imitatio Christi* in Twelfth-Century Crusade Spirituality', *Elite and Popular Religion*, ed. Kate Cooper and Jeremy Gregory (Woodbridge, 2006), pp. 54–64.
——, *Crusading Spirituality in the Holy Land and Iberia, c. 1095–c. 1187* (Woodbridge, 2008).
Racinet, P., 'Le depart et le retour du croisé. Arrangements matériels et spirituels avec les moines', *Occident et Orient IXe-XVe siècles: histoire et archéologie; actes du colloque d'Amiens, 8, 9 et 10 octobre 1998*, ed. R.-H. Bautier, G. Jehel, and J. Richard. Histoire mediévale et archéologie, 11 (Amiens, 2000), pp, 11–24.
Rawcliffe, C., 'Learning to Love the Leper: Aspects of Institutional Charity in Anglo-Norman England', *ANS*, 23 (2001), 231–50.
Renouard, Y., 'Essai sur le rôle de l'empire Angevin dans la formation de la France et de la civilisation française au XIIe et XIIIe siècles', *Revue historique*, 195 (1945), 289–304.
——,, *Bordeaux sous les rois d'Angleterre* (Bordeaux, 1965).
Reynolds, S., *Fiefs and Vassals: The Medieval Evidence Reinterpreted* (Oxford, 1994).
Richard, A., *Histoire des comtes de Poitou, 778-1204* (Paris, 1903).
Richard, J., 'Le financement des croisades', *Pouvoir et gestion. Cinquièmes rencontres – 29 et 30 novembre 1996*. Collection histoire, gestion, organisations, 5 (Toulouse, 1997), pp. 63–71.
——, 'Les Templiers et les Hospitaliers en Bourgogne et en Champagne méridionale (XIIe–XIIIe siécles)', *Vorträge und Forschungen: Die Geistlichen Ritterorden Europas*, Vol. 26, ed. J. Fleckenstein and M. Hellmann (1980), pp. 231–42.

Richemond, E.L., *Recherches généalogiques sur la famille des Seigneurs de Nemours*, Vol. 1 (Fontainebleau, 1907).

Ricouart, L., *Les biens de l'abbaye de Saint-Vaast dans les diocèses de Beauvais, de Noyon, de Soissons et d'Amiens* (Anzin, 1888).

Riley-Smith, J., *The Knights of St John in Jerusalem and Cyprus, c.1050–1310* (London, 1967).

——, *The First Crusade and the Idea of Crusading* (London, 1986).

——, *The Crusades - A Short History* (London, 1990).

——, 'Family Traditions and Participation in the Second Crusade', *The Second Crusade and the Cistercians*, ed. M. Gervers (New York, 1992), pp. 101–8.

——, 'Early Crusaders to the East and the Costs of Crusading 1095-1130', *Cross-Cultural Convergences in the Crusader Period: Essays Presented to Aryeh Grabois on his Sixty-Fifth Birthday*, ed. M. Goodich, S. Menache and S. Schein (New York, 1995).

——, *The First Crusaders, 1095–1131* (Cambridge, 1999).

——, *The Crusades: A History*. 3rd edition (London, 2014).

——, *What Were the Crusades?* 4th edition (Basingstoke, 2009).

Robinson, J. S., 'The Papacy 1122–1198', in *The New Cambridge Medieval History*, 5/2, ed. D. Luscombe and J. Riley-Smith (Cambridge, 2004), 317–83.

Rodger, N.A.M., *Safeguard of the Seas, a Naval History of Britain, 660–1649* (London, 1997).

Röhricht, R., *Beiträge zur Geschichte der Kreuzzüge* (Berlin, 1878).

——, *Die Deutschen in Heiligen Lande* (Innsbruck, 1894).

Roland, C.-G., *Histoire généalogique de la maison de Rumigny-Florennes* (Brussels, 1891).

Rose, S., *The Wine Trade in Medieval Europe, 1000–1500* (London and New York, 2011).

[M. Roserot, Note on genealogy of Villehardouin], *Revue de Champagne et de Brie*, 18 (1885), 392.

Round, J.H., *Geoffrey of Mandeville: A Study of the Anarchy* (London, 1892).

——, 'Some Crusaders of Richard I', *EHR*, 18 (1903), 467–81.

——, *The King's Serjeants and Officers of State* (London, 1911).

——, 'The Saladin Tithe', *EHR*, 31 (1916), 447–50.

——, 'The Counts of St Pol in Essex and Kent'; revised and completed by W.R. Powell, *Essex Archaeology & History*, 3rd series Vol. 27 (1996), pp. 193–201.

Rousseau, C.M., 'Home Front and Battlefield: The Gendering of Papal Crusading Policy, 1095–1221', *Gendering the Crusades*, ed. S.B. Edgington and S. Lambert (New York, 2001), pp. 31–44.

Rowlands, I.W., 'Warriors Fit for a Prince, Welsh Troops in Angevin Service, 1154–1216', *Mercenaries and Paid Men, The Mercenary Identity in the Middle Ages* (Leiden, 2008), pp. 207–30.

Royle, E., 'Introduction: Regions and Identities', *Issues of Regional Identity. In Honour of John Marshall*, ed. E. Royle (Manchester, 1998), pp. 1–13.

Ryan, V, 'Richard I and the Early Evolution of the Fourth Crusade', *The Fourth Crusade: Event, Aftermath, and Perceptions*, ed. T. Madden (Aldershot, 2008), pp. 3–14.

Sahlins, P., 'Natural Frontiers Revisited: France's Boundaries since the Seventeenth Century', *American Historical Review*, 95/5 (1990), 1423–51.

Salvioli, G., 'Il monachesimo occidentale e la sua storia economica', *Rivista italiana di sociologia*, 15 (1911), 123–56.

Sanders, I.J., *English Baronies: A Study of Their Origin and Descent (1086–1327)* (Oxford, 1960).

Sayers, J. 'English Charters from the Third Crusade', *Tradition and Change: Essays in Honour of Marjorie Chibnall Presented by Her Friends on the Occasion of Her Seventieth Birthday*, ed. D. Greenway, C. Holdsworth and J. Sayers (Cambridge, 1985), pp. 194–213.

——, *Innocent III: Leader of Europe, 1198–1216* (London and New York, 1994).

Serjeantson, R.M., and Adkins, W.R.D., *A History of the County of Northampton*, Vol. 2 (London, 1906).

Scammell, J., 'The Formation of the English Social Structure: Freedom, Knights, and Gentry, 1066–1300', *Speculum*, 68 (1993), 591–618.

Schenk, J., 'Forms of Lay Association with the Order of the Temple', *JMH*, 34 (2008), 79–103.

——, 'Nomadic Violence in the First Latin Kingdom of Jerusalem and the Military Orders', *Reading Medieval Studies*, 36 (2010), 39–55.

——, *Templar Families: Landowning Families and the Order of the Temple in France, c.1120–1307* (Cambridge, 2012).

Schmid, K., 'Zur Problematik von Familie, Sippe und Geschlecht, Haus und Dynastie beim mittealterlichen Adel: Vortragen zum Thema "Adel und Herrschaft in Mittelalter"', *Zeitschrift für die Geschichte des Oberrheins*, 105 (1957), 1–62.

——, 'Welfisches Selbstverständnis', *Adel und Kirche: Gerd Tellenbach zum 65 Geburtstag dargebracht von Freunden und Schülern*, ed. J. Fleckenstein and K. Schmid (Freiburg, 1968), pp. 390–416.

Schwennicke, D., *Europaische Stammtafeln*, New Series, Vol. 29 (Frankfurt, 2013).

Shepard, J., 'The English and Byzantium: A Study of Their Role in the Byzantine Army in the Later Eleventh Century', *Traditio*, 29 (1973), 53–92.

Sherif, M. and C.W., *An Outline of Social Psychology* (New York, 1956).

Sherif, M., *In Common Predicament: Social Psychology of Intergroup Conflict and Cooperation* (Boston, 1966).

Shideler, J.C., *A Medieval Catalan Noble Family: the Montcadas, 1000–1230* (Berkeley, CA, 1983).

Siberry, E., 'The Crusading Counts of Nevers', *Nottingham Medieval Studies*, 34 (1990), 64–70.

Sibert, G. de, *Histoire des Ordres Royaux, Hospitaliers-Militaires de Notre Dame du Mont Carmel et de Saint-Lazare de Jérusalem* (Paris, 1772).

Siebold, G.L., 'The Essence of Military Group Cohesion', *Armed Forces and Society*, 33/2 (2007), 286–95.

Simon, A.L., *The History of the Wine Trade in England*, Vol. 1 (London, 1964).

Simpkin, D., 'The Organisation of Chivalric Society', *A Companion to Chivalry*, ed. R.W. Jones and P. Coss (Woodbridge, 2019), pp. 39–56.

Simpson, G.G., 'The *Familia* of Roger de Quincy, Earl of Winchester and Constable

of Scotland', *Essays on the Nobility of Medieval Scotland*, ed. K.J. Stringer (Edinburgh, 1985), pp. 102–29.
Sinex, M., 'Echoic Irony in Walter Map's Satire against the Cistercians', *Comparative Literature*, 54/4 (2002), 275–90.
Skovgaard-Petersen, K., *A Journey to the Promised Land: Crusading Theology in the 'Historia de profectione Danorum in Hierosolymam', c.1200* (Copenhagen, 2001).
Slack, C., 'The Quest for Gain: Were the First Crusaders Proto-Colonists?', *Seven Myths of the Crusades*, ed. A.J. Andrea and A. Holt (Indianapolis, 2015), pp. 70–90.
Sladden, J.C., *Beside the Bright Stream: The Background and History of St Oswald's Church Lower Peover*, 4th edition (Altrincham, 1994).
Smith, B., *Colonisation and Conquest in Medieval Ireland: The English in Louth, 1170–1330* (Cambridge, 1999).
Smith, C., *Crusading in the Age of Joinville* (Aldershot, 2006).
Smith, K.A., 'Monastic Memories of the Early Crusading Movement', *Remembering the Crusades and Crusading*, ed. M. Cassidy-Welch (London, 2017), pp. 136–40.
Sorell, A., *Europe et la Revolution française, Vol. 1: Les Moeurs politiques et les traditions* (Paris, 1885).
Southern, R.W., *Western Society and the Church in the Middle Ages* (New York, 1970).
Spear, D.S., *The Personnel of the Norman Cathedrals During the Ducal Period, 911–1204* (London, 2006).
——, 'The Secular Clergy of Normandy and the Crusades', *Crusading and Pilgrimage in the Norman World*, ed. K. Hurlock and P. Oldfield (Woodbridge, 2015), pp. 81–103.
Stacey, R.C., *Politics, Policy and Finance under Henry III 1216–1245* (Oxford, 1987).
Stafford, P., 'La Mutation Familiale: A Suitable Case for Caution', *Community, the Family and the Saint: Patterns of Power in Early Medieval Europe*, ed. J. Hill and M. Swan (Turnhout, 1998), pp. 103–25.
Stanton, M.P., Dittmar, S.S., Jezewski, M.A., and Dickerson, S.S., 'Shared Experiences and Meanings of Military Nurse Veterans', *Image – the Journal of Nursing Scholarship*, 28/4 (1996), 343–7.
Stasson, M.F. and Bradshaw, S.D., 'Explanations of Individual–Group Performance Differences: What Sort of "Bonus" Can Be Gained Through Group Interaction?' *Small Group Research*, 26/2 (1995), 296–308.
Staunton, M., *The Historians of Angevin England* (Oxford, 2017).
Stenton, D.M., 'Roger of Howden and Benedict', *EHR*, 68 (1953), 574–82.
Stenton, F., *The First Century of English Feudalism, 1066–1166* (Oxford, 1961).
Stevenson, W.B., 'England, France and the Channel Islands, 1204–1259', *La Société Guernesiaise, Report and Transactions*, 19 (1976), 569–76.
——, 'English Rule in the Channel Isles in a Period of Transition, 1204–59', *Société Guernesiaise. Report and Transactions*, 20 (1977), 234–58.
Stone, L., 'Prosopography', *Historical Studies Today*, ed. F. Gilbert and S. Graubard (New York, 1972), pp. 107–40.
Stråth, B., 'A European Identity, To the Historical Limits of a Concept', *European Journal of Social Theory*, 5/4 (2002), 387–401.

Strayer, J.R., *The Administration of Normandy under Saint Louis* (Cambridge, MA, 1932).
Strickland, M., *War and Chivalry, The Conduct and Perception of War in England and Normandy, 1066–1215* (Cambridge, 1996).
——, *Henry the Young King, 1155–1183* (New Haven and London, 2016).
Stubbs, W., *The Constitutional History of England*, 4th edition (Oxford, 1883).
Studd, R., 'Reconfiguring the Angevin Empire, 1224–1259', *England and Europe in the Reign of Henry III (1216–1272)*, ed. B.K.U. Weiler and I.W. Rowlands (Aldershot, 2002), pp. 31–41.
Sturdza, M.D., *Dictionnaire historique et généalogique des grandes familles de Grèce, d'Albanie et de Constantinople*, 2nd edition (Paris, 1999).
Tanner, H.J., *Families, Friends and Allies: Boulogne and Politics in Northern France and England, c.879–1160* (Leiden, 2004).
Thomas, H.M., *The English and the Normans: Ethnic Hostility, Assimilation, and Identity 1066–c.1220* (Oxford, 2003).
Thompson, K., 'William Talvas, Count of Ponthieu, and the Politics of the Anglo-Norman Realm', *England and Normandy in the Middle Ages*, ed. D. Bates and A. Curry (London, 1994), pp. 169–84.
——, 'The Lords of L'Aigle: Ambition and Insecurity on the Borders of Normandy', *ANS*, 18 (1996), 177–99.
——, *Power and Border Lordship in Medieval France: the County of Perche, 1000–1226* (Woodbridge, 2000).
——, 'L'aristocratie anglo-normande et 1204', *1204: La Normandie entre Plantagenêts et Capétiens*, ed. A. Flambard-Héricher and V. Gazeau (Caen, 2003), pp. 179–87.
Tibble, S., *Crusader Armies* (New Haven and London, 2018).
Toowell, W., *Leicester Village History: Burton Lazars* (Melton Mowbray, 1882).
Touati, F.-O., *Maladie et société au moyen âge. La lèpre, les lépreux et les léproseries dans la province ecclésiastique de Sens jusqu'au milieu de XIVe siècle* (Paris, 1998).
Tout, T.F., *Chapters in the Administrative History of Medieval England*, Vol. 2 (Manchester, 1937).
Turner, R.V., 'Changing Perceptions of the New Administrative Class in Anglo-Norman and Angevin England: The *Curiales* and Their Conservative Critics', *Journal of British Studies*, 29 (1990), 93–177.
——, 'Richard Barre and Michael Belet: Two Angevin Civil Servants', *Judges, Administrators and the Common Law in Angevin England*, ed. R.V. Turner (London, 1994), pp. 180–98.
——, 'The Problem of Survival for the Angevin "Empire": Henry II's and his Sons' Vision Versus Late Twelfth Century Realities', *American Historical Review*, Vol. 100 (1995), 78–96.
——, 'Richard Lionheart and English Episcopal Elections', *Albion*, 29 (1997), 1–13.
——, 'The Households of the Sons of Henry II', *La cour Plantagenêt, 1154-1204*, ed. M. Aurell (Poitiers, 2000), pp. 49–62.
——, '*Ricardus Dux Aquitanorum et Comes Andegavorum*', *HSJ*, 13 (2004), 151–73.
——, *Eleanor of Aquitaine* (New Haven and London, 2009).
Turner, R.V., and Heiser, R.R., *The Reign of Richard the Lionheart, Ruler of the Angevin Empire, 1189–99* (Harlow, 2005).
Tyerman, C., *England and the Crusades, 1095–1588* (Chicago and London, 1988).

——, *The Invention of the Crusades* (Basingstoke, 2000).
——, *God's War: A New History of the Crusades* (London, 2006).
——, *How to Plan a Crusade: Religious War in the High Middle Ages* (London, 2015).
Vale, M., *The Angevin Legacy and the Hundred Years War, 1250–1340* (Oxford, 1990).
Vasselot de Régné, C. de, 'A Crusader Lineage from Spain to the Throne of Jerusalem: The Lusignans', *Crusades*, 16 (2017), 95–114.
Vellenga, B.A., and Christenson, J., 'Healing the Wounds of War: the Vietnam Veteran after Operation Desert Storm', *Perspectives in Psychiatric Care*, 31/4 (1995), 5–8.
Verbrugge, L.M., 'The Structure of Adult Friendship Choices', *Social Forces*, 56 (1997), 576–97.
Verbruggen, J.F., *The Art of Warfare in Western Europe During the Middle Ages*, 2nd revised edition, trans. S. Willard and R.W. Southern (Woodbridge, 1997).
Vercauteren, F., 'Une parenté dans la France du Nord aux XIe et XIIe siecles', *Le Moyen Age*, 69 (1963), 223–45.
Vicaire, M-H., '"L'affaire de paix et de foi" du Midi de la France', *Cahiers de Fanjeaux*, 4 (1968), 102–26.
Vielliard, F., 'Richard Coeur de Lion et son entourage normand: le témoignage de l'Estoire de la guerre sainte', *Bibliothèque de l'École des chartes*, 160 (2002), 7–26.
Vincent, N.C., *Peter des Roches: An Alien in English Politics 1205–1238* (Cambridge, 1996).
——, 'Twyford under the Bretons 1066–1250', *Nottingham Mediaeval Studies*, 41 (1997), 80–99.
——, 'The Borough of Chipping Sodbury and the Fat Men of France', *Transactions of the Bristol and Gloucestershire Record Society*, 116 (1998), 42–59.
——, 'Isabella of Angoulême: John's Jezebel', *King John, New Interpretations*, ed. S.D. Church (Woodbridge, 1999), pp. 165–219.
——, 'The Foundation of Wormegay Priory', *Norfolk Archaeology*, 43 (1999), 307–12.
——, 'Warin and Henry Fitz Gerald, the King's Chamberlains: the Origins of the FitzGeralds Revisited', *ANS* 21 (1999): 233–60.
——, 'Henry and the Poitevins', *La cour Plantagenêt, 1154-1204: Actes du Colloque tenu à Thouars du 30 avril au 2 mai 1999*, ed. M. Aurell (Poitiers, 2000), pp. 103–35.
——, 'William Marshal, King Henry II and the Honour of Châteauroux', *Archives*, 15 (2000), 1–15.
——, 'The Charters of Henry II: The Introduction of the Royal "Inspeximus" Revisited', *Dating Undated Medieval Charters*, ed. M. Gervers (Budapest/ Woodbridge 2000), pp. 97–120.
——, 'Conclusion', *Noblesses de l'espace Plantagenêt, 1154-1204*, ed. M. Aurell (Poitiers 2001), pp. 207–14.
——, 'Les Normands de l'entourage d'Henri II Plantagenêt', *La Normandie et l'Angleterre au Moyen Age*, ed. P. Bouet and V. Gazeau (Caen, 2003), pp. 75–88.
——, 'Regional Variations in the Charters of King Henry II (1154–89)', *Charters and Charter Scholarship in Britain and Ireland*, ed. M.T. Flanagan and J.A. Green (London 2005), pp. 70–106.
——, 'Patronage, Politics and Piety in the Charters of Eleanor of Aquitaine', *Plan-

tagenêts et Capétiens: confrontations et héritages, ed. M. Aurell and N.-Y. Tonnerre (Turnhout 2006), pp. 17–60.

——, 'Introduction: Henry II and the Historians', *Henry II: New Interpretations*, ed. C. Harper-Bill and N. Vincent (Woodbridge, 2007), pp.1–23.

——, 'The Court of Henry II', *Henry II, New Interpretations*, ed. C. Harper-Bill and N. Vincent (Woodbridge, 2007), pp. 335–61.

——, 'Did Henry II Have a Policy Towards the Earls?', *War, Government and Aristocracy in the British Isles, c.1150–1500. Essays in Honour of Michael Prestwich*, ed. C. Given-Wilson, A. Kettle, and L. Scales (Woodbridge, 2008).

——, 'Hugh de Gundeville (fl. 1147–1181)', *Records, Administration and Aristocratic Society in the Anglo-Norman Realm*, ed. N. Vincent (Woodbridge 2009), pp. 125–52.

Virgoe, R., 'Aspects of the County Community in the Fifteenth Century', *Profit, Piety and the Professions in Late Medieval England*, ed. M. Hicks (Gloucester, 1990), pp. 1–13.

Walker, D., 'Crown and Episcopacy under the Normans and the Angevins', *ANS*, 5 (1983), 220–33.

Walker, J., 'Crusaders and Patrons: The Influence of the Crusades on the Patronage of the Order of St. Lazarus in England', *The Military Orders, Vol. I: Fighting for the Faith and Caring for the Sick*, ed. M. Barber (Abingdon, 1994), pp. 327–32.

Wallace, W.L., *Student Culture: Social Structure and Continuity in a Liberal Arts College* (Chicago, 1966).

Warlop, E., *De Vlaamse adel vóór 1300* (Handzame, 1968).

——, *The Flemish Nobility before 1300*, 4 Vols (Kortrijk, 1975).

Warren, W.L., *King John*, 2nd edition (London, 1978).

Weiler, B.K.U., and Rowlands, I.R. (eds.), *England and the Continent in the Thirteenth Century* (Aldershot, 2002).

Werveke, H. van, 'La contribution de la Flandre et de Hainaut à la troisième croisade', *Le Moyen Age*, 78 (1972), 55–90.

West, F.J., *The Justiciarship of England, 1066-1232* (Cambridge, 1966).

Wetherell, C., 'Historical Social Network Analysis', *International Review of Social History*, 43 (1998), 125–44.

White, G.H., 'The Career of Waleran, Count of Meulan and Earl of Worcester (1104–66)', *Transactions of the Royal Historical Society*, Ser. 4, 17 (1934), 19–48.

White, S., *Custom, Kinship and Gifts to Saints: the* Laudatio Parentum *in Western France, 1050–1150* (Chapel Hill, NC, 1988).

Whitwell, R.J., 'English Monasteries and the Wool Trade in the 13th Century', *Vierteljahrschrift für Social-und-Wirtsschaftsgeschichte*, 2 (1904), 1–33.

Wightman, W.E., *The Lacy Family in England and Normandy, 1066–1194* (Oxford, 1966).

Wilkinson, B., 'The Government of England during the Absence of Richard I on Crusade', *Bulletin of the John Rylands Library*, 28 (1944), 485–509.

Williams, D.H., *The Cistercians in the Early Middle Ages* (Leominster, 1998).

Young, C.R., *Hubert Walter: Lord of Canterbury and Lord of England* (Durham, 1968).

Zacour, N.P. and Hazard, H.W., *A History of the Crusades. Vol. 5: The Impact of the Crusades on the Near East* (Madison, WI, 1985).

Zeller, G., 'La monarchie d'ancien régime et les frontières naturelles', *Revue d'histoire moderne*, 8 (1933), 305–33.

Zink, M., 'Autour de la Bataille des Vins de Henri d'Andeli: le blanc du prince, du pauvre et du poète', *L'Imaginaire du vin*, ed. M. Milner and M. Chatelain-Courtois (Marseille, 1989), pp. 111–21.

Unpublished PhD Theses

'The Coucher Book and Charter of Bolton Priory', ed. K.J. Legg (University of Sheffield, 2002).

Abram, A. 'The Augustinian Canons in the Diocese of Coventry and Lichfield and Their Benefactors, 1115–1320' (University of Wales, 2007).

Asmoui Ismail, D.C., 'A History of the Counts of Brienne, 950–1210' (Royal Holloway, University of London, 2013).

Benjamin, D., 'Support Structures in Crusading Armies, 1095–1241' (University of Leicester, 2015).

Bowie, C.M., 'The Daughters of Henry II and Eleanor of Aquitaine: a Comparative Study of Twelfth-Century Royal Women' (University of Glasgow, 2011).

Flynn, J., 'Sense and Sentimentality: The Soldier–Horse Relationship in the Great War' (University of Derby, 2016).

Fox, E.T., 'Piratical Schemes and Contracts: Pirate Articles and their Society, 1660–1730' (University of Exeter, 2013).

Gossman, R., 'The Financing of the Crusades' (University of Chicago, 1965).

Kane, J., 'The Impact of the Cross on Western Crusade Terminology' (University of Cambridge, 2016).

Poggioli, P.A., 'From Politics to Prelate: The Career of Walter of Coutances, Archbishop of Rouen, 1184–1207' (Johns Hopkins University, 1984).

Satchell, A.E.M., 'The Emergence of Leper-houses in Medieval England, 1100–1250' (University of Oxford, 1998).

Smith, N.J.C., '*Servicium Debitum* and Scutage in Twelfth Century England with Comparisons to the *Regno* of Southern Italy' (Durham University, 2010).

Villegas-Aristizábal, L., 'Norman and Anglo-Norman Participation in the Iberian Reconquista' (University of Nottingham, 2013).

Walker, J., 'The Patronage of the Templars and the Order of St Lazarus in England in the Twelfth and Thirteenth Centuries' (University of St Andrews, 1991).

Watson, R., 'The Counts of Angoulême from the 9th to the Mid 13th Century: with a Catalogue of Comital Documents from 882/3 to 1246' (University of East Anglia, 1976).

Web-based Sources

Cushing, D., 'Richard I and the Jewish "Servi Camarae" as a Funding Source for the Third Crusade': https://www.academia.edu/983627 [accessed 25 September 2020].

Diplomata Belgica. The Diplomatic Sources from the Medieval Southern Low Countries, ed. T. de Hemptinne, J. Deploige, J.-L. Kupper and W. Prevenier (Brussels, 2015): www.diplomata-belgica.be [accessed 25 September 2020].

Ferguson, N., 'The False Prophecy of Hyperconnection: How to Survive the Networked World', *Foreign Affairs* (October 2007): <https://www.foreignaffairs.com/articles/2017-08-15/false-prophecy-hyperconnection> [accessed 25 September 2020].

Stacey, R.C., 'Hubert Walter', *Oxford Dictionary of National Biography: https://www.oxforddnb.com/*

Revised Regesta Regni Hierosolymitani Database: http://crusades-regesta.com [accessed 25 September 2020]

Index

Acre (port, city)   21, 23–5, 61, 65–6, 81, 86, 137, 156, 170–1, 199, 204, 205 n.264–5, 209, 210
   Siege of (1189–91)   17, 22, 36–7, 46, 52, 54–61, 75–7, 82, 84, 100–2, 104–8, 110–11, 131, 137, 143, 157 n.197, 168, 175, 179, 181–2, 192, 202–03, 205, 209 n.291 and 294, 210, 213–4, 218
   Battle of (4 Oct 1189)   22, 151 n.167
   St Martin Offensive (12 Nov 1190)   17, 60–1, 175, 222–3, 242, 269, 303, 307, 340
Adam of Savoisy   45, 50, 237
Alan of Fontaine   145, 156 n.191, 276
Alan of Lille   29, 31–2, 34, 60
Alan Trenchemer   137, 193–5, 282, 361
Alan of Valoignes, sheriff of Kent   55, 110-11, 305–7, 379, 388
Alard Fleming   175–6, 188–9, 193, 294, 361
Alard I of Croisilles   46, 50, 265
Alexander of Arsic, lord of Cogges   156, 180–2, 324, 387
Alice of Courtenay   99, 101, 110, 215
Alice of Gant   76, 78–9, 82, 110
Ambroise   11, 24 n.90, 25, 296, 377
Andrew of Brienne, lord of Ramerupt   58 n.165, 100, 244, 250–1, 255, 272
Andrew of Chauvigny   25 n.96, 183, 185 n.155, 188, 196–7, 201, 287, 360, 372
Anjou (county)   2 n. 4, 27, 106 n.85, 185, 197, 280, 345, 364
Anseau IV of Garlande   98, 225
Anselm of Neuvilette   50, 266
Anselm III of Montréal   109, 136, 231–2
Anselm IV of Montréal   136, 231–2
Appares (associate justiciar)   76, 116 n.134, 166–7, 191, 357–8, 371
Aquitaine (duchy)   2 n. 4, 153, 161 n.9, 185, 197
Arbalester (archer, crossbowman)   180 n.128, 187
Armiger (arms-bearer)   173, 187, 282, 383
Arnold II of Guines   143–4, 351
Arnold III of Therouanne   145, 259–60
Arnold of IV Bois, lord of Thorpe   128, 201, 309

Arsuf, battle of (7 Sep 1191)   17, 65, 87 n.317, 93, 109, 174, 176–7
Ascalon (city)   152, 164, 171, 174, 177, 206
Aswalo II, lord of Seignelay   100, 107–08, 136, 252–4
Aubrey Clément, royal marshal   171 n.77, 224, 257
Aubrey de Vere, earl of Oxford, master chamberlain of England   172, 392, 396
Audita tremendi (papal bull)   8, 15, 31, 35, 90, 115, 118, 122, 159 n.2, 160 n.5, 213
Augustinians – see Order of Canons Regular of St Augustine

Baldwin of Forde, archbishop of Canterbury   5, 24, 33–5, 37, 49, 53–61, 181, 183 n.147, 186 n.159, 215, 303
Baldwin of Béthune   104 n.76, 124, 140, 143, 145, 156, 189, 191 n.180, 183, 192 n.193, 204–5, 206 n.269, 222, 259, 292, 373
Baldwin le Carron, lord of Rumes   XIII, 51 n.128, 57 n.161, 145, 156–7, 170, 174–7, 188–9, 191 n.183, 204–5, 206 n.269, 207 n.277, 223, 269–70, 385–6,
Baldwin II of Bailleul   143–5
Baldwin V, count of Hainaut   23, 93 n.14, 145, 153–4, 157, 174, 175 n.101, 181, 268–9, 273, 275–78, 285–6
Balian of Ibelin   59
Barbeau Abbey   16 n.67, 72, 220, 223
Barlings Abbey   76, 350
Bartholomew of Vignory   109, 244, 255–6
Barton Lazars Leprosarium   66, 81
Battle Abbey   51, 327
Beaulieu Abbey   149 n.153, 286–7, 289
Beaulieu Leprosarium (Grand-Beaulieu)   72, 87
Bec-Hellouin Abbey   64, 66, 74 n.239–40, 292
Benedictines – see Order of St Benedict
Berengaria of Navarre, queen of England   112, 278–9, 349
Bergues Abbey   63
Bernard of Clairvaux, Saint   32 n.20, 35–6, 102, 107, 113 n.122
Bernard II of St Valéry   105, 126, 143
Bertram III of Verdun   117, 167 n.50, 191 n.180, 206 n.269, 286, 363

Bertran of Born   153
Boigny Leprosarium   72, 81, 86 n.311, 220
Bonport Abbey   68, 278, 336
Bordesley Abbey   65, 84 n.302, 308, 326
Brabant (duchy)   2 n. 4, 154, 208, 261–2, 271
Brittany (duchy)   2 n. 4, 185, 192, 204
  Breton crusaders   185, 192, 337–8, 384
Butler (*Pincerna*)   62, 76 n.250, 110, 126, 144 n. 134, 163, 172–3, 228, 294, 306, 354, 361, 388

Castellan (castle constable)   55, 133 n.134, 143–4, 156, 164, 195 n.204, 209, 221, 260, 267, 271, 276, 282, 327, 342, 353, 357–8, 360, 365–72, 388
Chaloché Abbey   69, 287
Château-l'Abbaye Abbey   222, 390
Chamberlain (*camerarius*)   126, 128, 144 n.134, 146, 163, 167, 172–3, 181, 188, 199, 224, 246, 256, 260, 284, 289, 291, 293, 296, 308, 356, 360–2, 387, 392,
Champagne   27, 46, 57–8, 83–4, 98–100, 102, 136, 155, 157, 226–7, 231–2, 236, 242–3, 245–8, 256
Charité-sur-Loire Abbey   97, 225, 238–9
Charron Abbey   69, 295
Chertsey Abbey   69
Cheshire   204 n.256, 320, 368
Chivalry   6, 13, 95
Cistercians – see Order of Cistercians
Clarembaud of Châlon   176
Clarembaud of Noyers, lord of Noyers   106–7, 136, 250–2
Clarembold IV of Chappes   106, 109, 249–50, 253
Clement III, pope   9, 35, 37
Cleric, clerk   13, 21, 24–5, 40 n.61, 54 n.139, 55, 58, 61, 77 n.255, 132, 164 n.28, 173, 187, 196–7, 203, 289, 291–3, 297, 303, 313, 321, 348, 354–5, 362, 379
Conon of Béthune   142 n.119, 259, 271, 289, 292
Conon of Duras, count of Duras and Montaigu   48, 262
Constable (*comites stabularius*)   46, 50, 57, 58 n.164, 75 n.245, 84, 100, 102, 104 n.78, 116–7, 131, 143–4, 164, 168, 172, 181 n.132, 197, 199, 223–4, 243, 260, 284, 311, 315, 320, 328, 337, 359, 364, 367–8, 370, 372, 386–7
Conrad of Montferrat   22, 59–60, 125, 198, 204, 221, 243, 245–6, 250, 254, 256, 268, 289, 373, 386
Conroi   93, 158, 177, 181, 197, 217
Cornwall   2 n.4, 132–3, 217, 294, 319, 350
Croxton Abbey   65 n 203, 75, 286

Crusades
  First   1–2, 8–9, 11 n.38, 29, 30, 36, 37 n. 48, 44, 48, 57–8 n.165, 71, 77, 78 n.259, 90, 101, 102 n.65, 105, 109, 117 n.142, 119, 126, 148, 215
  Second   10, 27, 31, 33, 37–8, 41–2, 76, 77 n.25126, 4, 78–9, 81–2, 101–3, 105–6, 108–10, 112–15, 118, 199, 212, 215–16,
  of 1177   34, 78, 82 n. 288, 97, 99, 104–5, 112 n. 113, 175 n.96, 263, 265, 351, 357, 382,
  German   112, 261
  Fourth   15 n.61, 102, 108, 142 n. 119, 157, 216, 218, 237, 240, 246–9, 259, 264, 289, 374

Dalon Abbey   68, 71, 341
Darum (city), siege of (May 1192)   167, 188, 209–10, 278, 280, 287, 308, 342, 348, 357, 359, 376, 378
David of Scotland, earl of Huntington   157, 392
Dreux of Fontenil   128, 201, 309
Dreux IV of Merlo, lord of Saint-Bris, constable of France   17, 97, 136, 172, 223–5
Dunkeswell Abbey   76, 349
Durand of Outillé, lord of Valoignes   110, 306, 388

Eaucourt Abbey   47, 50, 265
Easby Abbey   45, 327
Eleanor of Aquitaine, queen of England   23, 77–8 n.258, 81, 106, 112–3, 126, 136, 137 n. 82, 166, 187–8, 215, 278–9, 282, 287, 304, 327, 349, 365, 369, 379
Engelram of Fiennes, lord of Martock   64–65 n.198, 148–9 n.153, 156, 264
Engelram of Préaux   157, 198
Ernald of Mandeville   103–04, 116, 130, 182, 310–11, 387
Esnecca (longship)   193–4
Eustacia of Croisilles   46–7, 265
Everard of Aulnay   49, 245–7
Everard I of Chacenay   58, 109, 115, 155 n.188, 232, 243–4, 250–1
Everard II of Brienne, count of Brienne   47, 58, 109, 114, 231–2, 243–5, 247–51, 255, 272

Falconer   188, 291–2, 363
Familia, familiares – see *mesnie*
Flanders (county)   2 n.4, 9 n.28, 98, 138–9, 144, 148, 153

Flemish crusaders 58, 61–3, 91, 93 n.14, 104, 142, 150, 156, 175, 189, 212, 260, 263–74
Floreffe Abbey 36, 52–3, 214, 267–8, 386
Fontenay Abbey 45
Forde Abbey 54, 74–6, 88, 121, 130, 304
Fontevraud Abbey 43, 284
Frederick Barbarossa, Emperor Frederick I 2, 9, 35, 59, 91, 183, 186 n.159, 213, 259, 261–2
Frederick of Seignelay 100, 107, 115, 136, 252–4
Fulk of Fontaine 145, 156 n.191, 276
Fulk of Rufford 44, 328

Garnier of Nablûs, master of the Hospitallers 172, 176, 346, 393
Geddington, Great Council of 35, 41, 54, 65, 67, 297, 350–1, 353, 357, 363, 367, 392–6
Geoffrey of Balliol 129, 217, 327
Geoffrey of Bois 129, 321, 378
Geoffrey of Brulon 156, 290, 382
Geoffrey Fitz-Peter 76, 116 n. 134, 166, 191 n.181, 349, 358
Geoffrey of Lusignan 58 n.165, 60, 106, 204, 206, 244, 339–41, 390
Geoffrey the Goldsmith 131, 323
Geoffrey III of Joinville, seneschal of Champagne 57–8, 108–9, 246, 247–8
Geoffrey III of Perche, count of Perche 47, 66 n.207, 97, 112, 238, 390
Geoffrey IV of Joinville 58, 243, 246–8, 108–9
Geoffrey IV of Rancon, lord of Taillebourg 106, 339–41, 390–1
Geoffrey Talbot of Heathfield 55, 75
Gerald of Wales, Gerald of Barri 24, 34, 40, 56, 62 n.184, 203, 209, 351–2
Gerard Talbot, lord of Linton 55, 75, 156, 191 n. 183, 192–3 n.193, 283, 374
Gregory VIII, pope 2, 8–9, 15, 31, 35–6, 90, 115, 118, 121, 213
Gilbert of Glanville, bishop of Rochester 54–5, 393
Gilbert of Pecche 44, 321
Gisors (town) 2, 9, 16–17, 54, 57, 62, 141, 174 n.93, 180, 183, 282–3, 364, 369, 392
Gîte (right to hospitality) 46
Gobert of Merchin 47, 50, 271
Godfrey of Bouillon, king of Jerusalem 10, 36, 48, 264
Godfrey of Lucy, bishop of Winchester 202, 393
Godfrey of Saint-Vérain 47, 50, 236
Godfrey of Villehardouin 245–8
Godescalc III of Morialmé 53, 264, 267–8

Guy of Chappes, lord of Jully 106, 109, 249–50,
Guy of Fontaine 145, 156 n.191, 276
Guy of Lusignan, king of Jerusalem 1, 22, 58–9, 106, 137, 204
Guy of Noyelles, lord of Noyelles 48, 116, 130, 222, 251
Guy of Noyers, Templar 107, 109, 252
Guy of Pierre-Perthius 107, 252
Guy of Vergy, lord of Vergy 97, 234–5
Guy II of Dampierre, constable of Champagne 57–8, 100, 102, 109, 115, 226, 232, 243–5, 247

Hagan of Ervy, lord of Ervy 44, 87–8, 136, 258
Hainaut (duchy) 2 n.4, 23, 33 n.25, 35–6, 98, 145–6, 153–4,
    Hainautian crusaders 52–3, 57 n. 161, 145, 157, 174–6, 189, 205, 268, 269, 272–8, 385–6
Haliwell Abbey 67, 68 n.215
Hattin, battle of (4 Jul 1187) 1, 31, 33 n.26, 52, 59, 78, 82 n.289, 85, 129,
Hautmont Abbey 47, 50, 271–2
Hellin of Wavrin, seneschal of Flanders 58, 143, 156, 270–1, 273
Henry Fitz-Nicholas 128, 310
Henry of Hastings 56 n.156, 105, 156 n.191, 315
Henry of Longchamp, sheriff of Herefordshire 156, 166, 191 n.183, 198–9, 353, 359, 365 – 6
Henry of Mailoc 128, 309
Henry of Marcy, cardinal-bishop of Albano 33, 35, 54 n.138, 57
Henry Pigot, seneschal 116, 131 n. 50, 144, 311, 387
Henry Pomeroy 55, 75, 130, 304
Henry the Young King 87, 113, 116, 151, 152 n.175, 154, 156, 162 n.15, 163–4, 173, 179–80, 185–6, 189–92, 198, 200, 205–06, 227, 289, 362
Henry I of Bar, count of Bar 56–7 n.158, 58, 114, 228–9, 243
Henry II of Trois, count of Champagne 98 n.42, 102, 114, 136, 213, 220, 222, 228, 242–3, 245–7, 250, 254, 256–7
Henry II, king of England 2, 12–13, 15–16 n.63, 33 n.26, 35, 40–3, 46, 54, 61–2, 64, 68 n.215, 69, 73, 81–2, 93 n.14, 99–100, 105–6, 112–3, 124–5, 127, 131, 136, 139–43, 145, 146 n.143, 152, 161–5, 167–8, 170, 173, 174–5, 179–81, 183, 187–8 n.160, 189–95, 197–201, 203, 205, 208–10, 214, 220, 229, 238, 280, 283, 289–92, 294–5, 297, 300,

302–03, 305–06, 308, 312, 315, 337, 348, 354–5, 357–66, 368–9, 371–5, 377, 379, 381–2, 384, 388–9, 392
Heraclius, Latin patriarch of Jerusalem 51, 56, 305, 358
Herman IV, margrave of Baden and Verona 103, 267
Holland (county) 2 n.4, 261–2
Holmcultram Abbey 64, 68 n.123, 74 n.239, 348
Holme Abbey 67, 68 n.215
Hospitallers – see Military Orders, Order of Knights of the Hospital of Saint John of Jerusalem
Household – see *mesnie*
Hubert Walter, bishop of Salisbury 49, 53 n.137, 54–6, 61, 76, 77 n.254, 87 n.317, 110, 132, 176, 180, 192, 202–03, 305, 307, 329, 362, 394
Hugh Bardolf, marshal 116 n.134, 166, 170, 191 n.181, 358, 367, 369
Hugh of Bourbonne 46, 50, 237
Hugh of Neville 23, 76, 295, 376
Hugh of Oyry 17, 57 n.161, 111, 223–4, 269
Hugh Peitevin 55 n.148, 116, 329
Hugh III of Broyes 114
Hugh III, duke of Burgundy 52, 101, 156, 171, 176, 214, 221, 230–2, 338–9
Hugh VI of Gournay, lord of Gourney 205
Hugh IV, count of St Pol 17, 47, 50, 146, 222, 240, 242, 251, 289, 292, 390
Humbert IV 'the young' of Beaujeau, lord of Beaujeau 101, 277
Humphrey IV of Toron, lord of Toron 59, 80, 86, 206, 386

Iberia 9, 14, 37–8, 131, 215
Imagined Communities 121–3, 147, 158
Imitatio Christi (Imitation of Christ, Life in Christ) 3, 25, 29–32, 37, 79, 118, 214, 216
Inheritance 26, 46, 51, 68 n.215–6, 92, 96–101, 108, 111, 120, 124–5, 128, 141, 145 n.138, 146, 153, 156, 175, 187 n.160, 191, 194 n.200, 199, 204, 214, 216, 227, 256, 291, 354, 362, 364, 369
Innocent III, pope 11, 14–15, 36–7, 40, 48, 111, 132, 216
Ireland (lordship) 2 n. 4, 388
    Irish crusaders 110–1, 186 n.159, 388

Jaffa (port, city) 50, 69 n.222, 129, 168, 197–8, 203, 280–1, 284, 286, 288, 290, 292, 296–9, 320–1, 327, 329, 336–7, 338–40, 347, 354–7, 360, 363, 372–6, 378–80, 382, 386–7, 390–1
    Peace of 69, 76 n.247, 85
    Siege/relief of (Jul–Aug 1192) 69, 76 n. 247, 77 n.257, 129, 164 n. 27, 173, 198, 204, 206, 244 258, 278–80, 285–8, 294–5, 298, 308, 321, 340, 345, 357, 362, 367, 372–3, 375–9, 386
James I Avesnes, lord of Avesnes 58–9, 93, 109, 145–6, 244, 260, 265, 268, 270, 272
Jerusalem (city) VIII, 1, 9–10, 22, 36, 43, 47–8, 69, 80, 111, 130, 141 n.111, 169
    Fall of (to Saladin 2 Oct 1187) 2, 26–7, 31, 35, 52, 57, 75, 80–1, 85, 88, 117, 119 n.151, 132, 142, 157, 160 n. 5, 213–4, 218
    Kingdom/Crown of VII, 1, 10, 31, 59, 61, 71 n.228, 219
    Recovery of (from Saladin) 14, 29–30, 32, 38, 53, 130, 160, 169, 213, 215
Joanna, queen of Sicily 112–3, 171, 198, 238, 242–3, 263, 278–9, 281, 287, 348–9, 360
John of Anagni, papal legate 43
John of Arcis-sur-Aube, lord of Arcis-sur-Aube 101 n.60, 107 n.92, 136, 232
John Fitz-Richard, constable of Chester 82, 84, 104, 117, 143, 320, 346, 368
John of Hessle 131, 330
John le Strange, lord of Ruyton 130, 325
John of Montmirail, lord of Montmirail 99, 110, 222, 226, 243
John Lackland, count of Mortain 84, 114, 167, 200 n.239, 210, 360
John of Penigeston 115, 329
John of Préaux, lord of Préaux 87, 156, 199, 286–7, 359, 362, 372
John I of Nesle, castellan of Bruges 42, 57 n.163, 143, 145, 221, 260
John I of Sées, count of Ponthieu 47, 48 n. 117, 50, 57 n. 161, 101, 112 n.112, 116, 126, 130, 180, 222, 251
Jordan of Le Hommet, constable of Séez 124 n.13, 143, 164, 167–8, 197 n.219, 199, 284, 367
Joscelin of Neville 44, 331
Jocelin III, lord of Mayenne 105–6, 125, 191–2, 337–8, 345, 388
Joscius of Tyre, archbishop of Tyre 2
Joseph of Exeter 24, 55, 303
Jus naufragii (right of shipwreck) 137
Justiciar 55, 111 n.110, 116 n.134, 165–6, 172, 188, 197, 279–81, 284, 291, 301, 305, 345, 353, 357, 359, 384

Kelso Abbey 48, 50, 343–4
Kinship 4, 7, 10, 16, 26–7, 90-103,

107–14, 118, 120, 190, 197, 199, 211, 215–7, 218
Knight – see *miles*

Leopold V of Austria, count of Austria 59
Lineage 26, 52, 90, 92, 94–8, 100–01, 106–07, 114, 120, 123, 129, 216–7,
London (port, city) 131, 140, 181–2, 217, 294, 297, 306, 313, 323–4, 347–8, 355, 371–2, 381, 395
Longpont Abbey 72 n.232, 135–6, 226
Ludwig III, landgrave of Thuringia 59

Maizières Abbey 97, 230, 234–5
Malmesbury Abbey 64, 67 n.210, 74 n.240, 348
Manasses, bishop of Langres 52, 84, 109, 231–2, 243–4
Marshal (*marah schalh*) 168–72, 174, 176–7, 189, 198, 224, 245–8, 257, 281, 288, 349–50, 357–8, 360–1, 379
Matthew Oisel 55, 75, 130, 304
Matthew of Walincourt 157, 278
Maud of Valoignes 55, 110–11, 215
Maurice II of Craon, constable of Ancenis 76, 192, 337–8, 364, 372, 375
Memory 5–6, 86 n.311, 91–4, 112, 217
Mesnie 11, 26, 48, 75 n.245, 94, 106, 119, 126–30, 156–7, 162–212
Messina (port, city) 17, 22, 48, 167, 182, 187, 198, 201, 203, 220, 222, 226, 229, 238, 244, 278–9, 283–4, 286, 289, 291, 296–7, 301, 308, 312, 321, 326, 334, 339, 341, 344–5, 350
Michael Belet, butler 62, 173, 361
Miles, Milites (caballero, chaveliers, ritter) 1, 11–13, 27, 30, 39–42, 54–6, 60, 65, 69–70, 77 n.254, 80–2, 84–6, 90, 93, 104, 109 n.100, 116, 126–9, 134, 140–2, 148–58, 162–4, 167–8, 170–92, 196–201, 204–09, 211, 241, 245, 267, 277, 344
Miles Beauchamp 116, 129, 301
Military Orders 26, 29, 38–9, 52, 63, 67, 70, 73–4, 78, 87–8, 152, 169, 183, 187, 216, 218
    Order of Knights of the Hospital of Saint John of Jerusalem, Hospitallers 17, 37, 42, 50–2, 55, 66–7, 72, 80–2, 84, 85 n.307, 87, 104 n.78, 169–77, 220–21, 234, 237, 243, 252, 254–5, 262, 267, 271, 313, 346, 351, 393
    Order of St Lazarus, Lazarines 3, 66, 70 n.224, 71–4, 78–88, 121, 216, 238, 278, 290, 311, 316, 348
    Poor Fellow-Soldiers of Christ and of the Temple of Solomon,

Templars VII, 10, 17, 24, 30, 33, 37, 39, 41 n.69, 42, 44 n.90, 46–7, 49–53, 60, 63–4, 67, 70, 72, 75, 77 – 80, 82 n.288–9, 83–5, 87, 92, 98, 105–07, 109–10, 146, 157, 169–71, 176–7, 197, 205, 220–2, 224, 226, 228–30, 233, 235–40, 243–5, 247–9, 252–4, 256, 258, 269, 278, 285, 290, 295, 305, 308, 317, 320, 322, 326, 332, 335, 341–2, 345–6, 348–9, 384, 389
Military retainers – see *mesnie*
Monachus, bishop of Caesarea 22, 25
Mortgaging of Property 39–42, 44–5, 48–50, 88, 129, 216, 272, 321, 343

Narjot II of Toucy, lord of Toucy 58, 108–09, 238, 243, 245
Normandy (duchy) 2 n. 4, 21, 39, 42 n.74, 58 n.165, 64, 73, 77 n.254, 86–7, 106 n.85, 116, 124–5, 128, 136, 146, 148, 153, 168, 175 n.96, 179–81, 185, 191, 201 n.244, 210
    Norman crusaders 10, 27, 43–4, 91, 146, 173, 184–5, 198–9, 282–7, 289, 292, 296–7, 299–300, 309–10, 312–14, 329, 332, 334–7
Newhouse Abbey 64 n.196, 68 n.215, 74, 280–1
Nigel of Mowbray 43, 55, 77 n.256, 78, 82, 110, 131, 290
Norbertines – see Order of Canons Regular of Prémontré
Nuclearisation (familial) 92, 94–5, 97, 119, 216

Odo of Merlo 97
Order of Canons Regular of Prémontré, Premonstratensians, Norbertines 17, 29, 36–7, 45, 50–2, 56–7, 62–3, 66–8, 70, 72, 74, 76, 78 n.263, 80, 88, 100, 138 n.94, 214, 216, 220–2, 229–30, 240, 242–5, 250–1, 253–4, 258, 263, 267–8, 271–2, 277, 280–3, 290, 295, 305, 307, 327, 331–2, 339, 345, 349–50, 390
Order of Canons Regular of St Augustine, Augustinians 17, 24, 50, 67, 69–70, 74, 220, 259, 265, 271, 278, 281, 300, 305–06, 308, 312, 325, 329–30, 337, 347–8, 357
Order of Cistercians 3, 16 n.67, 17, 29, 32–6, 39, 42–3, 45, 49–51, 53, 57, 61–78, 80, 82 n.288, 84, 87–8, 97, 102, 105 n.84, 134–5, 138–9, 216, 220–6, 228–35, 237, 240–6, 250–9, 262–3, 266, 268, 272, 286–7, 289–91, 295, 301–04, 308–09, 311–12, 320, 326, 328–9, 336–8, 340–2, 345–6, 349
Order of St Benedict, Benedictines 17, 22,

32, 44, 50, 57 n.159, 62 n.187, 63–4, 67, 69–71, 74, 97, 220, 222, 224–5, 227, 230, 238–43, 246, 249–52, 259–61, 263, 266–7, 271–3, 278–9, 283–5, 292, 295–6, 298, 303, 305–06, 308, 311, 315, 324, 326, 335, 338, 345, 347–9, 351
Order of Tiron, Tironensians   65–7, 285, 343–4
Osmund of Stuteville   77, 131, 146 n.141, 157, 182, 329, 387
Otto II of Trazegnies, lord of Trazegnies   52–3, 65, 145–6, 175 n.101, 204–7, 268, 386

Pax Dei (Peace of God)   147
Peter of Blois   33–4, 54, 304
Peter of Préaux   156, 173, 191 n.183, 192–3 n.193, 198, 200, 286–7, 359, 362, 372–3
Peter of Ross, archdeacon of Carlisle   77, 131, 291, 329, 331–2
Peter of Seignelay   100, 107, 115, 136, 252–4
Peter II of Courtenay, count of Nevers, Auxerre, and Tonnere   17, 57, 99–102, 110, 155, 220, 222, 226–7,
Philip Augustus, Philip II, king of France   2, 21, 23, 43, 46, 48, 56, 59, 61, 72–4, 76 n.250, 102, 108, 110, 125–6, 133–6, 142–3, 146, 155–6, 160, 165 n.35, 167–8, 172–4, 178, 180, 183, 195, 202–04, 209–10, 212, 213–15, 220–30, 238, 240, 243, 257, 270, 273, 278, 292, 348, 355, 364, 389
Philip of Alsace, count of Flanders   58, 62–3, 73, 78, 91, 104, 126, 139–43, 145, 150, 154, 156, 165 n.35, 174 – 5, 189 – 90, 213, 263–5, 269, 351, 357
Philip of Dreux, bishop of Beauvais   37, 56–9, 61, 101–02, 114, 155, 157, 215, 220–23, 226–27, 240, 243, 313
Philip of Kyme   76, 130–31, 322
Philip of Plessis   157, 346
Pipewell Abbey   65, 67–8, 202, 353, 392, 394–5
Poitiers (city)   43, 99, 344–5
Poitou (county)   2 n. 4, 21, 181, 185, 197, 279–80, 296, 339–40, 360, 364
Pontigny Abbey   88, 97, 134, 136, 218, 225, 231–2, 242–3, 251–4, 258
Portugal   38, 215
Preaching the Third Crusade   26, 30–5, 37–8, 40, 54, 57, 61, 63, 89, 91, 114, 118–20, 175 n.101, 186 n.159, 209, 214–6, 303, 392
Premonstratensians – see Order of Canons Regular of Prémontré
Preudomme, prodome   7, 13, 152, 155, 214

Rainard of Seignelay   100, 107, 115, 136, 252–4
Rainard III of Grancey, lord of Grancey   52, 233
Ralph of Arden   111, 129 n.39, 307, 388
Ralph of Aubigny   131, 331
Ralph of Chall   44–5, 50, 55 n.148, 327
Ralph of Mauleon   116, 204, 340, 386
Ralph of Ste-Marie   128, 310
Ralph of Tilly, constable to the archbishop of York   131, 305, 328, 330, 344
Ralph I, count of Clermont   9 n.28, 17, 57, 111, 222–3, 228–9
Ralph II of Fougères, lord of Fougères   82 n.288, 104 n.74, 124, 157, 191–2, 284, 311, 337, 384
Ralph III Tesson, lord of St-Savour-le-Viconte   44, 283, 285, 377
Ramla (city)   36
   Skirmish (6 Nov 1191)   125, 146, 205, 222, 268, 278, 287, 289, 361, 372–3, 386, 390
   Skirmish (1192)   128, 143, 201, 296, 299, 308–10, 356–7, 374, 376
Ranulf of Glanville, justiicar   37, 55–6, 76, 110–11, 129 n.39, 131, 176, 182, 192, 215, 305–07, 358–9, 388, 393
Raoul III of Nesle, count of Soissons   17, 57, 143, 157, 221, 260
Raoul I of Coucy, lord of Coucy   37, 57, 100, 106, 221, 239–40, 242
Raymond of Tripoli, count of Tripoli   80, 86
Raynald of Nevers, lord of Décize   100, 222, 227, 254
Reading Abbey   65–7, 74, 278, 311, 348, 351
Rievaulx Abbey   64 n.195, 68 n.213, 77–8, 123, 290, 329
Richard of Clare, lord of Saham   64, 129, 315
Richard Fitz-William of Langford, lord of Little Windsor   55, 75, 130, 304
Richard I, king of England, Richard the Lionheart   2–3, 15, 22–7, 37, 40 n.60, 43, 46–8, 51, 52 n.129, 54–56, 59, 61, 63–74, 76–8, 80, 82, 85–9, 99, 102 n.68, 104–06, 108, 111–14, 116–17, 124–6, 128–9, 131–33, 136–41, 143, 146, 149 n.154, 152, 150 n.159, 152, 154, 156, 159–212, 213, 215, 222, 238, 240, 242–3, 263, 268, 278–81, 283, 286–9, 291–4, 296–8, 308, 317, 325, 343, 348–50, 353–96
Richard of Templo   24–5
Richard of Vernon   69, 87 n.317, 284–5, 336
Robert of Beaurain   156, 278–9
Robert of Bois, rector of Claybrooke   128 n.33, 309

Robert of Cokefield, warden of St Edmonds 43, 314
Robert the Constable (of Halsham) 46, 50, 116, 144, 311, 387
Robert Corbet, lord of Caus 130, 325
Robert Fitz-Richard (Thesaurarius), prior of the Hospitallers in England 84, 104 n.78, 320, 346
Robert Hunaud 48, 50, 129, 343
Robert of Icklesham 50, 51 n.125, 129, 327
Robert Kent 48, 50, 129, 343
Robert of la Mare 129 n.39, 131, 156, 312–3, 365
Robert Neal 128, 310
Robert II of Newburgh, deputy chamberlain 128, 308–09, 361
Robert Pirou, preceptor of Temple Hurst 104–05
Robert of Quincy, lord of Buckley 117, 128, 164, 181–2, 199, 206, 308, 343, 386
Robert of Sablé, Lord of Sablé, master of the Templars 171, 295, 338, 345, 384
Robert Sablonières 98, 239
Robert of Thornham 76, 129 n.39, 172, 197, 280–1, 360, 363
Robert Tresgoz, constable of Salisbury Castle 156, 165, 178, 191 n.181, 183, 192–3 n.193, 371
Robert Trussebot 55, 77, 79, 87 n.317, 111, 131, 173, 181, 283, 329, 362
Robert I of Wavrin, seneschal of Flanders 143, 156, 270–1, 273
Robert II of Dreux, count of Dreux 17, 37, 56–8, 101–02, 114, 157, 220–2, 226–7, 229, 240, 243, 313
Robert II, abbot of Forde Abbey 54–5, 75, 304
Robert III (Fitz-Pernel), earl of Leicester, high steward of England 69, 83, 86, 105, 110, 117, 124, 128–9, 143, 183, 199, 201, 213, 218, 226, 308–09, 312, 341, 343, 357
Robert V of Béthune, advocate of Béthune 142, 144–5, 259, 289, 292
Roger of Glanville 111, 117, 305–07, 328, 330, 344, 358, 388
Roger of Harcourt, lord of Renneville
Roger of Howden 9 n.28, 21–2, 24, 46, 57 n.161, 68, 75, 131, 148 n.153, 164 n.28, 175, 181, 195, 203, 292, 355
Roger of Mowbray 43–4, 76–9, 81–2, 84, 86, 110, 124, 290
Roger Peitevin 116
Roger le Pole 117, 325
Roger of Préaux 156 n.191, 157, 161 n.11, 167, 191 n.183, 198, 286–7, 359, 372–3
Roger of Saceio 69, 287, 377

Roger of Tosny 105, 192, 284, 315, 338, 387
Roger of Wavrin, bishop of Cambrai 58, 143, 156, 270–1, 273
Ronald, son-in-law to Nicholas of Gôtentin 48, 50, 129, 343–4
Rotrou III, count of Perche 86, 97, 112, 125, 202, 238, 243, 389, 341
Routier 208–09
Rufford Abbey 62 n.187, 65

Saint-André-au-Bois Abbey 72 n.230, 220
Saint-Loup Abbey 47
St Botolph's Priory 69
Saladin, Salah ad-Din (Yusuf ibn Ayyub) 1, 31, 36, 57, 69, 75–6, 78, 85, 88, 92, 146 n.140, 157, 160 n.5, 164, 171, 176–8, 197–8, 206, 214, 248, 263–4, 305, 385
Saladin Tithe 26, 33, 39–46, 48–9, 51–3, 73, 78, 88, 129, 133, 215–6, 297, 303, 350, 353, 363, 392, 395
Saul of Bruil 128, 163 n.23, 200, 202, 299, 374
Scotland 48, 117 n.142, 129, 133, 136, 179, 217
   Scottish crusaders 48, 117, 127–30, 164, 181–2, 199, 206, 308, 343, 386
Scutage (shield tax) 56 n.156, 86 n.312, 117 n.142, 165 n.35, 179, 192 n.189, 326, 334
Scutifer (shield-bearer) 173 n.90
Sempringham Priory 50, 66, 74, 76–8, 88, 138 n.94, 281, 295, 337, 351
Seneschal – see steward
Serjeant 42, 44, 54, 86, 93, 126, 134, 150 n.163, 164, 168–9, 178, 182–3, 187–8, 194 n.200, 196 n.212, 210, 217, 354, 363
Servientes – see serjeant,
Sheriff, shrievalty 75, 77, 110–1, 117, 123, 133 n.64, 156, 160–1, 163–6, 170, 172, 173 n.89, 178, 186, 194–5, 199, 210, 291, 306, 317, 319, 327, 343, 354, 357–8, 360–1, 365–9, 372, 374, 378–9, 383, 388
Silves, siege of (Jul–Sep 1189) 58, 131, 221–3, 225–7, 229, 231, 243–4, 247, 323, 338
Squadron
   Cavalry 93, 152, 158, 177, 217
   Naval 137 n.83, 172, 195, 280–1, 363
Standard-bearer 77, 173–4, 198, 206, 266, 285, 287, 329, 362
Stephen of Brive 107, 252–4
Stephen of Longchamp 167, 171, 199, 280, 353, 359, 365–6, 372, 375
Stephen of Pierre-Perthuis 107, 252–4
Stephen of Sancerre, count of Sancerre 9 n.28, 57, 222, 228–9, 238, 242 – 3
Stephen of Thornham, marshal, treasurer 170–2, 190, 197–8, 280–1, 360, 363

Stephen of Tours   156 n.191, 168, 191 n. 180, 280, 379
Steward (*stiweard, dapifer*)   44, 52 n.134, 58, 84 n.304, 105 n.82, 106, 115–6, 117 n.142, 124, 126, 128, 143–4, 156, 163–4, 167–9, 171, 184, 186, 188, 191–2, 197, 199, 201–02, 211, 217, 222, 231, 247–8, 270, 280, 286, 303, 306, 308–09, 311, 315, 337, 357, 359–60, 364, 368, 371–2, 379, 384, 387, 389
Sven Thorkilsen   116
Swineshead Abbey   65

Taille (direct tax)   46
Templars – see Military Orders, Poor Fellow-Soldiers of Christ and of the Temple of Solomon
Theobald of Valoignes, lord of Parham, butler of Ireland   110-11, 186 n.159, 306-7, 388
Theobald V of Blois, count of Blois   2, 9, 17, 46, 57, 99, 220, 222–3, 224–5, 228–9, 243
Thierry of Montfauçon, archbishop of Besançon   109, 231–2, 243–4
Thomas Becket, Saint   41, 54, 75, 104, 131
Tiron Abbey   65–7
Tironensians – see Order of Tiron
Treuga Dei (Truce of God)   147
Troarn Abbey   47, 50, 62 n.187, 251
Trois-Fontaines Abbey   49, 186 n.159, 245–6
True Cross   2, 31, 34, 37–8, 52, 160, 205 n.261, 214
Tyre (port, city)   24, 36, 54, 59, 112, 198, 206, 240, 305, 320, 335, 343, 358–9, 362, 368, 386, 388

Urban III, pope   1

Val-Notre-Dame Abbey   68 n.217, 72, 257
Vauluisant Abbey   72
Vaux-de-Cernay Abbey   62 n.187, 72
Vézelay (city)   80–1, 97, 113, 187, 281–2, 291, 297, 350, 353–4, 355, 357
Vifgage (living usufructory pledge of property)   46–7, 50, 236–7
Vitry-aux-Loges Leprosarium   72

Wales   54, 56, 61, 128, 136, 138, 140, 166, 179, 195 n.204, 212, 303, 334, 368
    Welsh crusaders   186 n.159, 203, 209–10, 342, 351–2
Walkelin of Ferrers   87, 311–12, 381
Walter of Coutances, archbishop of Rouen   23, 113, 187, 203, 282, 350, 353, 369, 371, 379

Walter of Dunstanville   42
Walter the Englishman   137
Walter le Nair   46, 50, 329
Walter of Ross   77, 79, 131, 239–40, 291, 329, 331–2
Walter of Sombernon, lord of Sombernon   52, 237
Walter IV of Vienne, count of Salins, lord of Bourbon   157, 339
Warin II Fitz-Gerald, baron of the Exchequer   128, 143, 181 n.181, 199, 356
Warin Fitz-Simon   82, 316
Whitby Abbey   44, 71
William, count of Joigny   99–101, 110, 222, 227, 254
William Brewer   75–6, 116, 166–7, 191, 349, 358
William III of Braose, lord of Bamber   140, 166, 194–5, 210, 368
William of Bruil   128, 202, 299, 374
William of Cayeux, lord of Bouillancourt   125, 156–7, 191 n.183, 199, 204–06, 259, 289, 292, 373
William of Ferrers, earl of Derby   65–6, 79, 82, 87 n.317, 311, 389
William Fitz-Aldelin, sheriff of Cumberland   44, 167, 178, 191 n.181, 327, 365
William Fitz-Osbert   38, 44, 131, 323
William of Forz of Oléron   137, 172, 183, 188, 196, 201, 205 n.260, 279–80, 359
William of Longchamp, chancellor of England   23, 77, 113, 162, 166–7, 197 n.219, 199, 202–4, 298, 353, 358–9, 365–7, 369–72
William of Mandeville, earl of Essex   52, 66, 76, 104, 104, 116, 140–4, 162, 166, 183, 188 n.163, 311, 351, 357, 387
William Marshal, lord of Striguil, high marshal of England   116, 125, 128, 143, 149, 152 n.175, 154, 156–7, 166–7, 170, 173 n.85, 174 n.93, 178, 180, 183, 189, 190 n.178, 191–2, 197–8, 200–01, 204–7, 210, 218, 357, 361, 379,
William of Merchin   47
William of Merlo   97, 136, 223–5
William of Mowbray   79 n.264, 82, 84, 86, 124
William of Préaux   156–7, 191 n.183, 192–3 n.193, 198, 204, 286–7, 359, 362, 372–3
William of Reimes   76, 281, 381
William des Roches, lord of Sablé   69, 191 n.180, 295, 345, 377
William of Stuteville, sheriff of Northumberland   77, 139–40, 146 n.141, 366
William II, King of Sicily   112, 238

William II of Tancarville, chamberlain of Normandy   146, 173, 180–1, 194–5, 284–5, 336, 387
William IV des Barres   156–7, 226
William IV of Garlande, lord of Livry   98, 225
William IV, castellan of Saint-Omer   139, 144–5, 260, 272

Wroxall Priory   64, 67 n.210

Yorkshire   22, 55, 61, 64 n.195, 77–8, 99, 105, 111 n.110, 131, 139–40, 166–8, 173 n.91, 188, 202, 210, 217, 281, 290, 292, 306, 311, 327–32, 334, 360, 372, 379

Warfare in History

The Battle of Hastings: Sources and Interpretations, *edited and introduced by Stephen Morillo*

Infantry Warfare in the Early Fourteenth Century: Discipline, Tactics, and Technology, *Kelly DeVries*

The Art of Warfare in Western Europe during the Middle Ages, from the Eighth Century to 1340 (second edition), *J.F. Verbruggen*

Knights and Peasants: The Hundred Years War in the French Countryside, *Nicholas Wright*

Society at War: The Experience of England and France during the Hundred Years War, *edited by Christopher Allmand*

The Circle of War in the Middle Ages: Essays on Medieval Military and Naval History, *edited by Donald J. Kagay and L.J. Andrew Villalon*

The Anglo-Scots Wars, 1513–1550: A Military History, *Gervase Phillips*

The Norwegian Invasion of England in 1066, *Kelly DeVries*

The Wars of Edward III: Sources and Interpretations, *edited by Clifford J. Rogers*

The Battle of Agincourt: Sources and Interpretations, *Anne Curry*

War Cruel and Sharp: English Strategy under Edward III, 1327–1360, *Clifford J. Rogers*

The Normans and their Adversaries at War: Essays in Memory of C. Warren Hollister, *edited by Richard P. Abels and Bernard S. Bachrach*

The Battle of the Golden Spurs (Courtrai, 11 July 1302): A Contribution to the History of Flanders' War of Liberation, 1297–1305, *J.F. Verbruggen*

War at Sea in the Middle Ages and the Renaissance, *edited by John B. Hattendorf and Richard W. Unger*

Swein Forkbeard's Invasions and the Danish Conquest of England, 991–1017, *Ian Howard*

Religion and the Conduct of War, c.300–1215, *David S. Bachrach*

Warfare in Medieval Brabant, 1356–1406, *Sergio Boffa*

Renaissance Military Memoirs: War, History and Identity, 1450–1600, *Yuval Noah Harari*

The Place of War in English History, 1066–1214, *J.O. Prestwich, edited by Michael Prestwich*

War and the Soldier in the Fourteenth Century, *Adrian R. Bell*

German War Planning, 1891–1914: Sources and Interpretations, *Terence Zuber*

The Battle of Crécy, 1346, *Andrew Ayton and Sir Philip Preston*

The Battle of Yorktown, 1781: A Reassessment, *John D. Grainger*

Special Operations in the Age of Chivalry, 1100–1550, *Yuval Noah Harari*

Women, Crusading and the Holy Land in Historical Narrative, *Natasha R. Hodgson*

The English Aristocracy at War: From the Welsh Wars of Edward I to the Battle of Bannockburn, *David Simpkin*

The Calais Garrison: War and Military Service in England, 1436–1558, *David Grummitt*

Renaissance France at War: Armies, Culture and Society, c. 1480–1560, *David Potter*

Bloodied Banners: Martial Display on the Medieval Battlefield, *Robert W. Jones*

Alfred's Wars: Sources and Interpretations of Anglo-Saxon Warfare in the Viking Age, *Ryan Lavelle*

The Dutch Army and the Military Revolutions, 1588–1688, *Olaf van Nimwegen*

In the Steps of the Black Prince: The Road to Poitiers, 1355–1356, *Peter Hoskins*

Norman Naval Operations in the Mediterranean, *Charles D. Stanton*

Shipping the Medieval Military: English Maritime Logistics in the Fourteenth Century, *Craig L. Lambert*

Edward III and the War at Sea: The English Navy, 1327–1377, *Graham Cushway*

The Soldier Experience in the Fourteenth Century, *edited by Adrian R. Bell, Anne Curry, Adam Chapman, Andy King and David Simpkin*

Warfare in Tenth-Century Germany, *David S. Bachrach*

Chivalry, Kingship and Crusade: The English Experience in the Fourteenth Century, *Timothy Guard*

The Norman Campaigns in the Balkans, 1081–1108, *Georgios Theotokis*

Welsh Soldiers in the Later Middle Ages, 1282–1422, *Adam Chapman*

Merchant Crusaders in the Aegean, 1291–1352, *Mike Carr*

Henry of Lancaster's Expedition to Aquitaine, 1345–1346: Military Service and Professionalism in the Hundred Years War, *Nicholas A. Gribit*

Scotland's Second War of Independence, 1332–1357, *Iain A. MacInnes*

Military Communities in Late Medieval England: Essays in Honour of Andrew Ayton, *edited by Gary P. Baker, Craig L. Lambert and David Simpkin*

The Black Prince and the *Grande Chevauchée* of 1355, *Mollie M. Madden*

Military Society and the Court of Chivalry in the Age of the Hundred Years War, *Philip J. Caudrey*

Warfare in the Norman Mediterranean, *edited by Georgios Theotokis*

Chivalry and Violence in Late Medieval Castile, *Samuel A. Claussen*

The Household Knights of Edward III: Warfare, Politics and Kingship in Fourteenth-Century England, *Matthew Hefferan*

www.ingramcontent.com/pod-product-compliance
Lightning Source LLC
Chambersburg PA
CBHW070804300426
44111CB00014B/2418